WORLD HISTORY

SECOND EDITION

WORLD HISTORY

TO 1500

WILLIAM J. DUIKER

The Pennsylvania State University

JACKSON J. SPIELVOGEL

The Pennsylvania State University

WEST/WADSWORTH

I⊤P® an International Thomson Publishing company

Belmont, CA • Albany, NY • Bonn • Boston • Cincinnati • Detroit • Johannesburg • London • Los Angeles • Madrid
Melbourne • Mexico City • New York • Paris • Singapore • Tokyo • Toronto • Washington

History Editor　Clark Baxter
Senior Developmental Editor　Sharon Adams Poore
Editorial Assistant　Amy Guastello
Print Buyer　Barbara Britton
Marketing Manager　Jay Hu
Production Management　Heather Stratton/GTS Graphics
Composition and Color Separation　GTS Graphics
Maps　GeoSystems Global Corporation
Copy Editor　Patricia Lewis
Art and Photograph Research　Sarah Evertson/Image Quest
Text and Document Permissions Management　Lynn Reichel
Interior and Cover Design　Diane Beasley
Cover Art　By the tenth century C.E., Arab trade routes extended over half the globe (see Chapter 7).
　　　　Bibliotheque Nationale, Paris.
Printer　World Color, Taunton

Art, Photograph, Document, and Map credits appear in the rear of the book.

Printed in the United States of America
1 2 3 4 5 6 7 8 9 10

For more information contact Wadsworth Publishing Company, 10 Davis Drive, Belmont, CA 94002, or electronically at http://www.thomson.com/wadsworth.html

International Thomson Publishing Europe
Berkshire House 168-173
High Holborn
London, WC1V 7AA, England

Thomas Nelson Australia
102 Dodds Street
South Melbourne 3205
Victoria, Australia

Nelson Canada
1120 Birchmount Road
Scarborough, Ontario
Canada M1K 5G4

International Thomson Publishing GmbH
Königswinterer Strasse 118
53227 Bonn, Germany

International Thomson Editores
Campos Eliseos 385, Piso 7
Col. Polanco
11560 México D.F. México

International Thomson Publishing Asia
221 Henderson Road
#05-10 Henderson Building
Singapore 0315

International Thomson Publishing Japan
Hirakawacho Kyowa Building, 3F
2-2-1 Hirakawacho
Chiyoda-ku, Tokyo 102, Japan

International Thomson Publishing Africa
Building 19, Constantia Park
240 Old Pretoria Road
Halfway House, 1685 South Africa

ISBN 0-534-53120-2

About the Authors

William J. Duiker is Liberal Arts Professor Emeritus of East Asian studies at The Pennsylvania State University. A former U.S. diplomat with service in Taiwan, South Vietnam, and Washington, D.C., he received his doctorate in Far Eastern history from Georgetown University in 1968, where his dissertation dealt with the Chinese educator and reformer Cai Yuanpei. At Penn State, he has written widely on the history of Vietnam and modern China, including the widely acclaimed The Communist Road to Power in Vietnam *(revised edition, Westview Press, 1996), which was selected for a Choice Outstanding Academic Book Award in 1982–1983 and 1996–1997. Other recent books are* China and Vietnam: The Roots of Conflict *(Berkeley, 1987) and* Sacred War: Nationalism and Revolution in a Divided Vietnam *(McGraw-Hill, 1995). He is currently at work on a biography of the Vietnamese revolutionary Ho Chi Minh. While his research specialization is in the field of nationalism and Asian revolutions, his intellectual interests are considerably more diverse. He has traveled widely and has taught courses on the History of Communism and non-Western civilizations at Penn State. He is currently planning his fourth voyage around the world with the Semester at Sea Program.*

Jackson J. Spielvogel is associate professor of history at The Pennsylvania State University. He received his Ph.D. from The Ohio State University, where he specialized in Reformation history under Harold J. Grimm. His articles and reviews have appeared in such journals as Moreana, Journal of General Education, Catholic Historical Review, Archiv für Reformationsgeschichte, *and* American Historical Review. *He has also contributed chapters or articles to* The Social History of the Reformation, The Holy Roman Empire: A Dictionary Handbook, Simon Wiesenthal Center Annual of Holocaust Studies, *and* Utopian Studies. *His work has been supported by fellowships from the Fullbright Foundation and the Foundation for Reformation Research. At Penn State, he helped inaugurate the Western civilization courses as well as a popular course on Nazi Germany. His book* Hitler and Nazi Germany *was published in 1987 (third edition, 1996). He is the author of* Western Civilization, *published in 1991 (third edition, 1997). Professor Spielvogel has won five major university-wide teaching awards. During the year 1988–1989, he held the Penn State Teaching Fellowship, the university's most prestigious teaching award. In 1996, he won the Dean Arthur Ray Warnock Award for Outstanding Faculty Member, and in 1997, he became the first recipient of the Schreyer Institute's Student Choice Award for innovative and inspiring teaching.*

To Marion and Ginger,
the best of role models
W.J.D.

To Diane,
whose love and support made it all possible
J.J.S.

◆

Contents

CHAPTER 13

❖·❖·❖·❖·❖·❖·❖·❖·❖·❖·❖·❖·❖·❖

Crisis and Rebirth: Europe in the Fourteenth and Fifteenth Centuries   446

Maps

Chronologies

Preface

For several million years after primates first appeared on the surface of the earth, human beings lived in small communities, seeking to survive by hunting, fishing, and foraging in a frequently hostile environment. Then suddenly, in the space of a few thousand years, there was an abrupt change of direction as human beings in a few widely scattered areas of the globe began to master the art of cultivating food crops. As food production increased, the population in those areas rose correspondingly, and people began to congregate in larger communities. Governments were formed to provide protection and other needed services to the local population. Cities appeared and became the focal point of cultural and religious development. Historians refer to this process as the beginnings of civilization.

For generations, historians in Europe and the United States have pointed to the rise of such civilizations as marking the origins of the modern world. Courses on Western civilization conventionally begin with a chapter or two on the emergence of advanced societies in Egypt and Mesopotamia and then proceed to ancient Greece and the Roman Empire. From Greece and Rome, the road leads directly to the rise of modern civilization in the West.

There is nothing inherently wrong with this approach. Important aspects of our world today can indeed be traced back to these early civilizations, and all human beings the world over owe a considerable debt to their achievements. But all too often this interpretation has been used to imply that the course of civilization has been linear in nature, leading directly from the emergence of agricultural societies in ancient Mesopotamia to the rise of advanced industrial societies in Europe and North America. Until recently, most courses on world history taught in the United States routinely focused almost exclusively on the rise of the West, with only a passing glance at other parts of the world, such as Africa, India, and East Asia. The contributions made by those societies to the culture and technology of our own time were often passed over in silence.

Several reasons have been advanced to justify this approach. Some have argued that students simply are not interested in what is unfamiliar to them. Others have said that it is more important that young minds understand the roots of their own heritage than that of peoples elsewhere in the world. In many cases, however, the motivation for this Eurocentric approach has been the belief that since the time of Socrates and Aristotle Western civilization has been the sole driving force in the evolution of human society.

Such an interpretation, however, represents a serious distortion of the process. During most of the course of human history, the most advanced civilizations have been not in the West, but in East Asia or the Middle East. A relatively brief period of European dominance culminated with the era of imperialism in the late nineteenth century, when the political, military, and economic power of the advanced nations of the West spanned the globe. During recent generations, however, that dominance has gradually eroded, partly as the result of changes taking place within Western societies and partly because new centers of development are emerging elsewhere on the globe—notably in East Asia, where the growing economic strength of Japan and many of its neighbors has led to the now familiar prediction that the twenty-first century will be known as the Pacific Century.

World history, then, is not simply a chronicle of the rise of the West to global dominance, nor is it a celebration of the superiority of the civilization of Europe and the United States over other parts of the world. The history of the world has been a complex process in which many branches of the human community have taken an active part, and the dominance of any one area of the world has been a temporary rather than a permanent phenomenon. It will be our purpose in this book to present a balanced picture of this story, with all respect for the richness and diversity of the tapestry of the human experience. Due attention must be paid to the rise of the West, of course, since that has been the most dominant aspect of world history in recent centuries. But the contributions made by other peoples must be given adequate consideration as well, not only in the period prior to 1500 when the major centers of civilization were located in Asia, but also in our own day, where a multipolar picture of development is clearly beginning to emerge.

Anyone who wishes to teach or write about world history must decide whether to present the topic as an integrated whole or as a collection of different cultures. The world that we live in today, of course, is in many respects an interdependent one in terms of economics as well as culture and communications, a reality that is often expressed by the phrase "global village." The convergence of peoples across the surface of the earth into an integrated world system began in early times and intensified after the rise of capitalism in the early modern era. In growing recognition of this trend, historians trained in global history, as well as instructors in the growing number of world history courses, have now begun to speak and write of a "global approach" that turns attention away from the study of individual civilizations and focuses instead on the "big picture" or, as the world historian Fernand Braudel termed it, interpreting world history as a river with no banks.

On the whole, this development is to be welcomed as a means of bringing the common elements of the evolution of human society to our attention. But there is a risk involved in this approach. For the vast majority of their time on earth, human beings have lived in partial or virtually total isolation from each other. Differences in climate, location, and geographical features have created human societies very different from each other in culture and historical experience. Only in relatively recent times—the commonly accepted date has long been the beginning of the age of European exploration at the end of the fifteenth century, but some would now push it back to the era of the Mongol empire or even further—have cultural interchanges begun to create a common "world system," in which events taking place in one part of the world are rapidly transmitted throughout the globe, often with momentous consequences. In recent generations, of course, the process of global interdependence has been proceeding even more rapidly. Nevertheless, even now the process is by no means complete, as ethnic and regional differences continue to exist and to shape the course of world history. The tenacity of these differences and sensitivities is reflected not only in the rise of internecine conflicts in such divergent areas as Africa, India, and Eastern Europe, but also in the emergence in recent years of such regional organizations as the Organization of African Unity, the Association for the Southeast Asian Nations, and the European Economic Community. Political leaders in various parts of the world speak routinely of "Arab unity," the "African road to socialism," and the "Confucian path to economic development."

The second problem is a practical one. College students today are all too often not well informed about the distinctive character of civilizations such as China and India and, without sufficient exposure to the historical evolution of such societies, will assume all too readily that the peoples in these countries have had historical experiences similar to ours and will respond to various stimuli in a similar fashion to those living in Western Europe or the United States. If it is a mistake to ignore those forces that link us together, it is equally a mistake to underestimate those factors that continue to divide us and to differentiate us into a world of diverse peoples.

Our response to this challenge has been to adopt a global approach to world history while at the same time attempting to do justice to the distinctive character and development of individual civilizations and regions of the world. The presentation of individual cultures will be especially important in Parts I and II, which cover a time when it is generally agreed that the process of global integration was not yet far advanced. Later chapters will begin to adopt a more comparative and thematic approach, in deference to the greater number of connections that have been established among the world's peoples since the fifteenth and sixteenth centuries. Part V will consist of a series of chapters that will center on individual regions of the world while at the same time focusing on common problems related to the Cold War and the rise of global problems such as overproduction and environmental pollution. Moreover, sections entitled "Reflections" at the close of the five major parts of the book will attempt to link events together in a broad comparative and global framework.

We have sought balance in another way as well. Many textbooks tend to simplify the content of history courses by emphasizing an intellectual or political perspective or, most recently, a social perspective, often at the expense of sufficient details in a chronological framework. This approach is confusing to students whose high school social studies programs have often neglected a systematic study of world history. We have attempted to write a well-balanced work in which political, economic, social, religious, intellectual, cultural, and military history have been integrated into a chronologically ordered synthesis.

To enliven the past and let readers see for themselves the materials that historians use to create their pictures of the past, we have included primary sources (boxed documents) in each chapter that are keyed to the discussion in the text. The documents include examples of the religious, artistic, intellectual, social, economic, and political aspects of life in different societies and reveal in a vivid fashion what civilization meant to the individual men and women who shaped it by their actions.

Each chapter has a lengthy introduction and conclusion to help maintain the continuity of the narrative and to provide a synthesis of important themes. Time lines enable students to see the major developments of an era at a glance, while the more detailed chronologies reinforce the events discussed in the text. An annotated bibliography at the end of each chapter reviews the most recent literature on each period and also gives references to some of the older, "classic" works in each field. Extensive maps and illustrations serve to deepen the reader's understanding of the text. To facilitate comprehension of cultural movements, illustrations of artistic works discussed in the text are placed next to the discussions.

As preparation for revision of *World History*, we reexamined the entire book and analyzed the comments and reviews of many colleagues who have found the book to be a useful instrument for introducing their students to world history. In making revisions for the second edition, we sought to build upon the strengths of the first edition and, above all, to maintain the balance, synthesis, and narrative qualities that characterized the first edition. To keep up with the ever-growing body of historical scholarship, new or revised material has been added throughout the book. Throughout the revising process, we also worked to craft a book that we hope students will continue to find very readable. Headings and subheadings in every chapter were revised to give students a more vivid introduction to the content of the chapters. Moreover, we added anecdotes to the introductions in order to convey more dramatically the major theme or themes of each chapter.

To provide a more logical arrangement of the material, we also made some major revisions of the book. The material in the Prologue was incorporated into a revised Chapter 1. Part II was extensively reordered and revised. The chapter on "The New World" was moved to the beginning of Part II, while the material in Chapters 10, 12, and 13 was reorganized into two new chapters (Chapter 9, "The Expansion of Civilization in Southern Asia," and Chapter 11, "The East Asian Rimlands: Early Japan, Korea, and Vietnam"). Moreover, the two chapters on European civilization in the Middle Ages (8 and 9) have been condensed and reorganized to form a new Chapter 12, "The Making of Europe and the World of the Byzantine Empire, 500–1300." In Part IV, a new chapter, Chapter 25: "Nationalism, Revolution, and Dictatorship: Africa, Asia, and Latin America from 1919 to 1939," has been added. In Part V, Chapters 28 and 30 were reorganized and rewritten to form two new thematic chapters: Chapter 27, "In the Grip of the Cold War: The Breakdown of the Yalta System," and Chapter 28, "Brave New World: Communism." Moreover, all "Suggestions for Further Reading" at the end of each chapter were updated, and new illustrations were added to every chapter.

The enthusiastic response to the primary sources (boxed documents) led us to evaluate the content of each document carefully and add a number of new documents throughout the text. For the second edition, the maps have been revised where needed and, as in the first edition, are carefully keyed to all text references. New maps have also been added.

Because courses in world history at American and Canadian colleges and universities follow different chronological divisions, a one-volume comprehensive edition and a two-volume edition of this text are being made available to fit the needs of instructors. Teaching and learning ancillaries include:

Instructor's Manual/Test Bank. Contains chapter outlines, suggestions for lecture topics, essay and identification questions, discussion questions for the primary documents, and suggested films and musical selections. The textbook contains approximately 2,000 test questions.

Instructor's Manual on Disk. Contains the Instructor's Manual portion of the IM/TB Windows.

ESA Computerized Testing. The test bank in a computerized format is available in both Windows and Macintosh formats.

Full Color Transparency Acetates. Contains all the maps in the text as well as commentary on each map. The commentary, by James Harrison of Siena College, includes not only the text caption, but also additional points of interest about the map, what it shows, and its relevance to the study of world history. Possible discussion questions for student involvement are included. Available to qualified adopters.

Study Guide. Contains key terms, critical thinking questions, multiple choice questions, questions to help analyze primary documents, and chapter summaries.

Study Tips for World History. New to this edition, chapter outlines, study questions, and key terms and their pronunciations.

Document Exercise Workbooks. Prepared by Donna Van Raaphorst of Cuyahoga Community College. It provide a collection of exercises based on primary sources in history. Available in two volumes.

Map Exercise Workbooks. Prepared by Cynthia Kosso of Northern Arizona University, these feature approximately thirty map exercises in each volume. Designed to help students feel comfortable with maps by having them work with different kinds of maps and identify places.

World History Reader. New to this edition. Contains additional documents not found in the text and longer excerpts of documents that are included in the text.

Slide Set. A set of 200 slides, including 100 maps from the text and 100 images from the text.

PowerPoint. Acetate map images from the text in the PowerPoint format. Available in both Windows and Macintosh formats.

World History Videodiscs. Short, focused video clips, photos, artwork, animations, music, and dramatic readings are used to bring life to historical topics and events that are most difficult for students to appreciate from a textbook alone. For example, students will experience the grandeur of Versailles and the defeat felt by a German soldier at Stalingrad.

Video Library.

World History CD-ROM. For Windows. Eighteen interactive journeys.

Internet Guide for History. Prepared by Daniel Kurland and John Soares. Section One introduces students to the Internet, including tips for searching on the Web. Section Two introduces students to how history research can be done and lists URL sites by topic.

Web Page.

Acknowledgments

*B*oth authors gratefully acknowledge that without the generosity of many others, this project could not have been completed. William Duiker would like to thank Kumkum Chatterjee and On-cho Ng for their helpful comments about unfamiliar issues related to the history of India and premodern China. His longtime colleague Cyril Griffith, now deceased, was a cherished friend and a constant source of information about modern Africa. Art Goldschmidt has been of invaluable assistance in reading several chapters of the manuscript, as well as in unravelling many of the mysteries of Middle Eastern civilization. Finally, he remains profoundly grateful to his wife, Yvonne V. Duiker, Ph.D. She has not only given her usual measure of love and support when this appeared to be an insuperable task, but she has also contributed her own time and expertise to enrich the sections on art and literature, thereby adding life and sparkle

to this, as well as the first, edition of the book. To her, and to his daughters Laura and Claire, he will be forever thankful for bringing joy to his life.

Jackson Spielvogel would like to thank Art Goldschmidt, David Redles, and Christine Colin for their time and ideas and, above all, his family for their support. The gifts of love, laughter, and patience from his daughters, Jennifer and Kathryn, his sons, Eric and Christian, and his daughters-in-law, Liz and Michele, were invaluable. Diane, his wife and best friend, provided him with editorial assistance, wise counsel, and the loving support that made a project of this magnitude possible.

Thanks to West/Wadsworth's comprehensive review process, many historians were asked to evaluate our manuscript. We are grateful to the following for the innumerable suggestions that have greatly improved our work:

Charles F. Ames, Jr.
Salem State College

Nancy Anderson
Loyola University

Gloria M. Aronson
Normandale College

Charlotte Beahan
Murray State University

Doris Bergen
University of Vermont

Martin Berger
Youngstown State University

Deborah Biffton
University of Wisconsin/LaCrosse

Patricia J. Bradley
Auburn University at Montgomery

Dewey Browder
Austin Peay State University

Antonio Calabria
University of Texas at San Antonio

Alice-Catherine Carls
University of Tennessee-Martin

Yuan Ling Chao
Middle Tennessee State University

Mark W. Chavalas
University of Wisconsin

Hugh Clark
Ursinus College

Joan Coffey
Sam Houston State University

John Davis
Radford University

Ross Dunn
San Diego State University

Lane Earn
University of Wisconsin-Oshkosh

Edward L. Farmer
University of Minnesota

William W. Farris
University of Tennessee

Ronald Fritze
Lamar University

Joe Fuhrmann
Murray State University

Robert Gerlich
Loyola University

Marc J. Gilbert
North Georgia College

William J. Gilmore-Lehne
Richard Stockton College of New Jersey

Richard M. Golden
University of North Texas

Joseph M. Gowaskie
Rider College

Don Gustafson
Augsburg College

Deanna Haney
Lansing Community College

Ed Haynes
Winthrop College

Linda Kerr
University of Alberta at Edmonton

Zoltan Kramar
Central Washington University

Craig A. Lockard
University of Wisconsin-Green Bay

George Longenecker
Norwich University

Robert Luczak
Vincennes University

Patrick Manning
Northeastern University

Dolores Nason McBroome
Humboldt State University

John McDonald
Northern Essex Community College

Andrea McElderry
University of Louisville

Jeff McEwen
Chattanooga State Technical Community College

John A. Mears
Southern Methodist University

Marc A. Meyer
Berry College

Stephen S. Michot
Mississippi County Community College

John Ashby Morton
Benedict College

William H. Mulligan
Murray State University

Henry A. Myers
James Madison University

Sandy Norman
Florida Atlantic University

Patrick M. O'Neill
Broome Community College

Norman G. Raiford
Greenville Technical College

Jane Rausch
University of Massachusetts-Amherst

Dianna K. Rhyan
Columbus State Community College

Merle Rife
Indiana University of Pennsylvania

Patrice C. Ross
Columbus State Coimmunity College

John Rossi
LaSalle University

Keith Sandiford
University of Manitoba

Elizabeth Sarkinnen
Mt. Hood Community College

Bill Schell
Murray State University

Robert M. Seltzer
Hunter College

David Shriver
Cuyahoga Community College

Amos E. Simpson
University of Southwestern Louisiana

Wendy Singer
Kenyon College

Marvin Slind
Washington State University

Paul Smith
Washington State University

John Snetsinger
California Polytechnic State University

George Stow
LaSalle University

Patrick Tabor
Chemeketa Community College

Tom Taylor
Seattle University

John G. Tuthill
University of Guam

Joanne Van Horn
Fairmont State College

Pat Weber
University of Texas-El Paso

Douglas L. Wheeler
University of New Hampshire

David L. White
Appalachian State University

Elmira B. Wicker
Southern University-Baton Rouge

Glee Wilson
Kent State University

Harry Zee
Cumberland County College

The authors are truly grateful to the people who have helped us to produce this book. We especially want to thank Clark Baxter, whose faith in our ability to do this project was inspiring. Hal Humphrey, Production Services Coordinator at West/Wadsworth, was both patient and thoughtful as he guided us through the process of revision for the second edition of our book. Heather Stratton of GTS Graphics was as cooperative and cheerful as she was competent in matters of production. As usual, Pat Lewis was an outstanding copy editor. Lynn Reichel and Sarah Evertson provided valuable assistance in obtaining permissions for the boxed documents and illustrations.

A Note to Students about Languages and the Dating of Time

One of the most difficult challenges in studying world history is coming to grips with the multitude of names, words, and phrases in unfamiliar languages. Unfortunately, this problem has no easy solution. We have tried to alleviate the difficulty, where possible, by providing an English-language translation of foreign words or phrases. The issue is especially complicated in the case of Chinese, since two separate systems are commonly used to transliterate the spoken Chinese language into the Roman alphabet. The Wade-Giles system, invented in the nineteenth century, was the most frequently used until recent years, when the pinyin system was adopted by the People's Republic of China as its own official form of transliteration. We have opted to use the latter, since it appears to be gaining acceptance in the United States, but the initial use of a Chinese word is accompanied by its Wade-Giles equivalent in parentheses for the benefit of those who may encounter the term in their outside reading.

In our examination of world history, we need also to be aware of the dating of time. In recording the past, historians try to determine the exact time when events occurred. World War II in Europe, for example, began on September 1, 1939, when Adolf Hitler sent German troops into Poland, and ended on May 7, 1945, when Germany surrendered. By using dates, historians can place events in order and try to determine the development of patterns over periods of time.

If someone asked you when you were born, you would reply with a number, such as 1979. In the United States, we would all accept that number without question, because it is part of the dating system followed in the Western world (Europe and the Western Hemisphere). In this system, events are dated by counting backward or forward from the birth of Christ (assumed to be the year 1). An event that took place 400 years before the birth of Christ would most commonly be dated 400 B.C. (before Christ). Dates after the birth of Christ are labeled as A.D. These letters stand for the Latin words *anno domini*, which mean "in the year of the Lord" (or the year of the birth of Christ). Thus an event that took place 250 years after the birth of Christ is written A.D. 250, or in the year of the Lord 250. It can also be written as 250, just as you would not give your birth year as A.D. 1979, but simply 1979.

Some historians now prefer to use the abbreviations B.C.E. ("before the common era") and C.E. ("common era") instead of B.C. and A.D. This is especially true of world historians who prefer to use symbols that are not so Western or Christian oriented. The dates, of course, remain the same. Thus, 1950 B.C.E. and 1950 B.C. would be the same year, as would A.D. 40 and 40 C.E. In keeping with the current usage by many world historians, this book will use the terms B.C.E. and C.E.

Historians also make use of other terms to refer to time. A decade is 10 years; a century is 100 years; and a millennium is 1,000 years. The phrase fourth century B.C.E. refers to the fourth period of 100 years counting backward from 1, the assumed date of the birth of Christ. Since the first century B.C.E. would be the years 100 B.C.E. to 1 B.C.E., the fourth century B.C.E. would be the years 400 B.C.E. to 301 B.C.E. We could say, then, that an event in 350 B.C.E. took place in the fourth century B.C.E.

The phrase fourth century C.E. refers to the fourth period of 100 years after the birth of Christ. Since the first period of 100 years would be the years 1 to 100, the fourth period or fourth century would be the years 301 to 400. We could say, then, for example, that an event in 350 took place in the fourth century. Likewise, the first millennium B.C.E. refers to the years 1000 B.C.E. to 1 B.C.E.; the second millennium C.E. refers to the years 1001 to 2000.

The dating of events can also vary from people to people. Most people in the Western world use the Western calendar, also known as the Gregorian calendar after Pope Gregory XIII who refined it in 1582. The Hebrew calendar, on the other hand, uses a different system in which the year one is the equivalent of the Western year 3760 B.C.E., considered by Jews to be the date of the creation of the world. Thus, the Western year 2000 will be the year 5760 on the Jewish calendar. The Islamic calendar begins year 1 on the day Muhammad fled Mecca, which is the year 622 on the Western calendar.

WORLD HISTORY

The First Civilizations and the Rise of Empires

For several million years after the first appearance of primates on the surface of the earth, human beings lived in small communities, seeking to survive by hunting, fishing, and foraging in a frequently hostile environment. Then suddenly, in the space of a few thousand years, there was an abrupt change of direction, as human beings in a few widely scattered areas of the globe began to master the art of cultivating food crops. As food production increased, the population in these areas rose correspondingly, and people began to congregate in larger communities. Governments were formed to provide protection and other needed services to the local population. Cities appeared and became centers of cultural and religious development. Historians call this process the beginnings of civilization.

The first civilizations that emerged in Mesopotamia, Egypt, India, and China all shared a number of basic characteristics. Each developed in a river valley that was able to provide the agricultural resources needed to maintain a large population. Although agricultural practices varied considerably from civilization to civilization, in each civilization a part of the population lived in cities, which became the focal points for political, economic, social, cultural, and religious development. These cities were much larger than the Neolithic towns that preceded them, and the new configurations in turn gave rise to significant changes in political, military, social, and economic structures.

All of these early civilizations established some kind of organized government bureaucracy to meet the administrative demands of the growing population while armies were organized for protection and to gain land and power. A new social structure based on economic power arose. While kings and an upper class of priests, political leaders, and warriors dominated, there also existed a large group of free people (farmers, artisans, craftspeople) and at the very bottom, socially, a class

MIDDLE EAST

Agriculture and Neolithic towns

Sumerian civilization

INDIA

First agricultural settlements

Harappan civilization

CHINA

First settled agriculture

EGYPT AND THE MEDITERRANEAN

Agriculture in Nile valley

Flowering of Egyptian civilization

of slaves. Abundant agricultural yields in these regions created opportunities for economic specialization as a surplus of goods enabled some people to work in occupations other than farming. The demand of ruling elites for luxury items encouraged artisans and craftspeople to create new products. As urban populations exported finished goods in exchange for raw materials from neighboring populations, organized trade grew substantially.

The new urban civilizations were also characterized by significant religious and cultural developments. The gods were often deemed critical to a community's success, and professional priestly classes regulated relations with the gods. Writing was an important development in the new civilizations. Rulers, priests, merchants, and artisans used writing to keep records and even create new kinds of literary expression. New forms of artistic activity, including monumental architectural structures, occupied a prominent place in the new urban environments.

Although trade occasionally brought the new civilizations into contact with one another and in many cases led to the expansion of new technology from one region to another, by and large the early river valley civilizations developed independently with each grounded in local developments ultimately related to the new agricultural practices of the Neolithic Age. Taken together, however, the civilizations of Mesopotamia, Egypt, India, and China constituted nothing less than a revolutionary stage in the growth of human society.

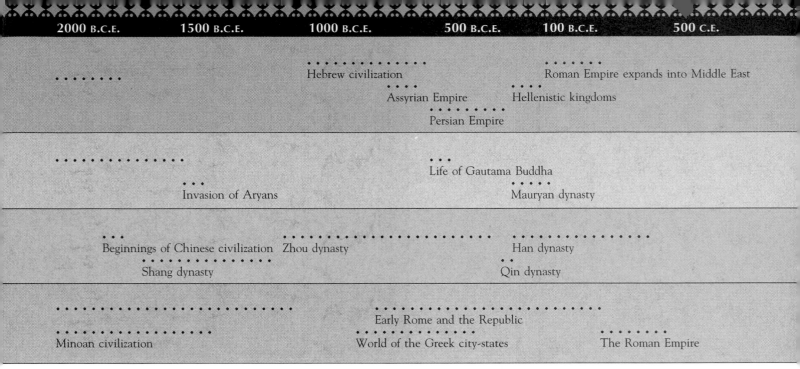

2000 B.C.E.	1500 B.C.E.	1000 B.C.E.	500 B.C.E.	100 B.C.E.	500 C.E.

Hebrew civilization

Roman Empire expands into Middle East

Assyrian Empire

Hellenistic kingdoms

Persian Empire

Life of Gautama Buddha

Invasion of Aryans

Mauryan dynasty

Beginnings of Chinese civilization   Zhou dynasty

Han dynasty

Shang dynasty

Qin dynasty

Early Rome and the Republic

Minoan civilization

World of the Greek city-states

The Roman Empire

From the beginnings of the first civilizations around 300 B.C.E., there was an ongoing movement toward the creation of larger territorial states with more sophisticated systems of control. This process reached a high point in the first millennium B.C.E. Between 1000 and 500 B.C.E., the Assyrians and Persians amassed empires that encompassed either large areas or all of the ancient Middle East. The conquests of Alexander the Great in the fourth century B.C.E. created an even larger, if short-lived, empire that was soon divided into the four Hellenistic kingdoms. Later, the western portion of the Hellenistic kingdoms as well as the Mediterranean world and much of western Europe fell subject to the mighty empire of the Romans. At the same time, much of India became part of the Mauryan Empire. Finally, in the last few centuries B.C.E., the Qin and Han dynasties of China created a unified Chinese state.

All of these empires exhibited some common characteristics. Each developed some kind of efficient administrative system that enabled it to control vast territories and to integrate diverse populations and regions. The administrative division of imperial lands into provinces directed by a centrally appointed governor and the collection of taxes in some form from subject populations enabled these vast empires to flourish. Of course, these empires were ultimately dependent on the effective use of military power. Each empire maintained some kind of professional standing army that enabled it to conquer new territories.

Moreover, military forces were used to maintain the new imperial frontiers, often buttressed by defensive frontier fortresses. The Great Wall of China still bears witness to the importance of these barriers. Roads, too, were an element in the administration of empires. A system of well-constructed roads enabled the Romans to communicate with the far-flung provinces of their empire. The Chinese dug canals that enabled the state to transport troops and supplies thousands of miles to the southern border of the empire.

These empires also concentrated enormous wealth in the hands of the ruling elites. The vast landed estates of the elite may no longer be evident, but the remaining ruins of immense imperial palaces and lavish public buildings erected by rulers are visible testaments to imperial wealth. They are also reminders that these empires ultimately relied on economic exploitation.

But empires also provided benefits to their inhabitants. Efficiently governed states often created favorable conditions for economic prosperity. Imperial regimes invested in public works projects—such as the construction of roads and harbors—that benefited the empire's subjects. Empires also facilitated the growth of manufacturing and trade as both raw materials and luxury goods flowed into the hands of the wealthy ruling elites. Trade also brought increasing contacts between empires. The Silk Road that linked the Chinese and Roman empires made it possible for wealthy Romans to have the precious silks of China.

For millions of people within the empires, religious and philosophical systems that seemed to give meaning to life provided a sense of cultural identity. Great religions, such as Hinduism and Buddhism, sought to encourage the right relationship between human beings and the higher powers of the universe. Greek philosophy, Confucianism, and Daoism (also known as Taoism) all sought to help people live in harmony with the universe by understanding the underlying patterns of reality. Moreover, both philosophical and religious systems provided ethical codes, often embodied in written scriptures, that provided guidelines for everyday life.

While examining the achievements and the challenges faced by these early civilizations, however, we must be careful not to ignore events taking place elsewhere on the globe. Beyond the islands of civilization that will be discussed in these early chapters, life was changing for peoples in other areas as well—in the steppes of Central Asia, on the Arabian peninsula, and in the Sahara. Here climatic changes were forcing peoples who had previously lived by hunting, fishing, and foraging to adopt new methods to survive. Some turned to agriculture, while others attempted to survive by trade or the domestication of cattle, sheep, or other mammals.

As time passed, contacts between such nomadic peoples and the settled civilizations became increasingly frequent. The dynamic relationship between these two types of societies became a crucial theme in the process of human evolution throughout the later course of history. In some ways, the relationship was a fruitful one, because it facilitated cross-cultural contacts and the exchange of new ideas and new technology. In other cases, the relationship was marked by tension and conflict, as pastoral and sedentary societies fought over territory. Nomadic warriors made periodic raids against settled communities, and the latter sent expeditions to pacify pastoral populations and bring them under control.

In the end, it was the failure of these two types of human society to establish an amicable relationship that brought an end to most of the ancient empires. Before the end of the first millennium B.C.E., both ancient Egypt and Mesopotamia had been overrun by nomadic peoples. A few centuries later, China and the Roman Empire would meet the same fate. But the fall of these ancient civilizations cannot be laid entirely at the feet of barbarians from beyond the frontier. Internal weaknesses were also a contributing factor. At the same time, however, these ancient civilizations left a legacy that soon gave birth to new forms of society, while spreading the concept of civilization to other parts of the globe.

CHAPTER 1

The First Civilizations: The Peoples of Western Asia and Egypt

In 1849, a daring young Englishman made a hazardous journey into the deserts and swamps of southern Iraq. Braving high winds and temperatures that reached 120 degrees Fahrenheit, William Loftus led a small expedition southward along the banks of the Euphrates River in search of the roots of civilization. As he said, "From our childhood we have been led to regard this place as the cradle of the human race."

Guided by native Arabs into the southernmost reaches of Iraq, Loftus and his small band of explorers were soon overwhelmed by what they saw. He wrote, "I know of nothing more exciting or impressive than the first sight of one of these great piles, looming in solitary grandeur from the surrounding plains and marshes." One of these piles, known to the natives as the mound of Warka, contained the ruins of Uruk, one of the first cities in the world and part of the world's first civilization.

Southern Iraq, known to ancient peoples as Mesopotamia, was one of the four areas in the world where civilization began. In the fertile valleys of the Tigris and Euphrates, the Nile, the Indus, and the Yellow River, in Mesopotamia, Egypt, India, and China, intensive agriculture became capable of supporting large groups of people. In these regions civilization was born. The first civilizations emerged in western Asia (now known as the Middle East) and Egypt, where people developed organized societies and created the ideas and institutions that we associate with civilization.

Before considering the early civilizations of western Asia and Egypt, however, we must

Emergence of Sumerian city-states   Babylonian kingdom   The Hebrews   Height of Persian power

Emergence of Egyptian civilization   Egypt—Old Kingdom   Egypt—Middle Kingdom   Egypt—New Kingdom

Great Pyramid   Code of Hammurabi   Age of prophets in Israel   Zoroastrianism

briefly examine humankind's prehistory and observe how human beings made the shift from hunting and gathering to agricultural communities and ultimately to cities and civilization.

The First Humans

Historians rely mostly on documents to create their pictures of the past, but no written records exist for the prehistory of humankind. In their absence, the story of early humanity depends upon archaeological and, more recently, biological information, which anthropologists and archaeologists use to formulate theories about our early past.

Although modern science has given us more precise methods for examining prehistory, much of our understanding of early humans still relies upon considerable conjecture. Given the rate of new discoveries, the following account of the current theory of early human life might well be changed in a few years. As the great British archaeologist Louis Leakey reminded us years ago, "Theories on prehistory and early man constantly change as new evidence comes to light."

The earliest humanlike creatures—known as hominids—lived in Africa some three to four million years ago. Known as Australopithecines, they flourished in East and South Africa and were the first hominids to make simple stone tools. The oldest known stone tool—a knife blade that is probably 2.6 million years old—was found in Africa.

A second stage in early human development occurred around 1.5 million years ago when *Homo erectus* ("upright human being") emerged. *Homo erectus* made use of larger and more varied tools and was the first hominid to leave Africa and move into both Europe and Asia.

Around 250,000 years ago, a third—and crucial—stage in human development began with the emergence of *Homo sapiens* ("wise human being"). By 100,000 B.C.E., two groups of *Homo sapiens* had developed. One type was the Neanderthal, whose remains were first found in the Neander valley in Germany. Their remains have since been found in both Europe and the Middle East and have been dated to between 100,000 and 30,000 B.C.E. Neanderthals relied on a variety of stone tools and were the first early people to bury their dead. Some scientists maintain that burial of the dead indicates a belief in an afterlife. Neanderthals in Europe made clothes from the skins of animals that they had killed for food.

The first anatomically modern humans, known as *Homo sapiens sapiens* ("wise, wise human being"), appeared in Africa between 200,000 and 150,000 years ago. Recent evidence indicates that they began to spread outside Africa around 100,000 years ago. Map 1.1 on p. 8 shows probable dates for different movements, although many of these are still controversial. By 30,000 B.C.E., *Homo sapiens sapiens* had replaced the Neanderthals, who had largely become extinct.

The movement of the first modern humans was rarely deliberate. Groups of people advanced beyond their old hunting grounds at a rate of only two to three miles per generation. This was enough, however, to populate the world in some tens of thousands of years. Based on recent evidence, some scholars have suggested that such advanced human creatures may have emerged independently in different parts of the world, rather than in Africa alone. In any case, by 10,000 B.C.E., members of the *Homo sapiens sapiens* species could be found throughout the world. By that time, it was the only human species left. All humans today, be they Europeans, Australian aborigines, or Africans, belong to the same subspecies of human being.

The Hunter-Gatherers of the Old Stone Age

One of the basic distinguishing features of the human species is the ability to make tools. The earliest tools were made of stone, and the term *Paleolithic* (Greek for "Old Stone") Age is used to designate this early period of human history (c. 2,500,000–10,000 B.C.E.).

For hundreds of thousands of years, humans relied on hunting and gathering for their daily food. Paleolithic peoples had a close relationship with the world around them, and over a period of time, they came to know which animals to hunt and which plants to eat. They did not know how to grow crops or raise animals, however. They gathered wild nuts, berries, fruits, and a variety of wild grains and green plants. Around the world, they hunted and consumed various animals, including buffalo, horses, bison, wild goats, and reindeer. In coastal areas, fish provided a rich source of food.

The hunting of animals and the gathering of wild plants no doubt led to certain patterns of living. Archaeologists and anthropologists have speculated that Paleolithic people lived in small bands of twenty or thirty people. They were nomadic (they moved from place to place) since they had no choice but to follow animal migrations and vegetation cycles. Hunting depended upon careful observation of animal behavior patterns and required a group effort to have any real chance of success. Over the years, tools became more refined and more useful. The invention of the spear, and later the bow and arrow, made hunting considerably easier. Harpoons and fishhooks made of bone increased the catch of fish.

Both men and women were responsible for finding food—the chief work of Paleolithic people. Since

✤ Map 1.1   The Spread of *Homo Sapiens Sapiens*.

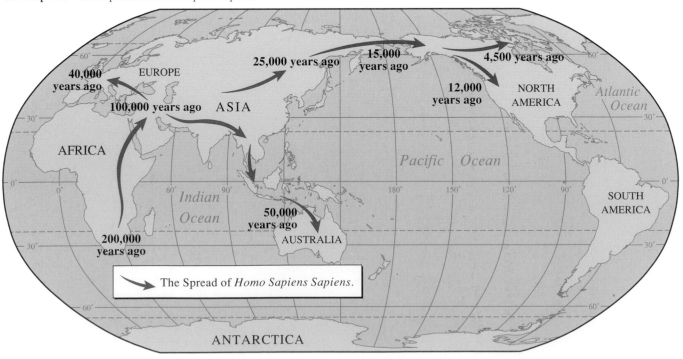

women bore and raised the children, they generally stayed close to the camps, but they played an important role in acquiring food, gathering berries, nuts, and grains. Men hunted the wild animals, an activity that took them far from camp. Because both men and women played important roles in providing for the band's survival, scientists have argued that a rough equality existed between men and women. Indeed, some speculate that both men and women made the decisions that governed the activities of the Paleolithic band.

These groups of Paleolithic peoples, especially those who lived in cold climates, found shelter in caves. Over time, they created new types of shelter as well. Perhaps the most common was a simple structure of wood poles or sticks covered with animal hides. Where wood was scarce, Paleolithic hunter-gatherers might use the bones of mammoths for the framework and cover it with animal hides. The systematic use of fire, which archaeologists believe began around 500,000 years ago, made it possible for the caves and human-made structures to have a source of light and heat. Fire also enabled early humans to cook their food, making it better tasting, longer lasting, and, in the case of some plants, such as wild grain, easier to chew and digest.

The making of tools and the use of fire—two important technological innovations of Paleolithic peoples—remind us how crucial the ability to adapt was to human survival. Changing physical conditions during periodic ice ages posed a considerable threat to human existence. Paleolithic peoples used their technological innovations—such as the ability to make tools and use fire—to change their physical environment. By working together, they found a way to survive. And by passing on their common practices, skills, and material products to their children, they ensured that later generations, too, could survive in a harsh environment.

But Paleolithic peoples did more than just survive. The cave paintings of large animals found in southwestern France and northern Spain bear witness to the cultural activity of Paleolithic peoples. A cave discovered in southern France in 1994 contains more than three hundred paintings of lions, oxen, owls, panthers, and other animals. Most of these are animals that Paleolithic people did not hunt, which suggests that the paintings were created for religious or even decorative purposes.

The Agricultural Revolution, c. 10,000–4000 B.C.E.

The end of the last ice age around 10,000 B.C.E. was followed by what is called the Neolithic Revolution; that is,

the revolution that occurred in the New Stone Age (the word *Neolithic* is Greek for "New Stone"). The name New Stone Age is misleading, however. Although Neolithic peoples made a new type of polished stone axes, this was not the major change that occurred after 10,000 B.C.E.

The real change was the shift from hunting animals and gathering plants for sustenance to producing food by systematic agriculture. The planting of grains and vegetables provided a regular supply of food while the taming of animals, such as sheep, goats, cattle, and pigs, added a steady source of meat, milk, and fibers such as wool for clothing. Larger animals could also be used as beasts of burden. The growing of crops and the taming of food-producing animals created a new relationship between humans and nature. Historians like to speak of this as an agricultural revolution. Revolutionary change is dramatic and requires great effort, but the ability to acquire food on a regular basis gave humans greater control over their environment. It also enabled them to give up their nomadic ways of life and begin to live in settled communities.

The shift to food producing from hunting and gathering was not as sudden as was once believed, however. The Mesolithic period ("Middle Stone Age," c. 10,000–7000 B.C.E.) saw a gradual transition from a food-gathering and hunting economy to a food-producing one and witnessed a gradual domestication of animals as well. Likewise, the

◆ **Paleolithic Cave Painting.** Cave paintings of large animals provide good examples of the cultural creativity of Paleolithic peoples. This scene is part of a large underground chamber found accidentally in 1940 at Lascaux, France, by some boys looking for their dog. This work is dated around 14,000 B.C.E.

movement toward the use of plants and their seeds as an important source of nourishment was also not sudden. Evidence seems to support the possibility that the Paleolithic hunters and gatherers had already grown crops to supplement their traditional sources of food. Moreover, throughout the Neolithic period, hunting and gathering as well as nomadic herding remained ways of life for many people around the world.

Systematic agriculture developed independently in different areas of the world between 8000 and 5000 B.C.E. Inhabitants of the Middle East began cultivating wheat and barley and domesticating pigs, cattle, goats, and sheep by 8000 B.C.E. From the Middle East, farming spread into the Balkans region of Europe by 6500 B.C.E. By 4000 B.C.E., it was well established in the south of France, central Europe, and the coastal regions of the Mediterranean. The cultivation of wheat and barley also spread from western Asia into the Nile valley of Egypt by 6000 B.C.E. and soon spread up the Nile to other areas of Africa, especially the Sudan and Ethiopia. In the woodlands and tropical forests of central Africa, a separate agricultural system emerged based on the cultivation of tubers or root crops such as yams and tree crops such as bananas. The cultivation of wheat and barley also eventually moved eastward into the highlands of northwestern and central India between 7000 and 5000 B.C.E. By 5000 B.C.E., rice was being cultivated in Southeast Asia, from where it spread into South China. In northern China, the cultivation of millet and the domestication of pigs and dogs seem well established by 6000 B.C.E. In the Western Hemisphere, Mesoamericans (inhabitants of present-day Mexico and Central America) domesticated beans, squash, and maize (or corn) as well as dogs and fowl between 7000 and 5000 B.C.E.

The growing of crops on a regular basis made possible the support of larger populations and gave rise to more permanent settlements, which historians refer to as Neolithic farming villages or towns. Although Neolithic villages appeared in Europe, India, Egypt, China, and Mesoamerica, the oldest and most extensive ones were located in the Middle East. Jericho, in Palestine near the Dead Sea, was in existence by 8000 B.C.E. and covered several acres by 7000 B.C.E. It had a wall several feet thick that enclosed houses made of sun-dried bricks. Çatal Hüyük, located in modern-day Turkey, was an even larger community. Its walls enclosed thirty-two acres, and its population probably reached six thousand inhabitants during its high point from 6700 to 5700 B.C.E. People lived in simple mudbrick houses that were built so close to one another that there were few streets. To get to their

�֎ Map 1.2   The Development of Agriculture.

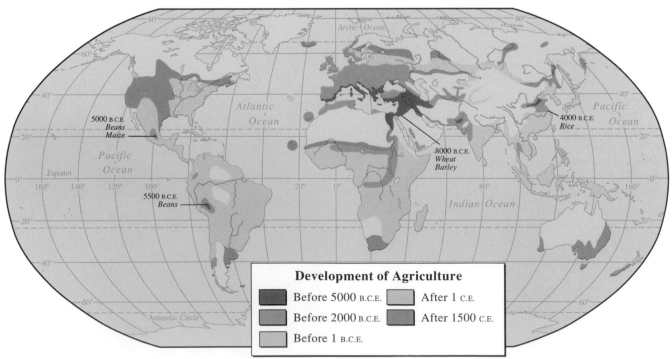

homes, people had to walk along the rooftops and then enter the house through a hole in the roof.

Archaeologists have discovered twelve cultivated products in Çatal Hüyük, including fruits, nuts, and three kinds of wheat. People grew their own food and stored it in storerooms in their homes. Domesticated animals, especially cattle, yielded meat, milk, and hides. Hunting scenes on the walls would indicate that the people of Çatal Hüyük hunted as well, but unlike earlier hunter-gatherers, they no longer relied on hunting to survive. Food surpluses also made it possible for people to do things other than farming. Some people became artisans and made weapons and jewelry that were traded with neighboring peoples, thus opening the inhabitants of Çatal Hüyük to the wider world around them.

Religious shrines housing figures of gods and goddesses have been found at Çatal Hüyük, as have a number of female statuettes. Molded with noticeably large breasts and buttocks, these "earth mothers" perhaps symbolically represented the fertility of both "our mother" earth and human mothers. Both the shrines and the statues point to the growing role of religion in the lives of these Neolithic peoples.

The Neolithic agricultural revolution had far-reaching consequences. Once people settled in villages or towns, they built houses for protection and other structures for the storage of goods. As organized communities stored food and accumulated material goods, they began to engage in trade. In the Middle East, for example, the new communities exchanged such objects as shells, flint, and semiprecious stones. People also began to specialize in certain crafts, and a division of labor developed. Pottery was made from clay and baked in fire to make it hard. The pots were used for cooking and to store grains. Woven baskets were also used for storage. Stone tools became refined as flint blades were used to make sickles and hoes for use in the fields. In the course of the Neolithic Age, many of the food plants still in use today came to be cultivated. Moreover, vegetable fibers from such plants as flax and cotton were used to make thread that was woven into cloth.

The change to systematic agriculture in the Neolithic Age also had consequences for the relationship between men and women. Men assumed the primary responsibility for working in the fields and herding animals, jobs that kept them away from the home. Women remained behind, caring for the children and weaving clothes, making cheese from milk, and performing other tasks that required considerable labor in one place. In time, as work outside the home was increasingly perceived as more important than work done at home, men came to play the more dominant role, a basic pattern that would persist until our own times.

Other patterns set in the Neolithic Age also proved to be enduring elements of human history. Fixed dwellings, domesticated animals, regular farming, a division of labor, men holding power, all of these are part of the human story. For all of our scientific and technological progress, human survival still depends on the growing and storing of food, an accomplishment of people in the Neolithic Age. The Neolithic Revolution was truly a turning point in human history.

Between 4000 and 3000 B.C.E., significant technical developments began to transform the Neolithic towns. The invention of writing enabled records to be kept while the use of metals marked a new level of human control over the environment and its resources. Already before 4000 B.C.E., artisans had discovered that metal-bearing rocks could be heated to liquefy the metal, which could then be cast in molds to produce tools and weapons that were more useful than stone instruments. Although copper was the first metal to be utilized in producing tools, after 4000 B.C.E., metalworkers in western Asia discovered that a combination of copper and tin created bronze, a far harder and more durable metal than copper. Its widespread use has led historians to speak of a Bronze Age from around 3000 to 1200 B.C.E., after which bronze was increasingly replaced by iron.

At first, Neolithic settlements were hardly more than villages, but as their inhabitants mastered the art of farming, the villages gradually began to give birth to more sophisticated and complex human societies. As wealth increased, these societies began to develop armies and to build walled cities. By the beginning of the Bronze Age, the concentration of larger numbers of people in the river valleys of Mesopotamia, Egypt, India, and China was leading to a whole new pattern for human life.

The Emergence of Civilization

As we have seen, early human beings formed small groups that developed a simple culture that enabled them to survive. As human societies grew and developed greater complexity, a new form of human existence—called civilization—came into being. A civilization is a complex culture in which large numbers of human beings share a number of common elements. Historians have identified a number of basic characteristics of civilization. These include (1) an urban revolution: cities became the focal points for political, economic, social, cultural, and religious development; (2) a distinct religious structure: the gods were deemed crucial to the community's success, and professional priestly classes, as stewards of the gods' property, regulated relations with the gods; (3) new political and military structures: an organized government bureaucracy arose to meet the administrative demands of the growing population while armies were organized to gain land and power; (4) a new social structure based on economic power: while kings and an upper class of priests, political leaders, and warriors dominated, there also existed a large group of free commoners (farmers, artisans, craftspeople) and at the very bottom, socially, a class of slaves; (5) the development of writing: kings, priests, merchants, and artisans used writing to keep records; (6) new forms of significant artistic and intellectual activity: monumental architectural structures, usually religious, occupied a prominent place in urban environments, while smaller examples of individual creativity also proliferated; and (7) the development of more complexity in a material sense: capital was accumulated and metals smelted to produce a variety of material objects.

Why early civilizations developed remains difficult to explain. Since civilizations developed independently in India, China, Mesopotamia, and Egypt, can general causes be identified that would explain why all of these civilizations emerged? A number of possible explanations of the beginning of civilization have been suggested. A theory of challenge and response maintains that challenges forced human beings to make efforts that resulted in the rise of civilization. Some scholars have adhered to a material explanation. Material forces, such as the growth of food surpluses, made possible the specialization of labor and development of large communities with bureaucratic organization. But some areas were not natu-

rally conducive to agriculture. Abundant food could only be produced with a massive human effort to carefully manage the water, an effort that created the need for organization and bureaucratic control and led to civilized cities. Some historians have argued that nonmaterial forces, primarily religious, provided the sense of unity and purpose that made such organized activities possible. Finally, some scholars doubt that we are capable of ever discovering the actual causes of early civilization.

Civilization in Mesopotamia

The Greeks spoke of the valley between the Tigris and Euphrates Rivers as Mesopotamia, the land "between the rivers." The region receives little rain, but the soil of the plain of southern Mesopotamia was enlarged and enriched over the years by layers of silt deposited by the two rivers. In late spring, the Tigris and Euphrates overflow their banks and deposit their fertile silt, but since this flooding depends upon the melting of snows in the upland mountains where the rivers begin, it is irregular and sometimes catastrophic. In such circumstances, farming could be accomplished only with human intervention in the form of irrigation and drainage ditches. A complex system was required to control the flow of the rivers and produce the crops. Large-scale irrigation made possible the expansion of agriculture in this region, and the abundant food provided the material base for the emergence of civilization in Mesopotamia.

The City-States of Ancient Mesopotamia

The creators of the first Mesopotamian civilization were the Sumerians, a people whose origins remain unclear. By 3000 B.C.E., they had established a number of independent cities in southern Mesopotamia, including Eridu, Ur, Uruk, Umma, and Lagash. As the cities expanded in size, they came to exercise political and economic control over the surrounding countryside, forming city-states. These city-states were the basic units of Sumerian civilization.

Sumerian cities were surrounded by walls. Uruk, for example, occupied an area of approximately a thousand acres encircled by a wall six miles long with defense towers located every thirty to thirty-five feet along the wall. City dwellings, built of sun-dried bricks, included both the small flats of peasants and the larger dwellings of the civic and priestly officials. Although Mesopotamia had little stone or wood for building purposes, it did have plenty of mud. Mudbricks, easily shaped by hand, were

◆ **The "Royal Standard" of Ur.** This series of panels is from the "Royal Standard" of Ur, a box dating from c. 2700 B.C.E. and discovered in a stone tomb from the royal cemetery of the Sumerian city-state of Ur. These scenes from the box depict the activities of the king and his court after a military victory. In the top panel, the king and his court drink wine while at the right a musician plays a bull-headed harp. The middle panel shows bulls, rams, and fish being brought to the banquet hall. The bottom panel shows booty from the king's victory.

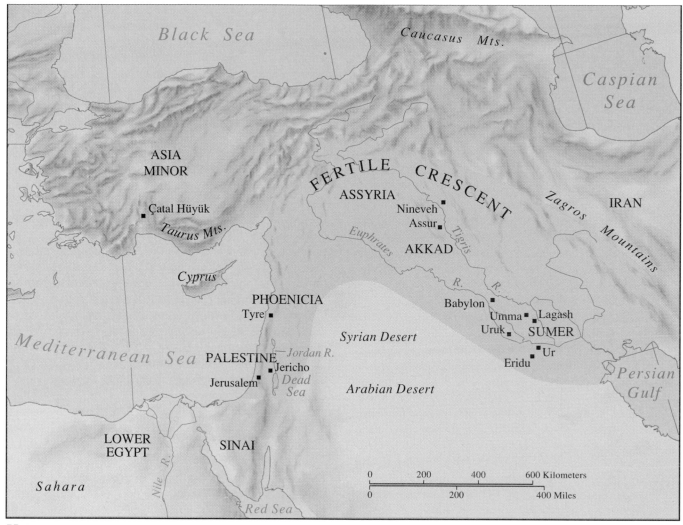

✳ **Map 1.3** Ancient Mesopotamia.

left to bake in the hot sun until they were hard enough to use for building. People in Mesopotamia were remarkably inventive with mudbricks, inventing the arch and the dome and constructing some of the largest brick buildings in the world. Mudbricks are still used in rural areas of the Middle East today.

The most prominent building in a Sumerian city was the temple, which was dedicated to the chief god or goddess of the city and often built atop a massive stepped tower called a ziggurat. The Sumerians believed that gods and goddesses owned the cities, and much wealth was used to build temples as well as elaborate houses for the priests and priestesses who served the gods. Priests and priestesses, who supervised the temples and their property, had much power. The temples owned much of the

city land and livestock and served not only as the physical center of the city, but also its economic and political center.

In fact, historians believe that in the early stages of the city-states, priests and priestesses played an important role in ruling. The Sumerians believed that the gods ruled the cities, making the state a theocracy (government by a divine authority). Eventually, however, ruling power passed into the hands of worldly figures known as kings.

Sumerians viewed kingship as divine in origin— kings, they believed, derived their power from the gods and were the agents of the gods. Regardless of their origins, kings had power—they led armies, initiated legislation, supervised the building of public works, provided courts, and organized workers for the irrigation projects upon which Mesopotamian agriculture depended. The army, the government bureaucracy, and the priests and priestesses all aided the kings in their rule. Befitting their power, Sumerian kings lived in large palaces with their wives and children.

The economy of the Sumerian city-states was primarily agricultural, but commerce and industry became important as well. The people of Mesopotamia produced woolen textiles, pottery, and the metalwork for which they were especially well known. Foreign trade, which was primarily a royal monopoly, could be extensive. Royal officials imported luxury items, such as copper and tin, aromatic woods, and fruit trees, in exchange for dried fish, wool, barley, wheat, and the metal goods produced by Mesopotamian craftspeople. Traders traveled by land to the eastern Mediterranean in the west and by sea to India in the east. The invention of the wheel around 3000 B.C.E. led to carts with wheels that made the transport of goods easier.

Sumerian city-states contained three major social groups—nobles, commoners, and slaves. Nobles included royal and priestly officials and their families. Commoners included the nobles' clients who worked for the palace and temple estates and other free citizens who worked as farmers, merchants, fishermen, scribes, and craftspeople. Probably 90 percent or more of the population were farmers. They could exchange their crops for the goods of the artisans in free town markets. Slaves belonged to palace officials, who used them mostly in building projects; temple officials, who used mostly female slaves to weave cloth and grind grain; and rich landowners, who used them for farming and domestic work.

Empires in Ancient Mesopotamia

As the number of Sumerian city-states grew and the states expanded, new conflicts arose as city-state fought city-state for control of land and water. The fortunes of various city-states rose and fell over the centuries. The constant wars, with their burning and sacking of cities, left many Sumerians in deep despair, as is evident in the words of this Sumerian poem from the city of Ur: "Ur is destroyed, bitter is its lament. The country's blood now fills its holes like hot bronze in a mold. Bodies dissolve like fat in the sun. Our temple is destroyed, the gods have abandoned us, like migrating birds. Smoke lies on our city like a shroud."

Located in the flat land of Mesopotamia, the Sumerian city-states were also open to invasion. To the north of the Sumerian city-states were the Akkadians. We call them a Semitic people because of the type of language they spoke (see Table 1.1). Around 2340 B.C.E., Sargon, leader of the Akkadians, overran the Sumerian city-states and established an empire that included most of Mesopotamia as well as lands westward to the Mediterranean. But the Akkadian empire eventually disintegrated, and its end by 2100 B.C.E. brought a return to the system of warring city-states until Ur-Nammu of Ur succeeded in reunifying most of Mesopotamia. But this final flowering of Sumerian culture collapsed with the coming of the Amorites. Under Hammurabi, the Amorites or Old Babylonians, a large group of Semitic-speaking seminomads, created a new empire.

Hammurabi (1792–1750 B.C.E.) employed a well-disciplined army of foot soldiers who carried axes, spears, and copper or bronze daggers. He learned to divide his opponents and subdue them one by one. Using such methods, he gained control of Sumer and Akkad and reunified Mesopotamia almost to the old borders established by Sargon of Akkad. After his conquests, he called himself "the sun of Babylon, the king who has made the four quarters of the world subservient," and established a new capital at Babylon, north of Akkad.

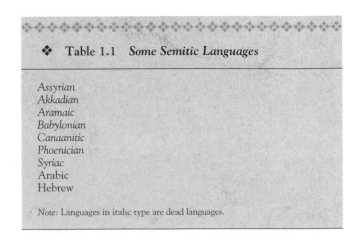

❖ **Table 1.1** *Some Semitic Languages*

Assyrian
Akkadian
Aramaic
Babylonian
Canaanitic
Phoenician
Syriac
Arabic
Hebrew

Note: Languages in italic type are dead languages.

Hammurabi, the man of war, was also a man of peace. He followed in the footsteps of previous conquerors by assimilating Mesopotamian culture with the result that Sumerian ways continued to exist despite the end of the Sumerians as a political entity. A collection of his letters, found by archaeologists, reveals that he took a strong interest in state affairs. He built temples, defensive walls, and irrigation canals; encouraged trade; and brought an economic revival. After his death, however, a series of weak kings were unable to keep Hammurabi's empire united, and it finally fell to new invaders.

THE CODE OF HAMMURABI

Hammurabi is best remembered for his law code, a collection of 282 laws (see the box on p. 16). For centuries, laws had regulated people's relationships with one another in the lands of Mesopotamia, but only fragments of these earlier codes survive. Hammurabi's collection provides considerable insight into almost every aspect of everyday life there and provides us a priceless glimpse of the values of this early society.

The Code of Hammurabi reveals a society with a system of strict justice. Penalties for criminal offenses were severe and varied according to the social class of the victim. A crime against a member of the upper class (a noble) by a member of the lower class (a commoner) was punished more severely than the same offense against a member of the lower class. Moreover, the principle of retaliation ("an eye for an eye, a tooth for a tooth") was fundamental to this system of justice. It was applied in cases where members of the upper class committed crimes against their social equals. For crimes against members of the lower classes, a money payment was made instead.

Hammurabi's code took seriously the responsibilities of public officials. The governor of an area and city officials were expected to catch burglars. If they failed to do so, the officials in the district where the crime was committed had to replace the lost property. If murderers were not found, the officials had to pay a fine to the relatives of the victim. Soldiers were likewise expected to fulfill their duties and responsibilities for the order and maintenance of the state. If a soldier hired a substitute to fight for him, he was put to death, and the substitute was given control of his estate. Laws also sheltered ordinary soldiers from the wrongful actions of their officers. An officer who forced someone to join his army, took the goods of his soldiers, or wronged them seriously was executed.

The law code also furthered the proper performance of work with what virtually amounted to consumer protec-

tion laws. Builders were held responsible for the buildings they constructed. If a house collapsed and caused the death of the owner, the builder was put to death. If the collapse caused the death of the son of the owner, the son of the builder was put to death. If goods were destroyed by

◆ **Stele of Hammurabi (Code of Hammurabi, King of Babylonia).** Although the Sumerians compiled earlier law codes, Hammurabi's code was the most famous in early Mesopotamian history. The code recognized three social classes in Babylonia (nobles, free commoners, and slaves) and included laws dealing with marriage and divorce, job performance, punishments for crime, and even sexual relations. The upper section of the stele depicts Hammurabi standing in front of the seated sun god Shamash, who orders the king to record the law. The lower section contains the actual code.

❧ The Code of Hammurabi ☙

Although there were earlier Mesopotamian law codes, Hammurabi's is the most complete. It was inscribed on a stele (stone) topped by a bas-relief depicting Hammurabi receiving the inspiration for the law code from the sun-god Shamash, who was also the god of justice. The law code emphasizes the principle of retribution ("an eye for an eye") and punishments that vary according to social status. Punishments could be severe. Marriage and family affairs also play a large role in the code. The following examples illustrate these concerns.

The Code of Hammurabi

25. If fire broke out in a free man's house and a free man, who went to extinguish it, cast his eye on the goods of the owner of the house and has appropriated the goods of the owner of the house, that free man shall be thrown into that fire.

129. If the wife of a free man has been caught while lying with another man, they shall bind them and throw them into the water. If the husband of the woman wishes to spare his wife, then the king in turn may spare his subject.

131. If a free man's wife was accused by her husband, but she was not caught while lying with another man, she shall make affirmation by god and return to her house.

196. If a free man has destroyed the eye of a member of the aristocracy, they shall destroy his eye.

198. If he has destroyed the eye of a commoner or broken the bone of a commoner, he shall pay one mina of silver.

199. If he has destroyed the eye of a free man's slave or broken the bone of a free man's slave, he shall pay one-half his value.

209. If a free man struck another free man's daughter and has caused her to have a miscarriage, he shall pay ten shekels of silver for her fetus.

210. If that woman has died, they shall put his daughter to death.

211. If by a blow he has caused a commoner's daughter to have a miscarriage, he shall pay five shekels of silver.

212. If that woman has died, he shall pay one-half mina of silver.

213. If he struck a free man's female slave and has caused her to have a miscarriage, he shall pay two shekels of silver.

214. If that female slave has died, he shall pay one-third mina of silver.

---

the collapse, they had to be replaced and the house itself reconstructed at the builder's expense.

The number of laws in Hammurabi's code dedicated to land tenure and commerce reveals the importance of agriculture and trade in the Mesopotamian economy. Numerous laws dealt with questions of landholding, such as the establishment of conditions for renting farmland and the division of produce between tenants and their landlords. Laws concerning land use and irrigation were especially strict, an indication of the danger of declining crop yields if the lands were used incompetently. Commercial activity was also carefully regulated. Rates of interest on loans were watched closely. If the lender raised his rate of interest after a loan was made, he lost the entire amount of the loan. The Code of Hammurabi even specified the precise wages of laborers and artisans, such as brickmakers and jewelers.

The largest category of laws in the Code of Hammurabi focused on marriage and the family. Parents arranged marriages for their children. After marriage, the parties involved signed a marriage contract; without it, no one was considered legally married. While the husband provided a bridal payment, the woman's parents were responsible for a dowry to the new husband. Dowries were carefully monitored and were governed by specific regulations.

As in many patriarchal societies, women possessed far fewer privileges and rights in the married relationship than men. A woman's place was in the home, and failure to fulfill her expected duties was grounds for divorce. If a woman was not able to bear children, her husband could divorce her, but he did have to return the dowry to her family. If a wife tried to leave home to engage in business, thus neglecting her house, her husband could divorce her and did not have to repay the dowry. Furthermore, a wife who was a "gadabout, . . . neglecting her house [and] humiliating her husband" could be drowned. We do know that in practice not all women remained at home. Some worked in business and were especially prominent in the running of taverns.

Women were guaranteed some rights, however. If a woman was divorced without good reason, she received the dowry back. A woman could seek divorce and get her dowry back if her husband was unable to show that she had done anything wrong. In theory, a wife was guaranteed use of her husband's legal property in the event of his death. The mother could also decide which of her sons would receive an inheritance.

Sexual relations were strictly regulated as well. Husbands, but not wives, were permitted sexual activity outside marriage. A wife caught committing adultery was pitched into the river, although her husband could ask the king to pardon her. Incest was strictly forbidden. If a father committed incestuous relations with his daughter, he would be banished. Incest between a son and mother resulted in both being burned.

Fathers ruled their children as well as their wives. Obedience was duly expected: "If a son has struck his father, they shall cut off his hand." If a son committed a serious enough offense, his father could disinherit him, although fathers were not permitted to disinherit their sons arbitrarily.

The Culture of Mesopotamia

A spiritual worldview was of fundamental importance to Mesopotamian culture. To the peoples of Mesopotamia, the gods were living realities who affected all aspects of life. It was crucial, therefore, that the correct hierarchies be observed. Leaders could prepare armies for war, but success really depended on a favorable relationship with the gods. This helps to explain the importance of the priestly class and is the reason why even the kings took great care to dedicate offerings and monuments to the gods.

THE IMPORTANCE OF RELIGION

The Mesopotamians viewed their city-states as earthly copies of a divine model and order. Each city-state was sacred since it was linked to a god or goddess. Hence, Nippur, the earliest center of Sumerian religion, was dedicated to Enlil, the god of wind. Moreover, located at the heart of each city-state was a temple complex. Occupying several acres, this sacred area consisted of a ziggurat with a temple at the top dedicated to the god or goddess who owned the city. The temple complex was the true center of the community. The main god or goddess dwelt there symbolically in the form of a statue, and the ceremony of dedication included a ritual that linked the statue to the god or goddess and thus supposedly harnessed the power of the deity for the city's benefit. Considerable wealth was poured into the construction of temples as well as other buildings used for the residences of priests and priestesses who served the gods. Although the gods literally owned the city, the temple complex used only part of the land and rented out the remainder. Essentially, the temples dominated individual and commercial life, an indication of the close relationship of Mesopotamian religion and culture.

The physical environment had an obvious impact on the Mesopotamian view of the universe. Ferocious floods, heavy downpours, scorching winds, and oppressive humidity were all part of the Mesopotamian climate. These conditions and the resulting famines easily convinced Mesopotamians that this world was controlled by supernatural forces and that the days of human beings "are numbered; whatever he may do, he is but wind," as *The Epic of Gilgamesh* put it. In the presence of nature, Mesopotamians could easily feel helpless, as this poem relates:

> *The rampant flood which no man can oppose,*
> *Which shakes the heavens and causes earth to tremble,*
> *In an appalling blanket folds mother and child,*
> *Beats down the canebrake's full luxuriant greenery,*
> *And drowns the harvest in its time of ripeness.*[1]

The Mesopotamians discerned cosmic rhythms in the universe and accepted its order, but perceived that it was not completely safe because of the presence of willful, powerful cosmic powers that they identified with gods and goddesses.

With its numerous gods and goddesses animating all aspects of the universe, Mesopotamian religion was polytheistic in nature. The four most important deities were An, Enlil, Enki, and Ninhursaga. An was the god of the sky and hence the most important force in the universe. Since his basic essence was authority, he was also viewed as the source or active principle of all authority, including the earthly power of rulers and fathers alike. Enlil, god of wind, was considered the second greatest power of the visible universe. In charge of the wind and thus an expression of the legitimate use of force, Enlil became the symbol of the proper use of force on earth as well. Enki was god of the earth. Since the earth was the source of life-giving waters, Enki was also god of rivers, wells, and canals. More generally, he represented the waters of creativity and was responsible for inventions and crafts. Ninhursaga began as a goddess associated with soil, mountains, and vegetation. Eventually, however, she was worshiped as a mother goddess, a "mother of all children," who manifested her power by giving birth to kings and conferring the royal insignia upon them.

Human beings' relationship with the gods was based on subservience since, according to Sumerian myth, human beings were created to do the manual labor the gods were unwilling to do for themselves. Moreover, humans were insecure because they could never be sure of the gods' actions. But humans did make attempts to circumvent or relieve their anxiety by discovering the intentions of the gods; these efforts gave rise to the development of the arts of divination.

Divination took a variety of forms. A common form, at least for kings and priests who could afford it, involved killing animals, such as sheep or goats, and examining their livers or other organs. Supposedly, features seen in the organs of the sacrificed animals foretold events to come. Thus, one handbook states that if the animal organ has shape x, then the outcome of the military campaign will be y. Private individuals relied on cheaper divinatory techniques. These included interpreting patterns of smoke from burning incense or the pattern formed when oil was poured into water. The Mesopotamian arts of divination arose out of the desire to discover the purposes of the gods. If people could decipher the signs that foretold events, the events would be predictable and humans could act wisely.

THE CULTIVATION OF NEW ARTS AND SCIENCES

The realization of writing's great potential was another aspect of Mesopotamian culture. The oldest Mesopotamian texts date to around 3000 B.C.E. and were written by the Sumerians, who used a cuneiform ("wedge-

◆ **The Development of the Cuneiform System of Writing.** This table shows the evolution of eighteen representative signs from c. 3000 B.C.E. to 600 B.C.E. Examples: No. 1 is a picture of a star. The sign for star also meant heaven, sky, or god. No. 11 is a picture of a stream of water. The sign for water was also used for the word "in" because the Sumerian words for "water" and "in" sounded alike. No. 12 combines a picture of a head emphasizing the mouth with the sign for water. The compound sign represents a Sumerian word meaning to eat.

shaped") system of writing. Using a reed stylus, they made wedge-shaped impressions on clay tablets, which were then baked or dried in the sun. Once dried, these tablets were virtually indestructible, and the several hundred thousand that have been found so far have provided a valuable source of information for modern scholars. Sumerian writing evolved from pictures of concrete objects to simplified and stylized signs, leading eventually to a phonetic system that made possible the written expression of abstract ideas.

Mesopotamian peoples used writing primarily for record keeping. The most common cuneiform tablets record transactions of daily life: tallies of cattle kept by herdsmen for their owners, production figures, lists of taxes and wage payments, accounts, contracts, and court decisions affecting business life. There are also monumental texts, documents that were intended to last forever, such as inscriptions etched in stone on statues and royal buildings.

Still another category of cuneiform inscriptions includes the large body of basic texts produced for teaching purposes. Schools for scribes were in operation by 2500 B.C.E. They were necessary because considerable time was needed to master the cuneiform system of writing. The primary goal of scribal education was to produce professionally trained scribes for careers in the temples and palaces, the military, and government service. Pupils were male and primarily from wealthy families. Gradually, the schools became important centers for culture because Mesopotamian literature was utilized for instructional purposes.

Writing was important because it enabled a society to keep records and maintain knowledge of previous practices and events. Writing also made it possible for people to communicate ideas in new ways, which is especially evident in Mesopotamian literary works. The most famous piece of Mesopotamian literature was *The Epic of Gilgamesh,* an epic poem that records the exploits of a legendary king of Uruk. Gilgamesh, wise, strong and perfect in body, part man, part god, befriends a hairy beast named Enkidu. Together, they set off in pursuit of heroic deeds. When Enkidu dies, Gilgamesh experiences the pain of mortality and enters upon a search for the secret of immortality. But his efforts fail (see the box on p. 20). Gilgamesh remains mortal. The desire for immortality, one of humankind's great searches, ends in complete frustration. "Everlasting life," as this Mesopotamian epic makes clear, is only for the gods.

Peoples in Mesopotamia also made outstanding achievements in mathematics and astronomy. In math, the Sumerians devised a number system based on 60, using combinations of 6 and 10 for practical solutions.

Geometry was used to measure fields and erect buildings. In astronomy, the Sumerians made use of units of 60 and charted the heavenly constellations. Their calendar was based on twelve lunar months and was brought into harmony with the solar year by adding an extra month from time to time.

Egyptian Civilization: "The Gift of the Nile"

Although contemporaneous with Mesopotamia, civilization in Egypt evolved along somewhat different lines. Of central importance to the development of Egyptian civilization was the Nile River. That the Egyptian people recognized its significance is apparent in this Hymn to the Nile (also see the box on p. 21): "The bringer of food, rich in provisions, creator of all good, lord of majesty, sweet of fragrance. . . . He who . . . fills the magazines, makes the granaries wide, and gives things to the poor. He who makes every beloved tree to grow. . . ."[2] Egypt, like Mesopotamia, was a river valley civilization.

The Nile is a unique river, beginning in the heart of Africa and coursing northward for thousands of miles. It is the longest river in the world. The Nile was responsible for creating an area several miles wide on both banks of the river that was fertile and capable of producing abundant harvests. The "miracle" of the Nile was its annual flooding. The river rose in the summer from rains in central Africa, crested in Egypt in September and October, and left a deposit of silt that created an area of rich soil. The Egyptians called this fertile land the "Black Land," because it was dark in color from the silt and the lush crops that grew on it. Beyond these narrow strips of fertile fields lay the deserts (the "Red Land").

Unlike the floods of Mesopotamia's rivers, the flooding of the Nile was gradual and usually predictable, and the river itself was seen as life enhancing, not life threatening. Although a system of organized irrigation was still necessary, the small villages along the Nile could make the effort without the massive state intervention that was required in Mesopotamia. Egyptian civilization, consequently, tended to remain more rural with many small population centers congregated along a narrow band on both sides of the Nile. About one hundred miles before it empties into the Mediterranean, the river splits into two major branches, forming the delta, a triangular-shaped territory called Lower Egypt to distinguish it from Upper Egypt, the land upstream to the south. Egypt's important cities developed at the tip of the delta. Even today, most of Egypt's people are crowded along the banks of the Nile River.

≽ The Great Flood ≼

The great epic poem of Mesopotamian literature, The Epic of Gilgamesh, includes an account by Utnapishtim (a Mesopotamian version of the later biblical Noah), who had built a ship and survived the flood unleashed by the gods to destroy humankind. In this selection, Utnapishtim recounts his story to Gilgamesh, telling how the god Ea advised him to build a boat and how he came to land the boat at the end of the flood.

The Epic of Gilgamesh

"In those days the world teemed, the people multiplied, the world bellowed like a wild bull, and the great god was aroused by the clamor. Enlil heard the clamor and he said to the gods in council, 'The uproar of mankind is intolerable and sleep is no longer possible by reason of the babel.' So the gods agreed to exterminate mankind. Enlil did this, but Ea [Sumerian Enki, god of the waters] because of his oath warned me in a dream. . . . 'tear down your house and build a boat, abandon possessions and look for life, despise worldly goods and save your soul alive. Tear down your house, I say, and build a boat. . . . then take up into the boat the seed of all living creatures. . . .' [Utnapishtim did as he was told and then the destruction came.]

"For six days and six nights the winds blew, torrent and tempest and flood overwhelmed the world, tempest and flood raged together like warring hosts. When the seventh day dawned the storm from the south subsided, the sea grew calm, the flood was stilled; I looked at the face of the world and there was silence, all mankind was turned to clay. The surface of the sea stretched as flat as a roof-top; I opened a hatch and the light fell on my face. Then I bowed low, I sat down and I wept, the tears streamed down my face, for on every side was the waste of water. I looked for land in vain, but fourteen leagues distant there appeared a mountain, and there the boat grounded; on the mountain of Nisir the boat held fast, she held fast and did not budge. . . . When the seventh day dawned I loosed a dove and let her go. She flew away, but finding no resting-place she returned. Then I loosed a swallow, and she flew away but finding no resting-place she returned. I loosed a raven, she saw that the waters had retreated, she ate, she flew around, she cawed, and she did not come back. Then I threw everything open to the four winds, I made a sacrifice and poured out a libation on the mountain top."

The surpluses of food that Egyptian farmers grew in the fertile Nile valley made Egypt prosperous. But the Nile also served as a unifying factor in Egyptian history. In ancient times, the Nile was the fastest way to travel through the land, making both transportation and communication easier. Winds from the north pushed sailboats south, and the current of the Nile carried them north. Often when they headed downstream (or north), people used long poles or paddles to propel their boats forward.

Unlike Mesopotamia, which was subject to constant invasion, Egypt was blessed by natural barriers that fostered isolation, protected it from invasion, and gave it a sense of security. These barriers included the deserts to the west and east, the cataracts (rapids) on the southern part of the Nile, which made defense relatively easy, and the Mediterranean Sea to the north. These barriers, however, did not prevent the development of trade. Indeed, there is evidence of very early trade between Egypt and Mesopotamia itself.

In essence, Egyptian geography and topography played important roles in the early history of the country. The regularity of the Nile floods and the relative isolation of the Egyptians created a sense of security that was accompanied by a feeling of changelessness. Egyptian civilization was characterized by a remarkable degree of continuity over thousands of years. It was certainly no accident that Egyptians believed in cyclical rather than linear progress. Just as the sun passed through its daily cycle and the Nile its annual overflow, Egyptian kings reaffirmed the basic, unchanging principles of justice at the beginning of each new cycle of rule.

The Old and Middle Kingdoms

The basic framework for the study of Egyptian history was provided by Manetho, an Egyptian priest and historian who lived in the early third century B.C.E. He divided Egyptian history into thirty-one dynasties of kings. Based on Manetho and other king lists, modern historians have

≳ The Significance of the Nile River and the Pharaoh ≲

Two of the most important sources of life for the ancient Egyptians were the Nile River and the pharaoh. Egyptians perceived that the Nile River made possible the abundant food that was a major source of their well-being. This Hymn to the Nile, probably from the nineteenth and twentieth dynasties in the New Kingdom, expresses the gratitude Egyptians felt for the Nile.

Hymn to the Nile

Hail to you, O Nile, that issues from the earth and comes to keep Egypt alive! . . .

He that waters the meadows which Re created, in order to keep every kid alive.

He that makes to drink the desert and the place distant from water: that is his dew coming down from heaven. . . .

The lord of fishes, he who makes the marsh-birds to go upstream. . . .

He who makes barley and brings emmer into being, that he may make the temples festive.

If he is sluggish, then nostrils are stopped up, and everybody is poor. . . .

When he rises, then the land is in jubilation, then every belly is in joy, every backbone takes on laughter, and every tooth is exposed.

The bringer of good, rich in provisions, creator of all good, lord of majesty, sweet of fragrance. . . .

He who makes every beloved tree to grow, without lack of them.

The Egyptian king, or pharaoh, was viewed as a god and the absolute ruler of Egypt. His significance and the gratitude of the Egyptian people for his existence are evident in this hymn from the reign of Sesotris III (c. 1880–1840 B.C.E.).

Hymn to the Pharaoh

He has come unto us that he may carry away Upper Egypt; the double diadem [crown of Upper and Lower Egypt] has rested on his head.

He has come unto us and has united the Two Lands; he has mingled the reed with the bee [symbols of Lower and Upper Egypt].

He has come unto us and has brought the Black Land under his sway; he has apportioned to himself the Red Land.

He has come unto us and has taken the Two Lands under his protection; he has given peace to the Two Riverbanks.

He has come unto us and has made Egypt to live; he has banished its suffering.

He has come unto us and has made the people to live; he has caused the throat of the subjects to breathe. . . .

He has come unto us and has done battle for his boundaries; he has delivered them that were robbed.

divided Egyptian history into three major periods known as the Old Kingdom, Middle Kingdom, and New Kingdom. These were periods of long-term stability characterized by strong monarchical authority, competent bureaucracy, freedom from invasion, much construction of temples and pyramids, and considerable intellectual and cultural activity. But between the periods of stability were times of political chaos known as the Intermediate periods, which were characterized by weak political structures and rivalry for leadership, invasions, a decline in building activity, and a restructuring of society.

According to the Egyptians' own tradition, their land consisted initially of numerous populated areas ruled by tribal chieftains. Around 3100 B.C.E., the first Egyptian royal dynasty, under a king called Menes, united both Upper and Lower Egypt into a single kingdom. Henceforth, the king would be called "King of Upper and King of Lower Egypt," and the royal crown would be a double diadem, signifying the unification of all Egypt. Just as the Nile served to unite Upper and Lower Egypt physically, kingship served to unite the two areas politically.

The Old Kingdom encompassed the third through sixth dynasties of Egyptian kings, lasting from around 2700 to 2200 B.C.E. It was an age of prosperity and splendor, made visible in the construction of the greatest and largest pyramids in Egypt's history. The capital of the Old Kingdom was located at Memphis, south of the delta.

Kingship was a divine institution in ancient Egypt and formed part of a universal cosmic scheme (see the box above): "What is the king of Upper and Lower Egypt?

He is a god by whose dealings one lives, the father and mother of all men, alone by himself, without an equal."[3] In obeying their king, subjects helped to maintain the cosmic order. A breakdown in royal power could only mean that citizens were offending divinity and weakening the universal structure. Among the various titles of Egyptian kings, that of pharaoh (originally meaning "great house" or "palace") eventually came to be the most common.

Although they possessed absolute power, Egyptian kings were not supposed to rule arbitrarily, but according to set principles. The chief principle was called *Ma'at*, a spiritual precept that conveyed the idea of truth and justice, but especially right order and harmony. To ancient Egyptians, this fundamental order and harmony had existed throughout the universe since the beginning of time. Pharaohs were the divine instruments who maintained it and were themselves subject to it.

Although theoretically absolute in their power, in practice Egyptian kings did not rule alone. Initially, members of the king's family performed administrative tasks, but by the fourth dynasty a bureaucracy with regular procedures had developed. Especially important was the office of vizier, "steward of the whole land." Directly responsible to

Map 1.4   Ancient Egypt.

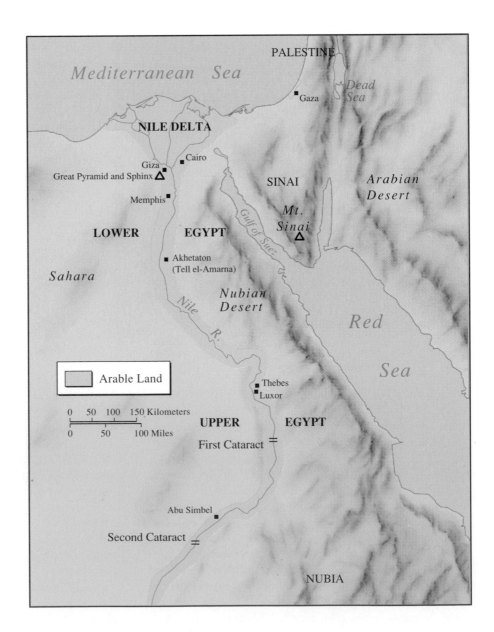

the king, the vizier was in charge of the bureaucracy with its numerous departments, such as police, justice, river transport, and public works. Agriculture and the treasury were the two most important departments. Agriculture was, of course, the backbone of Egyptian prosperity, and the treasury collected the taxes that were paid in kind. A careful assessment of land and tenants was undertaken to provide the tax base. For administrative purposes, Egypt was divided into provinces or nomes, as they were later called by the Greeks—twenty-two in Upper and twenty in Lower Egypt. A governor, called by the Greeks a nomarch, was head of each nome and was responsible to the king and vizier. Nomarchs, however, tended to build up large holdings of land and power within their nomes, creating a potential rivalry with the pharaohs.

Despite the theory of divine order, the Old Kingdom eventually collapsed, ushering in a period of chaos. Finally, a new royal dynasty managed to pacify all Egypt and inaugurated the Middle Kingdom, a new period of stability lasting from c. 2050 to 1652 B.C.E. Egyptians later portrayed the Middle Kingdom as a golden age, a clear indication of its stability. Several factors contributed to its vitality. The nome structure was reorganized. The boundaries of each nome were now settled precisely, and the obligations of the nomes to the state were clearly delineated. Nomarchs were confirmed as hereditary officeholders but with the understanding that their duties must be performed faithfully. These included the collection of taxes for the state and the recruitment of labor forces for royal projects, such as stone quarrying.

The Middle Kingdom was characterized by a new concern of the pharaohs for the people. In the Old Kingdom, the pharaoh had been viewed as an inaccessible god-king. Now he was portrayed as the shepherd of his people with the responsibility to build public works and provide for the public welfare. As one pharaoh expressed it: "He [a particular god] created me as one who should do that which he had done, and to carry out that which he commanded should be done. He appointed me herdsman of this land, for he knew who would keep it in order for him."[4]

Society and Economy in Ancient Egypt

Egyptian society had a simple structure in the Old and Middle Kingdoms; basically, it was organized along hierarchical lines with the god-king at the top. The king was surrounded by an upper class of nobles and priests who participated in the elaborate rituals of life that surrounded the pharaoh. This ruling class ran the government and managed its own landed estates, which provided much of its wealth.

Below the upper classes were merchants and artisans. Within Egypt, merchants engaged in an active trade up and down the Nile as well as in town and village markets. Some merchants also engaged in international trade; they were sent by the king to Crete and Syria where they obtained wood and other products. Expeditions traveled into Nubia for ivory and down the Red Sea to Punt for incense and spices. Egyptian artisans exhibited unusually

♦ **Pair Statue of King Menkaure and His Queen.** The period designated as the Old Kingdom began approximately four centuries after Egypt's unification (c. 3100 B.C.E.) and lasted until approximately 2200 B.C.E. The kings of Egypt (eventually called "pharaohs") were regarded as gods, divine instruments who maintained the fundamental order and harmony of the universe and wielded absolute power. This statue depicts King Menkaure and his queen (Dynasty IV).

The Egyptians

Early Dynastic (Dynasties 1–2)	c. 3100–2700 B.C.E.
Old Kingdom (Dynasties 3–6)	c. 2700–2200 B.C.E.
First Intermediate Period (Dynasties 7–10)	c. 2200–2050 B.C.E.
Middle Kingdom (Dynasties 11–12)	c. 2050–1652 B.C.E.
Second Intermediate Period (Dynasties 13–17)	c. 1652–1567 B.C.E.
New Kingdom (Dynasties 18–20)	c. 1567–1085 B.C.E.
Post-Empire (Dynasties 21–31)	c. 1085–30 B.C.E.

high standards of craftsmanship and physical beauty, while producing an incredible variety of goods: stone dishes; beautifully painted boxes made of clay; wooden furniture; gold, silver, and copper tools and containers; paper and rope made of papyrus; and linen clothes.

By far, the largest number of people in Egypt simply worked the land. In theory, the king owned all the land, but granted out portions of it to his subjects. Large sections were in the possession of nobles and the temple complexes. Moreover, although free farmers who owned their own land had once existed, by the end of the Old Kingdom, this group had disappeared. Most of the lower classes were serfs, or common people bound to the land, who cultivated the estates. They paid taxes in the form of crops to the king, nobles, and priests, lived in small villages or towns, and provided military service and forced labor for building projects.

The Culture of Egypt

Egypt produced a culture that dazzled and awed its later conquerors. The Egyptians' technical achievements alone, especially visible in the construction of the pyramids, demonstrated a measure of skill unequaled in the world at that time. To the Egyptians, all of these achievements were part of a cosmic order suffused with the presence of the divine.

SPIRITUAL LIFE IN EGYPTIAN SOCIETY

The Egyptians had no word for religion, because it was an inseparable element of the entire world order to which Egyptian society belonged. The Egyptians possessed a remarkable number of gods associated with heavenly bodies and natural forces. Two groups, sun gods and land gods, came to have special prominence, hardly unusual in view of the importance of the sun, the river, and the fertile land along its banks to Egypt's well-being. The sun was the source of life and hence worthy of worship. A sun cult developed, and the sun god took on different forms and names, depending on his specific function. He was worshiped as Atum in human form and as Re, who had a human body but the head of a falcon. The pharaoh took the title of "Son of Re," since he was regarded as the earthly embodiment of Re. Eventually, Re became associated with Amon, an air god of Thebes, as Amon-Re.

River and land deities included Osiris and Isis with their child Horus, who was related to the Nile and to the sun as well. Osiris became especially important as a symbol of resurrection or rebirth. A famous Egyptian myth told of the struggle between Osiris, who brought civilization to Egypt, and his evil brother Seth, who killed him, cut his body into fourteen parts, and tossed them into the Nile River. Osiris's faithful wife Isis found the pieces and, with help from other gods, restored Osiris to life. Their son Horus avenged his father by castrating Seth. As a symbol of resurrection and judge of the dead, Osiris took on an important role for the Egyptians. By identifying with Osiris, one could hope to gain new life, just as Osiris had done. The dead, embalmed and mummified, were placed in tombs (in the case of kings, in pyramidal tombs), given the name of Osiris, and, by a process of magical identification, became Osiris. Like Osiris, they would then be reborn. The flood of the Nile and the new life it brought to Egypt were symbolized by Isis gathering all of Osiris's parts together and were celebrated each spring in the festival of the new land.

Later Egyptian spiritual practice began to emphasize morality by stressing Osiris's role as judge of the dead. The dead were asked to give an account of their earthly deeds to show whether they deserved a reward. Other means were also employed to gain immortality. Magical incantations, preserved in the *Book of the Dead*, were used to ensure a favorable journey to a happy afterlife. Specific instructions explained what to do when confronted by the judge of the dead. These instructions had two aspects. The negative confession gave a detailed list of what one had not done:

What is said on reaching the Broad-Hall of the Two Justices [the place of the next-world judgment], absolving X [the name and title of the deceased] of every sin which he had committed. . . .

> I have not committed evil against men.
> I have not mistreated cattle.
> I have not blasphemed a god. . . .
> I have not done violence to a poor man.
> I have not done that which the gods abominate.
> I have not defamed a slave to his superior.
> I have not made anyone sick.
> I have not made anyone weep.
> I have not killed. . . .
> I have not caused anyone suffering. . . .
> I have not had sexual relations with a boy.
> I have not defiled myself. . . .[5]

Later the suppliant made a speech listing his good actions: "I have done that which men said and that with which gods are content. . . . I have given bread to the hungry, water to the thirsty, clothing to the naked, and a ferry-boat to him who was marooned. I have provided divine offerings for the gods and mortuary offerings for the dead."[6]

At first the Osiris cult was reserved for the very wealthy who could afford to take expensive measures to preserve the body after death. During the Middle Kingdom, however, the cult became "democratized"—extended to all Egyptians who aspired to an afterlife.

THE PYRAMIDS

One of the great achievements of Egyptian civilization, the building of pyramids, occurred in the time of the Old Kingdom. Pyramids were not built in isolation but as part of a larger complex dedicated to the dead, in effect, a city of the dead. The area included a large pyramid for the king's burial, smaller pyramids for his family, and mastabas, rectangular structures with flat roofs, as tombs for the pharaoh's noble officials. The tombs were well prepared for their residents. The rooms were furnished and stocked with numerous supplies, including chairs, boats, chests, weapons, games, dishes, and a variety of foods. The Egyptians believed that human beings had two bodies, a physical one and a spiritual one, which they called the *ka*. If the physical body was properly preserved (hence mummification) and the tomb furnished with all the various objects of regular life, the *ka* could return and continue its life despite the death of the physical body. A pyramid was not only the king's tomb, it was also an important symbol of royal power. It could be seen for miles

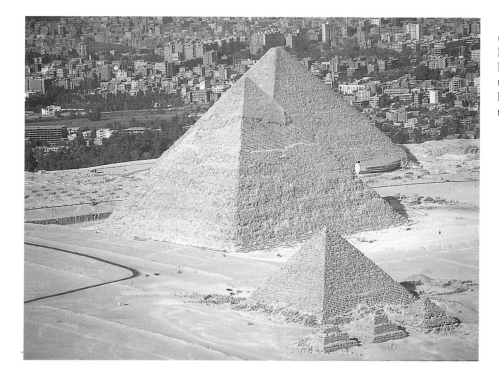

♦ **The Great Pyramid of Giza.** The three pyramids at Giza, across the Nile River from Cairo, are the most famous in Egypt. Pyramids served as tombs for both the king and his immediate family. The largest of the three pyramids at Giza is the Great Pyramid of Khufu.

away as a visible reminder of the glory and might of the ruler who was a living god on earth.

The largest and most magnificent of all the pyramids was built under King Khufu. Constructed at Giza around 2540 B.C.E., this famous Great Pyramid covers thirteen acres, measures 756 feet at each side of its base, and stands 481 feet high. Its four sides are almost precisely oriented to the four points of the compass. The interior included a grand gallery to the burial chamber, which was built of granite with a lidless sarcophagus for the pharaoh's body. The Great Pyramid still stands as a visible symbol of the power of Egyptian kings and the spiritual conviction that underlay Egyptian society. No pyramid built later ever matched its size or splendor.

ART AND WRITING

Commissioned by kings or nobles for use in temples and tombs, Egyptian art was largely functional. Wall paintings and statues of gods and kings in temples served a strictly spiritual purpose. They were an integral part of the performance of ritual, which was thought necessary to preserve the cosmic order and hence the well-being of Egypt. Likewise, the mural scenes and sculptured figures found in the tombs had a specific function. They were supposed to assist the journey of the deceased into the afterworld.

Egyptian art was also formulaic. Artists and sculptors were expected to observe a strict canon of proportions that determined both form and presentation. This canon gave Egyptian art a distinctive appearance for thousands of years. Especially characteristic was the convention of combining the profile, semiprofile, and frontal views of the human body in relief work and painting in order to represent each part of the body accurately. The result was an art that was highly stylized, yet still allowed distinctive features to be displayed.

Writing emerged in Egypt during the first two dynasties. The Greeks later labeled Egyptian writing hieroglyphics, meaning "priest-carvings" or "sacred writings." Hieroglyphs were sacred characters used as picture signs that depicted objects and had a sacred value at the same time. Although hieroglyphs were later simplified into two scripts for writing purposes, they never developed into an alphabet. Egyptian hieroglyphs were initially carved in stone, but later the two simplified scripts were written on papyrus, a paper made from the papyrus reed that grew along the Nile. Most of the ancient Egyptian literature that has come down to us was written on papyrus rolls and wooden tablets.

Chaos and a New Order: The New Kingdom

The Middle Kingdom came to an end in the midst of another period of instability. An incursion into the delta region by a people known as the Hyksos initiated this second age of chaos. The Hyksos were part of a larger group of peoples who spoke Semitic languages and originally lived in the Arabian peninsula. Some of these Semitic-speaking peoples had moved into northern Mesopotamia as well as Syria and Palestine. The Hyksos infiltrated Egypt in the seventeenth century B.C.E. and came to dominate much of the country. However, the presence of the Hyksos was not entirely negative for Egypt. They introduced Egypt to Bronze Age technology by teaching the Egyptians how to make bronze for use in new agricultural tools and weapons. More significantly, the Hyksos introduced new aspects of warfare to Egypt, including the horse-drawn war chariot, a heavier sword, and the compound bow. Eventually, a new line of pharaohs—the eighteenth dynasty—made use of the new weapons to throw off Hyksos domination, reunite Egypt, establish the New Kingdom (c. 1567–1085 B.C.E.), and launch the Egyptians along a new militaristic and imperialistic path. During the period of the New Kingdom, Egypt became the most powerful state in the Middle East. The Egyptians occupied Palestine and Syria, but permitted the local native princes to continue to rule under Egyptian control. Egyptian armies also moved westward into Libya. The achievements of the empire were made visible in the construction of magnificent new buildings and temples, especially the temple centers at Karnak and Luxor.

The eighteenth dynasty was not without its own troubles, however. Amenhotep IV (c. 1364–1347 B.C.E.) introduced the worship of Aton, god of the sun disk, as the chief god (see the box on p. 27) and pursued his worship with great enthusiasm. Changing his own name to Akhenaten ("It is well with Aton"), the pharaoh closed the temples of other gods and especially endeavored to lessen the power of Amon-Re and his priesthood at Thebes. Akhenaten strove to reduce their influence by replacing Thebes as the capital of Egypt with Akhetaton ("dedicated to Aton"), a new city located near modern Tell el-Amarna, two hundred miles north of Thebes.

Akhenaten's attempt at religious change proved to be a failure. It was too much to ask Egyptians to give up their traditional ways and beliefs, especially since they saw the destruction of the old gods as subversive of the very cosmic order upon which Egypt's survival and continuing prosperity depended. Moreover, the priests at Thebes were unalterably opposed to the changes, which had diminished their influence and power. At the same time, Akhenaten's preoccupation with religion caused him to

⇒ Akhenaten's Hymn to Aton ⇐

Amenhotep IV, more commonly known as Akhenaten, created a religious upheaval in Egypt by introducing the worship of Aton, god of the sun disk, as the sole god. Akhenaten's attitude to Aton is seen in this hymn. Some authorities have noted a similarity in spirit and wording to the 104th Psalm of the Old Testament.

Hymn to Aton

Your rays suckle every meadow.
When you rise, they live, they grow for you.
You make the seasons in order to rear all that you have
    made,
The winter to cool them,
And the heat that they may taste you.
You have made the distant sky in order to rise therein,
In order to see all that you do make.
While you were alone,
Rising in your form as the living Aton,
Appearing, shining, withdrawing or approaching,
You made millions of forms of yourself alone.

Cities, towns, fields, road, and river—
Every eye beholds you over against them,
For you are the Aton of the day over the earth. . . .
The world came into being by your hand,
According as you have made them.
When you have risen they live,
When you set they die.
You are lifetime your own self,
For one lives only through you.
Eyes are fixed on beauty until you set.
All work is laid aside when you set in the west.
But when you rise again,
Everything is made to flourish for the king, . . .
Since you did found the earth
And raise them up for your son,
Who came forth from your body:
    the King of Upper and Lower Egypt, . . .
    Akh-en-Aton, . . . and the Chief Wife of the King . . .
    Nefert-iti, living and youthful forever and ever.

---

ignore foreign affairs and led to the loss of both Syria and Palestine. Akhenaten's changes were soon undone after his death by those who influenced his successor, the boy-pharaoh Tutankhamon (1347–1338 B.C.E.). Tutankhamon returned the government to Thebes and restored the old gods. The Aton experiment had failed to take hold, and the eighteenth dynasty itself came to an end in 1333.

The nineteenth dynasty managed to restore Egyptian power one more time. Under Rameses II (c. 1279–1213 B.C.E.), the Egyptians regained control of Palestine but were unable to reestablish the borders of their earlier empire. New invasions in the thirteenth century by the "Sea Peoples," as Egyptians called them, destroyed Egyptian power in Palestine and drove the Egyptians back within their old frontiers. The days of Egyptian empire were ended, and the New Kingdom itself expired with the end of the twentieth dynasty in 1085. For the next thousand years, despite periodical revivals of strength, Egypt was dominated by Libyans, Nubians, Persians, and finally Macedonians after the conquest of Alexander the Great

(see Chapter 4). In the first century B.C.E., Egypt became a province in Rome's mighty empire. Egypt continued, however, to influence its conquerors by the richness of its heritage and the awesome magnificence of its physical remains.

Daily Life in Ancient Egypt: Family and Marriage

Ancient Egyptians had a very positive attitude toward daily life on earth and followed the advice of the wisdom literature, which suggested that people marry young and establish a home and family. Monogamy was the general rule, although a husband was allowed to keep additional wives if his first wife was childless. Pharaohs, of course, were entitled to harems. The queen was acknowledged, however, as the Great Wife with a status higher than that of the other wives. The husband was master in the house, but wives were very much respected and in charge of the household and education of the children. From a book of wise sayings (which the Egyptians called "instructions") came this advice:

> If you are a man of standing, you should found your household and love your wife at home as is fitting. Fill her belly; clothe her back. Ointment is the prescription for her body. Make her heart glad as long as you live. She is a profitable field for her lord. You should not contend with her at law, and keep her far from gaining control. . . . Let her heart be soothed through what may accrue to you; it means keeping her long in your house.[7]

Women's property and inheritance remained in their hands, even in marriage. Although most careers and public offices were closed to women, some did operate businesses. Peasant women worked long hours in the fields and at numerous domestic tasks. Upper-class women could function as priestesses, and some queens even became pharaohs in their own right. The most famous was Hatshepsut in the New Kingdom.

Little is known about marital arrangements and ceremonies although it does appear that marriages were arranged by parents. The primary concerns were family and property, and clearly the chief purpose of marriage was to produce children, especially sons. From the New Kingdom came this piece of wisdom: "Take to yourself a wife while you are [still] a youth, that she may produce a son for you."[8] Only sons could carry on the family name. Daughters were not slighted, however. Numerous tomb paintings show the close and affectionate relationship parents had with both sons and daughters. Although marriages were arranged, some of the surviving love poems from ancient Egypt suggest that some marriages included an element of romance. Here is the lament of a lovesick boy for his "sister" (lovers referred to each other as "brother" and "sister"):

> Seven days to yesterday I have not seen the sister, and a sickness has invaded me;
> My body has become heavy,
> And I am forgetful of my own self.
> If the chief physicians come to me,
> My heart is not content with their remedies. . . .
> What will revive me is to say to me: "Here she is!"
> Her name is what will lift me up. . . .
> My health is her coming in from outside:
> When I see her, then I am well.[9]

◆ **A Hunting Scene.**   A favorite pastime of the Egyptian upper classes was hunting waterfowl in the stands of papyrus reeds that grew along the riverbanks. This tomb painting shows a wealthy Egyptian with members of his family hunting geese with throwsticks.

Marriages could and did end in divorce, which was allowed, apparently with compensation for the wife. Adultery, however, was strictly prohibited with stiff punishments, especially for women who could have their noses cut off or be burned at the stake.

New Centers of Civilization

Our story of civilization so far has been dominated by Mesopotamia and Egypt. But significant developments were also taking place on the fringes of these civilizations. Farming had spread into the Balkan peninsula of Europe by 6500 B.C.E., and by 4000 B.C.E., it was well established in southern France, central Europe, and the coastal regions of the Mediterranean. Although migrating farmers from the Middle East may have brought some farming techniques into Europe, historians now believe that the Neolithic peoples of Europe domesticated animals and began to farm largely on their own.

One outstanding feature of late Neolithic Europe was the building of megalithic structures. Megalith is Greek for "large stone." Radiocarbon dating, a technique that allows scientists to determine the ages of objects, shows that the first megalithic structures were built around 4000 B.C.E., more than a thousand years before the great pyramids were built in Egypt. Between 3200 and 1500 B.C.E., standing stones that were placed in circles or lined up in rows were erected throughout the British Isles and northwestern France. Other megalithic constructions have been found as far north as Scandinavia and as far south as the islands of Corsica, Sardinia, and Malta. Some archaeologists have demonstrated that the stone circles were used as observatories to detect not only such simple astronomical phenomena as midwinter and midsummer sunrises, but also such sophisticated observations as the major and minor standstills of the moon.

By far, the most famous of these megalithic constructions is Stonehenge in England. Stonehenge consists of a series of concentric rings of standing stones. Its construction sometime between 2100 and 1900 B.C.E. was no small accomplishment. The eighty bluestones used at Stonehenge, for example, weighed four tons each and were transported to the site from their original source, 135 miles away. Like other megalithic structures, Stonehenge indicates a remarkable awareness of astronomy on the part of its builders, as well as an elaborate coordination of workers.

✦ **Stonehenge.** The Bronze Age in northwestern Europe is known for its "megaliths," or large standing stones. Between 3200 and 1500 B.C.E., standing stones placed in circles or lined up in rows were erected throughout the British Isles and northwestern France. By far, the most famous of these megalithic constructions was Stonehenge in England.

The Impact of the Indo-Europeans

In large part, both the details of construction and the purpose of the megalithic structures of Europe remain a mystery. Also puzzling is the role of the Indo-European peoples. The term *Indo-European* refers to people who used a language derived from a single parent tongue. Indo-European languages include Greek, Latin, Persian, Sanskrit, and the Germanic and Slavic languages (see Table 1.2). It has been suggested that the original Indo-European—speaking peoples were based somewhere in the steppe region north of the Black Sea or in southwestern Asia, in modern Iran or Afghanistan. Although there had been earlier migrations, around 2000 B.C.E. they began major nomadic movements into Europe (including present-day Italy and Greece), India, and western Asia. One group of Indo-Europeans who moved into Asia Minor and Anatolia (modern Turkey) around 1750 B.C.E. coalesced with the native peoples to form the Hittite kingdom with its capital at Hattusha (Bogazköy in modern Turkey).

Between 1600 and 1200 B.C.E., the Hittites created their own empire in western Asia and even threatened the power of the Egyptians. The Hittites were the first of the Indo-European peoples to make use of iron, enabling them to construct weapons that were stronger and cheaper to make because of the widespread availability of iron ore. But around 1200 B.C.E., new waves of invading Indo-European peoples destroyed the Hittite empire. The destruction of the Hittite kingdom and the weakening of Egypt around 1200 B.C.E. temporarily left no dominant powers in western Asia, allowing a patchwork of petty kingdoms and city-states to emerge, especially in the area of Syria and Palestine. The Phoenicians were one of these peoples.

The Phoenicians

A Semitic-speaking people, the Phoenicians lived in the area of Palestine along the Mediterranean coast on a narrow band of land 120 miles long. Their newfound political independence after the demise of Hittite and Egyptian power helped the Phoenicians expand the trade that was already the foundation of their prosperity. The chief cities of Phoenicia—Byblos, Tyre, and Sidon—were ports on the eastern Mediterranean, but they also served as distribution centers for the lands to the east in Mesopotamia. The Phoenicians themselves produced a number of goods for foreign markets, including purple dye, glass, wine, and lumber from the famous cedars of Lebanon. In addition, the Phoenicians improved their ships and became great international sea traders. They charted new routes, not only in the Mediterranean, but also in the Atlantic Ocean where they reached Britain and sailed south along the west coast of Africa. The Phoenicians established a number of colonies in the western Mediterranean, including settlements in southern Spain, Sicily, and Sardinia. Carthage, the Phoenicians' most famous colony, was located on the North African coast.

Culturally, the Phoenicians are best known as transmitters. Instead of using pictographs or signs to represent whole words and syllables as the Mesopotamians and Egyptians did, the Phoenicians simplified their writing by using twenty-two different signs to represent the sounds of their speech. These twenty-two characters or letters could be used to spell out all the words in the Phoenician language. Although the Phoenicians were not the only people to invent an alphabet, theirs would have special significance because it was eventually passed on to the Greeks. From the Greek alphabet was derived the Roman alphabet that we still use today. The Phoenicians achieved much while independent, but they ultimately fell subject to the Assyrians and Persians.

The Hebrews: The "Children of Israel"

To the south of the Phoenicians lived another group of Semitic-speaking people known as the Hebrews. Although they were a minor factor in the politics of the region, their religion—known as Judaism—influenced both Christianity and Islam and flourished as a world religion. The Hebrews had a tradition concerning their origins and history that was eventually written down as part of the Hebrew Bible, known to Christians as the Old Testament. The Hebrews' own tradition states that they were descendants of the patriarch Abraham who had migrated from Mesopotamia to the land of Palestine, where they became identified as the "Children of Israel." The Hebrews were a nomadic people, organized along tribal lines, who followed a lifestyle based on grazing flocks and herds rather than farming. According to tradition, because of drought the Hebrews migrated to Egypt where they lived peacefully until a pharaoh enslaved them. Thereafter, they remained in bondage until Moses led his

❖ **Table 1.2**   *Some Indo-European Languages*

Subfamily	Languages
Indo-Iranian	*Sanskrit*, Persian
Balto-Slavic	Russian, Serbo-Croatian, Czech, Polish, Lithuanian
Hellenic	Greek
Italic	*Latin*, romance languages (French, Italian, Spanish, Portuguese, Romanian)
Celtic	Irish, Gaelic
Germanic	Swedish, Danish, Norwegian, German, Dutch, English

Note: Languages in italic type are dead languages.

people out of Egypt in the well-known "exodus." Some historians believe this would have occurred in the first half of the thirteenth century B.C.E. The Hebrews then wandered for many years in the desert until they entered Palestine (possibly around 1220 B.C.E.), where they became involved in a lengthy conflict with the Canaanites, who were already settled there. Around 1000 B.C.E., under the pressure of the ongoing struggle with the Philistines, the Hebrews embarked upon the establishment of a monarchy.

The creation of a monarchy was not an easy task because many Hebrews were still accustomed to tribal life and tribal organization. By the time of King Solomon (c. 971–931 B.C.E.), however, the Hebrews had established control over all of Palestine and made Jerusalem into the capital of a united kingdom. The formerly nomadic Hebrews had become a settled community based on farming

Map 1.5 Ancient Palestine.

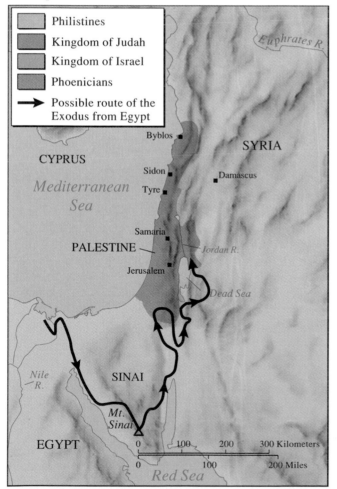

Philistines
Kingdom of Judah
Kingdom of Israel
Phoenicians
→ Possible route of the Exodus from Egypt

and urban life, and centralized political organization had replaced the independent ways of the twelve Hebrew tribes. Solomon did even more to strengthen royal power. He expanded the political and military establishments and was especially active in extending the trading activities of the Hebrews. Solomon is best known for his building projects, of which the most famous was the Temple in the city of Jerusalem. The Hebrews viewed the Temple as the symbolic center of their religion, and hence of the Hebrew kingdom itself. The Temple now housed the Ark of the Covenant, the holy chest containing the sacred relics of the Hebrew religion and, symbolically, the throne of the invisible God of Israel. Under Solomon, ancient Israel was at the height of its power, but his efforts to centralize royal power along the lines of Mesopotamian despotism led to dissatisfaction among his subjects, who believed that his actions threatened the old Hebrew tribal ties.

After Solomon's death, the tension between the northern and southern Hebrew tribes led to the establishment of two separate kingdoms—a kingdom of Israel, composed of the ten northern tribes with its capital at Samaria, and a southern kingdom of Judah, consisting of two tribes with its capital at Jerusalem. By the end of the ninth century, the independence of the kingdom of Israel was increasingly threatened by the rising power of the Assyrians. In 722 B.C.E., the Assyrians destroyed Samaria, overran the kingdom of Israel, and deported many Hebrews to other parts of the Assyrian Empire. These dispersed Hebrews (the "ten lost tribes") merged with neighboring peoples and gradually lost their identity.

The southern kingdom of Judah was also forced to pay tribute to Assyria but managed to retain its independence as Assyrian power declined. A new enemy, however, appeared on the horizon. The Chaldeans brought the final destruction of Assyria, conquered the kingdom of Judah, and completely destroyed Jerusalem in 586 B.C.E. Many upper-class Hebrews were deported to Babylonia; the memory of their exile is still evoked in the stirring words of Psalm 137:

> By the rivers of Babylon, we sat and wept when we
>   remembered Zion. . . .
> How can we sing the songs of the Lord while in a foreign
>   land?
> If I forget you, O Jerusalem, may my right hand forget its
>   skill.
> May my tongue cling to the roof of my mouth if I do not
>   remember you,
> if I do not consider Jerusalem my highest joy.[10]

But the Babylonian captivity of the Hebrew people did not last. A new set of conquerors, the Persians, destroyed the Chaldean kingdom and allowed the Hebrews to return to Jerusalem and rebuild their city and temple. The revived kingdom of Judah remained under Persian control until the conquests of Alexander the Great in the fourth century B.C.E. The people of Judah survived, even-

◆ **The King of Israel Pays Tribute to the King of Assyria.**
By the end of the ninth century B.C.E., the kingdom of Israel had been forced to pay tribute to the Assyrian Empire. The Assyrians overran the kingdom in 722 B.C.E. and destroyed the capital city of Samaria. In this scene from a black obelisk, Jehu, king of Israel, is shown paying tribute to the king of Assyria.

tually becoming known as the Jews and giving their name to Judaism, the religion of Yahweh, the Jewish God.

THE SPIRITUAL DIMENSIONS OF ISRAEL

The spiritual outlook of the earliest ancestors of the Hebrews was polytheistic, but by the time they had returned to Palestine after their captivity in Egypt, the Hebrew version of monotheism had begun to emerge. According to the Hebrew conception, there is but one God, whom the Hebrews called YHWH, which by convention is written Yahweh. God is the creator of the world and everything in it. Indeed, Yahweh means "he causes to be." All the gods of all other peoples were simply idols. The Hebrew God was totally sovereign and ruled the world; he was subject to nothing. All peoples were his servants, whether they knew it or not. This God was also transcendent. He had created nature, but was not in nature. The stars, moon, rivers, wind, and other natural phenomena were not divinities or suffused with divinity, but God's handiwork. All of God's creations could be admired for their awesome beauty, but not worshiped as God.

This omnipotent creator of the universe was not removed from the life he had created, however, but was a just and good God who expected goodness from his people. If they did not obey his will, they would be punished. But he was also a God of mercy and love: "The Lord is gracious and compassionate, slow to anger and rich in love. The Lord is good to all; he has compassion on all he has made."[11]

The Hebrew spiritual perspective also emphasized individual worth. Each person, possessed of moral freedom, had the ability to choose between good and evil. But an important condition was attached to this freedom. People could not simply establish their own ethical standards. Through Moses and other holy men, God had made known his commandments, his ideals of behavior. True freedom consisted of accepting God's ethical norms voluntarily. If people chose to ignore the good, then suffering and evil would follow. Despite the awesome dimensions of God as creator and sustainer of the universe, the Hebrew message also emphasized that each person could have a personal relationship with this powerful being. As the psalmist sang: "My help comes from the Lord, the Maker of heaven and earth. He will not let your foot slip—he who watches over you will not slumber."[12]

The Hebrew conception of God was closely related to three aspects of the Hebrew religious tradition that have special significance: the covenant, law, and the prophets. During the exodus from Egypt, when Moses led his peo-

≋ The Covenant and the Law: The Book of Exodus ≋

During the exodus from Egypt, the Hebrews supposedly made their covenant with Yahweh. They agreed to obey their God and follow his law. In return, Yahweh promised to take special care of his chosen people. This selection from the book of Exodus describes the making of the covenant and God's commandments to the Hebrews.

Exodus 19: 1–8

In the third month after the Israelites left Egypt—on the very day—they came to the Desert of Sinai. After they set out from Rephidim, they entered the desert of Sinai, and Israel camped there in the desert in front of the mountain. Then Moses went up to God, and the Lord called to him from the mountain, and said, "This is what you are to say to the house of Jacob and what you are to tell the people of Israel: 'You yourselves have seen what I did to Egypt, and how I carried you on eagles' wings and brought you to myself. Now if you obey me fully and keep my covenant, then out of all nations you will be my treasured possession. Although the whole earth is mine, you will be for me a kingdom of priests and a holy nation.' These are the words you are to speak to the Israelites." So Moses went back and summoned the elders of the people and set before them all the words the Lord had commanded him to speak. The people all responded together, "We will do everything the Lord has said." So Moses brought their answer back to the Lord.

Exodus 20: 1–3, 7–17

And God spoke all these words, "I am the Lord your God, who brought you out of Egypt, out of the land of slavery. You shall have no other gods before me. . . . You shall not misuse the name of the Lord your God, for the Lord will not hold anyone guiltless who misuses his name. Remember the Sabbath day by keeping it holy. Six days you shall labor and do all your work, but the seventh day is a Sabbath to the Lord your God. On it you shall not do any work, neither you, nor your son or daughter, nor your manservant or maidservant, nor your animals, nor the alien within your gates. For in six days the Lord made the heavens and the earth, the sea, and all that is in them, but he rested on the seventh day. Therefore the Lord blessed the Sabbath day and made it holy. Honor your father and your mother, so that you may live long in the land the Lord your God is giving you. You shall not murder. You shall not commit adultery. You shall not steal. You shall not give false testimony against your neighbor. You shall not covet your neighbor's house. You shall not covet your neighbor's wife, or his manservant or maidservant, his ox or donkey, or anything that belongs to your neighbor."

---

ple out of bondage into the promised land, a special event supposedly occurred that determined the Hebrew experience for all time. According to tradition, God entered into a covenant or contract with the tribes of Israel who believed that Yahweh had spoken to them through Moses (see the box above). The Hebrews promised to obey Yahweh and follow his law. In return, Yahweh promised to take special care of his chosen people, "a peculiar treasure unto me above all people."

This covenant between Yahweh and his chosen people could be fulfilled, however, only by Hebrew obedience to the law of God. Law became a crucial element of the Hebrew world and had a number of different dimensions. In some instances, it set forth specific requirements, such as payments for offenses. Most important, since the major characteristic of God was his goodness, were the ethical concerns that stood at the center of the law. Sometimes these took the form of specific standards of moral behavior: "You shall not murder. You shall not commit adultery. You shall not steal."[13] But these concerns were also expressed in decrees that regulated the economic, social, and political life of the community since God's laws of morality applied to all areas of life. These laws made no distinctions between classes and emphasized the protection of the poor, widows, orphans, and slaves.

The prophets were "holy men" who supposedly had special communion with God and felt called upon to serve as his voice to his people. In the ninth century B.C.E., the prophets were particularly vociferous about the tendency of the Hebrews to accept other gods, chiefly the fertility and earth gods of other peoples in Palestine. The prophets warned of the terrible retribution that God would exact from the Hebrews if they did not keep the covenant to remain faithful to him alone and just in their dealings with one another (see the box above).

⇒ The Hebrew Prophets: Isaiah and Amos ⇐

The Hebrew prophets warned the Hebrew people that they must obey God's commandments or face being punished for breaking their covenant with God. These selections from the prophets Isaiah and Amos make clear that God's punishment would fall upon the Hebrews for their sins. Even the Assyrians, as Isaiah indicated, would be used as God's instrument to punish them.

Isaiah 3: 14–17, 24–26

The Lord enters into judgment against the elders and leaders of his people: "It is you who have ruined my vineyard; the plunder from the poor is in your houses. What do you mean by crushing my people and grinding the faces of the poor?" declares the Lord, the Lord Almighty. The Lord says, "The women of Zion are haughty, walking along with outstretched necks, flirting with their eyes, tripping along with mincing steps, with ornaments jingling on their ankles. Therefore the Lord will bring sores on the heads of the women of Zion; the Lord will make their scalps bald. . . ." Instead of fragrance there will be a stench; instead of a sash, a rope; instead of well-dressed hair, baldness; instead of fine clothing, sackcloth; instead of beauty, branding. Your men will fall by the sword, your warriors in battle. The gates of Zion will lament and mourn; destitute, she will sit on the ground.

Isaiah 10: 1–6

Woe to those who make unjust laws, to those who issue oppressive decrees, to deprive the poor of their rights and withhold justice from the oppressed of my people, making widows their prey and robbing the fatherless. What will you do on the day of reckoning, when disaster comes from afar? To whom will you run for help? Where will you leave your riches? Nothing will remain but to cringe among the captives or fall among the slain. Yet for all this, his anger is not turned away, his hand is still upraised. "Woe to the Assyrian, the rod of my anger, in whose hand is the club of my wrath! I send him against a godless nation, I dispatch him against a people who anger me, to seize loot and snatch plunder, and to trample them down like mud in the streets."

Amos 3: 1–2

Hear this word the Lord has spoken against you, O people of Israel—against the whole family I brought up out of Egypt: "You only have I chosen of all the families of the earth; therefore I will punish you for all your sins."

The golden age of prophecy began in the mid-eighth century and continued during the time when the Hebrews were threatened by Assyrian and Chaldean conquerors. The "men of God" went through the land warning the Hebrews that they had failed to keep God's commandments and would be punished for breaking the covenant: "I will punish you for all your iniquities." Amos prophesied the fall of the northern kingdom of Israel to Assyria; twenty years later, Isaiah said the kingdom of Judah too would fall.

Out of the words of the prophets came new concepts that enriched the Hebrew tradition, including a notion of universalism and a yearning for social justice. Although Hebrew religious practices gave Jews a sense of separateness from other peoples, the prophets transcended this by embracing a concern for all humanity. All nations would someday come to the God of Israel: "all the earth shall worship thee." A universal community of all people under God would someday be established through Israel's efforts. This vision encompassed the elimination of war and the establishment of peace for all the nations of the world. In the words of the prophet Isaiah: "He will judge between the nations and will settle disputes for many people. They will beat their swords into plowshares and their spears into pruning hooks. Nation will not take up sword against nation, nor will they train for war anymore."[14]

The prophets also cried out against social injustice. They condemned the rich for causing the poor to suffer, denounced luxuries as worthless, and threatened Israel with prophecies of dire punishments for these sins. God's command was to live justly, share with one's neighbors, care for the poor and the unfortunate, and act with compassion. When God's command was not followed, the social fabric of the community was threatened. These proclamations by Israel's prophets became a source for universal ideals of social justice, even if they have never been perfectly realized.

UNIQUENESS OF THE HEBREW RELIGION

The Hebrew religion was unique among the religions of western Asia and Egypt. The most dramatic difference was the Hebrews' belief that there is only one God for all peoples (a true monotheism), but the Hebrews also differed in other significant ways. In virtually every religion in ancient Mesopotamia and Egypt, priests alone (and occasionally rulers) had access to the gods and their desires. In the Hebrew tradition, God's wishes, although communicated to the people through a series of special holy men, had all been written down. No Hebrew spiritual leader could claim that he alone knew God's will. It was accessible to anyone who could read Hebrew. Judaism was a religion initially of the spoken word and eventually of the written word. Finally, although the Hebrew prophets eventually developed a sense of universalism, the demands of the Hebrew religion (the need to obey their God) encouraged a separation between the Hebrews and their non-Hebrew neighbors. Unlike most other peoples of the Middle East, the Hebrews could not simply accept the gods of their conquerors and their neighbors and be amalgamated into a community. To remain faithful to the demands of their God, they might even have to refuse loyalty to political leaders.

The Rise of New Empires

An independent Hebrew state could exist only because there was a power vacuum in western Asia after the destruction of the Hittite kingdom and the weakening of the Egyptian empire. But this condition did not last; new empires soon arose that came to dominate vast stretches of the ancient world.

The Assyrian Empire

The first of these empires was formed in Assyria, located on the upper Tigris River, an area that brought it into both cultural and political contact with Mesopotamia. The Assyrians were a Semitic-speaking people who exploited the use of iron weapons to establish an empire by 700 B.C.E. that included Mesopotamia, parts of the Iranian plateau, sections of Asia Minor, Syria, Palestine, and Egypt down to Thebes. Ashurbanipal (669–626 B.C.E.) was one of the strongest Assyrian rulers, but during his reign it was already becoming apparent that the Assyrian Empire was greatly overextended. Internal strife intensified as powerful Assyrian nobles gained control of vast territories and waged their own private military campaigns. Moreover, subject peoples, such as the Babyloni-

ans, greatly resented Assyrian rule and rebelled against it. Soon after Ashurbanipal's reign, the Assyrian Empire began to disintegrate rapidly. The capital city of Nineveh fell to a coalition of Chaldeans and Medes in 612 B.C.E., and in 605 B.C.E., the rest of the empire was finally divided between the coalition powers.

At its height, the Assyrian Empire was ruled by kings whose power was considered absolute. Under their leadership, the Assyrian Empire came to be well organized. By eliminating governorships held by nobles on a hereditary basis and instituting a new hierarchy of local officials directly responsible to the king, the Assyrian kings gained greater control over the resources of the empire. The Assyrians also developed an efficient system of communication to administer their empire more effectively. A network of posting stages was established throughout the empire that used relays of horses (mules or donkeys in mountainous terrain) to carry messages. The system was so effective that a provincial governor anywhere in the empire (except Egypt) could send a question and receive an answer from the king in his palace within a week.

The ability of the Assyrians to conquer and maintain an empire was due to a combination of factors. Over many years of practice, the Assyrians developed effective military leaders and fighters. They were able to enlist and deploy troops numbering in the hundreds of thousands, although most campaigns were not on such a large scale. In 845 B.C.E., an Assyrian army of 120,000 men crossed the Euphrates on a campaign. Size alone was not decisive, however. The Assyrian army was extremely well organized and disciplined. It included a standing army of infantrymen as its core, accompanied by cavalry and horse-drawn war chariots that were used as mobile platforms for shooting arrows. Moreover, the Assyrians had the advantage of having the first large armies equipped with iron weapons. The Hittites had been the first to develop iron metallurgy, but iron came to be used extensively only after new methods for hardening it became common after 1000 B.C.E.

Another factor in the army's success was its ability to use different kinds of military tactics (see the box on p. 36). The Assyrian army was capable of waging guerrilla warfare in the mountains and set battles on open ground as well as laying siege to cities. The Assyrians were especially renowned for their siege warfare. They would hammer a city's walls with heavy, wheeled siege towers and armored battering rams, while sappers dug tunnels to undermine the walls' foundations and cause them to collapse. The besieging Assyrian armies learned to cut off supplies so effectively that if a city did not fall to them, the inhabitants could be starved into submission.

The Assyrian Military Machine

The Assyrians achieved a reputation for possessing a mighty military machine. They were able to use a variety of military tactics and were successful whether they were waging guerrilla warfare, fighting set battles, or laying siege to cities. In these three selections, Assyrian kings boast of their military conquests.

King Sennacherib (704–681 B.C.E.) Describes a Battle with the Elamites in 691

At the command of the god Ashur, the great Lord, I rushed upon the enemy like the approach of a hurricane. . . . I put them to rout and turned them back. I transfixed the troops of the enemy with javelins and arrows. . . . I cut their throats like sheep. . . . My prancing steeds, trained to harness, plunged into their welling blood as into a river; the wheels of my battle chariot were bespattered with blood and filth. I filled the plain with the corpses of their warriors like herbage. . . . As to the sheikhs of the Chaldeans, panic from my onslaught overwhelmed them like a demon. They abandoned their tents and fled for their lives, crushing the corpses of their troops as they went. . . . In their terror they passed scalding urine and voided their excrement into their chariots.

King Sennacherib Describes His Siege of Jerusalem (701 B.C.E.)

As to Hezekiah, the Jew, he did not submit to my yoke, I laid siege to 46 of his strong cities, walled forts and to the countless small villages in their vicinity, and con-

quered them by means of well-stamped earth-ramps, and battering-rams brought thus near to the walls combined with the attack by foot soldiers, using mines, breeches as well as sapper work. I drove out of them 200,150 people, young and old, male and female, horses, mules, donkeys, camels, big and small cattle beyond counting, and considered them booty. Himself I made a prisoner in Jerusalem, his royal residence, like a bird in a cage. I surrounded him with earthwork in order to molest those who were leaving his city's gate.

King Ashurbanipal (669–626 B.C.E.) Describes His Treatment of Conquered Babylon

I tore out the tongues of those whose slanderous mouths had uttered blasphemies against my god Ashur and had plotted against me, his god-fearing prince; I defeated them completely. The others, I smashed alive with the very same statues of protective deities with which they had smashed my own grandfather Sennacherib—now finally as a belated burial sacrifice for his soul. I fed their corpses, cut into small pieces, to dogs, pigs, . . . vultures, the birds of the sky and also to the fish of the ocean. After I had performed this and thus made quiet again the hearts of the great gods, my lords, I removed the corpses of those whom the pestilence had felled, whose leftovers after the dogs and pigs had fed on them were obstructing the streets, filling the places of Babylon, and of those who had lost their lives through the terrible famine.

A final factor in the effectiveness of the Assyrian military machine was its ability to create a climate of terror as an instrument of warfare. The Assyrians became famous for their terror tactics, although some historians believe that their policies were no worse than those of other conquerors. As a matter of regular policy, the Assyrians laid waste the land in which they were fighting, smashing dams, looting and destroying towns, setting crops on fire, and cutting down trees, particularly fruit trees. The Assyrians were especially known for committing atrocities on their captives. King Ashurnasirpal recorded this account of his treatment of prisoners:

> 3000 of their combat troops I felled with weapons. . . . Many of the captives taken from them I burned in a fire.

Many I took alive; from some of these I cut off their hands to the wrist, from others I cut off their noses, ears and fingers; I put out the eyes of many of the soldiers. . . . I burned their young men and women to death.

After conquering another city, the same king wrote: "I fixed up a pile of corpses in front of the city's gate. I flayed the nobles, as many as had rebelled, and spread their skins out on the piles. . . . I flayed many within my land and spread their skins out on the walls."[15] (Obviously, not a king to play games with!) It should be noted that this policy of extreme cruelty to prisoners was not used against all enemies, but was primarily reserved for those who were already part of the empire and then rebelled against Assyrian rule.

ASSYRIAN SOCIETY AND CULTURE

Unlike the Hebrews, the Assyrians were not fearful of mixing with other peoples. In fact, Assyrian deportation policies created a polyglot society in which ethnic differences were not very important. What gave identity to the Assyrians themselves was their language, although even that was akin to that of their southern neighbors in Babylonia who also spoke a Semitic language. Religion was also a cohesive force. Assyria was literally "the land of Ashur," a reference to its chief god. The king, as the human representative of the god Ashur, provided a final unifying focus.

Agriculture formed the principal basis of Assyrian life. Assyria was a land of farming villages with relatively few significant cities, especially in comparison to Mesopotamia. Unlike Mesopotamia, where farming required the minute organization of large numbers of people to control irrigation, Assyrian farms received sufficient moisture from regular rainfall.

Trade was second to agriculture in economic importance. For internal trade, metals, such as gold, silver, copper, and bronze, were used as a medium of exchange. Various agricultural products also served as a form of payment or exchange. Because of their geographical location, the Assyrians served as middlemen and participated in an international trade in which they imported timber, wine, and precious metals and stones while exporting textiles produced in palaces, temples, and private workshops.

The culture of the Assyrian Empire was essentially hybrid in nature. The Assyrians assimilated much of Mesopotamian civilization and saw themselves as guardians of Sumerian and Babylonian culture. Ashurbanipal, for example, established a large library at Nineveh that included the available works of Mesopotamian history. Assyrian kings also tried to maintain old traditions when they rebuilt damaged temples by constructing the new buildings on the original foundations, not in new locations. Assyrian religion reflected this assimilation of other cultures as well. Although the Assyrians had their own national god Ashur as their chief deity, virtually all of their remaining gods and goddesses were Mesopotamian.

Among the best-known objects of Assyrian art are the relief sculptures found in the royal palaces in three of the Assyrian capital cities, Nimrud, Nineveh, and Khorsabad. These reliefs, which were begun in the ninth century and reached their high point in the reign of Ashurbanipal in the seventh century, depicted two different kinds of subject matter: ritual or ceremonial scenes revolving around the person of the king and scenes of hunting and war. The latter show realistic action scenes of the king and his warriors engaged in battle or hunting animals, especially lions. These pictures depict a strongly masculine world where discipline, brute force, and toughness are the enduring values, indeed, the very values of the Assyrian military monarchy.

The Persian Empire

The Chaldeans, a Semitic-speaking people, had gained ascendancy in Babylonia by the seventh century and came to form the chief resistance to Assyrian control of Mesopotamia. After the collapse of the Assyrian Empire, the Chaldeans, under their king Nebuchadnezzar II (605–562 B.C.E.), restored Babylonia to its position as the leading state in western Asia. Nebuchadnezzar rebuilt Babylon as the center of his empire, giving it a reputation as one of the great cities of the ancient world. But the splendor of Chaldean Babylonia proved to be short-lived when Babylon fell to the Persians in 539 B.C.E.

The Persians were an Indo-European–speaking people who lived in southwestern Iran and fell subject to the ethnically related Medes. Primarily nomadic, the Persians were organized in tribes or clans led by petty kings assisted by a group of warriors who formed a class of nobles. At the beginning of the seventh century, the

◆ **King Ashurbanipal's Lion Hunt.** This relief, sculptured on alabaster as a decoration for the northern palace in Nineveh, depicts King Ashurbanipal engaged in a lion hunt. The relief sculpture, one of the best-known forms of Assyrian art, ironically reached its high point under Ashurbanipal at the same time that the Assyrian Empire began to disintegrate.

Achaemenid dynasty, based in Persis in southern Iran, managed to unify the Persians. One of the dynasty's members, Cyrus (559–530 B.C.E.), created a powerful Persian state that rearranged the political map of western Asia. In 550 B.C.E., he extended Persian control over the Medes, making Media the first Persian satrapy or province. Three years later, Cyrus defeated the prosperous Lydian kingdom in western Asia Minor, and Lydia became another Persian satrapy. Cyrus's forces then went on to conquer the Greek city-states that had been established on the Ionian coast. Cyrus then turned eastward, subduing the eastern part of the Iranian plateau, Sogdia, and even western India. His eastern frontiers secured, Cyrus entered Mesopotamia in 539 and captured Babylon. His treatment of Babylonia showed remarkable restraint and wisdom. Babylonia was made into a Persian province under a Persian satrap, but many government officials were kept in their positions. Cyrus took the title "King of All, Great King, Mighty King, King of Babylon, King of the Land of Sumer and Akkad, King of the Four Rims (of the Earth), the Son of Cambyses the Great King, King of Anshan"[16] and insisted that he stood in the ancient, unbroken line of Babylonian kings. By appealing to the vanity of the Babylonians, he won their loyalty. Cyrus also issued an edict permitting the Hebrews, who had been brought to Babylon in the sixth century B.C.E., to return to Jerusalem with their sacred temple objects and to rebuild their Temple as well.

To his contemporaries, Cyrus the Great was deserving of his epithet. The Greek historian Herodotus recounted that the Persians viewed him as a "father," a ruler who was "gentle, and procured them all manner of goods."[17] Certainly, Cyrus must have been an unusual ruler for his time, a man who demonstrated considerable wisdom and compassion in the conquest and organization of his empire. Cyrus attempted—successfully—to obtain the favor of the priesthoods in his conquered lands by restoring temples and permitting a wide degree of religious toleration. He won approval by using not only Persians, but also native peoples as government officials in their own states. Unlike the Assyrian rulers of an earlier empire, he had a reputation for mercy. Medes, Babylonians, Hebrews, all accepted him as their legitimate ruler. Indeed, the Hebrews regarded him as the anointed one of God: "I

✖ **Map 1.6** The Assyrian and Persian Empires.

am the Lord who says of Cyrus, 'He is my shepherd and will accomplish all that I please'; he will say of Jerusalem, 'Let it be rebuilt'; and of the temple, 'Let its foundations be laid.' This is what the Lord says to his anointed, to Cyrus, whose right hand I take hold of to subdue nations before him."[18] Cyrus had a genuine respect for ancient civilizations—in building his palaces, he made use of Assyrian, Babylonian, Egyptian, and Lydian practices. Indeed, Cyrus had a sense that he was creating a "world empire" that included peoples who had ancient and venerable traditions and institutions.

Cyrus's successors extended the territory of the Persian Empire. His son Cambyses (530–522 B.C.E.) undertook a successful invasion of Egypt and made it into a satrapy with Memphis as its capital. Darius (521–486 B.C.E.) added a new Persian province in western India that extended to the Indus River and moved into Europe proper, conquering Thrace and making the Macedonian king a vassal. A revolt of the Ionian Greek cities in 499 B.C.E. resulted in temporary freedom for these communities in western Asia Minor. Aid from the Greek mainland, most notably from Athens, encouraged the Ionians to invade Lydia and burn Sardis, center of the Lydian satrap. This event led to Darius's involvement with the mainland Greeks. After reestablishing control of the Ionian Greek cities, Darius undertook an invasion of the Greek mainland, which culminated in the famous Athenian victory in the Battle of Marathon in 490 B.C.E. (see Chapter 4).

GOVERNING THE EMPIRE

By the reign of Darius, the Persians had created the largest empire the world had yet seen. It not only included all the old centers of power in Egypt and western Asia, but also extended into Thrace and Asia Minor in the west and into India in the east. For administrative purposes, the empire had been divided into approximately twenty provinces called satrapies. Each province was ruled by a governor or satrap, literally a "protector of the Kingdom." Although Darius had not introduced the system of satrapies, he did see that it was organized more rationally. He created a sensible system for calculating the tribute that each satrapy owed to the central government and gave satraps specific civil and military duties. They collected tributes, were responsible for justice and security, raised military levies for the royal army, and normally commanded the military forces within their satrapies. In terms of real power, the satraps were miniature kings with courts imitative of the Great King's.

From the time of Darius on, satraps were men of Persian descent. The major satrapies were given to princes of

CHRONOLOGY

The Empires

The Assyrians	
Height of power	700 B.C.E.
Ashurbanipal	669–626 B.C.E.
Fall of Nineveh	612 B.C.E.
Assyrian Empire destroyed	605 B.C.E.
The Persians	
Unification under Achaemenid dynasty	600s B.C.E.
Persian control over Medes	550 B.C.E.
Conquests of Cyrus the Great	559–530 B.C.E.
Cambyses and conquest of Egypt	530–522 B.C.E.
Reign of Darius	521–486 B.C.E.

the royal family, and their position became essentially hereditary. The minor satrapies were placed in the hands of Persian nobles. Their offices, too, tended to pass from father to son. The hereditary nature of the governors' offices made it necessary to provide some checks to their power. Consequently, royal officials at the satrapal courts acted as spies for the Great King.

An efficient system of communication was crucial to sustaining the Persian Empire. Well-maintained roads facilitated the rapid transit of military and government personnel. One in particular, the so-called Royal Road, stretched from Sardis, the center of Lydia in Asia Minor, to Susa, the chief capital of the Persian Empire. Like the Assyrians, the Persians established staging posts equipped with fresh horses for the king's messengers.

In this vast administrative system, the Persian king occupied an exalted position. Although not considered to be a god in the manner of an Egyptian pharaoh, he was nevertheless the elect one or regent of the Persian god Ahuramazda (see Persian Religion later in this chapter). All subjects were the king's servants, and he was the source of all justice, possessing the power of life and death over everyone. Persian kings were largely secluded and not easily accessible. They resided in a series of splendid palaces. Darius in particular was a palace builder on a grand scale. His description of the construction of a palace in the chief Persian capital of Susa demonstrated what a truly international empire Persia was:

♦ Archers of the Persian Guard. One of the main pillars supporting the Persian Empire was the military. This frieze, composed of enamel brick, depicts members of the famous infantry force known as the Immortals, so called because their number was never allowed to drop below 10,000. Those killed would be replaced immediately. They carry the standard lance and bow and arrow of the infantry.

> This is the . . . palace which at Susa I built. From afar its ornamentation was brought. . . . The cedar timber was brought from a mountain named Lebanon; the Assyrians brought it to Babylon, and from Babylon the Carians and Ionians brought it to Susa. Teakwood was brought from Gandara and from Carmania. The gold which was used here was brought from Sardis and from Bactria. The stone—lapis lazuli and carnelian—was brought from Sogdiana. . . . The silver and copper were brought from Egypt. The ornamentation with which the wall was adorned was brought from Ionia. The ivory was brought from Ethiopia, from India, and from Arachosia. The stone pillars were brought from . . . Elam. The artisans who dressed the stone were Ionians and Sardians. The goldsmiths who wrought the gold were Medes and Egyptians. . . . Those who worked the baked brick (with figures) were Babylonians. The men who adorned the wall were Medes and Egyptians. At Susa here a splendid work was ordered; very splendid did it turn out.[19]

But Darius was unhappy with Susa. He did not really consider it his homeland, and it was oppressively hot in the summer months. He built another residence at Persepolis, a new capital located to the east of the old one and at a higher elevation.

The policies of Darius also tended to widen the gap between the king and his subjects. As the Great King himself said of all his subjects: "what was said to them by me, night and day it was done."[20] Over a period of time, the Great Kings in their greed came to hoard immense quantities of gold and silver in the various treasuries located in the capital cities. Both their hoarding of wealth and their later overtaxation of their subjects are considered crucial factors in the ultimate weakening of the Persian Empire.

In its heyday, however, the empire stood supreme, and much of its power depended upon the military. By the time of Darius, the Persian monarchs had created a standing army of professional soldiers. This army was truly international in character, composed of contingents from the various peoples who made up the empire. At its core was a cavalry force of 10,000 and an elite infantry force of 10,000 Medes and Persians known as the Immortals because they were never allowed to fall below 10,000 in number. When one was killed, he was immediately replaced. The Persians made effective use of their cavalry, especially for operating behind enemy lines and breaking up lines of communication.

PERSIAN RELIGION

Of all the Persians' cultural contributions, the most original was their religion. The popular religion of the Iranians before the advent of Zoroastrianism in the sixth century focused on the worship of the powers of nature, such as the sun, moon, fire, and winds. Mithra was an especially popular god of light and war who came to be viewed as a sun god. The people worshiped and sacrificed to these powers of nature with the aid of priests, known as Magi.

Zoroaster was a semilegendary figure who, according to Persian tradition, was born in 660 B.C.E. After a period of wandering and solitude, he experienced revelations that caused him to be revered as a prophet of the "true religion." It is difficult to know what Zoroaster's original teachings were since the sacred book of Zoroastrianism, the Zend Avesta, was not written down until the third century C.E. Scholars believe, however, that the earliest section of the Zend Avesta, known as the Yasna, consisting of seventeen hymns or gathas, contains the actual writings of Zoroaster. This enables us to piece together his message.

That spiritual message was grounded in a monotheistic framework. Although Ahuramazda was not a new god to the Iranians, to Zoroaster he was the only god and the religion he preached was the only perfect one. Ahuramazda (the "Wise Lord") was the supreme deity who brought all things into being:

This I ask of You, O Ahuramazda; answer me well:
Who at the Creation was the first father of Justice?—
Who assigned their path to the sun and the stars?—
Who decreed the waxing and waning of the moon, if it was
    not You?— . . .
Who has fixed the earth below, and the heaven above with its
    clouds that it might not be moved?—
Who has appointed the waters and the green things upon the
    earth?—
Who has harnessed to the wind and the clouds their
    steeds?— . . .
Thus do I strive to recognize in You, O Wise One,
Together with the Holy Spirit, the Creator of all things.[21]

According to Zoroaster, Ahuramazda also possessed abstract qualities or states that all humans should aspire to, such as Good Thought, Right, and Piety. Although Ahuramazda was supreme, he was not unopposed. Right is opposed by the Lie, Truth by Falsehood, Life by Death. At the beginning of the world, the good spirit of Ahuramazda was opposed by the evil spirit (in later Zoroastrianism, the evil spirit is identified with Ahriman). Although it appears that Zoroaster saw it as simply natural that where there is good, there will be evil, later followers had a tendency to make these abstractions concrete and overemphasize the reality of an evil spirit. Humans also played a role in this cosmic struggle between good and evil. Ahuramazda, the creator, gave all humans free will and the power to choose between right and wrong. The good person chooses the right way of Ahuramazda. Zoroaster taught that there would be an end to the struggle between good and evil. Ahuramazda would eventually triumph, and at the last judgment at the end of the world, the final separation of good and evil would occur. Zoroaster also provided for individual judgment as well. Each soul faced a final evaluation of its actions. If a person had performed good deeds, he or she would achieve paradise, the "House of Song" or the "Kingdom of Good Thought"; if evil deeds, then the soul would be thrown into an abyss, the "House of Worst Thought," where it would experience future ages of darkness, torment, and misery.

The spread of Zoroastrianism was due to its acceptance by the Great Kings of Persia. The inscriptions of Darius make clear that he believed Ahuramazda was the only god. Although Darius himself may have been a monotheist, as the kings and Magi, or priests of Persia, propagated Zoroaster's teachings on Ahuramazda, dramatic changes occurred. Zoroastrianism lost its monotheistic emphasis, and the old nature worship resurfaced. Hence, Persian religion returned to polytheism with Ahuramazda becoming only the chief of a number of gods of light. Mithra, the sun god, became a helper of Ahuramazda and later, in Roman times, the source of another religion. Persian kings were also very tolerant of other religions, and gods and goddesses of those religions tended to make their way into the Persian pantheon. Moreover, as frequently happens to the ideas of founders of religions, Zoroaster's teachings acquired concrete forms that he had never originally intended. The struggle between good and evil was taken beyond the abstractions of Zoroaster into a strong ethical dualism. The spirit of evil became an actual being who had to be warded off by the use of spells and incantations. Descriptions of the last judgment came to be filled with minute physical details. Some historians believe that Zoroastrianism, with its emphasis on good and evil, a final judgment, and individual judgment of souls, had an impact on Christianity, a religion that eventually surpassed it in significance.

Conclusion

The peoples of Mesopotamia and Egypt built the first civilizations. They developed cities and struggled with the problems of organized states. They developed writing to keep records and created literature. They constructed monumental architecture to please their gods, symbolize their power, and preserve their culture for all time. They developed new political, military, social, and religious structures to deal with the basic problems of human existence and organization. These first literate civilizations left detailed records that allow us to view how they grappled with three of the fundamental problems that humans have pondered: the nature of human relationships, the nature of the universe, and the role of divine forces in that cosmos. Although later peoples would provide different answers from those of the Mesopotamians and Egyptians, it was they who first posed the questions, gave answers, and wrote them down. Human memory begins with these two civilizations.

By the middle of the second millennium B.C.E., much of the creative impulse of the Mesopotamian and Egyptian civilizations was beginning to wane. Around 1200 B.C.E., the decline of the Hittites and Egyptians had created a power vacuum that allowed a number of small states to emerge and flourish temporarily. All of them were eventually overshadowed by the rise of the great empires of the Assyrians and Persians. The Assyrian Empire had been the first to unite almost all of the ancient Middle East. Even larger, however, was the empire of the Great Kings of Persia. Although it owed much to the administrative organization created by the Assyrians, the Persian Empire had its own peculiar strengths. Persian rule was tolerant as well as efficient. Conquered peoples were allowed to keep their own religions, customs, and methods of doing business. The many years of peace that the Persian Empire brought to the Middle East facilitated trade and the general well-being of its peoples. It is no

wonder that many peoples expressed their gratitude for being subjects of the Great Kings of Persia. Among these peoples were the Hebrews, who created no empire but nevertheless left an important spiritual legacy. The evolution of Hebrew monotheism created in Judaism one of the world's greatest religions; it influenced the development of both Christianity and Islam.

The Persians had also extended their empire to the Indus River, which brought them into contact with another ancient civilization that had developed independently of the civilizations in the Middle East and Egypt. It is to India that we must now turn.

CHAPTER NOTES

1. Quoted in Thorkild Jacobsen, "Mesopotamia," in Henri Frankfort et al., *Before Philosophy* (Baltimore, 1949), p. 139.
2. James B. Pritchard, *Ancient Near Eastern Texts*, 3d ed. (Princeton, N.J., 1969), p. 372.
3. Quoted in Milton Covensky, *The Ancient Near Eastern Tradition* (New York, 1966), p. 51.
4. Quoted in B. G. Trigger, B. J. Kemp, D. O'Connor, and A. B. Lloyd, *Ancient Egypt: A Social History* (Cambridge, 1983), p. 74.
5. Pritchard, *Ancient Near Eastern Texts*, p. 34.
6. Ibid., p. 36.
7. Ibid., p. 413.
8. Ibid., p. 420.
9. Quoted in John A. Wilson, *The Culture of Ancient Egypt* (Chicago, 1956), p. 264.
10. Psalms 137: 1, 4–6.
11. Psalms 145: 8–9.
12. Psalms 121: 2–3.
13. Exodus 20: 13–15.
14. Isaiah 2: 4.
15. Quoted in H. W. F. Saggs, *The Might That Was Assyria* (London, 1984), pp. 261–62.
16. Quoted in J. M. Cook, *The Persian Empire* (New York, 1983), p. 32.
17. Herodotus, *The Persian Wars*, trans. George Rawlinson (New York, 1942), p. 257.
18. Isaiah, 44: 28; 45:1.
19. Quoted in A. T. Olmstead, *History of the Persian Empire* (Chicago, 1948), p. 168.
20. Quoted in Cook, *The Persian Empire*, p. 76.
21. Yasna 44: 3–4, 7, as quoted in A. C. Bouquet, *Sacred Books of the World* (Harmondsworth, 1954), pp. 111–12.

SUGGESTED READINGS

For a beautifully illustrated introduction to the ancient world, see *Past Worlds: The Times Atlas of Archaeology* (Maplewood, N.J., 1988), written by an international group of scholars. The following works are of considerable value in examining the prehistory of humankind: R. Leakey, *The Making of Mankind* (London, 1981);

P. Mellars and C. Stringer, *The Human Revolution* (Edinburgh, 1989); and D. O. Henry, *From Foraging to Agriculture* (Philadelphia, 1989).

A fascinating introduction to the world of ancient Near Eastern studies can be found in W. D. Jones, *Venus and Sothis: How the Ancient Near East Was Rediscovered*

(Chicago, 1982). A very competent general survey primarily of the political history of Mesopotamia and Egypt is W. W. Hallo and W. K. Simpson, *The Ancient Near East: A History* (New York, 1971). Also valuable are A. B. Knapp, *The History and Culture of Ancient Western Asia and Egypt* (Chicago, 1987); H. J. Nissen, *The Early History of the Ancient Near East, 9000–2000 B.C.* (Chicago, 1988); and W. von Soden, *The Ancient Orient: An Introduction to the Study of the Ancient Near East* (Grand Rapids, Mich., 1994). H. W. F. Saggs, *Babylonians* (Norman, Okla., 1995) provides an overview of the people of ancient Mesopotamia. The fundamental collection of translated documents from the ancient Near East is J. B. Pritchard, *Ancient Near Eastern Texts*, 3d ed. with Supplement (Princeton, N.J., 1969).

General works on ancient Mesopotamia include A. L. Oppenheim, *Ancient Mesopotamia*, 2d ed. (Chicago, 1977); S. Lloyd, *The Archaeology of Mesopotamia*, rev. ed. (London, 1984); and M. E. Mallowan, *Early Mesopotamia and Iran* (New York, 1966). The world of the Sumerians has been well described in S. N. Kramer, *The Sumerians* (Chicago, 1963) and *History Begins at Sumer* (New York, 1959). See also the recent summary of the historical and archaeological evidence by H. Crawford, *Sumer and the Sumerians* (Cambridge, 1991). The fundamental work on the spiritual perspective of ancient Mesopotamia is T. Jacobsen, *The Treasures of Darkness: A History of Mesopotamian Religion* (New Haven, Conn., 1976).

For a good introduction to ancient Egypt, see the beautifully illustrated work by J. Baines and J. Málek, *The Cultural Atlas of the World: Ancient Egypt* (Alexandria, Va., 1991). A good survey is C. Hobson, *The World of the Pharaohs* (New York, 1987). For an interesting introduction to Egyptian history, see B. J. Kemp, *Ancient Egypt* (London, 1989). A new approach is attempted in B. G. Trigger, B. J. Kemp, D. O'Connor, and A. B. Lloyd, *Ancient Egypt: A Social History* (Cambridge, 1983). On Akhenaten and his religious changes, see D. Redford, *Akhenaten: The Heretic King* (Princeton, N.J., 1984). Egyptian religion is covered in S. Morenz, *Egyptian Religion* (London, 1973). The importance of the afterlife in Egyptian civilization is examined in A. Spencer, *Death in Ancient Egypt* (Harmondsworth, 1982). On culture in general, see J. A. Wilson, *The Culture of Ancient Egypt* (Chicago, 1956). The leading authority on the pyramids is I. E. S. Edwards, *The Pyramids*

of Egypt, rev. ed. (Harmondsworth, 1976). Daily life in ancient Egypt can be examined in J. White, *Everyday Life in Ancient Egypt* (London, 1963); and T. G. H. James, *Pharaoh's People: Scenes from Life in Imperial Egypt* (London, 1984). An important new study on women is G. Robins, *Women in Ancient Egypt* (Cambridge, Mass., 1993).

On the Sea Peoples, see the standard work by N. Sanders, *The Sea Peoples: Warriors of the Ancient Mediterranean* (London, 1978). A good introductory survey on the Hittites can be found in O. R. Gurney, *The Hittites*, 2d ed. (Harmondsworth, 1981).

For a good account of Phoenician domestic history and overseas expansion, see D. Harden, *The Phoenicians*, rev. ed. (Harmondsworth, 1980). There is an enormous literature on ancient Israel. Two good studies on the archaeological aspects are Y. Aharoni, *The Archaeology of the Land of Israel* (Philadelphia, 1982); and W. F. Albright, *The Archaeology of Palestine* (Harmondsworth, 1949). For historical narratives, see especially J. Bright, *A History of Israel*, 3d ed. (Philadelphia, 1981), a fundamental study; the survey by M. Grant, *The History of Ancient Israel* (New York, 1984); and H. Shanks, *Ancient Israel: A Short History from Abraham to the Roman Destruction of the Temple* (Englewood Cliffs, N.J., 1988). R. de Vaux, *Ancient Israel: Its Life and Institutions* (New York, 1961), is especially good on the social institutions of ancient Israel. For general studies on the religion of the Hebrews, see Y. Kaufmann, *The Religion of Israel* (Chicago, 1960); and H. Ringgren, *Israelite Religion* (London, 1966).

A recent detailed account of Assyrian political, economic, social, military, and cultural history is H. W. F. Saggs, *The Might That Was Assyria* (London, 1984). On one aspect of Assyrian culture, see R. D. Barnett, *Assyrian Sculpture* (Toronto, 1975). The Chaldean empire can be examined in J. Oates, *Babylon* (London, 1979).

The classic work on the Persian Empire is A. T. Olmstead, *History of the Persian Empire* (Chicago, 1948), but a recent work by J. M. Cook, *The Persian Empire* (New York, 1983), provides new material and fresh interpretations on the Persians. Also of value is B. Dicks, *The Ancient Persians* (Newton Abbott, 1979). On the history of Zoroastrianism, see especialy R. C. Zaehner, *The Dawn and Twilight of Zoroastrianism* (London, 1961). Also helpful is M. Boyce, *Zoroastrians: Their Religious Beliefs and Practices* (London, 1979).

Ancient India

Arjuna was despondent as he prepared for battle. In the opposing army were many of his friends and colleagues, some of whom he had known since childhood. In despair he turned for advice to Krishna, his chariot driver, who, unknown to Arjuna, was in actuality an incarnation of the Indian deity Vishnu. Do not despair of your duty, Krishna advised his friend:

> To be born is certain death,
>   to the dead, birth is certain.
> It is not right that you should sorrow
>   for what cannot be avoided. . . .
>
> If you do not fight this just battle
>   you will fail in your own law
> and in your honor,
>   and you will incur sin.

Krishna's advice to Arjuna is contained in the Bhagavadgita, one of India's most sacred classical writings, and reflects one of the key tenets in Indian philosophy—the belief in reincarnation, or rebirth of the soul. It also points up the importance of doing one's duty with detachment and without regard to the consequences. Arjuna was a warrior, and according to Aryan tribal tradition, he was obliged to follow the code of his class. "There is more joy in doing one's own duty badly," advised Krishna, "than in doing another man's duty well."

In advising Arjuna to fulfill his obligation as a warrior, the author of the Bhagavadgita, writing around the second century B.C.E. about a battle that took place almost a thousand years earlier, and antelope, while figures made of copper or terra-cotta show a lively sensitivity and a sense of grace and movement that is almost modern.

Presumably, the Indus valley peoples possessed a literature like their contemporaries to the west. Unfortunately, none has survived, and the only examples of Harappan writing are the pictographic symbols inscribed on the clay seals. The script contained more than four hundred characters, but most are too stylized to be identified by their shape, and scholars have thus far been unable to decipher them. Many of these seals appear to have been used by merchants to keep track of their commercial transactions, but some may also have been used as amulets or have had other religious significance. Several depict religious figures or ritualistic scenes of sacrifice. Until the script is deciphered, however, much about the Harappan civilization must remain, as one historian termed it, a fascinating enigma.

The Arrival of the Aryans

One of the great mysteries of Harappan civilization is how it came to an end. Archaeologists working at Mohenjo-Daro have discovered signs of first a gradual decay and then a sudden destruction of the city and its inhabitants sometime around 1500 B.C.E. Many of the surviving skeletons have been found in postures of running or hiding, reminiscent of the ruins of the Roman city of Pompeii, destroyed by the eruption of Mount Vesuvius in 79 C.E.

These tantalizing signs of flight before a sudden catastrophe have led some scholars to surmise that the city of Mohenjo-Daro (the name was applied by archaeologists and means "city of the dead"), and perhaps Harappan civilization as a whole, was destroyed by nomadic peoples from the north sometime around the middle of the second millennium B.C.E. These invaders, who called themselves Aryans, were part of an extensive group of Indo-European–speaking peoples who at that time inhabited vast areas in what is now Siberia and the steppes of Central Asia. Whereas other Indo-European–speaking peoples moved westward and eventually settled in Europe, the Aryan communities moved south across the Hindu Kush into the plains of northern India, where they replaced the Harappans and created a new society based on Aryan culture and institutions. Although the Aryans were almost certainly not as sophisticated in a cultural sense as the Harappans, like many nomadic peoples they excelled at the art of war. As in Mesopotamia and the Nile valley, the contact between pastoral and agricultural

◆ **Naked Dancer.** This five-inch bronze figure of a young dancer in repose is one of the few surviving metal sculptures from Mohenjo-Daro. The detail and grace of her stance reflect the skill of the Harappan artist four thousand years ago.

peoples proved to be unstable and ended in armed conflict.

This vision of an apocalyptic clash of cultures between the Harappan and Aryan peoples may be accurate in its broad outlines. Nevertheless, it is doubtful that the Aryan invaders were directly responsible for the final destruction of the city of Mohenjo-Daro. More likely, Harappan civilization had fallen on hard times, perhaps because of climatic changes in the Indus valley, and was already in a state of decline. Archaeologists have found clear signs of social decay, including evidence of trash in the streets, neglect of public services, and overcrowding in urban neighborhoods. The destruction of Mohenjo-Daro itself may have been the result of natural phenomena such as floods, an earthquake, or a shift in the course of the Indus River. If such is the case, the Aryans subjugated a people whose moment of greatness had already passed.

Whatever the truth of such conjectures, between 1500 and 1000 B.C.E. the Aryan peoples gradually advanced eastward from the Indus valley, across the fertile plain of the Ganges, and later southward into the Deccan Plateau, eventually extending their political mastery throughout the entire South Asian subcontinent. But although the Dravidian peoples, the probable descendants of the ancient Harappans, may have been subdued by the militarily more powerful Aryans, they were destined to survive as a prominent element in the civilization of traditional India, and their culture became a key element in the creation of modern Indian society.

The meeting of the two cultures, the Aryan and the Dravidian, provided the cultural intermingling and tension that have formed the basis for Indian society from ancient times to the present. The Aryans came to India with a strong class system based on a ruling warrior class. They apparently held the indigenous peoples in some contempt and assigned them to a lower position in society, providing the initial basis for the strong hierarchy of class status that developed into the caste system.

Historians know relatively little about the origins and early culture of the Aryans, except that they were a pastoral people who practiced some agriculture and were originally organized on a tribal basis. They had no written language, however, and left few physical remains in the form of settled cities or villages. Most of what is known is based on oral traditions passed on in the Rigveda, an ancient work that was eventually written down after the Aryans arrived in India (the Rigveda is one of several Vedas, or collections of sacred instructions and rituals).

Whatever their origins, after they settled in India, the Aryans gradually adapted to the geographical realities of their new homeland and abandoned the pastoral life for agricultural pursuits. They were assisted by the introduction of iron, which probably came from the Middle East, where it had first been introduced by the Hittites (see Chapter 1) about 1500 B.C.E. The invention of the iron plow, along with the development of irrigation, allowed the Aryans and their indigenous subjects to clear the dense jungle growth along the Ganges River and transform it into one of the richest agricultural regions in all South Asia. They also developed their first writing system and were thus able to transcribe the legends that previously had been passed down from generation to generation by memory.

But traditions die hard. Although little is known about the life of the Aryans in the period immediately following their arrival in India, early writings like the Rigveda and the Mahabharata, a vast epic of early Aryan society, chronicle an era of warring kingdoms and shifting tribal alliances. This pattern had undoubtedly originated in Central Asia and apparently continued long after they settled in India.

While warring groups squabbled for precedence in India, powerful new empires were rising to the west. First came Persia, with the empire of Cyrus and Darius. Then

◆ **The City of the Dead.**   Mohenjo-Daro (the City of the Dead) was one of the two major cities of the ancient Indus River civilization. In addition to rows on rows of residential housing, it had a ceremonial center, with a royal palace and a sacred bath that was probably used by the priests as a means of achieving ritual purity.

came the Greeks. After two centuries of sporadic rivalry and warfare, the Greeks temporarily achieved a brief period of regional dominance in the late fourth century B.C.E. with the rise of Macedonia under Alexander the Great. Alexander had heard of the riches of India, and in 330 B.C.E., after conquering Persia, he launched an invasion of the east (see Chapter 4). Like a bright meteor in a night sky, his armies crossed Persia, and in 326 they flashed across the plains of northwestern India. They departed almost as suddenly as they had come, leaving in their wake Greek administrators and a veneer of cultural influence that would affect the area for generations to come.

The Alexandrian conquest of India was only a brief interlude in the history of the subcontinent, but it played a formative role in Indian history, for on the heels of Alexander's departure came the rise of the first dynasty to control much of the region. The founder of the new state, who took the royal title Chandragupta Maurya (324–301 B.C.E.), drove out the Greek occupation forces after the departure of Alexander and solidified his control over the North Indian plain. He established the capital of his new Mauryan Empire at Pataliputra (modern Patna) in the Ganges valley. Little is known of his origins, although some sources have identified him as a certain Sandrocottus who had originally fought on the side of the invading Greek forces but then angered Alexander with his outspoken advice. Other sources say he may have been the illegitimate son of an Indian king whom he overthrew to form his own dynasty.

The Art of Statecraft in Ancient India: The Arthasastra

Little, too, is known of Chandragupta Maurya's empire. Most accounts of his reign rely on a work by the Greek ambassador Megasthenes that no longer exists. Megasthenes was an ambassador to the Mauryan court at Pataliputra in about 302 B.C.E. He was apparently a military officer who had previously served in Kandahar (today Afghanistan) and was replaced during the reign of Bindusara, Chandragupta's son and successor. Chandragupta Maurya was apparently advised by a brilliant court official named Kautilya, the reputed author of a treatise on politics called the *Arthasastra*. The work actually dates from a later time, but it may well reflect Kautilya's ideas, which constituted a revolutionary change in Indian political culture.

As noted previously, evidence about the institutions of the early Aryans is scanty, but historians have pieced together at least a partial picture of their politics and government. As in other Indo-European societies, political power among the Aryans was probably originally held by a chieftain, called a *raja* (prince). The chief was assisted by a council of elders composed of other leading members of the tribe, and like them, he was normally affiliated with a warrior class, called the *kshatriya*. The chief technically did not rule by divine right, but derived his power from a simple social contract based on his ability to protect the members of the tribe from rival groups. This social contract was embodied in a story related in the Mahabharata, one of the great epics of the Aryan peoples. According to this source, Brahman, the chief god of the Aryans, transformed Manu, the first man, into a king because of his ability to protect the people. Later rajas would claim that they were descended from Manu. Thus, although an early Aryan ruler could not claim to possess divine status, he could cite the Mahabharata to show that he was a "representative" of the gods.

These distinctions were of more than academic importance. Even after the position of chieftain was transformed into that of a king (usually called a *maharaja*, or great prince), the tradition that the ruler did not possess absolute authority remained strong. Like all human beings, the ruler was required to follow the *dharma*, a set of laws that set behavioral standards for all individuals and classes in Indian society (see the box on p. 52). According to the Mahabharata, revolt against an evil king was permissible, a concept that was also important in China (see Chapter 3).

As Aryan society grew in size and complexity after the conquest of India, the ruler began to take on more of the trappings of a royal personage, including the title of *maharaja*. This process was certainly well underway at the time of the rise of the Mauryan dynasty in the fourth century B.C.E. and is described in the *Arthasastra*.

In describing the science of statecraft in the India of his day, the author of the *Arthasastra* followed the Mahabharata and other Vedic texts in implying that the basis of kingship lay in an unwritten agreement between the ruler and the people, which made the king responsible for providing protection and material welfare to his subjects. The author asserts that the ruler must be energetic, endowed with a strong character, truthful, religious, intelligent, magnanimous toward his subjects, and willing to listen to his advisers (see the box on p. 53). The Aryan tradition is thus clear: the ruler is a man like other men and must conform to the laws of Heaven.

Although royal power was thus subject to at least theoretical constraints, the *Arthasastra* also asserts that when

⇒ Bits of Wisdom from Ancient India ⇐

The Mahabharata, the great epic of the early Aryan peoples, includes both moral exhortations for the ruling class and bits of simple wisdom that still touch us today. In this passage, a voice personifying the dharma, or code of behavior, tests the hero's worthiness to become king by posing riddles about the meaning of life. The questions are eternal ones that still have relevance in our own time. The use of riddles as a means of testing mental skills was common to many early societies, including ancient Greece and China.

The Mahabharata

"What is swifter than the wind?"
"The mind is swifter than the wind."
"What is more numerous than the blades of grass in a meadow?"
"Our thoughts number more than that."
"What is the best of all things that are praised?"
"Skill."
"What is the most valuable possession?"

"Knowledge."
"What is not thought of until it departs?"
"Health."
"What is the best happiness?"
"Contentment."
"What covers all the world?"
"Darkness."
"What keeps a thing from discovering itself?"
"That is also darkness."
"What enemy cannot be overcome?"
"That is anger."
"What is honesty?"
"That is to look and to see every living creature as yourself, bearing your own will to live, and your own fear of death."
"How may peace be false?"
"When it is tyranny."

the sacred law of the *dharma* and practical politics collide, the latter must take precedence:

> Whenever there is disagreement between history and sacred law or between evidence and sacred law, then the matter should be settled in accordance with sacred law. But whenever sacred law is in conflict with rational law, then reason shall be held authoritative. . . .[1]

The *Arthasastra* also emphasizes ends rather than means, achieved results rather than the methods employed. For this reason, it has often been compared to the famous political treatise of the Italian Renaissance, Machiavelli's *The Prince*, written over a thousand years later.

As in other ancient civilizations, the political system in ancient India had a pronounced elitist character. Early Aryan tribal rulers were usually members of a warrior class called the *kshatriya*. Normally, although not exclusively, the position of ruler was passed on within the royal family from father to oldest son in the practice called primogeniture. The *Arthasastra* reflected such views, noting that the ruler should be "born of a high family." But the *kshatriya* class was not exclusive, and from time to time commoners were admitted to its ranks. According to an Indian folk saying, "Whoever rules is a *kshatriya*," a

thought highly reminiscent of the Chinese proverb that "he who wins is the king; he who loses is the rebel" (see Chapter 3).

Admittedly, the first Indian empire, that of Chandragupta Maurya, was highly centralized and even despotic, at least as described in the *Arthasastra*: "It is power and power alone which, only when exercised by the king with impartiality, and in proportion to guilt, over his son or his enemy, maintains both this world and the next."[2] The king possessed a large army and a secret police responsible to his orders (according to the Greek ambassador Megasthenes, Chandragupta Maurya was chronically fearful of assassination, a not unrealistic concern for someone who had allegedly come to power by violence). Reportedly, all food was tasted in his presence, and he made a practice of never sleeping twice in the same bed in his sumptuous palace.

Nevertheless, the authority of the ruler was circumscribed in a number of practical ways. In the first place, early Indian kings probably inherited from tribal times the tradition of relying for advice on a privy council, a practice that by Mauryan times had evolved into a more sophisticated cabinet-type system with councillors for war, treasury, legal matters, and so forth. The author of the *Arthasastra* recommended that these advisers be selected on the basis of merit, although presumably most of

The Duties of a King

Kautilya, India's earliest known political philosopher, was an adviser to the Mauryan rulers. The Arthasastra, though written down at a later date, very likely reflects his ideas. This passage sets forth the necessary characteristics of a king, including efficiency, diligence, energy, compassion, and concern for the security and welfare of the state.

The Arthasastra

Only if a king is himself energetically active, do his officers follow him energetically. If he is sluggish, they too remain sluggish. And, besides, they eat up his works. He is thereby easily overpowered by his enemies. Therefore, he should ever dedicate himself energetically to activity.

He should divide the day as well as the night into eight parts. . . . During the first one-eighth part of the day, he should listen to reports pertaining to the organization of law and order and to income and expenditure. During the second, he should attend to the affairs of the urban and the rural population. During the third, he should take his bath and meal and devote himself to study. During the fourth, he should receive gold and the departmental heads. During the fifth, he should hold consultations with the council of ministers through correspondence and also keep himself informed of the secret reports brought by spies. During the sixth, he should devote himself freely to amusement or listen to the counsel of the ministers. During the seventh, he should inspect the military formations of elephants, cavalry, chariots, and infantry. During the eighth, he, together with the commander-in-chief of the army, should make plans for campaigns of conquest. When the day has come to an end he should offer the evening prayers.

During the first one-eighth part of the night, he should meet the officers of the secret service. During the second, he should take his bath and meals and also devote himself to study. During the third, at the sounding of the trumpets, he should enter the bed chamber and should sleep through the fourth and fifth. Waking up at the sounding of the trumpets, he should, during the sixth part, ponder over the teachings of the sciences and his urgent duties for the day. During the seventh, he should hold consultations and send out the officers of the secret service for their operations. During the eighth, accompanied by sacrificial priests, preceptors and the chaplain, he should receive benedictions; he should also have interviews with the physician, the kitchen-superintendent, and the astrologer. Thereafter, he should circumambulate by the right a cow with a calf and an ox and then proceed to the reception hall. Or he should divide the day and the night into parts in accordance with his own capacities and thereby attend to his duties.

A king should attend to all urgent business, he should not put it off. For what has been thus put off becomes either difficult or altogether impossible to accomplish.

The vow of the king is energetic activity, his sacrifice is constituted of the discharge of his own administrative duties; his sacrificial fee [to the officiating priests] is his impartiality of attitude toward all; his sacrificial consecration is his anointment as king.

In the happiness of the subjects lies the happiness of the king; in their welfare, his own welfare. The welfare of the king does not lie in the fulfillment of what is dear to him; whatever is dear to the subjects constitutes his welfare.

Therefore, ever energetic, a king should act up to the precepts of the science of material gain. Energetic activity is the source of material gain; its opposite, of downfall.

In the absence of energetic activity, the loss of what has already been obtained and of what still remains to be obtained is certain. The fruit of one's works is achieved through energetic activity—one obtains abundance of material prosperity.

them came either from the *kshatriya* or from the *brahmin* or priestly class, which had originally advised the king on religious matters. He also recommended that they be bold, articulate, enthusiastic, diligent, and endowed with foresight. Who could disagree with that list! The authority of the advisers was theoretically limited by a board of censors, officials who were empowered to investigate cases of possible malfeasance and incompetence within the bureaucracy.

Secondly, the ruler's authority beyond the confines of the capital may often have been limited. The empire was divided into provinces that were ruled by governors appointed by and reporting to the ruler. At first, most of these governors were probably relatives or military commanders in favor at court. Later, however, the position became hereditary, thus protecting them to some degree from arbitrary replacement by the monarch. The provinces themselves were divided into districts, each under a chief magistrate appointed by the governor. At the base of the government pyramid was the village, where the vast majority of the Indian people lived. The village was governed by a council of elders; membership in the council was normally hereditary and was shared by the wealthiest families in the village.

Caste and Class: Social Structures in Ancient India

As the Aryan peoples spread throughout northern India, they eventually abandoned their pastoral pursuits and took up settled farming. Nevertheless, the conquest of India by the Aryans was destined to have a lasting impact on Indian society, for out of that clash of conqueror and conquered evolved a set of social institutions and class divisions that has persisted with only minor changes down to the present day.

THE CASTE SYSTEM

At the base of the social system that emerged from the clash of cultures was the concept of the superiority of the invading peoples over their conquered subjects. In a sense, it became an issue of color, because the Aryan invaders, a primarily light-skinned people, were contemptuous of their subjects, who were dark. Light skin came to imply high status, while dark skin suggested the opposite.

The concept of color, however, was only the physical manifestation of a division that took place in Indian society on the basis of economic functions. Indian classes (called *varna*, literally "color" and commonly known as "castes" in English) did not simply reflect an informal division of labor. Instead, they were a set of rigid social classifications that determined not only one's occupation, but also one's status in society and one's hope for ultimate salvation (see Escaping the Wheel of Life later in this chapter). The term *caste* is from the Portuguese word for tribe or clan. There were five major castes in Indian society in ancient times. At the top were two castes, collectively viewed as the aristocracy, which clearly represented the ruling elites in Aryan society prior to their arrival in India: the priests and the warriors.

The priestly caste, known as the *brahmins*, was usually considered to be at the top of the social scale. Descended from a class of seers who had advised the ruler on religious matters in Aryan tribal society (*brahmin* meant "one possessed of *Brahman*," a term for the supreme god in the Hindu religion), they were eventually transformed into an official class after their religious role declined in importance. The Greek ambassador Megasthenes described this caste as follows:

> From the time of their conception in the womb they are under the care and guardianship of learned men who go to the mother, and under the pretense of using some incantations for the welfare of herself and her unborn child, in reality give her prudent hints and counsels, and the women who listen to them most willingly are thought to be the most fortunate in their offspring. After their birth the children are in the care of one person after another, and as they advance in years their masters are men of superior accomplishments. The philosophers reside in a grove in front of the city within a moderate-sized enclosure. They live in a simple style and lie on pallets of straw and [deer] skins. They abstain from animal food and sexual pleasures; and occupy their time in listening to serious discourse and in imparting knowledge to willing ears.[3]

The second caste was the *kshatriya*, or the warriors. Although often listed below the *brahmins* in social status, many *kshatriyas* were probably descended from the ruling warrior class in Aryan society prior to the conquest of India and thus may have originally ranked socially above the *brahmins*, although they were ranked lower in religious terms. Like the *brahmins*, the *kshatriyas* were originally identified with a single occupation—that of fighting—but as the character of Aryan society changed, they often switched to other forms of employment. At the same time, new conquering families from other castes were sometimes tacitly accepted into the ranks of the warriors.

The third-ranked caste in Indian society was the *vaisya* (literally, "commoner"). The *vaisyas* were usually viewed in economic terms as the merchant caste. Ac-

Social Classes in Ancient India

The Law of Manu is an early treatise on social organization and behavior in ancient India. It was probably written in the first or second century B.C.E. The following excerpt describes the various social classes in India and their prescribed duties.

The Law of Manu

For the sake of the preservation of this entire creation, the Exceedingly Resplendent One assigned separate duties to the classes which had sprung from his mouth, arms, thighs, and feet.

Teaching, studying, performing sacrificial rites, so too making others perform sacrificial rites, and giving away and receiving gifts—these he assigned to the [brahmins].

Protection of the people, giving away of wealth, performance of sacrificial rites, study, and nonattachment to sensual pleasures—these are, in short, the duties of a kshatriya.

Tending of cattle, giving away of wealth, performance of sacrificial rites, study, trade and commerce, usury, and agriculture—these are the occupations of a vaishya.

The Lord has prescribed only one occupation [karma] for a sudra, namely, service without malice of even these other three classes.

Man is stated to be purer above the navel than below it; hence His mouth has been declared to be the purest part by the Self-Existent One.

On account of his origin from the best limb of the Cosmic Person, on account of his seniority, and on account of the preservation by him of the Veda [brahman]—the brahman is in respect of dharma the lord of this entire creation.

The Self-Existent One, having performed penance, produced the brahman first of all, from his own mouth, for the sake of the conveying of the offerings intended for the gods and those intended for the ancestral spirits, and for the sake of the preservation of this entire universe.

What created being can be superior to him through whose mouth the gods always consume the obligations intended for them, and the ancestral spirits those intended for them?

Of created beings, those which are animate are the best; of the animate, those which subsist by means of their intellect; of the intelligent, men are the best; and of men, the [brahmins] are traditionally declared to be the best.

In this treatise there are expounded in entirely dharma, the merits and demerits of [human] actions, and the eternal code of conduct of the four classes.

The code of conduct—prescribed by scriptures and ordained by sacred tradition—constitutes the highest dharma; hence a twice-born person, conscious of his own Self [seeking spiritual salvation], should be always scrupulous in respect of it.

---

cording to Indian tradition, their primary duties were to tend cattle or to engage in commerce. Some historians have speculated that the *vaisyas* were originally guardians of the tribal herds, but that after settling in India many moved into commercial pursuits. The Greek observer Megasthenes noted that members of this caste "alone are permitted to hunt and keep cattle and to sell beasts of burden or to let them out on hire. In return for clearing the land of wild beasts and birds which infest sown fields, they receive an allowance of corn from the king. They lead a wandering life and dwell in tents."[4] Although this caste was ranked below the first two in social status, it shared with them the privilege of being considered "twice-born," a term referring to a ceremony at puberty whereby young males were initiated into adulthood and introduced into Indian society. After the ceremony, male members of the top three castes were allowed to wear the "sacred thread" for the remainder of their lives.

Below the three "twice-born" castes were the *sudras*, who represented the great bulk of the Indian population. The *sudras* were not considered fully Aryan, and the term probably originally referred to the conquered Dravidian population. Most *sudras* were peasants or artisans or worked at other forms of manual labor. They had only limited rights in society. One early Indian source says "The Lord has prescribed only one occupation [karma] for a sudra, namely service without malice of even these other three classes" (see the box above).

At the lowest level of Indian society, and in fact not even considered a legitimate part of the caste system itself, were the untouchables (also known as outcastes, or *pariahs*). The untouchables probably originated as a slave class consisting of prisoners of war, criminals, tribal minorities, and other groups considered outside Indian society. Even after slavery was outlawed, the untouchables were given menial and degrading tasks that other Indians would not accept, such as collecting trash, handling dead bodies, or serving as butchers or tanners (i.e., handling dead meat). According to the estimate of one historian, they may have comprised somewhat more than 5 percent of the total population of India in antiquity.

The life of the untouchables was extremely demeaning. They were not considered human, and their very presence was considered polluting to members of the other *varna*. No Indian would touch or eat food handled or prepared by an untouchable. Untouchables lived in special ghettos and were required to tap two sticks together to announce their presence when they traveled outside their quarters, so that others could avoid them.

Technically, these caste divisions were absolute. Individuals supposedly were born, lived, and died in the same caste. In practice, some upward or downward mobility probably took place in early times, and as time went on, there was undoubtedly some flexibility in economic functions. But throughout most of Indian history caste taboos remained strict. Members were generally not permitted to marry outside their caste (although, in practice, men were occasionally allowed to marry below their caste, but not above it). At first, attitudes toward the handling of food were relatively loose, but eventually that taboo grew stronger, and social mores dictated that sharing meals and marrying outside one's caste were unacceptable.

The people of ancient India did not belong to a particular caste as individuals, but as part of a larger kin group commonly referred to as the *jati*, a system of large extended families that originated in ancient India and still exists in somewhat changed form today. The origins of the *jati* system are unknown. Historians once assumed that it developed much later than the concept of *varna* and came into existence as a means of facilitating the assimilation of large tribal groups into the larger Indian society. Recent evidence, however, suggests that an early form of the segregated joint family may have existed in Harappan society. The dig at Mohenjo-Daro indicates that the city was rigidly divided into separate blocks based on occupation, which possibly reflected fears of pollution. If that is the case, the idea of the large joint family may have originally been a Dravidian concept that survived and adapted to the Aryan conquest. Whatever the truth of the matter, the *jati* eventually became

identified with a specific caste, living in a specific area and carrying out a specific function in society. Each caste was divided into thousands of separate *jatis*, each with its own separate economic function.

Caste was thus the basic social organization into which traditional Indian society was divided. Each *jati* was itself composed of hundreds if not thousands of individual nuclear families and was governed by its own council of elders. Membership in this ruling council was usually hereditary and was based on the wealth or social status of particular families within the community.

In theory, each *jati* was assigned a particular form of economic activity. Obviously, though, not all families in a given caste could take part in the same vocation, and as time went on, members of a single *jati* commonly engaged in several different lines of work. Sometimes an entire *jati* would have to move its location in order to continue a particular form of activity. In other cases, it would adopt an entirely new occupation in order to remain in a certain area. Such changes in habitat or occupation introduced the possibility of movement up or down the social scale. In this way, an entire *jati* could sometimes engage in upward mobility, even though it was not possible for individuals, who were tied to their caste identity for life, to do so.

The caste system may sound highly constricting, but there were persuasive social and economic reasons why it survived for so many centuries. In the first place, it provided an identity for individuals in a highly hierarchical society. Although an individual might rank lower on the social scale than members of other castes, it was always possible to find others ranked at a lower level. Caste was also a means for new groups, such as mountain tribal people, to achieve a recognizable place in the broader community. Perhaps equally important, caste was a primitive form of welfare system. Each *jati* was obliged to provide for any of its members who were poor or destitute. Caste also provided an element of stability in a society that, all too often, was in a state of political anarchy.

DAILY LIFE IN ANCIENT INDIA

Beyond these rigid social stratifications was the Indian family. Not only was life centered around the family, but the family, not the individual, was the most basic unit in society. The ideal was an extended family, with three generations living under the same roof. It was essentially patriarchal, except along the Malabar coast, near the southwestern tip of the subcontinent, where a matriarchal form of social organization prevailed down to mod-

ern times. In the rest of India, the oldest male traditionally possessed legal authority over the entire family unit.

The family was linked together in a religious sense by
a series of commemorative rites to ancestral members.
This ritual originated in the Vedic era and consisted of
family ceremonies to honor the departed and to link the
living and the dead. The male family head was responsible for leading the ritual. At his death, his eldest son had
the duty of conducting the funeral rites.

The importance of the father and the son in family ritual underlined the importance of males in Indian society.
Male superiority was expressed in a variety of ways.
Women could not serve as priests (although, in practice,
some were accepted as seers), nor were they normally
permitted to study the Vedas. In general, males had a
monopoly on education, since the primary goal of learning to read was to carry on family rituals. In high-class
families, young men, after having been initiated into the
sacred thread, began Vedic studies with a *guru* (teacher).
Some then went on to higher studies in one of the major
cities. The goal of such an education might be either professional or religious. Such young men were not supposed
to marry until after twelve years of study.

In general, only males could inherit property, except
in a few cases where there were no sons. According to
law, a woman was always considered a minor. Divorce
was prohibited, although it sometimes took place. According to the *Arthasastra,* a wife who had been deserted by her husband could seek a divorce. Polygamy
was fairly rare and apparently occurred mainly among
the higher classes, but husbands were permitted to take
a second wife if the first was barren. Producing children
was an important aspect of marriage, both because they
provided security for their parents in old age and because they were a physical proof of male potency. Child
marriage was common for young girls, whether because
of the desire for children or because daughters represented an economic liability to their parents. But perhaps the most graphic symbol of women's subjection to
men was the ritual of *sati* (often written *suttee*), which
required the wife to throw herself on her dead husband's funeral pyre. The Greek visitor Megasthenes reported "that he had heard from some persons of wives
burning themselves along with their deceased husbands
and doing so gladly; and that those women who refused
to burn themselves were held in disgrace." All in all, it
was undoubtedly a difficult existence. According to the
Law of Manu, women were subordinated to men, first to
their father, then to their husband, and finally to their
sons:

She should do nothing independently
 even in her own house.
In childhood subject to her father,
 in youth to her husband,
and when her husband is dead to her sons,
 she should never enjoy independence. . . .

She should always be cheerful,
 and skillful in her domestic duties,
with her household vessels well cleansed,
 and her hand tight on the purse-strings. . . .

In season and out of season
 her lord, who wed her with sacred rites,
ever gives happiness to his wife,
 both here and in the other world.

Though he be uncouth and prone to pleasure,
 though he have no good points at all,
the virtuous wife should ever
 worship her lord as a god.[5]

At the root of female subordination to the male was the
practical fact that, as in most agricultural societies, men
did most of the work in the fields. Females were viewed as
having little utility outside the home and indeed were
considered an economic burden, since parents were
obliged to provide a dowry to acquire a husband for a
daughter. Female children also appeared to offer little advantage in maintaining the family unit, since they joined
the families of their husbands after the wedding ceremony.

Despite all of these indications of female subjection to
the male, there are numerous signs that in some ways,
women often played an influential role in Indian society,
and the Hindu code of behavior stressed that they should
be treated with respect (see the box on p. 58). Indians appeared to be fascinated by female sexuality, and tradition
held that women often used their sexual powers to
achieve domination over men. The author of the Mahabharata complained that "the fire has never too many
logs, the ocean never too many rivers, death never too
many living souls, and fair-eyed woman never too many
men." Despite the legal and social constraints, women often played an important role within the family unit, and
many were admired and honored for their talents. It is
probably significant that paintings and sculpture from ancient and medieval India frequently show women in a
role equal to the men, and the tradition of the henpecked
husband is as prevalent in India as in many Western societies (see the box on p. 59).

⇒ *The Position of Women in Ancient India* ⇐

The ambivalence toward women in ancient India is apparent in this passage from the Law of Manu, *which states that men should respect women. At the same time, it also makes clear that women's place is in the home.*

The *Law of Manu*

Women must be honored and adorned by their father, brothers, husbands, and brothers-in-law who desire great good fortune.

Where women, verily, are honored, there the gods rejoice; where, however, they are not honored, there all sacred rites prove fruitless.

Where the female relations live in grief—that family soon perishes completely; where, however, they do not suffer from any grievance—that family always prospers. . . .

Her father protects her in childhood, her husband protects her in youth, her sons protect her in old age—a woman does not deserve independence.

The father who does not give away his daughter in marriage at the proper time is censurable; censurable is the husband who does not approach his wife in due season; and after the husband is dead, the son, verily, is censurable, who does not protect his mother.

Even against the slightest provocations should women be particularly guarded; for unguarded they would bring grief to both the families.

Regarding this as the highest dharma of all four classes, husbands, though weak, must strive to protect their wives.

His own offspring, character, family, self, and dharma does one protect when he protects his wife scrupulously. . . .

The husband should engage his wife in the collection and expenditure of his wealth, in cleanliness, in dharma, in cooking food for the family, and in looking after the necessities of the household. . . .

Women destined to bear children, enjoying great good fortune, deserving of worship, the resplendent lights of homes on the one hand and divinities of good luck who reside in the houses on the other—between these there is no difference whatsoever.

Homosexuality was not unknown in India. It was condemned in the lawbooks, however, and generally ignored by literature, which devoted its attention entirely to erotic heterosexuality. The *Kamasutra*, a textbook on sexual practices and techniques dating from the second century C.E. or slightly thereafter, mentions homosexuality briefly and with no apparent enthusiasm.

The Economy

Most people in ancient India, of course, were primarily concerned with survival. This was certainly true for the vast majority who lived on the land. The Aryan conquest did not drastically change the economic character of Indian society. Not only did most Aryans apparently abandon their pastoral existence and take up farming, but it is likely that agriculture expanded rapidly under Aryan rule with the invention of the iron plow and the spread of North Indian culture into the Deccan Plateau. One consequence of this process was to shift the focus of Indian culture from the Indus valley further eastward to the Ganges River valley, which even today is one of the most densely populated regions on earth. The flatter areas in the Deccan Plateau and in the coastal plains were also turned into cropland.

For most Indian farmers, life was harsh indeed. Among the most fortunate were those who owned their own land, although they were, of course, required to pay taxes. Many others were sharecroppers or landless laborers. They were subject to the vicissitudes of the market and often paid exorbitant rents to their landlord. Concentration of land in large holdings was limited by the tradition of dividing property among all the sons, but large estates worked by hired laborers or rented out to sharecroppers were not uncommon, particularly in areas where local *rajas* derived much of their wealth from their property.

Another problem for Indian farmers was the unpredictability of the climate. India is in the monsoon zone. The monsoon is a seasonal wind pattern in southern Asia that blows from the southwest during the summer months and from the northeast during the winter. The southwest monsoon is commonly marked by heavy rains as the moisture-laden winds pass over the Indian landmass. If the rains were late, as they frequently were, thousands would starve, particularly in the drier areas, which were especially dependent upon rainfall. Strong governments attempted to deal with such problems by building

⇒ The Henpecked Monk ⇐

This passage is from the Sutrakrtanga, one of the sacred books of the Jain religion. While the object of concern is technically not that familiar figure of ridicule, the henpecked husband, the passage indicates the concern that many men in ancient India felt when exposed to the wiles of their female contemporaries.

The *Sutrakrtanga*

A celibate monk shouldn't fall in love,
and though he hankers after pleasure he should hold
himself in check,
for these are the pleasures
which some monks enjoy.

If a monk breaks his vows,
and falls for a woman,
she upbraids him and raises her foot to him,
and kicks him on the head.

"Monk, if you won't live with me
as husband and wife,
I'll pull out my hair and become a nun,
for you shall not live without me!"

But when she has him in her clutches
it's all housework and errands!
"Fetch a knife to cut this gourd!"
"Get me some fresh fruit!"

"We want wood to boil the greens,
and for a fire in the evening!"
"Now paint my feet!"
"Come and massage my back". . .

"Get me my lip-salve!"
"Find my sunshade and slippers!"
"I want a knife to cut this string!"
"Take my robe and have it dyed blue!". . .

"Fetch me my tweezers and my comb!"
"Get me a ribbon to tie my hair!"
"Now pass me my looking-glass!"
"Put my toothbrush down beside me!". . .

"Fetch the pot and the drum and the rag-ball,
for our little boy to play with!"
"Monk, the rains are on the way,
patch the roof of the house and look to the stores!"

"Bring me the chair with the twine seat,
and my wooden-soled slippers to go out walking!"
So pregnant women boss their husbands,
just as though they were household slaves.

When a child is born, the reward of their labors,
she makes the father hold the baby.
And sometimes the fathers of sons
stagger under their burdens like camels.

They get up at night, as though they were nurses,
to lull the howling child to sleep,
and, though they are shamefaced about it,
scrub dirty garments, just like washermen. . . .

So, monks, resist the wiles of women,
avoid their friendship and company.
The little pleasure you get from them
will only lead you into trouble!

state-operated granaries and maintaining the irrigation works, but strong governments were rare and famine was probably all too common. The staple crops in the north were wheat, barley and millet, with wet rice common in the fertile river valleys. In the south, grain and vegetables were supplemented by various tropical products, cotton, and spices such as pepper, ginger, cinnamon, and saffron.

By no means were all Indians farmers. As time passed, India became one of the most advanced trading and manufacturing civilizations in the ancient world, although in isolated mountain areas people still lived by hunting and food gathering. As we saw earlier, regional trade had developed during the Harappan period, when prosperous merchants carried on lucrative commercial relations with neighboring Mesopotamia and probably even with Saba (Sheba) and other states in the region of the Red Sea (see Chapter 8).

After the rise of the Mauryas, India's role in regional trade began to expand, and the subcontinent became a major transit point in a vast commercial network that

◆ Female Earth Spirit. This 2,000-year-old female earth spirit carved from sandstone represents the ancient Indian fertility concept. Voluptuous and idealized, these spirits could allegedly cause a tree to blossom if they merely touched a branch with their arm or wrapped a leg around its trunk. Graceful and sensuous, she seems to be breathing and moving out of the stone.

extended from the rim of the Pacific to the Middle East and the Mediterranean Sea. This regional trade went both by sea and by camel caravan. Maritime trade across the Indian Ocean may have begun as early as the fifth century B.C.E. It extended eastward from the Red Sea as far as Southeast Asia and China and southward as far as the straits between Africa and the island of Madagascar. At first, most trading ships followed the coastline, but later navigators mastered the monsoon winds and struck directly across open water to their destination. Westward went spices, perfumes, jewels, textiles, precious stones and ivory, and wild animals. In return, India received gold, tin, lead, and wine.

India's expanding role as a manufacturing and commercial hub of the ancient world was undoubtedly a spur to the growth of the state. Under Chandragupta Maurya, the central government became actively involved in commercial and manufacturing activities. It owned mines and vast crown lands and undoubtedly earned massive profits from its role in regional commerce. Separate government departments were established for trade, agriculture, mining, and the manufacture of weapons, and the movement of private goods was vigorously taxed. Nevertheless, a significant private sector also flourished; it was dominated by great caste guilds, which monopolized key sectors of the economy. A money economy probably came into operation during the second century B.C.E., when copper and gold coins were introduced from the Middle East. This in turn led to the development of banking. But village trade continued to be conducted by means of cowry shells (a highly polished shell used as a medium of exchange throughout much of Africa and Asia) or barter throughout the ancient period.

*E*scaping the Wheel of Life: The Religious World of Ancient India

Many people in the West associate India with religion. One reason for this is that two of the world's great religions, Buddhism and Hinduism, and several smaller ones, such as Jainism and Sikhism, originated in India. Probably another factor is the otherworldly character that many observers ascribe to Indian religion. To most Westerners, for example, the primary symbols of Indian religion are gurus, ascetics, and the nonviolent ideas of Mahatma Gandhi, the reformer who played a major role in the twentieth-century struggle to free India from British colonial rule.

Gandhi, gurus, and ascetics are all a legitimate part of Indian religious thought and practice, but it is probably misleading to believe that they are typical or representative of all religious belief in India. In actuality, Indian religion is as complex and concerned with everyday practical matters as is religion in most countries, including those of the West.

One historical reason for this complexity is that, like Indian politics and society, Indian religion is a blend of Aryan and Dravidian culture. The clash and subsequent intermingling of those two civilizations gave rise to an extraordinarily complex set of religious beliefs and practices filled with diversity and contrast. Although the differences between the two forms of religion were substantial, a number of religious practices commonly associated with Hinduism, such as the practice of yoga, the presence of sacred animals, and phallic worship, were also present in the belief structure of the Harappan peoples.

Hinduism

Evidence about the earliest religious beliefs of the Aryan peoples comes primarily from sacred texts such as the Vedas, a set of four collections of hymns and religious ceremonies transmitted by memory through the centuries by Aryan priests. Many of these religious ideas were probably common to all of the Indo-European peoples before their separation into different groups at least four thousand years ago. Early Aryan beliefs were based on the common concept of a pantheon of gods and goddesses representing great forces of nature similar to the immortals of Greek mythology. The Aryan ancestor of the Greek father-god Zeus, for example, may have been the deity known in early Aryan tradition as Dyaus (see Chapter 4).

As in Greek mythology, however, the parent god Dyaus was a somewhat distant figure who was eventually overshadowed by other, more functional gods possessing more familiar human traits. For a while, the primary Aryan god was the great warrior god Indra. Indra summoned the Aryan tribal peoples to war and was represented in nature by thunder. Later, Indra declined in importance and was replaced by Varuna, lord of justice, who eventually evolved into the modern deity Vishnu. As in Greek mythology, there were gods and goddesses representing various forces of nature or the needs of human beings, such as fire, fertility, wealth, and so forth.

The concept of sacrifice was a key element in Aryan religious belief in Vedic times. As in many other ancient cultures, the practice may have begun as human sacrifice, but later animals were used as substitutes, although human sacrifice was practiced in some isolated communities

down to modern times. The priestly class, or *brahmins,* played a key role in these ceremonies.

Another element of Aryan religious belief in ancient times was the idea of asceticism. The concept of self-sacrifice or even self-mutilation as a means of achieving an understanding of underlying reality was alluded to briefly in Vedic hymns (those who took part in the practice were called "silent ones"). But it began to become increasingly common with the writing of the so-called Upanishads (a set of commentaries on the Vedas) in the sixth century B.C.E., when it replaced the concept of sacrifice as a means of placating or communicating with the gods. According to one ancient critic of the practice of sacrifice, for example:

> Unsteady, indeed, are these boats in the form of sacrifices, eighteen in number, in which is prescribed only the inferior work. The fools who delight in this sacrificial ritual as the highest spiritual good go again and again through the cycle of old age and death.
>
> Abiding in the midst of ignorance, wise only according to their own estimate, thinking themselves to be learned, but really hard-struck, these fools go around in a circle like blind men led by one who is himself blind.
>
> Abiding manifoldly in ignorance they, all the same, like immature children think to themselves: "We have accomplished our aim." Since the performers of sacrificial ritual do not realize the truth because of passion, therefore, they, the wretched ones, sink down from heaven when the merit which qualified them for the higher world becomes exhausted. . . .
>
> Those who practice penance and faith in the forest, the tranquil ones, the knowers of truth, living the life of wandering mendicancy—they depart, freed from passion, through the door of the sun, to where dwells, verily. . . .the imperishable Soul.[6]

Apparently, the original motive for asceticism was to achieve magical powers, but later it was seen as a means of spiritual meditation that would enable the practitioner to reach beyond material reality to a world of truth and bliss beyond earthly joy and sorrow. According to a passage from one of the Upanishads: "The Self who is free from evil, free from old age, free from death, free from grief, free from hunger, free from thirst, whose desire is the Real [*satya,* or truth], whose intention is the Real— he should be sought after, he should be desired to be comprehended."[7] It is possible that another motive was to permit those with strong religious convictions to communicate directly with metaphysical reality without having to rely on the priestly class at court.

Asceticism, of course, has been practiced in other religions including Christianity and Islam, but it seems particularly identified with Hinduism, the religion that

❧ The Origins of the Universe ❧

The origins of the universe are among the topics considered in the Rigveda, India's earliest and perhaps most sacred work. This passage shows the monistic character of early Indian metaphysical belief. "Prajapati" in the text means "Lord of Creation."

The Rigveda

A golden embryo (hiranyagarbha) evolved in the beginning. Born the lord of what has come to be, he alone existed. He established the earth and heaven here. To what god should we do homage with our oblation?

Who is the life-giver, the strength-giver, whose decree all [even] the gods, honor, whose shadow is immortality and death—to what god should we do homage with our oblation?

Who has become the sole king of the breathing, shimmering world in its greatness, who is lord of the two-footed and four-footed here—to what god should we do homage with our oblation?

Whose are these snow-covered mountains in their greatness, whose is the sea together with, they say, the [world-]stream, whose are these directions, whose the two sides—to what god should we do homage with our oblation?

By whom were the mighty earth and heaven made firm, by whom the sky, by whom was the vault of heaven made fast, who measures out the region of the mid-space—to what god should we do homage with our oblation?

To whom both lines, being held fast, looked for help, quivering in their hearts, as over them the risen sun shines—to what god should we do homage with our oblation?

When the deep waters came, carrying everything as an embryo and giving birth to the fire [of worship], then the life of the gods, the sole [existent], evolved—to what god should we do homage with our oblation?

Who surveyed the waters in their greatness, the waters that carried the skill [to sacrifice] and gave birth to worship, who, the god beyond the gods, alone existed—to what god should we do homage with our oblation?

[later addition]

Let not him, the father of earth, do us harm or him who, keeping his principles true, has produced heaven and who produced the shining, deep waters—to what god should we do homage with our oblation?

[still later addition]

Prajapati! None other than you has encompassed all these things that have been engendered. That for which we desire as we make oblation to you, let that be ours. May we be lords of riches.

---

emerged from early Indian religious tradition. Eventually, asceticism evolved into the modern practice of body training that we know as *yoga* (union), which is accepted today as a meaningful element of Hindu religious practice.

Much early Aryan religious belief, as we have seen, was an adaptation of spirit worship into a form of naturalistic polytheism. The overall practical purpose was to protect the tribe from the multitude of threats to its survival. Eventually, however, Indians began to move beyond such common elements of the Indo-European pastoral tradition and engaged in speculation about the nature of the cosmic order. What emerged was a growing belief in the existence of a single monistic force in the universe, a form of ultimate reality called *Brahman*. Today the early form of Hinduism is sometimes called Brahmanism (see the box above). In the Upanishads, the concept began to emerge as an important element of Indian religious belief. It was the duty of the individual self—called the *Atman*—to achieve an understanding of this ultimate reality so that after death the self would merge in spiritual form with *Brahman*. Sometimes *Brahman* was described in more concrete terms as a creator god—eventually known as Vishnu—but more often in terms of a shadowy ultimate reality. According to one of the Upanishads:

In the beginning, my dear, this world was just being, one only, without a second. Some people, no doubt, say: "In the beginning, verily, this world was just nonbeing, one only, without a second; from that nonbeing, being was produced." But how, indeed, my dear, could it be so? said he. How could being be produced from nonbeing?

On the contrary, my dear, in the beginning this world was being alone, one only, without a second. Being thought to itself: "May I be many, may I procreate." It produced fire. That fire thought to itself: "May I be many, may I procreate." It produced water. Therefore, whenever a person grieves or perspires, then it is from fire [heat] alone that water is produced. That water thought to itself: "May I be many; may I procreate." It produced food. Therefore, whenever it rains, then there is abundant food; it is from water alone that food for eating is produced. . . . That divinity (Being) thought to itself: "Well, having entered into these three divinities [fire, water, and food] by means of this living Self, let me develop names and forms. . . ."[8]

REINCARNATION

Another new concept also probably began to appear around the time the Upanishads were written—the idea of reincarnation. This is the idea that the individual soul is reborn in a different form after death and progresses through several existences on the wheel of life until it reaches its final destination in a union with the Great World Soul, known as *Brahman*. Because life is harsh, this final release is the objective of all living souls.

A key element in this process is the idea of *karma*—that one's rebirth in a next life is determined by one's *karma* (actions) in this life. Hinduism places all living species on a vast scale of existence, including the four classes and the untouchables in human society. The current status of an individual soul, then, is not simply a cosmic accident, but the inevitable result of actions that that soul has committed in a past existence.

At the top of the scale are the *brahmins* (the priestly caste), who by definition are closest to ultimate release from the law of reincarnation. The *brahmins* are followed in descending order by the other castes in human society and the world of the beasts. Within the animal kingdom, an especially high position is reserved for the cow, which even today is revered by Hindus as a sacred beast. Some have speculated that the unique role played by the cow in Hinduism derives from the value of cattle in Aryan pastoral society. But others have pointed out that cattle were a source of both money and food and suggest that the cow's sacred position may have descended from the concept of the sacred bull in Dravidian culture.

The concept of *karma* is governed by the *dharma*, or the Law. A law regulating human behavior, the *dharma* imposes different requirements on different individuals, depending on their status in society. Those high on the social scale, such as *brahmins* and *kshatriyas*, are held to a more strict form of behavior than are *sudras*. The *brahmin*, for example, is expected to abstain from eating meat, because that would entail the killing of another living being, thus interrupting its *karma*.

How the concept of reincarnation originated is not known, although it was apparently not unusual for early peoples to believe that the individual soul would be reborn in a different form in a later life. In any case, in In-

✦ **Dancing Siva.** The Hindu deity Siva is often presented in the form of a bronze statue, performing his cosmic dance in which he simultaneously creates and destroys the universe. While his upper right hand creates the cosmos, his upper left hand reduces it in flames, and the lower two hands offer eternal blessing. Siva's dancing statues present the visual message of his power and compassion to his followers.

dia the concept may have had practical causes as well as consequences. In the first place, it tended to provide religious sanction for the rigid class divisions that had begun to emerge in Indian society after the Aryan conquest, and it provided moral and political justification for the privileges of those on the higher end of the scale.

At the same time, the concept of reincarnation provided certain compensations for those lower on the ladder of life. For example, it gave hope to the poor that if they behaved properly in this life, they might improve their condition in the next. It also provided a means for unassimilated groups such as tribal peoples to find a place in Indian society while at the same time permitting them to maintain their distinctive way of life.

The ultimate goal of achieving "good" *karma*, as we have seen, was to escape the cycle of existence. Life for most Indians in ancient times, as for many today, was painful, brutish, and short. To the sophisticated, the nature of that release was a spiritual union of the individual soul with the Great World Soul, *Brahman,* described in the Upanishads as a form of dreamless sleep, free from earthly desires. Such a concept, however, was undoubtedly too ethereal for the average Indian, who needed a more concrete form of heavenly salvation, a place of beauty and bliss after a life of disease and privation.

It was probably for this reason that the Hindu religion—in some ways so otherworldly and ascetic—came to be peopled with a multitude of very human gods and goddesses. It has been estimated that the Hindu pantheon contains more than 33,000 deities. Only a small number are primary ones, however, notably the so-called trinity of gods—Brahman the Creator, Vishnu the Preserver, and Siva (originally the Vedic god Rudra) the Destroyer. Although Brahman (sometimes in his concrete form called Brahma) is considered to be the highest god, Vishnu and Siva take precedence in the devotional exercises of many Hindus, who can be roughly divided into Vishnuites and Saivites. In addition to the trinity of gods, all of whom have wives with readily identifiable roles and personalities, there are countless minor deities, each again with its own specific function, such as bringing good fortune, arranging a good marriage, or guaranteeing a son in childbirth.

The rich variety and earthy character of many Hindu deities are repugnant to many Christians and Muslims, to whom God is an all-seeing and transcendent deity. Many Hindus, however, regard the multitude of gods as simply different manifestations of one ultimate reality. The various deities also provide a useful means for ordinary Indians to personify their religious feelings. Even though some individuals among the early Aryans attempted to communicate with the gods through sacrifice or asceticism, most Indians undoubtedly sought to satisfy their own individual religious needs through devotion, which they expressed through ritual ceremonies and offerings at a Hindu temple. Such offerings were not only a way to seek salvation, but also a means of satisfying all the aspirations of daily life.

Over the centuries, then, Hinduism changed radically from its origins in Aryan tribal society and became a religion of the vast majority of the Indian people. Concern with a transcendental union between the individual soul and the World Soul contrasted with practical desires for material wealth and happiness; ascetic self-denial contrasted with an earthy emphasis on the pleasures and values of sexual union between marriage partners. All of these became aspects of Hinduism, the religion of 70 percent of the Indian people.

Buddhism: The Middle Path

In the sixth century B.C.E., a new doctrine appeared in northern India that soon began to rival Hinduism's popularity throughout the subcontinent. This new doctrine was called Buddhism. The historical founder of Buddhism, Siddhartha Gautama, was a native of a small principality in the foothills of the Himalaya Mountains in what is today southern Nepal. He was born in the mid-sixth century B.C.E., the son of a ruling *kshatriya* family. According to tradition, the young Siddhartha was raised in affluent surroundings and trained, like many other members of his class, in the martial arts. On reaching maturity, he married and began to raise a family. But, according to Buddhist tradition, at the age of twenty-nine he suddenly discovered the pain of illness, the sorrow of death, and the degradation caused by old age in the lives of ordinary people and exclaimed: "Would that sickness, age, and death might be for ever bound!" From that time on, he decided to dedicate his life to determining the cause and seeking the cure for human suffering.

To find the answers to these questions, Siddhartha abandoned his home and family and traveled widely. At first he tried to follow the model of the ascetics (a popular recourse at that time for sensitive upper-class Hindus disgusted with the hedonism of elite lifestyles), but he eventually decided that self-mortification did not lead to a greater understanding of life and abandoned the practice. Then one day after a lengthy period of meditation under a tree, he finally achieved enlightenment as to the meaning of life and spent the remainder of his life preaching it. His conclusions, as embodied in his teachings, became the philosophy (or, as some would have it, the religion) of Buddhism. According to legend, the Devil (the Indian term is Mara) attempted desperately to tempt him with political power and the company of beautiful girls. But Siddhartha Gautama resisted:

> *Pleasure is brief as a flash of lightning*
> *Or like an Autumn shower, only for a moment . . .*
> *Why should I then covet the pleasures you speak of?*
> *I see your bodies are full of all impurity:*
> *Birth and death, sickness and age are yours.*
> *I seek the highest prize, hard to attain by men—*
> *The true and constant wisdom of the wise.*[9]

How much the modern doctrine of Buddhism resembles the original teachings of Siddhartha Gautama is open to debate, since much time has elapsed since his death and original texts relating his ideas are lacking. Nor is it certain

≈ How to Achieve Enlightenment ≈

One of the most famous passages in Buddhist literature is the sermon at Benares, which Siddhartha Gautama delivered to his followers in a deer park outside the holy city of Varanasi (Benares). Here he set forth the key ideas that would define Buddhist beliefs for centuries to come.

The Sermon at Benares

Thus have I heard: at one time the Lord dwelt at Benares at Isipatana in the Deer Park. There the Lord addressed the five monks:—

"These two extremes, monks, are not to be practiced by one who has gone forth from the world. What are the two? That conjoined with the passions and luxury, low, vulgar, common, ignoble, and useless; and that conjoined with self-torture, painful, ignoble, and useless. Avoiding these two extremes the Tathagata has gained the enlightenment of the Middle Path, which produces insight and knowledge and tends to calm, to higher knowledge, enlightenment, Nirvana.

"And what, monks, is the Middle Path, of which the Tathagata has gained enlightenment, which produces insight and knowledge, and tends to calm, to higher knowledge, enlightenment, Nirvana? This is the noble Eightfold Way: namely, right view, right intention, right speech, right action, right livelihood, right effort, right mindfulness, right concentration. This, monks, is the Middle Path, of which the Tathagata has gained enlightenment, which produces insight and knowledge, and tends to calm, to higher knowledge, enlightenment, Nirvana.

1. "Now this, monks, is the noble truth of pain: birth is painful, old age is painful, sickness is painful, death is painful, sorrow, lamentation, dejection, and despair are painful. Contact with unpleasant things is painful, not getting what one wishes is painful. In short the five groups of graspings are painful.
2. Now this, monks, is the noble truth of the cause of pain: the craving, which tends to rebirth, combined with pleasure and lust, finding pleasure here and there; namely, the craving for passion, the craving for existence, the craving for non-existence.
3. Now this, monks, is the noble truth of the cessation of pain, the cessation without a remainder of craving, the abandonment, forsaking, release, non-attachment.
4. Now this, monks, is the noble truth of the way that leads to the cessation of pain: this is the noble Eightfold Way; namely, right view, right intention, right speech, right action, right livelihood, right effort, right mindfulness, right concentration.

"And when, monks, in these four noble truths my due knowledge and insight with its three sections and twelve divisions was well purified, then monks . . . I had attained the highest complete enlightenment. This I recognized. Knowledge arose in me, insight arose that the release of my mind is unshakable; this is my last existence; now there is no rebirth."

that Siddhartha Gautama even intended to found a new religion or doctrine. In some respects, his ideas could be viewed as a reformist form of Hinduism, much as Martin Luther saw Protestantism as a reformation of Christianity. Siddhartha accepted much of the belief system of Hinduism, if not all of its practices. For example, he accepted the concept of reincarnation and the role of *karma* as a means of influencing the movement of individual souls up and down in the scale of life. He followed Hinduism in praising nonviolence and borrowed the idea of living a life of simplicity and chastity from the ascetics. Moreover, his vision of metaphysical reality—commonly known as *Nirvana*—is closer to the Hindu concept of *Brahman* than it is to the Christian concept of heavenly salvation. *Nirvana,* which involves an extinction of selfhood and a final reunion with the Great World Soul, is sometimes likened to a dreamless sleep or to a kind of "blowing out" (as of a candle). Buddhists occasionally remark that someone who asks for a description does not understand the concept.

At the same time, the new doctrine differed from existing Hindu practices in a number of key ways. In the first place, Siddhartha denied the existence of an individual soul. To him, the Hindu concept of *Atman*—the individual soul—meant that the soul was subject to rebirth and thus did not achieve a complete liberation from the cares of this world. In fact, Siddhartha denied the ultimate reality of the material world in its entirety and taught that humans' physical surroundings are an illusion

✦ **A Buddhist Prayer Hall.** Carved out of solid rock cliffs during the Mauryan dynasty, these rock chambers served as small meditation halls for traveling Buddhist monks. By the first century C.E., they had evolved into elaborate temples, the greatest being this example at Karli. Measuring over 120 feet in length and 45 feet high, with pillars, an altar, and a vault, it is reminiscent of the Roman basilica in the West.

to be transcended. Siddhartha's idea of achieving *Nirvana* was based on his conviction that the pain, poverty, and sorrow that afflict human beings are caused essentially by their attachment to the things of this world. Once worldly cares are abandoned, pain and sorrow can be forgotten. With this knowledge comes *bodhi*, or wisdom (thus, the term Buddhism and the familiar name of Gautama Buddha, or Gautama the Wise, for Siddhartha Gautama).

Achieving this understanding is a key step on the road to *Nirvana*, which, as in Hinduism, is a form of release from the wheel of life. According to tradition, Siddhartha transmitted this message in a sermon to his disciples in a deer park at Sarnath, not far from the modern city of Benares (also known as Varanasi). Like so many messages, it is deceptively simple and is enclosed in Four Noble Truths: life is suffering; suffering is caused by desire; the way to end suffering is to end desire; and the way to end desire is to avoid the extremes of a life of vulgar materialism and a life of self-torture and to follow the "Middle Path." This Middle Path, which is also known as the Eightfold Path, calls for right knowledge, right purpose, right speech, right conduct, right occupation, right effort, right awareness, and right meditation (see the box on p. 65).

Buddhism also differed from Hinduism in its relative egalitarianism. Although Siddhartha accepted the idea of reincarnation (and thereby the idea that human beings differ as a result of *karma* accumulated in a previous existence), he rejected the Hindu division of humanity into rigidly defined castes based on previous reincarnations and taught that all human beings could aspire to *Nirvana* as a result of their behavior in this life. This egalitarian message undoubtedly proved advantageous for the new doctrine as it competed with the powerful traditional force of Hinduism for support among the downtrodden peoples at the lower end of the social scale.

Buddhism also differed from Hinduism in its simplicity. Siddhartha rejected the panoply of gods that had become identified with Hinduism and forbade his followers to worship his person or his image after his death. In fact, many Buddhists view Buddhism as a philosophy rather than as a religion, citing Siddhartha's alleged comment that to discuss metaphysics is like building a castle in the sand—it will be washed away at the first high tide.

In one respect, Siddhartha Gautama was unable to transcend the social prejudices of his day, at least as his life and thought have been interpreted in Buddhist texts. Like many of his contemporaries, he was reportedly reluctant to accept women as the equal of men. In a conversation with his disciple Ananda, he remarked: "Women are soon angered, Ananda; women are full of passion, Ananda; women are envious, Ananda; women are stupid, Ananda. That is the reason, Ananda, that the cause, why women have no place in public assemblies, do not carry on a business, and do not earn their living by any profession."

One reason for Gautama's suspicion of women was probably his concern that sexual desire could seriously undermine the monastic life and an individual's concentration on the search for wisdom. Spiritual manhood required an abandonment of man's sexual nature. When Ananda asked the Master, "how shall we behave before women?" their conversation proceeded as follows:

"You should shun their gaze, Ananda."
"But if we see them, master, what then are we to do?"
"Not speak to them, Ananda."
"But if we do speak to them, what then?"
"Then you must watch over yourselves, Ananda."[10]

As time went on, Ananda's appeals had some effect, and Siddhartha Gautama agreed to accept women into the monastic order, but their inferior position within the order had been established and characterized Buddhist attitudes toward women down to modern times. Still, the position of women tended to be better in Buddhist societies than it was elsewhere in ancient India.

After Siddhartha Gautama's death in 480 B.C.E., the Buddhist message was spread by dedicated disciples who traveled the length and breadth of India carrying his message. Buddhist monasteries were established throughout the subcontinent to promote his teaching and provide housing and training for monks dedicated to the simple life and the pursuit of wisdom, while temples and stupas (stone towers housing relics of the Buddha) sprang up like mushrooms in the countryside.

During the next centuries, Buddhism began to compete actively for followers with prevailing Hindu beliefs, as well as with another new faith known as Jainism. Jainism was founded by Mahavira, a contemporary of Siddhartha Gautama. Resembling Buddhism in its rejection of the reality of the material world, Jainism was more extreme in practice. Where Siddhartha Gautama called for the "middle way" between passion and luxury and pain and self-torture, Mahavira preached a doctrine of extreme simplicity to his followers, who kept no possessions and relied on begging for a living. Some even rejected clothing and wandered through the world naked. Per-

CHRONOLOGY

Ancient India

Harappan civilization	c. 3000–1500 B.C.E.
Arrival of the Aryans	c. 1500 B.C.E.
Life of Gautama Buddha	c. 560–480 B.C.E.
Invasion of India by Alexander the Great	326 B.C.E.
Mauryan dynasty founded	324 B.C.E.
Reign of Chandragupta Maurya	324–301 B.C.E.
Reign of Asoka	269–232 B.C.E.
Collapse of Mauryan dynasty	183 B.C.E.
Rise of Kushan kingdom	c. first century C.E.

haps because of its insistence on a life of poverty, Jainism failed to attract enough adherents to become a major doctrine and never received official support. According to tradition, however, Chandragupta Maurya accepted Mahavira's doctrine after abdicating the throne and fasted to death in a Jain monastery.

ASOKA, A BUDDHIST MONARCH

Buddhism, on the other hand, received an important boost when Asoka, greatest of the monarchs of the Mauryan dynasty, converted to Buddhism sometime in the third century B.C.E. Chandragupta Maurya had ruled successfully for a quarter century and then, according to legend, he retired to a monastery and turned over his throne to his son Bindusara. Little is known about Bindusara, but his son and successor, Asoka (269–232 B.C.E.), is generally considered to be the greatest ruler in the history of India. According to historical accounts, like many before and after him, Asoka began his reign conquering, pillaging, and killing. But after his conversion to Buddhism, which preaches the doctrine of nonviolence, the king began to regret his bloodthirsty past. From that time on, he attempted to rule by benevolent means. According to one of his edicts, which is still extant:

When the king, Beloved of the Gods and of Gracious Mien, had been consecrated eight years Kalinga was conquered, 150,000 people were deported, 100,000 were killed, and many times that number died. But after the conquest of Kalinga, the Beloved of the Gods began to follow Righteousness (*Dharma*), to love Righteousness, and to give instruction in Righteousness. . . . The participation of all men in common suffering is grievous to the Beloved of the Gods. . . .[11]

In general, Asoka appears to have lived up to his reputation. He directed that banyan trees and shelters be placed along the road to provide shade and rest for weary travelers. He sent Buddhist missionaries throughout India and ordered the erection of stone pillars with Buddhist inscriptions to instruct people in the proper way. According to tradition, his son (or, according to some, his brother) converted the island of Sri Lanka to Buddhism, and the peoples there accepted a tributary relationship with the Mauryan Empire.

The Rule of the Fishes: India after the Mauryas

After Asoka's death in 232 B.C.E., the Mauryan Empire began to decline. In 183 B.C.E., the last Mauryan ruler was overthrown by one of his military commanders, and India slipped back into disunity. A number of new kingdoms, some of them perhaps influenced by the memory of the Alexandrian conquests, arose along the fringes of the subcontinent in Bactria, known today as Afghanistan. In the first century C.E., Indo-European–speaking peoples fleeing from the nomadic Xiongnu warriors in Central Asia seized power in the area and proclaimed the new Kushan Kingdom (see Chapter 3). For the next two centuries, the Kushanas extended their political sway over northern India as far as the central Ganges valley, while other kingdoms scuffled for predominance elsewhere on the subcontinent. India would not see unity again for another five hundred years.

Why had Kautilya's dream of a vast centralized empire throughout the Indian subcontinent failed to endure? After all, despite the ethnic and caste divisions, most Indians by now had a common sense of culture that had penetrated to a certain degree from the Indus valley in the northwest to the southern part of the Deccan Plateau in the south. Nor were the geographical barriers insurmountable, as the Mauryan conquests had demonstrated. Moreover, Indian tradition contained a strong desire for order and regulation, expressed through the concept of an ancient Golden Age characterized by universal adherence to the sacred *dharma*, while disorder and chaos were strongly condemned.

Some historians suggest that a decline in regional trade during the first millennium C.E. may have con-

tributed to the growth of small land-based kingdoms, which drew their primary income from agriculture. Another possible reason might be the tenacity of the Aryan tribal tradition and its influence on the political behavior of Indian elites. This tradition, which traced back to the nomadic past, survived virtually intact into the Indian period. Although the Mauryan rulers tried to supplant tribal institutions with a more centralized pattern of organization, clan loyalties once again came to the fore after the collapse of the Mauryan dynasty. Despite the modern impression—fostered in part by the pacifist Mahatma Gandhi—that Indian society prizes nonviolence, Indian history has more often been characterized by the rule of force than by the rule of reason. Furthermore, the political behavior of the ruling class was characterized by what Indians call the "rule of the fishes," which glorified warfare as the natural activity of the king and the aristocracy. The *Arthasastra,* which sets forth a model of a centralized Indian state, assumed that war was the "sport of kings" (see the box on p. 53).

Whatever the reasons, the consequences for India were often unfortunate and sometimes tragic. Internal divisions not only undermined government efficiency and social stability, but also opened the door to foreign conquest. Up to the twentieth century, India would rarely be united under the rule of its own indigenous leaders.

The Exuberant World of Indian Culture

Few cultures in the world are as rich and varied as that of India. Most societies excel in some forms of artistic and literary achievement and not in others, but India in its time has produced great works in almost all fields of cultural endeavor—art and sculpture, science, architecture, literature, and even music.

Literature

Few ancient societies can match the quality of India's literary achievement. Early India produced not only great religious literature like the Vedas and the Upanishads, but also great historical epics like the Mahabharata and the Ramayana, as well as drama and poetry.

There is no little irony in this vast output, considering that the written language of the early Harappans has not yet been deciphered, while the Aryan peoples had no written language at all prior to their arrival in the Indian subcontinent. The earliest known Indian literature comes from the Aryan tradition in the form of the four Vedas, which were passed down orally from generation to generation until they were finally written down after the conquest of India. The earliest of the Vedas, the Rigveda, dates from the second millennium B.C.E. and consists of over a thousand hymns that were used at religious ceremonies in Aryan tribal society. The other three Vedas were written considerably later and contain instructions for performing ritual sacrifices and other ceremonies connected with Aryan religious beliefs. Two other major religious works, the Brahmanas and the Upanishads, served as commentaries on the Vedas.

The language of the Vedas was Sanskrit, a member of the Indo-European family of languages, which descended from a common language spoken about four thousand years ago in southern Russia. After the Aryan conquest of India, Sanskrit gradually declined as the spoken language of the Aryan peoples and was replaced in northern India by a simpler tongue known as Prakrit. Nevertheless, Sanskrit continued to be used as the language of the bureaucracy and literary expression for many centuries after that and, like Latin in medieval Europe, served as a common language of communication (*lingua franca*) between various regions of India. In the south, a variety of Dravidian languages continued to be spoken.

As early as the fifth century B.C.E., Indian grammarians had already codified Sanskrit in order to preserve the authenticity of the Vedas for the spiritual edification of future generations. A famous grammar written by the

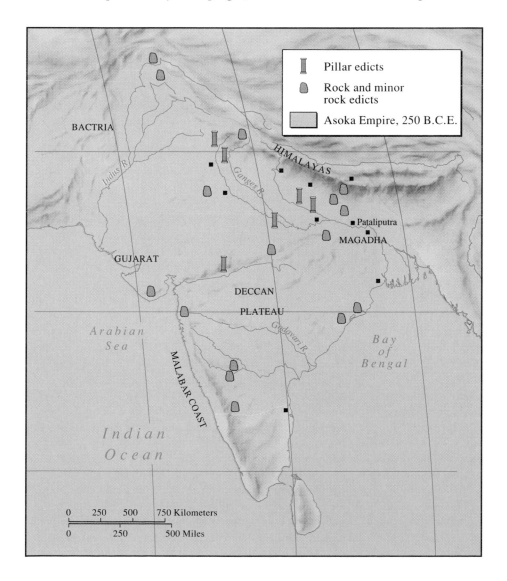

�֍ **Map 2.3**   The Empire of Asoka.

◆ **Asoka's Pillar.** Stone pillars like this polished sandstone column, which is thirty-two feet high, were erected during the reign of Emperor Asoka in the third century B.C.E. Commemorating events in the life of the Buddha or marking routes to the holy sites, they were placed on major trunk roads throughout the Indian subcontinent. The massive size of these pillars, some of which weighed up to fifty tons, is a testimony to the engineering skills of the peoples of ancient India.

scholar Panini in the fourth century B.C.E. set forth four thousand grammatical rules prescribing the correct usage of the spoken and written language. This achievement is particularly impressive in that Europe did not have a science of linguistics until the nineteenth century, when it was developed partly as a result of the discovery of the works of Panini and later Indian linguists.

After the undeciphered script of the Harappan culture, the first sign of a new written language appears with the edicts of the Mauryan emperor Asoka in the third century B.C.E. Those edicts, inscribed on stone columns erected throughout the empire, were written in a phonetic script that eventually evolved into the so-called Devanagari script, which is used by many of the major Indian languages today, including Hindi, the major language spoken in the Ganges valley. In the south, the Dravidian languages used their own phonetic scripts, which, to the untutored eye, look similar to Devanagari. The South Indian scripts were later used as a basis for the creation of written alphabets for several languages in Southeast Asia, including Thai and Khmer.

After the development of a writing system some time in the first millennium B.C.E., India's holy literature was probably inscribed on palm leaves stitched together into a book somewhat similar to the bamboo strips used during the same period in China. Also put into written form for the first time were India's great historical epics, the Mahabharata and the Ramayana. Among the greatest writings of antiquity, both of these epics may have originally been recited at sacrificial ceremonies by Aryan priests, but they are essentially historical writings that recount the martial exploits of great Aryan rulers and warriors.

The Mahabharata, consisting of more than 90,000 stanzas, is considered to be the longest poem in any written language. It was probably written about 100 B.C.E. and describes in great detail a war between cousins in Aryan tribal society for control of the kingdom about 1000 B.C.E. Interwoven in the narrative are many fantastic legends of the Hindu gods. Above all, the Mahabharata is a tale of moral confrontations and an elucidation of the ethical precepts of the *dharma*. The most famous section of the book is the so-called Bhagavadgita, a sermon by the legendary Indian figure Krishna on the eve of a major battle. In this sermon Krishna sets forth one of the key ethical maxims of Indian society: in taking action, one must be indifferent to success or failure and consider only the moral rightness of the act itself (see the box on p. 71).

The Ramayana, written at about the same time, is much shorter than the Mahabharata. It is an account of a semilegendary ruler named Rama who, as the result of a palace intrigue, is banished from the kingdom and forced to live as a hermit in the forest. Later, he fights the demon-king of Sri Lanka (Ceylon), who has kidnapped his beloved wife Sita. Like the Mahabharata, the Ramayana is strongly imbued with religious and moral significance. Rama himself is portrayed as the ideal Aryan hero, a perfect ruler and an ideal son, while Sita projects the supreme duty of female chastity and wifely loyalty to her husband. The Ramayana is a story of the triumph of good over evil, duty over self-indulgence, and generosity over selfishness. It combines filial and erotic love, conflicts of human passion, character analysis, and poetic descriptions of nature.

The Ramayana also has all the ingredients of an enthralling adventure: giants, wondrous flying chariots, invincible arrows and swords, and magic potions and mantras. The relationships among the gods, human beings, and animals are a particularly intriguing feature. One of the real heroes of the story is the monkey-king Hanuman, who flies from India to Sri Lanka to set the

The Dilemma of Arjuna

The Bhagavadgita is a short section of the long epic poem Mahabharata. It describes the dilemma faced by the legendary hero Arjuna as he debated the moral contradiction involved in killing human beings in order to achieve a worthy end. In this famous passage, Krishna (the god Vishnu in human form) exhorts Arjuna to recognize that in some instances, the end justifies the means.

The Bhagavadgita

The Blessed Lord said:

Just as the unwise act, being attached to their action, even so should the wise act, O Bharata, but without attachment, and only with a view to promoting the solidarity of society.

One should not create any conflict in the minds of the ignorant who are attached to action. On the contrary the wise man, himself acting in accordance with the technique of the yoga of action, should induce them willingly to undertake all [prescribed] actions.

Actions of every kind are actually done by the dispositions of matter; and, still, a person whose mind is deluded by the ego thinks: "I am the doer [of those actions]."

But he, O Mighty-Armed One, who knows the truth of the distinctness of the soul from the dispositions of matter and from the actions [resulting therefrom], does not become attached [to the results of actions], realizing that the dispositions operate upon the dispositions.

Those who are deluded by the dispositions of matter become attached to the disposition and the actions [resulting from them]. One who knows the whole truth should not make such dullards, who do not know the whole truth, falter [by himself renouncing all action].

Renouncing into Me all actions, with your mind fixed on the Self, and becoming free from desire and all sense of "my-ness," do you fight, freed from your spiritual fever.

What is action? What is inaction?—as to this even the wise sages are confounded. I will expound action to you, knowing which you will be liberated from evil.

One has to realize what is action; similarly, one has to realize what is wrong action; and one has also to realize what is inaction. Inscrutable, indeed, is the way of action.

He who sees inaction in action and action in inaction, he is discerning among men, expert in the technique of karmayoga, the doer of the entire action [enjoined by his dharma].

He whose undertakings are all devoid of motivating desires and purposes and whose actions are consumed by the fire of knowledge—him the wise call a man of learning.

Renouncing all attachment to the fruits of actions, ever content, independent—such a person even if engaged in action does not do anything whatever.

Action alone is your concern, never at all its fruits. Let not the fruits of action be your motive, nor let yourself be attached to inaction.

Steadfast in Yoga, engage yourself in actions, Dhananjaya, abandoning attachment and becoming even-minded in success and failure. Such even-mindedness is called yoga.

Far inferior is mere action to action done according to the technique of karmayoga, O Dhananjaya. Seek refuge in the [right] mental attitude. Wretched are those who are motivated by the fruits of action. One who acts according to the technique of karmayoga casts off, in this world, the consequences of both his good acts and his bad acts. Therefore take to this yoga. Yoga is skill in actions.

great battle in motion. Although the theme is a serious one, there are many humorous moments, such as a description of bears and monkeys drunk on honey-wine. Another is Hanuman's nocturnal visit to King Ravana's palace (see the box on p. 72). It is no wonder that the Ramayana became a popular favorite among Indians of all age groups and the source of folk tales and dramas that have been recited in Indian villages for centuries.

Architecture and Sculpture

After literature, the greatest achievements of early Indian civilization were in architecture and sculpture. It is appropriate to discuss these two types of artistic creativity together, since they were almost always fused in practice and had the common objective of serving the purposes of religion. Some of the earliest examples of Indian architecture stem from the time of Emperor Asoka, when

⇒ The Monkey-King in Sri Lanka ⇐

In the famous classic, the Ramayana, Rama is assisted in his effort to free his wife from Ravana, the king of Sri Lanka, by the monkey-king Hanuman. In this passage, Hanuman unexpectedly intrudes into the royal harem.

The Ramayana

That was the entrance to Ravana's bedroom. Hanuman ducked under the left corner of the draw-curtain and stood just inside with his back to the wall, looking out at a huge floor lit by flaming lamps of gold and covered with sleeping women so tumbled together that Hanuman could not tell where one lady left off and the next began.

There was hardly space to step anywhere. Those were the countless wives of the Demon King asleep in disarray, lying all over each other, women beautiful and bright as flashes of lightning now locked fast in Sleep's embrace. Hanuman thought, "When even the form of a heavenly star is less than enough, virtue's divine reward for a good life must be to receive such fair shapes and lovely limbs as these!"

Once arriving in that room of women, it would be harder for any man to remember who he was or where he stood or why, than to fly across the sea in the first place. And though Hanuman was not a man, still when he looked at each one he thought no other woman could be fairer, and when he saw the next sleeper she was in turn the best and most beautiful as he looked at her. Truly, among those magnificent women the rays of the one's beauty showed off the charms of another; they slept deeply after an evening of drinking and dancing and playing music. Their fragrant hair was loosened and their bracelets scattered; their beauty marks of sandal paste were smudged and their colored robes unclasped and their waist-chains ran loosely straying to the side; their hazy garlands were disbanded and their pearls had gone and their earrings were lost.

Even the bedroom lamps looked openly out at all those women while they had the chance, as Ravana slept. Hanuman picked his way among the love-skilled Queens of Lanka who were draped over the floor and looked at their faces. They smiled or frowned or sighed in their sleep; their pillows were others' arms and legs and laps; they pulled each other's robes and wrapped themselves in them. With their eyes lashed shut in sleep they were desirable as closed flowers; when they touched each other they smiled and drew closer, believing they pressed Ravana with their breasts. Even asleep the dancers moved enticingly; the girl musicians slept embracing drums and hugging lutes like their long-absent lovers.

The golden lamps on the walls watched over them unblinking, and in their light the gold and jewels of those Queens made a river of lights and colors and shimmering waves of gold and silver. Their pearl necklaces were white water-birds asleep between their breasts, rising and falling; their strings of turquoise were families of blue teal and their hips were the waves and the riverbanks; their faces of golden or white or deep blue skin were the lotuses; when they stirred sleepily, the small bells sewn on their silken clothes were the ripples moving with little sounds; and the bruises and scratches of love on their tender breasts were signs of where the lion and tiger had come to drink.

Buddhism became the religion of the state. The desire to propagate the ideas of Gautama Buddha inspired the great architecture of the Mauryan dynasty and the period that immediately followed.

Until the time of the Mauryas, Aryan buildings and other structures had been constructed of wood. With the rise of the empire, stone began to be used, as artisans arrived in India seeking official employment after the destruction of the Persian Empire by Alexander. Many of these stone carvers accepted the patronage of Emperor Asoka, who used them to spread Buddhist ideas throughout the subcontinent.

There were three main types of religious structure: the pillar, the stupa, and the rock chamber. The pillars are probably the most famous. During Asoka's reign, many stone columns were erected alongside roads to commemorate the events in the Buddha's life and mark pilgrim routes to holy places. Weighing up to fifty tons each and rising as high as thirty feet, these polished sandstone pillars were topped with a carved capital, usually depicting lions uttering the Buddha's message. Ten remain standing today.

A stupa was originally meant to house a relic of the Buddha, such as a lock of his hair or a branch of the famous Bodhi tree, and was constructed in the form of a burial mound (the pyramids in Egypt and similar holy edifices throughout the ancient world also derived from burial mounds). Eventually, the stupa became a place for devotion and the most familiar form of Buddhist architecture. It rose to considerable heights and was surmounted with a spire, possibly representing the stages of existence en route to *Nirvana*. According to legend, Asoka ordered the construction of 84,000 stupas throughout India to promote the Buddha's message. A few survive today, including the famous stupa at Sanchi, begun under Asoka and completed two centuries later.

The final form of early Indian architecture is the rock chamber carved out of a cliff on the side of a mountain. Asoka began the construction of these chambers to provide rooms to house monks or wandering ascetics and to serve as halls for religious ceremonies. Their construction was expanded under the Shungas, who succeeded briefly to power after the collapse of the Mauryan dynasty in the second century B.C.E. The chambers were rectangular in form, with pillars, an altar, and a vault, reminiscent of the Roman basilica in the West. The three most famous chambers of this period are at Bhaja, Karli, and Ajanta; the latter contains twenty-nine rooms.

These three forms of architecture were embellished with decorations that are among India's most treasured sculptures. Consisting of detailed reliefs and free-standing statues of deities, other human figures, and animals, they are permeated with a sense of nature and the vitality of life. Many reflect an amalgamation of popular and sacred themes, of Buddhist, Vedic, and pre-Aryan religious motifs, such as male and female earth spirits. Until the second century C.E., Siddhartha Gautama was represented only through symbols, such as the wheel of life, the Bodhi tree, and the footprint, perhaps because artists felt that it was impossible to render a visual impression of the Buddha in the state of *Nirvana*. After the spread of Mahayana Buddhism in the second century, when the Buddha was portrayed as a god, his image begins to appear in stone.

By this time, India had established its own unique religious art. The art is permeated by sensuousness and exuberance and is often overtly sexual. These scenes are meant to express otherworldly delights, not the pleasures of this world. They portray not earthly but heavenly splendor, the divine rewards of the gods, kings, and heroes described in the Sanskrit epics. The sensuous paradise that adorned the religious art of ancient India represented salvation and fulfillment for the ordinary Indian.

◆ **The Lions of Sarnath.** Their beauty and Buddhist symbolism make the Lions of Sarnath the most famous of the capitals topping Asoka's pillars. Sarnath, located just north of the city of Varanasi, was the holy site where Siddhartha Gautama first preached, and these roaring lions echo the proclamation of Buddhist teachings to the four corners of the world. The wheel not only represents Buddha's law but also proclaims Asoka's imperial legitimacy as the enlightened Indian ruler.

Our knowledge of the achievements of Indian science is limited by the paucity of written sources, but it is evident that ancient Indians had amassed an impressive amount of scientific knowledge in a number of areas. Especially notable was their work in astronomy, where they charted the movements of the heavenly bodies and recognized the spherical character of the earth at an early date. Their ideas of physics were similar to those of the Greeks; matter was divided into the five elements of earth, air, fire, water, and ether. Much of their early knowledge of metallurgy and medicine seems to have come from abroad, but many of their technological achievements are impressive, notably in the quality of their textiles and the massive stone pillars erected during the reign of Asoka. The pillars weighed up to fifty tons each and were transported by unknown means from many miles away to their final destination. The most important Indian contribution to the world of science was probably in the field of mathematics, but most of their achievements in this sphere took place during the first millenium C.E. and will be discussed in a later chapter.

Conclusion

While the peoples of North Africa and the Middle East were actively building the first civilizations, a similar process was getting underway in the Indus River valley. Unfortunately, we know much less about Harappan society than about its counterparts further to the west. Because of the continuing inability of scholars to decipher the script, archaeologists are reduced to sifting through the mute evidence found at the sites of the two ancient cities of Harappa and Mohenjo-Daro and their environs. Much has been learned about the nature of the Indus valley civilization in recent years, but without written records there are inherent limits to our understanding. How did the Harappan people deal with those fundamental human problems that were mentioned at the close of the previous chapter? The answers remain tantalizingly elusive.

As often happened elsewhere, however, the collapse of Harappan civilization did not lead to the total disappearance of its culture. The fall of Harappa led to

◆ **Sanchi Gate and Stupa.**   First constructed during the reign of Emperor Asoka, in the third century B.C.E., the stupa at Sanchi was enlarged over time, eventually becoming the greatest Buddhist monument in the entire Indian subcontinent. Originally intended to house a relic of the Buddha, the stupa became a holy place for devotion and a familiar form of Buddhist architecture. Sanchi's four elaborately carved stone gates, each over forty feet high, display exciting statues of Buddhist symbolism, including both animals and human figures.

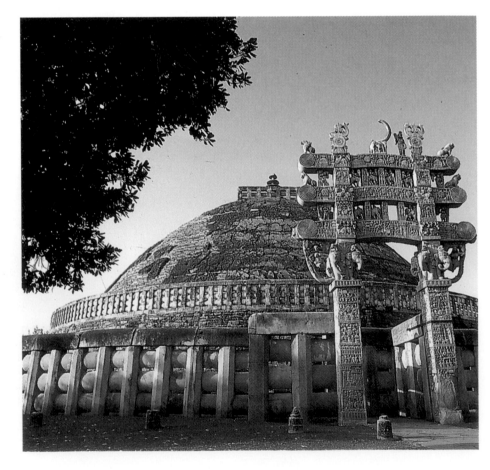

the rise of another civilization represented by the Aryans. While our understanding of the process is still highly imperfect, the new society that eventually emerged throughout the subcontinent was clearly the product of an amalgam of two highly distinctive cultures, Aryan and Dravidian, each of which made a significant contribution to the politics, the social institutions, and the creative impulse of ancient Indian civilization.

With the rise of the Mauryan dynasty in the fourth century B.C.E., the distinctive features of a great civilization begin to be clearly visible. It was extensive in its scope, embracing the entire Indian subcontinent and eventually, in the form of Buddhism and Hinduism,

spreading to China and Southeast Asia. But the underlying ethnic, linguistic, and cultural diversity of the Indian people posed a constant challenge to the unity of the state. After the collapse of the Mauryas, the subcontinent would not come under a single authority again for several hundred years.

In the meantime, another great experiment was taking place far to the northeast, across the Himalaya Mountains. Like many other civilizations of antiquity, the first Chinese state was concentrated on a major river system. And like them, too, its political and cultural achievements eventually spread far beyond their original habitat. In the next chapter, we turn to the civilization of ancient China.

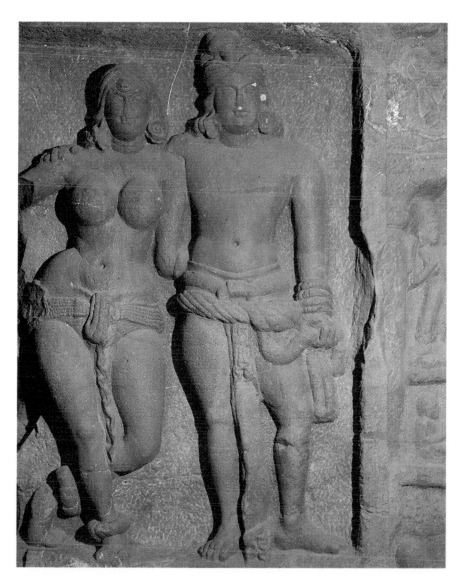

◆ **The Ideal Buddhist Couple.**   This stylized couple, who welcome the faithful to the Buddhist rock temple at Karli, symbolize the essence of human life, at harmony with both the temporal and spiritual worlds. Reminiscent of ancient Indian earth spirits, such figures later were featured in Hindu structures.

CHAPTER NOTES

1. Quoted in Richard Lannoy, *The Speaking Tree: A Study of Indian Culture and Society* (London, 1971), p. 318.
2. The quotation is from ibid., p. 319. Note also that the *Law of Manu* says that "punishment alone governs all created beings. . . . The whole world is kept in order by punishment, for a guiltless man is hard to find. . . ."
3. Strabo's *Geography*, Book 15, quoted in Michael Edwardes, *A History of India: From the Earliest Times to the Present Day* (London, 1961), p. 55.
4. Ibid., p. 54.
5. From the *Law of Manu*, quoted in A. L. Basham, *The Wonder That Was India* (London, 1961), pp. 180–81.
6. *Mundaka Upanishad*, 1:2, quoted in William Theodore de Bary, et al., eds. *Sources of Indian Tradition* (New York, 1966), pp. 28–29.
7. *Chandogya Upanishad*, 8:7–12 and *passim*, in ibid., pp. 30–31.
8. *Chandogya Upanishad*, 6:1–3, 12–14 and *passim*, in ibid., pp. 33–35.
9. Quoted in Ananda K. Coomaraswamy, *Buddha and the Gospel of Buddhism* (New York, 1964), p. 34.
10. Ibid., pp. 160–62.
11. De Bary, *Sources of Indian Tradition*, p. 146, from the Thirteenth Rock Edict.

SUGGESTED READINGS

For easy reference to the history and archaeology of India, see the colorful and schematic *Past Worlds: The Times Atlas of Archaeology* (Maplewood, N.J., 1988). Several standard histories of India are available today, all of which provide a good overview of the ancient period. One of the most readable and reliable is S. Wolpert, *New History of India,* 3d ed. (New York, 1989). V. A. Smith's edition of *The Oxford History of India,* 4th ed. (Oxford, 1981), although somewhat out of date, contains a wealth of information on various aspects of early Indian history. For a discussion of the Mauryan period directed to the lay reader, see M. Edwardes, *A History of India* (London, 1961). Also of note is H. H. Dodwell, ed., *The Cambridge History of India,* 6 vols. (Cambridge, 1922–1953).

By far the most informative and readable narrative on the history of India in premodern times is still A. L. Basham, *The Wonder That Was India* (London, 1961), which contains informative sections on prehistory, economy, language, art and literature, society, and everyday life. Also useful is A. L. Basham, ed., *A Cultural History of India* (Oxford, 1975). For a stimulating analysis of Indian culture and society in general, consult R. Lannoy, *The Speaking Tree* (London, 1971). R. Tha-

par, *Interpreting Early India* (Delhi, 1992), provides a view by an Indian historian.

Because of the relatively recent nature of archaeological exploration in South Asia, evidence for the Harappan period is not as voluminous as for areas such as Mesopotamia and the Nile valley. Some of the best work has been written by scholars who actually worked at the sites. For example, R. E. M. Wheeler's *Civilization of the Indus Valley and Beyond* (London, 1966) is a short, readable account of the Harappan era. A somewhat more extensive study is A. and B. Allchin, *The Birth of Indian Civilization, India and Pakistan before 500 B.C.* (Harmondsworth, 1968). For a detailed and well-illustrated analysis, see G. L. Possehlt, ed., *Harappan Civilization: A Contemporary Perspective* (Warminster, 1982). Commercial relations between Harappa and its neighbors are treated in S. Ratnagar, *Encounters: The Westerly Trade of the Harappan Civilization* (Oxford, 1981). See also *The Cultural Heritage of India,* vol. 1, *The Early Phase* (Calcutta, 1958) and J. Marshall's classic *Mohenjo-Daro and the Indus Civilization,* 3 vols. (London, 1931).

On the Mauryan period, see D. D. Kosambi, *The Culture and Civilization of Ancient India* (London, 1965) and R. Thapar, *Asoka and the Decline of the Mauryas* (Oxford, 1961).

There are a number of good books on the introduction of Buddhism into Indian society. Buddha's ideals are presented in A. K. Coomaraswamy, *Buddha and the Gospel of Buddhism* (London, 1916; revised, New York, 1964) and E. Conze, *Buddhism: Its Essence and Development* (Oxford, 1951). For a short summary, see E. A. Burtt, *The Teachings of the Compassionate Buddha* (New York, 1955). H. Akira, *A History of Indian Buddhism: From Sakyamuni to Early Mahayana* (Hawaii, 1990) provides a detailed analysis of early activities by Siddhartha Gautama and his followers. The intimate relationship between Buddhism and commerce is discussed in Liu Hsin-ju, *Ancient India and Ancient China: Trades and Religious Exchanges* (Oxford, 1988).

Hinduism, its origins and development, is the subject of S. Radhakrishnan, *The Hindu View of Life* (Oxford, 1926) and B. Walker, *Hindu World*, 2 vols. (London 1969). For a more general treatment, see S. N. Dasgupta, *A History of Indian Philosophy*, 5 vols. (Cambridge, 1922–55) and S. Radhakrishnan, *Indian Philosophy*, revised ed., 2 vols. (London, 1958).

There are a number of excellent surveys of Indian art, including the comprehensive S. L. Huntington, *The Art of Ancient India: Buddhist, Hindu, Jain* (New York, 1985) and B. Gray, *The Art of India* (Ithaca, N.Y., 1981). See also the standard survey in the Pelican History of Art series by B. Rowland, *The Art and Architecture of India: Buddhist, Hindu, Jain,* 3d ed., revised (Baltimore, 1967) and the concise *Indian Art* (London, 1976) by R. Craven. For specific information on the development of the stupa, see S. Dutt, *The Buddha and Five Centuries* (London, 1957). For texts with beautiful illustrations, consult C. Sivaramamurti, *The Art of India* (New York, 1977).

Few general surveys of Indian literature exist, perhaps because of the magnitude and diversity of India's literature. A good textbook for college students is E. C. Di-

mock, *The Literatures of India: An Introduction* (Chicago, 1974), which traces Indian literary achievement from the epics to the modern Hindi film. Also of interest is K. Chaitanya, *A New History of Sanskrit Literature* (Bombay, 1962). The most comprehensive by far is the work of A. K. Warder, still in progress; see his *Indian Kavya Literature*, 5 vols. (Delhi, 1972–1988). For background and analysis of the Bhagavadgita, see G. Feuerstein, *The Bhagavad Gita: Its Philosophy and Cultural Setting* (Wheaton, Ill., 1974). J. L. Brockington, *Righteous Rama: The Evolution of an Epic* (Oxford, 1985) sets the Ramayana in its total context with linguistic, cultural, and historical background.

Many editions of Sanskrit literature are available in English translation. Many are available in the multivolume *Harvard Oriental Series*. For a one-volume annotated anthology of selections from the Indian classics, consult S. N. Hay, ed., *Sources of Indian Tradition*, 2 vols. (New York, 1988), or J. B. Alphonso-Karkala, *An Anthology of Indian Literature*, 2d revised ed. (New Delhi, 1987), put out by the Indian Council for Cultural Relations.

Reading Sanskrit literature in translation is difficult for the uninitiated, due both to the length of the works and to the nature of Indian literature itself, which can be perceived as alien to Western aesthetics. The following works provide a good introduction. *Hymns from the Rig-Veda* (New York, 1975) by J. Le Mee and I. Gruttner is an accessible presentation of some of the hymns, with beautiful photographs expressing the Aryan awe of existence and the sense of oneness with the beauties and mysteries of the cosmos. The Mahabharata and Ramayana have been rewritten for 2,500 years. Fortunately, the vibrant versions, retold by William Buck and condensed to 400 pages each, reproduce the spirit of the originals and enthrall today's imagination. See W. Buck, *Mahabharata* (Berkeley, 1973) and *Ramayana* (Berkeley, 1976).

China in Antiquity

The Master said: "If the government seeks to rule by decree, and to maintain order by the use of punishment, the people will seek to evade punishment and have no sense of shame. But if government leads by virtue and governs through the rules of propriety, the people will feel shame and seek to correct their mistakes."

That statement is from the Analects, a collection of remarks by the Chinese philosopher Confucius that were gathered together by his disciples and published after his death in the fifth century B.C.E. Confucius (Chinese name Kung Fuci, or Master Kung) lived at a time when Chinese society was in a state of growing disarray. The political principles that had governed society since the founding of the Zhou dynasty six centuries earlier were widely ignored, and squabbling principalities scuffled for primacy as the power of the Zhou court steadily declined. The common people groaned under the weight of an oppressive manorial system that left them at the mercy of their feudal lords.

In the midst of this confusion, Confucius traveled the length of the kingdom observing events and seeking employment as a political counselor. Although he had little success in his job search, Confucius attracted a number of disciples, to whom he proposed a set of ideas that in later years served as the guiding principles for the Chinese empire. Some of his ideas are strikingly modern in their thrust. Among them is the revolutionary proposition that government depends on the will of the people.

Shang dynasty

Qin dynasty

Zhou dynasty

Han dynasty

First settled agriculture

Bronze Age begins

Invention of iron plow

Origins of Silk Road

Invention of writing system

Life of Confucius

Qin Shi Huangdi's tomb

"Hundred Schools" of ancient philosophy

The civilization that produced Confucius had originated more than fifteen hundred years earlier along the two great river systems of East Asia, the Yellow and the Yangtze. This vibrant new civilization, which we know today as ancient China, expanded gradually over its neighboring areas. By the third century B.C.E., it had emerged as a great empire, as well as the dominant cultural and political force in the entire region.

Like Sumer, Harappa, and Egypt, the civilization of ancient China began as a collection of autonomous villages cultivating food crops along a major river system. Improvements in agricultural techniques led to a food surplus and the growth of an urban civilization characterized by more complex political and social institutions, as well as new forms of artistic and intellectual creativity.

Like its counterparts elsewhere, ancient China faced the challenge posed by the appearance of pastoral peoples on its borders. Unlike Harappa, Sumer, and Egypt, however, ancient China was able to avoid destruction at the hands of the in-vaders and survived intact down to the formation of the Chinese empire in 221 B.C.E. The institutions and cultural values that had taken shape at the dawn of Chinese history were inherited by the empire and formed the foundation of traditional China until the beginning of the twentieth century. For that reason, Chinese civilization is sometimes described as the oldest continuous civilization on earth.

The Land and People of China

According to Chinese legend, Chinese society was founded by a series of rulers who brought the first rudiments of civilization to the region nearly five thousand years ago. The first of these was Fu Xi (Fu Hsi), the ox-tamer, who "knotted cords for hunting and fishing," domesticated animals, and introduced the beginnings of family life. The second was Shen Nong (Shen Nung), the divine farmer, who "bent wood for plows and hewed wood for plowshares." He was the first to teach the people the techniques of agriculture. Last came Huang Di (Huang Ti), the Yellow Emperor, who "strung a piece of wood for the bow, and whittled little sticks of wood for the arrows." Legend credits Huang Di with creating the Chinese system of writing, as well as with inventing the bow and arrow.[1]

Modern historians, of course, do not accept the literal accuracy of such legends, but view them instead as part of the process whereby early peoples attempt to make sense of the world and their role in it. Nevertheless, such re-creations of a mythical past often contain an element of truth and an allegorical explanation of the founding of the civilization.

Such is the case with the legendary "three sovereigns" of prehistoric China. Although there is no clear evidence that any of them actually existed as historical figures, their achievements symbolize some of the major characteristics that would define Chinese civilization throughout history: the interaction between nomadic and agricultural peoples, the importance of the family as the basic unit of Chinese life, and the development of a unique system of writing.

Human communities have existed in China for several hundred thousand years. At first, like their contemporaries throughout the world, the early Chinese lived a simple existence, fishing, hunting, and gathering food. Eventually, however, perhaps driven by the growing aridity of the climate in northern China, they began to settle along riverbanks in the transitional zone between the forested areas and the grasslands. There, sometime around the eighth millennium B.C.E., these early Chinese began to master the cultivation of crops. A number of these early agricultural settlements were in the neighborhood of the Yellow River, where they gave birth to two Neolithic societies known to archaeologists as the Yang-Shao and the LongShan cultures (sometimes identified in terms of their pottery as the painted and black pottery cultures).

Historians once thought that these Neolithic settlements were the earliest farming communities in China and that civilization, including such characteristics as organized government and a written language, spread gradually from this nuclear area to other regions of China. Recently, however, archaeologists have discovered the remains of similar agricultural settlements in the Yangtze valley in central China and along the coast to the south. These settlements were based on the cultivation of rice rather than dry crops such as millet, barley, and wheat, but they are as old as those in the north. Thus, agriculture, and perhaps other elements of early civilization, may have developed spontaneously in several areas of China rather than radiating outward from one central nuclear region.

At first, these simple Neolithic settlements were hardly more than villages, but as the inhabitants mastered the rudiments of agriculture, the little communities gradually gave rise to more sophisticated and complex societies. In a pattern that we have already seen elsewhere, civilization gradually spread from these nuclear settlements in the valleys of the Yellow and the Yangtze Rivers to other lowland areas of eastern and central China. Government emerged, along with a writing system and other forms of technology. As wealth increased, the societies began to amass armies and build walled cities. The process took several thousand years and finally reached a climax in the third century B.C.E. with the creation of the first state unifying most of China under a single ruler, the Qin (Ch'in) Empire.

The two great river valleys, then, can be considered the core regions in the development of Chinese civilization, and it was in these densely cultivated valleys that East Asia began to emerge as one of the great food-producing areas of the ancient world. But China is not just a land of fertile fields. In fact, only 12 percent of the total land area is arable, compared with 23 percent in the United States. Much of the remainder consists of mountains and deserts that ring the country on its northern and western frontiers.

This often arid and forbidding landscape is a dominant feature of Chinese life and has played a significant role in Chinese history. The geographical barriers served to isolate the Chinese people from advanced agrarian societies in other parts of Asia. The frontier regions in the Gobi Desert, Central Asia, and the Tibetan plateau were themselves sparsely inhabited by peoples of Mongolian, Indo-European, or Turkish extraction. Most were pastoral societies, and as was the case in the other river valley civilizations, their contacts with the Chinese were often characterized by mutual distrust and conflict. Although fewer in number than the Chinese, many of these peoples, like other nomadic societies throughout the steppes of Central Asia, possessed impressive skills in war and were sometimes aggressive in seeking wealth or territory in the settled regions south of the Gobi Desert. Over the next two thousand years, the northern frontier became one of the great faultlines of conflict in Asia, as Chinese armies attempted to protect precious farmlands from marauding peoples from beyond the frontier. As in other areas where pastoral and agricultural peoples came into contact, the struggle was a continual one, and the outcome at any given time depended on the ability of the settled peoples to fend off the threats of the invaders. When China was unified and blessed with capable rulers, it could usually keep the nomadic intruders at bay and even bring them under a loose form of Chinese administration. But in times of internal weakness, China was vulnerable to attack from the north, and on several occasions, nomadic peoples succeeded in overthrowing native Chinese rulers and setting up their own dynastic regimes.

From other directions, China normally had little to fear. To the east lay the China Sea, a lair for pirates and the source of powerful typhoons that occasionally ravaged the Chinese coast, but otherwise rarely a source of concern. South of the Yangtze River was a hilly region inhabited by a mixture of peoples of varied language and ethnic stock who lived by farming, fishing, or food gathering. They were gradually absorbed in the inexorable expansion of Chinese civilization.

The Dawn of Chinese Civilization: The Shang Dynasty

Historians of China have traditionally dated the beginning of Chinese civilization to the founding of the Xia (Hsia) dynasty more than four thousand years ago. Although the precise date for the rise of the Xia is in dispute, legend maintains that the founder was a ruler named Yu, who is also credited with introducing irrigation and draining the floodwaters that periodically threatened to inundate the North China plain (see the box on p. 82). The Xia dynasty, in turn, was replaced by a second dynasty, the Shang, in the eighteenth century B.C.E. Unlike its predecessor, the Shang has been historically confirmed, since its capital at Anyang, just north of the Yellow River in north-central China, has been located and excavated by archaeologists. Among the finds at the Anyang dig were thousands of so-called oracle bones, ox and chicken bones or turtle shells that were used by Shang rulers for divination and to communicate with the gods. The inscriptions on these oracle bones are generally considered to be the earliest form of Chinese writing and provide much of our information about the beginnings of civilization in China. They describe a culture gradually emerging from the Neolithic to the early Bronze Age.

Political Organization

According to the available evidence, China under the Shang dynasty was a predominantly agricultural society ruled by an aristocratic class whose major occupation was war. One ancient chronicler complained that "the big affairs of state consist of sacrifice and soldiery."[2] Combat was carried on by means of two-horse chariots. The appearance of chariots in China in the mid-second millennium B.C.E. coincides roughly with similar developments elsewhere, leading some historians to suggest that the Shang ruling class may originally have invaded China from elsewhere in Asia. But items found in Shang burial

mounds are similar to Longshan pottery, implying that the Shang ruling elites were linear descendants of the indigenous Neolithic peoples in the area. If that was the case, the Shang may have acquired their knowledge of horse-drawn chariots through contact with the peoples of neighboring regions.

Some recent support for that assumption has come from evidence unearthed in the sandy wastes of Xinjiang, China's far northwestern province. There Chinese archaeologists have discovered corpses dating back as early as the second millennium B.C.E. with physical characteristics that are clearly European. They are also clothed in textiles similar to those worn at the time in Europe, suggesting that they may have been members of an Indo-European migration from areas much further to the west. If that is the case, it is not improbable that they were familiar with advances in chariot making that had occurred at least five thousand years ago in southern Russia and Kazakstan (see Chapter 1). By about 2000 B.C.E. spoked wheels were being deposited at gravesites in Ukraine and

◆ **Shell and Bone Writing.** The earliest known form of writing in China dates back to the early Shang dynasty and was inscribed on shells or animal bones. Messages to the gods were scratched on bones, which cracked after being exposed to fire. The cracks were then interpreted by sorcerers. Originally composed of pictographs and ideographs 4,000 years ago, Chinese writing has evolved into an elaborate system of stylized symbols still in use today.

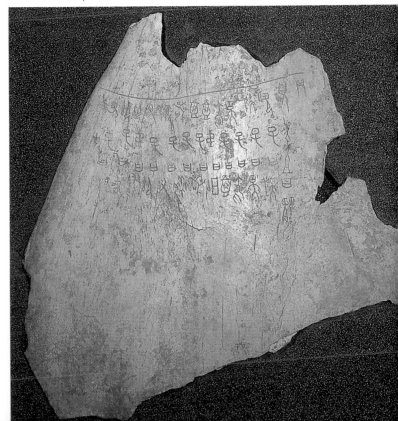

❧ A Treatise on the Yellow River and Its Canals ❧

Sima Qian (Szu-ma Ch'ien) was a famous historian of the Han dynasty who lived during the second and first centuries B.C.E. In his most famous work, entitled Historical Records, *he describes the public works projects undertaken during the Xia dynasty to convert the dangerous waters of the Yellow River to human use. Although the identification of irrigation with Yu may be apocryphal, China later became one of the foremost hydraulic societies in the ancient world.*

Sima Qian, *Historical Records*

The documents on the Hsia dynasty tell us that Emperor Yu spent thirteen years controlling and bringing an end to the floods, and during that period, though he passed by the very gate of his own house, he did not take the time to enter. On land he traveled in a cart and on water in a boat; he rode a sledge to cross the mud and wore cleated shoes in climbing the mountains. In this way he marked out the nine provinces, led the rivers along the bases of the mountains, decided what tribute was appropriate for each region in accordance with the quality of its soil, opened up the nine roads, built embankments around the nine marshes, and made a survey of the nine mountains.

Of all the rivers, the Yellow River caused the greatest damage to China by overflowing its banks and inundating the land, and therefore he turned all his attention to controlling it. Thus he led the Yellow River in a course from Chi-shih past Lung-men and south to the northern side of Mount Hua; from there eastward along the foot of Ti-chu Mountain, past the Meng Ford and the confluence of the Lo River to Ta-p'ei. At this point Emperor Yu decided that, since the river was descending from high ground and the flow of the water was rapid and fierce, it would be difficult to guide it over level ground without danger of frequent disastrous breakthroughs. He therefore divided the flow into two channels, leading it along the higher ground to the north, past the Chiang River and so to Ta-lu. There he spread it out to form the Nine Rivers, brought it together again to make the Backward-flowing River [i.e., tidal river], and thence led it into the Gulf of Pohai. When he had thus opened up the rivers of the nine provinces and fixed the outlets of the nine marshes, peace and order were brought to the lands of the Hsia and his achievements continued to benefit the Three Dynasties which followed.

---

also in the Gobi Desert, just north of the great bend of the Yellow River. It is thus not unlikely that the new technology became available to the founders of the Shang dynasty and may have aided their rise to power in northern China.

Unfortunately, we still do not know much about the nature of government under the Shang. From tantalizing hints provided by the oracle bones and other scattered evidence unearthed at Anyang and other nearby sites, it seems clear that under the Shang a sophisticated and relatively centralized monarchy was already in the process of creation. The Shang king ruled with the assistance of a central bureaucracy in the capital city. His realm was divided into a number of territories governed by aristocratic chieftains, but the king's power was evident in that he appointed these chieftains and could apparently depose them at will. He was also responsible for the defense of the realm and controlled large armies that often fought on the fringes of the kingdom. The transcendent importance of the ruler was graphically displayed in the ritual

sacrifices undertaken at his death, when hundreds of his retainers were buried with him in the royal tomb.

As the inscriptions on the oracle bones make clear, the Chinese ruling elite believed in the existence of supernatural forces beyond the power of human beings and thought that they could communicate with those forces to obtain divine intervention on matters pertaining to this world. In fact, the purpose of the oracle bones was to communicate with the gods. Messages were scratched on the bones. When the bones were exposed to fire, they would develop cracks that were interpreted by sorcerers as responses to questions posed to the gods. The questions inscribed on the bones often expressed practical concerns: Will it rain? Will the king be victorious in battle? Will he recover from his illness?

This evidence also suggests that the king, through his court sorcerers, was already being viewed as an intermediary between Heaven and Earth. In fact, an early Chinese character for king (王) consists of three horizontal lines connected by a single vertical line; the middle horizontal line represents the king's place between human society and the divine forces in nature.

The early Chinese also had a clear sense of life in the hereafter. Though some of the human sacrifices discovered in the royal tombs were presumably intended to propitiate the gods, others were meant to accompany the king or members of his family on the journey to the next world. From this conviction would come the concept of the veneration of ancestors (commonly known in the West as "ancestor worship") and the practice, which continues to the present day in many Chinese communities, of burning replicas of physical objects to accompany the departed on their journey to the next world.

One further point is worthy of mention. The Chinese also believed that divine forces, including a god of the harvest, existed in objects of nature. In fact, spirit worship in various forms has survived in China down to the present century. But Shang dynasty Chinese had already come to believe in the existence of one transcendent god, known as Shang Di (Supreme Emperor). Thus, like peoples of other ancient civilizations, they were gradually turning to a form of anthropomorphism.

Social Structures

In the Neolithic period, the farm village was apparently the basic social unit of China, at least in the core region of the Yellow River valley. Villages were organized by clans rather than by nuclear family units, and all residents probably took the common clan name of the entire village. In some cases, a village may have included more than one clan. At Banpo (Pan P'o), an archaeological site near modern-day Xian that dates back at least eight thousand years, the houses in the village are separated by a ditch, which some scholars think may have served as a divider between two clans. The individual dwellings at Banpo housed nuclear families, but a larger building in the village was apparently used as a clan meeting hall. The tribal origins of Chinese society may help to explain the continued importance of the joint family in traditional China, as well as the relatively small number of family names in Chinese society. Even today there are only about four hundred commonly used family names in a society of more than one billion people.

By Shang times, the classes were becoming increasingly differentiated. It is likely that some poorer peasants did not own their farms, but were obliged to work the land of the chieftain and other elite families in the village (see the box on p. 84). The aristocrats not only made war and served as officials (indeed, the first Chinese character for official originally meant warrior), they were also the primary landowners. In addition to the aristocratic elite and the peasants, there were also a small number of merchants and artisans, as well as slaves, probably consisting primarily of criminals or prisoners taken in battle.

The Shang are perhaps best known for their mastery of the art of bronze casting. Utensils, weapons, and ritual objects made of bronze have been found in royal tombs in urban centers throughout the area known to be under Shang influence (see Metalwork and Sculpture later in this chapter). It is also clear that the Shang had achieved a fairly sophisticated writing system; the oracle bones provide concrete evidence of the existence of a system of ideographs and pictographs that is the direct ancestor of the written language used in China today.

The Zhou Dynasty

In the late twelfth century B.C.E., the Shang dynasty was overthrown by an aggressive young state located somewhat to the west of Anyang, the Shang capital, and near the great bend of the Yellow River as it begins to flow directly eastward to the sea. The new dynasty, which called itself the Zhou (Chou), survived for more than nine hundred years and was thus the longest-lived dynasty in the history of China. Like their predecessors, the Zhou rulers were apparently the direct descendants of the Neolithic civilization that had emerged earlier throughout the Yellow River valley and ruled over a frontier region on the western fringes of the Shang state. According to tradition, the last of the Shang rulers was a tyrant who

Map 3.1 Shang China.

Major regions of the late Shang state

≽ Life in the Fields ≼

*T*he following passage is from the Book of Songs, a famous classic that was written sometime during the early Zhou dynasty. This excerpt describes the calendar of peasant life on an estate in ancient China and indicates the various types of service that peasants provided for their lord.

The Book of Songs

In the seventh month the Fire Star passes the meridian;
In the ninth month clothes are given out.
In the days of [our] first month, the wind blows cold;
In the days of [our] second, the air is cold.
Without coats, without garments of hair,
How could we get to the end of the year?
In the days of [our] third month we take our plows in
    hand;
In the days of [our] fourth we make our way to the fields.
Along with wives and children,
We eat in those south-lying acres.
The surveyor of the fields comes and is glad.

In the seventh month the Fire Star passes the meridian;
In the ninth month clothes are given out.
With the spring days the warmth begins,
And the oriole utters its song.
The young women take their deep baskets
And go along the small paths,
Looking for the tender [leaves of the] mulberry trees
As the spring days lengthen out,
They gather in crowds the white southern wood.
The girl's heart is wounded with sadness,
For she will soon be going with one of the young lords.

. . .

In the eighth month spinning is begun;
We make dark fabrics and yellow,
"With our red dye so bright,
We make robes for our young lords."

In the ninth month we prepare the stockyard,
And in the tenth we bring in the harvest.
The millets, the early and the late,
Together with paddy and hemp, beans and wheat.

. . .

Now we go up to work in the manor.
"In the day you gather the thatch-reeds;
In the evening twist them into rope;
Go quickly on to the roofs;
Soon you are to sow the grain."

In the days of [our] second month we cut the ice with
    tingling blows;
In the days of [our] third month [it is] stored in the
    icehouse.
In the days of [our] fourth month, very early,
A lamb with scallions is offered in sacrifice.
In the ninth month are shrewd frosts;
In the tenth month the stockyard is cleared.
With twin pitchers we hold the feast,
Killed for it is a young lamb.
Up we go into the lord's hall,
Raise the cup of buffalo-horn;
"Long life for our lord; may he live for ever and ever!"

oppressed the people (Chinese sources assert that he was a degenerate who built "ponds of wine" and ordered the composing of lustful music that "ruined the morale of the nation"), leading the ruler of the principality of Zhou to revolt and establish a new dynasty.[3]

The Zhou located their capital in their home territory, near the present-day city of Xian. Later they established a second capital city at modern-day Luoyang, farther to the east, to administer new territories captured from the Shang. This established a pattern of eastern and western capitals that would endure off and on in China for nearly two thousand years.

Political Structures

The Zhou dynasty (1122–221 B.C.E.) adopted the political system of its predecessors with some changes. The Shang practice of dividing the kingdom into a number of territories governed by officials appointed by the king was continued under the Zhou. At the apex of the government hierarchy was the Zhou king, who was served by a bureaucracy of growing size and complexity. It now included several ministries responsible for rites, education, law, and public works. Beyond the capital, the Zhou kingdom was divided into a number of principalities called *guo (kuo)*, which is now the Chinese word for a state or nation. As under the Shang, the governing officials of these territories were members of the hereditary aristocracy, but they were appointed by the king and were at least theoretically subordinated to his authority. At least in the beginning, many were members of the royal family, and the Zhou king, in a symbolic sense, was like the head of a large extended family, with each individual princely official owing a loose allegiance to his lord. Each was assisted by his own smaller regional bureaucracy. Like his predecessors, the Zhou king was in charge of defense and controlled armies that served under his command throughout the country.

But the Zhou kings also introduced some innovations. As described by the *Rites of Zhou*, one of the oldest surviving documents on statecraft, the Chinese now began to develop a theory of government. According to this document, the duke of Zhou, brother of the founder of the Zhou dynasty, asserted that the Zhou house ruled China because it possessed the "mandate of Heaven." According to this concept, Heaven (viewed as an impersonal law of nature rather than as an anthropomorphic deity) maintained order in the universe through the Zhou king, who thus ruled over all humanity (the Chinese term *tian xia* literally means "all under Heaven") by a mandate from Heaven. The king, who was selected to rule because of his talent and virtue, was then responsible for governing the people with compassion and efficiency. The duke of Zhou used such ideas to justify the Zhou conquest of the Shang, since the last Shang ruler had allegedly mistreated the people. Eventually, the concept of the heavenly mandate would become a cardinal principle of Chinese statecraft.[4]

But, as one historian has noted, the mandate of Heaven was double-edged. The king was expected to rule according to the proper "Way" (called the *Dao* and roughly reminiscent of the Hindu concept of *dharma*). It was his duty to propitiate the gods in order to protect the people from natural calamities or a bad harvest. Later this role would be embodied in a ritual ceremony conducted once each year by the Chinese emperor at the Temple of Heaven in Beijing. If he failed to rule effectively, theoretically at least he could be overthrown and replaced by a new ruler. Such a concept, of course, had first been asserted by the duke of Zhou.

This theory has strong political implications, because it not only sets forth a "right of revolution" to overthrow a corrupt or evil ruler, but also makes clear that the king, though serving as a representative of Heaven, is not a divine being himself. In practice, of course, each founder of a new dynasty would routinely assert that he had earned the mandate of Heaven, and who could disprove it except by overthrowing the king? The pragmatic Chinese would later enshrine this view in an ironic proverb: "He who wins is the king; he who loses is the rebel."

Later Chinese would regard the period of the early Zhou dynasty, as portrayed in the *Rites of Zhou* (which, of course, is no more an unbiased source than any modern government document), as a Golden Age, when there was harmony in the world and all was right under Heaven. And the key to that harmony lay in the character of the ruler, who operated as an intermediary between Heaven

◆ **Shang Bronzes.** The most significant artistic contributions of the Shang dynasty were undoubtedly its bronze ritual vessels. Used initially as food containers in ceremonial rites for ancestral devotion by the emperors, these magnificent objects were the product of an advanced technology unmatched by any contemporary civilization. Sought out by museums everywhere, Shang bronzes are still considered one of the art wonders of the world. Note the stylized face of a dragon, known as a Taotie, that is a characteristic of Shang bronze objects.

and Earth (as we have seen, the early Chinese character for king was a graphic representation of that concept). If the king failed to carry out his responsibilities, Heaven could show its displeasure by calling forth a natural disaster, such as a drought or a flood.

Whether the system functioned in such an ideal manner, of course, is open to question. In any case, the Golden Age did not last, whether because it never existed in practice or because of the increasing complexity of Chinese civilization. Perhaps, too, its disappearance was a consequence of the intellectual and moral decline of the rulers of the Zhou royal house. The power of the central government began to disintegrate, giving rise to bitter internal rivalries among the various principalities. Whereas the *Rites of Zhou* had described a monarch who was both strong and benevolent, in actuality by the sixth century B.C.E., the officials who governed had succeeded in making their positions hereditary at the expense of the king. They had amassed the enormous power of the principalities in a society that was characterized by a rigid demarcation between powerful nobles and a downtrodden peasantry.

Economy and Society

During the Zhou dynasty, the essential characteristics of Chinese economic and social institutions began to take shape. The Zhou inherited and continued the pattern of land ownership that had existed under the Shang. According to the ideal described by Confucian scholars of a later day, the peasants worked on lands owned by their lord, but also had land of their own that they cultivated for their own use. The practice was called the "well field system," since the Chinese character for well (井) resembles a simplified picture of the division of the farmland into nine separate segments. Each peasant family tilled an outer plot for its own use and then joined with other families to work the inner one for the hereditary lord (see the box on p. 84). How widely this system was used is unclear, but Communist historians would later cite it as an early form of Chinese socialism. As the following poem indicates, life for the average farmer was a difficult one. The "big rat" is probably a reference to the high taxes imposed on the peasants by the government or lord.

> *Big rat, big rat*
> *Do not eat my millet!*
> *Three years I have served you,*
> *But you will not care for me.*

> *I am going to leave you*
> *And go to that happy land;*
> *Happy land, happy land,*
> *Where I will find my place.*

> *Big rat, big rat,*
> *Do not eat my sprouts!*
> *Three years I have served you*
> *But you give me no comfort.*
> *I am going to leave you*
> *And go to those happy fields;*
> *Happy fields, happy fields;*
> *Who there shall long moan?*

In addition to the nobles and the peasants, there was a class of artisans and merchants, living in walled towns under the direct control of the local lord. A passage in a classical text called the *Book of Changes* remarked that the rulers in ancient times set up markets and ordered "all the people under Heaven to gather their goods there for exchange and then to return home, in order that all goods might find their appropriate destinations."[5]

At first, commerce was limited to the exchange of local products in daily use, but eventually trade expanded to include goods imported from distant regions, such as salt, iron, cloth and various luxury goods. Merchants did not operate independently as autonomous individuals, but were considered the property of the local lord and on occasion could even be bought and sold like chattels.

There was also a class of slaves, who performed a variety of menial tasks and perhaps worked on local irrigation projects. Most of them were probably prisoners of war captured during conflicts with the neighboring principalities. Scholars do not know how extensive slavery was in ancient times, but slaves probably did not comprise a large proportion of the total population.

The period from the sixth to the third centuries B.C.E. was an era of rapid change. This period was marked by the growth of large autonomous states owing only a loose allegiance to the Zhou ruling house. As these states grew in size and power, they began to regulate the local economy and seek reliable sources of revenue for their expanding armies, such as a uniform tax system and government monopolies on key commodities such as salt and iron.

Behind such political developments, an economic revolution was taking place. The period of the later Zhou was an era of significant economic growth and technological innovation, especially in agriculture. During the Neolithic period, farmers were still dependent upon rainfall to water their crops. In the Yellow River valley and other areas of North China, for the most part they grew millet and other dry crops that could survive on little moisture. Further south, in the Yangtze River delta or along the southern coast, farmers grew rice in marshy regions or along the riverbanks. Historians are not certain when or where irrigation was first practiced—there are indications that it was used in limited fashion during the Shang—but it was certainly in wide use by the sixth century B.C.E. During that time, large-scale water control projects were undertaken to regulate the flow of rivers and distribute water evenly to the fields, as well as to construct canals to facilitate the transport of goods from one region to another (see the box on p. 82).

Perhaps the most impressive technological achievement of the period was the construction of the massive water control project on the Min River, a tributary of the Yangtze just above the city of Chengdu (Ch'eng-tu) in Sichuan (Szechwan) Province. This system of canals and spillways, which was put into operation by the state of Qin a few years prior to the end of the Zhou dynasty, diverted excess water from the river into the local irrigation network and watered an area populated by as many as five million people. The system is still in use today, over two thousand years later.

Food production was also stimulated by a number of advances in farm technology. By the mid-sixth century B.C.E., the introduction of iron had led to the development of iron plowshares, which were more advanced than those used elsewhere and permitted deep plowing for the first time. Other innovations dating from the later Zhou were the use of natural fertilizer, the collar harness, and the technique of leaving land fallow to preserve or replenish nutrients in the soil (see the box on p. 88).

The advances in agriculture, which enabled the population of China to rise as high as 20 million people during the late Zhou era, were also undoubtedly a major factor in the growth of commerce and manufacturing. During the later Zhou, economic wealth began to replace noble birth as the prime source of power and influence. Utensils made of iron became more common, and trade developed in a variety of useful commodities, such as cloth, salt, and various manufactured goods.

One of the most important items of trade in ancient China was silk. There is evidence of silkworm raising as early as the Neolithic period. Remains of silk material have been found on Shang bronzes, and a large number of fragments have been recovered in tombs dating from the mid-Zhou era. Silk cloth was used not only for clothing and quilts, but also to wrap the body of the dead prior to burial. Fragments have been found throughout Central Asia and as far away as Athens, suggesting that the famous "Silk Road" was in operation as early as the fifth century B.C.E. (for a discussion of the Silk Road, see Chapter 10).

With the development of trade and manufacturing, China began to move toward a money economy. The first form of money may have been seashells (the Chinese character for goods or property contains the ideographic symbol for "shell"), but by the Zhou dynasty iron money had developed in the form of pieces of iron shaped like a knife or round coins with a hole in the middle so they could be carried in strings of a thousand coins. Most ordinary Chinese were not involved in the money economy, however, but simply used a system of barter. Even taxes and rents, as well as the salaries of government officials, were normally paid in grain.

The Hundred Schools of Ancient Philosophy

In China, as in other great river valley societies, the birth of civilization was accompanied by the emergence of an organized effort to comprehend the nature of the cosmos and the role of human beings within it. As civilization evolves, people cease to observe nature with awe and wonderment and begin to seek an explanation for the forces at work in the universe and their effects on human lives. This search, of course, marks the birth of religion and philosophy. In ancient China, speculation over such questions began in the very early stages of the rise of civilization and culminated at the end of the Zhou era in the "hundred schools" of ancient philosophy, a wide-ranging debate over the nature of human beings, society, and the universe.

The first hint of the nature of religious belief in ancient China comes from relics found in royal tombs in Neolithic times. By then, the Chinese had already developed a religious sense beyond the primitive belief in the existence of spirits in nature. As we have seen, the Shang had already begun to believe in the existence of one transcendent god, known as Shang Di, who presided over all the forces of nature. As time went on, the Chinese concept of religion began to evolve from the idea of a vaguely anthropomorphic god to a somewhat more impersonal symbol of universal order known as Heaven (*Tian*, or *T'ien*). There was also much speculation among Chinese intellectuals about the nature of the cosmic order. One of the earliest ideas was that the universe was divided into two primary forces of good and evil, light and dark, male and female, called the *yang* and the *yin*, represented symbolically by the sun (*yang*) and the moon (*yin*). According

Environmental Concerns in Ancient China

Even in antiquity, China possessed a large population that often stretched the limits of the productive potential of the land. In the following excerpt, the late Zhou philosopher Mencius appeals to his sovereign to adopt policies that will conserve precious resources and foster the well-being of his subjects. Clearly, Mencius was concerned that environmental needs were being neglected. Unfortunately, his advice has not always been followed, as environmental degradation remains a problem in China today. The destruction of the forests, for example, has deprived China of much of its wood resources, and the present government has launched an extensive program to plant trees.

The Book of Mencius

If you do not interfere with the busy season in the fields, then there will be more grain than the people can eat; if you do not allow nets with too fine a mesh to be used in large ponds, then there will be more fish and turtles than they can eat; if hatchets and axes are permitted in the forests on the hills only in the proper seasons, then there will be more timber than they can use. When the people have more grain, more fish and turtles than they can eat, and more timber than they can use, then in the support of their parents when alive and in the mourning of them when dead, they will be able to have no regrets over anything left undone. This is the first step along the Kingly way.

If the mulberry is planted in every homestead of five mu of land, then those who are fifty can wear silk; if chickens, pigs and dogs do not miss their breeding season, then those who are seventy can eat meat; if each lot of a hundred mu is not deprived of labor during the busy seasons, then families with several mouths to feed will not go hungry. Exercise due care over the education provided by the village schools, and discipline the people by teaching them the duties proper to sons and younger brothers, and those whose heads have turned gray will not be carrying loads on the roads. When those who are seventy wear silk and eat meat and the masses are neither cold nor hungry, it is impossible for their prince not to be a true King.

Now when food meant for human beings is so plentiful as to be thrown to dogs and pigs, you fail to realize that it is time for garnering, and when men drop dead from starvation by the wayside, you fail to realize that it is time for distribution. When people die, you simply say, "It is none of my doing. It is the fault of the harvest." In what way is that different from killing a man by running him through, while saying all the time, "It is none of my doing. It is the fault of the weapon." Stop putting the blame on the harvest and the people of the whole Empire will come to you.

---

to this theory, which is reminiscent of similar ideas developing in the Middle East and southern Europe, life was a dynamic process of interaction between the forces of *yang* and *yin*. Early Chinese could attempt only to understand the process and perhaps to have some minimal effect on its operation. They could not hope to reverse it. It is sometimes asserted that this belief has contributed to the heavy element of fatalism in Chinese popular wisdom. The Chinese have traditionally believed that bad times will be followed by good times, and vice versa.

The belief that there was some mysterious "law of nature" that could be interpreted by human beings, a carryover from the Shang period when sorcerers used oracle bones to seek communication with the gods, undoubtedly encouraged the practice of divination and other attempts to predict the future. Philosophers invented various ways to interpret the will of nature, while shamans,

playing a role similar to the *brahmins* in India, were employed at court to assist the emperor in his policy deliberations until at least the fifth century C.E. One of the most famous manuals used for this purpose was the *Yi Jing (I Ching)*, known in English as the *Book of Changes*.

CONFUCIANISM

Such efforts to divine the mysterious purposes of Heaven notwithstanding, Chinese thinking about metaphysical reality also contained a strain of pragmatism, which is readily apparent in the ideas of the great philosopher Confucius. Confucius (the Latin form of his honorific title Kung Fuci, or K'ung Fu-tzu, meaning Master Kung) was born in the state of Lu (in the modern province of Shandong) in 551 B.C.E. After reaching maturity, he apparently hoped to find employment as a political adviser in one of the principalities into which China was divided at that time, but he had little success in finding a patron. Nevertheless, he made an indelible mark on history as an independent (and somewhat disgruntled) political and social philosopher.

In conversations with his disciples contained in the *Analects* (a collection of his sayings preserved by his disciples), Confucius often adopted a detached and almost skeptical view of Heaven. "You are unable to serve man," he commented on one occasion, "how then can you hope to serve the spirits? While you do not know life, how can you know about death?" In many instances, he appeared to advise his followers to revere the deities and the ancestral spirits, but to keep them at a distance. Confucius believed it was useless to speculate too much about metaphysical questions. Better by far to assume that there was a rational order to the universe and then concentrate one's attention on ordering the affairs of this world.[6]

Confucius's interest in philosophy, then, was essentially political and ethical. The universe was constructed in such a way that if human beings could act harmoniously in accordance with its purposes, their own affairs would prosper. Much of his concern was with human behavior. The key to proper behavior was to behave in accordance with the *Dao* (Way). Confucius assumed that all human beings had their own *Dao*, depending on their individual role in life, and it was their duty to follow it. Even the ruler had his own *Dao*, and as we have seen, he ignored it at his peril. The idea of the *Dao* is reminiscent of the concept of *dharma* in ancient India and played a similar role in governing the affairs of society.

Two elements in the Confucian interpretation of the *Dao* are particularly worthy of mention. The first is the concept of duty. It was the responsibility of all individuals to subordinate their own interests and aspirations to the broader need of the family and the community. This concept of duty is often expressed in the form of a "work ethic" similar to the so-called Puritan work ethic that allegedly characterized popular attitudes in Europe and North America during the seventeenth and eighteenth centuries. Confucius assumed that if each individual worked hard to fulfill his or her assigned destiny, the affairs of society as a whole would surely prosper as well. In this respect, it was important for the ruler to set a good example. If he followed his "kingly way," the beneficial effects would radiate throughout society.

A second key element in the Confucian interpretation of *Dao* is the idea of humanity, sometimes translated as "human heartedness." This concept involves a sense of compassion and empathy for others. It is similar in some ways to Christian concepts, but with a subtle twist.

Where Christian teachings call on human beings to "behave toward others as you would have them behave toward you," the Confucian maxim is put in a different way: "Do not do unto others what you would not wish done to yourself." To many Chinese, this attitude symbolizes an element of tolerance in the Chinese character that has not always been practiced in other societies.[7]

Confucius may have considered himself a failure because he never attained the position he wanted, but his ideas were undoubtedly appealing to many of his contemporaries, and in the generations after his death, his message spread widely throughout China. Confucius was an outspoken critic of his times, and like many a conservative in our own days, he lamented the disappearance of the Golden Age of the early Zhou (see the box on p. 90).

In fact, however, Confucius was not just another disgruntled Chinese conservative mourning the passing of the good old days, but a revolutionary thinker, many of whose key ideas looked forward rather than backward. Perhaps his most striking political idea was that the government should not be limited solely to those of noble birth, but should be open to all men of superior quality. As one of his disciples reports in the *Analects*: "The Master said, by nature, men are nearly alike; by practice, they get to be wide apart."[8] Confucius undoubtedly had himself in mind as one of those "superior" men, but the rapacity of the hereditary lords must have added strength to his convictions.

The concept of rule by merit was, of course, not an unfamiliar idea in the China of his day; the *Rites of Zhou* had clearly stated that the king himself deserved to rule because of his talent and virtue, rather than as the result of noble birth. In practice, however, aristocratic privilege must have been a determining factor in opening the doors to political influence, and many of Confucius's contemporaries must have regarded his appeal for government by talent as both exciting and dangerous. Confucius did not explicitly question the right of the hereditary aristocracy to play an active and leading role in the political process, nor did his ideas have much effect in his lifetime. Still, they opened the door to a new concept of the art of statecraft that was later implemented in the form of a bureaucracy selected through a civil service examination (see the section on Confucianism and the State later in this chapter).

Confucius's ideas, passed on to later generations through the *Analects* as well as through other writings allegedly written by Confucius, had a strong impact on Chinese political thinkers of the late Zhou period at a time when the existing system was in disarray and open to serious question. But like most great thinkers,

≽ The Way of the Great Learning ≼

Unfortunately, few texts exist today that were written by Confucius himself. Most were written or edited by his disciples. The following text, entitled The Great Learning, was probably written two centuries after Confucius's death, but it illustrates his view that good government begins with the cultivation of individual morality and proper human relationships at the basic level. This conviction that "to bring peace to the world, cultivate your own person" continued to win general approval down to modern times.

The Great Learning

The Way of the Great Learning consists in clearly exemplifying illustrious virtue, in loving the people, and in resting in the highest good.

Only when one knows where one is to rest can one have a fixed purpose. Only with a fixed purpose can one achieve calmness of mind. Only with calmness of mind can one attain serene repose. Only in serene repose can one carry on careful deliberation. Only through careful deliberation can one have achievement. Things have their roots and branches; affairs have their beginning and end. He who knows what comes first and what comes last comes himself near the Way.

The ancients who wished clearly to exemplify illustrious virtue throughout the world would first set up good government in their states. Wishing to govern well their states, they would first regulate their families. Wishing to regulate their families, they would first cultivate their persons. Wishing to cultivate their persons, they would first rectify their minds. Wishing to rectify their minds, they would first seek sincerity in their thoughts. Wishing for sincerity in their thoughts, they would first extend their knowledge. The extension of knowledge lay in the investigation of things. For only when things are investigated is knowledge extended; only when knowledge is extended are thoughts sincere; only when thoughts are sincere are minds rectified; only when minds are rectified are our persons cultivated; only when our persons are cultivated are our families regulated; only when families are regulated are states well governed; and only when states are well governed is there peace in the world.

From the emperor down to the common people, all, without exception, must consider cultivation of the individual character as the root. If the root is in disorder, it is impossible for the branches to be in order. To treat the important as unimportant and to treat the unimportant as important—this should never be. This is called knowing the root; this is called the perfection of knowledge. . . .

Confucius's ideas were sufficiently ambiguous to be interpreted in very contradictory ways. Some, like the philosopher Mencius (370–290 B.C.E.), stressed the humanistic side of Confucian ideas, arguing that human beings were by nature good and thus could be taught their civic responsibilities by example. He also stressed that the ruler had a duty to govern with compassion:

> It was because Chieh and Chou lost the people that they lost the empire, and it was because they lost the hearts of the people that they lost the people. Here is the way to win the empire: win the people and you win the empire. Here is the way to win the people: win their hearts and you win the people. Here is the way to win their hearts: give them and share with them what they like, and do not do to them what they do not like. The people turn to a human ruler as water flows downward or beasts take to wilderness.[9]

Here is a prescription for political behavior that could win wide support in our own day. Other thinkers, however, rejected Mencius's rosy view of human nature and argued for a different approach.

LEGALISM

One school of thought that became quite popular during the "hundred flowers" era in ancient China was the philosophy of Legalism. Taking issue with the view of Mencius and other disciples of Confucius that human nature was essentially good, the Legalists argued that human beings were by nature evil and would follow the correct path only if coerced by harsh laws and stiff punishments. They were referred to as the "School of Law," because they rejected the Confucian view that government by "superior men" could solve society's problems and argued instead for a system of impersonal laws.

The Legalists disagreed with the Confucian belief that the universe has a moral core. They therefore believed that only firm action by the state could bring about social order. Because human nature was essentially corrupt, officials could not be trusted to carry out their duties in a fair and evenhanded manner, and only a strong ruler could create an orderly society. All human actions should be subordinated to the effort to create a strong and prosperous state subject to his will.

Both the Legalists and the author of the Indian treatise *Arthasastra* (see Chapter 2) focused on the importance of the ruler within the political culture, but the latter tempered his utilitarian concern for the needs of the state by asserting that the ruler and his officials must display a true compassion for the needs of the people. The Legalists, however, countered that fear of harsh punishment, more than the promise of material reward, could best motivate the common people to serve the interests of the ruler. Legalism bears a superficial resemblance to modern Western democratic society in its emphasis on the need for impartial laws to govern human behavior, but it is closer to modern totalitarian doctrines in its conviction that the ultimate objective of the political process is not the welfare of the individual, but the needs of the state.

DAOISM

One of the most popular alternatives to Confucianism was the philosophy of Daoism (frequently spelled Taoism). According to Chinese tradition, the Daoist school was founded by a contemporary of Confucius popularly known as Lao Tzu (Lao Zi), or the Old Master. Many modern scholars are skeptical that Lao Tzu actually existed. Nevertheless, the ideas that are attributed to him attained popularity during the centuries before the founding of the Han dynasty and became a worthy rival to the Confucian school of philosophy.

Obtaining a clear understanding of the original concepts of Daoism is difficult because the primary document containing its principles, a short treatise known as the *Dao De Jing* (sometimes translated as *The Way of the Tao*), is an enigmatic book whose correct interpretation has baffled scholars for centuries. The opening line, for example, explains less what the *Dao* is than what it is not: "The Tao [Way] that can be told of is not the eternal Tao. The name that can be named is not the eternal name."[10]

Nevertheless, the basic concepts of Daoism, as they have been transmitted through the ages by followers of the doctrine, are not especially difficult to understand. Like Confucianism, Daoism does not anguish over the underlying meaning of the cosmos. Rather, it attempts to set forth proper forms of behavior for human beings here on earth.

In most other respects, however, Daoism presents a view of life and its ultimate meaning that is almost diametrically opposed to the one adopted by Confucius and his followers. Where Confucian doctrine asserts that it is the duty of human beings to work hard to improve life here on earth, Daoists contend that the true way to interpret the will of Heaven is not action, but inaction (*wu wei*). The best way to act in harmony with the universal order is to act spontaneously and let nature take its course (see the box on p. 92).

Such a message could be very appealing to those who were uncomfortable with the somewhat rigid flavor of the Confucian work ethic and preferred a more individualistic approach. This image would eventually find graphic expression in the long tradition of Chinese landscape painting, which in its classical form would depict naturalistic scenes of mountains, water, and clouds and underscore the fragility and smallness of individual human beings.

Daoism achieved considerable popularity in the waning years of the Zhou dynasty and competed for favor with the various other doctrines that flourished at the time. It was especially popular among intellectuals, who may have found it appealing as an escapist antidote in a world characterized by growing disorder.

POPULAR BELIEFS

Daoism also played a second role as a somewhat loose framework for popular spiritualistic and animistic beliefs among the common people. Popular Daoism was less a philosophy than a religion; it comprised a variety of rituals and forms of behavior that were regarded as a means of achieving heavenly salvation or even a state of immortality on earth. Daoist sorcerers practiced various types of mind or body-training exercises in the hope of achieving power, sexual prowess, and long life. It was primarily in this form that Daoism would survive into a later age.

The philosophical forms of Confucianism and Daoism did not provide much meaning to the mass of the population, for whom philosophical debate over the ultimate meaning of life was not as important as the daily struggle for survival. For most Chinese, in ancient as well as in modern times, Heaven was not a vague impersonal law of nature, as it was for many Confucian and Daoist intellectuals, but a terrain peopled with innumerable gods and spirits of nature, both good and evil. As in Western societies, popular religion grew out of primitive beliefs in the existence of spirits in nature—in trees, mountains, and streams as well as the heavenly bodies. As human beings

The Dao De Jing (The Way of the Dao) *is the great classic of philosophical Daoism (Taoism). Traditionally attributed to the legendary Chinese philosopher Lao Tzu (Old Master), it was probably written sometime during the era of Confucius. This opening passage illustrates two of the key ideas that characterize Daoist belief: it is impossible to define the nature of the universe, and "inaction" (not Confucian "action") is the key to ordering the affairs of human beings.*

The Way of the Dao

The Tao that can be told of is not the eternal Tao;
The name that can be named is not the eternal name.
The Nameless is the origin of Heaven and Earth;
The Named is the mother of all things.

Therefore let there always be non-being, so we may see their subtlety.
And let there always be being, so we may see their outcome.
The two are the same,
But after they are produced, they have different names.
They both may be called deep and profound.
Deeper and more profound,
The door of all subtleties!

When the people of the world all know beauty as beauty,
There arises the recognition of ugliness.
When they all know the good as good,
There arises the recognition of evil.
Therefore:
Being and non-being produce each other;
Difficult and easy complete each other;
Long and short contrast each other;
High and low distinguish each other;
Sound and voice harmonize each other;
Front and behind accompany each other.

Therefore the sage manages affairs without action
And spreads doctrines without words.
All things arise, and he does not turn away from them.
He produces them but does not take possession of them.
He acts but does not rely on his own ability.
He accomplishes his task but does not claim credit for it.
It is precisely because he does not claim credit that his accomplishment remains with him.

mastered the techniques of farming, they called on divine intervention to guarantee a good harvest. Other gods were responsible for the safety of fishermen, transportation workers, or prospective mothers.

Another aspect of popular religion was the belief that the spirits of deceased human beings lived in the atmosphere for a time before ascending to Heaven or descending to Hell. During that period of purgatory, surviving family members had to care for the spirits through proper ritual, or they would become evil spirits and haunt the survivors.

Thus, in ancient China, a multiplicity of doctrines and beliefs offered human beings a variety of interpretations of the nature of the universe. Confucianism satisfied the need for a rational doctrine of nation building and social organization at a time when the existing political and social structure was beginning to disintegrate.

Philosophical Daoism provided an alternative to Confucianism and a framework for a set of diverse animistic beliefs at the popular level. But neither could provide an effective response to the deeper emotional needs that sometimes inspire the human spirit. Neither could effectively provide solace in a time of sorrow or the hope of a better life in the hereafter. Something else would be needed to fill the gap.

The Rise of the Chinese Empire: The Qin and the Han

During the last two centuries of the Zhou dynasty (the fourth and third centuries B.C.E.), the authority of the king became increasingly nominal, and several of the small principalities into which the Zhou kingdom had been divided began to evolve into powerful states that presented a potential challenge to the Zhou ruler himself. Chief among these were Qu (Ch'u) in the central Yangtze valley, Wu in the Yangtze delta, and Yue (Yueh) along the southeastern coast. At first, their mutual rivalries had been kept in check, but by the late fifth century B.C.E., competition had intensified into civil war, giving birth to an era known in Chinese historical records as the "Period of the Warring States" (see the box on p. 94). Powerful principalities vied with each other for preeminence and largely ignored the now purely titular authority of the Zhou court. New forms of warfare also emerged with the invention of iron weapons and the introduction of the foot soldier. Cavalry, too, made its first appearance, armed with the powerful crossbow. According to an ancient Chinese text, the invention of the crossbow can be attributed to a resident of the state of Qu as early as the seventh century B.C.E.:

> Mr. Ch'in [Qin] considered . . . that the bow and arrow was no longer sufficient to keep the world in obedience, for in his time all the feudal lords were fighting against one another with weapons, and could not be controlled by ordinary archery. He therefore added at right-angles to the bow a stock and established a trigger-mechanism with a box or housing, thus increasing its strength. In this way all the feudal lords could be subdued. Mr. Ch'in transmitted his invention to the Three Lords of Ch'u. . . . Before their time the men of Ch'u had for several generations guarded their frontiers only with bows of peachwood and arrows of thorn.[11]

Eventually, the relatively young state of Qin, located in the area originally occupied by the Zhou rulers several centuries earlier, became a key player in the game. Benefiting from a strong defensive position in the mountains to the west of the great bend of the Yellow River, as well as from their control of the rich Sichuan plains as an economic base, the Qin gradually subdued their main rivals through conquest or diplomatic maneuvering. In 221 B.C.E., the Qin ruler declared the establishment of a new dynasty, the first truly unified government in Chinese history.

The Qin Dynasty (221–206 B.C.E.)

One of the primary reasons for the triumph of the Qin was probably the character of the Qin ruler, known to history as Qin Shi Huangdi (Ch'in Shih Huang Ti), or the First Qin Emperor. A man of forceful personality and

✖ **Map 3.2**   China during the period of the Warring States.

The Art of War

With the possible exception of the nineteenth-century German military strategist Karl von Clausewitz, there is probably no more famous or respected writer on the art of war than the ancient Chinese thinker Sun Tzu. Yet surprisingly little is known about him. Recently discovered evidence suggests that he lived sometime in the fifth century B.C.E., during the chronic conflict of the Period of Warring States of the late Zhou era, and that he was an early member of an illustrious family of military strategists who advised Zhou rulers for more than two hundred years. But despite the mystery surrounding his life, there is no doubt of his influence on later generations of military planners. Among his most avid followers in our century have been the revolutionary leaders Mao Zedong and Ho Chi Minh, as well as the Japanese military strategists who planned the attacks on Port Arthur and pearl Harbor.

The following brief excerpt from his classic The Art of War provides a glimmer into the nature of his advice, still so timely today.

Selections from Sun Tzu

Sun-tzu said:

"In general, the method for employing the military is this: . . . Attaining one hundred victories in one hundred battles is not the pinnacle of excellence. Subjugating the enemy's army without fighting is the true pinnacle of excellence. . . .

"Thus the highest realization of warfare is to attack the enemy's plans; next is to attack their alliances; next to attack their army; and the lowest is to attack their fortified cities.

"This tactic of attacking fortified cities is adopted only when unavoidable. Preparing large movable protective shields, armored assault wagons, and other equipment and devices will require three months. Building earthworks will require another three months to complete. If the general cannot overcome his im-

patience but instead launches an assault wherein his men swarm over the walls like ants, he will kill one-third of his officers and troops, and the city will still not be taken. This is the disaster that results from attacking [fortified cities].

"Thus one who excels at employing the military subjugates other people's armies without engaging in battle, captures other people's fortified cities without attacking them, and destroys others people's states without prolonged fighting. He must fight under Heaven with the paramount aim of 'preservation.' . . .

"In general, the strategy of employing the military is this: If your strength is ten times theirs, surround them; if five, then attack them; if double, then divide your forces. If you are equal in strength to the enemy, you can engage him. If fewer, you can circumvent him. If outmatched, you can avoid him. . . .

"Thus there are five factors from which victory can be known:
"One who knows when he can fight, and when he cannot fight, will be victorious.
"One who recognizes how to employ large and small numbers will be victorious.
"One whose upper and lower ranks have the same desires will be victorious.
"One who, fully prepared, awaits the unprepared will be victorious.
"One whose general is capable and not interfered with by the ruler will be victorious.
"These five are the Way (Tao) to know victory. . . .

"Thus it is said that one who knows the enemy and knows himself will not be endangered in a hundred engagements. One who does not know the enemy but knows himself will sometimes be victorious, sometimes meet with defeat. One who knows neither the enemy nor himself will invariably be defeated in every engagement."

immense ambition, Qin Shi Huangdi had ascended to the throne of Qin (during the Period of the Warring States, the rulers of the various principalities had begun to refer to themselves as *wang*, or king) in 246 B.C.E. at the age of thirteen. Described by the famous Han dynasty historian Sima Qian as having "the chest of a bird of prey, the voice of a jackal, and the heart of a tiger," the

new king of Qin found the Legalist views of his adviser Li Su (Li Ssu) only too appealing. In 221 B.C.E., he defeated the last of Qin's rivals and founded a new dynasty with himself as emperor.

The Qin dynasty transformed Chinese politics. Philosophical doctrines about the art of statecraft that had proliferated during the late Zhou period were prohibited,

Memorandum on the Burning of Books

*L*i Su, the author of the following passage, was a chief
minister of the First Qin Emperor. An exponent of Legalism, Li Su hoped to eliminate all rival theories on government. His recommendation to the emperor on the subject
was recorded by the Han dynasty historian Sima Qian. The
emperor approved the proposal and ordered all books contrary to the spirit of Legalist ideology to be destroyed on pain
of death. Fortunately, some texts were preserved by being
hidden, or even memorized by their owners, and were thus
available to later generations. For centuries afterward, the
First Qin Emperor and his minister were singled out for criticism because of their intolerance and their effort to control
the very minds of their subjects. Totalitarianism, it seems, is
not exclusively a modern concept.

Sima Qian, *Historical Records*

In earlier times the empire disintegrated and fell into
disorder, and no one was capable of unifying it. Thereupon the various feudal lords rose to power. In their discourses they all praised the past in order to disparage
the present and embellished empty words to confuse
the truth. Everyone cherished his own favorite school
of learning and criticized what had been instituted by
the authorities. But at present Your Majesty possesses a
unified empire, has regulated the distinctions of black
and white, and has firmly established for yourself a position of sole supremacy. And yet these independent
schools, joining with each other, criticize the codes of
laws and instructions. Hearing of the promulgation of a
decree, they criticize it, each from the standpoint of

his own school. At home they disapprove of it in their
hearts; going out they criticize it in the thoroughfare.
They seek a reputation by discrediting their sovereign;
they appear superior by expressing contrary views, and
they lead the lowly multitude in the spreading of slander. If such license is not prohibited, the sovereign
power will decline above and partisan factions will form
below. It would be well to prohibit this.

Your servant suggests that all books in the imperial
archives, save the memoirs of Ch'in, be burned. All
persons in the empire, except members of the Academy
of Learned Scholars, in possession of the *Book of Odes*,
the *Book of History*, and discourses of the hundred
philosophers should take them to the local governors
and have them indiscriminately burned. Those who
dare to talk to each other about the *Book of Odes* and
the *Book of History* should be executed and their bodies
exposed in the market place. Anyone referring to the
past to criticize the present should, together with all
members of his family, be put to death. Officials who
fail to report cases that have come under their attention
are equally guilty. After thirty days from the time of issuing the decree, those who have not destroyed their
books are to be branded and sent to build the Great
Wall. Books not to be destroyed will be those on medicine and pharmacy, divination by the tortoise and milfoil, and agriculture and arboriculture. People wishing
to pursue learning should take the officials as their
teachers.

and Legalism was adopted as the official ideology. Those
who opposed the policies of the new regime were punished and sometimes executed, while books presenting
ideas contrary to the official orthodoxy were publicly put
to the torch, perhaps the first example of book burning in
history (see the box above).

Legalistic theory gave birth to a number of fundamental administrative and political developments, some of
which would survive the Qin and serve as a model for future dynasties. In the first place, unlike the Zhou the Qin
was a highly centralized state. The central bureaucracy
was divided into three primary ministries: a civil authority, a military authority, and a censorate, whose inspectors surveyed the efficiency of officials throughout the

system. This would later become standard administrative
procedure for future Chinese dynasties.

Below the central government were two levels of administration—commanderies (provinces) and counties.
Unlike the Zhou system, officials at these levels did not
inherit their positions, but were appointed by the court
and were subject to dismissal at the emperor's whim. Apparently, some form of merit system was used, although
there is no evidence that selection was based on performance in an examination. The civil servants may have
been chosen on the recommendation of other government officials. A penal code was instituted that provided
for harsh punishments for all wrongdoers. Officials were
watched by the censors, who reported directly to the

throne. Those guilty of malfeasance in office were executed.

Qin Shi Huangdi, who had a passion for centralization, unified the system of weights and measures, standardized the monetary system and the written forms of Chinese characters, and ordered the construction of a system of roads extending throughout the entire empire. He also attempted to eliminate the remaining powers of the landed aristocrats and divided their estates among the peasants, who were now taxed directly by the state. He thus eliminated potential rivals and secured tax revenues for the central government. Members of the aristocratic clans were required to live in the capital city at Xianyang (Hsien-yang), just north of modern-day Xian, so that the court could monitor their activities. Such a system may not have been advantageous to the peasants in all respects, however, since the central government could now collect taxes more effectively and mobilize the peasants for military service and for various public works projects.

The Qin dynasty was equally unsympathetic to the merchants, whom it viewed as parasites. Private commercial activities were severely restricted and heavily taxed, while many of the more vital forms of commerce and manufacturing, such as mining, wine making, and the distribution of salt, were placed under a government monopoly.

Qin Shi Huangdi was equally aggressive in foreign affairs. His armies continued the gradual advance to the south that had taken place during the final years of the Zhou dynasty, extending the border of China to the edge of the Red River in modern-day Vietnam. To supply the Qin armies operating in the area, a canal was dug that provided direct inland navigation from the Yangtze River in central China to what is now the modern city of Guangzhou (Canton) in the south.

BEYOND THE FRONTIER: THE NOMADIC PEOPLES AND THE GREAT WALL OF CHINA

The main area of concern for the Qin emperor, however, was in the north, where a nomadic people, known to the Chinese as the Xiongnu (Hsiung-nu) and possibly related to the Huns (see Chapter 5), had become increasingly active in the area of the Gobi Desert. The area north of the Yellow River had been sparsely inhabited since prehistoric times. At that time, the climate of North China was somewhat milder and moister than it is today, and parts of the region may have been heavily forested. The local population probably lived by hunting and fishing, practicing limited forms of agriculture, or herding animals such as cattle or sheep.

As the climate throughout northeastern Asia gradually became drier, such peoples faced a severe ecological challenge and were forced to rely increasingly on animal husbandry as a means of livelihood. Their response was to master the art of riding on horseback and adopt the nomadic life. Organized loosely into tribes consisting of a number of individual kinship groups, they ranged far and wide in search of pasture for their herds of cattle, goats, or sheep. As they moved seasonally from one pasture to another, they often traveled several hundred miles carrying their goods and their circular felt tents, called *yurts*, with them.

But the new way of life presented its own challenges. Increased food production led to a growing population, which in times of drought outstripped the available resources. Rival tribes then competed for the best pastures. After they mastered the art of fighting on horseback sometime during the middle of the first millennium B.C.E., territorial warfare became commonplace throughout the entire frontier region from the Pacific Ocean to Central Asia.

Contact between the pastoral peoples and the sedentary Chinese communities near the frontier region undoubtedly took place throughout this period, and Chinese sources indicate that tensions between them were not unknown. At the end of the Zhou dynasty in the third century B.C.E., the nomads, in the form of the Xiongnu, posed a serious threat to the security of China's northern frontier, and a number of Chinese principalities in the area began to build walls and fortifications to keep them out. But warriors on horseback possessed significant advantages over the infantry battalions of the Chinese. Recounting the situation a few generations later, the famous Chinese historian Sima Qian remarked wistfully that "the little boys start out by learning to ride sheep and shoot birds and rats with a bow and arrow, and when they get a little older they shoot foxes and hares, which are used for food. Thus all the young men are able to use a bow and act as armed cavalry in time of war."

Qin Shi Huangdi's answer to the problem was to strengthen the walls to keep the marauders out. In Sima Qian's words:

> [The] First Emperor of the Ch'in dispatched Meng T'ien to lead a force of a hundred thousand men north to attack the barbarians. He seized control of all the lands south of the Yellow River and established border defenses along the river, constructing forty-four walled district cities overlooking the river and manning them with convict laborers transported to the border for garrison duty. Thus he utilized the natural mountain barriers to establish the border defenses, scooping out the valleys and constructing ram-

parts and building installations at other points where they were needed. The whole line of defenses stretched over ten thousand *li* [a *li* is one-third of a mile] from Lin-t'ao to Liao-tung and even extended across the Yellow River and through Yang-shan and Pei-chia.[12]

Today, of course, we know Qin Shi Huangdi's project as the Great Wall. Children are taught that the Great Wall is more than two thousand years old and extends nearly four thousand miles from the sandy wastes of Central Asia to the sea. It is constructed of massive granite blocks and is wide enough on top to provide a roadway for horse-drawn chariots. Its size and length are so massive that it is the only human-made object that can be seen from outer space.

Unfortunately, only a part of this romantic tale is true. The wall that we know today from films and photographs was not built at the order of the First Qin Emperor, but was constructed fifteen hundred years later by an emperor of the Ming dynasty. Some of the walls built by the Qin do indeed remain standing, but many of them were constructed of loose stone, sand, or piled rubble and are barely visible from an airliner flying at 30,000 feet. Finally, the Qin did not begin the construction of the wall, but only joined sections of walls that had existed in various parts of North China for decades, if not centuries.

This is not to say, of course, that the wall was not a massive project. It undoubtedly required the efforts of thousands of laborers, many of whom met their deaths there and, according to legend, are now buried within the wall. And, to many Chinese at the time, Qin Shi Huangdi's action must have made sense, since it must have seemed inevitable that once the nomads possessed military superiority, they would use it for the purposes of conquest. According to Sima Qian: "It is their custom to herd their flocks in times of peace and make their living by hunting, but in periods of crisis they take up arms and go off on plundering and marauding expeditions. This seems to be their inborn nature."[13]

As we have seen, the answer is not quite that simple. In some cases, pastoral peoples are driven to seek new pastures by overpopulation or the desiccation of their usual lands. Some scholars point out that nomadic tribes sometimes resort to warfare when their trade with neighboring agricultural communities is threatened. Undoubtedly, all of these hypotheses contain some truth (see Chapter 12). Perhaps a more accommodating attitude on the part of the Zhou and the Qin would have alleviated some of the tension along the border. Qin Shi Huangdi, however, was hardly inclined toward accommodation and adopted a hard line. He did enjoy some success in fending off the potential threat from the north, but the

victory was a temporary one. Over the next two thousand years, the northern frontier became one of the great faultlines of conflict in Asia.

THE FALL OF THE QIN

The Legalist system put in place by the First Qin Emperor was designed to achieve maximum efficiency as well as total security for the state. It did neither. Qin Shi Huangdi was apparently aware of the dangers of factionalism within the imperial family and established a class of eunuchs (males whose testicles have been removed) who served as personal attendants for himself and for female

◆ **Qin Shi Huangdi.** Qin Shi Huangdi, the First Emperor of Qin, who reigned from 221 to 206 B.C.E., was one of the most influential figures in the history of China. Although considered ruthless by many historians, he created the first unified Chinese state, ordered the construction of a system of roads throughout the country, standardized the Chinese currency and written language, and brought together the scattered defensive battlements into what we now know as the "Great Wall."

members of the royal family. The original idea may have been to restrict the influence of male courtiers, and the eunuch system later became a standard feature of the Chinese imperial system. But eunuchs were clearly in a position of influence because of their role as confidential advisers to the royal family. The rivalry between the "inner" imperial court and the "outer" court of bureaucratic officials led to tensions that became a source of chronic difficulties that persisted until the end of the imperial system.

By ruthlessly gathering control over the empire into his own hands, Qin Shi Huangdi had hoped to establish a rule that, in the words of Sima Qian, "would be enjoyed by his sons for ten thousand generations." In fact, his centralizing zeal alienated many key groups. Landed aristocrats and Confucian intellectuals, as well as the common people, groaned under the censorship of thought and speech, harsh taxes, and forced labor projects. "He killed men," recounted the historian, "as though he thought he could never finish, he punished men as though he were afraid he would never get around to them all, and the whole world revolted against him."[14] Shortly after the emperor died in 210 B.C.E., the dynasty quickly descended into factional rivalry, and four years later it was overthrown.

The disappearance of the Qin brought an end to an experiment in absolute rule that later would be viewed by

♦ **The Great Wall.** The section of the Great Wall that is often visited by tourists today is not the work of the First Emperor of Qin, but was built at the order of a Ming ruler many centuries later. The original walls were often composed of loose stone, dirt, or piled rubble, and posed little obstacle to invading nomads from the north. The section illustrated here is located north of the city of Duahuang in Central Asia.

Chinese historians as a betrayal of humanistic Confucian principles. But in another sense, the Qin system was a response—though somewhat extreme—to the real and growing problems of administering a large and increasingly complex society. Although later rulers would denounce Legalism and enthrone Confucianism as the new state orthodoxy, in practice they would make use of a number of the key tenets of Legalism as a means of administering the empire and controlling the behavior of their subjects.

The Glorious Han Dynasty (202 B.C.E.–221 C.E.)

The fall of the Qin was followed by a brief period of civil strife as aspiring successors competed for hegemony. But China did not revert to the pattern of warring states that had characterized the last years of the Zhou. To the contrary, it gave rise to one of the greatest and most durable dynasties in Chinese history—the Han. The Han dynasty would later become so closely identified with the advance of Chinese civilization that even today the Chinese sometimes refer to themselves as "people of Han" and to their language as the "language of Han."

The founder of the Han dynasty was Liu Bang (Liu Pang), a commoner of peasant origin who would be known historically by his title of Han Gaozu (Han Kao Tsu, or Exalted Emperor of Han). Under his strong rule and that of his successors, the new dynasty quickly moved to consolidate its control over the empire and promote the welfare of its subjects. Efficient and benevolent, at least by the standards of the time, Gaozu maintained the centralized political institutions of the Qin but abandoned the harsh Legalistic approach to law enforcement that had characterized his predecessor. Han rulers also reversed the effort by the First Qin Emperor to enforce a single ideology and discovered in Confucian principles a useful foundation for the creation of a new state philosophy. Under the Han, Confucianism began to take on the character of an official ideology.

CONFUCIANISM AND THE STATE

The integration of Confucian doctrine with Legalist practice did not take long to accomplish. Although the founding Han ruler declared his intention to discard the harsh methods adopted by the Qin and return to the ideal principles of the Golden Age, he and his successors found it convenient to retain many of the institutions and practices introduced by the First Qin Emperor. For example, they borrowed the tripartite division of the central government into civilian and military authorities and a censorate. The government was headed by what would eventually emerge as a Grand Council including representatives from all three segments of government. The Han also retained the system of local government, dividing the empire into provinces and districts. The term *commandery*, with its military connotations, was eventually discarded, however.

Finally, and perhaps most important, the Han continued the Qin system of selecting government officials on the basis of merit rather than birth. Shortly after founding the new dynasty, Emperor Gaozu decreed that local officials would be asked to recommend promising candidates for public service. Thirty years later, in 165 B.C.E., the first known civil service examination was administered to candidates for positions in the bureaucracy. Shortly after that, an academy was established to train such candidates.

Nevertheless, this trend toward rule by merit was still limited. Available information suggests that the first can-

didates were almost all from aristocratic or other wealthy families, and the Han bureaucracy itself was still dominated by the traditional hereditary elite. Still, the principle of selecting officials on the basis of talent had been established and would eventually become standard practice.

The decision by the Han dynasty to combine Confucian principles and Legalistic practices, creating a system that is generally known as State Confucianism, may well have been a sound one, given the prevailing circumstances. China under the Han dynasty was a vast empire that required a strong central bureaucracy to survive. The population increased rapidly—by some estimates rising from about 20 million to over 60 million at the height of the dynasty—creating a growing need for a large and efficient bureaucracy to maintain the state in proper working order. Unfortunately, the Han were unable to resolve all of the problems left over from the past. Factionalism at court remained a serious problem and undermined the efficiency of the central government. Equally important,

Map 3.3   The Han Empire.

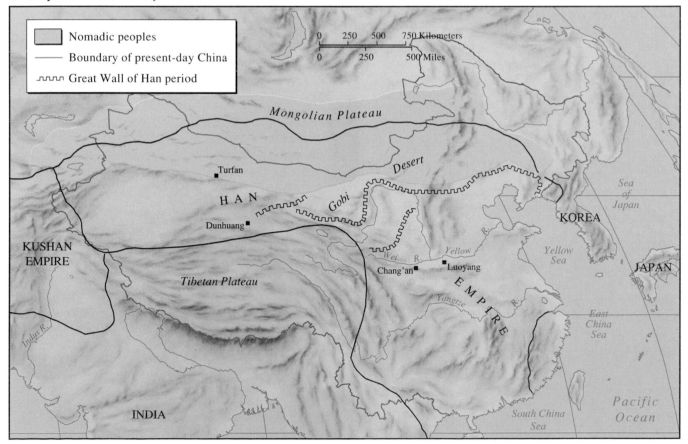

despite their efforts, the Han rulers were never able to limit sufficiently the power of the great aristocratic families, who continued to play a dominant role in political and economic affairs. The failure to curb the power of the wealthy clans eventually became a major factor in the final collapse of the dynasty.

SOCIETY AND ECONOMY IN THE HAN EMPIRE

As in the realm of politics, Han rulers saw some value in the economic and social policies followed by their predecessors. In particular, they saw that a free peasantry paying taxes directly to the state would both limit the wealth and power of the great noble families and increase the state's revenues. Given the relatively looser control over society maintained by the Han, however, the central government had difficulty preventing the recurrence of the economic inequities that had characterized the last years of the Zhou. Although the land taxes on free farmers were relatively light, there were a number of other exactions, including military service and forced labor of up to one month annually. Although the use of iron tools brought new lands under the plow and food production increased steadily, the trebling of the population under the Han eventually reduced the average size of the individual farm plot to about one acre per capita, barely enough for survival. As time went on, many poor peasants were forced to sell their land and become tenant farmers paying rents ranging up to half of the annual harvest. Thus, land once again came to be concentrated in the hands of the powerful landed clans, which often owned thousands of acres worked by tenants and mustered their own military forces to bully free farmers into becoming tenants.

Although such economic problems contributed to the eventual downfall of the dynasty, in general the Han era was one of unparalleled productivity and prosperity. The

◆ **Han Gentlemen.** Some of the customs of the Chinese of 2,000 years ago can be seen in paintings found in Han dynasty tombs. One can still eavesdrop on these dignified gentlemen, in their elegant robes, as they discuss some serious matter.

CHRONOLOGY

Ancient China

Xia (Hsia) dynasty	?–1766? B.C.E.
Shang dynasty	1766–1122? B.C.E.
Zhou (Chou) dynasty	1122?–221 B.C.E.
Life of Confucius	551–479 B.C.E.
Period of the Warring States	403–221 B.C.E.
Life of Mencius	370–290 B.C.E.
Qin (Ch'in) dynasty	221–206 B.C.E.
Life of the Qin First Emperor	259–210 B.C.E.
Formation of Han dynasty	202 B.C.E.
Wang Mang interregnum	9–23 C.E.
Collapse of Han dynasty	221 C.E.

period was marked by a major expansion of trade, both domestic and foreign. This was not necessarily due to official encouragement. In fact, the Han were as suspicious of private merchants as their predecessors had been and passed discriminatory laws and levied stiff taxes on trade in an effort to limit commercial activities. Merchants were also subject to severe social disabilities. They were disqualified from seeking office, restricted in their place of residence, and viewed in general as parasites providing little true value to Chinese society.

Despite such restrictions, trade and manufacturing prospered in Han times and contributed to the general rise in prosperity that marked much of the period. Much of this activity was directed by the state, including shipyards, the manufacture of weapons, mining, and the operation of granaries. The government also moved cautiously into foreign trade, mostly with neighboring areas in Central and Southeast Asia, although trade relations were established with countries as far away as India and the Mediterranean. Some of this long-distance trade was carried by sea through southern ports like Quangzhou, but more was transported by overland caravans on the Silk Road (see Chapter 10) and other similar routes through the vast deserts and plateaus that led westward into Central Asia. Some of the trade was organized in the form of tribute missions, with neighboring countries providing local specialties like tropical products and precious stones in return for Chinese silks, glazed pottery (an early form of porcelain), and various manufactured products. China often gave more than it received to ensure that neighboring monarchs would accept China's benevolent protection and not harbor its enemies.

New technology contributed to the economic prosperity of the Han era. Significant progress was achieved in such areas as textile manufacturing, water mills, and iron casting; the latter led to the invention of steel a few centuries later. Paper was invented under the Han, while the invention of the rudder and fore-and-aft rigging permitted ships to sail into the wind for the first time. Thus equipped, Chinese merchant ships carrying heavy cargoes could sail throughout the islands of Southeast Asia and into the Indian Ocean.

Finally, the Han emperors continued the process of territorial expansion and consolidation that had begun under the Zhou and the Qin. Han rulers, notably the martial Han Wudi (Han Wu Ti, or Martial Emperor of Han), successfully completed the assimilation into the empire of the southern regions below the Yangtze River, including the Red River delta in what is today northern Vietnam. Han armies were also sent westward into Central Asia, where they penetrated as far as the Caspian Sea, pacifying nomadic tribal peoples and extending China's boundary far beyond its previous extent. The Han continued to have problems working out an

Map 3.4   Trade Routes of the Ancient World.

◆ **Jade Burial Suit.** During the Han dynasty, members of the imperial family were buried in jade body suits such as this one, which dates from the second century B.C.E. It is composed of jade squares that were sewn together with gold thread. Extremely expensive to produce, they were eventually banned by the court as too extravagant.

effective relationship with the Xiongnu beyond the Great Wall to the north. Han Gaozu had attempted military pacification, but that failed and nomadic raids on Chinese territory continued, once reaching almost to the gates of the capital city, now located at Chang'an (Ch'ang An, or Eternal Peace), located on the site of modern-day Xian. A successor, Han Wendi (Han Wen Ti), tried conciliation, and a treaty was signed dividing authority between the Chinese and the Xiongnu at the Great Wall. But some people at court argued that the Celestial Emperor should not be forced to deal on equal terms with barbarians, and conflict continued intermittently to the end of the dynasty.

THE DECLINE AND FALL OF THE HAN

In 9 C.E., a reformist official Wang Mang, who was troubled by the plight of the peasants, seized power from the Han court and declared the foundation of a new Xin (New) dynasty. In the years prior to his seizure of power,

the empire had begun to fall into decay. As frivolous or depraved rulers amused themselves with the pleasures of court life, the power and influence of the central government began to wane, and the great noble families filled the vacuum, amassing vast landed estates and transforming free farmers into tenants. Wang Mang may have genuinely hoped to improve the lot of the common people and restore China to the glories of its past. He nationalized the land and tried to confiscate the great estates. He attempted to restore the ancient well field system and abolish slavery. In so doing, however, he alienated powerful interests, who conspired to overthrow him. In 23 C.E., beset by administrative chaos and a collapse of the frontier defenses, Wang Mang was put to death in a coup d'etat.

For a time, strong leadership revived some of the glory of the early Han. The court did attempt to reduce land taxes and carry out land resettlement programs. The growing popularity of nutritious crops like rice and soybeans, along with the introduction of new crops such as alfalfa and grapes, helped to boost food production. But the monopoly of land and power by the great landed families continued. Weak rulers were isolated within their imperial chambers and dominated by eunuchs and other powerful figures at court. Official corruption and the concentration of land in the hands of the wealthy led to widespread peasant unrest. The population of the empire, which had been estimated at about 60 million in China's first census in the year 2 C.E., shrank to less than 20 million two hundred years later. In the early third century C.E., the dynasty was finally brought to an end when power was seized by Cao Cao (Ts'ao Ts'ao), a general well known to millions of later Chinese as one of the main characters in the famous Chinese epic, *The Romance of the Three Kingdoms*. One Chinese source bitterly describes the conditions of the times:

> The houses of the powerful are compounds where several hundreds of ridgebeams are linked together. Their fertile fields fill the countryside. Their slaves throng in thousands, and their military dependents can be counted in tens of thousands. Their boats, carts and merchants are spread throughout the four quarters. Their stocks of goods held back for speculation fill up the principal cities. Their great mansions cannot contain their precious stones and treasure. The upland valleys cannot hold their horses, cattle, sheep, and swine. Their elegant apartments are full of seductive lads and lovely concubines. Singing-girls and courtesans are lined up in their deep halls.[15]

The great achievements of the Han could not hide the internal weaknesses, and the dynasty was unable to survive Cao Cao's coup d'etat. But Cao Cao was unable to consolidate his power, and China entered a period of almost constant anarchy and internal division, compounded by invasions of northern tribal peoples. The next great dynasty did not arise until the beginning of the seventh century, four hundred years later.

Daily Life in Ancient China

Of all the social institutions that have appeared in organized human societies, few have been as closely identified with China as the family. As in most agricultural civilizations, the family served as the basic economic and social unit in society. In traditional China, however, it took on an almost sacred quality as a microcosm of the entire social order.

It is difficult to locate the precise origins of the family system in ancient China. In Neolithic times, the farm village, organized around the clan, was the basic social unit in China, at least in the core region of the Yellow River valley. Even then, however, there were signs that the smaller family unit was becoming more important, at least among the nobility, who attached considerable significance to the ritual veneration of their immediate ancestors. A noble lineage, of course, was a prerequisite for high social status in those early times and a ladder of upward mobility into positions of civilian or military leadership.

The concept of family took on growing importance during the Zhou dynasty, not only for the great noble families but among the population at large. Certainly, it was already well established by the time of Confucius in the sixth and fifth centuries B.C.E. Through the writings of Confucius and his disciples, the family system took on the symbolic as well as the practical quality that it has retained to our own day. Loyalty to family members was considered even more important than loyalty to the broader community or the state. In one significant passage in the *Analects,* Confucius remarked that a son should protect his father even if the latter had committed a crime against the community. That, he asserted, is the mark of a civilized society.

At the crux of the concept of family in China was the idea of filial piety, which called on all members of the family to subordinate their needs and desires to the patriarchal head of the family. More broadly, it created a hierarchical system in which every family member had his or her place. All Chinese learned the "five relationships" that were the key to a proper social order. The son was subordinate to the father, the wife to her husband, the younger brother to the older brother, and all were subject to their king. The final relationship was the proper one between friend and friend. Only if all members of the family and the community as a whole behaved in a properly filial manner would society function effectively.

What explains the importance of the family and the concept of filial piety in ancient China? Certainly, the need for cooperation in agriculture was a significant factor. In ancient times as today, farming in China was highly labor-intensive, especially the cultivation of rice, which, due to its productivity and nutritive qualities, had become the primary crop in the region of the Yangtze River and the provinces to the south. Rice cultivation requires unceasing hard work. First, rice seedlings are planted in several inches of water in a nursery bed, while the farmer plows the larger paddy fields in preparation for planting. During the rainy season, the plants are transferred individually by back-breaking labor to the paddy fields after they have flooded. After the transplanting, the irrigation network bringing water into and through the fields must be kept in operation, and the plants themselves protected from pests. When the crop is ripe for harvesting, the stalks must be cut, and the kernels separated from the stalks and husks and brought to the house where the rice is prepared for sale to the rice miller.

◆ **Flooded Rice Fields.**   Rice is a very labor-intensive crop, which requires many workers to plant the seedlings and organize the distribution of water. Initially, the fields are flooded to facilitate the rooting of the rice seedlings and to add nutrients to the soil. Fish breeding in the flooded fields help keep mosquitoes and other insects in check. As the plants mature, the fields are drained, and the plants complete their four-month growing cycle in dry soil.

Under such circumstances, it is hardly surprising that the subordination of the individual to the needs of the family was a matter of supreme importance in traditional China. Children were essential to the productivity of the family, not only during their youthful years, but even later when sons were expected to take over the burden of physical labor on the family plots and provide for the security of their parents.

A stable family system based on obedient and hardworking members can serve as a bulwark for an efficient government, but putting loyalty to the family and the clan over loyalty to the state can also present a threat to a centralizing monarch. For that reason, the Qin dynasty attempted to destroy the clan system in China and assert the primacy of the state. According to one historian, Legalists even imposed heavy taxes on any family with more than two adult sons in order to break down the family concept. The Qin reportedly also originated the practice of organizing several family units into larger groups of five and ten families that would exercise mutual control and surveillance. Later dynasties continued the practice under the name of the *Bao-jia* (*Pao-chia*) system.

But the efforts of the Qin to eradicate or at least reduce the importance of the family system ran against tradition and the dynamics of the Chinese economy, and under the Han the family revived and increased in importance. Under the Han, the family system began to take on the character that it would possess until our own day. The family was not only the basic economic unit, it was also the basic social unit for education, religious observances, and training in ethical principles. According to a popular Confucian aphorism, to ensure proper behavior, it was necessary to begin in the family and then extend outward to the broader community and "all under Heaven" (see the box on p. 90).

We know much more about the lifestyle of the elites than of the common people in ancient China. According to tradition, the Yellow Emperor first taught the people to build houses in the late third millennium B.C.E. Early examples probably consisted of two rooms, with a main hall in front and living quarters in the back. The first houses were probably constructed of wooden planks, but later Chinese mastered the art of building in tile and brick. By the first millennium B.C.E., most public buildings and the houses of the wealthy were probably constructed in this manner.

Few examples of the homes of the common people have survived aside from a few archaeological sites such as Banpo village near Xian in central China. In the beginning, according to the author of the *Book of Changes*, "man dwelt in the cave and lived out in the field. Later

on, the sages substituted houses with ridge-poles and roofs to protect them from the rain." By Han times, most Chinese probably lived in simple houses of mud, wooden planks, or brick with thatch or occasionally tile roofs. But in some areas of China, cave dwelling remained common down to modern times, especially in the loess (pronounced "less," a type of soil common in North China) areas of North China, where the yellow soil is soft and provides good protection from the heat and cold. The most famous cave-dweller of modern times was Mao Zedong, who lived in a cave in Yan'an during his long struggle against Chiang Kai-shek.

Chinese houses usually had little furniture; most people squatted or sat with their legs spread out on the packed mud floor. Chairs were apparently not introduced until the sixth or seventh centuries C.E. Clothing was simple, consisting of cotton trousers and shirts in the summer and wool or burlap in the winter.

The cooking of food had been introduced in early times, with the staple foods being millet or other dry crops in the north and rice in the south. Other common vegetable crops were wheat, barley, mustard greens, and bamboo shoots. In early times, such foods were often consumed in the form of porridge, but by the Zhou dynasty, stir-frying in a *wok* was becoming common. Where possible, the Chinese family would vary its diet of grain foods with vegetables, fruit (including pears, peaches, apricots, and plums), and fish or meat, but for most, such additions to the daily plate of rice, millet, or soybeans were a rare luxury.

Alcohol in the form of ale was drunk at least by the higher classes and by the early Zhou era had already begun to inspire official concern. According to the *Book of History*, "King Wen admonished and admonished the young nobles who were charged with office, or in any employment, that they should not ordinarily use spirits; and throughout all the states he required that they should be drunk only on occasion of sacrifices, and that then virtue should preside so that there might be no drunkenness."[16]

Most Chinese, then as now, lived in the countryside. But as time went on, cities began to play a larger role in Chinese society. The first towns were little more than forts for the local aristocracy; they were small in size and limited in population. By the Zhou era, however, larger towns, usually located on the major trade routes, began to combine administrative with economic functions, serving as regional markets or manufacturing centers. Such cities were usually surrounded by a wall and a moat, and a raised platform might be built within the walls to provide a place for ritual ceremonies and housing for the ruler's family.

By the Han, the major city in China was Chang'an,

the imperial capital. The city covered a total area of nearly forty square kilometers and was surrounded by a twelve-foot wall of rammed yellow earth. The wall, which was probably built with conscript labor, was surrounded by a moat. Twelve gates provided entry into the city, and eight major avenues ran east-west or north-south. Each avenue was forty-five meters wide; a center strip in each avenue was reserved for the emperor, whose palace and gardens occupied nearly half the southern and central part of the city.

The Humble Estate: Women in Ancient China

Male dominance was a key element in the social system of ancient China. As in many traditional societies, the male was considered of transcendent importance because of his role as food procurer or, in the case of farming communities, food producer. In ancient China, men worked in the fields and women raised children and served in the home. This differential in sexual roles goes back to prehistoric times and is embedded in Chinese creation myths. According to legend, Fu Xi's wife Nu Wa assisted her husband in organizing society by establishing the institution of marriage and the family. Yet Nu Wa was not just a household drudge. After Fu Xi's death, she became China's first female sovereign.

During ancient times, women apparently did not normally occupy formal positions of authority, but they often became a force in politics, especially at court where wives of the ruler or other female members of the royal family were often influential in palace intrigues. Such activities were frowned on, however, as the following passage from the *Book of Songs* attests:

> *A clever man builds a city,*
> *A clever woman lays one low;*
> *With all her qualifications, that clever woman*
> *Is but an ill-omened bird.*
> *A woman with a long tongue*
> *Is a flight of steps leading to calamity;*
> *For disorder does not come from heaven,*
> *But is brought about by women.*
> *Among those who cannot be trained or taught*
> *Are women and eunuchs.*[17]

The nature of gender relationships was also graphically demonstrated in the Chinese written language. The character for man (**男**) combines the symbols for strength and a rice field, while the character for woman (**女**) represents a person in a posture of deference and respect. The character for peace (**安**) is a woman under a roof. A wife is symbolized by a woman with a broom. Male chauvinism has deep linguistic roots in China.

Confucian thought, while not denigrating the importance of women as mothers and homemakers, accepted the dual roles of men and women in Chinese society. Men governed society. They carried on family ritual through the veneration of ancestors. They were the warriors, scholars, and ministers. It is not surprising that women were taught to accept their secondary role in life. Ban Zhao, a prominent female historian of the Han dynasty whose own career was an exception to the rule, described that role as follows:

> To be humble, yielding, respectful and reverential; to put herself after others . . . these qualities are those exemplifying woman's low and humble estate. To retire late and rise

◆ **Han Pottery House.**   During the Han Dynasty, the Chinese people thought that even in heaven one could still be surrounded by one's earthly possessions, such as family, servants, and house. Since such material goods could not accompany one directly into the afterworld, pottery models such as the one shown here were made and then placed in tombs with the dead.

early; not to shirk exertion from dawn to dark . . . this is called being diligent. To behave properly and decorously in serving her husband; to be serene and self-possessed, shunning jests and laughter . . . this is called being worthy of continuing the husband's lineage. If a woman possess the above mentioned three qualities, then her reputation shall be excellent.[18]

Ban Zhao was the younger sister of the famous historian Ban Gu, who became the official historian of the Han dynasty. In writing the official history of the Han era, Ban Gu initiated a tradition that would be followed for centuries until the final collapse of the dynastic system in the early twentieth century.

The World of Culture

Modern knowledge about artistic achievements in ancient civilizations is limited because often little has survived the ravages of time. Fortunately, many of the advanced cultures of the ancient world, such as Egypt and Mesopotamia, were located in relatively arid areas where many artifacts of early civilizations were preserved, even over thousands of years. In more humid regions, such as China and Southeast Asia, the cultural residue left by the civilizations of antiquity has been adversely affected by climate.

As a result, relatively little remains of the cultural achievements of the ancient Chinese aside from the Neolithic pottery of Banpo, Yangshao, and Longshan in the Yellow River valley and the historical relics found at the site of the Shang dynasty capital at Anyang. In recent years, a rich trove from the time of the Qin Empire has been unearthed near the tomb of Qin Shi Huangdi near Xian in central China and at Han tombs nearby. But little remains of the literature of ancient China and almost none of the painting, architecture, and music.

Metalwork and Sculpture

Discoveries at archaeological sites indicate that ancient China was a society rich in cultural achievement. The pottery found at Neolithic sites such as Banpo, Longshan, and Yangshao exhibits a freshness and vitality of form and design that is appealing to the modern viewer, while the ornaments, such as rings and beads, show a strong aesthetic sense.

The pace of Chinese cultural development began to quicken during the Shang dynasty, which ruled in North China from the eighteenth to the twelfth century B.C.E. At that time, objects cast in bronze, which are among the most extraordinary and admired creations of Chinese art, began to appear. Some scholars have speculated that the Chinese learned the art of bronze working from other cultures, but recent finds at early Shang sites suggest that the technology was developed indigenously, perhaps as early as the Xia era.

Bronze casting may have originally been used in the manufacture of weapons, but the Shang later transferred the art to making bronze ritual vessels for sacrificial purposes. Not much is known about Shang religious beliefs, but in noble families, the veneration of ancestors was important, as the souls of the dead had to be kept alive to protect their descendants. The bronze vessels, which were produced in great variety, were used as ceremonial instruments for preparing and serving food and drink in the ancestral rites. Later they were used for decoration or for dining at court.

Shang bronzes, with their highly sophisticated and intricate relief work, are technically unequaled and are considered one of the highest cultural achievements of antiquity. The designs incorporate complex religious symbols, reflecting awe at the power of nature and concerns over the problems of life and death. The most important decoration of Shang bronzes is the so-called *taotie* (t'ao-t'ieh) mask with two large globular eyes, nostrils, fangs, and sometimes claws and horns. It is normally presented as the silhouette of two dragons face to face, so that each forms half the mask. Although fierce in appearance, to the Han peoples the *taotie* represented a guardian force against the evil spirits they so dreaded.

One reason for the extraordinary quality of Shang bronze work is the method of casting used. Bronze workers in most ancient civilizations used the lost wax method, where a model was first made in wax. After a clay mold had been formed around it, the model was heated so that the wax would disappear, and the empty space was filled with molten metal. In China, clay molds composed of several sections were tightly fit together prior to the introduction of the liquid bronze. This technique, which had evolved from ceramic techniques used during the Neolithic period, enabled the artisans to apply the design directly to the mold and thus contributed to the clarity of line and rich surface decoration of the Shang bronzes.

Bronze casting became a large-scale business, and more than ten thousand vessels of an incredible variety of form and design survive today. The art of bronze working continued into the Zhou and the Han dynasties, but the quality and originality declined, and the Shang bronzes remain the pinnacle of creative art in ancient China.

As in other parts of the world, one reason for the decline of bronze casting in China was the rise in popularity of iron. The first evidence of human-made iron in ancient China dates back to the ninth or eighth centuries B.C.E., with the appearance of ritual vessels and tools made of wrought iron. Iron-making thus developed much later in China than in the Middle East, where it had been mastered almost a millennium earlier. Once familiar with the process, however, the Chinese quickly moved to the forefront. Iron workers in Europe and the Middle East, lacking the technology to achieve the high temperatures necessary to melt iron ore for casting, were forced to work with wrought iron, a cumbersome and expensive process. The Chinese, however, invented the technique of the blast furnace, powered by a person operating a bellows, by the fourth century B.C.E. They were therefore able to manufacture cast iron ritual vessels and agricultural tools centuries before an equivalent technology appeared in the West.

One of the reasons for the deterioration of the bronze-casting tradition was the development of lacquerware and ceramics. Lacquer, obtained from a resinous substance deposited on trees by the *lac* insect, had been produced since Neolithic times, and by the Han it had become a popular method of applying a hard coating to objects made of wood or fabric. Pottery, too, had existed since early times, but technological advances during the Han led to the production of a high-quality form of pottery covered with a brown or gray-green glaze, the latter known popularly as celadon. During the Han, both lacquerware and pottery replaced bronze in popularity and value.

Unlike the bronzes, not much sculpture from the ancient period has survived, and historians once thought that Chinese sculpture prior to the Han dynasty was limited to small animals carved in wood or bone and surface decorations on furniture and other household items. But recent archaeological evidence has demonstrated the error of that assumption. In 1974, farmers digging a well about thirty-five miles east of Xian unearthed a number of terra-cotta figures in an underground pit about one mile east of the burial mound of the First Qin Emperor. Chinese archaeologists sent to work at the site discovered a vast terra-cotta army that they believed was a re-creation of Qin Shi Huangdi's imperial guard, which was to accompany the emperor on his journey to the next world.

One of the astounding features of the terra-cotta army is its size. The army is enclosed in four pits that were originally encased in a wooden framework, which has since disintegrated. More than a thousand figures have already been unearthed in the first pit, along with horses, wooden chariots, and seven thousand bronze weapons.

◆ **A Bronze Horse.** This horse from a second-century C.E. Han tomb is a beautiful example of Chinese bronze sculpture. Poised on a swallow, it suggests the divine power that the Chinese of this time attributed to horses.

Archaeologists estimate that there are more than six thousand figures in that pit alone.

Equally impressive is the quality of the work. Slightly larger than life-size, the figures were molded of finely textured clay, then fired and painted. The detail on the uniforms is realistic and sophisticated, but the most striking feature is the individuality of the facial features of the soldiers. Apparently, ten different head shapes were used and were then modeled further by hand to reflect the variety of ethnic groups and personality types in the army.

The discovery of the terra-cotta army also shows that the Chinese had come a long way from the human sacrifices that had taken place at the death of Shang sovereigns more than a thousand years earlier. But the project must have been ruinously expensive and is additional evidence of the burden the Qin ruler imposed on his subjects. One historian has estimated that one-third of the national income in Qin and Han times may have been spent on preparations for the ruler's afterlife. The emperor's mausoleum has not yet been unearthed, but it is enclosed in a mound seventy-six meters in height and is surrounded by a rectangular wall six kilometers in circumference. According to the Han historian Sima Qian, the ceiling is a replica of the heavens, while the floor contains a relief model of the entire Qin kingdom, with rivers flowing in mercury. According to tradition, traps were set within the mausoleum to prevent intruders, and

◆ **Qin Shi Huangdi's Tomb.** The First Emperor of Qin ordered the construction of an elaborate mausoleum, an underground palace complex protected by an army of terra-cotta soldiers and horses to accompany him on his journey to the afterlife. This massive formation of 6,000 life-sized armed soldiers, discovered accidentally by farmers in 1974, reflects the grandeur and power that was Qin Shi Huangdi's.

the workers putting in the final touches were buried alive in the tomb with its secrets.

Qin Shi Huangdi's ambitious effort to provide for his immortality became a pattern for his successors during the Han dynasty, although apparently on a somewhat more modest scale. In 1990, Chinese workers discovered a similar underground army for a Han emperor of the second century B.C.E. Like the imperial guard of the First Qin Emperor, the underground soldiers were buried in parallel pits and possessed their own weapons and individual facial features. But they were smaller—only one-third the height of the average human adult—and were armed with wooden weapons and were dressed in silk clothing, now decayed. A burial pit nearby indicates that as many as ten thousand workers, probably slaves or prisoners, died in the process of building the emperor's mausoleum, which took an estimated ten years to construct.

Language and Literature

While the famous Shang bronzes and the recently discovered terra-cotta army have deservedly earned high acclaim, perhaps the most important cultural contribution of ancient China to later Chinese society was the invention and development of the Chinese written language. Unfortunately, we can only speculate about the origins of the famous system of Chinese characters, one of the earliest and perhaps the most fascinating and aesthetically pleasing form of writing invented by human beings.

Legend attributes the invention of writing to Cang Jie, an official at the court of Huang Di, the Yellow Emperor, in the mid-third millennium B.C.E. According to a scholar writing many centuries later, "in the olden days of history, there were many scholars who devoted themselves to the invention of written languages. However, only the one invented by Ts'ang Chieh (Cang Jie) has been transmitted to posterity, because of its uniformity."[19]

In all likelihood, the invention of the Chinese written language was the product not of a single mind, but of the genius of the people. Scratches found on pottery at the Neolithic village of Banpo are almost certainly a primitive form of writing, but whether they are an early form of the modern Chinese character is unclear.

By Shang times, as the oracle bones demonstrate, the Chinese had developed a simple but functional script that is the recognizable ancestor of the highly complex and beautiful written language of today. Like many other languages of antiquity, it was primarily ideographic and pictographic in form. Symbols, usually called "characters," were created to represent an idea or to form a picture of the object to be represented. For example, the Chinese characters for mountain (山), the sun (日), and the moon (月) were meant to represent the objects themselves. Other characters, such as "big" (大) (a man with his arms outstretched), represent an idea. The word "east" (東) symbolizes the sun coming up behind the trees.

Each character, of course, would be given a sound by the speaker when pronounced. In other cultures, this process led to the abandonment of the system of ideographs and the adoption of a written language based on phonetic symbols, such as the Roman alphabet or the *devanagari* in India. The Chinese, too, eventually began to attach phonetic meaning to some of their symbols, and it is sometimes possible for Chinese speakers to guess the pronunciation of a character they have not seen before. But although the Chinese language has evolved continuously over a period of more than four thousand years, it has never entirely abandoned its original ideographical format, although the phonetic element has developed into a significant part of the individual character. In that sense, the Chinese written language is virtually unique in the world today.

Certainly, one reason the language retained its ideographic quality must have been the aesthetic quality of the written characters. By the time of the Han dynasty, if not earlier, the written language came to be seen as an art form as well as a means of communication, and calligraphy became one of the most prized forms of painting in China. In fact, the art of writing Chinese characters with a brush undoubtedly exerted considerable influence on the evolution of Chinese painting as a whole (see Chapter 10).

More important in shaping the evolution of the Chinese written language, however, was probably its role as a useful tool in facilitating communication and promoting national unity. If the written language had developed in the direction of a phonetic alphabet, it could no longer have served as the written system for all the peoples of an expanding civilization. Although the vast majority spoke a tongue derived from a parent Sinitic language (a system distinguished by its tonal nature, a characteristic that gives Chinese its lilting quality even today), the languages spoken in various regions of the country differed from each other in pronunciation and to a lesser degree in vocabulary and syntax; for the most part, they were (and are today) mutually unintelligible. For example, natives of the current capital city of Beijing in North China could not converse in their own language with residents of the industrial city of Shanghai in the lower Yangtze valley, and neither group could speak intelligibly with someone from the city of Guangzhou (formerly Canton) in the south.

The Chinese answer to this problem was to give all the spoken languages the same writing system. Although any character might be pronounced differently in different regions of China, that character would be written the same way (after the standardization undertaken under the Qin) no matter where it was written. The development of a single writing system was the cement that helped to create and maintain a sense of unity and common identity in a multilinguistic empire. Like Latin in the Roman Empire, the writing system permitted people of diverse linguistic and cultural backgrounds to communicate by means of the written word.

This system of written characters could be read by educated Chinese from one end of the country to the other. It became the language of the bureaucracy and the vehicle for the transmission of Chinese culture to all Chinese from the Great Wall to the southern border and even beyond. It has sometimes been observed, with pardonable exaggeration, that the Chinese written language is the one predominant feature of Chinese culture, the tool that brought together the various peoples and transformed what otherwise would have been a highly diverse region of the world into a single nationality and a single culture.

The written language, however, was not identical with the spoken. In China, the language of the bureaucracy—in later years informally labeled "the language of officials"—evolved a totally separate vocabulary and grammatical structure from the spoken tongues. As a result, those who used it required special training.

◆ **Tomb Soldier (Qin Shi Huangdi's Tomb).** This is one of the 6,000 soldiers guarding the underground palace complex of Emperor Qin Shi Huangdi's tomb. Incredibly, each soldier has individualized facial features and expressions. Originally, they carried real weapons and their uniforms were painted in brilliant colors. They are a most majestic and foreboding sight.

The language of the bureaucracy, known as "literary Chinese," became the vehicle for literary creativity in traditional China. The earliest extant form of Chinese literature dates from the Zhou dynasty, although it probably originated a few centuries earlier. It was written on silk or strips of bamboo and consisted primarily of historical records such as the *Rites of Zhou*, philosophical treatises such as the *Analects* and *The Way of the Dao*, and poetry, as recorded in the *Book of Songs* and the *Song of the South*. Poetry was particularly prized in ancient China. Perhaps the tonal quality of the Chinese spoken language lends itself to poetic expression, and poetry, like music, was considered a useful tool in training a gentleman. In later years, when Confucian principles had been elevated into a state ideology, the key works identified with the Confucian School were integrated into a set of so-called Confucian Classics. These works became required reading for generations of Chinese schoolchildren and introduced them to the forms of behavior that would be required of them as adults (see the box on p. 110).

◈ Love Spurned in Ancient China ◈

The Books of Songs is an anthology of about three hundred poems written during the early Zhou dynasty. According to tradition, they were selected by Confucius from a much larger collection. In later years, many were given political interpretations. The poem reprinted here, however, expresses a very human cry of love spurned.

The Book of Songs: The Odes

You seemed a guileless youth enough,
Offering for silk your woven stuff;
But silk was not required by you;
I was the silk you had in view.
With you I crossed the ford, and while
We wandered on for many a mile
I said, "I do not wish delay,
But friends must fix our wedding-day …
Oh, do not let my words give pain,
But with the autumn come again."

And then I used to watch and wait
To see you passing through the gate;
And sometimes, when I watched in vain,
My tears would flow like falling rain;
But when I saw my darling boy,
I laughed and cried aloud for joy.
The fortune-tellers, you declared,
Had all pronounced us duly paired;
"Then bring a carriage," I replied,
"And I'll away to be your bride."

The mulberry-tree upon the ground,
Now sheds its yellow leaves around.

Three years have slipped away from me
Since first I shared your poverty;
And now again, alas the day!
Back through the ford I take my way.

My heart is still unchanged, but you
Have uttered words now proved untrue;
And you have left me to deplore
A love that can be mine no more.

For three long years I was your wife,
And led in truth a toilsome life;
Early to rise and late to bed,
Each day alike passed o'er my head.
I honestly fulfilled my part,
And you—well, you have broke my heart.
The truth my brothers will not know,
So all the more their gibes will flow.
I grieve in silence and repine
That such a wretched fate is mine.

Ah, hand in hand to face old age!—
Instead, I turn a bitter page.
O for the river-banks of yore;
O for the much-loved marshy shore;
The hours of girlhood, with my hair
Ungathered, as we lingered there.
The words we spoke, that seemed so true,
I little thought that I should rue;
I little thought the vows we swore
Would some day bind us two no more.

The Han dynasty continued the pattern set during the long Zhou era. While poetry and philosophical essays continued to be popular, historical writing became the primary form of literary creativity. The major histories of the Han period, such as the works by Sima Qian and Ban Gu, set a model for future dynastic histories up to the modern day. They combined political and social history with biographies of key figures. Like so much literary work in China, their primary purpose was moral and political—to instruct their readers on the underlying reasons for the rise and fall of individual human beings and dynasties.

By its nature, Chinese literature was not only didactic but elitist. Since only a minority of the population could read and write—and that minority was almost exclusively male—books, and even the Chinese written characters, acquired an almost sacred quality, even among ordinary Chinese. For them, as for ordinary people the world over in ancient times, culture was transmitted orally in the form of folktales and morality plays. Later, such early types of popular literature evolved into histories in epic form such as the famous *Romance of the Three Kingdoms*, a swashbuckling tale of intrigue and derring-do after the collapse of the Han dynasty. Still later, such tales evolved into the Chinese novel.

Music

Because of its social importance, no discussion of ancient Chinese culture can be complete without a brief reference to music. According to a historian writing in the Han dynasty, Fu Xi's wife Nu Wa invented the first musical instrument, a set of bamboo pipes called the *sheng*. Inside each pipe were several reeds that would vibrate to sound a musical note when the musician blew on the spout and fingered the appropriate keyhole for that reed. Other musical instruments invented in ancient China included the flute, various stringed instruments, bells and chimes, the drum, and the gourd. Bells cast in bronze were first used in the Shang period and were hung in rows and then struck with a wooden mallet. The finest were produced during the mid-Zhou era and are considered to be among the best examples of early bronze work in China.

From early times, music was viewed not just as an aesthetic pleasure, but as a means of achieving political order and refining the human character. In fact, music may have originated as a means of accompanying sacred ritual at the royal court. According to the *Historical Records*, a history written during the Han dynasty: "When our sage-kings of the past instituted rites and music, their objective was far from making people indulge in the enjoyment of delicious food and the amusements of singing and dancing. . . . Music is produced to purify the heart, and rites introduced to rectify the behavior. When one's behavior is rectified, one attains solemnity and respectfulness in character, which give one stateliness and dignity in appearance."

The correlation between ritual and music was clearly recognized in ancient China: "Music is what can not be done away with in man's emotional life; rites is what can not be replaced in his intellectual life." And "music is introduced to purify the hearts, and rites introduced to rectify the behavior." Eventually, however, music began to be appreciated for its own sake as well as for singing and dancing:

> Music is the rhythmic movement in man's heart, while musical notes are its outward expression in sounds. When one feels pleased, one would speak of it at great length. While speaking of it at great length does not suffice, one would be sighing for it in singing. And while sighing for it still does not suffice, one would wield one's arms and swing one's legs in dancing.[20]

By the late Zhou era, bells had begun to give way as the instrument of choice to strings and wind instruments, while the purpose of music shifted from ceremony to entertainment. This led conservative critics to rail against the onset of an age of debauchery.

Ancient historians stressed the relationship between music and court life, but it is highly probable that music, singing, and dancing were equally popular among the common people. The *Book of History*, purporting to describe conditions in the late third millennium B.C.E., suggests that ballads emanating from the popular culture were welcomed at court. Nevertheless, court music and popular music differed in several respects. Among other things, popular music was more likely to be motivated by the desire for pleasure than for the purpose of law and order and moral uplift. Those differences continued to be reflected in the evolution of music in China down to modern times.

Conclusion

Of the great classical civilizations discussed in Part I of this book, China was the last to come into full flower. By the time the Shang began to display the first signs of emerging as an organized state, the societies in Mesopotamia and the Nile valley had already reached an advanced level of civilization. Unfortunately, not enough is known about the early stages of any of these civilizations to allow us to determine why some developed earlier than others, but one likely reason for China's late arrival was that it was virtually isolated from other emerging centers of culture elsewhere in the world and thus was compelled to develop essentially on its own. Although there are tantalizing hints that early Chinese may have learned the technology of chariot making through links with Indo-European–speaking peoples in Central Asia, only at the end of the first millennium B.C.E. did the Han dynasty come into regular contact with other civilizations in South Asia, the Middle East, and the Mediterranean.

Once embarked on its own path toward the creation of a complex society, however, China achieved results that were in all respects the equal of its counterparts elsewhere. During the glory years of the Han dynasty, China extended the boundaries of its empire far into the sands of Central Asia and southward along the coast of the South China Sea into what is modern-day Vietnam. The doctrine of State Confucianism provided an effective ideology for the state, and Chinese culture appeared unrivaled. In many respects, its scientific and technological achievements were unsurpassed.

One reason for China's striking success undoubtedly was that, unlike its contemporary civilizations, it long was able to fend off the danger from nomadic peoples along the northern frontier. By the end of the second century B.C.E., however, the Xiongnu were looming ominously, and tribal warriors began to nip at the borders of the empire. While the dynasty was strong, the problem was manageable, but when internal difficulties began to corrode the unity of the state, China became increasingly vulnerable to the threat from the north and entered its own time of troubles.

During the glory years of the Han, another great civilization was beginning to take form on the northern shores of the Mediterranean Sea. Unlike China and the other ancient societies discussed thus far, this new civilization in Europe was based as much on trade as it was on agriculture. Yet the political and cultural achievements of ancient Greece were the equal of any of the great human experiments that had preceded it and soon began to exert a significant impact on the rest of the ancient world.

CHAPTER NOTES

1. *Book of Changes*, quoted in Chang Chi-yun, *Chinese History of Fifty Centuries*, vol. 1, *Ancient Times* (Taipei, 1962), pp. 15, 31, and 65.
2. Ibid., p. 381.
3. Quoted in E. N. Anderson, *The Food of China* (New Haven, Conn., 1988), p. 21.
4. According to Chinese tradition, the *Rites of Zhou* was written by the duke of Zhou himself near the time of the founding of the Zhou dynasty. Modern historians believe that it was written much later, perhaps as late as the fourth century B.C.E., as speculation on what the Golden Age must have been like.
5. Quoted in Chang Chi-yun, *Chinese History of Fifty Centuries*, p. 39. The poem about "big rat" is in *The Book of Songs*, quoted in Sebastian de Grazia, ed., *Masters of Chinese Political Thought: From the Beginnings to the Han Dynasty* (New York, 1973), pp. 40–41.
6. *Confucian Analects* (Lun Yu), ed. James Legge (Taipei, 1963), 11:11 and 6:20.
7. Ibid., 15:23.
8. *Confucian Analects*, 17:2.
9. *Book of Mencius (Meng Zi)*, 4 A:9, quoted in William Theodore de Bary et al., eds., *Sources of Chinese Tradition*, (New York, 1960), p. 107.
10. Quoted in de Bary, *Sources of Chinese Tradition*, p. 53.
11. Cited in Robert Temple, *The Genius of China: 3,000 Years of Science, Discovery, and Invention* (New York, 1986), p. 219.
12. Burton Watson, *Records of the Grand Historian of China* (New York, 1961), vol. 2, pp. 155, 160.
13. Ibid., p. 155.
14. Ibid., pp. 32, 53.
15. Quoted in Mark Elvin, *The Pattern of the Chinese Past* (Stanford, Calif., 1973), p. 32.
16. Clae Waltham, *Shu Ching: Book of History* (Chicago, 1971), p. 154.
17. Quoted in Herbert A. Giles, *A History of Chinese Literature* (New York, 1923), p. 19.
18. Lloyd E. Eastman, *Family, Fields, and Ancestors: Constancy and Change in China's Social and Economic History, 1550–1949* (New York, 1988), p. 19.
19. Chang Chi-yun, *Chinese History of Fifty Centuries*, quoting *Hsun Tzu*, p. 99.
20. Ibid., p. 186–87.

SUGGESTED READINGS

There are several general histories of China that provide a useful overview of the period of antiquity. Perhaps the best known is the classic *East Asia: Tradition and Transformation* (Boston, 1973) by J. K. Fairbank, E. O. Reis-

chauer, and A. M. Craig. Also of use are C. Schirokauer, *A Brief History of Chinese and Japanese Civilizations*, 2d ed. (San Diego, 1989); and M. Elvin, *The Pattern of the Chinese Past* (Stanford, Calif., 1973), which presents a provocative interpretation of key issues in Chinese history. For an easy capsulated overview of ancient China, enjoy the colorful *Past Worlds: The Times Atlas of Archaeology* (Maplewood, N.J., 1988) and *The Times Atlas of World History* (Maplewood, N.J., 1978). Political and social maps of China can be found in A. Herrmann, *An Historical Atlas of China* (Chicago, 1966).

The period of the Neolithic era and the Shang dynasty has received increasing attention in recent years. For an impressively documented and annotated overview, see Kwang-chih Chang, *Shang Civilization* (New Haven, Conn., 1980) and *Studies in Shang Archaeology* (New Haven, Conn., 1982). D. Keightley, *The Origins of Chinese Civilization* (Berkeley, 1983) presents a number of interesting articles on selected aspects of the period. An older but still interesting work is H. Maspero, *China in Antiquity* (Amherst, Mass., 1988), a translation of his *La Chine Antique*.

The Zhou and Qin dynasties have also received considerable attention. The former is exhaustingly analyzed in Cho-yun Hsu and J. M. Linduff, *Western Zhou Civilization* (New Haven, Conn., 1988) and Li Xueqin, *Eastern Zhou and Qin Civilizations* (New Haven, Conn., 1985). The latter is a translation of an original work by a mainland Chinese scholar and is especially interesting for its treatment of the development of the silk industry and the money economy in ancient China. Also of interest is the study of Qin Shi Huangdi by A. Cotterell, *The First Emperor of China* (New York, 1981). On bronze casting, see E. L. Shaughnessy, *Sources of Eastern Zhou History* (Berkeley, 1991). Also of value for its treatment of the formation of social classes is Cho-yun Hsu, *Ancient China in Transition* (Stanford, Calif., 1965).

There are a number of useful books on the Han dynasty. Zhongshu Wang, *Han Civilization* (New Haven, Conn., 1982) presents new evidence from the mainland on recent excavations from Han tombs and the old imperial capital of Chang'an. M. Loewe, *Everyday Life in Early Imperial China during the Han Period, 202 BC–220 AD* (London, 1968) contains useful material on religious beliefs and the development of social classes during the Han. Also, see the lavishly illustrated *The Han Civilization of China* (Oxford, 1982) by M. P. Serstevens. For a firsthand view, see B. Watson, *Records of the Grand Historian of China* (New York, 1961), a translation of key passages from Sima Qian's history of the period. For the historian's life, consult *Ssu-ma Ch'ien: Grand Historian of China* (New York, 1958).

The philosophy of ancient China has attracted considerable attention from Western scholars. Some standard works include A. Waley, *Three Ways of Thought in Ancient China* (New York, 1939); H. G. Creel, *Chinese Thought: From Confucius to Mao Tse-Tung* (Chicago, 1953); Feng Yu-Ian, *A Short History of Chinese Philosophy* (New York, 1960); and F. Mote, *Intellectual Foundations of China*, 2d ed. (New York, 1989). On Confucius, see Liu Wu-chi, *A Short History of Confucian Philosophy* (Middlesex, 1955); and H. G. Creel, *Confucius: The Man and the Myth* (London, 1951). The latter is a sympathetic treatment that emphasizes the humanistic side of Confucian philosophy. S. de Grazia, ed., *Masters of Chinese Political Thought: From the Beginnings to the Han Dynasty* (New York, 1973) includes passages from the ancient philosophers that deal with the political realm.

For works on general culture and science, consult the illustrated work by R. Temple, *The Genius of China: 3000 Years of Science, Discovery, and Invention* (New York, 1986); and J. Needham, *Science in Traditional China: A Comparative Perspective* (Boston, 1981). See also E. N. Anderson, *The Food of China* (New Haven, Conn., 1988).

The most comprehensive collection of original writings is W. T. de Bary, *Sources of Chinese Tradition* (New York, 1969), which includes excerpts from most of the ancient texts. The complete translations of the Confucian classics are in J. Legge, *The Chinese Classics*, 5 vols. (Hong Kong, 1960) with critical and exegetical notes. For a modernized edition of the *Book of History*, see C. Waltham, *Shu Ching: Book of History* (Chicago, 1971). For an annotated version of Lao Tzu, see Wing-Tsit Chan, *The Way of Lao Tzu* (Indianapolis, 1963).

For a comprehensive introduction to Chinese art, consult M. Sullivan, *The Arts of China*, 3d ed. (Berkeley, 1984) with good illustrations in color. Also, see M. Tregear, *Chinese Art* (Oxford, 1980) and L. Sickman and A. Sopor, *Art and Architecture of China*, 3d. ed. (Middlesex, 1968). For a discussion of the ancient art of China, see J. Rawson, *Ancient China: Art and Archaeology* (New York, 1980). Many beautifully illustrated volumes on Chinese art in general and several series on ancient Chinese art are available. See the four-volume series entitled *Chinese Art* by the Universe Library of Antique Art (New York, 1960–1965) and the first two volumes of *Art in China* (Tokyo, 1968 and 1969) by Japanese scholars, coordinated by M. Tregear, on Neolithic cultures and the arts of the Buddhist cave temples. See also B. Smith and Wan-go Wang, *China: A History of Art* (New York, n. d.), a beautifully illustrated one-volume survey. Finally, see D. L. Goldschmidt and J. C. Moreau-Gobard, *Chinese Art* (New York, 1962), which presents ancient Chinese art treasures from private collections.

CHAPTER

4

The Civilization of the Greeks

In 431 B.C.E., war erupted in Greece as two very different Greek city-states—Athens and Sparta—fought for domination of the Greek world. The people of Athens felt secure behind their walls and in the first winter of the war held a public funeral to honor those who had died in battle. On the day of the ceremony, the citizens of Athens joined in a procession, with the relatives of the dead wailing for their loved ones. As was the custom in Athens, one leading citizen was asked to address the crowd, and on this day it was Pericles who spoke to the people. He talked about the greatness of Athens and reminded the Athenians of the strength of their political system: "Our constitution," he said, "is called a democracy because power is in the hands not of a minority but of the whole people. When it is a question of settling private disputes, everyone is equal before the law. . . . Just as our political life is free and open, so is our day-to-day life in our relations with each other. . . . Here each individual is interested not only in his own affairs but in the affairs of the state as well."

In this famous Funeral Oration, Pericles gave voice to the ideal of democracy and the importance of the individual. It was the Greeks who laid the intellectual foundations of Western civilization. They asked some basic questions about human life that still dominate intellectual pursuits: What is the nature of the universe? What is the purpose of human existence? What is our relationship to divine forces? What constitutes a community? What constitutes a state? What is true education? What are the true sources of

Mycenaean Greece · · · · · · · · · · · · · Age of Expansion · · · · · · · · · · · · · Hellenistic kingdoms · · · · · · · · · · · · · · · ·

Classical Age · · · · · · · · · · ·

Lycurgan reforms in Sparta · · · · · · · Great Peloponnesian War · ·

Battle of Marathon · Conquests of Alexander the Great · ·

Homer · · Parthenon · · · Plato and Aristotle · · · · · Flourishing of Hellenistic science · · · · · · · · ·

Greek drama (Aeschylus, Sophocles, Euripides) · · · · · · ·

---

law? What is truth itself and how do we realize it? The Greeks not only gave answers to these questions; they proceeded to create a system of logical, analytical thought in order to examine them.

The story of ancient Greek civilization is a remarkable one that begins with the first arrival of the Greeks around 1900 B.C.E. By the eighth century B.C.E., the characteristic institution of ancient Greek life, the polis or city-state, had emerged. Greek civilization flourished and reached its height in the classical era of the fifth century B.C.E., which has come to be closely identified with the achievements of Athenian democracy. But the inability of the Greek states to end their fratricidal warfare eventually left them vulnerable to the Macedonian king Philip II and helped to bring an end to the Greek world of independent city-states.

Although the Greek city-states were never the same after their defeat by the Macedonian monarch, it did not bring an end to the influence of the Greeks. Philip's son Alexander led the Macedonians and Greeks on a spectacular conquest of the Persian Empire and opened the door to the spread of Greek culture throughout the Middle East. We use the term Hellenistic to designate this new period of Greek history. The Hellenistic world was the world of Greeks and non-Greeks, and it resulted, in its own way, in a remarkable series of accomplishments.

Early Greece

Geography played an important role in the evolution of Greek history. Compared to the landmasses of Mesopotamia and Egypt, Greece occupied a small area. It was a mountainous peninsula that encompassed only 45,000 square miles of territory, about the size of the state of Louisiana. The mountains and the sea played especially significant roles in the development of Greek history. Much of Greece consists of small plains and river valleys surrounded by mountain ranges 8,000–10,000 feet high. The mountainous terrain had the effect of isolating Greeks from one another. Consequently, Greek communities tended to follow their own separate paths and develop their own way of life. Over a period of time, these communities became so fiercely attached to their independence that they were unwilling to join into larger units of organization and only too willing to fight one another to gain advantage. No doubt the small size of these independent Greek communities fostered participation in political affairs and unique cultural expressions, but the rivalry among these communities also led to the internecine warfare that ultimately devastated Greek society.

The sea also influenced the evolution of Greek society. Greece had a long seacoast, dotted by bays and inlets that provided numerous harbors. The Greeks also inhabited a number of islands to the west, south, and particularly to the east of the Greek mainland. It is no accident that the Greeks became seafarers who sailed out into the Aegean and the Mediterranean Seas first to make contact with the outside world and later to establish colonies that would spread Greek civilization throughout the Mediterranean world.

Greek topography helped to determine the major territories into which Greece was ultimately divided. South of the Gulf of Corinth was the Peloponnesus, virtually an island as seen on a map. Consisting mostly of hills, mountains, and small valleys, the Peloponnesus was the location of Sparta, as well as the site of Olympia where the famous athletic games were held. Northeast of the Peloponnesus was the Attic peninsula (or Attica), the home of Athens, hemmed in by mountains to the north and west and surrounded by the sea to the south and east. Northwest of Attica was Boeotia in central Greece with its chief city of Thebes. To the north of Boeotia was Thessaly, which contained the largest plains and became

a great producer of grain and horses. To the north of Thessaly lay Macedonia, which was not of much importance in Greek history until 338 B.C.E. when the Macedonian king Philip II conquered the Greeks.

Minoan Crete

By 2800 B.C.E., a Bronze Age civilization that used metals, especially bronze, in the construction of weapons had been established in the area of the Aegean Sea. The early Bronze Age settlements on the Greek mainland, created by non-Greek-speaking peoples, were overshadowed by another Bronze Age civilization on the large island of Crete, southeast of the Greek mainland.

The civilization of Minoan Crete was first discovered by the English archaeologist Arthur Evans, who named it Minoan after Minos, the legendary king of Crete. Evans's excavations on Crete at the beginning of the twentieth century led to the discovery of an enormous palace complex at Knossus near modern Heracleion. The remains revealed a rich and prosperous culture with Knossus as the probable center of a far-ranging "sea empire," probably largely commercial in nature. Because

◆ **The Minoan Sport of Bull Leaping.**   Minoan bull games were held on festival days in the great palaces on the island of Crete. As seen in this fresco from the east wing of the palace at Knossus, women and men acrobats (the man in red) somersaulted over the back of the bull. Another person waited behind the bull to catch the leapers.

Evans found few military fortifications for the defense of Knossus itself, he assumed that Minoan Crete had a strong navy. We do know from archaeological remains that the people of Minoan Crete were accustomed to sea travel and had made contact with the more advanced civilization of Egypt. Egyptian products have been found in Crete and Cretan products in Egypt.

The Minoan civilization reached its height between 2000 and 1450 B.C.E. The palace at Knossus, the royal seat of the kings, demonstrates the obvious prosperity and power of this civilization. It was an elaborate structure built around a central courtyard and included numerous private living rooms for the royal family and workshops for making decorated vases, small sculptures, such as ivory figurines, and jewelry. Even bathrooms, with elaborate drains, formed part of the complex. The rooms were decorated with frescoes in bright colors showing sporting events and naturalistic scenes that have led some to assume that the Cretans had a great love of nature. Storerooms in the palace held enormous jars of oil, wine, and grain, presumably paid as taxes in kind to the king. The kings were apparently assisted by a large bureaucracy that kept detailed records of the payments.

The centers of Minoan civilization on Crete suffered a sudden and catastrophic collapse around 1450 B.C.E. The cause of this destruction has been vigorously debated. Some historians believe that a tsunami triggered by a powerful volcanic eruption on the island of Thera was responsible for the devastation. Most historians, however, maintain that the destruction was the result of invasion and pillage by mainland Greeks known as the Mycenaeans.

The Mycenaean Greeks

The term *Mycenaean* is derived from Mycenae, a remarkable fortified site first excavated by the amateur German archaeologist Heinrich Schliemann. In a series of shaft graves, Schliemann discovered an incredible collection of gold masks, cups, jewelry, bronze weapons, and pottery, all belonging to the Mycenaean Greek civilization, which flourished between 1600 and 1100 B.C.E. The Mycenaean Greeks were part of the Indo-European family of peoples (see Chapter 1) who spread from their original location into southern and western Europe, India, and Iran. One group entered the territory of Greece from the north around 1900 B.C.E. and, over a period of time, managed to gain control of the Greek mainland and develop a civilization.

Mycenaean civilization, which reached its high point between 1400 and 1200 B.C.E., consisted of a number of powerful monarchies based in fortified palace complexes,

♦ **The So-Called Death Mask of Agamemnon.** This death mask of thin gold was one of the first objects found by Heinrich Schliemann in his excavation of a series of shaft graves at Mycenae. Schliemann claimed that he had found the mask of Agamemnon, king of Mycenae in Homer's *Iliad*. The excited archaeologist wrote to the king of Greece: "Today I have looked on the face of Agamemnon."

which were built on hills and surrounded by gigantic stone walls, such as those found at Mycenae, Tiryns, Pylos, Thebes, and Orchomenos. These various centers of power probably formed a loose confederacy of independent states with Mycenae the strongest. Next in importance to the kings in these states were the army commanders, the priests, and the bureaucrats who kept careful records. The free citizenry included peasants, soldiers, and artisans with the lowest rung of the social ladder consisting of serfs and slaves.

The Mycenaeans were, above all, a warrior people who prided themselves on their heroic deeds in battle. Archaeological evidence indicates that the Mycenaean monarchies also developed an extensive commercial network. Mycenaean pottery has been found throughout the Mediterranean basin, in Syria and Egypt to the east and Sicily and southern Italy to the west. But some scholars also believe that the Mycenaeans, led by Mycenae itself, spread outward militarily, conquering Crete and making it part of the Mycenaean world. The most famous of all their supposed military adventures has come down to us in the epic poetry of Homer (see Homer later in this chapter). Did the Mycenaean Greeks, led by Agamemnon, king of Mycenae, sack the city of Troy on the northwestern coast of Asia Minor around 1250 B.C.E.? Since the excavations of Heinrich Schliemann, begun in 1870, scholars have debated this question. Many do believe in the basic authenticity of the Homerian legend, even if the details have become shrouded in mystery.

By the late thirteenth century, Mycenaean Greece was showing signs of serious trouble. Mycenae itself was torched around 1190 B.C.E., reinhabited, and finally abandoned around 1125 B.C.E. Other Mycenaean centers show similar patterns of destruction. By 1100 B.C.E., the Mycenaean culture was coming to an end.

Modern scholars have proposed a number of theories to explain the collapse of Mycenaean civilization. According to the Greeks' own legend, their mainland was invaded from the north by another Greek-speaking people who were less civilized than the Mycenaeans. Called the Dorians, these invaders supposedly destroyed the old centers of Mycenaean power and ultimately established themselves in the Peloponnesus. But there is little archaeological evidence to support the idea of massive Dorian invasions. Other historians argue that internal conflict among the Mycenaean kings and major earthquakes were more important factors in the Mycenaean decline. What is certain is that by 1100 B.C.E., the Greek world had entered a new period of considerable insecurity.

The Greeks in a Dark Age (c. 1100–c. 750 B.C.E.)

After the collapse of Mycenaean civilization, Greece entered a difficult era of declining population and falling food production. Moreover, we have few records to help us reconstruct what happened in this period. Because of the difficult conditions and our lack of knowledge about the period, historians refer to it as a Dark Age. Not until 850 B.C.E. did farming revive. At the same time, some new developments were forming the basis for a revived Greece.

During the Dark Age, large numbers of Greeks left the mainland and migrated across the Aegean Sea to various islands, and especially to the western shores of Asia Minor, a strip of territory that came to be called Ionia. Based on their dialect, the Greeks who resided there were called Ionians. Two other major groups of Greeks settled in established parts of Greece. The Aeolian Greeks who were located in northern and central Greece colonized the large island of Lesbos and the adjacent territory of the mainland. The Dorians established themselves in southwestern Greece, especially in the Peloponnesus, as well as on some of the south Aegean islands, including Crete.

Other important activities occurred in this Dark Age as well. There was a revival of some trade and some economic activity besides agriculture. Iron came into use for the construction of weapons. And at some point in the eighth century B.C.E., the Greeks adopted the Phoenician alphabet to give themselves a new system of writing. Near the very end of this so-called Dark Age appeared the work of Homer, who has come to be viewed as one of the truly great poets of all time.

Homer

The origins of the *Iliad* and the *Odyssey*, the first great epics of early Greece, are to be found in the oral tradition of reciting poems recounting the deeds of heroes of the Mycenaean age. It is generally assumed that early in the eighth century B.C.E., Homer made use of these oral traditions to compose the *Iliad*, his epic of the Trojan War. The war was caused by an act of Paris, a prince of Troy. By kidnapping Helen, wife of the king of the Greek state of Sparta, he outraged all the Greeks. Under the leadership of the Spartan king's brother, Agamemnon of Mycenae, the Greeks attacked Troy. Ten years later, the Greeks finally won and sacked the city.

But the *Iliad* is not so much the story of the war itself as it is the tale of the Greek hero Achilles and how the "wrath of Achilles" led to disaster. As is true of all great literature, the *Iliad* abounds in universal lessons. Underlying them all is the clear message, as one commentator has observed, that "men will still come and go like the generations of leaves in the forest; that he will still be weak, and the gods strong and incalculable; that the quality of a man matters more than his achievement; that violence and recklessness will still lead to disaster, and that this will fall on the innocent as well as on the guilty." [1]

Although the *Odyssey* has long been considered Homer's other masterpiece, some scholars believe that it was composed later than the *Iliad* and was probably not the work of Homer. The *Odyssey* is an epic romance that recounts the journeys of one of the Greek heroes, Odysseus, after the fall of Troy and his ultimate return to his wife. But there is a larger vision here as well: the testing of the heroic stature of Odysseus until, by both cunning and patience, he prevails. In the course of this testing, the underlying moral message is "that virtue is a better policy than vice." [2]

⇒ Homer's Ideal of Excellence ⇐

The Iliad and the Odyssey, which the Greeks believed were both written by Homer, were used as basic texts for the education of Greeks for hundreds of years during antiquity. This passage from the Iliad, describing the encounter between Hector, prince of Troy, and his wife Andromache, illustrates the Greek ideal of gaining honor through combat. At the end of the passage, Homer also reveals the Greek attitude toward women.

Homer, *Iliad*

Hector looked at his son and smiled, but said nothing. Andromache, bursting into tears, went up to him and put her hand in his. "Hector," she said, "you are possessed. This bravery of yours will be your end. You do not think of your little boy or your unhappy wife, whom you will make a widow soon. Some day the Achaeans [Greeks] are bound to kill you in a massed attack. And when I lose you I might as well be dead. . . . I have no father, no mother, now. . . . I had seven brothers too at home. In one day all of them went down to Hades' House. The great Achilles of the swift feet killed them all. . . .

"So you, Hector, are father and mother and brother to me, as well as my beloved husband. Have pity on me now; stay here on the tower; and do not make your boy an orphan and your wife a widow. . . ."

"All that, my dear," said the great Hector of the glittering helmet, "is surely my concern. But if I hid myself like a coward and refused to fight, I could never face the Trojans and the Trojan ladies in their trailing gowns. Besides, it would go against the grain, for I have

trained myself always, like a good soldier, to take my place in the front line and win glory for my father and myself. . . ."

As he finished, glorious Hector held out his arms to take his boy. But the child shrank back with a cry to the bosom of his girdled nurse, alarmed by his father's appearance. He was frightened by the bronze of the helmet and the horsehair plume that he saw nodding grimly down at him. His father and his lady mother had to laugh. But noble Hector quickly took his helmet off and put the dazzling thing on the ground. Then he kissed his son, dandled him in his arms, and prayed to Zeus and the other gods: "Zeus, and you other gods, grant that this boy of mine may be, like me, pre-eminent in Troy; as strong and brave as I; a mighty king of Ilium. May people say, when he comes back from battle, 'Here is a better man than his father.' Let him bring home the bloodstained armor of the enemy he has killed, and make his mother happy."

Hector handed the boy to his wife, who took him to her fragrant breast. She was smiling through her tears, and when her husband saw this he was moved. He stroked her with his hand and said, "My dear, I beg you not to be too much distressed. No one is going to send me down to Hades before my proper time. But Fate is a thing that no man born of woman, coward or hero, can escape. Go home now, and attend to your own work, the loom and the spindle, and see that the maidservants get on with theirs. War is men's business; and this war is the business of every man in Ilium, myself above all."

Although the *Iliad* and the *Odyssey* supposedly deal with the heroes of the Mycenaean age of the thirteenth century B.C.E., many scholars believe that they really describe the social conditions of the Dark Age. According to the Homeric view, Greece was a society based on agriculture in which a landed warrior-aristocracy controlled much wealth and exercised considerable power. There is no doubt that Homer's society was divided along class lines with the warrior-aristocrats as the dominant group. Homer's world reflects the values of aristocratic heroes.

This, of course, explains the importance of Homer to later generations of Greeks. Homer did not so much record history: he made it. The Greeks regarded the *Iliad*

and the *Odyssey* as authentic history and as the works of one poet, Homer. These masterpieces gave the Greeks an ideal past with a legendary age of heroes and came to be used as standard texts for the education of generations of Greek males. As one Athenian stated, "My father was anxious to see me develop into a good man . . . and as a means to this end he compelled me to memorize all of Homer." [3] The values Homer inculcated were essentially the aristocratic values of courage and honor (see the box above). It was important to strive for the excellence befitting a hero, which the Greeks called *arete*. In the warrior-aristocratic world of Homer, *arete* is won in struggle or contest. Through his willingness to fight, the hero protects his family and friends, preserves and expands his own honor and that of his family, and earns his reputation. To later generations of Greek males, these heroic values formed the core of aristocratic virtue, a fact that explains the tremendous popularity of Homer as an educational tool. Homer gave to the Greeks a single universally accepted model of heroism, honor, and nobility. But in time, as a new world of city-states emerged in Greece, new values of cooperation and community also transformed what the Greeks learned from Homer.

The World of the Greek City-States (c. 750–c. 500 B.C.E.)

In the eighth century B.C.E., Greek civilization burst forth with new energies. Two major developments stand out in this era: the evolution of the *polis* as the central institution in Greek life and the Greeks' colonization of the Mediterranean and Black Seas.

The Polis

The origins of the Greek *polis* (plural *poleis*) are not very clear. It developed slowly during the Dark Age following the upheavals that brought a close to the Mycenaean age, and by the eighth century B.C.E., it had emerged as a truly unique and fundamental institution in Greek society. In the most basic sense, a *polis* could be defined as a small but autonomous political unit in which all major political, social, and religious activities were carried out at one central location.

In a physical sense, the *polis* encompassed a town or city or even a village and its surrounding countryside. But the town or city or village served as the focus or central point where the citizens of the *polis* could assemble for political, social, and religious activities. In some *poleis*, this central meeting point was a hill, like the Acropolis at Athens, which could serve as a place of refuge during an attack and later in some sites came to be the religious center on which temples and public monuments were erected. Below the acropolis would be an *agora*, an open space that served both as a place where citizens could assemble and as a market. Citizens resided in town and country alike, but the town remained the center of political activity.

Poleis could vary greatly in size, from a few square miles to a few hundred square miles. The larger ones were the product of consolidation. The territory of Attica, for example, had once had twelve *poleis*, but eventually became a single *polis* (Athens) through a process of amalgamation. Athens grew to have a population of more than 300,000 by the fifth century B.C.E., with an adult male citizen body of about 43,000. Most *poleis* were considerably smaller than Athens, however.

The *polis* was much more than just a political institution. It was, above all, a community of citizens in which all political, economic, social, cultural, and religious activities were focused. As a community, the *polis* consisted of citizens with political rights (adult males), citizens with no political rights (women and children), and noncitizens (slaves and resident aliens). All citizens of a *polis* possessed fundamental rights, but these rights were coupled with responsibilities. The Greek philosopher Aristotle argued that the citizen did not just belong to himself: "we must rather regard every citizen as belonging to the state." The unity of citizens was important and often meant that states would take an active role in directing the patterns of life.

The system of the *polis* also relied on local patriotism, which was encouraged by the veneration of a god or goddess as patron of the community. But local patriotism also had a negative side. It tended to foster mutual suspicion and divide Greece into a large number of tiny sovereign units. In the long run, the division of Greece into fiercely patriotic sovereign units helped to bring its ruin. The cultural unity of the Greeks, reinforced by a common language and common gods, did not mean much politically.

The development of the *polis* was paralleled by the emergence of a new military system. Greek fighting had previously been dominated by aristocratic cavalrymen, who reveled in individual duels with enemy soldiers. But by the end of the eighth century and beginning of the seventh century B.C.E., the hoplite infantry formation—the phalanx—came into being. Hoplites were heavily armed infantrymen, who wore bronze or leather helmets, breastplates, and greaves (shin guards). Each carried a round shield, short sword, and a thrusting spear about nine feet long. Hoplites advanced into battle as a unit, forming a phalanx (a rectangular formation) in tight order, usually eight ranks deep. As long as the hoplites kept their order, were not outflanked, and did not break, they either secured victory or, at the very least, suffered no harm. The phalanx was easily routed, however, if its order broke.

The hoplite force had political as well as military repercussions. The aristocratic cavalry was now outdated. Since each hoplite provided his own armor, men of property, both aristocrats and small farmers, made up the new phalanx. Those who could become hoplites and fight for the state could also challenge aristocratic control.

◆ **The Hoplite Forces.** The Greek hoplites were infantrymen equipped with large round shields and long thrusting spears. In battle they advanced in tight phalanx formation and were dangerous opponents as long as this formation remained unbroken. This vase painting of the seventh century B.C.E. shows two groups of hoplite warriors engaged in battle. The piper on the left is leading another line of soldiers preparing to enter the fray.

Colonization and the Rise of Tyrants

Between 750 and 550 B.C.E., the Greek people left their homeland in large numbers to settle in distant lands. Poverty and land hunger created by the growing gulf between rich and poor, overpopulation, and the development of trade were all factors that led to the establishment of colonies. Greek colonies varied in purpose and organization. Some were simply trading posts or centers for the transshipment of goods to Greece. Most were larger settlements that included good agricultural land taken from the native populations in the area. Each colony was founded as a *polis* and was usually independent of the mother *polis* (hence the word *metropolis*) that had established it. Invariably, the colony saw itself as an independent entity whose links to the mother city were not political, but were based on sharing common social, economic, and especially religious practices.

In the western Mediterranean, new Greek settlements were established along the coastline of southern Italy, southern France, eastern Spain, and northern Africa west of Egypt. To the north, the Greeks set up colonies in Thrace, where they sought good agricultural lands to grow grains. Greeks also settled along the shores of the Black Sea and secured the approaches to it with cities on the Hellespont and Bosphorus, most notably Byzantium, site of the later Constantinople (Istanbul). By establishing these settlements, the Greeks spread their culture throughout the Mediterranean basin. Colonization also led to increased trade and industry. The Greeks sent their pottery, wine, and olive oil to the colonies; in return, they received grains and metals from the west and fish, timber, wheat, metals, and slaves from the Black Sea region. In many *poleis*, the expansion of trade and industry created a new group of rich men who desired political privileges commensurate with their wealth, but found them impossible to gain because of the power of the ruling aristocrats.

The aspirations of the newly rising industrial and commercial groups opened the door to the rise of tyrants in the seventh and sixth centuries B.C.E. They were not necessarily oppressive or wicked as our word *tyrant* connotes. Greek tyrants were rulers who came to power in an unconstitutional way; a tyrant was not subject to the law. Many tyrants were actually aristocrats who opposed the control of the ruling aristocratic faction in their cities. The support for the tyrants, however, came from the new rich who made their money in trade and industry as well as from poor peasants who were becoming increasingly indebted to landholding aristocrats. Both groups were opposed to the domination of political power by aristocratic oligarchies.

Tyrants usually achieved power by a local coup d'etat and maintained it by using mercenary soldiers. Once in power, they promoted public works projects, such as the construction of new marketplaces, temples, and walls, that not only glorified the city but also enhanced their own popularity. Tyrants also favored the interests of merchants and traders. Despite these achievements, however, tyranny was largely extinguished by the end of the sixth century B.C.E. Its very nature as a system outside the law seemed contradictory to the ideal of law in a Greek community. Although tyranny did not last, it played a significant role in the evolution of Greek history by ending the rule of narrow aristocratic oligarchies. Once the

✖ Map 4.1   Classical Greece.

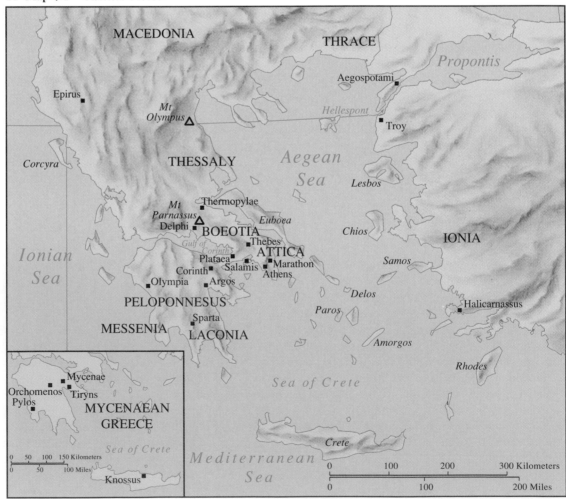

tyrants were eliminated, the door was opened to the participation of new and more people in governing the affairs of the community. Although this trend culminated in the development of democracy in some communities, in other states expanded oligarchies of one kind or another managed to remain in power. Greek states exhibited considerable variety in their governmental structures; this can perhaps best be seen by examining the two most famous and most powerful Greek city-states, Sparta and Athens.

Sparta

The Greeks of Sparta and Athens spoke different dialects and developed different political systems. The Spartans sought stability and conformity and emphasized order. The Athenians allowed for individual differences and stressed freedom. Although Athens and Sparta shared a common heritage, their differences grew so large in the minds of their citizens that the two states were ultimately willing to engage in a life-and-death struggle to support their separate realities. When they did so, the entire Greek world was the real loser.

Located in the southeastern Peloponnesus, Sparta, like other Greek states, faced the problem of land hunger. Rather than solving this problem by colonization, Sparta looked for land nearby and, beginning around 740 B.C.E., undertook the conquest of neighboring Messenia despite its larger size and population. After the conquest, Sparta subjected the Messenians, although greatly outnumbered by them (7 to 1), to serfdom. Known as helots, they were bound to the land for Sparta's benefit. Initially, this imperialistic venture had little apparent effect on Sparta. But in the seventh century, the Messenians revolted. Although Sparta succeeded in quelling the revolt, the struggle was so long and hard that the Spartans made a conscious decision to create a military state so that they could dominate Messenia for ages to come.

After 600 B.C.E., the Spartans instituted a series of reforms that are associated with the name of the lawgiver Lycurgus (see the box on p. 124). Although historians are not sure of his historicity, there is no doubt about the results of these reforms. By the end of the sixth century B.C.E., Sparta had been transformed into a perpetual military camp.

The lives of Spartans were now rigidly organized. At birth, each child was examined by state officials who decided whether it was fit to live. Those judged unfit were exposed to die. Boys were taken from their mothers at the age of seven and put under control of the state. They lived in quasi-military barracks, where they were sub-

jected to harsh discipline to make them tough and given an education that stressed military training and obedience to authority. At twenty, Spartan males were enrolled in the army for regular military service. Although allowed to marry, they continued to live in the barracks and ate all their meals in public dining halls with their fellow soldiers. Meals were simple; the famous Spartan black broth consisted of a piece of pork boiled in blood, salt, and vinegar, causing a visitor who ate in a public mess to remark that he now understood why Spartans were not afraid to die. At thirty, Spartan males were recognized as mature and allowed to vote in the assembly and live at home, but they remained in military service until the age of sixty.

While their husbands remained in military barracks until age thirty, Spartan women lived at home. Because of this separation, Spartan women had greater freedom of movement and greater power in the household than was common for women elsewhere in Greece. They were encouraged to exercise and remain fit to bear and raise healthy children. Like the men, Spartan women engaged in athletic exercises in the nude. At solemn feasts, the young women marched naked in processions, and in the presence of the young men, they sang songs about those who had showed special gallantry or cowardice on the battlefield. Many Spartan women upheld the strict Spartan values, expecting their husbands and sons to be brave in war. The story is told that as a Spartan mother was burying her son, an old woman came up to her and said, "You poor woman, what a misfortune." "No," replied the other, "because I bore him so that he might die for Sparta and that is what has happened, as I wished." [4]

The so-called Lycurgan reforms also reorganized the Spartan government. The political structure combined monarchical, aristocratic, and democratic elements. The executive branch of the Spartan state originally consisted of two kings from different families. They were primarily responsible for military affairs, served as the leaders of the Spartan army on its campaigns, and played some role in foreign policy. Probably in the early eighth century, the domestic role of the kings was superseded by a college of five men who were elected annually and became responsible for the education of youth and the conduct of all citizens. A council of elders, composed of the two kings and twenty-eight citizens over the age of sixty, constituted the aristocratic element in the Spartan constitution. The council's primary task was to determine the issues that would be presented to the assembly of all male citizens, which provided the democratic element in the state. The assembly did not debate, but only voted on the issues put before it by the council of elders.

≋ *The Lycurgan Reforms* ≋

In order to maintain their control over the conquered Messenians, the Spartans instituted the reforms that created their military state. In this account of the supposed lawgiver Lycurgus, the Greek historian Plutarch discusses the effect of these reforms on the treatment and education of boys.

Plutarch, *Lycurgus*

Lycurgus was of another mind; he would not have masters bought out of the market for his young Spartans, . . . nor was it lawful, indeed, for the father himself to breed up the children after his own fancy; but as soon as they were seven years old they were to be enrolled in certain companies and classes, where they all lived under the same order and discipline, doing their exercises and taking their play together. Of these, he who showed the most conduct and courage was made captain; they had their eyes always upon him, obeyed his orders, and underwent patiently whatsoever punishment he inflicted; so that the whole course of their education was one continued exercise of a ready and perfect obedience. The old men, too, were spectators of their performances, and often raised quarrels and disputes among them, to have a good opportunity of finding out their different characters, and of seeing which would be valiant, which a coward, when they should come to more dangerous encounters. Reading and writing they gave them, just enough to serve their turn; their chief care was to make them good subjects, and to teach them to endure pain and conquer in battle. To this end, as they grew in years, their discipline was proportionately increased; their heads were close-clipped, they were accustomed to go barefoot, and for the most part to play naked.

After they were twelve years old, they were no longer allowed to wear any undergarments, they had one coat to serve them a year; their bodies were hard and dry, with but little acquaintance of baths and unguents; these human indulgences they were allowed only on some few particular days in the year. They lodged together in little bands upon beds made of the rushes which grew by the banks of the river Eurotas, which they were to break off with their hands with a knife; if it were winter, they mingled some thistle-down with their rushes, which it was thought had the property of giving warmth. By the time they were come to this age there was not any of the more hopeful boys who had not a lover to bear him company. The old men, too, had an eye upon them, coming often to the grounds to hear and see them contend either in wit or strength with one another, and this as seriously . . . as if they were their fathers, their tutors, or their magistrates; so that there scarcely was any time or place without someone present to put them in mind of their duty, and punish them if they had neglected it.

[Spartan boys were also encouraged to steal their food.] They stole, too, all other meat they could lay their hands on, looking out and watching all opportunities, when people were asleep or more careless than usual. If they were caught, they were not only punished with whipping, but hunger, too, being reduced to their ordinary allowance, which was but very slender, and so contrived on purpose, that they might set about to help themselves, and be forced to exercise their energy and address. This was the principal design of their hard fare.

To guarantee the continuity of their new military state, the Spartans deliberately turned their backs on outside society and cultural amenities. Foreigners were discouraged from visiting Sparta to prevent the importation of novel ideas. Nor were Spartans, except for military reasons, encouraged to travel abroad where they might pick up new ideas. Trade and commerce were likewise minimized. With their material needs provided for by the helots who worked the land, Spartan citizens were expected to dedicate themselves to their duties as a ruling class. The Spartan government discouraged them from pursuing philosophy, literature, the arts, or any subject that might foster the creation of novel thoughts dangerous to the stability of the state.

In the sixth century, Sparta used its military might and the fear it inspired to gain greater control of the Peloponnesus by organizing an alliance of almost all the Peloponnesian states. Sparta's strength enabled it to dominate this Peloponnesian League and determine its policies. By 500 B.C.E., the Spartans had organized a powerful military state that maintained order and stability in the Peloponnesus. Raised from early childhood to believe that total loyalty to the Spartan state was the basic reason for existence, the Spartans viewed their strength as justification for their militaristic ideals and regimented society.

Athens

By 700 B.C.E., Athens had established a unified *polis* on the peninsula of Attica. Although early Athens had been ruled by a monarchy, by the seventh century B.C.E., it had fallen under the control of its aristocrats. They possessed the best land and controlled political and religious life by means of a council of nobles, assisted by a board of nine archons. Although there was an assembly of full citizens, it possessed few powers.

Near the end of the seventh century B.C.E., Athens was experiencing political and social discontent stemming from the development of rival factions within the aristocracy and serious economic problems. Increasing numbers of Athenian farmers found themselves sold into slavery when they were unable to repay the loans they had borrowed from their aristocratic neighbors, pledging themselves as collateral. Repeatedly, revolutionary cries for cancellation of debts and a redistribution of land were heard.

Hoping to avoid tyranny, the ruling Athenian aristocrats responded to this crisis by choosing Solon, a reform-minded aristocrat, as sole archon in 594 B.C.E. and giving him full power to make changes. Solon's reforms dealt with both the economic and political problems. He canceled all current land debts, outlawed new loans based on humans as collateral, and freed people who had fallen into slavery for debts. He refused, however, to carry out the redistribution of the land and hence failed to deal with the basic cause of the economic crisis. This failure, however, was overshadowed by the commercial and industrial prosperity that Athens began to experience in the following decades.

Like his economic reforms, Solon's political measures were also a compromise. Though by no means eliminating the power of the aristocracy, they opened the door to the participation of new people, especially the nonaristocratic wealthy, in the government. But Solon's reforms, though popular, did not truly solve Athens's problems. Aristocratic factions continued to vie for power, and the poorer peasants resented Solon's failure to institute land redistribution. Internal strife finally led to the very institution Solon had hoped to avoid—tyranny. Pisistratus, an aristocrat, seized power in 560 B.C.E. Pursuing a foreign policy that aided Athenian trade, Pisistratus remained popular with the mercantile and industrial classes. But the Athenians rebelled against his son and ended the tyranny in 510 B.C.E. Although the aristocrats attempted to reestablish an aristocratic oligarchy, Cleisthenes, another aristocratic reformer, opposed this plan and, with the backing of the Athenian people, gained the upper hand in 508 B.C.E. The reforms of Cleisthenes now established the basis for Athenian democracy.

A major aim of Cleisthenes' reforms was to weaken the power of traditional localities and regions, which had provided the foundation for aristocratic strength. He enrolled all citizens in ten new tribes, each of which contained inhabitants located in the country districts of Attica, the coastal areas, and Athens itself. The ten tribes thus contained a cross section of the population and reflected all of Attica, a move that diminished local interests and increased loyalty to the *polis*. Each of the ten tribes chose fifty members by lot each year for a new council of 500, which was responsible for the administration of both foreign and financial affairs and prepared the business that would be handled by the assembly. This assembly of all male citizens had final authority in the passing of laws after free and open debate; thus, Cleisthenes' reforms had reinforced the central role of the assembly of citizens in the Athenian political system.

The reforms of Cleisthenes created the foundations for Athenian democracy. More changes would come in the fifth century when the Athenians themselves would begin to use the word *democracy* to describe their system (our word *democracy* comes from the Greek words *demos* [people] and *kratia* [power]). By 500 B.C.E., Athens was more united than it had been and was on the verge of playing a more important role in Greek affairs.

The High Point of Greek Civilization: Classical Greece

Classical Greece is the name given to the period of Greek history from around 500 B.C.E. to the conquest of Greece by the Macedonian king Philip II in 338 B.C.E. It was a period of brilliant achievement, much of it associated with the flowering of democracy in Athens under the leadership of Pericles. Many of the lasting contributions of the Greeks occurred during this period. The age began with a mighty confrontation between the Greek states and the mammoth Persian Empire.

The Challenge of Persia

As Greek civilization grew and expanded throughout the Mediterranean, it was inevitable that it would come into contact with the Persian Empire to the east. The Ionian Greek cities in western Asia Minor had already fallen

CHRONOLOGY

◆◆◆◆◆◆◆◆◆◆◆◆◆◆◆◆◆◆◆◆◆◆

The Persian Wars

Rebellion of Greek cities in Asia Minor	499–494 B.C.E.
Battle of Marathon	490 B.C.E.
Xerxes invades Greece	480–479 B.C.E.
Battles of Thermopylae and Salamis	480 B.C.E.
Battle of Plataea	479 B.C.E.

subject to the Persian Empire by the mid-sixth century B.C.E. An unsuccessful revolt by the Ionian cities in 499 B.C.E.—assisted by the Athenian navy—led the Persian ruler Darius to seek revenge by attacking the mainland Greeks in 490 B.C.E. The Persians landed an army on the plain of Marathon, only twenty-six miles from Athens. There a mostly Athenian army, though clearly outnumbered, went on the attack and defeated the Persians decisively. Although a minor defeat to the Persians, the Battle of Marathon was of great importance to the Athenians, who had proved that the Persians could be beaten.

Xerxes, the new Persian monarch after the death of Darius in 486 B.C.E., vowed revenge and renewed the invasion of Greece. In preparation for the attack, some of the Greek states formed a defensive league under Spartan leadership, while the Athenians pursued a new military policy by developing a navy. By the time of the Persian invasion in 480 B.C.E., the Athenians had produced a fleet of about 200 vessels.

Xerxes led a massive invasion force into Greece: close to 150,000 troops, almost 700 naval ships, and hundreds of supply ships to keep the large army fed. The Greeks decided to fight a delaying action at the pass of Thermopylae along the main road into central Greece, probably to give the Greek fleet of 300 ships the chance to fight the Persian fleet. The Greeks knew that the Persian army was dependent on the fleet for supplies. A Greek force numbering close to 9,000, under the leadership of a Spartan king and his contingent of 300 Spartans, managed to hold the Persian army for two days until a Greek traitor told the Persians of a mountain path that enabled them to outflank the Greek force. Although some of the Greeks retreated when they became aware of the Persian movement, the Spartans fought to the last man.

The Athenians, now threatened by the onslaught of the Persian forces, abandoned their city. While the Per-

sians sacked and burned Athens, the Greek fleet remained offshore near the island of Salamis and challenged the Persian navy to fight. Although the Greeks were outnumbered, they managed to outmaneuver the Persian fleet and utterly defeated it. A few months later, early in 479 B.C.E., the Greeks formed the largest Greek army seen up to that time and decisively defeated the Persian army at Plataea, northwest of Attica. The Greeks had won the war and were now free to pursue their own destiny.

The Growth of an Athenian Empire in the Age of Pericles

After the defeat of the Persians, Athens stepped in to provide new leadership against the Persians by forming a confederation called the Delian League. Organized in the winter of 478–477 B.C.E., the Delian League was dominated by the Athenians from the beginning. Its main headquarters was on the island of Delos, but its chief officials, including the treasurers and commanders of the fleet, were Athenian. Under the leadership of the Athenians, the Delian League pursued the attack against the Persian Empire. Virtually all of the Greek states in the Aegean were liberated from Persian control. Arguing that the Persian threat was now over, some members of the Delian League wished to withdraw. But the Athenians forced them to remain in the league and to pay tribute. "No secession" became Athenian policy. The Delian League was rapidly becoming the nucleus of an Athenian empire.

At home, Athenians favored the new imperial policy, especially after 461 B.C.E., when a political faction, led by a young aristocrat named Pericles, triumphed. Under Pericles, who was a dominant figure in Athenian politics until 429 B.C.E., Athens embarked upon a policy of expanding democracy at home while severing its association with Sparta and expanding its new empire abroad. This period of Athenian and Greek history, which historians have subsequently labeled the age of Pericles, witnessed the height of Athenian power and the culmination of its brilliance as a civilization.

In the age of Pericles, the Athenians became deeply attached to their democratic system. The sovereignty of the people was embodied in the assembly, which consisted of all male citizens over eighteen years of age. In the 440s, that was probably a group of about 43,000. Not all attended, however, and the number present at the meetings, which were held every ten days on a hillside east of the Acropolis, seldom reached 6,000. The assembly passed all laws and made final decisions on war and

Athenian Democracy: The Funeral Oration of Pericles

*I*n his History of the Peloponnesian War, *the Greek historian Thucydides presented his reconstruction of the eulogy given by Pericles in the winter of 431/430* B.C.E. *to honor the Athenians killed in the first campaigns of the Great Peloponnesian War. It is a magnificent, idealized description of Athenian democracy at its height.*

Thucydides, *History of the Peloponnesian War*

Our constitution is called a democracy because power is in the hands not of a minority but of the whole people. When it is a question of settling private disputes, everyone is equal before the law; when it is a question of putting one person before another in positions of public responsibility, what counts is not membership of a particular class, but the actual ability which the man possesses. No one, so long as he has it in him to be of service to the state, is kept in political obscurity because of poverty. And, just as our political life is free and open, so is our day-to-day life in our relations with each other. We do not get into a state with our next-door neighbor if he enjoys himself in his own way, nor do we give him the kind of black looks which, though they do no real harm, still do hurt people's feelings. We are free and tolerant in our private lives; but in public affairs we keep to the law. This is because it commands our deep respect.

We give our obedience to those whom we put in positions of authority, and we obey the laws themselves, especially those which are for the protection of the oppressed, and those unwritten laws which it is an acknowledged shame to break. . . . Here each individual is interested not only in his own affairs but in the affairs of the state as well: even those who are mostly occupied with their own business are extremely well-informed on general politics—this is a peculiarity of ours: we do not say that a man who takes no interest in politics is a man who minds his own business; we say that he has no business here at all. We Athenians, in our own persons, take our decisions on policy or submit them to proper discussions: for we do not think that there is an incompatibility between words and deeds; the worst thing is to rush into action before the consequences have been properly debated. . . . Taking everything together then, I declare that our city is an education to Greece, and I declare that in my opinion each single one of our citizens, in all the manifold aspects of life, is able to show himself the rightful lord and owner of his own person, and do this, moreover, with exceptional grace and exceptional versatility. And to show that this is no empty boasting for the present occasion, but real tangible fact, you have only to consider the power which our city possesses and which has been won by those very qualities which I have mentioned.

foreign policy. Pericles expanded the Athenians' involvement in their democracy (see the box above) by making lower-class citizens eligible for public offices formerly closed to them and introducing state pay for officeholders, including those who served on the large Athenian juries. Poor citizens could now afford to participate in public affairs.

A large body of city magistrates, usually chosen by lot without regard to class, handled routine administrative tasks. The overall directors of policy, a board of ten officials known as generals, were elected by public vote and were usually wealthy aristocrats, even though the people were free to select otherwise. The generals could be reelected, enabling individual leaders to play an important political role. Pericles, for example, was elected to the generalship thirty times between 461 and 429 B.C.E. But all public officials were subject to scrutiny and could be deposed from office if they lost the people's confidence. The Athenians had also devised the practice of ostracism to protect themselves against overly ambitious politicians. Members of the assembly could write on a broken pottery fragment (*ostrakon*) the name of the person they most disliked or considered most harmful to the *polis*. A person who received a majority (if at least 6,000 votes were cast) was exiled for ten years.

The Athenian pursuit of democracy at home was coupled with increasing imperialism abroad as the voluntary allies of the Delian League were converted into the involuntary subjects of an Athenian naval empire. Citing the threat of the Persian fleet in the Aegean, the Athenians moved the treasury of the league from the island of Delos to Athens itself in 454 B.C.E. Members were, in effect, charged a fee (tribute) for the Athenian claim of protection. Pericles also used the money in the league treasury, without the approval of its members, to build new temples in Athens, an arrogant reminder that the Delian League had become the Athenian empire. But Athenian imperialism alarmed the other Greek states, and soon all Greece was confronted with a new war.

The Great Peloponnesian War and the Decline of the Greek States

During the forty years after the defeat of the Persians, the Greek world came to be divided into two major camps: Sparta and its supporters and the Athenian maritime em-

◆ **Pericles: Roman Copy of Fifth-Century Bronze Original.** Pericles dominated Athenian politics from 461 B.C.E. until 429 B.C.E. In addition to increasing the Athenians' participation in their own democratic system, he also pursued an imperialistic policy, expanding the Athenian empire both on the Greek mainland and abroad. Largely with funds taken from the treasury of the Delian League, Pericles also initiated a number of beautification projects for Athens.

pire. In his classic *History of the Peloponnesian War*, the great Greek historian Thucydides pointed out that the fundamental, long-range cause of the Peloponnesian War was the fear that the growing Athenian empire aroused in Sparta and its allies. Then, too, Athens and Sparta had created two very different kinds of societies, and neither state was able to tolerate the other's system. A series of disputes finally led to the outbreak of war in 431 B.C.E.

At the beginning of the war, both sides believed they had winning strategies. The Athenian plan was based on the navy. The citizens of Attica would be brought into the city and remain behind the protective walls of Athens and the port of Piraeus, while the overseas empire and the navy kept them supplied. Pericles knew perfectly well that the Spartans and their allies could beat the Athenians in pitched battles, which, of course, formed the focus of the Spartan strategy. The Spartans and their allies invaded Attica and ravaged the fields and orchards, hoping that the Athenians would send out their army to fight beyond the walls. But Pericles was convinced that Athens was secure behind its walls and retaliated by sending out naval excursions to ravage the seacoast of the Peloponnesus. In the second year of the war, however, plague devastated the crowded city of Athens and wiped out possibly one-third of the Athenian population. Pericles himself died the following year (429 B.C.E.), a severe loss to Athens. Despite the losses from the plague, the Athenians fought on in a struggle that witnessed numerous instances of futile destruction. War weariness finally led to a truce in 421 B.C.E., but it proved to be short-lived.

The Athenians initiated a second phase of the war in 415 B.C.E., when they decided to invade the island of Sicily, believing that its conquest would give them a strong source of support to carry on a lengthy war. But the "great expedition" of the Athenians suffered a massive defeat outside the city of Syracuse. All of the Athenians were killed or sold into slavery. Despite the disaster, the Athenians refused to give up, but raised new armies and sent out new fleets. The final crushing blow came, however, in 405 B.C.E., when the Athenian fleet was destroyed at Aegospotami on the Hellespont. Athens was besieged and surrendered in 404 B.C.E. Its walls were torn down, the navy disbanded, and the Athenian empire destroyed. The great war was finally over.

The Great Peloponnesian War weakened the major Greek states and certainly destroyed any possibility of cooperation among the Greek states. The next seventy years of Greek history are a sorry tale of efforts by Sparta, Athens, and Thebes, a new Greek power, to dominate

Greek affairs. In continuing their petty wars, the Greek states remained oblivious to the growing power of Macedonia to their north and demonstrated convincingly that the genius of the Greeks did not lie in politics. Culture, however, was quite a different story.

The Culture of Classical Greece

Classical Greece saw a period of remarkable intellectual and cultural growth throughout the Greek world. Historians agree, however, that Periclean Athens was the most important center of classical Greek culture. Indeed, the eighteenth-century French philosopher and writer Voltaire listed the Athens of Pericles as one of four happy ages "when the arts were brought to perfection and which, marking an era of the greatness of the human mind, are an example to posterity."[5]

THE WRITING OF HISTORY

History as we know it, as the systematic analysis of past events, was a Greek creation. Herodotus (c. 484–c. 425 B.C.E.), an Ionian Greek from Asia Minor, was the author of the *History of the Persian Wars*, a work commonly regarded as the first real history in Western civilization. It is indeed the earliest lengthy Greek prose work to have survived intact. The Greek word *historia* (from which we derive our word *history*) means "research" or "investigation," and it is in the opening line of Herodotus's *History* that we find the first recorded use of the word:

> These are the researches [*historia*] of Herodotus of Halicarnassus, which he publishes, in the hope of thereby preserving from decay the remembrance of what men have done, and of preventing the great and wonderful actions of the Greeks and the Barbarians from losing their due meed of glory; and withal to put on record what were their ground of feud.[6]

The central theme of Herodotus's work is the conflict between the Greeks and the Persians, which he viewed as a struggle between Greek freedom and oriental despotism. His account demonstrates a remarkable range of interests, including geography, politics, social structures, economics, religion, and even psychology. Herodotus traveled extensively for his information and was dependent for his sources on what we today would call oral history. Although he was a master storyteller and sometimes included considerable fanciful material, Herodotus was also capable of exhibiting a critical attitude toward the materials he used. Regardless of its weaknesses, Herodotus's *History* is an important source of information

on the Persians and certainly our chief source for the Persian Wars themselves.

Thucydides (c. 460–c. 400 B.C.E.) was, by far, the better historian; in fact, historians consider him the greatest historian of the ancient world. Thucydides was an Athenian and a participant in the Peloponnesian War. He had been elected a general, but a defeat in battle led the fickle Athenian assembly to send him into exile, which gave him the opportunity to write his *History of the Peloponnesian War*.

Unlike Herodotus, Thucydides was not concerned with underlying divine forces or gods as explanatory causal factors in history. He saw war and politics in purely rational terms, as the activities of human beings. He examined the long-range and immediate causes of the Peloponnesian War in a clear, methodical, objective fashion. Thucydides placed much emphasis on accuracy and the precision of his facts. As he stated:

> And with regard to my factual reporting of the events of the war I have made it a principle not to write down the first story that came my way, and not even to be guided by my own general impressions; either I was present myself at the events which I have described or else I heard of them from eye-witnesses whose reports I have checked with as much thoroughness as possible.[7]

Thucydides also provided remarkable insight into the human condition. He believed that human nature was a constant: "It will be enough for me, however, if these words of mine are judged useful by those who want to understand clearly the events which happened in the past and which (human nature being what it is) will, at some time or other and in much the same ways, be repeated in the future."[8] He was not so naive as to believe in an exact repetition of events, but felt that political situations recur in similar fashion and that the study of history is of great value in understanding the present.

The Great Peloponnesian War

Invasion of Attica	431 B.C.E.
Athenian invasion of Sicily	415–413 B.C.E.
Battle of Aegospotami	405 B.C.E.
Surrender of Athens	404 B.C.E.

GREEK DRAMA

Drama, as we know it, was created by the Greeks. Tragedy was clearly intended to do more than entertain. It was used to educate citizens and was supported by the state for that reason. Its origins, however, are unclear. Many historians assume that it developed out of religious ritual, and its performance was certainly connected to religious festivals. In Athens, tragedy was given its initial form by Thespis, who wrote tragedies that had one actor and a chorus and were performed at the festival of the City Dionysia instituted by the tyrant Pisistratus beginning in the 530s B.C.E. For some time, the form of Greek tragedy remained rather stable, with the chorus speaking the important lines, but eventually a second and later a third actor were added, creating more dialogue with the chorus as background. Action was very limited. Content was generally based on myths or legends that the audience already knew. In fact, early Greek tragedy derived many of its themes from Homer along with its basic preoccupation with the sufferings of the tragic hero.

Aeschylus (525–456 B.C.E.) is the first tragedian whose plays are known to us. Although he wrote ninety tragedies, only seven have survived. As was customary in Greek tragedy, his plots are simple, and the characters are primarily embodiments of a single passion. The entire drama focuses on a single tragic event and its meaning. At the City Dionysia, Greek tragedies were supposed to be presented in a trilogy (a set of three plays) built around a common theme. The only complete trilogy we possess, called the Oresteia, was written by Aeschylus. The theme of this trilogy is derived from Homer. Agamemnon, the king of Mycenae, returns a hero from the defeat of Troy. His wife Clytemnestra revenges the sacrificial death of her daughter Iphigenia by murdering Agamemnon, who had been responsible for Iphigenia's death. In the second play of the trilogy, Agamemnon's son Orestes avenges his father by killing his mother. Orestes is now pursued by the avenging furies who torment him for killing his mother. Evil acts breed evil acts and suffering is one's lot, suggests Aeschylus. But Orestes is put on trial and acquitted by Athena, the patron goddess of Athens. Personal vendetta has been eliminated and law has prevailed. Reason has triumphed over the forces of evil.

Sophocles (c. 496–406 B.C.E.) added a third actor to his plays and diminished the role of the chorus. Only 7 of his 123 plays have survived. Probably his most famous play was Oedipus the King. The oracle of Apollo foretells how a man (Oedipus) will kill his own father and marry his mother. Despite all attempts at prevention, the tragic events occur. Although it appears that Oedipus suffered the fate determined by the gods, Oedipus also accepts that he himself as a free man must bear responsibility for his actions: "It was Apollo, friends, Apollo, that brought this bitter bitterness, my sorrows to completion. But the hand that struck me was none but my own."[9]

The third outstanding Athenian tragedian, Euripides (c. 485–406 B.C.E.), moved beyond his predecessors in creating more realistic characters. His plots also became more complex with a greater interest in real-life situations. Perhaps the greatest of all his plays was The Bacchae, which dealt with the introduction of the hysterical rites associated with Dionysus, god of wine. Euripides is often seen as a skeptic, who questioned traditional moral and religious values. Euripides was also critical of the traditional view that war was glorious. He portrayed war as brutal and barbaric and expressed deep compassion for the women and children who suffered from it.

Greek tragedies dealt with universal themes still relevant to our day. They probed such problems as the nature of good and evil, the conflict between spiritual values and the demands of the state or family, the rights of the individual, the nature of divine forces, and the nature of human beings. Over and over again, the tragic lesson was repeated: humans were free and yet could operate only within limitations imposed by the gods. The real task was to cultivate the balance and moderation that led to awareness of one's true position. But the pride in human accomplishment and independence is real. As the chorus chants in Sophocles' Antigone: "Is there anything more wonderful on earth, our marvelous planet, than the miracle of man?"[10]

Competitions for Greek comedy developed later than those for tragedy. We first see comedies organized at the festival of Dionysus in Athens in 488/487 B.C.E. The plays of Aristophanes (c. 450–c. 385 B.C.E.), who used both grotesque masks and obscene jokes to entertain the Athenian audience, are examples of Old Comedy. But comedy in Athens was also more clearly political than tragedy. It was used to attack or savagely satirize both politicians and intellectuals. In The Clouds, for example, Aristophanes characterized the philosopher Socrates as the operator of a thought factory where people could learn deceitful ways of handling other people. Later plays gave up the element of personal attack and featured contemporary issues. Of special importance to Aristophanes was his opposition to the Peloponnesian War. Lysistrata, performed in 411 B.C.E., at a time when Athens was in serious danger of losing the war, had a comic but effective message against the war (see the box on p. 131).

⇒ *Athenian Comedy: Sex as an Antiwar Instrument* ⇐

Greek comedy became a regular feature of the dramatic presentations at the festival of Dionysus in Athens beginning in 488/487 B.C.E. Aristophanes used his comedies to present political messages, especially to express his antiwar sentiments. The plot of Lysistrata centers on a sex strike by wives in order to get their husbands to end the Peloponnesian War. In this scene from the play, Lysistrata (whose name means "she who dissolves the armies") has the women take a special oath. The oath involves a bowl of wine offered as a libation to the gods.

Aristophanes, *Lysistrata*

Lysistrata: Lampito: all of you women: come, touch the bowl, and repeat after me: I WILL HAVE NOTHING TO DO WITH MY HUSBAND OR MY LOVER

Kalonike: I will have nothing to do with my husband or my lover

Lysistrata: THOUGH HE COME TO ME IN PITIABLE CONDITION

Kalonike: Though he come to me in pitiable condition (Oh, Lysistrata! This is killing me!)

Lysistrata: I WILL STAY IN MY HOUSE UNTOUCHABLE

Kalonike: I will stay in my house untouchable

Lysistrata: IN MY THINNEST SAFFRON SILK

Kalonike: In my thinnest saffron silk

Lysistrata: AND MAKE HIM LONG FOR ME.

Kalonike: And make him long for me.

Lysistrata: I WILL NOT GIVE MYSELF

Kalonike: I will not give myself

Lysistrata: AND IF HE CONSTRAINS ME

Kalonike: And if he constrains me

Lysistrata: I WILL BE AS COLD AS ICE AND NEVER MOVE

Kalonike: I will be as cold as ice and never move

Lysistrata: I WILL NOT LIFT MY SLIPPERS TOWARD THE CEILING

Kalonike: I will not lift my slippers toward the ceiling

Lysistrata: OR CROUCH ON ALL FOURS LIKE THE LIONESS IN THE CARVING

Kalonike: Or crouch on all fours like the lioness in the carving

Lysistrata: AND IF I KEEP THIS OATH LET ME DRINK FROM THIS BOWL

Kalonike: And if I keep this oath let me drink from this bowl

Lysistrata: IF NOT, LET MY OWN BOWL BE FILLED WITH WATER.

Kalonike: If not, let my own bowl be filled with water.

Lysistrata: You have all sworn?

Myrrhine: We have.

THE ARTS: THE CLASSICAL IDEAL

The arts of the Western world have been largely dominated by the artistic standards established by the Greeks of the classical period. Classical Greek art did not aim at experimentation for experiment's sake, but was concerned with expressing eternally true ideals. Its subject matter was basically the human being, but presented harmoniously as an object of great beauty. The classic style, based on the ideals of reason, moderation, symmetry, balance, and harmony in all things, was meant to civilize the emotions.

In architecture the most important form was the temple dedicated to a god or goddess. Because Greek religious ceremonies were held at altars in the open air, temples were not used to enclose the faithful, as modern churches are. At the center of Greek temples were walled rooms that housed the statues of deities and treasuries in which gifts to the gods and goddesses were safeguarded. These central rooms were surrounded by a screen of columns that made Greek temples open structures rather than closed ones. The columns were originally made of wood, but changed to limestone in the seventh century and to marble in the fifth century B.C.E. The most significant formal element in Greek temples was the shape and size of the columns in combination with the features above and below the column. The Doric order, which evolved first in the Dorian Peloponnesus, consisted of thick, fluted columns with simple capitals resting directly on a platform without a base. Above the capitals was a fairly complex entablature. The Greeks considered the Doric order grave, dignified, and masculine. The Ionic style was first developed in western Asia Minor and consisted of slender columns with a more elaborate base and

✦ **Doric, Ionic, and Corinthian Orders.** This illustration depicts the Doric, Ionic, and Corinthian orders of columns. The size and shape of a column constituted one of the most important aspects of Greek temple architecture. The Doric order, with plain capitals and no base, developed first in the Dorian Peloponnesus and was rather simple in comparison to the slender Ionic column, which had an elaborate base and spiral-shaped capitals, and the Corinthian column, which featured leaf-shaped capitals.

✦ **The Parthenon.** The arts in classical Greece were designed to express the eternal ideals of reason, moderation, symmetry, balance, and harmony. In architecture, the most important form was the temple, and the classical example of this kind of architecture is the Parthenon, built between 447 and 432 B.C.E. The Parthenon, located on the Acropolis, was dedicated to Athena, the patron goddess of Athens, but it also served as a shining example of the power and wealth of the Athenian empire.

volute or spiral-shaped capitals. The Greeks characterized the Ionic order as slender, elegant, and feminine in principle. Corinthian columns, with their more detailed capitals modeled after acanthus leaves, came later, near the end of the fifth century B.C.E.

Some of the finest examples of Greek classical architecture were built in fifth-century Athens. The development of Athenian architecture was aided tremendously by the massive rebuilding program funded from the treasury of the Delian League and instituted almost a half-century after the Persians destroyed Athens in the Persian Wars. The most famous building, regarded as the greatest example of the classical Greek temple, was the Parthenon, built between 447 and 432 B.C.E. The master builders Ictinus and Callicrates directed the construction of this temple consecrated to Athena, the patron goddess of Athens. We could say, however, that the Parthenon, an expression of Athenian enthusiasm, was also dedicated to the glory of Athens and the Athenians. The Parthenon typifies the principles of classical architecture: the search for calmness, clarity, and freedom from superfluous detail. The individual parts of the temple were constructed in accordance with certain mathematical ratios also found in natural phenomena. The architects' concern with these laws of proportion is paralleled by the attempt of Greek philosophers to understand the general laws underlying nature.

Greek sculpture also developed a classical style that differed significantly from the artificial stiffness of the figures of an earlier period. Statues of the male nude, the favorite subject of Greek sculptors, now exhibited more relaxed attitudes; their faces were self-assured, their bodies flexible and smooth-muscled. Although the figures possessed natural features that made them lifelike, Greek sculptors sought to achieve not realism, but a standard of ideal beauty. Polyclitus, a fifth-century sculptor, authored a treatise (now lost) on a canon of proportions that he illustrated in a work known as the *Doryphoros*. His theory maintained that the use of ideal proportions, based on mathematical ratios found in nature, could produce an ideal human form, beautiful in its perfected and refined features. This search for ideal beauty was the dominant feature of the classical standard in sculpture.

THE GREEK LOVE OF WISDOM

Philosophy is a Greek word that originally meant "love of wisdom." Although influenced by the cosmology and theology of the Near East, early Greek philosophers went their own way in seeking "wisdom." They were concerned with the development of critical or rational thought about the nature of the universe and the place of divine forces and souls in it. Many Greeks, however, were simply not interested in such speculations. The Sophists were a group of philosophical teachers in the fifth century who rejected such speculation as foolish; they argued that understanding the universe was beyond the reach of the human mind. It was more important for individuals to improve themselves, so the only worthwhile object of study was human behavior. The Sophists were wandering scholars who sold their services as professional teachers to the young men of Greece, especially those of Athens. The Sophists stressed the importance of rhetoric (the art of persuasive oratory) in winning debates and swaying an audience, a skill that was especially valuable in democratic Athens. The Sophists tended to be skeptics who questioned the traditional values of their societies. Their skepticism was often intertwined with relativism, the belief that there are no absolute values or beliefs. There was, for example, no absolute right or wrong—what was right for one individual might be wrong for another. Consequently, true wisdom consisted of being able to perceive one's own good and to pursue its acquisition.

✦ **Doryphoros.**   This statue, known as the *Doryphoros*, or spear-carrier, is by the fifth-century sculptor Polyclitus, who believed it illustrated the ideal proportions of the human figure. Classical Greek sculpture moved away from the stiffness of earlier figures, but retained the young male nude as the favorite subject matter. The statues became more lifelike, with relaxed poses and flexible, smooth-muscled bodies. The aim of sculpture, however, was not simply realism, but rather the expression of ideal beauty.

Many people, however, viewed the Sophists as harmful to the traditional values of society and especially dangerous to the values of young people.

In classical Greece, Athens became the foremost intellectual and artistic center. Its reputation is perhaps strongest of all in philosophy. After all, Socrates, Plato, and Aristotle raised basic questions that have been debated for two thousand years; these are still largely the same philosophical questions we wrestle with today.

Socrates (469–399 B.C.E.) left no writings, but we know about him from his pupils, especially his most famous one, Plato. By occupation, Socrates was a stonemason, but his true love was philosophy. He taught a number of pupils, but not for pay, because he believed that the goal of education was only to improve the individual. He made use of a teaching method that is still known by his name. The "Socratic method" utilizes a question-and-answer technique to lead pupils to see things for themselves by using their own reason. Socrates believed that all real knowledge is within each person; only critical examination was needed to call it forth. This was the real task of philosophy since "the unexamined life is not worth living."

Socrates' questioning of authority and public demonstration of others' lack of knowledge led him into trouble. Athens had had a tradition of free thought and inquiry, but its defeat in the Peloponnesian War had created an environment intolerant of open debate and soul-searching. Socrates was accused and convicted of corrupting the youth of Athens by his teaching. An Athenian jury sentenced him to death.

One of Socrates' disciples was Plato (c. 429–347 B.C.E.), considered by many the greatest philosopher of Western civilization. Unlike his master Socrates, who wrote nothing, Plato wrote a great deal. In his dialogues, he used Socrates as his chief philosophical debater.

Plato's philosophical thought focused on the essence of reality and was centered in the concept of Ideas or ideal Forms. According to Plato, a higher world of eternal, unchanging Ideas or Forms has always existed. To know these Forms is to know truth. These ideal Forms constitute reality and can only be apprehended by a trained mind, which, of course, is the goal of philosophy. The objects that we perceive with our senses are simply reflections of the ideal Forms. Hence, they are shadows while reality is found in the Forms themselves.

Plato's ideas of government were set out in his dialogue entitled *The Republic*. Based on his experience in Athens, Plato had come to distrust the workings of democracy. It was obvious to him that individuals could not attain an ethical life unless they lived in a just and rational state. Plato's search for the just state led him to construct an ideal state. *The Republic* is often considered the first major work of utopian literature. In his ideal state, the population was divided into three basic groups. At the top was an upper class, a ruling elite, the famous

philosopher-kings: "Unless either philosophers become kings in their countries or those who are now called kings and rulers come to be sufficiently inspired with a genuine desire for wisdom; unless, that is to say, political power and philosophy meet together . . . there can be no rest from troubles . . . for states, nor yet, as I believe, for all mankind."[11] The second group were those who showed courage; they would be the warriors who protected the society. All the rest made up the masses, essentially people driven, not by wisdom or courage, but by desire. They would be the producers of society—the artisans, tradesmen, and farmers.

In Plato's ideal state, each group fulfilled its assigned role, creating a society that functioned harmoniously. The needs of the community, rather than the happiness of the individual, were Plato's concern, and he focused on the need for the guardians or rulers, above all, to be removed from any concerns for wealth or prestige so that they could strive for what was best for the community. To rid the guardians of these desires, Plato urged that they live together, forgoing both private property and family life. Plato believed that women, too, could be rulers; in this, he departed radically from the actual practices of the Greek states.

Plato established a school at Athens known as the Academy. One of his pupils, who studied there for twenty years, was Aristotle (384–322 B.C.E.), who later became a tutor to Alexander the Great. Aristotle differed significantly from his teacher in that he did not accept Plato's theory of ideal Forms. Like Plato, Aristotle believed in universal principles or forms, but he thought that form and matter were inseparable. By examining individual objects, we can perceive their form and arrive at universal principles, but they do not exist as a separate higher world of reality beyond material things, but are a part of things themselves. Aristotle's interests, then, lay in analyzing and classifying things based on thorough research and investigation. His interests were wide-ranging, and he wrote treatises on an enormous number of subjects: ethics, logic, politics, poetry, astronomy, geology, biology, and physics.

Like Plato, Aristotle wished for an effective form of government that would rationally direct human affairs. Unlike Plato, he did not seek an ideal state based on the embodiment of an ideal Form of justice, but tried to find the best form of government by a rational examination of existing governments. For his *Politics*, Aristotle examined the constitutions of 158 states and arrived at general categories for organizing governments. He identified three good forms of government: monarchy, aristocracy, and constitutional government. But based on his examination, he warned that monarchy can easily turn into tyranny, aristocracy into oligarchy, and constitutional government into radical democracy or anarchy. He favored constitutional government as the best form for most people.

With Aristotle's death, the great age of classical Greek philosophy came to an end. By 322 B.C.E., the world of the small city-state was also coming to a close, and a time for new empires had arrived. Philosophical thought began to move into new channels.

Greek Religion

The emphasis on rationalism and the role of human beings in Greek literature and thought might lead some to believe that a spiritual perspective was not important to the Greeks. This is simply not true. Greek religion was intricately connected to every aspect of daily life; it was both social and practical. Public festivals, which originated from religious practices, served specific functions: boys were prepared to be warriors, girls to be mothers. Since religion was related to every aspect of life, citizens had to have a proper attitude to the gods. Religion was a civic cult necessary for the well-being of the state. Temples dedicated to a god or goddess were the major buildings in Greek cities. Proper ritual rather than belief formed the crucial part of Greek religion. It had no official body of priests enunciating dogma and controlling religious matters. Although there were priests and priestesses to care for certain religious shrines, most religious ceremonies were led by civilians serving as priests, and priesthoods were civic offices.

The epic poetry of Homer contained a coherent theogony or genealogy of the gods that provided Greek religion with a definite structure. Over a period of time, all Greeks came to accept a common Olympian religion. There were twelve chief gods who supposedly lived on Mount Olympus, the highest mountain in Greece. Among the twelve were Zeus, the chief deity and father of the gods; Athena, goddess of wisdom and crafts; Apollo, god of the sun and poetry; Aphrodite, goddess of love; and Poseidon, brother of Zeus and god of the seas and earthquakes.

The twelve Olympian gods were common to all Greeks, who thus shared a basic polytheistic religion. Each *polis* usually singled out one of the twelve Olympians as a guardian deity of the community. Athena was the patron goddess of Athens, for example. But each *polis* also had its own local deities who remained important to the community as a whole, and each family had

patron gods as well. Because it was desirable to have the gods look favorably upon one's activities, ritual assumed enormous proportions in Greek religion. Prayers were often combined with gifts to the gods based on the principle, "I give so that you [the gods] will give [in return]." Ritual also meant sacrifices, whether of animals or agricultural products. Animal victims were burned on an altar in front of a temple or a small altar in front of a home. The Greeks maintained religious calendars (lists of sacrifices) specifying what a god or goddess should receive and on what day it should be given.

Festivals also developed as a way to honor the gods and goddesses. Some of these (the Panhellenic celebrations) came to have international significance and were held at special locations, such as those dedicated to the worship of Zeus at Olympia or to Apollo at Delphi. Numerous events were held in honor of the gods at the great festivals, including athletic competitions to which all Greeks were invited. The first such games were held at the Olympic festival in 776 B.C.E. and then were held every four years thereafter to honor Zeus. Initially, the Olympic contests consisted of foot races and wrestling, but later, boxing, javelin throwing, and various other contests were added.

As another practical side of Greek religion, Greeks wanted to know the will of the gods. One possibility was to consult seers who obtained omens from dreams, the flight of birds, or the entrails of sacrificial animals. But perhaps the most famous method of divining the will of the gods was to visit an oracle, a sacred shrine dedicated to a god or goddess who revealed the future. The most famous was the oracle of Apollo at Delphi, located on the side of Mount Parnassus, overlooking the Gulf of Corinth. At Delphi, a priestess listened to questions while in a state of ecstasy that was believed to be induced by Apollo. Her responses were interpreted by the priests and given in verse form to the person asking questions. Representatives of states and individuals traveled to Delphi to consult the oracle of Apollo. States might inquire whether they should undertake a military expedition; individuals might raise such questions as, "Heracleidas asks the god whether he will have offspring from the wife he has now." Responses were often enigmatic and at times even politically motivated. Croesus, the king of Lydia in Asia Minor who was known for his incredible wealth, sent messengers to the oracle at Delphi, asking "whether he shall go to war with the Persians." The oracle replied that if Croesus attacked the Persians, he would destroy a mighty empire. Overjoyed to hear these words, Croesus made war on the Persians but was crushed by his enemy. A mighty empire—that of Croesus—was destroyed.

Daily Life in Classical Athens

The Greek city-state was, above all, a male community: only adult male citizens took part in public life. In Athens, this meant the exclusion of women, slaves, and foreign residents, or roughly 85 percent of the total population in Attica. There were probably 150,000 citizens in Athens, of whom about 43,000 were adult males who exercised political power. Resident foreigners, who numbered about 35,000, received the protection of the laws, but were also subject to some of the responsibilities of citizens, namely, military service and the funding of festivals. The remaining social group, the slaves, numbered around 100,000.

◆ **Women in the Loom Room.** In Athens, women were considered to be citizens and could participate in religious cults and festivals, but they had no rights and were barred from any political activity. Women were thought to belong in the house, caring for the children and the needs of the household. A principal activity of Greek women was the making of clothes. This vase shows two women working on a warp-weighted loom.

Slavery was a common institution in the ancient world. Economic needs dictated the desirability of owning at least one slave, although the very poor in Athens did not own any. The really wealthy might own large numbers, but those who did usually employed them in industry. Most often, slaves in Athens performed domestic tasks, such as being cooks and maids, or worked in the fields. Few peasants could afford more than one or two. Other slaves worked as unskilled and skilled labor. Those slaves who worked in public construction were paid the same as citizens. In many ways, as some historians have argued, although Athens was a slave-owning society, the economy was not dependent on the use of slaves. Slavery in most instances was a substitute for wage labor, which was frowned upon by most freedom-loving Athenians.

The Athenian economy was largely agricultural, but highly diversified as well. Agriculture consisted of growing grains, vegetables, and fruit trees for local consumption; raising vines and olive trees for wine and olive oil, which were exportable products; and grazing sheep and goats for wool and milk products. Given the size of the population in Attica and the lack of abundant fertile land, Athens had to import between 50 and 80 percent of its grain, a staple in the Athenian diet. Trade was thus highly important to the Athenian economy. The building of the port at Piraeus and the Long Walls (a series of defensive walls four and one-half miles long connecting Athens and Piraeus) created the physical conditions that made Athens the leading trade center in the fifth-century Greek world.

Artisans were more important to the Athenian economy than their relatively small numbers might suggest. In particular, Athens was the chief producer of high-quality painted pottery in the fifth century. Other crafts had moved beyond the small workshops into the factory through the use of slave labor. The shield factory of Lysias, for example, employed 120 slaves. Public works projects also provided considerable livelihood for Athenians. The building program of Pericles, financed from the Delian League treasury, made possible the hiring of both skilled and unskilled labor.

The Athenian lifestyle was basically simple. Athenian houses were furnished with necessities bought from artisans, such as beds, couches, tables, chests, pottery, stools, baskets, and cooking utensils. Wives and slaves made clothes and blankets at home. The Athenian diet was rather plain and relied on such basic foods as barley, wheat, millet, lentils, grapes, figs, olives, almonds, bread made at home, vegetables, eggs, fish, cheese, and chicken. Olive oil was widely used, not only for eating,

⮞ Household Management and the Role of the Athenian Wife ⮜

In fifth-century Athens, a woman's place was in the home. She had two major responsibilities: the bearing and raising of children and the management of the household. In his dialogue on estate management, Xenophon relates the advice of an Attican gentleman on how to train a wife.

Xenophon, Oeconomicus

[Ischomachus addresses his new wife] For it seems to me, dear, that the gods with great discernment have coupled together male and female, as they are called, chiefly in order that they may form a perfect partnership in mutual service. For, in the first place, that the various species of living creatures may not fail, they are joined in wedlock for the production of children. Secondly, offspring to support them in old age is provided by this union, to human beings, at any rate. Thirdly, human beings live not in the open air, like beasts, but obviously need shelter. Nevertheless, those who mean to win stores to fill the covered place, have need of someone to work at the open-air occupations; since ploughing, sowing, planting and grazing are all such open-air employments; and these supply the needful food. . . . For he made the man's body and mind more capable of enduring cold and heat, and journeys and campaigns; and therefore imposed on him the outdoor tasks. To the woman, since he has made her body less capable of such endurance, I take it that God has assigned the indoor tasks. And knowing that he had created in the woman and had imposed on her the nourishment of the infants, he meted out to her a larger portion of affection for new-born babes than to the man. . . . Now since we know, dear, what duties have been assigned to each of us by God, we must endeavor, each of us, to do the duties allotted to us as well as possible. . . .

Your duty will be to remain indoors and send out those servants whose work is outside, and superintend those who are to work indoors, and to receive the incomings, and distribute so much of them as must be spent, and watch over so much as is to be kept in store, and take care that the sum laid by for a year be not spent in a month. And when wool is brought to you, you must see that cloaks are made for those that want them. You must see too that the dry corn is in good condition for making food. One of the duties that fall to you, however, will perhaps seem rather thankless: you will have to see that any servant who is ill is cared for.

---

but for lighting lamps and rubbing on the body after washing and exercise. Although country houses kept animals, they were used for reasons other than their flesh: oxen for ploughing, sheep for wool, and goats for milk and cheese.

The family was an important institution in ancient Athens. It was composed of husband, wife, and children (a nuclear family), although other dependent relatives and slaves were regarded as part of the family economic unit. The family's primary social function was to produce new citizens. Strict laws of the fifth century had stipulated that a citizen must be the offspring of a legally acknowledged marriage between two Athenian citizens whose parents were also citizens.

Women who were citizens could participate in most religious cults and festivals, but were otherwise excluded from public life. They could not own property beyond personal items and always had a male guardian. The function of the Athenian woman as wife was very clear. Her foremost obligation was to bear children, especially male children who would preserve the family line. The marriage formula that Athenians used put it succinctly: "I give this woman for the procreation of legitimate children." Secondly, a wife was to take care of her family and her house, either doing the household work herself or supervising the slaves who did the actual work (see the box above).

Women were kept under strict control. Since they were married at fourteen or fifteen, they were taught about their responsibilities at an early age. Although many managed to learn to read and play musical instruments, they were often cut off from any formal education. And women were expected to remain at home out of sight unless they attended funerals or festivals. If they left the house, they were to be accompanied. A woman working alone in public was either poverty-stricken or not a citizen.

Male homosexuality was also a prominent feature of Athenian life. The Greek homosexual ideal was a relationship between a mature man and a young male. It is

♦ **Bust of Alexander the Great.**   This bust of Alexander the Great is a Roman copy of the head of a statue, possibly by Lysippus. Although he aspired to be another Achilles, the tragic hero of Homer's *Iliad*, Alexander also sought more divine honors. He claimed to be descended from Heracles, a Greek hero worshiped as a god, and as pharaoh of Egypt, he gained recognition as a living deity.

most likely that this was an aristocratic ideal and not one practiced by the common people. While the relationship was frequently physical, the Greeks also viewed it as educational. The older male (the "lover") won the love of his "beloved" by his value as a teacher and by the devotion he demonstrated in training his charge. In a sense, this love relationship was seen as a way of initiating young males into the male world of political and military dominance. The Greeks did not feel that the coexistence of homosexual and heterosexual predilections created any special problems for individuals or their society.

The Rise of Macedonia and the Conquests of Alexander

While the Greek city-states were continuing their fratricidal warfare, to their north a new and ultimately powerful kingdom was emerging in its own right. Although a Greek-speaking people, the Macedonians were viewed as barbarians by their southern neighbors, the Greeks. The Macedonians were mostly rural folk, organized in tribes, not city-states, and not until the end of the fifth century B.C.E. did Macedonia emerge as an important kingdom. When Philip II (359–336 B.C.E.) came to the throne, he built an efficient army and turned Macedonia into the chief power of the Greek world. He was soon drawn into the internecine conflicts of the Greeks.

The Greeks had mixed reactions to Philip's growing strength. Some viewed Philip as a savior who would rescue the Greeks from themselves by uniting them. Many Athenians, however, especially the orator Demosthenes, portrayed Philip as ruthless, deceitful, treacherous, and barbaric and called upon the Athenians to undertake a struggle against him. Demosthenes' repeated calls for action, combined with Philip's rapid expansion, finally spurred Athens into action. Allied with a number of other Greek states, Athens fought the Macedonians at the Battle of Chaeronea, near Thebes, in 338 B.C.E. The Macedonian army crushed the Greeks, and Philip was now free to consolidate his control over the Greek peninsula. The independent Greek *polis*, long the basic political unit of the Greek world, came to an end as Philip formed a league of the Greek states. Although Philip allowed the Greek city-states autonomy in domestic affairs, he retained the general direction of their foreign affairs. Many Greeks still objected to being subject to the less civilized master from the north, but Philip insisted that the Greek states end their bitter rivalries and cooperate with him in a war against Persia. Before Philip could undertake his invasion of Asia, however, he was assassinated, leaving the task to his son Alexander.

Alexander the Great

Alexander was only twenty when he became king of Macedonia. The illustrious conqueror was, in many ways, prepared for kingship by his father, who had taken Alexander along on military campaigns and, indeed, had given him control of the cavalry at the important battle of Chaeronea. After his father's assassination, Alexander moved quickly to assert his authority, securing the Macedonian frontiers and smothering a rebellion in Greece. He then turned to his father's dream, the invasion of the Persian Empire.

There is no doubt that Alexander was taking a chance in attacking the Persian Empire. Although weakened in some respects, it was still a strong state. Alexander's fleet was inferior to that of the Persians, and his finances were shaky at best. In the spring of 334 B.C.E., Alexander entered Asia Minor with an army of some 37,000 men. About half were Macedonians, the rest being Greeks and other allies. The cavalry, which would play an important role as a striking force, numbered about 5,000. The army was accompanied by architects, engineers, historians, and scientists, a clear indication of Alexander's grand vision and positive expectations at the beginning of his campaign.

His first confrontation with the Persians, at a battle at the Granicus River in 334 B.C.E., almost cost him his life, but resulted in a major victory. By spring of 333 B.C.E., the entire western half of Asia Minor was in Alexander's hands, and the Ionian Greek cities of western Asia Minor had been "liberated" from the Persian oppressor. Meanwhile, the Persian king Darius III mobilized his forces to stop Alexander's army. Although the Persian troops outnumbered Alexander's, the Battle of Issus was fought on a narrow field that canceled the advantage of superior numbers and resulted in another Macedonian success. After his victory at Issus in 333 B.C.E., Alexander turned south, and by the winter of 332, Syria, Palestine, and Egypt were under his domination. He took the traditional title of pharaoh of Egypt and founded the first of a series of cities named after him (Alexandria) as the Greek administrative capital of Egypt. It became (and re-

mains today) one of Egypt's and the Mediterranean world's most important cities.

In 331 B.C.E., Alexander renewed his offensive, moved into the territory of the ancient Mesopotamian kingdoms, and fought the decisive battle with the Persians at Gaugamela, not far from Babylon. After his victory, Alexander entered Babylon and then proceeded to the Persian capitals at Susa and Persepolis where he acquired the Persian treasuries and took possession of vast quantities of gold and silver (see the box on p. 140). By 330, Alexander was again on the march, pursuing Darius. After Darius was killed by one of his own men, Alexander took the title and office of the Great King of the Persians. But he was not content to rest with the spoils of the Persian Empire. Over the next three years, he moved east and northeast, as far as modern Pakistan. By summer 327 B.C.E., he had entered India. But two more years of fighting in an exotic and difficult terrain exhausted his troops, who mutinied and refused to go on. Reluctantly, Alexander turned back, leading his men across the arid lands of southern Iran. Conditions in the desert were appalling; the blazing sun and lack of water led to thousands of

✖ Map 4.2 The Conquests of Alexander the Great.

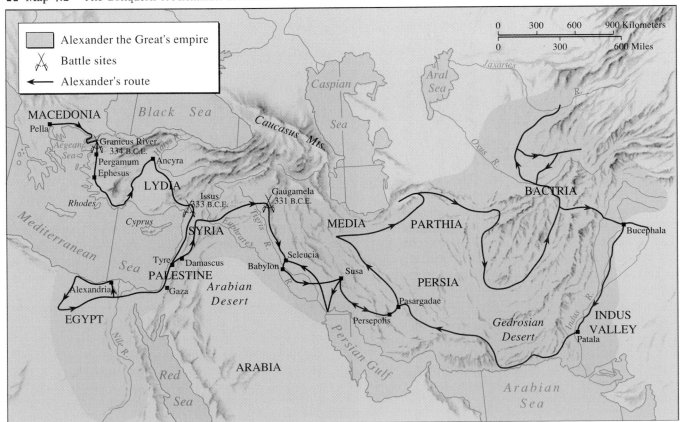

The Destruction of the Persian Palace at Persepolis

After Alexander's decisive victory at Gaugamela, he moved into Persia where he captured the chief Persian cities. At Persepolis, he burned the Persian grand palace to the ground. The ancient historians Arrian and Diodorus of Sicily gave different explanations for this act: one argues that it was a deliberate act of revenge for the Persian invasion of Greece in the fifth century; the other that the burning resulted from a wild drinking party. Modern historians do not agree on which version is more plausible. Arrian was a Greek-speaking Roman senator of the second century C.E. Diodorus of Sicily lived in the first century B.C.E.

Arrian, *The Life of Alexander the Great*

Thence he marched to Persepolis with such rapidity that the garrison had no time to plunder the city's treasure before his arrival. He also captured the treasure of Cyrus the First at Pasargadae. . . . He burnt the palace of the Persian kings, though this act was against the advice of Parmenio, who urged him to spare it for various reasons, chiefly because it was hardly wise to destroy what was now his own property, and because the Asians would, in his opinion, be less willing to support him if he seemed bent merely upon passing through their country as a conqueror rather than upon ruling it securely as a king. Alexander's answer was that he wished to punish the Persians for their invasion of Greece; his present act was retribution for the destruction of Athens, the burning of the temples, and all the other crimes they had committed against the Greeks.

Diodorus of Sicily, *Library of History*

Alexander held games in honor of his victories. He performed costly sacrifices to the gods and entertained his friends bountifully. While they were feasting and the drinking was far advanced, as they began to be drunken a madness took possession of the minds of the intoxicated guests. At this point one of the women present, Thaïs by name and Attic by origin, said that for Alexander it would be the finest of all his feats in Asia if he joined them in a triumphal procession, set fire to the palaces, and permitted women's hands in a minute to extinguish the famed accomplishments of the Persians. This was said to men who were still young and giddy with wine, and so, as would be expected someone shouted out to form the procession and light torches, and urged all to take vengeance for the destruction of the Greek temples. Others took up the cry and said that this was a deed worthy of Alexander alone. When the king had caught fire at their words, all leaped up from their couches and passed the word along to form a victory procession in honor of Dionysus [god of wine and religious ecstasy].

Promptly many torches were gathered. Female musicians were present at the banquet, so the king led them all out for the procession to the sound of voices and flutes and pipes, Thaïs the courtesan leading the whole performance. She was the first, after the king, to hurl her blazing torch into the palace. As the others all did the same, immediately the entire palace area was consumed, so great was the conflagration. It was most remarkable that the impious act of Xerxes, king of the Persians, against the acropolis at Athens should have been repaid in kind after many years by one woman, a citizen of the land which had suffered it, and in sport.

deaths before Alexander and his remaining troops reached Babylon. Alexander planned still more campaigns, but in June 323 B.C.E., weakened from wounds, fever, and probably excessive alcohol, he died at the young age of thirty-two.

THE LEGACY OF ALEXANDER

Alexander is one of the most puzzling great figures in history. Historians relying on the same sources give vastly different pictures of him. Some portray him as an idealistic visionary and others as a ruthless Machiavellian. How did Alexander the Great view himself? We know that he sought to imitate Achilles, the hero of Homer's *Iliad*, destroyer of Hector and Troy. He also claimed to be descended from Heracles, the Greek hero who came to be worshiped as a god. No doubt, Alexander aspired to divine honors; as pharaoh of Egypt, he became a living god according to Egyptian tradition and at one point even sent instructions to the Greek cities to "vote him a god."

Regardless of his ideals, motives, or views about himself, one fact stands out: Alexander truly created a new age, the Hellenistic era. The word *Hellenistic* is derived from a Greek word meaning "to imitate Greeks." It is an appropriate way, then, to describe an age that saw the extension of the Greek language and ideas to the non-Greek world of the Middle East. Alexander's destruction of the Persian monarchy had extended Greco-Macedonian rule over an enormous area. It created opportunities for Greek engineers, intellectuals, merchants, soldiers, and administrators. While the Greeks on the mainland might remain committed to the ideals of their city-states, those who followed Alexander and his successors participated in a new political unity based on the principle of monarchy. Alexander had transformed his army from a Macedonian force into an international one, owing loyalty only to himself. His successors used force to establish military monarchies that dominated the Hellenistic world after his death. Autocratic power, based on military strength and pretensions of divine rule, became a regular feature of those Hellenistic monarchies and was part of Alexander's political legacy to the Hellenistic world. His vision of empire no doubt inspired the Romans, who were, of course, the real heirs of Alexander's legacy.

But Alexander also left a cultural legacy. As a result of his conquests, Greek language, art, architecture, and literature spread throughout the Middle East. The urban centers of the Hellenistic age, many founded by Alexander and his successors, became springboards for the diffusion of Greek culture. Alexander had established a number of cities and military colonies named Alexandria to guard strategic points and supervise wide areas. Most of the settlers were Greek mercenaries. It has been estimated that, in the course of his campaigns, Alexander summoned some 60,000 to 65,000 additional mercenaries from Greece, at least 36,000 of whom took up residence in the garrisons and new cities. While the Greeks spread their culture in the east, they were also inevitably influenced by eastern ways. Thus, Alexander's legacy created one of the basic characteristics of the Hellenistic world: the clash and fusion of different cultures.

The World of the Hellenistic Kingdoms

The united empire that Alexander created by his conquests disintegrated soon after his death. All too soon, the most important Macedonian generals were engaged in a struggle for power. By 300 B.C.E., any hope of unity was dead, and eventually four Hellenistic kingdoms emerged as the successors to Alexander: Macedonia under the Antigonid dynasty, Syria and the east under the

Seleucids, the Attalid kingdom of Pergamum in western Asia Minor, and Egypt under the Ptolemies. All were eventually conquered by the Romans.

The Hellenistic monarchies created a semblance of stability for several centuries, even though Hellenistic kings refused to accept the new status quo and periodically engaged in wars to alter it. At the same time, an underlying strain always existed between the new Greco-Macedonian ruling class and the native populations. Together these factors created a certain degree of tension that was never truly ended until the vibrant Roman state to the west stepped in and imposed a new order.

The Hellenistic kingdoms shared a common political system that represented a break with their Greek past. To the Greeks, monarchy was an institution for barbarians, associated in their minds with people like the Persians. While they retained democratic forms of government in their cities, at the same time the Greeks of the Hellenistic world were forced to accept monarchy as a new fact of political life.

Although Alexander the Great apparently had planned to fuse Greeks and easterners—he used Persians as administrators, encouraged his soldiers to marry easterners, and did so himself—Hellenistic monarchs relied primarily on Greeks and Macedonians to form the new ruling class. It has been estimated that in the Seleucid kingdom, for example, only 2.5 percent of the people in authority were non-Greek and most of them were commanders of local military units. Those who did advance

Map 4.3   The World of the Hellenistic Monarchs.

to important administrative posts had learned Greek (all government business was transacted in Greek) and had become hellenized in a cultural sense. The policy of excluding non-Greeks from leadership positions, it should be added, was not due to the incompetence of the natives, but to the determination of the Greek ruling class to maintain its privileged position. It was the Greco-Macedonian ruling class that provided the only unity in the Hellenistic world.

Since the hellenizing process was largely an urban phenomenon, the creation of new Greek cities is an especially important topic. In his conquests, Alexander had founded a series of new cities and military settlements, and Hellenistic kings did likewise. The new population centers varied considerably in size and importance. Military settlements were meant to maintain order and might consist of only a few hundred men strongly dependent upon the king. But there were also new independent cities with thousands of inhabitants. Alexandria in Egypt was the largest city in the Mediterranean region by the first century B.C.E.

Hellenistic rulers encouraged this massive spread of Greek colonists to the Middle East because of their intrinsic value to the new monarchies. Greeks (and Macedonians) provided not only a recruiting ground for the army, but also a pool of civilian administrators and workers who would contribute to economic development. Even architects, engineers, dramatists, and actors were in demand in the new Greek cities. Many Greeks and Macedonians were quick to see the advantages of moving to the new urban centers and gladly sought their fortunes in the Middle East. Greeks of all backgrounds joined the exodus, at least until around 250 B.C.E. when the outpouring began to slow significantly.

Many of the new urban centers were completely dominated by Greeks while the native populations remained cut off from all civic institutions. The Greeks' belief in their own cultural superiority provided an easy rationalization for their political dominance of the eastern cities. But Greek control of the new cities of the Middle East was also necessary because the kings frequently used the cities as instruments of government, enabling them to rule considerable territory without an extensive bureaucracy. At the same time, for security reasons, the Greeks needed the support of the kings. After all, the Hellenistic cities were islands of Greek culture in a sea of non-Greeks. The relationship between rulers and cities, therefore, was a symbiotic one that bore serious consequences for the cities.

The Greek cities of the Hellenistic era were the chief agents for the spread of Hellenic culture in the Middle East, as far, in fact, as modern Afghanistan and India. These Greek cities were also remarkably vibrant despite their subordination to the Hellenistic monarchies and persisted in being a focal point for the loyalty of their citizens.

Economic and Social Trends

Agriculture was still of primary importance to both the native populations and the new Greek cities of the Hellenistic world. The Greek cities continued their old agrarian patterns. A well-defined citizen body owned land and worked it with the assistance of slaves. But their farms were isolated units in a vast area of land ultimately owned by the king or assigned to large estate owners and worked by native peasants dwelling in villages. Overall, then, neither agricultural patterns nor methods of production underwent significant changes.

Few new products or manufacturing methods were introduced during the Hellenistic era, but the centers of manufacturing shifted significantly. Industry spread from Greece to the east—especially to Asia Minor, Rhodes, and Egypt. New textile centers were set up at Pergamum, while glass and silver crafts were developed in Syria. And busiest of all the cities in manufacturing was Alexandria in Egypt, a center for the production of parchment, textiles, linens, oil, metalwork, and glass.

Commerce experienced considerable expansion in the Hellenistic era. Indeed, trading contacts linked much of the Hellenistic world together. The decline in the number of political barriers encouraged more commercial traffic. Although Hellenistic monarchs still fought wars, the conquests of Alexander and the policies of his successors made possible greater trade between east and west. An incredible variety of products were traded: gold and silver from Spain; salt from Asia Minor; timber from Macedonia; ebony, gems, ivory, and spices from India; frankincense (used on altars) from Arabia; slaves from Thrace, Syria, and Asia Minor; fine wines from Syria and western Asia Minor; olive oil from Athens; and numerous exquisite foodstuffs, such as the famous prunes of Damascus. The greatest trade, however, was in the basic staple of life—grain.

One of the more noticeable features of social life in the Hellenistic world was the emergence of new opportunities for women—at least, for upper-class women—especially in the economic area. Documents show increasing numbers of women involved in managing slaves, selling property, and making loans. Even then, legal contracts in which women were involved had to include their official male guardians, although in numerous instances these men no longer played an important function but were only listed to satisfy legal requirements. Only in Sparta were women free to control their own economic affairs. Many Spartan women were noticeably wealthy; females owned 40 percent of Spartan land.

Spartan women, however, were an exception, especially on the Greek mainland. Women in Athens, for example, still remained highly restricted and supervised. Although a few philosophers welcomed female participation in men's affairs, many philosophers rejected equality between men and women and asserted that the traditional roles of wives and mothers were most satisfying for women.

But the opinions of philosophers did not prevent upper-class women from making gains in areas other than the economic sphere (see the box on p. 144). New possibilities for females arose when women in some areas of the Hellenistic world were allowed to pursue education in the traditional fields of literature, music, and even athletics. Education, then, provided new opportunities for women: female poets appeared in the third century, and there are instances of women involved in both scholarly and artistic activities.

The creation of the Hellenistic monarchies, which represented a considerable departure from the world of the city-state, also gave new scope to the role played by the monarchs' wives, the Hellenistic queens. In Macedonia, a pattern of alliances between mothers and sons provided openings for women to take an active role in politics, especially in political intrigue. In Egypt, opportunities for royal women were even greater because the Ptolemaic rulers reverted to an Egyptian custom of kings marrying their own sisters. Of the first eight Ptolemaic rulers, four wed their sisters. Ptolemy II and his sister-wife Arsinoë II were both worshiped as gods in their lifetimes. Arsinoë played an energetic role in government and was involved in the expansion of the Egyptian navy. She was also the first Egyptian queen whose portrait appeared on coins with her husband. Hellenistic queens also showed an intense interest in culture. They wrote poems, collected art, and corresponded with intellectuals.

≽ A New Autonomy for Women ≼

Upper-class women in Hellenistic society enjoyed no-ticeable gains, and even in the lives of ordinary women, a new assertiveness came to the fore despite the continuing domination of society by men. The first selection is taken from the letter of a wife to her husband, complaining about his failure to return home. In the second selection, a father complains that his daughter has abandoned him, contrary to an Egyptian law providing that children who have been properly raised should support their parents.

Letter from Isias to Hephaistion, 168 B.C.E.

If you are well and other things are going right, it would accord with the prayer that I make continually to the gods. I myself and the child and all the household are in good health and think of you always. When I received your letter from Horos, in which you announce that you are in detention in the Serapeum at Memphis, for the news that you are well I straightway thanked the gods, but about your not coming home, when all the others who had been secluded there have come, I am ill-pleased, because after having piloted myself and your child through such bad times and been driven to every extremity owing to the price of wheat, I thought that now at least, with you at home, I should enjoy some respite, whereas you have not even thought of coming home nor given any regard to our circumstances, remembering how I was in want of everything while you were still here, not to mention this long lapse of time and these critical days, during which you have sent us nothing. As, moreover, Horos who delivered the letter has brought news of your having been released from detention, I am thoroughly ill-pleased. Notwithstanding, as your mother also is annoyed, for her sake as well as for mine please return to the city, if nothing more pressing holds you back. You will do me a favor by taking care of your bodily health. Farewell.

Letter from Ktesikles to King Ptolemy, 220 B.C.E.

I am wronged by Dionysios and by Nike my daughter. For though I raised her, my own daughter, and educated her and brought her to maturity, when I was stricken with bodily ill-health and was losing my eyesight, she was not minded to furnish me with any of the necessities of life. When I sought to obtain justice from her in Alexandria, she begged my pardon, and in the eighteenth year she swore me a written royal oath to give me each month twenty drachmas, which she was to earn by her own bodily labor. . . . But now corrupted by Dionysios, who is a comic actor, she does not do for me anything of what was in the written oath, despising my weakness and ill-health. I beg you, therefore, O king, not to allow me to be wronged by my daughter and by Dionysios the actor who corrupted her, but to order Diophanes the strategus [a provincial administrator] to summon them and hear us out; and if I am speaking the truth, let Diophanes deal with her corrupter as seems good to him and compel my daughter Nike to do justice to me. If this is done I shall no longer be wronged but by fleeing to you, O king, I shall obtain justice.

Culture in the Hellenistic World

Although the Hellenistic kingdoms encompassed vast territories and many diverse peoples, the Greeks provided a sense of unity as a result of the diffusion of Greek culture throughout the Hellenistic world. The Hellenistic era was a period of considerable cultural accomplishment in many areas—literature, art, science, and philosophy. Although these achievements occurred throughout the Hellenistic world, certain centers, especially the great Hellenistic cities of Alexandria and Pergamum, stood out. In both cities, cultural developments were encouraged by the rulers themselves. Rich Hellenistic kings had considerable resources with which to patronize culture.

New Directions in Literature and Art

The Hellenistic age produced an enormous quantity of literature, most of which has not survived. Hellenistic monarchs, who held literary talent in high esteem, subsidized writers on a grand scale. The Ptolemaic rulers of Egypt were particularly lavish. The combination of their largess and a famous library with over 500,000 scrolls drew a host of scholars and authors to Alexandria, including a circle of poets. Theocritus (c. 315–250 B.C.E.), originally a native of the island of Sicily, wrote "little poems" or idylls dealing with erotic subjects, lovers' complaints, and, above all, pastoral themes expressing his love of nature and his appreciation of nature's beauties. In writing short poems, Theocritus was following the advice of Greek literary scholars who argued that Homer could never be superseded and urged writers to stick to well-composed, short poems instead.

In the Hellenistic era, Athens remained the theatrical center of the Greek world. While little remained of tragedy, a New Comedy developed, which completely rejected political themes and sought only to entertain and amuse. The Athenian playwright Menander (c. 342–291 B.C.E.) was perhaps the best representative of New Comedy. Plots were simple: typically, a hero falls in love with a not-really-so-bad prostitute who turns out eventually to be the long-lost daughter of a rich neighbor. The hero marries her and they live happily ever after.

The Hellenistic period saw a great outpouring of historical and biographical literature. The chief historian of the Hellenistic age was Polybius (c. 203–c. 120 B.C.E.), a Greek who lived for some years in Rome. He is regarded by many historians as second only to Thucydides among Greek historians. His major work consisted of forty books narrating the history of the "inhabited Mediterranean world" from 221 to 146 B.C.E. Only the first five books are extant although long extracts from the rest of the books survive. His history focuses on the growth of Rome from a city-state to a vast empire. It is apparent that Polybius understood the significance of the Romans' achievement. He followed Thucydides in seeking rational motives for historical events. He also approached his sources critically and used firsthand accounts.

In addition to being patrons of literary talent, the Hellenistic monarchs were eager to spend their money to beautify and adorn the cities within their states. The founding of new cities and the rebuilding of old ones provided numerous opportunities for Greek architects and sculptors. Hellenistic architects laid out their new cities on the rectilinear grid model first used by Hippodamus of Miletus in the fifth century B.C.E. The buildings of the Greek homeland—gymnasia, baths, theaters, and, of course, temples—lined the streets of these cities. Most noticeable in the construction of temples was the use of the more ornate Corinthian order, which became especially popular during the Hellenistic age.

Sculptors were patronized by Hellenistic kings and rich citizens. Thousands of statues, many paid for by the people honored, were erected in towns and cities all over the Hellenistic world. Hellenistic sculptors traveled throughout this world, attracted by the material rewards offered by wealthy patrons. As a result, although distinct styles developed in Alexandria, Rhodes, and Pergamum,

◆ **Portrait of Queen Arsinoë II.**   Arsinoë II, sister and wife of King Ptolemy II, played an active role in Egyptian political affairs. This statue from around 270–240 B.C.E. shows the queen in the traditional style of a pharaoh.

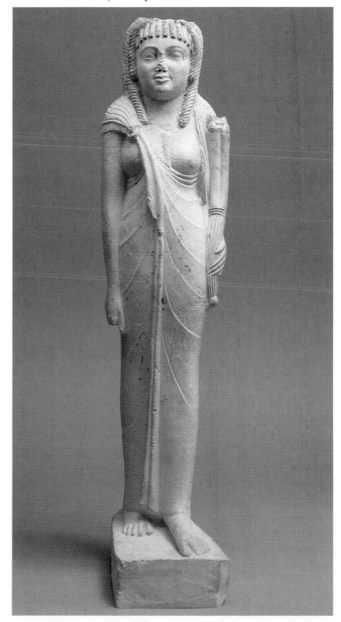

Hellenistic sculpture was characterized by a considerable degree of uniformity. While maintaining the technical skill of the classical period, Hellenistic sculptors moved away from the idealism of fifth-century classicism to a more emotional and realistic art, seen in numerous statues of old women, drunks, and little children at play.

A Golden Age of Science

The Hellenistic era witnessed a more conscious separation of science from philosophy. In classical Greece, what we would call the physical and life sciences had been divisions of philosophical inquiry. Nevertheless, by the time of Aristotle, the Greeks had already established an important principle of scientific investigation, empirical research or systematic observation as the basis for gener-

◆ **Old Market Woman.**   Greek architects and sculptors were highly valued throughout the Hellenistic world, as kings undertook projects to beautify the cities of their kingdoms. Unlike the sculptors of the classical period, Hellenistic sculptors no longer tried to capture ideal beauty in their sculptures, but moved toward a more emotional and realistic art. This statue of an old market woman is typical of this new trend in art.

alization. In the Hellenistic age, the sciences tended to be studied in their own right. While Athens remained the philosophical center, Alexandria and Pergamum, the two leading cultural centers of the Hellenistic world, played a significant role in the development of Hellenistic science.

By far the most famous scientist of the period, Archimedes (287–212 B.C.E.) of Syracuse, came from the western Mediterranean region. Archimedes was especially important for his work on the geometry of spheres and cylinders, for establishing the value of the mathematical constant pi, and for creating the science of hydrostatics. Archimedes was also a practical inventor. He may have devised the so-called Archimedean screw used to pump water out of mines and to lift irrigation water as well as a compound pulley for transporting heavy weights. During the Roman siege of his native city of Syracuse, he constructed a number of devices to thwart the attackers. According to Plutarch's account, the Romans became so frightened "that if they did but see a little rope or a piece of wood from the wall, instantly crying out, that there it was again, Archimedes was about to let fly some engine at them, they turned their backs and fled."[12] Archimedes' accomplishments inspired a wealth of semilegendary stories. Supposedly, he discovered specific gravity by observing the water he displaced in his bath and became so excited by his realization that he jumped out of the water and ran home naked, shouting, "Eureka" ("I have found it"). He is said to have emphasized the importance of levers by proclaiming to the king of Syracuse: "Give me a lever and a place to stand and I will move the earth." The king was so impressed that he encouraged Archimedes to lower his sights and build defensive weapons instead.

Philosophy: New Schools of Thought

While Alexandria and Pergamum became the renowned cultural centers of the Hellenistic world, Athens remained the prime center for philosophy. After Alexander the Great, the home of Socrates, Plato, and Aristotle continued to attract the most illustrious philosophers from the Greek world who chose to establish their schools there. While Plato's Academy and Aristotle's Lyceum continued to exist and attract some students, new schools of philosophical thought (the Epicureans and Stoics) reinforced Athens's reputation as a philosophical center.

Epicurus (341–270 B.C.E.), the founder of Epicureanism, established a school in Athens near the end of the fourth century B.C.E. Epicurus's famous belief in a doctrine of "pleasure" began with his view of the world. Though he did not deny the existence of the gods, he did not believe they played any active role in the world. The universe ran on its own. This left human beings free to follow self-interest as a basic motivating force. Happiness was the goal of life, and the means to achieve it was the pursuit of pleasure, the only true good. But the pursuit of pleasure was not meant in a physical, hedonistic sense:

> When, therefore, we maintain that pleasure is the end, we do not mean the pleasures of profligates and those that consist in sensuality, as is supposed by some who are either ignorant or disagree with us or do not understand, but freedom from pain in the body and from trouble in the mind. For it is not continuous drinkings and revellings, nor the satisfaction of lusts, nor the enjoyment of fish and other luxuries of the wealthy table, which produce a pleasant life, but sober reasoning, searching out the motives for all choice and avoidance, and banishing mere opinions, to which are due the greatest disturbance of the spirit.

Pleasure was not satisfying one's desire in an active, gluttonous fashion, but freedom from emotional turmoil, freedom from worry, the freedom that came from a mind at rest. To achieve this passive pleasure, one had to free oneself from public activity: "We must release ourselves from the prison of affairs and politics." They were too strenuous to give peace of mind. But this was not a renunciation of all social life, for to Epicurus, a life could only be complete when it was centered on the basic ideal of friendship: "Of all the things which wisdom acquires to produce the blessedness of the complete life, far the greatest is the possession of friendship."[13] Epicurus's own life in Athens was an embodiment of his teachings. He and his family created their own private community where they could pursue their ideal of true happiness.

Epicureanism was eventually overshadowed by another school of thought known as Stoicism, which became the most popular philosophy of the Hellenistic world and later flourished in the Roman Empire as well. It was the product of a teacher named Zeno (335–263 B.C.E.), who came to Athens and began to teach in a public colonnade known as the Painted Portico (the *Stoa Poikile*—hence Stoicism). Like Epicureanism, Stoicism was concerned with how individuals find happiness. But Stoics took a radically different approach to the problem. To them, happiness, the supreme good, could be found only in virtue, which meant essentially living in harmony with the will of God: "And this very thing constitutes the virtue of the happy man and the smooth current of life, when all actions promote the harmony of the spirit dwelling in the individual man with the will of him who

orders the universe."[14] One achieved happiness by choosing to follow the will of God through the free exercise of one's own will. To the Stoics, the will of God was the same thing as the will of nature because nature was simply a manifestation or expression of God. "Living according to nature," therefore, meant following the will of God or the natural laws that God established to run the universe.

Virtuous living, then, was living in accordance with the laws of nature or submitting to the will of God (see the box on p. 148). This led to the acceptance of whatever one received in life since God's will for us was by its very nature good. By accepting God's law, people mastered themselves and gained inner peace. Life's problems could not disturb such individuals, and they could bear whatever life offered (hence our word *stoic*). The Stoics did not believe that it was difficult to know the will of God. This knowledge could be derived through the senses, or what the Stoics called the "perception conveying direct apprehension." Sense perceptions of overwhelming strength had to be a revelation of God's standards.

Unlike Epicureans, Stoics did not believe in the need to separate oneself from the world and politics. Public service was regarded as noble. The real Stoic was a good citizen and could even be a good government official. Because Stoics believed that a divine principle was present throughout the universe, each human being also contained a divine spark. This led to a belief in the oneness of humanity. The world constituted a single society of equal human beings. Although they were not equal in the outer world, because each contained the divine spark, all were free to follow God's will (what was best for each individual). All persons then, even slaves, though unfree in body, were equal at the level of the soul.

Epicureanism and especially Stoicism appealed to large numbers of people in the Hellenistic world. Both of these philosophies focused primarily on the problem of human happiness. Their popularity would suggest a fundamental change in the character of the Greek lifestyle. In the classical Greek world, the happiness of individuals and the meaning of life were closely associated with the life of the *polis*. One found fulfillment within the community. In the Hellenistic kingdoms, although the *polis* continued to exist, the sense that one could find satisfaction and fulfillment through life in the *polis* had weakened. Not only did individuals seek new philosophies that offered personal happiness, but in the cosmopolitan world of the Hellenistic states with their mixtures of peoples, a new openness to thoughts of universality could also emerge. For some people, Stoicism embodied this larger sense of community. The appeal of new philosophies in the Hellenistic era can also be explained by the apparent decline in certain aspects of traditional religion, which we can see by examining the status of Hellenistic religion.

Religion in the Hellenistic World

The spread of Greek civilization to the Hellenistic kingdoms of the Middle East made an impact on Greek religion, but not necessarily to the advantage of the Greeks. In religious life, the Greeks took more from the Middle East than they gave. When the Greeks spread throughout the Hellenistic kingdoms, they took their gods with them. Although the construction of temples may have been less important than in classical times, there were still many demonstrations of a lively religious faith. But over a period of time, there was a noticeable decline in the vitality of the traditional Greek Olympian religion. Much of Greek religion had always revolved around ritual, but the civic cults based on the traditional gods no longer seemed sufficient to satisfy people's emotional needs.

The decline in traditional Greek religion left Greeks receptive to the numerous religious cults of the eastern world. The Greeks were always tolerant of other religious institutions. Hence, in the Hellenistic cities of the Middle East, the traditional civic cults of their own gods and foreign cults existed side by side. Alexandria had cults of the traditional Greek gods, Egyptian deities, such as Isis and Horus, the Babylonian Astarte, and the Syrian Atargatis. The eastern religions that appealed most to Greeks, however, were the mystery religions. What was the source of their attraction?

The normal forms of religious worship in Hellenistic communities had lost some of their appeal. The practices of traditional, ritualized Greek religion in the civic cults seemed increasingly meaningless. For many people, the search for personal meaning remained unfulfilled, and they sought alternatives. Among educated Greeks, the philosophies of Epicureanism and especially Stoicism offered help. Another source of solace came in the form of mystery religions.

Mystery cults, with their secret initiations and promises of individual salvation, were not new to the Greek world. But the Greeks of the Hellenistic era were also strongly influenced by eastern mystery cults, such as those of Egypt, which offered a distinct advantage over the Greek mystery religions. The latter had usually been connected to specific locations (such as Eleusis), which meant that a would-be initiate had to undertake a pilgrimage in order to participate in the rites. In contrast, the eastern mystery religions were readily available since temples to their gods and goddesses were located throughout the Greek cities of the east.

All of the mystery religions were based on the same fundamental premises. Individuals could pursue a path to salvation and achieve eternal life by being initiated into a union with a savior god or goddess who had died and risen again. The ritual of initiation, by which the seeker identified with the god or goddess, was, no doubt, a highly emotional experience.

The Egyptian cult of Isis was one of the most popular of the mystery religions. The cult of Isis was very ancient, but became truly universal in Hellenistic times. Isis was the goddess of women, marriage, and children; as one of her hymns states: "I am she whom women call goddess. I ordained that women should be loved by men: I brought wife and husband together, and invented the marriage contract. I ordained that women should bear children. . . ."[15] Isis was also portrayed as the giver of civilization who had brought laws and letters to all humankind. The cult of Isis offered a precious commodity to its initiates—the promise of eternal life. In many ways, the cult of Isis and the other mystery religions of the Hellenistic era helped to pave the way for the coming and the success of Christianity.

Conclusion

The civilization of the ancient Greeks was the fountainhead of Western culture. Socrates, Plato, and Aristotle established the foundations of Western philosophy. Western literary forms are largely derived from Greek poetry and drama. Greek notions of harmony, proportion, and beauty have remained the touchstones for all subsequent Western art. A rational method of inquiry, so important to modern science, was conceived in ancient Greece. Many political terms are Greek in origin, and so too are concepts of the rights and duties of citizenship, especially as they were conceived in Athens, the first great democracy the world had seen. Especially during their classical period, the Greeks raised and debated the fundamental questions about the purpose of human existence, the structure of human society, and the nature of the universe that have concerned thinkers ever since.

All of these achievements came from a group of small city-states in ancient Greece. And yet there remains an element of tragedy about Greek civilization. For all of their brilliant accomplishments, the Greeks were unable to rise above the divisions and rivalries that caused them to fight each other and undermine their own civilization. Of course, their cultural contributions have outlived their political struggles. And the Hellenistic era, which emerged after the Greek city-states had lost their independence, made possible the spread of Greek ideas to larger areas.

♦ **The Cult of Isis.** The cult of Isis was one of the most popular mystery religions in the Hellenistic world. This fresco from Herculaneum in Italy depicts a religious ceremony in front of the temple of Isis. At the top, a priest holds a golden vessel while below him another priest leads the worshipers with a staff. A third priest fans the flames at the altar.

The Hellenistic period was a vibrant one. New cities arose and flourished. New philosophical ideas captured the minds of many. Significant achievements were made in art, literature, and science. Greek culture spread throughout the Middle East and made an impact wherever it was carried. But serious problems remained. Hellenistic kings continued to engage in inconclusive wars. Much of the formal culture was the special preserve of the Greek conquerors whose attitude of superiority kept them largely separated from the native masses of the Hellenistic kingdoms. Although the Hellenistic world achieved a degree of political stability, by the late third century B.C.E. signs of decline were beginning to multiply. Some of the more farsighted perhaps realized the danger the growing power of Rome presented to the Hellenistic world. The Romans would ultimately inherit Alexander's empire, and we must now turn to them and try to understand what made them such successful conquerors.

CHAPTER NOTES

1. H. D. F. Kitto, *The Greeks* (Harmondsworth, 1951), p. 64.
2. Homer, *Odyssey*, trans. E. V. Rieu (Harmondsworth, 1946), p. 337.
3. Xenophon, *Symposium*, trans. O. J. Todd (Harmondsworth, 1946), III, 5.
4. These words from Plutarch are quoted in E. Fantham, H. P. Foley, N. B. Kampen, S. B. Pomeroy, and H. A. Shapiro, *Women in the Classical World* (New York, 1994), p. 64.
5. Voltaire, *The Age of Louis XIV*, trans. Martyn Pollack (London, 1926), p. 1.
6. Herodotus, *The Persian Wars*, trans. George Rawlinson (New York, 1942), p. 3.
7. Thucydides, *The Peloponnesian War*, trans. Rex Warner (Harmondsworth, 1954), p. 24.
8. Ibid.
9. Sophocles, *Oedipus the King*, trans. David Grene (Chicago, 1959), pp. 68–69.
10. Sophocles, *Antigone*, trans. Don Taylor (London, 1986), p. 146.
11. Plato, *The Republic*, trans. F. M. Cornford (New York, 1945), pp. 178–79.
12. Plutarch, *Life of Marcellus*, trans. John Dryden (New York, n.d.), p. 378.
13. *Epicurus: The Extant Remains*, trans. Cyril Bailey (Oxford, 1926), pp. (in order of quotations) 89–91, 115, 101.
14. Diogenes Laertius, *Life of Zeno*, vol. 2, trans. R. D. Hicks (London, 1925), p. 195.
15. Quoted in W. W. Tarn, *Hellenistic Civilization* (London, 1930), p. 324.

SUGGESTED READINGS

The standard one-volume reference work for Greek history remains J. B. Bury and R. Meiggs, *A History of Greece to the Death of Alexander the Great*, 4th ed. (New York, 1975). Other good, general introductions to Greek history include *The Oxford History of the Classical World*, ed. J. Boardman, J. Griffin, and O. Murray (Oxford, 1986), pp. 19–385; N. G. L. Hammond, *A History of Greece to 322 B.C.*, 3d ed. (Oxford, 1986); and R. Sowerby, *The Greeks* (London, 1995). For a general survey of economic and social aspects, see P. Naquet, *Economic and Social History of Ancient Greece: An Introduction* (Berkeley, Calif., 1978).

Early Greek history is examined in O. Murray, *Early Greece* (London, 1980); and L. W. Taylor, *The Mycenaeans*, rev. ed. (London, 1983). For Dark Age Greece, see A. M. Snodgrass, *The Dark Age of Greece* (Edinburgh, 1971). For a good introduction to Homer and the Homeric problem, see J. Griffin, *Homer* (Oxford, 1980).

A good general work on the Greek age of expansion is A. M. Snodgrass, *Archaic Greece* (London, 1980). Economic and social history of the period is covered in C. Starr, *The Economic and Social Growth of Early Greece, 800–500 B.C.* (Oxford, 1977). On colonization, see J. Boardman, *The Greeks Overseas*, rev. ed. (Baltimore, 1980). The best work on tyranny is A. Andrewes, *The Greek Tyrants* (New York, 1963). On Sparta, see W. Forrest, *A History of Sparta, 950–121 B.C.*, 2d ed. (London, 1980). On early Athens, see the still valuable A. Jones, *Athenian Democracy* (London, 1957) and R. Osborne, *Demos* (Oxford, 1985). The Persian Wars are examined in A. Burn, *Persia and the Greeks: The Defense of the West*, rev. ed. (Stanford, Calif., 1984).

A general history of classical Greece can be found in S. Hornblower, *The Greek World, 479–323 B.C.* (London, 1983). Important works on Athens include W. R. Connor, *The New Politicians of Fifth-Century Athens* (Princeton, N.J., 1971) and D. Kagan, *Pericles of Athens and the Birth of Democracy* (New York, 1991). On the development of the Athenian Empire, see M. F. McGregor, *The Athenians and Their Empire* (Vancouver, 1987). The best way to examine the Great Peloponnesian War is to read the work of Thucydides, *History of the Peloponnesian War*, trans. R. Warner (Harmondsworth, 1954).

For a comprehensive history of Greek art, see M. Robertson, *A History of Greek Art*, 2 vols. (Cambridge, 1975). A good, brief study is J. Boardman, *Greek Art* (London, 1985). On sculpture, see G. M. A. Richter,

Sculpture and Sculptors of the Greeks (Oxford, 1971). A basic survey of architecture is H. W. Lawrence, *Greek Architecture*, rev. ed. (Harmondsworth, 1983). On Greek drama, see the general work by A. Lesky, *History of Greek Literature* (London, 1966). On Greek philosophy, a detailed study is available in W. K. C. Guthrie, *A History of Greek Philosophy*, 6 vols. (Cambridge, 1962–1981). A short, general study on Greek religion is W. Guthrie, *The Greeks and Their Gods* (Boston, 1965). Also of value is J. D. Mikalson, *Athenian Popular Religion* (Chapel Hill, N.C., 1983).

For general accounts of daily life in classical Athens, see T. B. L. Webster, *Everyday Life in Classical Athens* (London, 1969). On the family and women, see S. C. Humphreys, *The Family, Women and Death* (London, 1983); S. B. Pomeroy, *Goddesses, Whores, Wives, and Slaves* (New York, 1975), the best general book on women; and E. Fantham, H. P. Foley, N. B. Kampen, S. B. Pomeroy, and H. A. Shapiro, *Women in the Classical World* (New York, 1994). On slavery, see M. I. Finley, ed., *Slavery in Classical Antiquity* (Cambridge, 1960). On homosexuality, see E. Cantarella, *Bisexuality in the Ancient World* (New Haven, Conn., 1992).

A brief but excellent guide to recent trends in scholarship on the Hellenistic era can be found in C. Starr, *Past and Future in Ancient History* (Lanham, Md., 1987), pp. 19–32. The best general survey is F. W. Walbank, *The Hellenistic World* (London, 1981). For a good introduction to the early history of Macedonia, see E. N. Borza, *In the Shadow of Olympus: The Emergence of Macedon* (Princeton, N.J., 1990). Philip of Macedon is covered well in N. Hammond and G. Griffith, *A History of Macedonia*, vol. 2, *550–336* B.C. (Oxford, 1979). There are considerable differences of opinion on Alexander the Great. The best biographies include R. L. Fox, *Alexander the Great* (London, 1973); J. R. Hamilton, *Alexander the Great* (London, 1973); and P. Green, *Alexander of Macedon* (Berkeley, Calif., 1991).

The various Hellenistic monarchies can be examined in N. G. L. Hammond and F. W. Walbank, *A History of Macedonia*, vol. 3, *336–167* B.C. (Oxford, 1988). On the theory of Hellenistic kingship, see G. J. D. Aalders, *Political Thought in Hellenistic Times* (Amsterdam, 1975). On economic and social trends, see the classic and still indispensable M. I. Rostovtzeff, *Social and Economic History of the Hellenistic World*, 3 vols., 2d ed. (Oxford, 1953). Hellenistic women are examined in two works by S. B. Pomeroy, *Goddesses, Whores, Wives, and Slaves* (New York, 1975), pp. 120–48, and *Women in Hellenistic Egypt* (New York, 1984).

For a general introduction to Hellenistic culture, see J. Onians, *Art and Thought in the Hellenistic Age* (London, 1979). The best general survey of Hellenistic philosophy is A. A. Long, *Hellenistic Philosophy: Stoics, Epicureans, Skeptics*, 2d ed. (London, 1986). A superb work on Hellenistic science is G. E. R. Lloyd, *Greek Science after Aristotle* (London, 1973). On one facet of Hellenistic religion, see R. E. Witt, *Isis in the Graeco-Roman World* (London, 1971). On the entry of Rome into the Hellenistic world, see the basic work by E. S. Gruen, *The Hellenistic World and the Coming of Rome*, 2 vols. (Berkeley, Calif., 1984).

CHAPTER
5

The Roman World

Early Roman history is filled with legendary stories that tell of the heroes who made Rome great. One of the best known is the story of Horatius at the bridge. Threatened by attack from the neighboring Etruscans, Roman farmers abandoned their fields and moved into the city, where they would be protected by the walls. One weak point in the Roman defenses, however, was a wooden bridge over the Tiber River. Horatius was on guard at the bridge when a sudden assault by the Etruscans caused many Roman troops to throw down their weapons and flee. Horatius urged them to make a stand at the bridge behind him while he held the Etruscans back. Astonished at the sight of a single defender, the confused Etruscans threw their spears at Horatius, who caught them on his shield and barred the way. By the time the Etruscans had regrouped and were about to overwhelm the lone defender, the Roman soldiers brought down the bridge. When Horatius heard the bridge crash into the river behind him, he dove fully armed into the water and swam safely to the other side through a hail of arrows. Rome had been saved by the courageous act of a Roman who knew his duty and was determined to carry it out. Courage, duty, determination—these qualities would also serve the many Romans who believed that it was their mission to rule nations and peoples.

In the first millennium B.C.E., a group of Latin-speaking people established a small community on a plain called Latium on the Italian peninsula. This community, called Rome, was merely one of numerous Latin-speaking commu-

Republic begins   Early Empire   Fall of Rome

Conquest of Italy and Mediterranean

Twelve Tables   Decline and collapse of Republic   Roman citizenship to all
                                                                         free inhabitants of empire
Struggle of the orders

Augustan poets   Jesus of Nazareth   Constantine legalizes Christianity
(Virgil, Horace, Ovid)

Silver Age of Latin literature

nities in Latium, and the Latin speakers, in turn, constituted only some of the many peoples in Italy. Roman history is basically the story of the Romans' conquest of the plain of Latium, then Italy, and finally the entire Mediterranean world. Why were the Romans able to do this? Scholars do not really know all the answers. The Romans made the right decisions at the right time, which is to say the Romans were a people distinguished by a high degree of political wisdom.

The Romans were also a practical people. Unlike the Greeks, who reserved their citizenship for small, select groups, the Romans often offered their citizenship to the peoples they conquered, thus laying the basis for a strong, integrated empire. The Romans knew that they were inferior to the Greeks in the intellectual sphere and did not hesitate to borrow ideas and culture from them. Roman strength lay in government, law, and engineering. The Romans knew how to govern people, establish legal structures, and construct the roads that took them to the ends of the known world. Throughout their empire, they carried their law, their political institutions, their engineering skills, and their Latin language. And

even after the Romans were gone, those same gifts continued to play an important role in the civilizations that came after them.

The Emergence of Rome

Italy is a peninsula extending about 750 miles from north to south. It is not very wide, however, averaging about 120 miles across. The Apennines traverse the peninsula from north to south, forming a ridge down the middle that divides west from east. Nevertheless, Italy has some fairly large fertile plains ideal for farming. Most important were the Po valley in the north, probably the most fertile agricultural area; the plain of Latium, on which Rome was located; and Campania to the south of Latium. To the east of the Italian peninsula is the Adriatic Sea and to the west the Tyrrhenian Sea with the nearby large islands of Corsica and Sardinia. Sicily lies just west of the toe of the boot-shaped Italian peninsula.

Geography had an impact on Roman history. Although the Apennines bisected Italy, they were less rugged than the mountain ranges of Greece and did not divide the peninsula into many small isolated communities. Italy also possessed considerably more productive agricultural land than Greece, enabling it to support a large population. Rome's location was favorable from a geographical point of view. Located eighteen miles inland on the Tiber River, Rome had access to the sea and yet was far enough inland to be safe from pirates. Built on the famous seven hills, it was easily defended. Situated where the Tiber could be readily forded, Rome became a natural crossing point for north-south traffic in western Italy. All in all, Rome had a good central location in Italy from which to expand.

♦ **Etruscan Married Couple.** This sculpture, dating from 550 B.C.E., depicts a wealthy Etruscan married couple reclining on a couch. The Etruscans greatly influenced the early development of Rome and had an impact on Roman religion, sporting events, and military institutions.

Moreover, the Italian peninsula juts into the Mediterranean, making it an important crossroads between the western and eastern Mediterranean. Once Rome had unified Italy, involvement in Mediterranean affairs was natural. And after the Romans had conquered their Mediterranean empire, governing it was made considerably easier by Italy's central location.

The Greeks and Etruscans

We know little about the Indo-European peoples who moved into Italy during the second half of the second millennium B.C.E. By the first millennium B.C.E., other peoples had also settled in Italy—the two most notable being the Greeks and the Etruscans. The Greeks arrived on the Italian peninsula in large numbers during the age of Greek colonization (750–550 B.C.E.—see Chapter 4). Initially, the Greeks settled in southern Italy and then crept around the coast and up the peninsula as far as Brindisi (Brundisium). They also occupied the eastern two-thirds of Sicily. Ultimately, the Greeks had considerable influence on Rome. They cultivated the olive and the vine, passed on their alphabetic system of writing,

and provided artistic and cultural models through their sculpture, architecture, and literature. Indeed, many historians view Roman culture as a continuation of Greek culture. While Greek influence initially touched Rome indirectly through the Etruscans, the Roman conquest of southern Italy and Sicily brought them into direct contact with the Greeks.

The initial development of Rome, however, was influenced most by a people known as the Etruscans, who were located north of Rome in Etruria. The origins of the Etruscans are not clear, but after 650 B.C.E., they expanded in Italy and became the dominant cultural and economic force in a number of areas. To the north, they moved into north-central Italy, including the Po valley. To the south, according to Roman tradition and archaeological evidence, they controlled Rome and possibly all of Latium. From Latium they moved south and came into direct conflict with Greek colonists in southern Italy. In the sixth century B.C.E., the Etruscans were at the height of their power. But by 480 B.C.E., Etruscan power had begun to decline, and by 400 B.C.E., the Etruscans had been limited to Etruria itself. Later, they were invaded by the Gauls and then conquered by the Romans. Nevertheless, the Etruscans had had an impact. By transforming villages into towns and cities, they brought urbanization to northern and central Italy (the Greeks brought urbanization to southern Italy). Rome was, of course, the Etruscans' most famous product.

Early Rome

According to Roman legend, Rome was founded by the twin brothers, Romulus and Remus, in 753 B.C.E., and archaeologists have found that by the eighth century B.C.E. there was a settlement consisting of huts on the tops of Rome's hills. The early Romans, basically a pastoral people, spoke Latin, which, like Greek, belongs to the Indo-European family of languages (see the table in Chapter 1). The Roman historical tradition also maintained that early Rome (753–509 B.C.E.) had been under the control of seven kings and that two of the last three had been Etruscans. Some historians believe that the king list may have some historical accuracy. What is certain is that Rome did fall under the influence of the Etruscans for about a hundred years during the period of the kings. The Etruscans found Rome a pastoral community but left it a city.

By the beginning of the sixth century, under Etruscan influence, Rome began to emerge as an actual city. The Etruscans were responsible for an outstanding building program. They constructed the first roadbed of the chief

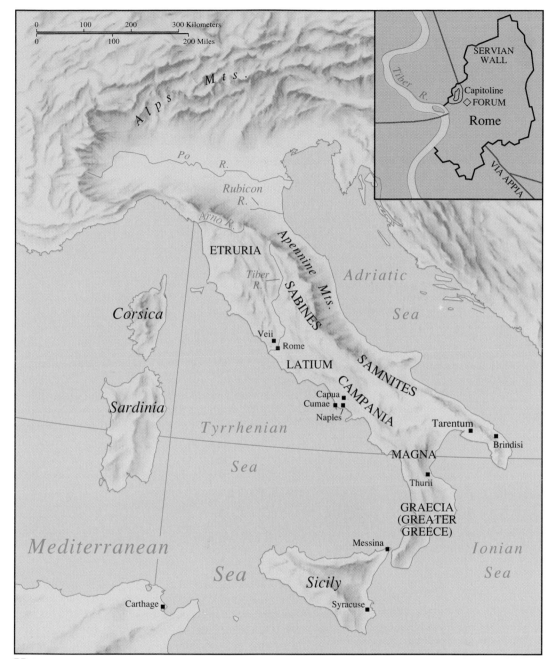

Map 5.1 Ancient Italy and the City of Rome.

street through Rome—the Sacred Way—before 575 B.C.E. and oversaw the development of temples, markets, shops, streets, and houses. By 509 B.C.E., the date when the monarchy supposedly was overthrown and a republican form of government established, a new Rome had emerged, essentially a result of the fusion of Etruscan and native Roman elements.

The Roman Republic

The transition from monarchy to a republican government was not easy. Rome felt threatened by enemies from every direction and, in the process of meeting these threats, embarked on a military course that led to the conquest of the entire Italian peninsula.

⇒ Cincinnatus Saves Rome: A Roman Morality Tale ⇐

There is perhaps no better account of how the virtues of duty and simplicity enabled good Roman citizens to prevail during the travails of the fifth century B.C.E. than Livy's account of Cincinnatus. He was chosen dictator, supposedly in 457 B.C.E., to defend Rome against the attacks of the Aequi. The position of dictator was a temporary expedient used only in emergencies; the consuls would resign and a leader with unlimited power would be appointed for a limited period (usually six months). In this account, Cincinnatus did his duty, defeated the Aequi, and returned to his simple farm in just fifteen days.

Livy, The Early History of Rome

The city was thrown into a state of turmoil, and the general alarm was as great as if Rome herself were surrounded. Nautius was sent for, but it was quickly decided that he was not the man to inspire full confidence; the situation evidently called for a dictator, and, with no dissentient voice, Lucius Quinctius Cincinnatus was named for the post.

Now I would solicit the particular attention of those numerous people who imagine that money is everything in this world, and that rank and ability are inseparable from wealth: let them observe that Cincinnatus, the one man in whom Rome reposed all her hope of survival, was at that moment working a little three-acre farm . . . west of the Tiber, just opposite the spot where the shipyards are today. A mission from the city found him at work on his land—digging a ditch, maybe, or ploughing. Greetings were exchanged, and he was

asked—with a prayer for divine blessing on himself and his country—to put on his toga and hear the Senate's instructions. This naturally surprised him, and, asking if all were well, he told his wife Racilia to run to their cottage and fetch his toga. The toga was brought, and wiping the grimy sweat from his hands and face he put it on; at once the envoys from the city saluted him, with congratulations, as Dictator, invited him to enter Rome, and informed him of the terrible danger of Municius's army. A state vessel was waiting for him on the river, and on the city bank he was welcomed by his three sons who had come to meet him, then by other kinsmen and friends, and finally by nearly the whole body of senators. Closely attended by all these people and preceded by his lictors he was then escorted to his residence through streets lined with great crowds of common folk who, be it said, were by no means so pleased to see the new Dictator, as they thought his power excessive and dreaded the way in which he was likely to use it.

[Cincinnatus proceeds to raise an army, march out, and defeat the Aequi.]

In Rome the Senate was convened by Quintus Fabius the City Prefect, and a decree was passed inviting Cincinnatus to enter in triumph with his troops. The chariot he rode in was preceded by the enemy commanders and the military standards, and followed by his army loaded with its spoils. . . . Cincinnatus finally resigned after holding office for fifteen days, having originally accepted it for a period of six months.

The Roman Conquest of Italy

At the beginning of the Republic, Rome was surrounded by enemies, including the Etruscans to the north and the Sabines, Volscians, and Aequi to the east and south. The Latin communities on the plain of Latium posed an even more immediate threat. If we are to believe Livy, one of the chief ancient sources for the history of the early Roman Republic, Rome was engaged in almost continuous warfare with the Volscians, Sabines, Aequi, and others for the next hundred years.

In his account of these years, the historian Livy provided a detailed narrative of Roman efforts. Many of

Livy's stories were legendary in character and indeed were modeled after events in Greek history. But Livy, writing in the first century B.C.E., used such stories to teach Romans the moral values and virtues that had made Rome great. These included tenacity, duty, courage, and especially discipline (see the box above). Indeed, Livy recounted stories of military leaders who executed their own sons for leaving their place in battle, a serious offense, since the success of the hoplite infantry depended on maintaining a precise order. These stories had little basis in fact, but like the story of George Washington and the cherry tree in American history, they provided mythical images to reinforce Roman patriotism.

The early successes of the Romans against their neighbors seemed to be in vain when, in 387 B.C.E., the Celts, known to the Romans as the Gauls, a people from north of the Alps who had previously moved into northern Italy, defeated the Romans in a battle outside Rome. The Gauls conquered Rome and sacked large parts of the city. Rome was left in shambles. But Roman tenacity won out. The Romans rebuilt the city and with new determination began again.

In 340 B.C.E., Rome crushed the Latin states in Latium and inaugurated a new system that ultimately became the basis for organizing the entire Italian peninsula: the Roman confederation, formed in 338 B.C.E. Under this system, Rome established treaties with the defeated members of the Latin states whereby these communities were related to Rome in one of three ways. The first category included only five or six privileged states in which all the citizens were given full Roman citizenship. A second category of communities acquired municipal status, which entitled their citizens to make legal contracts and intermarry with Romans, but not to vote or hold office in Rome. The remaining communities were made allies and bound to Rome by special treaties specifying their relations with Rome. All three categories of states retained considerable autonomy over their domestic affairs, but were required to provide soldiers for Rome. In the Roman confederation, Rome created a system that could be expanded, as it eventually was, to the rest of Italy. Moreover, the Romans did not regard the status of the conquered states as permanent. Loyal allies could improve their status and even hope to become Roman citizens. Thus, the Romans had found a way to give conquered states a stake in Rome's success.

Between 343 and 290 B.C.E., the Romans waged a fierce struggle with the Samnites, a hill people from the central Apennines, some of whom had settled in Campania, south of Rome. Rome was victorious and incorporated Campania and the Samnite states of central Italy into an expanded Roman confederation as Italian allies. These communities agreed to provide military aid (cavalry and infantry soldiers) to Rome and to allow Rome to control their foreign policy. Otherwise, they were free to govern themselves and maintain their own laws and political institutions.

The conquest of the Samnites gave Rome considerable control over a large part of Italy and also brought it into direct contact with the Greek communities of southern Italy. Soon the Romans were involved in hostilities with some of these Greek cities and by 267 B.C.E.

had completed their conquest of southern Italy and added the Greek states to the Roman confederation. Their relationship to Rome was the same as the Italian allies, except that the Greeks were required to furnish naval assistance—warships and sailors—instead of infantry and cavalry. After crushing the remaining Etruscan states to the north in 264 B.C.E., Rome had conquered all of Italy, except the extreme north.

The Romans' conquest of Italy can hardly be said to be the result of a direct policy of expansion. Much of it was opportunistic. The Romans did not hesitate to act once they felt their security threatened. And surrounded by potential enemies, Rome in a sense never felt secure. Yet once embarked on a course of expansion, the Romans pursued consistent policies that help to explain their success. The Romans were superb diplomats who excelled at making the correct diplomatic decisions. While firm and even cruel when necessary—rebellions were crushed without mercy—they were also shrewd in extending their citizenship and allowing autonomy in domestic affairs. In addition, the Romans were not only good soldiers, but persistent ones. The loss of an army or a fleet did not cause them to quit, but spurred them on to build new armies and new fleets. Finally, the Romans had a practical sense of strategy. As they conquered, they settled Romans and Latins in new communities outside Latium. By 264 B.C.E., the Romans had established colonies—fortified towns—at all strategic locations. By building roads to these settlements and connecting them, the Romans assured themselves of an impressive military and communications network that enabled them to rule effectively and efficiently. By insisting upon military service from the allies in the Roman confederation, Rome essentially mobilized the entire military manpower of all Italy for its wars.

The Roman State

During the period of Roman expansion in Italy, the Roman Republic developed political institutions that were, in many ways, determined by the social divisions that existed within the community. In law and politics, as in conquest, the Romans took a practical approach. They did not concern themselves with the construction of an ideal government, but instead fashioned political institutions in response to problems as they arose.

The chief executive officers of the Roman Republic were the consuls and praetors. Two consuls, chosen annually, administered the government and led the Roman army into battle. They possessed *imperium*, or "the right to command." In 366 B.C.E., a new office, that of the praetor, was created. The praetor also possessed *imperium* and could govern Rome when the consuls were away from the city and could also lead armies. The praetor's primary function, however, was the execution of justice. He was in charge of the civil law as it applied to Roman citizens. In 242 B.C.E., reflecting Rome's growth, another praetor was added to judge cases in which one or both people were noncitizens. The Roman state also had a number of administrative officials who handled specialized duties, such as the administration of financial affairs and supervision of the public games of Rome.

The Roman senate came to hold an especially important position in the Roman Republic. The senate or council of elders was a select group of about 300 men who served for life. The senate was not a legislative body and could only advise the magistrates. This advice of the senate was not taken lightly, however, and by the third century B.C.E. had virtually the force of law. No doubt the prestige of the senate's members furthered this development. But it also helped that the senate met continuously, while the chief magistrates changed annually and the popular assemblies were slow in operation and met only periodically.

The Roman Republic possessed a number of popular assemblies. By far the most important was the centuriate assembly, essentially the Roman army functioning in its political role. Organized by classes based on wealth, it was structured in such a way that the wealthiest citizens always had a majority. The centuriate assembly elected the chief magistrates and passed laws. Another assembly, the council of the plebs, came into being in 471 B.C.E. as a result of the struggle of the orders.

THE STRUGGLE OF THE ORDERS: SOCIAL DIVISIONS IN THE ROMAN REPUBLIC

The most noticeable element in the social organization of early Rome was the division between two groups—the patricians and the plebeians. The patrician class in Rome consisted of those families who were descended from the original senators appointed during the period of the kings. Their initial emergence was probably due to their wealth as great landowners. Thus, patricians constituted an aristocratic governing class. Only they could be consuls, other magistrates, and senators. Through their patronage of large numbers of dependent clients, they controlled the centuriate assembly and many other facets of Roman life. The plebeians constituted the considerably

larger group of "independent, unprivileged, poorer and vulnerable men" as well as nonpatrician large landowners, less wealthy landholders, craftsmen, merchants, and small farmers. Although they were citizens, they did not possess the same rights as the patricians. Both patricians and plebeians could vote, but only the patricians could be elected to governmental offices. Both had the right to make legal contracts and marriages, but intermarriage between patricians and plebeians was forbidden. At the beginning of the fifth century B.C.E., the plebeians began a struggle to seek both political and social equality with the patricians.

The first success of the plebeians came in 494 B.C.E., when they withdrew physically from the state. The patricians, who by themselves could not defend Rome, were forced to compromise. Two new officials known as tribunes of the plebs were instituted (later raised to five and then ten in number) who were given the power to protect plebeians against arrest by patrician magistrates. Moreover, after a new popular assembly for plebeians only, called the council of the plebs, was created in 471 B.C.E., the tribunes became responsible for convoking it and placing proposals before it. If adopted, these measures became *plebiscita* ("it is the opinion of the plebs"), but they were binding only on the plebeians, not the patricians. Nevertheless, the council of the plebs gave the plebeians considerable political leverage. After 445 B.C.E., when a law allowed patricians and plebeians to intermarry, the division between the two groups became less important. In the fourth century B.C.E., the consulship was opened to the plebeians. The climax of the struggle between the orders came in 287 B.C.E. with the passage of a law that stipulated that all *plebiscita* passed by the council of the plebs had the force of law and were binding on the entire community, both plebeians and patricians.

The struggle between the orders, then, had a significant impact on the development of the Roman constitution. Plebeians could now hold the highest offices of state, they could intermarry with the patricians, and they could pass laws binding on the entire Roman community. Although the struggle had been long, the Romans had handled it by compromise, not violent revolution. Theoretically, by 287 B.C.E., all Roman citizens were equal under the law, and all could strive for political office. But in reality, as a result of the right of intermarriage, a select number of patrician and plebeian families formed a new senatorial aristocracy that came to dominate the political offices. The Roman Republic had not become a democracy.

The Roman Conquest of the Mediterranean (264–133 B.C.E.)

After their conquest of the Italian peninsula, the Romans found themselves face-to-face with a formidable Mediterranean power—Carthage. Founded around 800 B.C.E. by Phoenicians from Tyre, Carthage in North Africa was located in a favorable position for commanding Mediterranean trade routes and had become an important commercial center. It had become politically and militarily strong as well. By the third century B.C.E., the Carthaginian empire included the coast of northern Africa, southern Spain, Sardinia, Corsica, and western Sicily. With its monopoly of western Mediterranean trade, Carthage was the largest and richest state in the area. The presence of Carthaginians in Sicily made the Romans apprehensive about Carthaginian encroachment on the Italian coast. In 264 B.C.E., mutual suspicions drove the two powers into a lengthy struggle for control of the western Mediterranean.

The Punic Wars

The First Punic War (264–241 B.C.E.) began when the Romans decided to intervene in a struggle between two Sicilian cities and sent an army to Sicily. The Carthaginians, who considered Sicily within their own sphere of influence, considered this just cause for war. In going to war, both sides determined on the conquest of Sicily. The Romans realized that the war would be long and drawn out if they could not supplement their land operations with a navy and promptly developed a substantial naval fleet. The Carthaginians, on the other hand, had difficulty finding enough mercenaries to continue the fight. After a long struggle in which both sides lost battles in North Africa and Sicily, a Roman fleet defeated the Carthaginian navy off Sicily, and the war quickly came to an end. In 241 B.C.E., Carthage gave up all rights to Sicily and had to pay an indemnity to Rome.

After the war, Carthage made an unexpected recovery and extended its domains in Spain to compensate for the territory lost to Rome. The Carthaginians proceeded to build up a formidable land army in the event of a second war with Rome, because they realized that defeating Rome on land was essential to victory. When the Romans encouraged one of Carthage's Spanish allies to revolt against Carthage, Hannibal, the greatest of the Carthaginian generals, struck back, beginning the Second Punic War (218–201 B.C.E.)

◆ **A Roman Legionary.** The Roman legionaries, with their legendary courage and tenacity, made possible the creation of the Roman Empire. This picture shows a bronze figure of a Roman legionary in full dress at the time of the height of the empire in the second century C.E. The soldier's cuirass is constructed of overlapping metal bands.

This time the Carthaginian strategy aimed at bringing the war home to the Romans and defeating them in their own backyard. Hannibal crossed the Alps with an army of 30,000–40,000 men and 6,000 horses and elephants and inflicted a series of defeats on the Romans. At Cannae in 216 B.C.E., the Romans lost an army of almost 40,000 men. Rome seemed on the brink of disaster but refused to give up, raised yet another army, and gradually recovered. Although Hannibal remained free to roam in Italy, he had neither the men nor the equipment to lay

The Roman Conquest of Italy and the Mediterranean

Sack of Rome by the Gauls	387 B.C.E.
Rome crushes Latin revolt	340 B.C.E.
Creation of the Roman confederation	338 B.C.E.
Samnite Wars	343–290 B.C.E.
The First Punic War	264–241 B.C.E.
The Second Punic War	218–201 B.C.E.
Battle of Cannae	216 B.C.E.
Rome completes seizure of Spain	206 B.C.E.
Battle of Zama	202 B.C.E.
The Third Punic War	149–146 B.C.E.
Macedonia made a Roman province	148 B.C.E.
Destruction of Carthage	146 B.C.E.
Kingdom of Pergamum deeded to Rome	133 B.C.E.

siege to the major cities, including Rome itself. The Romans began to reconquer some of the Italian cities that had rebelled against Roman rule after Hannibal's successes. More important, the Romans pursued a strategy aimed at undermining the Carthaginian empire in Spain. By 206 B.C.E., the Romans had pushed the Carthaginians out of Spain.

The Romans then took the war directly to Carthage, forcing the Carthaginians to recall Hannibal from Italy. At the Battle of Zama in 202 B.C.E., the Romans decisively defeated Hannibal's forces, and the war was over. By the peace treaty signed in 201 B.C.E., Carthage lost Spain, agreed to pay an indemnity, and promised not to go to war without Rome's permission. Spain was made into another Roman province. Rome had become the dominant power in the western Mediterranean.

Fifty years later, the Romans fought their third and final struggle with Carthage. The Carthaginians had technically broken their peace treaty with Rome by going to war against one of Rome's North African allies who had been encroaching on Carthage's home territory. The Romans used this opportunity to carry out the complete destruction of Carthage in 146 B.C.E., a policy advocated by a number of Romans, especially the conservative politi-

cian Cato, who ended every speech he made to the senate with the words, "And I think Carthage must be destroyed" (see the box on p. 161). The territory of Carthage became a Roman province called Africa.

The Eastern Mediterranean

During the Punic Wars, Rome had become acutely aware of the Hellenistic states of the eastern Mediterranean when the king of Macedonia made an alliance with Hannibal after the Roman defeat at Cannae. But Rome was preoccupied with the Carthaginians, and it was not until after the defeat of Carthage that Rome became involved in the world of Hellenistic politics as an advocate of the freedom of the Greek states. This support of the Greeks brought the Romans into conflict with both Macedonia and the kingdom of the Seleucids. Roman military victories and diplomatic negotiations rearranged the territorial boundaries of the Hellenistic kingdoms and brought the Greek states their freedom in 196 B.C.E. For fifty years, Rome tried to be a power broker in the affairs of the Greeks without assuming direct control of their lands. When these efforts failed, the Romans changed their policy.

In 148 B.C.E., Macedonia was made a Roman province, and when some of the Greek states rose in revolt against Rome's restrictive policies, Rome acted decisively. The city of Corinth, leader of the revolt, was destroyed in 146 B.C.E. to teach the Greeks a lesson, and Greece was placed under the control of the Roman governor of Macedonia. Thirteen years later, in 133 B.C.E., the king of Pergamum deeded his kingdom to Rome, giving Rome its first province in Asia. Rome was now master of the Mediterranean Sea.

The Nature of Roman Imperialism

Rome's empire was built in three stages: the conquest of Italy, the conflict with Carthage and expansion into the western Mediterranean, and the involvement with and domination of the Hellenistic kingdoms in the eastern Mediterranean. The Romans did not possess a master plan for the creation of an empire. Much of their expansion was opportunistic; once involved in a situation that threatened their security, the Romans did not hesitate to act. And the more they expanded, the more threats to their security appeared on the horizon, involving them in yet more conflicts. Indeed, the Romans liked to portray themselves as declaring war only for defensive reasons or to protect allies. That is only part of the story, however. It is likely, as some historians have recently suggested, that tween these two types of aristocratic leaders and their supporters engulfed the first century in political turmoil.

Of course, the aristocrats formed only a tiny minority of the Roman people. The backbone of the Roman state and army had traditionally been the small farmers. But economic changes that began in the period of the Punic Wars increasingly undermined the position of that group. Their lands had been severely damaged during the Second Punic War when Hannibal invaded Italy. Moreover, in order to win the wars, Rome had to increase the term of military service from two to six years. When they returned home, many farmers found their farms so deteriorated that they chose to sell out instead of remaining on the land. By this time, capitalistic agriculture was also increasing rapidly. Landed aristocrats had been able to develop large estates (called *latifundia*) by taking over state-owned land and by buying out small peasant owners. These large estates relied on slave and tenant labor and frequently concentrated on cash crops, such as grapes for wine, olives, and sheep for wool, which small farmers could not afford to do. Thus, the rise of *latifundia* contributed to the decline in the number of small citizen farmers. Since the latter group traditionally provided the foundation of the Roman army, the number of men available for military service declined. Moreover, many of these small farmers drifted to the cities, especially Rome, forming a large class of day laborers who possessed no property. This new urban proletariat was a highly unstable mass with the potential for causing much trouble in depressed times. Thus, Rome's economic, social, and political problems were serious and needed attention.

In 133 B.C.E., Tiberius Gracchus, himself a member of the aristocracy and a new tribune, came to believe that the underlying cause of Rome's problems was the decline of the small farmer. Consequently, Tiberius bypassed the senate, where he knew his rivals would oppose his proposal, and had the council of the plebs pass a land-reform bill that authorized the government to reclaim public land held by large landowners and to distribute it to landless Romans. Many senators, themselves large landowners whose estates included large tracts of public land, were furious, and a group of senators took the law into their own hands and assassinated Tiberius.

The efforts of Tiberius Gracchus were continued by his brother Gaius, elected tribune for both 123 and 122 B.C.E. Gaius, too, pushed for the distribution of land to displaced farmers. But he broadened his reform program with measures that would benefit the equestrian order, a rising group of wealthy people who wanted a share in the political power held by the ruling aristocracy. Many senators, hostile to Gaius's reforms and fearful of his growing popularity, instigated mob action that resulted in the

CHRONOLOGY

The Decline and Fall of the Republic

Reforms of Tiberius Gracchus	133 B.C.E.
Reforms of Gaius Gracchus	123–122 B.C.E.
Marius: First consulship	107 B.C.E.
Marius: Consecutive consulships	104–100 B.C.E.
Sulla as dictator	82–79 B.C.E.
First Triumvirate (Caesar, Pompey, Crassus)	60 B.C.E.
Caesar as dictator	47–44 B.C.E.
Octavian defeats Antony at Actium	31 B.C.E.

death of the reformer and many of his friends in 121 B.C.E. The attempts of the Gracchi brothers to bring reforms had opened the door to more instability and further violence.

A New Role for the Roman Army: Marius and Sulla

In the closing years of the second century B.C.E., a series of military disasters gave rise to a fresh outburst of popular anger against the old leaders of the senate. Military defeats in North Africa under a senatorial-appointed general encouraged Marius—a "new man" from the equestrian order—to run for the consulship on a "win the war" campaign slogan. Marius won and became a consul for 107 B.C.E. Marius then took command of the army in Africa and brought the war to a successful conclusion. He was then called upon to defeat the Celts who threatened an invasion of Italy. Marius was made consul for five years, from 104 to 100 B.C.E., raised a new army, and decisively defeated the Celts, leaving him in a position of personal ascendency in Rome.

In raising a new army, Marius initiated military reforms that proved to have drastic consequences. The Roman army had traditionally been a conscript army of small landholders. Marius recruited volunteers from both the urban and the rural proletariat who possessed no property. These volunteers swore an oath of loyalty to the general, not the senate, and thus inaugurated a professional-type army that might no longer be subject to the state. Moreover, to recruit these men, a general would promise them land, so that generals had to play politics in order to get legislation passed that would provide the land for their veterans. Marius left a powerful legacy. He had created a new system of military recruitment that placed much power in the hands of the individual generals.

Lucius Cornelius Sulla was the next general to take advantage of the new military system. The senate had placed him in charge of a war in Asia Minor, but when the council of the plebs tried to transfer the command to Marius, a civil war ensued. Sulla won and seized Rome itself in 82 B.C.E. He forced the senate to grant him the title of dictator to "reconstitute the Republic." After conducting a reign of terror to wipe out all opposition, Sulla revised the constitution to restore power to the senate and eliminate most of the powers of the popular assemblies and the tribunes of the plebs. In 79 B.C.E., believing that he had created a firm foundation for the traditional Republic governed by a powerful senate, he retired. But his real legacy was quite different from what he had intended. His example of using an army to seize power would prove most attractive to ambitious men.

◆ **Caesar.**   Conqueror of Gaul and member of the First Triumvirate, Julius Caesar is perhaps the best-known figure of the late Republic. Caesar became dictator of Rome in 47 B.C.E. and, after his victories in the civil war, was made dictator for life. Some members of the senate who resented his power assassinated him in 44 B.C.E. Pictured is a marble copy of the bust of Caesar.

The Collapse of the Republic

For the next fifty years, Roman history would be characterized by two important features: the jostling for power by a number of powerful individuals and the civil wars generated by their conflicts. Three powerful individuals came to hold enormous military and political power—Crassus, Pompey, and Julius Caesar. Crassus, who was known as the richest man in Rome, had successfully put down a major slave rebellion. Pompey had returned from a successful military command in Spain in 71 B.C.E. and been hailed as a military hero. Julius Caesar had been a spokesman for the *populares* from the beginning of his political career and had a military command in Spain. In 60 B.C.E., Caesar joined with Crassus and Pompey to form a coalition that historians called the First Triumvirate.

Though others had made political deals before, the combined wealth and power of these three men was enormous, enabling them to dominate the political scene and achieve their basic aims: Pompey received lands for his veterans and a command in Spain; Crassus was given a command in Syria; and Caesar was granted a special military command in Gaul (modern France). When Crassus was killed in battle in 53 B.C.E., his death left two powerful men with armies in direct competition. Caesar had used his time in Gaul wisely. He had conquered all of Gaul and gained fame, wealth, and military experience as well as an army of seasoned veterans who were loyal to him. When leading senators fastened on Pompey as the least harmful to their cause and voted for Caesar to lay down his command and return as a private citizen to Rome, Caesar refused and marched on Rome, thus guaranteeing a civil war between his forces and those of Pompey and his allies. The defeat of Pompey's forces left Caesar in complete control of the Roman government.

Caesar had officially been made dictator in 47 B.C.E., and in 44 B.C.E., he was made dictator for life. Although his ultimate intentions are a matter of speculation, he did institute a number of reforms designed to solve problems that ambitious senators like himself had previously exploited. In this way he hoped to ensure his continued control unchallenged. He increased the senate to 900 members by filling it with many of his supporters and granted citizenship to a number of people in the provinces who had provided assistance to him. He planned much more in the way of building projects and military adventures in the east, but in 44 B.C.E., a group of leading senators who resented his domination assassinated him in the belief that they had struck a blow for republican liberty (see the box on p. 165). In truth, they had set the stage for another civil war that delivered the death blow to the Republic.

The Assassination of Julius Caesar

When it quickly became apparent that Julius Caesar had no intention of restoring the Republic as they conceived it, about sixty senators, many of them his friends or pardoned enemies, formed a conspiracy to assassinate the dictator. It was led by Gaius Cassius and Marcus Brutus, who naively imagined that this act would restore the traditional Republic. The conspirators set the Ides of March (March 15), 44 B.C.E. as the date for the assassination. Caesar was in the midst of preparations for a campaign in the eastern part of the empire. Although informed that there was a plot against his life, he chose to disregard the warning. This account of Caesar's death is taken from his biography by the Greek writer Plutarch.

Plutarch, *Life of Caesar*

Fate, however, is to all appearance more unavoidable than unexpected. For many strange prodigies and apparitions are said to have been observed shortly before this event. . . . One finds it also related by many that a soothsayer bade him [Caesar] prepare for some great danger on the Ides of March. When this day was come, Caesar, as he went to the senate, met this soothsayer, and said to him by way of raillery, "The Ides of March are come," who answered him calmly, "Yes, they are come, but they are not past. . . ."

All these things might happen by chance. But the place which was destined for the scene of this murder, in which the senate met that day, was the same in which Pompey's statue stood, and was one of the edifices which Pompey had raised and dedicated with his theater to the use of the public, plainly showing that there was something of a supernatural influence which guided the action and ordered it to that particular place. Cassius, just before the act, is said to have looked toward Pompey's statue, and silently implored his assistance. . . . When Caesar entered, the senate stood up to show their respect to him, and of Brutus's confederates, some came about his chair and stood behind it, others met him, pretending to add their petitions to those of Tillius Cimber, in behalf of his brother, who was in exile; and they followed him with their joint applications till he came to his seat. When he was sat down, he refused to comply with their requests, and upon their urging him further began to reproach them severely for their importunities, when Tillius, laying hold of his robe with both his hands, pulled it down from his neck, which was the signal for the assault. Casca gave him the first cut in the neck, which was not mortal nor dangerous, as coming from one who at the beginning of such a bold action was probably very much disturbed; Caesar immediately turned about, and laid his hand upon the dagger and kept hold of it. And both of them at the same time cried out, he that received the blow, in Latin, "Vile Casca, what does this mean?" and he that gave it, in Greek to his brother, "Brother, help!" Upon this first onset, those who were not privy to the design were astonished, and their horror and amazement at what they saw were so great that they dared not fly nor assist Caesar, nor so much as speak a word. But those who came prepared for the business enclosed him on every side, with their naked daggers in their hands. Which way soever he turned he met with blows, and saw their swords leveled at his face and eyes, and was encompassed like a wild beast in the toils on every side. For it had been agreed they should each of them make a thrust at him, and flesh themselves with his blood: for which reason Brutus also gave him one stab in the groin. Some say that he fought and resisted all the rest, shifting his body to avoid the blows, and calling out for help, but that when he saw Brutus's sword drawn, he covered his face with his robe and submitted, letting himself fall, whether it were by chance or that he was pushed in that direction by his murderers, at the foot of the pedestal on which Pompey's statue stood, and which was thus wetted with his blood. So that Pompey himself seemed to have presided, as it were, over the revenge done upon his adversary, who lay here at his feet, and breathed out his soul through his multitude of wounds, for they say he received three-and-twenty. And the conspirators themselves were many of them wounded by each other, whilst they all leveled their blows at the same person.

Within a few years after Caesar's death, two men had divided the Roman world between them—Octavian, Caesar's heir and grandnephew, taking the west and Antony, Caesar's ally and assistant, the east. But the empire of the Romans, large as it was, was still too small for two masters, and Octavian and Antony eventually came into conflict. Antony allied himself with the Egyptian queen Cleopatra VII, with whom, like Caesar before him, he fell deeply in love. Octavian began a propaganda campaign, accusing Antony of catering to Cleopatra and giving away Roman territory to this "whore of the east." Finally, at the Battle of Actium in Greece in 31 B.C.E., Octavian's forces smashed the army and navy of Antony and Cleopatra. Both fled to Egypt where, according to the account of the Roman historian Florus, they committed suicide a year later:

> Antony was the first to commit suicide, by the sword. Cleopatra threw herself at Octavian's feet, and tried her best to attract his gaze: in vain, for his self-control was impervious to her beauty. It was not her life she was after, for that had already been granted, but a portion of her kingdom. When she realized this was hopeless and that she had been earmarked to feature in Octavian's triumph in Rome, she took advantage of her guard's carelessness to get herself into the mausoleum, as the royal tomb is called. Once there, she put on the royal robes which she was accustomed to wear, and lay down in a richly perfumed coffin beside her Antony. Then she applied poisonous snakes to her veins and slipped into death as though into a sleep.[1]

Octavian, at the age of thirty-two, stood supreme over the Roman world. The civil wars were ended. And so was the Republic.

The Age of Augustus (31 B.C.E.–14 C.E.)

In 27 B.C.E., Octavian proclaimed the "restoration of the Republic." He understood that only traditional republican forms would satisfy the senatorial aristocracy. At the same time, Octavian was aware that the Republic could not be fully restored and managed to arrive at a compromise that worked at least during his lifetime. In 27 B.C.E., the senate awarded him the title of Augustus—"the revered one." He preferred the title princeps, meaning chief citizen or first among equals. The system of rule that Augustus established is sometimes called the principate, conveying the idea of a constitutional monarch as co-ruler with the senate. But while Augustus worked to maintain this appearance, in reality, power was heavily weighted in favor of the princeps.

In the new constitutional order that Augustus created, the basic governmental structure consisted of a princeps (Augustus) and an aristocratic senate. Augustus retained the senate as the chief deliberative body of the Roman state. Its decrees, screened in advance by the princeps, now had the effect of law. The title of princeps—first citizen of the state—carried no power in itself, but Augustus also held the office of consul each year until 23 B.C.E., when he assumed the power of a tribune, which enabled him to propose laws and veto any item of public business. By observing proper legal forms for his power, Augustus proved to be highly popular. As the Roman historian Tacitus commented, "Indeed, he attracted everybody's goodwill by the enjoyable gift of peace. . . . Opposition did not exist."[2] No doubt, the ending of the civil wars had greatly bolstered Augustus's popularity. At the same time, his continuing control of the army, while making possible the Roman peace, was a crucial source of his power.

Augustus was especially eager to stabilize the military and administrative structures of the Roman Empire. The peace of the empire depended on the army and so did the security of the princeps. While primarily responsible for guarding the frontiers of the empire, the army was also used to maintain domestic order within the provinces. Augustus maintained a standing army of twenty-eight legions or about 150,000 men. Roman legionaries were recruited only from the citizenry and, under Augustus, largely from Italy. Augustus also maintained a large contingent of auxiliary forces—around 130,000—enlisted from the subject peoples. Augustus was also responsible for establishing the praetorian guard. Although nominally a military reserve, these "nine cohorts of elite troops," roughly 9,000 men, had the important task of guarding the person of the princeps. Eventually, the praetorian guard would play a weighty role in making and deposing emperors.

The role of the princeps as military commander gave rise to a title by which this ruler eventually came to be known. When victorious, a military commander was acclaimed by his troops as imperator. Augustus was so acclaimed on a number of occasions. Imperator is our word emperor. Although this title was applied to Augustus and his successors, Augustus himself preferred to use the title of princeps.

Augustus inaugurated a new system for governing the provinces. Under the Republic, the senate had appointed the provincial governors. Now, certain provinces were allotted to the princeps, who assigned deputies known as legates to govern them. These legates were from the senatorial class and held office as long as the emperor chose.

The senate continued to name the governors of the remaining provinces, but the authority of Augustus enabled him to overrule the senatorial governors and establish a uniform imperial policy.

Augustus also stabilized the frontiers of the Roman Empire. He conquered the central and maritime Alps and then expanded Roman control of the Balkan peninsula up to the Danube River. His attempt to conquer Germany failed when three Roman legions were massacred in 9 C.E. in the Teutoburg Forest by a coalition of German tribes. The defeat severely dampened Augustus's enthusiasm for continued expansion in central Europe. Thereafter, the Romans were content to use the Rhine as the frontier between the Roman province of Gaul and the German tribes to the east. In fact, Augustus's difficulties had convinced him that "the empire should not be extended beyond its present frontiers."[3] His defeats in Germany taught Augustus that Rome's power was not unlimited.

Augustan Society

Roman society in the Early Empire was characterized by a system of social stratification, inherited from the Republic, in which Roman citizens were divided into three basic classes: the senatorial, equestrian, and lower classes. Although each class had its own functions and opportunities, the system was not completely rigid. There were possibilities for mobility from one group to another.

Augustus had accepted the senatorial order as a ruling class for the empire. Senators filled the chief magistracies of the Roman government, held the most important military posts, and governed the provinces. One needed to possess property worth 1,000,000 sesterces (an unskilled laborer in Rome received 3 sesterces a day; a Roman legionary 900 sesterces a year in pay) to belong to the senatorial order. The equestrian order was expanded under Augustus and given a share of power in the new imperial state. The equestrian order was open to all Roman citizens of good standing who possessed property valued at 400,000 sesterces. They, too, could now hold military and governmental offices, but the positions open to them were less important than those of the senatorial order.

Those citizens not of the senatorial or equestrian orders belonged to the lower classes, who obviously constituted the overwhelming majority of the free citizens. The diminution of the power of the Roman assemblies ended whatever political power they may have possessed earlier in the Republic. Many of these people were provided with free grain and public spectacles to keep them from creating disturbances. Nevertheless, by gaining wealth

◆ **Augustus.** Octavian, Caesar's adopted son, emerged victorious from the civil conflict that rocked the Republic after Caesar's assassination. Augustus operated through a number of legal formalities to ensure that control of the Roman state rested firmly in his hands. This marble statue from Prima Porta depicts the *princeps* Augustus.

and serving as lower officers in the Roman legions, it was sometimes possible for them to advance to the equestrian order.

Augustus's belief that Roman morals had been corrupted during the late Republic led him to initiate social legislation to arrest the decline. He thought that increased luxury had undermined traditional Roman frugality and simplicity and caused a decline in morals, evidenced by easy divorce, a falling birthrate among the upper classes, and lax behavior manifested in hedonistic parties and the love affairs of prominent Romans with fashionable women and elegant boys.

Through his new social legislation, Augustus hoped to restore respectability to the upper classes and reverse the declining birthrate as well. Sumptuary legislation limited expenditures for feasts. Other laws made adultery a criminal offense. In fact, Augustus's own daughter Julia was exiled for adultery. Augustus also revised the tax laws to penalize bachelors, widowers, and married persons who had fewer than three children. The laws were enforced, but there is little evidence that they had much effect.

The Augustan Age was a lengthy one. Augustus died in 14 C.E. after dominating the Roman world for forty-five years. He had created a new order while placating those who yearned for the old by restoring and maintaining traditional values, a fitting combination for a leader whose favorite maxim was "make haste slowly." By the time of his death, his new order was so well established that few agitated for an alternative. Indeed, as the Roman historian Tacitus pointed out, "Actium had been won before the younger men were born. Even most of the older generation had come into a world of civil wars. Practically no one had ever seen truly Republican government. . . . Political equality was a thing of the past; all eyes watched for imperial commands."[4] The Republic was now only a memory and, given its last century of warfare, an unpleasant one at that. The new order was here to stay.

The Early Empire (14–180)

There was no serious opposition to Augustus's choice of his stepson Tiberius as his successor. Nevertheless, the designation of a family member as *princeps* was tantamount to accepting the principle of dynastic rule, hardly appropriate to the image Augustus had tried to create of the *princeps* as only the "first citizen of the state." By his actions, Augustus established the Julio-Claudian dynasty; the next four successors of Augustus were related either to his own family or that of his wife, Livia.

Several major tendencies emerged during the reigns of the Julio-Claudians (14–69 C.E.). In general, more and more of the responsibilities that Augustus had given to the senate tended to be taken over by the emperors, who also instituted an imperial bureaucracy, staffed by talented freedmen, to run the government on a daily basis. As the Julio-Claudian successors of Augustus acted more openly as real rulers rather than as "first citizens of the state," the opportunity for arbitrary and corrupt acts also increased. Nero (54–68) freely eliminated people he wanted out of the way, including his own mother, whom he had murdered. Without troops, the senators proved unable to oppose these excesses. However, Nero's extravagances did provoke a revolt of the Roman legions. Abandoned by his guards, Nero chose to commit suicide by stabbing himself in the throat after uttering his final words, "What an artist the world is losing in me." A new civil war erupted in 69, known as the year of the four emperors (see the box on p. 169). The significance of the year 69 was summed up precisely by Tacitus when he stated that "a well-hidden secret of the principate had been revealed: it was possible, it seemed, for an emperor to be chosen outside Rome."[5]

The Five "Good Emperors" (96–180)

At the beginning of the second century, however, a series of five so-called good emperors created a period of peace and prosperity that lasted for almost one hundred years. These rulers treated the ruling classes with respect, cooperated with the senate, ended arbitrary executions, maintained peace throughout the empire, and supported domestic policies generally beneficial to the empire. Though absolute monarchs, they were known for their tolerance and diplomacy. By adopting capable men as their successors, the first four good emperors reduced the chances of succession problems.

Under the five good emperors, the powers of the emperor continued to be extended at the expense of the senate. Increasingly, imperial officials appointed and directed by the emperor took over the running of the government. The good emperors also extended the scope of imperial administration to include areas previously untouched by the imperial government. Trajan (98–117) implemented the establishment of an alimentary program that provided state funds to assist poor parents in raising and educating their children.

The good emperors were widely praised by their subjects for their extensive building programs. Trajan and Hadrian (117–138) were especially active in constructing public works—aqueducts, bridges, roads, and harbor facilities—throughout the provinces and in Rome. Trajan built a new forum in Rome to provide a setting for his celebrated victory column. Hadrian's Pantheon, a temple of "all the gods," is one of the grandest ancient buildings surviving in Rome.

The Fate of Cremona in the Year of the Four Emperors

After the death of Nero in 68 C.E., a power struggle ensued that resulted in a year of confusion with four different emperors, each the leader of a field army. Galba replaced Nero and was in turn succeeded by Otho who was then defeated by Vitellius. Finally, Vespasian established a new dynasty. Some of the Italian cities suffered greatly in these struggles between Roman legions loyal to their commanders. This excerpt is from Tacitus's account of the destruction of Cremona by the forces that had declared for Vespasian.

Tacitus, The Histories

Forty thousand armed men forced their way into the city. . . . Neither rank nor years saved the victims from an indiscriminate orgy in which rape alternated with murder and murder with rape. Graybeards and frail old women, who had no value as loot, were dragged off to raise a laugh. But any full-grown girl or good-looking lad who crossed their path was pulled this way and that in a violent tug-of-war between the would-be captors, and finally drove them to destroy each other. A single looter trailing a hoard of money or temple-offerings of massive gold was often cut to pieces by others who were stronger. Some few turned up their noses at the obvious finds and inflicted flogging and torture on the owners in order to rummage after hidden valuables and dig for buried treasure. In their hands they held firebrands, which, once they had got their spoil away, they wantonly flung into the empty houses and rifled temples. It is not surprising that, in an army of varied tongues and conventions, including Romans, allies and foreigners [auxiliaries], there was a diversity of wild desires, differing conceptions of what was lawful, and nothing barred. Cremona lasted them four days. While all its buildings, sacred and secular, collapsed in flames, only the temple of Mefitis [goddess of pestilential vapors] outside the walls remained standing, defended by its position or the power of the divinity.

The Roman Empire at Its Height: Frontiers and the Provinces

Although Trajan broke with Augustus's policy of defensive imperialism by extending Roman rule into Dacia (modern Romania), Mesopotamia, and the Sinai peninsula, his conquests represent the high-water mark of Roman expansion. His successors recognized that the empire was overextended and pursued a policy of retrenchment. Hadrian withdrew Roman forces from much of Mesopotamia. Although he retained Dacia and Arabia, he went on the defensive in his frontier policy by reinforcing the fortifications along a line connecting the Rhine and Danube Rivers and building a defensive wall eighty miles long across northern Britain to keep the Scots out of Roman Britain. By the end of the second century, the vulnerability of the empire had become apparent. Frontiers were stabilized, and the Roman forces were established in permanent bases behind the frontiers. But when one frontier was attacked, troops had to be drawn from other frontiers, leaving them vulnerable to attack. The empire lacked a real strategic reserve, and in the next century its weakness would be ever more apparent.

At its height in the second century, the Roman Empire was one of the greatest states the world had seen. It covered about three and a half million square miles and had a population that has been estimated at more than 50 million. While the emperors and the imperial administration provided a degree of unity, considerable leeway was given to local customs, and the privileges of Roman citizenship were extended to many people throughout the empire. In 212, the emperor Caracalla completed the process by giving Roman citizenship to every free inhabitant of the empire. Latin was the language of the western part of the empire while Greek was used in the east. Although Roman culture spread to all parts of the empire, there were limits to romanization since local languages persisted and many of the empire's residents spoke neither Latin nor Greek.

The administration and cultural life of the Roman Empire depended greatly upon cities and towns. A provincial governor's staff was not large, so local city officials were expected to act as Roman agents in carrying out many government functions, especially those related to taxes. Most towns and cities were not large by modern standards. The largest was Rome, but there were also some large cities in the east: Alexandria in Egypt numbered over 300,000 inhabitants, Ephesus in Asia Minor had 200,000, Antioch in Syria around 150,000. In the west, cities were usually small, with only a few thousand inhabitants. Cities were important in the spread of

✖ Map 5.3 The Roman Empire from 14 to 117.

Roman culture, law, and the Latin language. They were also uniform in physical appearance with similar temples, markets, amphitheaters, and other public buildings.

Magistrates and town councillors chosen from the ranks of the wealthy upper classes directed municipal administration. These municipal offices were unsalaried, but were nevertheless desired by wealthy citizens because they received prestige and power at the local level as well as Roman citizenship. Roman municipal policy effectively tied the upper classes to Roman rule and ensured that these classes would retain control over the rest of the population.

The process of romanization in the provinces was reflected in significant changes in the governing classes of the empire. In the course of the first century, there was a noticeable decline in the number of senators from Italian families. By the end of the second century, Italian sena-

tors made up less than 50 percent of the total. Increasingly, the Roman senate was being recruited from wealthy provincial equestrian families. The provinces also provided many of the legionaries for the Roman army and, beginning with Trajan, supplied many of the emperors.

Prosperity in the Early Empire

The Early Empire was a period of considerable prosperity. Internal peace resulted in unprecedented levels of trade. Merchants from all over the empire came to the chief Italian ports of Puteoli on the Bay of Naples and Ostia at the mouth of the Tiber. Trade extended beyond the Roman boundaries and included even silk goods from China. But the patterns of trade were somewhat unbalanced. The importation of large quantities of grain to feed the populace of Rome and an incredible quantity of luxury items for the wealthy upper classes in the west led to a steady drainage of gold and silver coins from Italy and the west to the eastern part of the empire.

Increased trade helped to stimulate manufacturing. The cities of the east still produced the items made in Hellenistic times. The first two centuries of the empire also witnessed the high point of industrial development in Italy. Some industries became concentrated in certain areas, such as bronze work in Capua and pottery in Arretium in Etruria. Other industries, such as brickmaking, were pursued in rural areas as by-products of large landed estates. Much industrial production remained small scale and was done by individual artisans, usually freedmen or slaves. In the course of the first century, Italian centers of industry began to experience increasing competition from the provinces.

Despite the extensive trade and commerce, agriculture remained the chief occupation of most people and the underlying basis of Roman prosperity. While the large landed estates called *latifundia* still dominated agriculture, especially in southern and central Italy, small peasant farms persisted, particularly in Etruria and the Po valley. Although large estates concentrating on sheep and cattle raising used slaves, the lands of some *latifundia* were worked by free tenant farmers who paid rent in labor, produce, or sometimes cash.

In considering the prosperity of the Roman world, it is important to remember the enormous gulf between rich and poor. The development of towns and cities, so important to the creation of any civilization, is based in large degree upon the agricultural surpluses of the countryside. In ancient times, the margin of surplus produced by each farmer was relatively small. Therefore, the upper classes and urban populations had to be supported by the labor of a large number of agricultural producers who never found it easy to produce much more than they needed for themselves. In lean years, when there were no surpluses, the townspeople often took what they wanted, leaving little for the peasants.

Culture and Society in the Roman World

One of the most noticeable characteristics of Roman culture and society is the impact of the Greeks. By the end of the third century B.C.E., Greek civilization played an ever-increasing role in Roman culture. Greek ambassadors, merchants, and artists traveled to Rome and spread Greek thought and practices. After their conquest of the Hellenistic kingdoms, Roman military commanders shipped Greek manuscripts and artworks back to Rome. Multitudes of educated Greek slaves labored in Roman households. Virtually every area of Roman life, from literature and philosophy to religion and education, was affected by Greek models. Rich Romans hired Greek tutors and sent their sons to Athens to study. As the Roman poet Horace said, "captive Greece took captive her rude conqueror." Greek thought captivated the less sophisticated Roman minds, and the Romans became willing transmitters of Greek culture—not, however, without some resistance from Romans who had nothing but contempt for Greek politics and feared that Greek notions would put an end to the old Roman values. Even those who favored Greek culture blamed the Greeks for Rome's new vices, including luxury and homosexual practices.

◆ **The Shipping of Grain.** Trade was an important ingredient in the prosperity of the Early Empire. This tomb painting from Ostia, the port of Rome at the mouth of the Tiber, shows workers loading grain onto the *Isis Giminiana*, a small merchant ship, for shipment upriver to Rome. The captain of the ship stands by the rudder. Next to him is Abascantus, the ship's owner.

Roman Literature

The Romans produced little literature before the third century B.C.E., and the Latin literature that emerged in that century was strongly influenced by Greek models. The demand for plays at public festivals eventually led to a growing number of native playwrights. One of the best known was Plautus (c. 254–184 B.C.E.), who borrowed plots from Greek New Comedy (see Chapter 4) for his own plays. The actors wore Greek costumes and Greek masks and portrayed the same basic stock characters: lecherous old men, clever slaves, prostitutes, and young men in love. Plautus wrote for the masses and became a very popular playwright in Rome.

In the last century of the Republic, the Romans began to produce a new poetry, less dependent on epic themes and more inclined to personal expressions. Latin poets were now able to use various Greek forms to express their own feelings about people, social and political life, and love. The finest example of this can be seen in the work of Catullus (c. 87–54 B.C.E.), the "best lyric poet" Rome produced and one of the greatest in world literature.

Catullus became a master at adapting and refining Greek forms of poetry to express his emotions. He wrote a variety of poems on, among other things, political figures, social customs, the use of language, the death of his brother, and the travails of love. Catullus became infatuated with Clodia, the promiscuous sister of a tribune and wife of a provincial governor, and addressed a number of poems to her (he called her Lesbia), describing his pas-

sionate love and hatred for her (Clodia had many other lovers besides Catullus):

> Lesbia for ever on me rails;
> To talk of me, she never fails.
> Now, hang me, but for all her art
> I find that I have gained her heart.
> My proof is this: I plainly see
> The case is just the same with me;
> I curse her every hour sincerely,
> Yet, hang me, but I love her dearly.[6]

The ability of Catullus to express in simple fashion his intense feelings and curiosity about himself and his world had a noticeable impact on later Latin poets.

The development of Roman prose was greatly aided by the practice of oratory. Romans had great respect for oratory because the ability to persuade people in public debate meant success in politics. Oratory was brought to perfection in a literary fashion by Cicero (106–43 B.C.E.), the best exemplar of the literary and intellectual interests of the senatorial elite of the late Republic and, indeed, the greatest prose writer of that period. For Cicero, oratory was not simply skillful speaking. An orator was a statesman, a man who achieved his highest goal by pursuing an active life in public affairs.

Later, when the turmoil of the late Republic forced him into semiretirement politically, Cicero became more interested in the writing of philosophical treatises. He was not an original thinker, but performed a valuable service for Roman society by popularizing and making understandable the works of Greek philosophers. In his philosophical works, Cicero, more than anyone else, transmitted the classical intellectual heritage to the Western world. Cicero's original contributions came in the field of politics. His works On the Laws and On the Republic provided fresh insights into political thought. His emphasis on the need to pursue an active life to benefit and improve humankind would later greatly influence the Italian Renaissance.

From a cultural point of view, the late Republic is closely linked to the Augustan Age. Some of the great literary talents of the Augustan Age matured during the final phases of the Republic. Traditionally, Roman aristocrats had provided financial support for artists and poets in order to gain prestige and enhance their own reputations. Augustus continued this tradition. He perceived the publicity value of literature and art and became the most important patron of the arts during his principate. The literary accomplishments of the Augustan Age were such that the period has been called the "golden age" of Latin literature.

◆ **Roman Theater: Rehearsal of a Greek Play.** This mosaic found at Pompeii shows Roman actors preparing to present a Greek play. The seated figure is the chorus master who observes two actors dancing to the music of a pipe.

The most distinguished poet of the Augustan Age was Virgil (70–19 B.C.E.). The son of a small landholder in northern Italy, he proved to be only the first of a series of literary figures in the Augustan Age who welcomed the rule of Augustus. Virgil's masterpiece was the epic poem, the *Aeneid*, clearly meant to rival the work of Homer and fulfill an earlier promise made to Augustus to write a great work in his honor. The connection between Troy and Rome is made explicitly. Aeneas, the son of Anchises of Troy, survives the destruction of Troy and eventually settles in Latium; hence, Roman civilization is linked to Greek history. The character of Aeneas is portrayed in terms that remind us of the ideal Roman—his virtues are duty, piety, and faithfulness. Virgil's overall purpose was to show that Aeneas had fulfilled his mission to establish the Romans in Italy and thereby start Rome on its divine mission to rule the world.

> Let others fashion from bronze more lifelike, breathing
>   images—
> For so they shall—and evoke living faces from marble;
> Others excel as orators, others track with their instruments
> The planets circling in heaven and predict when stars will
>   appear.
> But, Romans, never forget that government is your medium!
> Be this your art:—to practice men in the habit of peace,
> Generosity to the conquered, and firmness against
>   aggressors.[7]

As Virgil expressed it, ruling was Rome's gift.

Another prominent Augustan poet was Horace (65–8 B.C.E.), a friend of Virgil. He was also close to Augustus and had a strong sense of identification with Italy. Horace was a very sophisticated writer whose overriding concern seems to have been to point out to his contemporaries the "follies and vices of his age." In the *Satires*, a medley of poems on a variety of subjects, Horace is revealed as a detached observer of human weaknesses. He directed his attacks against movements, not living people, and took on such subjects as sexual immorality, greed, and job dissatisfaction ("How does it happen, Maecenas, that no man alone is content with his lot?"[8]). Horace mostly laughs at the weaknesses of humankind and calls for forbearance: "Supposing my friend has got liquored and wetted my couch, . . . is he for such a lapse to be deemed less dear as a friend, or because when hungry he snatched up before me a chicken from my side of the dish?"[9] In his final work, the *Epistles*, Horace used another Greek form—the imaginary letter in verse—to provide a portrait of his friends and society and those things he held most dear: a simple life, good friends, and his beloved countryside.

Ovid (43 B.C.E.–18 C.E.) was the last of the great poets of the golden age. He belonged to a youthful, privileged social group in Rome that liked to ridicule old Roman values. In keeping with the spirit of this group, Ovid wrote a series of frivolous love poems known as the *Amores*. Intended to entertain and shock, they achieved their goal. Ovid's most popular work was the *Metamorphoses*, a series of fifteen complex mythological tales involving transformations of shapes, such as the change of chaos into order. A storehouse of mythological information, the *Metamorphoses* inspired many painters, sculptors, and writers, including Shakespeare.

Another of Ovid's works was *The Art of Love*. This was essentially a takeoff on didactic poems. Whereas authors of earlier didactic poems had written guides to farming, hunting, or some such subject, Ovid's work was a handbook on the seduction of women (see the box on p. 174). *The Art of Love* appeared to applaud the loose sexual morals of the Roman upper classes at a time when Augustus was trying to clean up the sexual scene in upper-class Rome. The *princeps* was not pleased. Ovid chose to ignore the wishes of Augustus and paid a price for it. In 8 C.E., he was implicated in a sexual scandal, possibly involving the emperor's daughter Julia, and was banished to a small town on the coast of the Black Sea where he died in exile.

The most famous Latin prose work of the golden age was written by the historian Livy (59 B.C.E.–17 C.E.). Livy's masterpiece was the *History of Rome* from the foundation of the city to 9 B.C.E. Only 35 of the original 142 books have survived, although we do possess brief summaries of the whole work from other authors. Livy perceived history in terms of moral lessons. He stated in the preface that

> The study of history is the best medicine for a sick mind; for in history you have a record of the infinite variety of human experience plainly set out for all to see; and in that record you can find for yourself and your country both examples and warnings: fine things to take as models, base things, rotten through and through, to avoid.[10]

For Livy, human character was the determining factor in history.

Livy's history celebrated Rome's greatness. He included scene upon scene that not only revealed the character of the chief figures but also demonstrated the virtues that had made Rome great. Of course, he had serious weaknesses as a historian. He was not always concerned about the factual accuracy of his myriad stories and was not overly critical of his sources. But he did tell a good story, and his work became the standard history of Rome for a long time.

⇒ Ovid and the Art of Love ⇐

Ovid has been called the last great poet of the Augustan golden age of literature. One of his most famous works was The Art of Love, a guidebook on the seduction of women. Unfortunately for Ovid, the work appeared at a time when Augustus was anxious to improve the morals of the Roman upper class. Augustus considered the poem offensive, and Ovid soon found himself in exile.

Ovid, *The Art of Love*

Now I'll teach you how to captivate and hold the woman of your choice. This is the most important part of all my lessons. Lovers of every land, lend an attentive ear to my discourse; let goodwill warm your hearts, for I am going to fulfill the promises I made you.

First of all, be quite sure that there isn't a woman who cannot be won, and make up your mind that you will win her. Only you must prepare the ground. Sooner would the birds cease their song in the springtime, or the grasshopper be silent in the summer . . . than a woman resist the tender wooing of a youthful lover. . . .

Now the first thing you have to do is to get on good terms with the fair one's maid. She can make things easy for you. Find out whether she is fully in her mistress's confidence, and if she knows all about her secret dissipations. Leave no stone unturned to win her over. Once you have her on your side, the rest is easy. . . .

In the first place, it's best to send her a letter, just to pave the way. In it you should tell her how you dote on her; pay her pretty compliments and say all the nice things lovers always say. . . . Even the gods are moved by the voice of entreaty. And promise, promise, promise. Promises will cost you nothing. Everyone's a millionaire where promises are concerned. . . .

If she refuses your letter and sends it back unread, don't give up; hope for the best and try again. . . .

Don't let your hair stick up in tufts on your head; see that your hair and your beard are decently trimmed. See also that your nails are clean and nicely filed; don't have any hair growing out of your nostrils; take care that your breath is sweet, and don't go about reeking like a billy-goat. All other toilet refinements leave to the women or to perverts. . . .

When you find yourself at a feast where the wine is flowing freely, and where a woman shares the same couch with you, pray to that god whose mysteries are celebrated during the night, that the wine may not overcloud your brain. 'Tis then you may easily hold converse with your mistress in hidden words whereof she will easily divine the meaning. . . .

By subtle flatteries you may be able to steal into her heart, even as the river insensibly overflows the banks which fringe it. Never cease to sing the praises of her face, her hair, her taper fingers and her dainty foot. . . .

Tears, too, are a mighty useful resource in the matter of love. They would melt a diamond. Make a point, therefore, of letting your mistress see your face all wet with tears. Howbeit, if you can't manage to squeeze out any tears—and they won't always flow just when you want them to—put your finger in your eyes.

In the history of Latin literature, the century and a half after Augustus is often labeled the "silver age" to indicate that the literary efforts of the period, while good, were not equal to the high standards of the Augustan "golden age." The popularity of rhetorical training encouraged the use of clever and ornate literary expressions at the expense of original and meaningful content. A good example of this trend can be found in the works of Seneca.

Educated in Rome, Seneca (c. 4 B.C.E.–65 C.E.) became strongly attached to the philosophy of Stoicism. He was a prolific writer, producing nine tragedies, 124 philosophical letters, seven books of *Natural Questions*, and a number of philosophical dialogues. In letters written to a young friend, he expressed the basic tenets of Stoicism: living according to nature, accepting events dispassionately as part of the divine plan, and a universal love for all humanity. Thus, "the first thing philosophy promises us is the feeling of fellowship, of belonging to mankind and being members of a community. . . . Philosophy calls for simple living, not for doing penance, and the simple way of life need not be a crude one."[11] Viewed in retrospect, Seneca displays some glaring inconsistencies. While preaching the virtues of simplicity, he amassed a fortune and was ruthless at times in protecting it. His letters show humanity, benevolence, and fortitude, but his sentiments are often undermined by an attempt to be clever with words.

The greatest historian of the silver age was Tacitus (c. 56–120). His main works included the *Annals* and *Histories*, which presented a narrative account of Roman history from the reign of Tiberius through the assassination of Domitian (14–96). Tacitus believed that history had a moral purpose: "It seems to me a historian's foremost duty to ensure that merit is recorded, and to confront evil deeds and words with the fear of posterity's denunciations."[12] As a member of the senatorial class, Tacitus was disgusted with the abuses of power perpetrated by the emperors. Forced to be silent in the reign of Domitian, he was determined that the "evil deeds" of wicked men would not be forgotten. Many historians believe he went too far in projecting back into his account of the past the evils of his own day. His work *Germania* is especially important as a source of information about the early Germans. But it too is colored by Tacitus's attempt to show the Germans as noble savages in comparison to the decadent Romans.

Art

The Romans were also dependent on the Greeks for artistic inspiration. During the third and second centuries B.C.E., they adopted many features of the Hellenistic style of art. The Romans developed a taste for Greek statues, which they placed not only in public buildings, but in their private houses. Once demand outstripped the supply of original works, reproductions of Greek statues became fashionable. The Romans' own portrait sculpture was characterized by an intense realism that included even unpleasant physical details. Wall paintings and frescoes in the houses of the rich realistically depicted landscapes, portraits, and scenes from mythological stories.

The Romans excelled in architecture, a highly practical art. Although they continued to utilize Greek styles and made use of colonnades, rectangular structures, and post and lintel construction, the Romans were also innovative. They made considerable use of curvilinear forms: the arch, vault, and dome. The Romans were also the first people in antiquity to use concrete on a massive scale. By combining concrete and curvilinear forms, they were able to construct massive buildings—public baths, such as those of Caracalla, and amphitheaters, the most famous of which was the Colosseum in Rome, capable of seating 50,000 spectators. These large buildings were made possible by Roman engineering skills. These same skills were put to use in constructing roads (the Romans built a network of 50,000 miles of roads throughout their empire), aqueducts (in Rome, almost a dozen aqueducts kept a population of one million supplied with water), and bridges.

✦ **Interior of the Colosseum of Rome.** The Colosseum was a large amphitheater constructed under the emperor Vespasian and his son Titus. The amphitheaters in which the gladiatorial contests were held varied in size throughout the empire. The Roman emperors understood that gladiatorial shows and other forms of entertainment helped to divert the poor and destitute from any political unrest.

Roman Law

One of Rome's chief gifts to the Mediterranean world of its day and to succeeding generations was its development of law. The Twelve Tables of 450 B.C.E. were the first codification of Roman law and, although inappropriate for later times, were never officially abrogated and were still memorized by schoolboys in the first century B.C.E. Civil law derived from the Twelve Tables proved inadequate for later Roman needs, however, and gave way to corrections and additions by the praetors. Upon taking office, a praetor issued an edict listing his guidelines for dealing with different kinds of legal cases. The praetors were knowledgeable in law, but they also relied on Roman jurists—amateur legal experts—for advice in preparing their edicts. The interpretations of the jurists, often embodied in the edicts of the praetors, created a body of legal principles.

In 242 B.C.E., the Romans appointed a second praetor who was responsible for suits involving a Roman and a non-Roman as well as between two non-Romans. The Romans found that although some of their rules of law could be used in these cases, special rules were often needed. These rules gave rise to a body of law known as the law of nations, defined by the Romans as "that part of the law which we apply both to ourselves and to foreigners." In the late Republic, the influence of Greek philosophy, primarily Stoicism, led the Romans to develop the idea of the law of nature—or universal divine law

⇒ Cato the Elder on Women ⇐

During the Second Punic War, the Romans enacted the Oppian Law, which limited the amount of gold women could possess and restricted their dress and use of carriages. In 195 B.C.E., an attempt to repeal the law was made, and women demonstrated in the streets on behalf of this effort. According to the Roman historian Livy, the conservative Roman official Cato the Elder spoke against repeal and against the women favoring it. Although the words are probably not Cato's own, they do reflect a traditional male Roman attitude toward women.

Livy, *The History of Rome*

"If each of us, citizens, had determined to assert his rights and dignity as a husband with respect to his own spouse, we should have less trouble with the sex as a whole; as it is, our liberty, destroyed at home by female violence, even here in the Forum is crushed and trodden underfoot, and because we have not kept them individually under control, we dread them collectively. . . . But from no class is there not the greatest danger if you permit them meetings and gatherings and secret consultations. . . .

"Our ancestors permitted no women to conduct even personal business without a guardian to intervene in her behalf; they wished them to be under the control of fathers, brothers, husbands; we (Heaven help us!) allow them now even to interfere in public affairs, yes, and to visit the Forum and our informal and formal sessions. What else are they doing now on the streets and at the corners except urging the bill of the tribunes and voting for the repeal of the law? Give loose rein to their uncontrollable nature and to this untamed creature and expect that they will themselves set bounds to their license; unless you act, this is the least of the things enjoined upon women by custom or law and to which they submit with a feeling of injustice. It is complete liberty or, rather, if we wish to speak the truth, complete license that they desire.

"If they win in this, what will they not attempt? Review all the laws with which your forefathers restrained their license and made them subject to their husbands; even with all these bonds you can scarcely control them. What of this? If you suffer them to seize these bonds one by one and wrench themselves free and finally to be placed on a parity with their husbands, do you think that you will be able to endure them? The moment they begin to be your equals, they will be your superiors. . . .

"Now they publicly address other women's husbands, and, what is more serious, they beg for a law and votes, and from sundry men they get what they ask. In matters affecting yourself, your property, your children, you, Sir, can be importuned; once the law has ceased to set a limit to your wife's expenditures you will never set it yourself. Do not think, citizens, that the situation which existed before the law was passed will ever return. . . ."

derived from right reason. The Romans came to view their law of nations as derived from or identical to this law of nature, thus giving Roman jurists a philosophical justification for systematizing Roman law according to basic principles.

Great progress was made in the study and codification of the law during the Early Empire. The second and early third centuries C.E. witnessed the "classical age of Roman law," a period in which a number of great jurists classified and compiled basic legal principles. Most jurists emphasized the emperor as the source of law: "What has pleased the emperor has the force of law."

The Roman Family

At the heart of the Roman social structure stood the family, headed by the *paterfamilias*—the dominant male. The household also included the wife, sons with their wives and children, unmarried daughters, and slaves. A family was virtually a small state within the state, and the power of the *paterfamilias* was parallel to that of the state magistrates over the citizens. Like the Greeks, Roman males believed that the weakness of the female sex necessitated male guardians (see the box above). The *paterfamilias* exercised that authority; upon his death, sons or nearest male relatives assumed the role of guardians. By the late Republic, however, although the rights of male guardians remained legally in effect, upper-class women found numerous ways to circumvent the power of their guardians.

Fathers arranged the marriages of their daughters, although there are instances of mothers and daughters having influence on the choice. In the Republic, women married "with legal control" passing from father to husband. By the mid-first century B.C.E., the dominant practice had changed to "without legal control," which meant that married daughters officially remained within the father's legal power. Since the fathers of most married women were dead, not being in the "legal control" of a husband entailed independent property rights that forceful women could translate into considerable power within the household and outside it. Traditionally, Roman marriages were intended to be for life, but divorce was introduced in the third century and became relatively easy to obtain since either party could initiate it and no one needed to prove the breakdown of the marriage. Divorce became especially prevalent in the first century B.C.E.—a period of political turmoil—when marriages were used to cement political alliances.

Some parents in upper-class families provided education for their daughters. Some had private tutors and others may have gone to primary schools. But, at the age when boys were entering secondary schools, girls were pushed into marriage. The legal minimum age was twelve, although fourteen was a more common age in practice. Although some Roman doctors warned that pregnancy could be dangerous for young girls, early marriages persisted due to the desire to benefit from the dowries as soon as possible and the reality of early mortality. A good example is Tullia, Cicero's beloved daughter. She was married at sixteen, widowed at twenty-two, remarried one year later, divorced at twenty-eight, remarried at twenty-nine, and divorced at thirty-three. She died at thirty-four, not unusual for females in Roman society.

By the second century C.E., significant changes were occurring in the Roman family. The foundations of the authority of the *paterfamilias* over his family, which had already begun to weaken in the late Republic, were further undermined. The *paterfamilias* no longer had absolute authority over his children; he could no longer sell them into slavery or have them put to death. Moreover, the husband's absolute authority over his wife also disappeared, a trend that had begun in the late Republic. In the Early Empire, the idea of male guardianship continued to weaken significantly, and by the late second century, though guardianships had not been abolished, they had become a formality.

Upper-class Roman women in the Early Empire had considerable freedom and independence. They had acquired the right to own, inherit, and dispose of property. Wives were not segregated from males in the home, but were appreciated as enjoyable company and were at the center of household social life. Upper-class women could attend the races, the theater, and events in the amphitheater, although in the latter two places they were forced to sit in separate female sections. Moreover, ladies of rank were still accompanied by maids and companions when they went out. Some women operated businesses, such as shipping firms. Women could not participate in politics, but the Early Empire saw a number of important women who influenced politics through their husbands, including Livia, the wife of Augustus, Agrippina, the mother of Nero, and Plotina, the wife of Trajan.

Slaves and Their Masters

Although slavery was a common institution throughout the ancient world, no people possessed more slaves or relied so much on slave labor as the Romans eventually did. Before the third century B.C.E., a small Roman farmer might possess one or two slaves who would help farm his few acres and perform domestic chores. These slaves would most likely be from Italy and be regarded as part of the family household. Only the very rich would have large numbers of slaves.

The Roman conquest of the Mediterranean brought a drastic change in the use of slaves. Large numbers of foreign slaves were brought back to Italy. During the Republic, Rome's wars were the chief source of slaves, followed by piracy; the children of slaves also became slaves. While some Roman generals brought back slaves to be sold to benefit the public treasury, ambitious generals of the first century, such as Pompey and Caesar, made

◆ **A Roman Lady.** Roman women, especially those of the upper class, developed comparatively more freedom than women in classical Athens despite the persistent male belief that women required guardianship. This mural decoration was found in the remains of a villa destroyed by the eruption of Mount Vesuvius.

The lowest stratum of the Roman population consisted of slaves. They were used extensively in households, at the court, as artisans in industrial enterprises, as business managers, and in numerous other ways. Although some historians have argued that slaves were treated more humanely during the Early Empire, these selections by the Roman historian Tacitus and the Roman statesman Pliny indicate that slaves still rebelled against their masters because of mistreatment. Many masters continued to live in fear of their slaves as witnessed by the saying, "As many enemies as you have slaves."

Tacitus, *The Annals of Imperial Rome*

Soon afterwards the City Prefect, Lucius Pedanius Secundus, was murdered by one of his slaves [61 C.E.]. Either Pedanius had refused to free the murderer after agreeing to a price, or the slave, in a homosexual infatuation, found competition from his master intolerable. After the murder, ancient custom required that every slave residing under the same roof must be executed. But a crowd gathered, eager to save so many innocent lives; and rioting began. The senate-house was besieged. Inside, there was feeling against excessive severity, but the majority opposed any change. Among the latter was Gaius Cassius Longinus, who when his turn came spoke as follows. . . .

'An ex-consul has been deliberately murdered by a slave in his own home. None of his fellow-slaves prevented or betrayed the murderer, though the senatorial decree threatening the whole household with execution still stands. Exempt them from the penalty if you like. But then, if the City Prefect was not important enough to be immune, who will be? Who will have enough slaves to protect him if Pedanius' four hundred were too few? Who can rely on his household's help if even fear for their own lives does not make them shield us?'

[The sentence of death was carried out.]

Pliny the Younger to Acilius

This horrible affair demands more publicity than a letter—Larcius Macedo, a senator and ex-praetor, has fallen a victim to his own slaves. Admittedly he was a cruel and overbearing master, too ready to forget that his father had been a slave, or perhaps too keenly conscious of it. He was taking a bath in his house at Formiae when suddenly he found himself surrounded; one slave seized him by the throat while the others struck his face and hit him in the chest and stomach and—shocking to say—in his private parts. When they thought he was dead they threw him onto the hot pavement, to make sure he was not still alive. Whether unconscious or feigning to be so, he lay there motionless, thus making them believe that he was quite dead. Only then was he carried out, as if he had fainted with the heat, and received by his slaves who had remained faithful, while his concubines ran up, screaming frantically. Roused by their cries and revived by the cooler air he opened his eyes and made some movement to show that he was alive, it being now safe to do so. The guilty slaves fled, but most of them have been arrested and a search is being made for the others. Macedo was brought back to life with difficulty, but only for a few days; at least he died with the satisfaction of having revenged himself, for he lived to see the same punishment meted out as for murder. There you see the dangers, outrages, and insults to which we are exposed. No master can feel safe because he is kind and considerate; for it is their brutality, not their reasoning capacity, which leads slaves to murder masters.

---

personal fortunes by treating slaves captured by their armies as their own private property.

The Romans used slaves in many ways. The rich, of course, owned the most and the best. In the late Republic, it became a badge of prestige to be attended by many slaves. Greeks were in much demand as household slaves where they served as tutors, musicians, doctors, and artists. Many slaves of all nationalities were used as menial household workers, such as cooks, valets, waiters, cleaners, and gardeners. Roman businessmen would employ slaves as shop assistants or artisans. Slaves were also used as farm laborers; in fact, huge gangs of slaves worked the large landed estates under pitiful conditions. Cato the Elder argued that it was cheaper to work slaves to death and then replace them than to treat them favorably. In addition, the roads, aqueducts, and public buildings were constructed by contractors utilizing slave labor. The total number of slaves is difficult to judge—estimates range from two to four free men to every slave.

It is also difficult to generalize about the treatment of Roman slaves. There are numerous instances of humane treatment by masters and situations where slaves even protected their owners from danger out of gratitude and esteem. But there are also examples of slaves murdering their owners, causing some Romans to live in unspoken fear of their slaves (see the box on p. 178). Slaves were also subject to severe punishments, torture, abuse, and hard labor that drove some to run away or even revolt against their owners. The Romans had stringent laws against aiding a runaway slave. The murder of a master by a slave might mean the execution of all the other household slaves. Near the end of the second century B.C.E., large-scale slave revolts occurred in Sicily where enormous gangs of slaves were subjected to horrible working conditions on large landed estates. Slaves were branded, beaten, fed inadequately, worked in chains, and housed at night in underground prisons. It took three years (from 135 to 132 B.C.E.) to crush a revolt of 70,000 slaves, and the great revolt on Sicily (104–101 B.C.E.) involved most of the island and took a Roman army of 17,000 men to suppress it. The most famous revolt on the Italian peninsula occurred in 73 B.C.E. Led by a Thracian gladiator named Spartacus, the revolt broke out in southern Italy and involved 70,000 slaves. Spartacus managed to defeat several Roman armies before he was finally trapped and killed in southern Italy in 71 B.C.E. Six thousand of his followers were crucified, the traditional form of execution for slaves.

The number of slaves probably peaked in the Early Empire. The defensive imperial policies pursued after Augustus led to a decline in the supply of slaves from foreign conquest. Manumission also contributed to the decline in the number of slaves. It had been customary in Rome for "good masters" to free their slaves, especially well-educated ones or good workers. While freedmen became Roman citizens, they were not given full rights of citizenship. They could vote but not run for office.

Imperial Rome

At the center of the colossal Roman Empire was the ancient city of Rome. Truly a capital city, Rome had the largest population of any city in the empire. It is estimated that its population was close to one million by the time of Augustus. For anyone with ambitions, Rome was the place to be. A magnet to many people, Rome was extremely cosmopolitan. Nationalities from all over the empire resided there with entire sections inhabited by specific groups, such as Greeks and Syrians.

Rome was, no doubt, an overcrowded and noisy city. Because of the congestion, cart and wagon traffic was banned from the streets during the day. The noise from the resulting vehicular movement at night often made

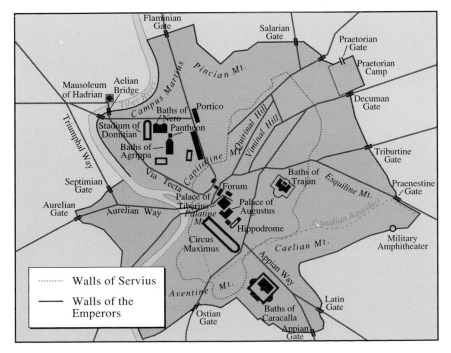

✖ **Map 5.4** Imperial Rome.

≈ The Public Baths of the Roman Empire ≈

The public baths in Rome and other cities played an important role in urban life. Introduced to Rome in the second century B.C.E. as a result of Greek influence, the number of public baths grew at a rapid pace in the Early Empire as the emperors contributed funds for their construction. The public baths were especially noisy near the end of the afternoon when Romans stopped in after work to use the baths before dinner. The following description is by Lucian, a traveling lecturer who lived in the second century and wrote satirical dialogues in Greek. This selection is taken from Hippias, or the Bath.

Lucian, *Hippias, or the Bath*

The building suits the magnitude of the site, accords well with the accepted idea of such an establishment, and shows regard for the principles of lighting. The entrance is high, with a flight of broad steps of which the tread is greater than the pitch, to make them easy to ascend. On entering, one is received into a public hall of good size, with ample accommodations for servants and attendants. On the left are the lounging rooms, also of just the right sort for a bath, attractive, brightly lighted retreats. Then, besides them, a hall, larger than need be for the purposes of a bath, but necessary for the reception of richer persons. Next, capacious locker rooms to undress in, on each side, with a very high and bril-liantly lighted hall between them, in which are three swimming pools of cold water; it is finished in Laconian marble, and has two statues of white marble in the ancient style. . . .

On leaving this hall, you come into another which is slightly warmed instead of meeting you at once with fierce heat; it is oblong, and has an apse on each side. Next to it, on the right, is a very bright hall, nicely fitted up for massage. . . . Then near this is another hall, the most beautiful in the world, in which one can stand or sit with comfort, linger without danger, and stroll about with profit. It also is refulgent with Phrygian marble clear to the roof. Next comes the hot corridor, faced with Numidian marble. The hall beyond it is very beautiful, full of abundant light and aglow with color like that of purple hangings. It contains three hot tubs.

When you have bathed, you need not go back through the same rooms, but can go directly to the cold room through a slightly warmed chamber. Everywhere there is copious illumination and full indoor daylight. . . . Why should I go on to tell you of the exercising floor and of the cloak rooms? . . . Moreover, it is beautiful with all other marks of thoughtfulness—with two toilets, many exits, and two devices for telling time, a water clock that makes a bellowing sound and a sundial.

---

sleep difficult. Evening pedestrian travel was dangerous. Although Augustus had organized a police force, lone travelers might be assaulted, robbed, or soaked by filth thrown out of the upper-story windows of Rome's massive apartment buildings.

An enormous gulf existed between rich and poor in the city of Rome. While the rich had comfortable villas, the poor lived in apartment blocks called *insulae*, which might be six stories high. Constructed of concrete, they were often poorly built and not infrequently collapsed. The use of wooden beams in the floors and movable stoves, torches, candles, and lamps within the rooms for heat and light made the danger of fire a constant companion. Once started, fires were extremely difficult to put out. The famous conflagration of 64, which Nero was unjustly accused of starting, devastated a good part of the city. Besides the hazards of collapse and fire, living conditions were also poor. High rents forced entire families into one room. The absence of plumbing, central heating, and open fireplaces made life so uncomfortable that poorer Romans spent most of their time outdoors in the streets.

Fortunately for these people, Rome boasted public buildings unequaled anywhere in the empire. Its temples, fora, markets, baths, theaters, triumphal arches, governmental buildings, and amphitheaters gave parts of the city an appearance of grandeur and magnificence (see the box above).

Though the center of a great empire, Rome was also a great parasite. Beginning with Augustus, the emperors accepted responsibility for providing food for the urban populace, with about 200,000 people receiving free grain. Even with the free grain, conditions were grim for the poor. Early in the second century C.E., a Roman doctor claimed that rickets was common among children in the city.

In addition to food, entertainment was provided on a grand scale for the inhabitants of Rome. The poet Juvenal said of the Roman masses: "But nowadays, with no vote to sell, their motto is 'Couldn't care less.' Time was when their plebiscite elected generals, heads of state, commanders of legions: but now they've pulled in their horns, there's only two things that concern them: Bread and Circuses."[13] Public spectacles were provided by the emperor and other state officials as part of the great festivals—most of them religious in origin—celebrated by the state. Over one hundred days a year were given over to these public holidays. The festivals included three major types of entertainment. At the Circus Maximus, horse and chariot races attracted hundreds of thousands, while dramatic and other performances were held in theaters. But the most famous of all the public spectacles were the gladiatorial shows.

The Gladiatorial Shows

The gladiatorial shows were an integral part of Roman society. They took place in amphitheaters, with the first permanent one having been constructed at Rome in 29 B.C.E. Perhaps the most famous was the Flavian amphitheater, called the Colosseum, constructed at Rome to seat 50,000 spectators. Amphitheaters were not limited to the city of Rome but were constructed throughout the empire. They varied greatly in size with capacities ranging from a few thousand to tens of thousands. Considerable resources and ingenuity went into building them, especially in the arrangements for moving wild beasts efficiently into the arena. In most cities and towns, amphitheaters came to be the biggest buildings, rivaled only by the circuses for races and the public baths. Where a society invests its money gives an idea of its priorities. Since the amphitheater was the primary location for the gladiatorial games, it is fair to say that public slaughter was an important part of Roman culture.

Gladiatorial games were held from dawn to dusk. Contests to the death between trained fighters formed the central focus of these games. Most gladiators were slaves or condemned criminals, although some free men lured by the hope of popularity and patronage by wealthy fans participated voluntarily. They were trained for combat in special gladiatorial schools.

Gladiatorial games included other forms of entertainment as well. Criminals of all ages and both sexes were sent into the arena without weapons to face certain death from wild animals who would tear them to pieces. Numerous kinds of animal contests were also staged: wild beasts against each other, such as bears against buffalo; staged hunts with men shooting safely from behind iron bars; and gladiators in the arena with bulls, tigers, and lions. Reportedly, five thousand beasts were killed in one

◆ **The Gladiatorial Games.**   Although some gladiators were free men enticed by the possibility of rewards, most were condemned criminals, slaves, or prisoners of war who were trained in special schools. A great gladiator could win his freedom through the games. The more bizarre an event, the more popular it was with the spectators. The fresco pictured here shows a captured tribesman exposed to a wild beast while gladiators are fighting with animals.

❧ Christian Ideals: The Sermon on the Mount ❧

Christianity was simply one of many religions competing for attention in the Roman Empire during the first and second centuries. The rise of Christianity marked a fundamental break with the value system of the upper-class elites who dominated the world of classical antiquity. As these excerpts from the Sermon on the Mount in the Gospel of Saint Matthew illustrate, Christians emphasized humility, charity, brotherly love, and a belief in the inner being and a spiritual kingdom superior to this material world. These values and principles were not those of classical Greco-Roman civilization as exemplified in the words and deeds of its leaders.

The Gospel according to Saint Matthew

Now when he saw the crowds, he went up on a mountainside and sat down. His disciples came to him, and he began to teach them, saying:

Blessed are the poor in spirit: for theirs is the kingdom of heaven.
Blessed are those who mourn: for they will be comforted.
Blessed are the meek: for they will inherit the earth.
Blessed are those who hunger and thirst for righteousness: for they will be filled.
Blessed are the merciful: for they will be shown mercy.
Blessed are the pure in heart: for they will see God.
Blessed are the peacemakers: for they will be called sons of God.
Blessed are those who are persecuted because of righteousness: for theirs is the kingdom of heaven. . . .

You have heard that it was said, 'Eye for eye, and tooth for tooth.' But I tell you, Do not resist an evil person. If someone strikes you on the right cheek, turn to him the other also. . . .

You have heard that it was said, 'Love your neighbor, and hate your enemy.' But I tell you, Love your enemies and pray for those who persecute you. . . .

Do not store up for yourselves treasures on earth, where moth and rust destroy, and where thieves break in and steal. But store up for yourselves treasures in heaven, where moth and rust do not destroy, and where thieves do not break in and steal. For where your treasure is, there your heart will be also. . . .

No one can serve two masters. Either he will hate the one and love the other, or he will be devoted to the one and despise the other. You cannot serve both God and Money.

Therefore I tell you, do not worry about your life, what you will eat or drink; or about your body, what you will wear. Is not life more important than food, and the body more important than clothes? Look at the birds of the air; they do not sow or reap or store away in barns, and yet your heavenly Father feeds them. Are you not much more valuable than they? . . . So do not worry, saying, What shall we eat? or What shall we drink? or What shall we wear? For the pagans run after all these things, and your heavenly Father knows that you need them. But seek first his kingdom and his righteousness, and all these things will be given to you as well.

ethical concepts—humility, charity, and brotherly love—that would form the basis for the value system of medieval Western civilization.

Although some people welcomed Jesus as the Messiah who would save Israel from oppression and establish God's kingdom on earth, Jesus spoke of a heavenly kingdom, not an earthly one: "My kingdom is not of this world."[19] Consequently, he disappointed the radicals. On the other hand, conservative religious leaders believed Jesus was undermining respect for traditional Jewish religion. To the Roman authorities of Palestine and their local allies, the Nazarene was a potential revolutionary who might transform Jewish expectations of a messianic kingdom into a revolt against Rome. Therefore, Jesus found himself denounced on many sides and was given over to the Roman authorities. The procurator Pontius Pilate ordered his crucifixion. But that did not solve the problem. A few loyal followers of Jesus spread the story that Jesus had overcome death and had been resurrected. He was then labeled *Christos* ("the anointed one") and hailed as the Messiah who would return and usher in the kingdom of God on earth.

Christianity began, then, as a religious movement within Judaism and was viewed that way by Roman authorities for many decades. Although tradition holds that one of Christ's disciples, Peter, founded the Christian church at Rome, the most important figure in early Christianity after Christ was Paul of Tarsus (c. 5–c. 67). Paul reached out to non-Jews and transformed Christianity from a Jewish sect into a world religion.

Called the "second founder of Christianity," Paul was a Jewish Roman citizen who had been strongly influenced by Hellenistic Greek culture. He believed that the message of Christ should be preached not only to Jews but to Gentiles (non-Jews) as well. Paul was responsible for founding Christian communities throughout Asia Minor and along the shores of the Aegean.

Paul provided a universal foundation for the spread of Christ's ideas. He taught that Christ was, in effect, a savior-god, the son of God, who had come to earth to save all humans who were basically sinners as a result of Adam's original sin of disobedience against God. By his death, Christ had atoned for the sins of all humans and made possible a new beginning for all men and women, with the potential for individual salvation. By accepting Christ as their savior, they too could be saved.

At first, Christianity spread slowly. Although it was disseminated mostly by the preaching of convinced Christians, written materials also appeared. Among them were series of letters or epistles written by Paul outlining Christian beliefs for different Christian communities. Some of Christ's disciples may also have preserved some of the sayings of the master in writing and would have passed on personal memories that became the basis of the written gospels—the "good news" concerning Christ—which attempted to give a record of Christ's life and teachings and formed the core of the New Testament. Although Jerusalem was the first center of Christianity, its destruction by the Romans in 70 C.E. dispersed the Christians and left individual Christian churches with considerable independence. By 100, Christian churches had been established in most of the major cities of the east and in some places in the western part of the empire. Many early Christians came from the ranks of Hellenized Jews and the Greek-speaking populations of the east. But in the second and third centuries, an increasing number of followers came from Latin-speaking people. A Latin translation of the Greek New Testament that appeared soon after 200 aided this process.

Although some of the fundamental values of Christianity differed markedly from those of the Greco-Roman world, the Romans initially did not pay much attention to the Christians, whom they regarded at first as simply another sect of Judaism. The structure of the Roman Empire itself aided the growth of Christianity. Christian missionaries, including some of Christ's original twelve disciples or apostles, used Roman roads to travel throughout the empire spreading their "good news."

As time passed, however, the Roman attitude toward Christianity began to change. The Romans were tolerant of other religions except when they threatened public order or public morals. Many Romans came to view Christians as harmful to the order of the Roman state. Since Christians held their meetings in secret and seemed to be connected to Christian groups in other areas, the government could view them as potentially dangerous to the state.

Some Romans felt that Christians were overly exclusive and hence harmful to the community and public order. The refusal of Christians to recognize other gods meant that they abstained from public festivals that honored these divinities. Finally, Christians refused to participate in the worship of the state gods and imperial cult. Since the Romans regarded these as important to the state, the Christians' refusal undermined the security of the state and hence constituted an act of treason, punishable by death. But to the Christians, who believed there was only one real god, the worship of state gods and the emperors was idolatry and would endanger their own salvation.

Nevertheless, Roman persecution of Christians in the first and second centuries was only sporadic and local, never systematic. Persecution began during the reign of Nero. After the fire that destroyed much of Rome, the emperor used the Christians as scapegoats, accusing them of arson and hatred of the human race and subjecting them to cruel deaths in Rome. In the second century, Christians were largely ignored as harmless. By the end of the reigns of the five good emperors, Christians still represented a small minority, but one of considerable strength.

The Decline and Fall of the Roman Empire

In the course of the third century, the Roman Empire came near to collapse. Military monarchy under the Severan rulers (193–235), which restored order after a series of civil wars, was followed by military anarchy. For a period of almost fifty years, from 235 to 284, the Roman Empire was mired in the chaos of continual civil war. The imperial throne was occupied by anyone who had the military strength to seize it. In these almost fifty years, there were twenty-two emperors, only two of whom did not meet a violent death. At the same time, the empire was beset by a series of invasions, no doubt exacerbated by the civil wars. In the east, the Sassanid Persians made inroads into Roman territory. Germanic tribes also poured into the empire. The Goths overran the Balkans and moved into Greece and Asia Minor. The Franks advanced into Gaul and Spain. Not until the reign of Aurelian (270–275) were most of the boundaries restored.

Invasions, civil wars, and plague came close to causing an economic collapse of the Roman Empire in the third century. The population declined drastically, possibly by as much as one-third. There was a noticeable decline in trade and small industry. The labor shortage created by the plague affected both military recruiting and the economy. Farm production deteriorated significantly. Fields were ravaged by Germanic tribes, but even more often by the defending Roman armies. Provincial governors seemed powerless to stop these depredations, and some even joined in the extortion. The monetary system began to show signs of collapse as a result of debased coinage and the beginnings of serious inflation.

Armies were needed more than ever, but financial strains made it difficult to pay and enlist the necessary soldiers. Whereas in the second century the Roman army had been recruited among the inhabitants of frontier provinces, by the mid-third century, the state had to rely on hiring Germans to fight under Roman commanders. These soldiers had no understanding of Roman traditions and no real attachment to either the empire or the emperors.

The Reforms of Diocletian and Constantine

At the end of the third and beginning of the fourth centuries, the Roman Empire gained a new lease on life through the efforts of two strong emperors, Diocletian and Constantine, who restored order and stability. The Roman Empire was virtually transformed into a new state: the so-called Late Empire, which included a new governmental structure, a rigid economic and social system, and a new state religion—Christianity.

Believing that the empire had grown too large for a single ruler, Diocletian (284–305) divided it into four administrative units. Despite the appearance of four-man rule, however, Diocletian's military seniority enabled him to claim a higher status and hold the ultimate authority. Constantine (306–337) continued and even expanded the autocratic policies of Diocletian. Both rulers greatly strengthened and enlarged the administrative bureaucracies of the Roman Empire. Henceforth, civil and

military bureaucracies were sharply separated. Each contained a hierarchy of officials who exercised control at the various levels. The emperor presided over both hierarchies of officials and served as the only link between them. New titles of nobility—such as *illustres* ("illustrious ones") and *illustrissimi* ("the most illustrious ones")—were instituted to dignify the holders of positions in the civil and military bureaucracies.

Additional military reforms were also inaugurated. The army was enlarged to 500,000 men, including German units. Mobile units were established that could be quickly moved to support frontier troops where the borders were threatened.

Constantine's biggest project was the construction of a new capital city in the east on the site of the Greek city of Byzantium on the shores of the Bosporus. Eventually renamed Constantinople (modern Istanbul), it was developed for defensive reasons: it had an excellent strategic location. Calling it his "New Rome," Constantine endowed the city with a forum, large palaces, and a vast amphitheater.

The political and military reforms of Diocletian and Constantine greatly enlarged two institutions—the army and civil service—that drained most of the public funds. Though more revenues were needed to pay for the army and bureaucracy, the population was not growing, so the tax base could not be expanded. Diocletian and Constantine devised new economic and social policies to deal with these financial burdens, but like their political policies, these measures were all based on coercion and loss of individual freedom. To fight inflation, Diocletian resorted to issuing a price edict in 301 that established maximum wages and prices for the entire empire, but despite severe penalties, it was unenforceable and failed to work.

Coercion also came to form the underlying basis for numerous occupations in the Late Roman Empire. In order to ensure the tax base and keep the empire going despite the shortage of labor, the emperors issued edicts that forced people to remain in their designated vocations. Hence, basic jobs, such as bakers and shippers, became hereditary. Free tenant farmers continued to decline and soon found themselves bound to the land by large landowners who took advantage of depressed agricultural conditions to enlarge their landed estates.

In general, the economic and social policies of Diocletian and Constantine were based on an unprecedented degree of control and coercion. Though temporarily successful, such authoritarian policies in the long run stifled the very vitality the Late Empire needed to revive its sagging fortunes.

✖ **Map 5.5**   Divisions of the Restored Roman Empire.

The Triumph of Christianity

The Romans' sporadic persecution of Christians in the first and second centuries had done nothing to stop the growth of Christianity. It had, in fact, served to strengthen Christianity as an institution in the second and third centuries by causing it to shed the loose structure of the first century and move toward a more centralized organization of its various church communities. Crucial to this change was the emerging role of the bishops, who began to assume more control over church communities. The Christian church was creating a well-defined hierarchical structure in which the bishops and clergy were salaried officers separate from the laity or regular church members.

Christianity grew slowly in the first century, took root in the second, and by the third had spread widely. Why was Christianity able to attract so many followers? Certainly, the Christian message had much to offer the Roman world. The promise of salvation, made possible by Christ's death and resurrection, made a resounding impact on a world full of suffering and injustice. Christianity seemed to imbue life with a meaning and purpose beyond the simple material things of everyday reality. Secondly, Christianity was not entirely unfamiliar. It could be viewed as simply another eastern mystery religion, offering immortality as the result of the sacrificial death of a savior-god. At the same time, it offered advantages that the other mystery religions lacked. Christ had been a human figure, not a mythological one, such as

CHRONOLOGY

◆◆◆◆◆◆◆◆◆◆◆◆◆◆◆◆◆◆◆◆◆◆◆◆◆◆◆◆◆

The Late Empire—Chief Rulers and Events

Military monarchy (Severan dynasty)	193–235
Military anarchy	235–284
Diocletian	284–305
Constantine	306–337
Edict of Milan	313
Theodosius "the Great"	378–395
Visigoths sack Rome	410
Vandals sack Rome	455
Romulus Augustulus is deposed	476

Mithras. Moreover, Christianity had universal appeal. Unlike Mithraism, it was not restricted to men. Furthermore, it did not require a painful or expensive initiation rite as other mystery religions did. Initiation was accomplished simply by baptism—a purification by water—through which one entered into a personal relationship with Christ. In addition, Christianity gave new meaning to life and offered what the Roman state religions could not—a personal relationship with God and connection to higher worlds.

Finally, Christianity fulfilled the human need to belong. Christians formed communities bound to one another in which people could express their love by helping each other and offering assistance to the poor, sick, widows, and orphans. Christianity satisfied the need to belong in a way that the huge, impersonal, and remote Roman Empire could never do.

Christianity proved attractive to all classes. The promise of eternal life was for all—rich, poor, aristocrats, slaves, men, and women. As Paul stated in his Epistle to the Colossians: "And [you] have put on the new self, which is being renewed in knowledge in the image of its Creator. Here there is no Greek nor Jew, circumcised or uncircumcised, barbarian, Scythian, slave or free, but Christ is all, and is in all."[20] Although it did not call for revolution or social upheaval, Christianity emphasized a sense of spiritual equality for all people.

As the Christian church became more organized, some emperors in the third century responded with more systematic persecutions, but their schemes failed to work.

The last great persecution was by Diocletian at the beginning of the fourth century. But even he had to admit what had become apparent in the course of the third century—Christianity had become too strong to be eradicated by force.

In the fourth century, Christianity prospered as never before after the Emperor Constantine became the first Christian emperor. Although he was not baptized until the end of his life, in 313 Constantine issued the famous Edict of Milan officially tolerating the existence of Christianity. Under Theodosius "the Great" (378–395), it was made the official religion of the Roman Empire. Christianity had triumphed.

The Fall of the Western Roman Empire

The restored empire of Diocletian and Constantine limped along for more than a century. After Constantine, the empire continued to divide into western and eastern parts. The west came under increasing pressure from the invading Germanic tribes. The major breakthrough into the Roman Empire came in the second half of the fourth century. Ferocious warriors from Asia, known as Huns, moved into eastern Europe and put pressure on the Germanic Visigoths who in turn moved south and west, crossed the Danube into Roman territory, and settled down as Roman allies. But the Visigoths soon revolted, and the Roman attempt to stop them at Adrianople in 378 led to a crushing defeat.

Increasing numbers of Germans now crossed the frontiers. In 410, the Visigoths sacked Rome. Vandals poured into southern Spain and Africa, Visigoths into Spain and Gaul. The Vandals crossed into Italy from North Africa and sacked Rome in 455. Twenty-one years later, the western emperor Romulus Augustulus (475–476) was deposed, and a series of Germanic kingdoms replaced the Roman Empire in the west while an Eastern Roman Empire continued with its center at Constantinople.

The end of the Roman Empire has given rise to numerous theories that attempt to provide a single, all-encompassing reason for the "decline and fall of the Roman Empire." These include the following: Christianity's emphasis on a spiritual kingdom undermined Roman military virtues and patriotism; traditional Roman values declined as non-Italians gained prominence in the empire; lead poisoning through leaden water pipes and cups caused a mental decline; plague decimated the population; Rome failed to advance technologically because of slavery; and Rome was unable to achieve a workable political system. There may be an element of truth in each of these theories, but each of them has also been challenged. History is an intricate web of relationships, causes, and effects. No single explanation will ever suffice to explain historical events. One thing is clear. Weakened by a shortage of manpower, the Roman army in the west was simply not able to fend off the hordes of people invading Italy and Gaul. In contrast, the Eastern Roman Empire, which would survive for another thousand years, remained largely free of invasion.

Conclusion

In the eighth and seventh centuries B.C.E., the pastoral community of Rome developed into an actual city. Between 509 and 264 B.C.E., the expansion of this city led to the union of almost all of Italy under Rome's control. Even more dramatically, between 264 and 133 B.C.E., Rome expanded to the west and east and became master of the Mediterranean Sea. Ultimately, the Roman Empire was one of the largest empires in antiquity. Rome's republican institutions proved inadequate for the task of ruling an empire, however, and after a series of bloody civil wars, Octavian created a new order that would rule the empire in an orderly fashion. His successors established a Roman imperial state.

Using their practical skills, the Romans made achievements in language, law, engineering, and government that were bequeathed to the future. The Romance languages of today (French, Italian, Spanish, Portuguese, and Romanian) are based on Latin. Western practices of impartial justice and trial by jury owe much to Roman law. As great builders, the Romans left monuments to their skills throughout Europe, some of which, such as aqueducts and roads, are still in use today. Aspects of Roman administrative practices survived in the Western world for centuries. The Romans also preserved the intellectual heritage of the ancient world. While we are justified in praising the empire, it is also important to remember its other side: the enormous gulf between rich and poor, the dependence upon enslaved or otherwise subject human beings, the bloodthirsty spectacles in the amphitheaters, and the use of institutionalized terror to maintain the order for which the empire is so often praised. In its last two hundred years, as Christianity spread, a slow transformation of the Roman world took place. The Germanic invasions greatly accelerated this process, and while many aspects of the Roman world would continue, a new civilization was emerging that would carry on yet another stage in the development of human society.

CHAPTER NOTES

1. Florus, *Epitome of Roman History*, trans. E. S. Forster (Cambridge, Mass., 1961), IV, ii, 149–51.
2. Tacitus, *The Annals of Imperial Rome*, trans. Michael Grant (Harmondsworth, 1956), p. 30.
3. Ibid., p. 37.
4. Ibid., p. 31.
5. Tacitus, *The Histories*, trans. Kenneth Wellesley (Harmondsworth, 1964), p. 23.
6. Michael Grant, ed., *Roman Readings* (Harmondsworth, 1958), p. 86.
7. Virgil, *The Aeneid*, trans. C. Day Lewis (Garden City, N.Y., 1952), p. 154.
8. Horace, *Satires*, in *The Complete Works of Horace*, trans. Lord Dunsany and Michael Oakley (London, 1961), 1.1, p. 139.
9. Ibid., 1.3, p. 151.
10. Livy, *The Early History of Rome*, trans. Aubrey de Selincourt (Harmondsworth, 1960), p. 18.
11. Seneca, *Letters from a Stoic*, trans. Robin Campbell (Harmondsworth, 1969), Letter 5.
12. Tacitus, *The Annals of Imperial Rome*, p. 147.
13. Juvenal, *The Sixteen Satires*, trans. Peter Green (Harmondsworth, 1967), Satire 10, p. 207.
14. Tacitus, *A Dialogue on Oratory*, in *The Complete Works of Tacitus*, trans. Alfred Church and William Brodribb (New York, 1942), 29, p. 758.
15. Quoted in Chester Starr, *Past and Future in Ancient History* (Lanham, Md., 1987), pp. 38–39.
16. Matthew 5: 17.
17. Matthew 7: 12.
18. Mark 12: 30–31.
19. John 18: 36.
20. Colossians 3: 10–11.

SUGGESTED READINGS

For a general account of Roman history, see J. Boardman, J. Griffin, and O. Murray, eds., *The Oxford History of the Classical World* (Oxford, 1986), pp. 384–828. A brief, but excellent guide to recent trends in scholarship can be found in C. Starr, *Past and Future in Ancient History* (Lanham, Md., 1987), pp. 33–57. A standard one-volume reference on the Roman Republic is M. Cary and H. H. Scullard, *A History of Rome Down to the Reign of Constantine*, 3d ed. (New York, 1975). Good surveys of the Roman Republic include M. H. Crawford, *The Roman Republic* (London, 1978); H. H. Scullard, *History of the Roman World, 753–146 B.C.*, 4th ed. (London, 1978); and A. Kamm, *The Romans* (London, 1995). For a beautifully illustrated survey, see J. F. Drinkwater and A. Drummond, *The World of the Romans* (New York, 1993).

Aspects of the Roman political structure can be studied in A. N. Sherwin-White, *The Roman Citizenship*, 2d ed. (Oxford, 1973). Changes in Rome's economic life can be examined in J. H. D'Arms, *Commerce and Social Standing in Ancient Rome* (Cambridge, Mass., 1981). On the Roman social structure, see G. Alfoeldy, *The Social History of Rome* (London, 1985).

General accounts of Rome's expansion in the Mediterranean world are provided by R. M. Errington, *The Dawn of Empire: Rome's Rise to World Power* (Ithaca, N.Y., 1971) and J. Heurgon, *The Rise of Rome to 264 B.C.*, trans. J. Willis (Berkeley, Calif., 1973). Especially important works on Roman expansion and imperialism include W. V. Harris, *War and Imperialism in Republican Rome* (Oxford, 1979) and E. Badian, *Roman Imperialism in the Late Republic* (Oxford, 1968).

An excellent account of basic problems in the late Republic can be found in M. Beard and M. H. Crawford, *Rome in the Late Republic* (London, 1984). The classic work on the fall of the Republic is R. Syme, *The Roman Revolution* (Oxford, 1960). A more recent work is E. S. Gruen, *The Last Generation of the Roman Republic* (Berkeley, Calif., 1974). Also valuable is C. Nicolet, *The World of the Citizen in Republican Rome* (London, 1980).

Good surveys of the early Roman Empire include P. Garnsey and R. Saller, *The Roman Empire: Economy, Society and Culture* (London, 1987); C. Wells, *The Roman Empire* (Stanford, Calif., 1984); and J. Wacher, *The Roman Empire* (London, 1987). A fundamental work on Roman government and the role of the emperor is F. Millar, *The Emperor in the Roman World* (London, 1977).

The Roman army is examined in G. Webster, *The Roman Imperial Army of the First and Second Centuries A.D.*, 2d ed. (London, 1979) and J. B. Campbell, *The Emperor and the Roman Army* (Oxford, 1984). On the provinces and Roman foreign policy, see E. N. Luttwak, *The Grand Strategy of the Roman Empire from the First Century A.D. to the Third* (Baltimore, 1976).

A good survey of Roman literature can be found in R. M. Ogilvie, *Roman Literature and Society* (Harmondsworth, 1980). A brief survey of Roman art can be found in J. M. C. Toynbee, *Art of the Romans* (London and New York, 1965). General studies of daily life in Rome include F. Dupont, *Daily Life in Ancient Rome* (Oxford, 1994) and J. P. V. D. Balsdon, *Life and Leisure in Ancient Rome* (London, 1969). On Roman cities, see J. E. Stambaugh, *The Ancient Roman City* (Baltimore, 1988). Roman women are examined in J. P. V. D. Balsdon, *Roman Women*, rev. ed., (London, 1974); S. Pomeroy, *Goddesses, Whores, Wives, and Slaves: Women in Classical Antiquity* (New York, 1976), pp. 149–226; and J. F. Gardner, *Women in Roman Law and Society* (Bloomington, Ind., 1986). On various aspects of Roman law, see H. F. Jolowicz and B. Nicholas, *Historical Introduction to Roman Law* (Cambridge, 1972). On slavery, see K. R. Bradley, *Slavery and Rebellion in the Roman World* (Bloomington, Ind., 1989).

Roman religion can be examined in J. Liebeschuetz, *Continuity and Change in Roman Religion* (Oxford, 1979). An introduction to the problems relating to the religious history of the imperial period is E. R. Dodds, *Pagan and Christian in an Age of Anxiety* (Cambridge, 1965). Useful works on early Christianity include W. A. Meeks, *The First Urban Christians* (New Haven, Conn., 1983); W. H. C. Frend, *The Rise of Christianity* (Philadelphia, 1984); and R. MacMullen, *Christianizing the Roman Empire* (New Haven, Conn., 1984).

The classic work on the "decline and fall" of the Roman Empire is Edward Gibbon, *Decline and Fall of the*

Roman Empire, J. B. Bury edition (London, 1909–14). An excellent survey is P. Brown, *The World of Late Antiquity* (London, 1971). Also valuable are R. Mac-Mullen, *The Roman Government's Response to Crisis,* A.D. *235–337* (New Haven, Conn., 1976) and *Corruption and the Decline of Rome* (New Haven, Conn., 1988). On the fourth century, see T. D. Barnes, *The New Empire of Diocletian and Constantine* (Cambridge, Mass., 1982) and M. Grant, *Constantine the Great: The Man and His Times* (New York, 1993). Recent studies analyzing the aristocratic circles, the barbarian invasions, and the military problem include E. A. Thompson, *Romans and Barbarians* (Madison, Wis., 1982) and A. Ferrill, *The Fall of the Roman Empire: The Military Explanation* (London, 1986).

The First Civilizations and the Rise of Empires

*I*n Part I of this book, we have focused our attention on the emergence of the first civilizations during the ancient era. As we have seen, each civilization developed somewhat independently of the others, and we have therefore treated them as distinct entities, each with its own pattern of development. But clearly, these civilizations encountered a number of similar experiences, and contacts between the civilizations sometimes played a significant role in their development. Let us now retrace our steps and evaluate the process in a comparative perspective. How and why did these first civilizations arise? What were the effects of their appearance on the human experience? What role did cross-cultural contacts play in their development? What was the nature of the relationship between these sedentary societies and nonagricultural peoples living elsewhere in the world, and how did each influence the other? Finally, what brought about the demise of these early civilizations, and what legacy did they leave for their successors in the region?

How and why the first civilizations arose has long been a matter of debate. In his classic work entitled *The Study of History*, historian Arnold Toynbee explained the origins of social change through the concept of challenge and response. Challenges, posed either by the environment or by actions taken by other peoples, compel human beings to make efforts that sometimes result in technological innovations that help to overcome the challenge. The world historian William McNeill carries the idea further, suggesting that encounters with strangers, especially stronger ones, are the primary factor provoking innovation and thus "the principal drive wheel of historic change."

Such theories are undoubtedly helpful to historians as general explanations for the process of social change, but we need to be more specific if we wish to find an explanation for the rise of the first civilizations. Why did some societies transform themselves into civilizations, while others did not? What factors determined how they responded? Although the answers to such questions are elusive, the evidence from the examples discussed here suggests that an important stimulus behind the rise of all of these early civilizations was the development of settled agriculture, which unleashed a series of changes in the organization of human communities that culminated in the rise of large ancient empires.

The exact time and place that crops were first cultivated successfully is uncertain. Many prehistorians believe that farming may have emerged independently in several different areas of the world when small human communities, driven by increasing population and a decline in available food resources, began to plant seeds in the ground in an effort to guarantee their survival. The first farmers, who may have lived as long as 10,000 years ago, used simple techniques, clearing and burning the underbrush in lightly wooded areas to provide nutrients for their crops. When the soil was exhausted, the community had to move on to a new area and begin the process all over again.

The first phase of the agricultural revolution thus probably had relatively little impact on the nature of human society and organization. Food production was still limited, and most communities that practiced agricultural techniques undoubtedly relied primarily on other forms of food production, such as hunting, foraging, or pastoralism. The real breakthrough took place when farmers began to cultivate crops along the floodplains of river systems. The advantage was that crops grown in such areas were not as dependent upon rainfall and therefore produced a more reliable harvest. An additional benefit was that the sediment carried by the river waters deposited nutrients in the soil, thus enabling the farmer to cultivate a single plot of ground for many years without moving to a new location. Thus, the first truly sedentary societies were born. As time went on, such communities gradually learned how to direct the flow of water to enhance the productive capacity of the land, while the introduction of the iron plow eventually led to the cultivation of heavy soils not previously susceptible to agriculture.

The spread of this river valley agriculture in isolated parts of Asia and Africa was the decisive factor in the rise of the first civilizations. The increase in food production in these regions led to a significant growth in population, while efforts to control the flow of water to maximize the irrigation of cultivated areas and to protect the local inhabitants from hostile forces outside the community provoked the first steps toward cooperative activities on a large scale. The need to oversee the entire process brought about the emergence of an elite that was eventually transformed into a government.

As we have seen, the first clear steps in the rise of the first civilizations occurred in the fourth and third millennia B.C.E. in Mesopotamia, North Africa, India, and China. How the first governments took shape in these areas is not certain, but anthropologists studying the evolution of human communities in various parts of the world have discovered that one common stage in the process is the emergence of what are called "big people" within a single village or a collection of villages. By means of their military prowess, dominant personalities, or political acumen, these people gradually emerge as the leaders of their communities. In time, the "big people" begin to assume formal symbols of authority and to pass on that authority to others within their own family. As the communities continue to grow in size and material wealth, the "big people" become hereditary monarchs, and their allies and family members are transformed into a hereditary monarchy.

The appearance of these sedentary societies had a major impact on the social organizations, religious beliefs, and way of life of the peoples living within their boundaries. With the increase in population and the development of centralized authority came the emergence of cities. While some of these urban centers were identified with a particular economic function, such as proximity to gold or iron deposits or a strategic location on a major trade route, others served primarily as administrative centers or the site of temples for the official cult or other ritual observances. Within these cities, new forms of livelihood appeared to satisfy the growing need for social services and consumer goods. Some people became artisans or merchants while others became warriors, scholars, or priests. The vast majority of the population in these first civilizations, however, were undoubtedly peasants or slaves working on the lands of the wealthy.

Within these civilizations, the nature of social organization also began to change. As the concept of private property spread, people were less likely to live in large kinship groups, and the concept of the nuclear family became increasingly prevalent. Sex roles increasingly came to be differentiated, with men working in the fields or at various specialized occupations and women remaining in the home. Wives were less likely to be viewed as partners and more often as under the control of their husbands.

With the increase in the availability of food, people were now living longer. At the same time, increasingly crowded conditions in the emerging cities led to a higher incidence of disease. Some reached epidemic proportions and wiped out a high percentage of the population. As the danger of illness increased, families began having large numbers of children to protect themselves in their old age. As a result of these countervailing trends, it is estimated that the overall population of the world may have increased by about four times between the beginning of sustained growth in the Sumerian population around 3500 B.C.E. and the end of the second millennium B.C.E.

These new civilizations were also the scene of significant religious and cultural developments. All of them gave birth to new religions as a means of explaining the functioning of the forces of nature. The approval of the gods was deemed critical to a community's chances of success, and a professional class of priests emerged to govern relations with the divine world. Temples were built as places for worship or sacrifice, and painting and sculpture were invented as ritualistic means of portraying the deities or other forces in the natural world.

Writing was an important development in the evolution of these new civilizations. In China and Egypt, priests used it to communicate with the gods. In Mesopotamia and the Indus River civilization, merchants relied on writing to maintain their accounts. Eventually, all of these civilizations used it as a means of creative expression. Other forms of artistic activity included sculpture, painting, and the building of monumental architectural structures.

At first, the authority of these new civilizations was probably restricted to the area immediately adjacent to the river valleys where they had originated, and they had relatively little contact with peoples in the surrounding regions. But there is growing evidence that a pattern of regional trade had begun to develop in the Middle East, and probably in South Asia and East Asia as well, at a very early date. As the population increased, the volume of trade undoubtedly rose with it, and the new civilizations began to move outward to acquire new lands and access to needed resources. As they expanded, they began to encounter peoples along the periphery of their growing empires.

Not much evidence has survived to chronicle the nature of these first encounters, but it is likely that the results varied widely according to time and place. In some cases, the growing civilizations found it relatively easy to absorb isolated communities of agricultural or food-gathering peoples whom they encountered. Such was the case in South China and in the southern part of the

South Asian peninsula. But in other instances, notably among the nomadic or seminomadic peoples in Central and northeastern Asia, the problem was more complicated and often resulted in bitter and extended conflict.

To the sedentary societies, the peoples living along the frontier appeared hostile and warlike, motivated solely by the desire for plunder and lacking in the basic attributes of civilization. Historians, most of whom have lived in civilizations themselves, have generally accepted that assessment. But to the dispassionate observer, the argument is not always wholly on the side of the settled societies. Often peoples living on the periphery of civilizations were residing in areas of marginal economic utility and were forced to seek their livelihood through a mixture of farming, food gathering, and hunting. As the climate throughout much of Central Asia became increasingly dry after the third millennium B.C.E., many of these communities were forced to adapt to changing circumstances by migrating to new areas or by domesticating animals, such as the horse. Some, like the Hyksos, the Hebrews, and the Indo-European peoples, began to live by a combination of farming and herding. Others, like the Scythians and Xiongnu, took up the purely nomadic life. Such communities had not generally emerged into a phase of statehood and operated as a fluid mixture of semiautonomous tribes, each under its own chieftain.

Contacts between these nomadic or seminomadic peoples and settled civilizations probably developed gradually over an extended period of time. Often the relationship, at least at the outset, was mutually beneficial. Nomadic peoples in Central Asia began to carry goods over long distances as early as 3,000 B.C.E. At first, the trade was carried by donkeys, but later the camel became the preferred means of transportation. Overland trade throughout southwestern Asia was already well established by the third and second millennia B.C.E. As we have seen, the silk route between China and the Mediterranean became an important avenue of long-distance commerce during the first millennium B.C.E.

Eventually, for reasons that are not always clear, the relationship between the settled peoples and the nomadic peoples became increasingly characterized by conflict. In some cases, the expanding sedentary empires attempted to drive the nomadic peoples off their land or to deprive them of access to trade with settled populations. In other cases, the increasing desiccation of the land may have deprived the peripheral peoples of their livelihood and forced them into desperate measures to find new means of survival. Sometimes the conflict may simply have been a consequence of the increasing aggressiveness of the nomadic peoples, as better techniques of warfare,

such as the ability to fight on horseback, gave them new advantages over their rivals. Taking advantage of their military superiority, nomadic peoples often raided settled areas, terrorized the inhabitants, and pillaged their belongings.

Where conflict occurred, the governments of the sedentary civilizations used a variety of techniques to resolve the problem, including negotiations, conquest, or alliance with other pastoral peoples to isolate their primary tormentors. We have seen all of these techniques at work in China, where the Qin and the Han tried a variety of the carrot and the stick to pacify the frontier and bring these unruly peoples under control. The Romans did not hesitate to ally with one Germanic tribe to ward off another.

As it turned out, few of these techniques had any lasting effect. The relationship along the frontier was inherently unstable and in the end was disastrous for the settled empires, all of which were eventually destroyed or seriously weakened as the result of invasion from beyond the frontier. The first to experience such a fate was the Harappan civilization in the Indus River valley, which was brought down at least in part as a result of the intrusion by Indo-European Aryan peoples along the northern frontier. Several hundred years later, the peoples of Mesopotamia fell at the hands of the Assyrians, who were, in turn, conquered by the Indo-European–speaking Persians. The empire of the pharaohs was conquered by the Hyksos, while the Roman Empire was brought to its knees as the result of constant pressure from the Germanic tribes to the north. Although the empire of the Han was not overthrown by the Xiongnu, pressure along the northern frontier contributed to the weakening of the dynasty, and after its collapse in the early third century B.C.E., the entire northern part of the country was overrun by peoples from beyond the Great Wall.

The nomadic peoples along the frontier understandably sparked fear among peoples in settled areas of the ancient world, but in broad historical terms, they played an important role in the development of the first civilizations and the later evolution of humankind. Not only were they the crucial link in the growing trade relationship between the Mediterranean, the Middle East, and far-off China, but they were also the means of introducing new technology to sedentary societies. The Assyrians probably introduced the knowledge of iron to the settled peoples of Mesopotamia, while the Hyksos played a similar role in Egypt. The pastoral peoples were the first to domesticate the horse and the camel, both destined ultimately to become useful forms of transportation for settled societies, and probably introduced the chariot to several sedentary civilizations throughout the Eurasian supercontinent. Although their unruly behavior undoubtedly posed a serious threat to settled societies, the nomadic peoples were a vital factor in the creation of the first global civilization in the Old World.

The increasing evidence that nomadic peoples outside the bounds of settled civilization played an important role in spreading technological advances throughout the inhabited world has brought about a significant change in the way historians view the classical empires. Until recently, national pride tended to reinforce the view that each of these civilizations evolved essentially on its own. In the last few years, however, there is a growing recognition that "cultural diffusion," as these exchanges of technology and ideas are labeled, played a major role in the emergence of the classical civilizations.

At the same time, it is also increasingly evident that these early civilizations were brought down not just by nomadic invasions, but by their own weaknesses, which made them increasingly vulnerable to attacks along the frontier. In the Roman Empire, bloated bureaucracies as well as excessive taxation to support them, an inability to achieve a workable political system, evident in frequent military struggles over succession to the throne, the decline of Roman military virtues and a reliance on noncitizen mercenaries, and population decline caused in part by plague all played a role in undermining Rome's ability to protect itself. In China, growing internal strains within the Han society, more than depredations along the frontier, caused the collapse of the Han Empire.

Another possible factor in the decline and collapse of the first civilizations was the role of the environment. Although proof is still lacking, much evidence suggests that ecological changes caused severe difficulties for peoples in the ancient world. Floods or drought may have brought an end to the Harappan empire, while the infes-tation of salt water may have leached the nutrients from the soils of the Fertile Crescent. Imperial Rome may have suffered food shortages as a result of the desiccation of the wheat fields of North Africa, while the flooding of mines in Spain may have brought about a shortage of silver and the debased coinage of the empire.

The fall of the ancient empires, of course, did not mark the end of civilization. Although the immediate consequences of the fall of Rome and the Han dynasty were a precipitous drop in world trade and a general decline in prosperity throughout the known world, new societies eventually rose on the ashes of the ancient empires. Although many were different in key respects from those they replaced, they still carried the legacy of their predecessors. In the meantime, the forces that had been unleashed in the civilizations of antiquity sent out strands of influence that were laying the basis for new societies elsewhere in the world: south of the Sahara in West and East Africa, where new societies were beginning to take shape; beyond the Alps in central Europe, where the Germanic peoples were in the process of forming a new society; in Southeast Asia, where the influence of India and China was beginning to help shape new societies among the trading and agricultural societies in the region; and across the Sea of Japan in the Japanese Islands, where native rulers would import Chinese ideas to form a new civilization uniquely their own. In the meantime, new civilizations were on the verge of creation in the New World, across the oceans in the continents of North and South America. Isolated from contact with the Old World since their migration across the Bering Strait at the end of the Ice Age, the peoples of America were beginning to form civilizations of their own. It is to this new stage of human development, marked by a broadening of global contacts, that we will turn in Part II of this book.

PART

II

New Patterns of Civilization

*I*n Part I of this book, we discussed the emergence of the great civilizations of antiquity. Based primarily in the great river valleys from North Africa and the Middle East to India and China and then spreading to the shores of the Mediterranean, these early civilizations realized great achievements, not only in building sound political and economic institutions, but also in the realm of religion and culture. But by the beginning of the first millennium C.E., these early states were mostly in a state of decline. Some were even at the point of collapse. One factor in that decline was invasion by nomadic peoples from beyond their borders, but another was internal decay.

On the ruins of these ancient empires, new patterns of civilization began to take shape between 400 and 1500 C.E. In some cases, these new societies were built on the political and cultural foundations of their predecessors. The Tang dynasty in China and the Guptas in India both looked back to the ancient period to find an ideological model for their own time. The Byzantine Empire carried on aspects of the classical Greek tradition while also adopting the powerful creed of Christianity from the Roman Empire. In other cases, new states incorporated some elements of the former classical civilizations while embarking in markedly different directions, as in the new European civilization of the Middle Ages and the Arabic societies of the Middle East.

In the meantime, complex societies were also beginning to appear in a number of other parts of the world—in Japan, in Southeast Asia, in sub-Saharan Africa, and across the Atlantic in the Americas. Except for the latter, which were developing in isolation, all of these civilizations were influenced to a greater or lesser degree by older or more powerful empires in the region, and all were increasingly linked by commercial and cultural contacts into what some world historians are beginning to call the first "global civilization." At the same time, each was able to supplement borrowed ideas with indigenous characteristics.

300 C.E.	400 C.E.	500 C.E.	600 C.E.	700 C.E.	800 C.E.	900 C.E.

INDIA AND THE MIDDLE EAST

Gupta dynasty in India

Foundation of
Abbasid caliphate

Arrival of Islam

Life of Muhammad

AFRICA

Conquest of Kush by Axum

Spread of Islam across North Africa

First states appear in West Africa

Arab takeover of lower Nile valley

EAST AND SOUTHEAST ASIA

Rise of Yamato state in Japan

Golden Age of the Silk Road

Rise of kingdom of Angkor

Tang dynasty in China

AMERICAS

Teotihuacán civilization

Moche culture in South America

Decline of the Mayas

EUROPE

The Germanic kingdoms

Charlemagne and the Carolingian Empire

Growth of feudalism

Like their classical predecessors, most of these new states obtained much of their wealth from agriculture. India, China, and medieval Europe were all predominantly agricultural societies. But what is most striking about the period is the growing importance of trade as a factor in national and global development. It was during the first millennium C.E. that the great trade routes of the traditional world—the Silk Road from China to the Middle East and then on to the Mediterranean, the caravan trade across the Sahara, and the commercial network that stretched across the Indian Ocean—all reached their maturity. Commercial links probably also existed among the various societies in the Americas.

What accounts for this surge in commercial activity? Certainly, technology is one answer. The technological revolution resulted in a vast increase in the variety and amount of goods available to buy and sell. By helping to increase agricultural production, it also created wealth that is an essential part of commercial transactions. It also contributed to improvements in transportation in such areas as ship construction in northern India

Conquest of Baghdad
by the Mongols

Ottoman Turks
seize Constantinople

Portuguese ships explore
West African coast

Kingdom of Zimbabwe

Spread of Mongols across East Asia

Beginning of Ming dynasty in China

Civilization of Chimor

Kingdom of the Aztecs

Rise of European kingdoms

The Black Death

The Renaissance in Italy

and navigational techniques. The mastery of monsoon patterns
and the introduction of the camel to the Sahara also aided the rise
in trade.

The growth of commerce had a number of important consequences.
First, it led to an increasing diversification of social and economic
classes in world societies. Although most of the great civilizations
remained primarily agrarian, each had thriving commercial and manufacturing sectors, some of which derived almost their entire livelihood
from their participation in regional trade networks. With the growth in
manufacturing and commerce came a corresponding rise in the number
and size of cities; some—like Mecca, Baghdad, and Canton—owed
their importance almost entirely to their strategic location on the trade
routes.

The expansion of regional and global trade also led to the spread of
ideas. Commerce brought Buddhism to China and Southeast Asia and
Islam to sub-Saharan Africa and the Indonesian archipelago. At first
the impact was felt primarily in the cities, but eventually the new

CHAPTER
6

The New World

In August 1519, five hundred Spanish soldiers of fortune left their anchorage near the modern city of Veracruz and began the long trek from the coast across the dusty plateau of Mexico to the capital of the Aztecs. At their head was Hernán Cortés, a Spanish conquistador who had just burned their ship to ensure that his followers would not launch a mutiny and sail back to Europe. In Tenochtitlán, the Aztec capital located in what is now Mexico City, Emperor Moctezuma received the news of the foreigners' presence and awaited their arrival with anticipation. According to Aztec legend, one of their ancestors, the godlike Quetzalcoatl, had left the area hundreds of years earlier, vowing to return one day to reclaim his heritage. Could this stranger with his band of men be Quetzalcoatl or his representative? When Cortés and his forces, now accompanied by a crowd of people they had encountered en route, reached the vicinity of Moctezuma's capital, the two men met face to face. With this encounter, the last barrier between the Old World and the previously unknown civilizations in the Western Hemisphere had been bridged, and a new era dawned.

The Aztecs were only the latest in a series of sophisticated societies that had sprung up at various locations in North and South America since human beings first crossed the Bering Strait several millennia earlier. Scholars are not certain precisely when or how the first human beings arrived in America, but most believe that migrations began during or at the end of the last Ice Age, more than 10,000 years ago, when peoples

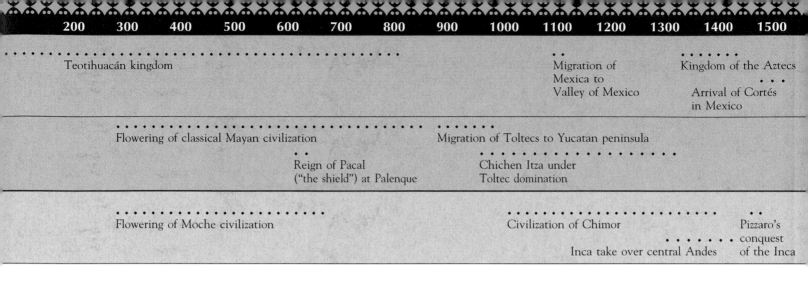

| 200 | 300 | 400 | 500 | 600 | 700 | 800 | 900 | 1000 | 1100 | 1200 | 1300 | 1400 | 1500 |

Teotihuacán kingdom

Migration of Mexica to Valley of Mexico

Kingdom of the Aztecs

Arrival of Cortés in Mexico

Flowering of classical Mayan civilization

Migration of Toltecs to Yucatan peninsula

Reign of Pacal ("the shield") at Palenque

Chichen Itza under Toltec domination

Flowering of Moche civilization

Civilization of Chimor

Pizzaro's conquest of the Inca

Inca take over central Andes

from northeastern Asia began to move across the Bering Strait into Alaska and then continued down into the plains of North America.

Most of these early peoples, today often referred to as Amerindians, lived by hunting and fishing or by food gathering. But by the second and first millennia B.C.E., the first organized societies began to take root in Central and South America. One key area of development was on the plateau of central Mexico. Another was in the lowland regions along the Gulf of Mexico and extending into modern-day Guatemala. A third was in the central Andes Mountains, adjacent to the Pacific coast. Others were just beginning to emerge in the river valleys and great plains of North America.

For the next two millennia, these societies developed in apparently total isolation from their counterparts elsewhere in the world. This lack of contact with other human beings deprived them of access to technological and cultural developments taking place in Africa, Asia, and Europe. They did not know of the wheel, for example, and their written languages were rudimentary compared to equivalents in complex civilizations in other parts of the globe. But in other respects, their cultural achievements were the equal of those realized elsewhere. When the first European explorers arrived in the New World at the turn of the sixteenth century, they described much that they observed in glowing terms.

Unfortunately for their own needs, one technological development that the peoples of America lacked was the knowledge of firearms. In a few short years, tiny bands of Spanish conquistadors were able to conquer the magnificent civilizations that we know today as the Aztecs, the Maya, and the Inca and turn them into ruins. Still, enough archaeological evidence remains to enable us to appreciate their impressive achievements.

The First Americans

When the first human beings arrived in the New World has long been a matter of dispute. In the first centuries following the voyages of Christopher Columbus, speculation centered on the possibility that the first settlers to reach the American continents had crossed the Atlantic Ocean. Were they the lost tribes of Israel? Were they Phoenician seafarers from Carthage? Or were they refugees from the legendary lost continent of Atlantis? In all cases, the assumption was that they were relatively recent arrivals.

By the mid-nineteenth century, under the influence of the new Darwinist concept of evolution, a new theory developed. It proposed that the peopling of America had taken place much earlier as a result of the migration of small communities across the Bering Strait. According to this hypothesis, early peoples might have crossed the narrow passage of water by canoe or perhaps traveled on foot at a time when low sea levels had created a land bridge between the Asian and North American continents.

Recent evidence, including numerous physical similarities between early Americans and contemporary peoples living in northeastern Asia, has confirmed this hypothesis. The debate on when the migrations began continues, however. Archaeologist Louis Leakey, one of the pioneers in the search for the origins of humankind in Africa, suggested that the first hominids may have arrived in America as long as 100,000 years ago. Others point out the lack of evidence for such early migrations and estimate that the first Americans were members of *Homo sapiens sapiens* who crossed from Asia by foot between 10,000 and 15,000 years ago in pursuit of herds of bison and caribou that moved into the area in search of grazing land as the glaciers receded from the North American continent. Recently obtained genetic evidence, however, suggests the possibility of an earlier date, perhaps as early as 29,000 years ago. Clearly, the question has not yet been definitively answered.

In any case, it is now generally accepted that human beings were living in the New World at least 15,000 years ago. They gradually spread throughout the North American continent and had penetrated almost to the tip of South America by about 10,000 B.C.E. These first Americans were hunters and food gatherers, who lived in small nomadic communities close to the source of their food supply. It is not known when agriculture was first practiced, but the cultivation of maize, and perhaps other crops as well, appears to have been underway as early as 5000 B.C.E. in the Tehuacan valley in the southern portion of the central plateau of Mexico. A similar process may have been underway in the lowland regions near the modern-day city of Veracruz and in the Yucatán peninsula further to the east. There, in the region that archaeologists call Mesoamerica, the first civilizations in the New World began to appear.

Map 6.1a   Peoples and Cultures of North America.

Early Civilizations in Central America

The first signs of civilization in Mesoamerica appeared in the first millennium B.C.E., with the emergence of what is called Olmec culture in the hot and swampy lowlands along the coast of the Gulf of Mexico south of Veracruz.

Olmec civilization was characterized by intensive agriculture along the muddy riverbanks in the area and by the carving of stone ornaments, tools, and monuments at sites such as San Lorenzo and La Venta. The site at La Venta includes a ceremonial precinct with a thirty-foot-high earthen pyramid, the largest of its date in all

Map 6.1b Peoples and Cultures of Central and Latin America.

Mesoamerica. The Olmec peoples organized a widespread trading network, carried on religious rituals, and devised an as yet undeciphered system of hieroglyphics that is similar in some respects to later Mayan writing (see Mayan Hieroglyphics later in this chapter) and may be the ancestor of the first true writing systems in the New World.

Olmec society apparently consisted of several classes, including a class of skilled artisans who produced a series of massive stone heads, some of which are more than ten feet high. The Olmec peoples supported themselves primarily by cultivating crops, such as corn and beans, but also engaged in fishing and hunting. The Olmec apparently played a ceremonial game on a stone ball court, a ritual that would later be widely practiced throughout the region (see The Maya later in this chapter).

Eventually, Olmec civilization began to decline, and apparently collapsed around the fourth century B.C.E. During its heyday, however, it extended from Mexico City to El Salvador and perhaps to the shores of the Pacific Ocean.

In the meantime, parallel developments were taking place at Monte Alban, on a hillside overlooking the modern city of Oaxaca in central Mexico. Around the middle of the first millennium B.C.E., the Zapotec peoples created an extensive civilization that flourished for several hundred years in the highlands. Like the Olmec sites, the site at Monte Alban contains a number of temples and pyramids, but they are located in much more awesome surroundings on a massive stone terrace atop a 1,200-foot-high mountain overlooking the Oaxaca valley. The majority of the population, estimated at about 20,000, dwelled on terraces cut into the sides of the mountain.

Teotihuacán: America's First Metropolis

The first major metropolis in Mesoamerica was the city of Teotihuacán, capital of an early kingdom that arose sometime around the third century B.C.E. and flourished for nearly a millennium until it collapsed under mysterious circumstances about 800 C.E. Located about thirty miles northeast of Mexico City, Teotihuacán covered an area of at least eight square miles and had as many as 150,000 inhabitants during its heyday; in size and sophistication, it rivaled its contemporary, the city of Rome. Along the main thoroughfare were temples and palaces, all dominated by a massive Pyramid of the Sun rising in four tiers to a height of more than two hundred feet. Under the pyramid, archaeologists have discovered the remains of sacrificial victims, probably put to death during the dedication of the structure. In the vicinity are the remains of a large market where goods from distant regions as well as agricultural produce grown by farmers in the vicinity were exchanged. The products traded included cacao, rubber, feathers, and various types of vegetables and meat. Pulque, a liquor extracted from the agave plant, was used in religious ceremonies. An obsidian mine nearby may explain the location of the city (see the next section).

◆ **The Pyramid of the Sun, Teotihuacán.** The first major metropolis in Central America was Teotihuacán, which was inhabited by as many as 150,000 people during its zenith sometime after 400 C.E. The ceremonial center of Teotihuacán, which contained more than five thousand structures, was laid out in a north-south and an east-west axis; it was dominated by the Pyramid of the Sun, rising in four tiers to a height of over two hundred feet.

Most of the city consisted of one-story stucco apartment compounds; some were as large as 35,000 square feet, sufficient to house more than a hundred people. Each apartment was divided into several rooms, while the compounds were covered by flat roofs made of wooden beams, poles, and stucco. The compounds were separated by wide streets laid out on a rectangular grid and were entered through narrow alleys. Ethnic groups from various parts of the region apparently established their own ghettos and embellished their dwellings with their own style of art and architecture.

Living within the fertile Valley of Mexico, an upland plateau surrounded by magnificent snowcapped mountains, the inhabitants of Teotihuacán probably obtained the bulk of their wealth from agriculture. At that time, the valley floor was filled with swampy lakes containing the water runoff from the surrounding mountains. The combination of fertile soil and adequate water combined to make the valley one of the richest farming areas in Mesoamerica.

Sometime during the eighth century, for unknown reasons the wealth and power of the city began to decline, and eventually its ruling class departed, with the priests carrying stone images of local deities on their backs. The next two centuries were a time of troubles throughout the region, as feuding principalities fought over limited farmland. The problem was compounded in later centuries when peoples from surrounding areas, attracted by the rich farmlands in the Valley of Mexico, migrated into the area and began to compete for territory with small city-states already established there. As the local population expanded, farmers began to engage in more intensive agriculture. To maintain their subsistence living, they drained the lakes to build *chinampas*, swampy islands crisscrossed by canals that provided water for their crops and easy transportation to local markets for their excess produce.

The Mysterious Maya

Far to the east of the Valley of Mexico, another major civilization had taken form in what one scholar has described as the "great green thumb" of the Yucatán peninsula, a vast limestone shelf that emerged from the sea millions of years ago. This was the civilization of the Maya, which was older and equally as sophisticated as the society at Teotihuacán.

Unlike the civilization of the Aztecs, Mayan civilization was not at its height when the Spaniards arrived, but had effectively come to an end centuries before the arrival of the Europeans. The area was conquered by Spain

in the mid-sixteenth century, and early Spanish visitors, such as the Catholic bishop Diego de Landa, were impressed by the remains of late Mayan cities that they found in the northern part of the peninsula. But the true glories of classical Mayan civilization, from a period several hundred years prior to the Spanish conquest, remained hidden in the dense undergrowth of the peninsula until the mid-nineteenth century. At that time, an American, John Lloyd Stephens, and a British photographer, Frederick Catherwood, who had heard reports of unexplored ruins in the Yucatán wilderness, visited the area and brought them to the attention of the general public.

Who were the people who built these impressive cities? Early speculation centered on an Old World or even extraterrestrial origin for the inhabitants, but it eventually became clear that the builders of this civilization were the ancestors of the Mayan peoples still living in the area. Like the Aztecs and their predecessors at Teotihuacán, the Maya trace their origins to the parent Olmec civilization in the lowlands along the Gulf of Mexico. It is not known when human beings first inhabited the peninsula, but peoples contemporaneous with the Olmecs were already cultivating such crops as corn, yams, and manioc in the area during the first millennium B.C.E. As the population increased, an early civilization began to emerge along the Pacific coast directly to the south of the peninsula and in the highlands of modern-

� **Map 6.2**   The Heartland of Mesoamerica.

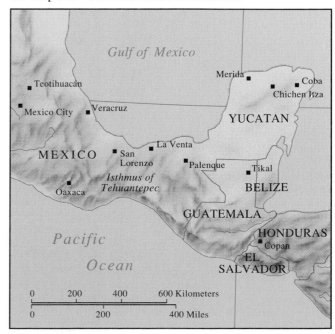

day Guatemala. Contacts were already established with the Olmec to the west.

Since the area was a source for cacao trees and the volcanic glass obsidian, the inhabitants soon developed relations with other early civilizations in the region. Used for tools, mirrors, and the blades of sacrificial knives, obsidian was much prized throughout Mesoamerica. Cacao trees were the source of chocolate, which was used as a beverage by the upper classes, while cocoa beans, the fruit of the cacao tree, were a common form of currency in markets throughout the region.

As the population in the area increased, the inhabitants began to migrate into the central Yucatán peninsula to the north. The overcrowding forced farmers in the lowland areas to shift from slash-and-burn cultivation to swamp agriculture of the type practiced in the lake region of the Valley of Mexico. By the middle of the first millennium C.E., the entire area was honeycombed with a patchwork of small city-states competing with each other for land and resources. The most important were probably Tikal and Copan, but it is doubtful that any were sufficiently powerful to dominate the entire area.

Mayan civilization during the classical era possessed a number of similarities with contemporaneous cultures to the west, and some scholars have speculated that for a time the ruling class was composed of aristocratic elites who had migrated from Teotihuacán. But recent archaeological finds suggest that most of the rulers of the Mayan city-states emerged from local lineage heads (often termed "big men") who gradually gained in influence over their rivals and eventually transformed themselves into hereditary rulers who then buttressed their authority by claiming the ability to communicate with divine forces. At Copan, this transformation apparently took place in the fifth century C.E., when the population of the surrounding valley reached nearly five thousand people.

Mayan religion was polytheistic. Although the names of the deities were different from those used elsewhere in the region, Mayan gods shared many of the same characteristics as deities of nearby cultures. The supreme god was named Itzamna (Lizard House). Deities were ranked in order of importance, and some, like the jaguar god of night, were evil rather than good. Some scholars believe that many of the nature deities may have been viewed as manifestations of one supreme godhead (see the box on p. 209). As at Teotihuacán, human sacrifice (normally by decapitation) was practiced to propitiate the heavenly forces.

Scenes from paintings and rock carvings depict a society preoccupied with war and the seizure of captives for sacrifice. Physically, the Mayan cities were built around a ceremonial core dominated by a central pyramid surmounted by a shrine to the gods. Nearby were other temples, palaces, and a sacred ball court.

The ball court was a rectangular space surrounded by vertical walls with metal rings through which the contestants attempted to drive a hard rubber ball. Although the rules of the game are only imperfectly understood, it apparently had religious significance, and the vanquished players were sacrificed in ceremonies held after the close of the game. Similar courts have been found at sites throughout Mesoamerica.

◆ **Preparing for Sacrifice.**   This copy of a wall painting from the 800 C.E. Mayan temple at Bonampak shows a ruler accepting a human sacrifice, which was offered to appease the anger of the deities. The Maya went on raids for victims and then sacrificed them in elaborate rites with ornate costumes and dancing. Here nobles wearing the pelts and the headdress of jaguars, the symbol of power and rank, preside over the ceremonial preparation of the victim.

The Creation of the World: A Mayan View

Popul Vuh, a sacred work of the ancient Maya, is an account of Mayan history and religious beliefs. No written version in the original Mayan script is extant, but shortly after the Spanish conquest, it was written down in Quiche (the spoken language of the Maya), using the Latin script, apparently from memory. This version was later translated into Spanish. The following excerpt from the opening lines of Popul Vuh recounts the Mayan myth of the creation.

Popul Vuh: The Sacred Book of the Maya

This is the account of how all was in suspense, all calm, in silence; all motionless, still, and the expanse of the sky was empty.

This is the first account, the first narrative. There was neither man, nor animal, birds, fishes, crabs, trees, stones, caves, ravines, grasses, nor forests; there was only the sky.

The surface of the earth had not appeared. There was only the calm sea and the great expanse of the sky.

There was nothing brought together, nothing which could make a noise, nor anything which might move, or tremble, or could make noise in the sky.

There was nothing standing; only the calm water, the placid sea, alone and tranquil. Nothing existed.

There was only immobility and silence in the darkness, in the night. Only the Creator, the Maker, Tepeu, Gucumatz, the Forefathers, were in the water surrounded with light. They were hidden under green and blue feathers, and were therefore called Gucumatz. By nature they were great sages and great thinkers. In this manner the sky existed and also the Heart of Heaven, which is the name of God and thus He is called.

Then came the word. Tepeu and Gucumatz came together in the darkness, in the night, and Tepeu and Gucumatz talked together. They talked then, discussing and deliberating; they agreed, they united their words and their thoughts.

Then while they meditated, it became clear to them that when dawn would break, man must appear. Then they planned the creation, and the growth of the trees and the thickets and the birth of life and the creation of man. Thus it was arranged in the darkness and in the night by the Heart of Heaven who is called Huracan.

The first is called Caculha Huracan. The second is Chipi-Caculha. The third is Raxa-Caculha. And these three are the Heart of Heaven.

So it was that they made perfect the work, when they did it after thinking and meditating upon it.

At one time, archaeologists believed that Mayan society probably had only two classes—the royal-priestly class and the peasants who served them. The power of the ruler was certainly impressive. One of the monarchs at Copan—known to scholars as "18 rabbit" from the hieroglyphs composing his name—ordered the construction of a grand palace requiring more than 30,000 person-days of labor. But the picture of society that is now emerging is more complex. Around the ruler was a class of aristocrats, lineage heads whose wealth was probably based on the ownership of land farmed by their poorer relatives. Eventually, many of the aristocrats became priests or scribes at the royal court or adopted honored professions as sculptors or painters. As the society's wealth grew, so did the need for artisans and traders, who began to form a small middle class. Although the size of the larger cities is difficult to estimate, urban centers such as Tikal may have had as many as 100,000 inhabitants at their height.

The majority of the population on the peninsula, however (estimated at roughly three million at the height of Mayan power), were undoubtedly farmers. They lived on their *chinampa* plots or on terraced hills in the highlands. There are some indications that the basic unit of society was the extended family, consisting on average of ten to twenty persons. Houses were built of adobe and thatch and probably resembled the houses of the majority of the population in the area today. There was a fairly clear-cut division of labor along sexual lines. The men were responsible for fighting and hunting, and the women for homemaking and the preparation of cornmeal, the staple food of much of the population.

MAYAN HIEROGLYPHICS

In some ways, Mayan culture was more advanced than the later Aztec civilization in the Valley of Mexico. The Maya, for example, created a writing system much more sophisticated than the relatively primitive system used by the Aztecs (see the box on p. 210). Unfortunately, the Spanish conquerors made no attempt to decipher the language with the assistance of natives familiar with the

≽ A Sample of Mayan Writing ≼

*T*he Maya were the only Mesoamerican people to devise a complete written language. Like the Sumerian and Egyptian scripts, the Mayan system was composed of a mixture of ideographs and phonetic symbols, which were written in double columns to be read from left to right and top to bottom. The language was rudimentary in many ways. It had few adjectives or adverbs, and the numbering system comprised only three symbols: a shell for zero, a dot for one, and a bar for five.

During the classical era from 300 to 900 C.E., the Maya used the script to record dynastic statistics with deliberate precision, listing the date of the ruler's birth, his accession to power, and his marriage and death, while highlighting victories in battle, the capture of prisoners, and ritual ceremonies. The symbols were carved on stone panels, stelae, and funerary urns or were painted with a brush on folding screen books made of bark paper; only four of these books from the late period remain extant today. Having developed an extremely sophisticated astrological system, the Maya incorporated it into their historical records. The complexity of Mayan hieroglyphs and

astronomical calculations have long baffled scholars, but great strides have been made in deciphering the script in recent years. It is now clear, for example, that the Maya ascribed great importance to the planet Venus, and its appearance determined the date of many important battles.

A sample of Mayan hieroglyphics is shown below.

"birth of . ."   "accession of . ."

"death of . ."   bloodletting rite

warfare   *chucah* "he captured . ."   "captor of . ."

Mayan Hieroglyphics

script. Bishop Diego de Landa, otherwise an astute and sympathetic observer of Mayan culture, remarked: "We found a large number of books in these characters and, as they contained nothing in which there were not to be seen superstition and lies of the devil, we burned them all, which they regretted to an amazing degree, and which caused them much affliction."[1]

The Mayan hieroglyphs remained undeciphered until scholars discovered that many passages contained symbols that recorded dates in the Mayan calendar known to specialists as the "Long Count." This calen-

dar, which measures time back to a particular date in August 3114 B.C.E., required a sophisticated understanding of astronomical events and mathematics to compile. Starting with these known symbols as a foundation, modern scholars have gradually deciphered the script.

Until recently, scholars had assumed that the Mayan hieroglyphs had no phonetic meaning and dealt almost exclusively with mathematical or astronomical matters related to the calendar. But as various glyphs were deciphered, scholars discovered that, like the scripts of the

◆ **A Ball Court.**   Throughout Mesoamerica a dangerous game was played on ball courts such as this one. A large ball of solid rubber was propelled from the hip at such tremendous speed that players had to wear extensive padding. More than an athletic contest, the game had religious significance. The court is thought to have represented the cosmos and the ball the sun, and the losers were sacrificed to the gods in postgame ceremonies.

Sumerians and ancient Egyptians, the Mayan hieroglyphs were both ideographic and phonetic in nature and, in fact, were becoming more phonetic as time passed. Moreover, as the meaning of extant passages was uncovered, it became clear that many of them document important events in the history of the state or the life of an individual ruler. They thus provide scholars with an important tool for learning more about this fascinating civilization.

One of the most important repositories of Mayan hieroglyphs is at Palenque, an archaeological site deep in the jungles in the neck of the Mexican peninsula, considerably to the west of the Yucatán. In a chamber located under the Temple of Inscriptions, archaeologists discovered a royal tomb and a massive limestone slab covered with hieroglyphs. By deciphering the message on the slab, archaeologists for the first time identified a historical figure in Mayan history. He was a ruler named Pacal, known from his glyph as "the shield"; Pacal ordered the construction of the Temple of Inscriptions in the mid-seventh century, and it was his body that was buried in the tomb.

As befits their intense interest in the passage of time, the Maya also had a sophisticated knowledge of astronomy and kept voluminous records of the movements of the heavenly bodies. There were practical reasons for their concern. The arrival of the planet Venus in the evening sky, for example, was a traditional time to prepare for war. The Temple of Inscriptions was oriented so that an observer could stand on the platform at the spring equinox and watch the setting of the sun.

THE MYSTERY OF MAYAN DECLINE

Sometime in the eighth or ninth century, the classical Mayan civilization in the central Yucatán peninsula began to decline. At Copan, for example, it ended abruptly in 822 C.E., when work on various stone sculptures ordered by the ruler suddenly ceased. The end of Palenque, a rival state to the west, soon followed. Whether the decline was caused by overuse of the land, invasion, internal revolt, or a natural disaster such as a volcanic eruption is a question that has puzzled archaeologists for decades. Recent evidence supports the theory that overcultivation of the land due to a growing population gradually reduced crop yields. Another theory is that a long drought, which lasted for almost two centuries in the ninth and tenth centuries C.E., may have played a major role. Certainly, the period was characterized by an increase in internecine war among the states and the rise of powerful nobles.

Whatever the case, cities like Tikal and Palenque were abandoned to the jungles, while newer urban centers in the northern part of the peninsula, like Uxmal and Chichen Itza, survived and continued to prosper. According to local history, this latter area was taken over by peoples known as the Toltecs led by a man known as Kukulcan ("feathered serpent"), who migrated to the peninsula from Tula in central Mexico sometime in the tenth century. Some scholars believe this flight was associated with the legend of the departure of Quetzalcoatl, the feathered serpent who promised that he would someday return to reclaim his homeland.

The Toltecs apparently controlled the upper peninsula from their capital at Chichen Itza for several centuries, and then they too declined. When the Spaniards arrived, the area was divided into a number of small principalities, while the former cities such as Uxmal and Chichen Itza had been abandoned.

The Aztecs

Among the groups moving into the Valley of Mexico after the fall of Teotihuacán were the Mexica (pronounced Mesheeca). No one knows the origins of these people, although folk legend held that their original homeland was an island in a lake called Aztlan. From that legendary homeland comes the name Aztec, by which they are known to the modern world. Sometime during the early twelfth century, these peoples left their original habitat and, carrying an image of their patron deity Huitzilopochtli, began a lengthy migration that climaxed with their arrival in the Valley of Mexico sometime late in the century.

Less sophisticated than many of their neighbors, the Aztecs at first were forced to seek alliances with stronger city-states in the region. They were renowned as excellent warriors, however, and (in a process reminiscent of the rise of Sparta in ancient Greece and the state of Qin in Zhou dynasty China) had become the leading city-state in the lake region by the early fifteenth century. Establishing their capital at Tenochtitlán on an island in the middle of Lake Texcoco, they set out to bring the entire region under their domination.

✦ **The Palace at Palenque.**   The civilization of the Maya of eastern Mexico was older but equally as sophisticated as that of the Aztecs. By the middle of the first millennium C.E., Mayan culture extended south as far as modern-day Guatemala. Here we see the seventh-century palace at Palenque, which had both sacred and secular functions; the tower was used for astronomy. Abandoned soon after, Palenque remained hidden in the jungle until the mid-nineteenth century.

For the remainder of the fifteenth century, the Aztecs consolidated their control over much of what is modern Mexico, from the Atlantic to the Pacific Ocean and as far south as the Guatemalan border. The new kingdom was not a centralized state but a collection of semiautonomous territories governed by local lords who were confirmed in their authority by the Aztec ruler in return for the payment of tribute. To provide an ideological focus for the kingdom, the Aztecs promoted their patron god Huitzilopochtli as the guiding deity of the entire population, which now numbered several million.

POLITICS AND SOCIETY

Like all great empires in ancient times, the Aztec state was authoritarian in nature. Power was vested in the hands of the monarch, whose authority had both a divine and a secular character. The Aztec ruler claimed descent

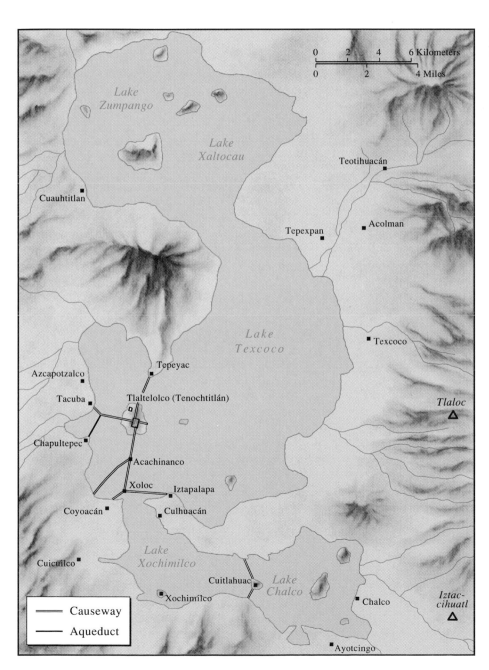

✖ **Map 6.3**   The Valley of Mexico Under Aztec Rule.

from the gods and served as an intermediary between the material and the metaphysical worlds. Unlike many of his counterparts in the Old World, however, the monarch did not obtain his position by a rigid law of succession. On the death of the ruler, his successor was selected from within the royal family by a small group of senior officials, who were also members of the family and were therefore eligible for the position. Once placed on the throne, the Aztec ruler was advised by a small council of lords, headed by a prime minister who served as the chief executive of the government, and a bureaucracy. Beyond the capital, the power of the central government was limited. As we have seen, rulers of territories conquered by or otherwise made subject to the Aztecs were allowed considerable autonomy in return for the payment of tribute, in the form of goods or captives, to the central government. The most important government officials in the provinces were the tax collectors, who collected the tribute. They used the threat of military action against those who failed to carry out their tribute obligations and understandably were not popular with the taxpayers. According to Bernal Díaz, a Spaniard who accompanied Hernán Cortés on his expedition to Tenochtitlán in 1519:

> . . . all these towns complained about Montezuma [the Aztec ruler at the time of the Cortés expedition] and his tax-collectors, speaking in private so that the Mexican ambassadors should not hear them, however. They said these officials robbed them of all they possessed, and that if their wives and daughters were pretty they would violate them in front of their fathers and husbands and carry them away. They also said that the Mexicans [that is, the representatives from the capital] made the men work like slaves, compelling them to carry pine-trunks and stone and firewood and maize overland and in canoes, and to perform other tasks, such as planting maize-fields, and that they took away the people's lands as well for the service of their idols.[2]

Positions in the government bureaucracy were the exclusive privilege of the hereditary nobility, all of whom traced their lineage to the founding family of the Aztec clan. Male children in noble families were sent to temple schools, where they were exposed to a harsh regimen consisting of manual labor, military training, and the memorization of information about Aztec society and religion. On reaching adulthood, they would select a career in the military service, the government bureaucracy, or the priesthood. As a reward for their services, senior officials received large estates from the government, and they alone had the right to hire communal labor.

Separated from the hereditary aristocracy was the remainder of the population, consisting of commoners, indentured workers, and slaves. The last two categories apparently accounted for a fairly small number of the inhabitants. Most indentured workers were landless laborers who contracted to work on the nobles' estates, while slaves served in the households of the wealthy. Slavery was not an inherited status, and the children of slaves were considered to be free citizens. The first Spanish visitors reported that both male and female slaves were sold in the markets. Some were chained to prevent them from escaping, while others were allowed to walk freely. Commoners might sell themselves into slavery when in debt and then later purchase their freedom.

The vast majority of the population were commoners. All commoners were members of large kinship groups called *calpullis*. Each *calpulli*, often consisting of as many as a thousand members, was headed by an elected chief, who was responsible for running the day-to-day affairs of the organization and serving as an intermediary with the central government. Each *calpulli* was responsible for providing taxes (usually in the form of goods) and conscript labor to the state.

Beyond such responsibilities, a *calpulli* was essentially self-governing. Each maintained its own temples and schools and administered the land held by the community. Farmland within the *calpulli* was held in common and could not be sold, although it could be inherited within the family. Within the cities, each *calpulli* occupied a separate neighborhood, where its members often performed a particular function, such as metalworking, stonecutting, weaving, carpentry, or commerce. Apparently, a large proportion of the population engaged in some form of trade, at least in the densely populated Valley of Mexico, where an estimated half of the people lived in an urban environment. Many farmers apparently brought their goods to the markets via the canals and sold them directly to retailers (see the box on p. 215).

The *calpulli* compounds themselves were divided into smaller family units. Most were nuclear in nature, although there were apparently some joint families comprising up to twenty people or more. Individual families lived in small flat-roofed dwellings containing one or two rooms. Each house was separate from its neighbors and had direct access to the surrounding streets and canals. The houses of farmers living on the *chinampas* were set on raised dirt platforms built above the surrounding fields to prevent flooding.

Sex roles within the family were rigidly stratified. Male children were trained for war and were expected to serve in the army on reaching adulthood. Women were expected to work in the home, weave textiles, and raise children, although like their brothers they were permitted to enter the priesthood. According to Bernal Díaz, a

⇒ Markets and Merchandise in Aztec Mexico ⇐

One of our most valuable descriptions of Aztec civilization is The Conquest of New Spain *written by Bernal Díaz, a Spaniard who accompanied Hernán Cortés on his expedition to Mexico in 1519. In the following passage, Díaz describes the great market at Tenochtitlán.*

Bernal Díaz, *The Conquest of New Spain*

Let us begin with the dealers in gold, silver, and precious stones, feathers, cloaks, and embroidered goods, and male and female slaves who are also sold there. They bring as many slaves to be sold in that market as the Portuguese bring Negroes from Guinea. Some are brought there attached to long poles by means of collars round their necks to prevent them from escaping, but others are left loose. Next there were those who sold coarser cloth, and cotton goods and fabrics made of twisted thread, and there were chocolate merchants with their chocolate. In this way you could see every kind of merchandise to be found anywhere in New Spain, laid out in the same way as goods are laid out in my own district of Medina del Campo, a center for fairs, where each line of stalls has its own particular sort. So it was in this great market. There were those who sold sisal cloth and ropes and the sandals they wear on their feet, which are made from the same plant. All these were kept in one part of the market, in the place assigned to them, and in another part were skins of tigers and lions, otters, jackals, and deer, badgers, mountain cats, and other wild animals, some tanned and some untanned, and other classes of merchandise.

There were sellers of kidney-beans and sage and other vegetables and herbs in another place, and in yet another they were selling fowls, and birds with great dewlaps, also rabbits, hares, deer, young ducks, little dogs, and other such creatures. Then there were the fruiterers; and the women who sold cooked food, flour and honey cake, and tripe, had their part of the market. Then came pottery of all kinds, from big water-jars to little jugs, displayed in its own place, also honey, honey-paste, and other sweets like nougat. Elsewhere they sold timber too, boards, cradles, beams, blocks, and benches, all in a quarter of their own.

Then there were the sellers of pitch-pine for torches, and other things of that kind, and I must also mention, with all apologies, that they sold many canoe-loads of human excrement, which they kept in the creeks near the market. This was for the manufacture of salt and the curing of skins, which they say cannot be done without it. I know that many gentlemen will laugh at this, but I assure them it is true. I may add that on all the roads they have shelters made of reeds or straw or grass so that they can retire when they wish to do so, and purge their bowels unseen by passers-by, and also in order that their excrement shall not be lost.

But why waste so many words on the goods in their great market? If I describe everything in detail I shall never be done. . . . I am forgetting the sellers of salt and the makers of flint knives, and how they split them off the stone itself, and the fisherwomen and the men who sell small cakes made from a sort of weed which they get out of the great lake, which curdles and forms a kind of bread which tastes rather like cheese. They sell axes too, made of bronze and copper and tin, and gourds and brightly painted wooden jars.

female deity presided over the rites of marriage. As in most traditional societies, chastity and obedience were desirable female characteristics. Bernardino de Sahagun, a Catholic missionary who compiled oral histories of the Aztec people in the sixteenth century, noted that a noblewoman was expected to be "patient, gentle, kind, benign, hard-working. . . . She governs, leads, provides for one, arranges well, administers peacefully."[3]

Although women in Aztec society enjoyed more legal rights than women in some traditional Old World civilizations, they were still not equal to men. Women were permitted to own and inherit property and to enter into contracts. Marriage was normally monogamous, although noble families sometimes practiced polygyny. Wedding partners were normally selected from within the lineage group, but not the immediate family. As in most societies at the time, parents usually selected their child's spouse, often for purposes of political or social advancement.

Classes in Aztec society were rigidly stratified. Commoners were not permitted to enter the nobility, although some occasionally rose to senior positions in the army or the priesthood as the result of exemplary service. As in medieval Europe, such occupations often provided a route of upward mobility for ambitious commoners.

LAND OF THE FEATHERED SERPENT: AZTEC RELIGION AND CULTURE

The Aztecs, like their contemporaries throughout Mesoamerica, lived in an environment populated by a multitude of gods. Scholars have identified more than a hundred deities in the Aztec pantheon; some of them were nature spirits, like the rain god Tlaloc, and some were patron deities, like the symbol of the Aztecs themselves, Huitzilopochtli. As in Indian religion, there was a supreme deity, called Ometeotl, who represented the all-powerful and omnipresent forces of the heavens, but he was rather remote, and other gods, notably the feathered serpent Quetzalcoatl, had a more direct impact on the lives of the people. Representing the forces of creation, virtue, and learning and culture, Quetzalcoatl bears a distinct similarity to Siva in Hindu belief. According to Aztec tradition, this godlike being had left his homeland in the Valley of Mexico in the tenth century, promising to return in triumph (see The Mystery of Mayan Decline earlier in this chapter).

Aztec cosmology was based on a belief in the existence of two worlds, the material and the divine. The earth was the material world and took the form of a flat disc surrounded by water on all sides. The divine world, which consisted of both heaven and hell, was the abode of the gods. Human beings could aspire to a form of heavenly salvation, but first had to pass through a transitional stage, somewhat like purgatory, before reaching their final destination, where the soul was finally freed from the body. To prepare for the final day of judgment, as well as to help them engage in proper behavior through life, all citizens underwent religious training at temple schools during adolescence and took part in various rituals throughout their lives. The most devout were encouraged to study for the priesthood. Once accepted, they served at temples ranging from local branches at the *calpulli* level to the highest shrines in the ceremonial precinct at Tenochtitlán.

Aztec religion contained a distinct element of fatalism that was inherent in their creation myth, which described an unceasing struggle between the forces of good and evil throughout the universe. This struggle led to the creation and destruction of four worlds, or suns. The world was now living in the time of the fifth sun. But that world, too, was destined to end with the destruction of this earth and all that is within it. The following poem, allegedly by a ruler of one of the states in the lake region, is an example of this fatalistic element in Aztec religious belief:

> *Even jade is shattered,*
> *Even gold is crushed,*
> *Even quetzal plumes are torn . . .*
> *One does not live forever on this earth:*
> *We endure only for an instant!*[4]

In an effort to postpone the day of reckoning, the Aztecs practiced human sacrifice. The Aztecs believed that by appeasing the sun god Huitzilopochtli with sacrifices, they could bring about a delay in the final destruction of their world. Victims were prepared for the ceremony through elaborate rituals and then brought to the holy shrine, where their hearts were ripped out of their chests and presented to the gods as a holy offering. It was

◆ **Quetzalcoatl.** Quetzalcoatl was one of the favorite deities of the Central American peoples. His visage of a plumed serpent, as shown here, was prominent in the royal capital of Teotihuacán. According to legend, Quetzalcoatl, the leader of the Toltecs, was tricked into drunkenness and humiliated by a rival god. In disgrace he left his homeland, but promised to return. In 1519, the Aztec monarch Moctezuma welcomed Hernán Cortés, the leader of the Spanish expedition, believing he was a representative of Quetzalcoatl.

⇒ Aztec Religion through Spanish Eyes ⇐

*A*lthough early Spanish visitors were impressed with many aspects of Aztec culture, they were revolted by its religious beliefs and practices. The following passage from Father Diego Duran's History of the Indies of New Spain *describes the ritual of human sacrifice that was a central part of Aztec religion. The Aztecs believed that only the gift of human hearts would appease their god Huitzilopochtli and prevent him from bringing disaster to their civilization.*

Diego Duran, *History of the Indies of New Spain*

When the day of the feast arrived, Moteczoma and Tlacaelel blackened their bodies with soot and applied it in such a way that it caught the light. . . . They placed crowns of fine feathers, adorned with gold and precious stones, upon their heads, and on each arm they wore a sheath of gold reaching from the elbow to the shoulder. On their feet were richly worked jaguar skin sandals, inlaid with gold and gems. They also were robed in splendid royal mantles and loincloths done in the same manner as the mantles. . . . Jeweled plugs were attached to holes in their noses, and both these lords carried flint knives in their hands.

The king and Tlacaelel now appeared before the assembly and went to stand upon the stone which was the likeness and image of the sun, one having ascended by one staircase and the other by another. The five priests of sacrifice followed them. They were to hold down the feet, hands and heads of the victims, and they were painted all over with red ocher, even their loincloths and tunics. Upon their heads they wore paper crowns surmounted by little shields which hung to the middle of their foreheads, also painted in ocher. On the top of their heads they wore long stiff feathers which had been tied to their hair and which stood straight up. On their feet were very common, worthless sandals. . . .

The five priests entered and claimed the prisoner who stood first in the line at the skull rack. Each prisoner they took to the place where the king stood and,

when they had forced him to stand upon the stone which was the figure and likeness of the sun, they threw him upon his back. One took him by the right arm, another by the left, one by his left foot, another by his right, while the fifth priest tied his neck with a cord and held him down so that he could not move.

The king lifted the knife on high and made a gash in his breast. Having opened it he extracted the heart and raised it high with his hand as an offering to the sun. When the heart had cooled he tossed it into the circular depression, taking some of the blood in his hand and sprinkling it in the direction of the sun. In this way the sacrificers killed four, one by one; then Tlacaelel came and killed another four in his turn. And so, four by four, the prisoners were slain, till every last man that had been brought from the Mixteca had perished.

When the sacrifice had ended the priests took from the shrine of Huitzilopochtli a paper serpent coiled about a pole, adorned with feathers. . . . A priest carried the snake, twisted about the pole. He then set it on fire and walked about the stone incensing it with the smoke. While it was burning, he climbed to the top of the monolith and threw the still smoldering serpent upon all the blood which bathed the stone. At this moment a great paper mantle was brought and cast upon the stone. It burned together with the serpent until the blood was consumed and dried.

Once the fire had gone out Moteczoma and Tlacaelel descended and, with the kings of Texcoco and Tacuba, withdrew to the royal seats. They anointed the royal guests, dressed them and adorned them with headdresses, mantles, arm-bands, loincloths and nose-plugs, all of these ornaments being of the same type used by the sacrificers. Everyone then took part in a solemn banquet with great festivities to commemorate the first use of the stone which was the image and likeness of the sun.

an honor to be chosen for sacrifice, and captives in particular were often used as sacrificial victims, since they represented valor, the trait the Aztecs prized most. One of the few descriptions we have of the ceremonies comes from the pen of Father Diego Duran, a Dominican friar who lived in Mexico during the mid-sixteenth century and left a description of the civilization of the Aztecs (see the box above).

Aztec art, like much of Aztec life, was permeated with religion. This characteristic can be traced back to pre-Aztec peoples like the Olmec and the civilization at Teotihuacán. Especially impressive to most modern viewers is the monumental architecture. Although much has been destroyed by the ravages of the Spanish conquerors and the passage of time, sufficient evidence remains to demonstrate that by the first millennium B.C.E.

the Olmec peoples had both the capacity and the will to construct massive structures in stone. An early example is at La Venta, not far from the modern city of Coatzalcoacos, where a rectangular ceremonial precinct, consisting of altars, colossal stone heads, and a thirty-foot-high pyramid, was erected to venerate the gods. Ornaments and figurines of jade and other semiprecious stone, bas-relief rock carvings, and multicolored cave paintings have been found at other Olmec sites. Virtually all of this art was imbued with religious significance and it depicted the deities (most of them combining human with animal forms) or religious ceremonies or served as votive offerings.

Many of the characteristics already visible in Olmec art and architecture were passed on to later peoples in the area. We have already discussed the ceremonial precincts at Monte Alban and Teotihuacán. Teotihuacán, in particular, demonstrated a massiveness of form and delicacy of technique that is in some respects the equal of its counterparts in the Old World.

These characteristics, supplemented by others reflecting the character of their own society and religion, were taken over by the Aztec peoples. At the center of the capital city of Tenochtitlán was the sacred precinct, dominated by the massive pyramid dedicated to Huitzilopochtli and the rain god Tlaloc. According to Bernal Díaz, at its base the pyramid was equal to the plots of six large European town houses and tapered from there to the top, which was surmounted by a platform containing shrines to the gods and an altar for performing human sacrifices. From ground level to the platform rose a stairway of 114 steps. At the top the viewer could take in a breathtaking panorama of the entire city, dotted with shrines and smaller pyramids and surrounded by the vast lake covered with canoes and crisscrossed by causeways coming from the mainland. The entire pyramid was covered with brightly colored paintings and sculptures, while the surrounding area was paved with burnished white flagstones and bordered with smaller shrines and dormitories for the priests. The imperial palace and the homes of senior officials were located nearby. The entire scene struck the Spanish visitor Díaz with awe (see the box on p. 219).

Like the art of the Olmecs, most Aztec art and sculpture had religious significance. Although little painting survives, it was evidently of high quality. Bernal Díaz compared the best work with that of Michelangelo. Artisans now worked not only with stone, but also with soft metals such as gold and silver, which they cast with the lost wax technique. They did not have the knowledge of making implements in bronze or iron, however. Stone working consisted primarily of representations of the gods and bas-reliefs depicting religious ceremonies. Among the most famous is the massive Stone of the Sun, carved for use at the central pyramid at Tenochtitlán and now housed in the National Museum of Anthropology in Mexico City. The carving takes the form of a disc portraying the perpetual struggle between the forces of good and evil in the universe, with an image of the sun god in the center.

The Aztecs did not possess a written literature, but had devised a form of writing based on hieroglyphs that represented an object or a concept. Such symbols, called glyphs, had no phonetic significance and did not constitute a writing system as such, but could give the sense of a message and were probably used by civilian or religious officials as notes or memoranda for their orations. Although many of the notes simply recorded dates in the complex calendar that had evolved since Olmec times,

◆ **The Stone of the Fifth Sun.**   This basaltic disc, which weighs twenty-six tons, recorded the Aztec view of the cosmos. It portrays the perpetual struggle between forces of good and evil in the universe; in the center is an intimidating image of the sun god clutching human hearts with his talons. Having previously traversed the creation and destruction of four worlds, the Aztecs believed they were living in the world of the fifth and final sun—hence this stone carving that was found in the central pyramid at Tenochtitlán.

⇒ A Description of Tenochtitlán ⇐

The Aztec capital of Tenochtitlán was built on an island in the Lake of Mexico. After the Spanish conquest, the lake was drained, and the area became the foundation of the modern capital of Mexico, Mexico City. Here Díaz describes the city as he viewed it from the top of the Temple of the Sun. The Spaniards razed the temple and built a cathedral in its place.

Bernal Díaz, *The Conquest of New Spain*

When we arrived near the great temple and before we had climbed a single step, the great Montezuma sent six *papas* [priests] and two chieftains down from the top, where he was making his sacrifices, to escort our Captain; and as he climbed the steps, of which there were one hundred and fourteen, they tried to take him by the arms to help him up in the same way as they helped Montezuma, thinking he might be tired, but he would not let them near him.

The top of the *cue* [pyramid] formed an open square on which stood something like a platform, and it was here that the great stones stood on which they placed the poor Indians for sacrifice. Here also was a massive image like a dragon, and other hideous figures, and a great deal of blood that had been spilled that day. Emerging in the company of two *papas* from the shrine which housed his accursed images, Montezuma made a deep bow to us all and said: "My lord Malinche, you must be tired after climbing this great *cue* of ours." And Cortés replied that none of us was ever exhausted by anything. Then Montezuma took him by the hand, and told him to look at his great city and all the other cities standing in the water, and the many others on the land round the lake; and he said that if Cortés had not had a good view of the great market-place he could see it better from where he now was. So we stood there looking, because that huge accursed *cue* stood so high that it dominated everything. We saw the three causeways that led into Mexico: the causeway of Iztapalapa by which we had entered four days before, and that of Tacuba along which we were afterwards to flee on the night of our great defeat, when the new prince Cuitlahuac drove us out of the city (as I shall tell in due course), and that of Tepeaqualla. We saw the fresh water which came from Chapultepec to supply the city, and the bridges that were constructed at intervals on the causeways so that the water could flow in and out from one part of the lake to another. We saw a great number of canoes, some coming with provisions and others returning with cargo and merchandise; and we saw too that one could not pass from one house to another of that great city and the other cities that were built on the water except over wooden drawbridges or by canoe. We saw *cues* and shrines in these cities that looked like gleaming white towers and castles: a marvelous sight. All the houses had flat roofs, and on the causeways were other small towers and shrines built like fortresses.

Having examined and considered all that we had seen, we turned back to the great market and the swarm of people buying and selling. The mere murmur of their voices talking was loud enough to be heard more than three miles away. Some of our soldiers who had been in many parts of the world, in Constantinople, in Rome, and all over Italy, said that they had never seen a market so well laid out, so large, so orderly, and so full of people.

others provide insight into the daily lives of the Aztec peoples. A trained class of scribes carefully painted the notes on paper made from the inner bark of fig trees. Unfortunately, many of them were destroyed by the Spaniards as part of their effort to eradicate all aspects of Aztec religion and culture.

THE DESTRUCTION OF AZTEC CIVILIZATION

For a century, the Aztec kingdom dominated much of central Mexico from the Atlantic to the Pacific coast, and its influence penetrated as far south as present-day Guatemala. Most local officials had accepted the sovereignty of the king in Tenochtitlán, but in the region of Tlaxcallan to the east, the authorities were restive under Aztec rule and sought a greater degree of independence.

In 1519, a Spanish expedition under the command of Hernán Cortés landed at Veracruz, on the Gulf of Mexico (see Chapter 14). Marching to Tenochtitlán at the head of a small contingent of troops, Cortés received a friendly welcome from the Aztec monarch Moctezuma Xocoyotzin (often called simply Montezuma), who initially believed his visitor was a representative of Quetzalcoatl, the godlike "feathered serpent" who had departed from his homeland centuries before (see the box on p. 220). But tensions soon erupted between the Spaniards

☙ Moctezuma's Greeting to Hernán Cortés ❧

As his small party arrived in the Aztec capital of Tenochtitlán, Cortés was greeted by King Moctezuma, who was under the impression that Cortés was the representative of Quetzalcoatl, the Aztec deity who had departed centuries earlier with a promise that he would one day return. In this letter to Queen Isabella of Spain, Cortés describes the welcoming ceremony and King Moctezuma's opening address. As Moctezuma would soon discover, he had been deceived as to his visitor's identity and intentions.

Hernán Cortés, Letter from Mexico

Close to the city there is a wooden bridge ten paces wide across a breach in the causeway to allow the water to flow, as it rises and falls. . . .

After we had crossed this bridge, Mutezuma came to greet us and with him some two hundred lords, all barefoot and dressed in a different costume, but also very rich in their way and more so than the others. They came in two columns, pressed very close to the walls of the street, which is very wide and beautiful and so straight that you can see from one end to the other. It is two-thirds of a league long and has on both sides very good and big houses, both dwellings and temples.

[After an exchange of gifts, Mutezuma then] addressed me in the following way:

"For a long time we have known from the writings of our ancestors that neither I, nor any of those who dwell in this land, are natives of it, but foreigners who came from very distant parts; and likewise we know that a chieftain, of whom they were all vassals, brought our people to this region. And he returned to his native land and after many years came again, by which time all those who had remained were married to native women and had built villages and raised children. And when he wished to lead them away again they would not go nor even admit him as their chief; and so he departed. And we have always held that those who descended from him would come and conquer this land and take us as their vassals. So because of the place from which you claim to come, namely, from where the sun rises, and the things you tell us of the great lord or king who sent you here, we believe and are certain that he is our natural lord, especially as you say that he has known of us for some time. So be assured that we shall obey you and hold you as our lord in place of that great sovereign of whom you speak; . . . I know full well of all that has happened to you from Puntunchan to here, and I also know how those of Cempoal and Tascalteca have told you much evil of me; believe only what you see with your eyes, for those are my enemies, and some were my vassals, and have rebelled against me at your coming and said those things to gain favor with you. I also know that they have told you the walls of my houses are made of gold, and that the floor mats in my rooms and other things in my household are likewise of gold, and that I was, and claimed to be, a god; and many other things besides. The houses as you see are of stone and lime and clay."

Then he raised his clothes and showed me his body, saying, as he grasped his arms and trunk with his hands, "See that I am of flesh and blood like you and all other men, and I am mortal and substantial. See how they have lied to you? It is true that I have some pieces of gold left to me by my ancestors; anything I might have shall be given to you whenever you ask. Now I shall go to other houses where I live, but here you shall be provided with all that you and your people require, and you shall receive no hurt, for you are in your own land and your own house."

and the Aztecs, provoked in part by demands by Cortés that the Aztecs denounce their native beliefs and accept Christianity. When the Spanish took Moctezuma hostage and began to destroy Aztec religious shrines, the local population revolted and drove the invaders from the city. Receiving assistance from the state of Tlaxcallan, Cortés managed to fight his way back into the city. Meanwhile the Aztecs were beginning to suffer the first effects of the diseases brought by the Europeans, which would eventually wipe out the majority of the local population. In a battle that to many Aztecs must have seemed to symbolize the dying of the legendary fifth sun, the Aztecs were finally vanquished. Within months, their magnificent city and its temples, believed by the conquerors to be the work of Satan, had been destroyed.

The First Civilizations in South America

South America is a vast continent, characterized by extremes in climate and geography. The north is dominated by the vast Amazon River, which flows through dense tropical jungles carrying a larger flow of water than any other river system in the world. Further to the south, the jungles are replaced by prairies and steppes stretching westward to the Andes Mountains, which extend the entire length of the continent from the Isthmus of Panama to the Strait of Magellan far to the south. Along the Pacific coast, on the western slopes of the mountains, are some of the driest desert regions in the world.

South America has been inhabited by human beings for at least 12,000 years. Wall paintings recently discovered at the "cavern of the painted rock" in the Amazon region suggest to some archaeologists that Stone Age peoples in the area were the contemporaries of hunting communities on the plains of western North America at least 11,000 years ago. Evidence of human settlement has been found on the Tierra del Fuego, at the southern tip of the continent, that dates back to 9500 B.C.E. Early peoples were hunters and food gatherers, but there are indications that irrigated farming was practiced in the northern fringe of the Andes Mountains as early as 2000 B.C.E. Other farming communities of similar age have been discovered in the Amazon River valley and on the western slopes of the Andes Mountains, where evidence of terraced agriculture dates back about four thousand years.

The first signs of civilization, in the form of social organizations above the village level, are found in the central Andes Mountains, in the region of modern-day Peru, Bolivia, and Ecuador. Archaeologists have discovered permanent settlements along the Peruvian coast that date back as far as 6000–5000 B.C.E. These settlements contain the remains of ceremonial precincts, complete with temples, ancestral tombs, and pyramids, similar to those of Mesoamerica. Archaeological evidence suggests that these peoples initially lived primarily by fishing but eventually practiced early forms of irrigated agriculture (burial sites indicate that many males suffered from a mild bone condition often experienced as the result of frequent immersion in cold water) and carried on an exchange of goods with peoples living further to the east in the Andes Mountains.

This early Andes civilization reached its height during the first millennium B.C.E. with the emergence of what is called the Chavin style, named for a site near the modern city of Chavin de Huantar, in the central mountains of modern-day Peru. Although the Chavin site was not the largest settled community in the area, it clearly marked the apex of the Andes civilization at that time and was probably a major religious center for peoples in the area. The ceremonial precinct at the site contained an impressive stone temple complete with interior galleries, a

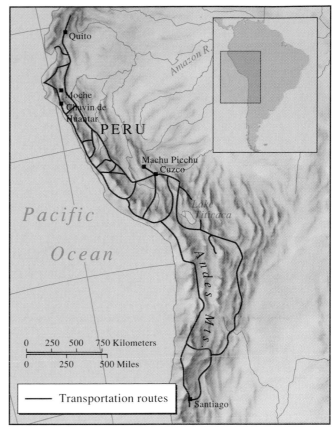

�֎ Map 6.4 The Inca Empire about 1500 C.E.

stone-block ceiling, and a system of underground canals that probably channeled water into the temple complex for ritualistic purposes. The structure was surrounded by stone figures depicting various deities and two pyramids, possibly dedicated to the sun and the moon. Artifacts of stone, bone, and gold were found at Chavin and related sites. Evidence of gold working has been found at gravesites dating back to the mid-second millennium B.C.E.

Early in the first millennium C.E., another advanced civilization appeared near the Pacific coast not far south of the border of Ecuador. At Moche, near the modern city of Trujillo, a major urban center arose amid irrigated fields in the valley of the Moche River, which flows from the foothills of the Andes Mountains into the Pacific Ocean. Farmers in the area grew maize, peanuts, potatoes, and cotton and probably supplied much of the food for peoples living throughout the region.

In all likelihood, Moche was the capital of a powerful state. Mochica art and architectural styles, characterized by a high quality of craftsmanship, were imitated at river valley sites throughout the surrounding area, which suggests that the authority of the Moche rulers may have extended as far as four hundred miles along the coast. Although many of the artifacts, such as stone and ceramic figures, woven textile goods, and household utensils, were clearly meant to be used for religious purposes, they often portray scenes related to daily life. Because the people of Moche, like other pre-Columbian societies in South America, lacked a written language, such artifacts provide us with tantalizing hints of the interests, occupations, and religious concerns of the people. Among other things, they indicate that the people at Moche, like those in Central America, were preoccupied with warfare. Paintings and pottery as well as other artifacts in stone, metal, and ceramics frequently portray warriors, prisoners, and sacrificial victims.

The Moche were also fascinated by the heavens, and much of their art consisted of celestial symbols and astronomical constellations. The nearby Nazca peoples drew immense pictures of animals (known as the "Nazca lines") in the desert near the coast. These drawings, which presumably had cosmological significance, have fascinated specialists and amateurs alike.

The area around the Moche River valley is extremely arid, receiving less than an inch of rain annually. The peoples in the area compensated, however, by building a sophisticated irrigation system to carry water from the river to the parched fields. At its zenith, Moche culture was spectacular. By the eighth century C.E., however, the civilization was in a state of collapse, the irrigation canals had been abandoned, and the remaining population suffered from severe malnutrition.

What had happened to bring Moche culture to this untimely end? Archaeologists speculate that environmental changes, perhaps brought on by changes in the water temperature known as El Niño, led to major flooding of coastal regions and the advance of sand dunes into the irrigated fields.

After the collapse of Moche civilization in the eighth century, a period of decline apparently set in until the rise of a new power about three hundred years later. With its capital at Chanchan, at the mouth of the Moche River, the kingdom of Chimor dominated the area for nearly four centuries until it too declined just before the Spaniards arrived in the early sixteenth century.

Chanchan itself was one of the largest cities in pre-Columbian South America. Built almost entirely of adobe, it housed an estimated 30,000 residents in an area of over twelve square miles and included a number of palace compounds surrounded by walls nearly thirty feet high. On the adobe walls were carved friezes depicting sea creatures and animals, various supernatural figures, and geometrical designs. One compound contained an intricate labyrinth that wound its way progressively inward until it ended in a central chamber, probably occupied by the ruler, at the heart of the building.

Like the Moche before them, the people of Chimor relied on irrigation to funnel the water from the river into their fields. An elaborate system of canals brought the water through hundreds of miles of hilly terrain to the fields near the coast. Channels of different shapes controlled the water flow to prevent erosion or stagnation,

◆ **A Gold Diadem.**　One of the most impressive achievements of the early civilizations in South America was the high quality of their metalwork. Much of their finest craftsmanship is found in the manufacture of delicate gold ornaments. Unfortunately, many of these artifacts were later melted down by Spanish Conquistadors. Illustrated here is a gold headpiece found at a site near Lake Titicaca and dating from the first millennium C.E.

either of which could have destroyed the entire system. Nevertheless, by the fifteenth century, Chimor, too, had disappeared, a victim of floods and a series of earthquakes that destroyed the intricate irrigation system that had been the basis of its survival.

The Inca

The Chimor kingdom was eventually succeeded in the late fifteenth century by an invading force from the mountains far to the south. In the late fourteenth century, the Incas were only a small community in the area of Cuzco, a city located at an altitude of 10,000 feet in the mountains of southern Peru. In the 1440s, however, under the leadership of their powerful ruler Pachakuti (sometimes called Pachacutec, or "he who transforms the world"), the Inca peoples launched a campaign of conquest that eventually brought the entire region under their authority. A classic empire builder, Pachakuti created a highly centralized state. The capital of Cuzco was transformed from a city of mud and thatch into an imposing metropolis of stone. The most impressive structure in the city was a temple dedicated to the sun, which a Spanish observer described as follows:

> It is built of smooth masonry, very level and smooth. The high altar (I use the term to make myself clear, though the Indians did not, of course, have altars) was at the east end. The roof was of wood and very lofty so that there would be plenty of air. It was covered with thatch: they had no tiles. All four walls of the temple were covered from top to bottom with plates and slabs of gold. Over what we have called the high altar they had the image of the Sun on a gold plate twice the thickness of the rest of the wall-plates. The image showed him with a round face and beams and flames of fire all in one piece, just as he is usually depicted by painters. It was so large that it stretched over the whole of that side of the temple from wall to wall.[5]

Under Pachakuti and his immediate successors, Topa Inca and Huayna Inca (the word *Inca* means "ruler"), the boundaries of the kingdom were extended as far as Ecuador, central Chile, and the edge of the Amazon basin.

THE WORLD OF THE FOUR QUARTERS:
INCA POLITICS AND SOCIETY

With a stunning concern for mathematical precision, Pachakuti divided his empire into provinces and districts. Each province was ruled by a governor related to the royal family and contained about 10,000 residents (at least in theory). Excess inhabitants were transferred to

CHRONOLOGY

Early America

Arrival of human beings in America	At least 15,000 years ago
First organized societies in the Andes	c. 6000 B.C.E.
Agriculture first practiced	c. 5000 B.C.E.
Rise of Olmec culture	First millennium B.C.E.
Origins of Mayan civilization	First millennium C.E.
Teotihuacán civilization	c. 300 B.C.E.–800 C.E.
Moche civilization	c. 150 C.E.–800 C.E.
Decline of the Maya	c. ninth century
Civilization of Chimor	c. 1100–1450
Migration of Mexica to Valley of Mexico	Late twelfth century
Kingdom of the Aztecs	Fifteenth century
Inca take over central Andes	Fifteenth century
Arrival of Hernán Cortés in Mexico	1519
Pizarro's conquest of the Inca	1532

other locations for economic or security purposes. The capital of Cuzco was also divided into four quarters, or residential areas, and the social status and economic functions of the residents of each quarter were rigidly defined. The name of the empire itself—Tahuantinsuyu—meant "the world of the four quarters" in the local Quechua language. Clearly, Pachakuti, who claimed descent from the sun god, intended to be a universal emperor.

The state was built on forced labor, using what has been called the "Inca mode of production." Laborers, often with their entire communities, were moved according to need from one part of the country to another to take part in the opening of virgin lands or other types of construction projects. In return, they may have been provided with food and drink and perhaps even with housing (see the box on p. 224). Conscripts probably built the buildings and monuments of the capital city of Cuzco, which was constructed of close-fitting stones that were a wonder to early European visitors. A Spanish traveler estimated that it might have taken twenty men up to one year to prepare the largest stones for placement.

Another major construction project was a system of 24,800 miles of highways and roads that extended from

⇒ Pachakuti, Reformer of the World ⇐

Garcilaso de la Vega, El Inca, who was of mixed Incan and Spanish blood, was born shortly before the Spanish conquest in the Inca capital of Cuzco. His Royal Commentaries of the Incas *was an account of Incan civilization and history. This excerpt describes the massive efforts of the Incan ruler Pachakuti (here Pachacutec) to regulate the lives of his subjects. It represents an effort of social engineering that seems eerily familiar.*

Garcilaso de la Vega,
Royal Commentaries of the Incas

On the death of Viracocha Inca, who was worshiped by the Indians with their gods, he was succeeded by his son, the great Titu, known as Manco Capac, a name he used until his father gave him the title of pachacutec, "reformer of the world." . . . He governed his empire with such industry, prudence, and fortitude in both peace and war that he not only extended the boundaries of all four parts of the kingdom they call Tahuantinsuyu, but also issued many laws and statutes, which have been very willingly confirmed by our Catholic kings, apart from such as refer to the worship of idols and to illicit marriages. . . . He increased the number of instructors and tutors, bade all the lords of vassals, the captains, and their children, and the Indians at large, whatever their occupation, whether soldiers or those of inferior rank, use the language of Cuzco: no post of authority, dignity, or command was to be given to anyone who did not know it well. . . .

This Inca ordered his people to eat with great frugality, though they had more liberty in drinking, whether princes or plebeians. He established that there should be special judges to suppress idleness, and desired that everyone should busy himself at his trade or serve his parents or masters or work for the good of the commonwealth; even boys and girls of five, six, or seven were made to occupy themselves in some task suitable for their years. The blind, the lame and the dumb who were able to work with their hands were given various tasks. The old were required to scare birds off the tilled fields, and all drew ample supplies of food and clothing from the public stores. Lest they should be wearied and distressed by continuous toil, he made a law that there should be three days' holiday every month (which was counted by the moon), on which occasion various games of no great interest were played. He ordered there to be three fairs each month, one every nine days, so that the villagers and field workers, after spending eight days at their tasks, could come to market in the city on the ninth, where they would see and hear whatever the Inca or his Council ordained.

---

the border of modern-day Colombia to a point south of modern-day Santiago, Chile. Two major roadways extended in a north-south direction, one through the Andes Mountains and the other along the coast with connecting routes between them. Rest houses and storage depots were placed along the roads, and various types of bridges, including some of the finest examples of suspension bridges in premodern times, were built over ravines and waterways. Use of the highways, however, was restricted to official and military purposes. Trained runners carried messages rapidly from one way station to another, enabling information to travel up to 140 miles in a single day.

The lives of women were as regimented as other aspects of Inca society. Marriage was strictly regulated, and men and women were required to select a marriage partner from within the immediate tribal group. After marriage, women's main duties were to care for the children and to weave cloth. Spanish visitors noted that women carried their weaving utensils wherever they went, even on visits to a friend's home.

There was one escape from a life of domestic servitude. Fortunate maidens were selected to serve as "chosen virgins" in temples throughout the country. Noblewomen were eligible to compete for service in the Temple of the Sun at Cuzco, while commoners might hope to serve in temples in the provincial capitals. Punishment for breaking the vow of chastity was harsh, and few evidently took the risk. Beautiful women from nonaristocratic families might also be selected as concubines of the ruler.

In rural areas, the population lived mainly by farming. In the mountains, the most common form was terraced agriculture, watered by irrigation systems that carried precise amounts of water into the fields, which were planted with maize, potatoes, and other crops. The plots were tilled by collective labor regulated by the state. The houses of the farmers, built of stone or adobe with thatched roofs, were located nearby. Villages were con-

≽ An Incan Aide-Mémoire ≼

*T*he Inca did not possess a written script. To record events and other aspects of their lives that they wished to remember, they used an ingenious system of knotted strings, called quipu. Here Garcilaso de la Vega, author of the Royal Commentaries of the Incas, provides us with a description of the process.

Garcilaso de la Vega, *Royal Commentaries of the Incas*

These men recorded on their knots all the tribute brought annually to the Inca, specifying everything by kind, species, and quality. They recorded the number of men who went to the wars, how many died in them, and how many were born and died every year, month by month. In short they may be said to have recorded on their knots everything that could be counted, even mentioning battles and fights, all the embassies that had come to visit the Inca, and all the speeches and arguments the king had uttered. But the purpose of the embassies or the contents of the speeches, or any other descriptive matter could not be recorded on the knots, consisting as it did of continuous spoken or written prose, which cannot be expressed by means of knots, since these can give only numbers and not words. To supply this want they used signs that indicated historical events or facts or the existence of any embassy, speech, or discussion in time of peace or war. Such

speeches were preserved by the *quipucamayus* by memory in a summarized form of a few words: they were committed to memory and taught by tradition to their successors and descendants from father to son. This was especially practiced in the villages or provinces where the event in question had occurred: there naturally such traditions were preserved better than elsewhere, because the natives would treasure them. Another method too was used for keeping alive in the memory of the people their deeds and the embassies they sent to the Inca and the replies he gave them. The *amautas* who were their philosophers and sages took the trouble to turn them into stories, no longer than fables, suitable for telling to children, young people, and the rustics of the countryside: they were thus passed from hand to hand and age to age, and preserved in the memories of all. Their stories were also recounted in the form of fables of an allegorical nature, some of which we have mentioned, while others will be referred to later. Similarly the *harauicus*, who were their poets, wrote short, compressed poems, embracing a history, or an embassy, or the king's reply. In short, everything that could not be recorded on the knots was included in these poems, which were sung at their triumphs and on the occasion of their greater festivals, and recited to the young Incas when they were armed knights. Thus they remembered their history.

---

nected by roads and paths that snaked through the mountainous terrain, sometimes crossing vast ravines on suspension bridges made of braided fiber and fastened to stone abutments on the opposite banks. Nothing is more indicative of the architectural genius of the Inca peoples than the ruins of the abandoned city of Machu Picchu, built on a lofty hilltop surrounded by mountain crags far above the Urubamba River.

INCA CULTURE

Like many other civilizations in pre-Columbian Latin America, the Inca state was built on war. Soldiers for the 200,000-man Inca army, the largest and best armed in the region, were raised by universal male conscription. Military units were moved rapidly along the highway system and were housed in the rest houses located along the roadside. Since the Inca had no wheeled vehicles, supplies were car-

ried on the backs of llamas. Once an area was placed under Incan authority, the local inhabitants were instructed in the Quechua language, which became the *lingua franca* of the state, and were introduced to the state religion. The Inca had no writing system, but kept records using a system of knotted strings called *quipu* (see the box above).

As in the case of the Aztecs and the Maya, the lack of a fully developed writing system did not prevent the Inca from realizing a high level of cultural achievement. Most of what survives was recorded by the Spanish and consists of entertainment for the elites. The Inca had a highly developed tradition of court theater, including both tragic and comic works. Productions often involved the recounting of valiant deeds and other historical events, and the actors were not professionals, but members of the nobility or senior officials who memorized their parts. There was also some poetry, composed in blank verse and often accompanied by music, which was usually played on reed instruments.

◆ **The Stones of Cuzco.** By the mid-fifteenth century C.E., the Inca had established a large empire in present-day Peru with their capital at Cuzco. Like other early peoples in the Americas, the Incas revered sacred stones and leveled terraces from a mountain above Cuzco to create a giant altar or throne. Guarding the sacred mountain are fifty-foot-high walls, which were built without mortar, a testimony to the excellence of Inca stonework.

THE CONQUEST OF THE INCA

The Inca empire was still in existence when the first Spanish expeditions arrived in the central Andes. The leader of the Spanish invaders, Francisco Pizarro, was accompanied by only a few hundred companions, but like Hernán Cortés he possessed steel weapons, gunpowder, and horses, none of which were familiar to his hosts. In the meantime, internal factionalism, combined with the onset of contagious diseases spread unknowingly by the Europeans, had weakened the ruling elite, and the empire fell rapidly to the Spanish forces in 1532. The last Inca ruler was tried by the Spaniards and executed. Pre-Columbian South America's greatest age was over.

Stateless Societies in the New World

The civilizations that we have discussed thus far in this chapter were only the most advanced of many evolving societies in North and South America. Beyond Central America and the high ridges of the Andes Mountains, on the Great Plains of North America, along the Amazon River in South America, and on the islands of the Caribbean Sea, other communities of Amerindians were beginning to master the art of agriculture and to build organized societies.

Although human beings had occupied much of the continent of North America during the early phase of human settlement in the New World, the switch to farming as a means of survival did not occur until the third

millennium B.C.E. at the earliest, and not until much later in most areas of the continent. Until that time, most Amerindian communities in what archaeologists call the Archaic period (from about 10,000 B.C.E. to the first millennium B.C.E.) lived by hunting, fishing, or foraging. The first hunters had trekked to the New World in pursuit of the bison, caribou, and mammoth that had crossed the land bridge of the Bering Strait at the end of the last Ice Age. As the supply of large animals began to diminish, they turned to smaller game and to fishing and foraging for wild plants, fruits, and nuts.

It was probably during the third millennium B.C.E. that peoples in selected parts of North America began to cultivate indigenous plants for food in a systematic way. As was the case elsewhere, early agriculture was often combined with traditional forms of subsistence such as hunting and food gathering, but as the population grew, wild game and food became scarce, forcing some communities to place more emphasis on cultivating crops. This shift first occurred in the Mississippi River valley from Ohio, Indiana, and Illinois down to the Gulf of Mexico. Among the most commonly cultivated crops were maize, squash, beans, and various types of grasses.

As the population in the area increased, people began to congregate in villages, and sedentary communities began to develop in the alluvial lowlands where the soil could be cultivated for many years at a time because of the nutrients deposited by the river water. As the communities grew, village councils were established to adjudicate disputes, and in a few cases several villages banded together under the authority of a local chieftain. Such chieftains may have claimed divine powers, for clear signs of human sacrifices have been found inside the main burial mounds. Urban centers began to appear, some of them inhabited by as many as 10,000 people or more. At the same time, regional trade increased. The people of the Hopewell culture in Ohio ranged from the shores of Lake Superior to the Appalachian Mountains and the Gulf of Mexico in search of metals, shells, obsidian, and manufactured items to support their economic needs and religious beliefs.

At the site of Cahokia, near the modern city of East St. Louis, Illinois, archaeologists found a burial mound more than ninety-eight feet high with a base larger than that of the Great Pyramid in Egypt. A hundred smaller mounds were also found in the vicinity. The town itself, which covered almost 300 acres and was surrounded by a wooden stockade, was apparently the administrative capital of much of the surrounding territory until its decline in the thirteenth century C.E. Cahokia carried on extensive trade with other communities throughout the region, and there are some signs of regular contacts with the civilizations in Mesoamerica, such as the presence of ball courts in the Central American style. But there are also indications that wars were not uncommon. It was apparently in an effort to bring an end to the constant warfare that the Iroquois, who inhabited much of the modern states of Pennsylvania and New York as well as parts of southern Canada, created a tribal alliance called the League of Iroquois.

West of the Mississippi River basin, most Amerindian peoples lived by hunting or food gathering. During the first millennium C.E., knowledge of agriculture gradually spread up the rivers to the Great Plains, and farming was practiced as far west as southwestern Colorado, where the Anasazi peoples (Navajo for "alien ancient ones") established an extensive agricultural community in an area extending from northern New Mexico and Arizona to southwestern Colorado and parts of southern Utah.

This part-time farming culture, based primarily on the cultivation of maize, first appeared about the beginning of the first millennium C.E. Although they apparently never discovered the wheel or used beasts of burden, the Anasazi eventually created a system of roads that facilitated an extensive exchange of technology, products, and ideas throughout the region. By the ninth century, they had mastered the art of irrigation, which allowed them to expand their productive efforts to squash and beans, and eventually created an important urban center at Chaco Canyon, in southern New Mexico. In the heart of a canyon at Pueblo Bonito, they built a walled city with dozens of three-story adobe houses with timbered roofs. Community religious functions were carried out in two large circular chambers called kivas. Clothing was made from hides or cotton cloth. At its height, Pueblo Bonito contained several hundred compounds housing several thousand residents. Roads extended out in all directions, permitting trade with other societies as far away as central Mexico. Another urban community was established along a cliff face at Mesa Verde, in southwestern Colorado.

Sometime during the late twelfth and thirteenth centuries, however, these settlements were suddenly abandoned, as the inhabitants migrated southward. Their descendants, the Zuni and the Hopi, now occupy pueblos in central Arizona and New Mexico. For years, archaeologists surmised that a severe drought was the root cause of the migration, but in recent years new evidence has raised doubts that decreasing rainfall, by itself, was a sufficient explanation. An increase in internecine warfare, perhaps brought about by climatic changes, may also have played a role in the decision to relocate. In any event, with increasing aridity and the importation of the horse by the Spanish in the sixteenth century (a native version of the horse had died out thousands of years ear-

♦ **Machu Picchu.** Situated in the Andes in modern-day Peru, Machu Picchu reflects the glory of Inca civilization. To farm such rugged terrain, the Incas constructed terraces and stone aqueducts. The most revered of the many temples and stone altars at Machu Picchu was the thronelike "hitching post of the sun" at the left, so called because of its close proximity to the sun god.

lier), hunting revived, and mounted nomads like the Apache and the Navajo came to dominate much of the southwest.

East of the Andes Mountains in South America, other Amerindian societies were beginning to make the transition to organized states. Perhaps the most prominent were the Arawak, a people living along the Orinoco River in modern-day Venezuela. Having begun to cultivate manioc (a tuber used today in the manufacture of tapioca) along the banks of the river, they gradually migrated down to the coast and then proceeded to move

Conclusion

The first human beings did not arrive in the New World until quite late in the prehistorical period. For the next several millennia, their descendants were forced to respond to the challenges of the environment in total isolation from other parts of the world. Nevertheless, around 5000 B.C.E., farming settlements began to appear in river valleys and upland areas in both Central and South America. Not long afterward—at least in historical time—organized communities located along the coast of the Gulf of Mexico and the western slopes of the central Andes Mountains embarked on the long march to civilization.

What is perhaps most striking about these developments is how closely the process in the New World paralleled that in the old. Although the civilizations in Central and South America were less advanced in terms of technology (the lack of iron and the wheel, for example, and the absence of a sophisticated writing system), in many other respects the states in Central America and the Andes were the equal of those that we will discuss in later chapters. One need only point to the awed comments of early Spanish visitors who said that the cities of the Aztecs were the equal of Seville and the other great metropolitan centers of Spain.

What was most repugnant to those early European visitors were the religious beliefs and practices of the civilizations that they encountered. They were repelled, of course, by the worship of strange idols, but even more by the human sacrifices on a massive scale. Before rushing to judgment, however, we should remember that similar practices had been carried out in many societies of the Old World, including the ancient civilizations of Egypt, India, and China. The Spaniards were perhaps most surprised to discover that civilizations that in other respects had achieved such a high degree of culture also practiced human sacrifice.

In recent years, some scholars have speculated that the peoples in the Americas were more peaceful than their counterparts in the Old World. The bulk of the evidence, however, suggests that the Amerindian peoples were every bit as addicted to the "war of the fishes" (see Chapter 2) as were those of the ancient empires of Africa and Asia. Yet in both hemispheres it appears that the first civilizations formed by the human species were brought to an end as much by environmental changes as by war. In the next chapter, we shall return to the Old World, where new civilizations were in the process of replacing the ancient empires.

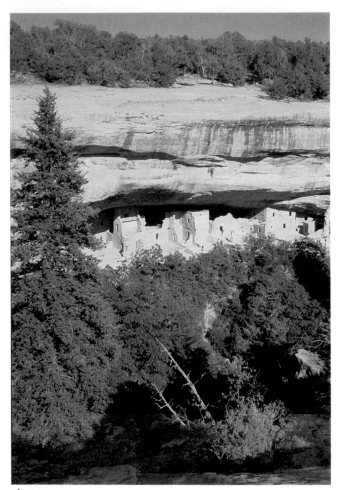

◆ **Cliff Palace at Mesa Verde.**   Mesa Verde is one of the best-developed sites of the Anasazi peoples in Southwestern North America. At one time they were farmers who tilled the soil atop the mesas, but eventually they were forced to build their settlements in more protected locations. At Cliff Palace shown here, adobe houses were hidden on the perpendicular face of the mesa. Access was achieved only by a perilous descent via indented finger and toeholds on the rockface.

eastward along the northern coast of the continent. Some occupied the islands of the Caribbean Sea. In their new island habitat, they lived by a mixture of fishing, hunting, and cultivating maize, beans, manioc, and squash, as well as other crops such as peanuts, peppers, and pineapples. As the population increased, a pattern of political organization above the village level appeared, along with recognizable social classes headed by a chieftain whose authority included control over the economy. The Arawak practiced human sacrifice, and some urban centers contained ball courts, suggesting the possibility of contacts with Mesoamerica.

CHAPTER NOTES

1. Quoted in Sylvanus Morley and George W. Brainerd, *The Ancient Maya* (Stanford, Calif., 1983), p. 513.
2. Bernal Díaz, *The Conquest of New Spain* (Harmondsworth, 1975), p. 210.
3. Quoted in Brian M. Fagan, *The Aztecs* (New York, 1984), p. 141.
4. Michael Coe, Dean Snow, and Elizabeth Benson, *Atlas of Ancient America* (New York, 1988), p. 149.
5. Garcilaso de la Vega, El Inca, *Royal Commentaries of the Incas and General History of Peru,* Part I, trans. Harold V. Livermore (Austin, Tex., 1966), p. 180.

SUGGESTED READINGS

For a profusely illustrated and informative overview of the early civilization of the Americas, see M. Coe, D. Snow, and E. Benson, *Atlas of Ancient America* (New York, 1988). The first arrival of human beings in the New World is discussed in J. D. Jennings, ed., *Ancient Native Americans* (San Francisco, 1978); and B. Fagan, *The Great Journey: The Peopling of Ancient America* (London, 1987).

For a recent overview of Aztec civilization in Mexico, see B. Fagan, *The Aztecs* (New York, 1984). S. D. Gillespie, *The Aztec Kings: The Construction of Rulership in Mexican History* (Tucson, 1989) is an imaginative effort to uncover the symbolic meaning in Aztec traditions. On the Olmecs and the Zapotecs, see E. P. Benson, *The Olmec and Their Neighbors* (Washington, D.C., 1981); M. D. Coe and R. A. Diehl, *In the Land of the Olmec* (Austin, Tex., 1980); and R. E. Blanton, *Monte Alban: Settlement Patterns at the Ancient Zapotec Capital* (New York, 1978).

For an early classical work on Mayan civilization, see S. G. Morley and G. W. Brainerd, *The Ancient Maya* (Stanford, Calif., 1983). N. Hammond, *Ancient Maya Civilization* (New Brunswick, N.J., 1982) provides a general survey for the nonspecialist. See also M. D. Coe, *The Maya* (London, 1993). For a richly illustrated general survey, see G. E. Stuart and G. S. Stuart, *The Mysterious Maya* (Washington, D.C., 1977).

Much of our information about the lives of the peoples of ancient Central America comes from Spanish writers who visited or lived in the area during the sixteenth and seventeenth centuries. For the original Spanish conquest of Mexico, see H. Cortés, *Letters from Mexico* (New Haven, Conn., 1986); and B. Díaz, *The Conquest of New Spain* (Harmondsworth, 1975). See also Fray D. Duran, *The Aztecs: The History of the Indies of New Spain* (New York, 1964).

On the Inca and their predecessors, see R. W. Keatinge, ed., *Peruvian Prehistory: An Overview of Pre-Inca and Inca Society* (Cambridge, 1988); G. Bankes, *Peru before Pizarro* (Oxford, 1977); and E. P. Lanning, *Peru before the Incas* (Englewood Cliffs, N.J., 1967). The arrival of the Spanish is chronicled in C. Howard, *Pizarro and the Conquest of Peru* (New York, 1967). For an extended account of Inca civilization, see G. de la Vega, El Inca, *Royal Commentaries of the Incas and General History of Peru* (Austin, Tex., 1966).

On the art and culture of the ancient Americas, see E. Pasztory, *Aztec Art* (New York, 1983); E. Henning and J. Raney, *Monuments of the Inca* (Boston, 1982); and L. Schele and M. E. Miller, *The Blood of Kings: A New Interpretation of Maya Art* (Austin, Tex., 1986). Writing systems are discussed in D. H. Kelley, *Deciphering the Maya Script* (Austin, Tex., 1976), and J. E. S. Thompson, *Maya Hieroglyphic Writing: An Introduction* (Norman, Okla., 1971).

CHAPTER

7

The World of Islam

In the year 570, in the Arabian city of Mecca, there was born a child named Muhammad whose life changed the course of world history. The son of a merchant, Muhammad grew to maturity in a time of transition. Old empires that had once ruled the entire Middle East were only a distant memory. The region was now divided into many separate states, and the people adhered to many different faiths.

Within a few decades of Muhammad's death, the Middle East was united once again. The initial triumph was primarily political and military. Arab armies marched westward across North Africa and eastward into Mesopotamia and Persia, imposing their authority and creating a new empire that stretched from the Iberian peninsula to the Indus valley. But Arab rule also brought with it a new religion and a new culture—that of Islam.

Islamic beliefs and Islamic culture exerted a powerful influence in all areas occupied by Arab armies. Initially, Arab beliefs and customs, as reflected through the prism of Muhammad's teachings, transformed the societies and cultures of the peoples living within the new empire. But eventually the distinctive political and cultural forces that had long characterized the region began to reassert themselves. Factional struggles led to the decline and then the destruction of the Arab empire. Invading forces from Central Asia established their control over the great mercantile cities of the region, while Christian crusaders attacked the empire from the west. New states

Life of Muhammad · Founding of Abbasid caliphate · · · Mongols destroy city of Baghdad

Reign of Harun al-Rashid

Muhammad's flight to Medina · · Election of Ali to caliphate

Conquest of Mecca · · · · · · · · · · Spread of Islam to Spain and northwestern India

Construction of city of Baghdad · Seljuk Turks seize Baghdad · Ottoman Turks seize Constantinople

Conquest of Anatolia by Seljuk Turks

formed in Spain, North Africa, and Persia and began to put their own stamp on the cultures of the region. Like the empires that had preceded it, the Arab empire, with its capital at Baghdad, became a thing of the past.

Still, the Arab conquest left a powerful legacy that survived the decline of Arab political power. The ideological and emotional appeal of Islam remained strong throughout the Middle East and even extended into areas not occupied by Arab armies, such as the Indian subcontinent, Southeast Asia, and sub-Saharan Africa. At the same time, the political unification of the entire region, although temporary, provided an environment conducive to the revival and expansion of long-distance trade and the exchange of culture and ideas that had taken place before the collapse of the classical empires at the beginning of the first millennium B.C.E. Although the vision of regional political and cultural unity that had inspired Muhammad and his followers was never realized, Islam remained a powerful force that provided a measure of religious and cultural unity for the region.

The Rise of Islam

The Arabs were a Semitic-speaking people of the Near East with a long history. They were mentioned in Greek sources of the fifth century B.C.E. and even earlier in the Old Testament. The Greek historian Herodotus had applied the name Arab to the entire peninsula, calling it Arabia. A kingdom called Nabataea was established there during the last centuries of the first millennium B.C.E. In 106 B.C.E., the Romans extended their authority to the Arabian peninsula, transforming it into a province of their growing empire.

During Roman times, the region was inhabited primarily by the Bedouins, nomadic peoples who came originally from the northern part of the peninsula. Although some peoples of the area engaged in trade, especially in the small settlements that sprang up around the major oases, the majority were poor Bedouins, and as time passed, the term *Arab* tended to be reserved for them.

Bedouin society was organized on a tribal basis. The ruling member of the tribe was called the *sheikh* and was selected from one of the leading families by a council of elders called the *majlis*. The *sheikh* ruled the tribe with the consent of the council. Each tribe was autonomous, but felt a general sense of allegiance to the larger unity of all the clans in the region. In early times, the Bedouins had supported themselves primarily by sheepherding or by raiding caravans passing through the desert, but after the domestication of the camel during the first millennium B.C.E., they began to participate in the caravan trade themselves and became major carriers of goods between the Persian Gulf and the Mediterranean Sea.

The Arabs of pre-Islamic times were polytheistic, with a supreme god known as Allah presiding over a community of spirits. It was a communal faith, involving all members of the tribe, and had no priesthood. The supreme deity was symbolized by a sacred stone. Each tribe possessed its own stone, but all worshiped a massive black meteorite, which was located in a central shrine called the *Ka'aba* in the commercial city of Mecca.

In the fifth and sixth centuries C.E., the economic importance of the Arabian peninsula began to increase. As a result of the political disorder in Mesopotamia—a consequence of the constant wars between the Byzantine and Persian Empires—and in Egypt, the trade routes that ran directly across the peninsula or down the Red Sea became increasingly risky, and a third route, which passed from the Mediterranean through Mecca to Yemen and then by ship across the Indian Ocean, became more popular. The communities in that part of the peninsula benefited from the change and took a larger share of the caravan trade between the Mediterranean and the countries on the other side of the Indian Ocean. As a consequence, relations between the Bedouins of the desert and the increasingly wealthy merchant class of the towns began to become strained.

Into this intense world stepped Muhammad, a man whose spiritual visions unified the Arab world with a speed no one would have suspected possible. Born in Mecca to a merchant family and orphaned at the age of six, Muhammad (570–632) grew up to become a caravan manager and eventually married a rich widow who was also his employer. For several years he lived in Mecca as a merchant, but was apparently troubled by the growing gap between the Bedouin moral values of honesty and generosity (he himself was a member of the local Hashemite clan of the Quraishi tribe) and the acquisitive behavior of the affluent commercial elites in the city.

✴ Map 7.1 The Middle East in the Time of Muhammad.

Deeply concerned, he began to visit the nearby hills to meditate in isolation.

On one of those occasions, he experienced visions and heard a voice that he was convinced was inspired by Allah. According to tradition, the message was conveyed by the angel Gabriel, who commanded Muhammad to recite. When the latter asked for clarification of what he was to do, the angel replied:

> Recite in the name of your Lord who created, created man from clots of blood! Recite! Your Lord is a most bountiful one, who by the pen taught man what he did not know.[1]

Muhammad was acquainted with Jewish and Christian beliefs and came to believe that while Allah had already revealed himself in part through Moses and Jesus—and thus through the Hebraic and Christian traditions—the final revelations were now being given to him. Out of his revelations, which were eventually dictated to scribes, came the Koran or Qur'an, the holy scriptures of Islam (meaning "submission to the will of Allah"). The Koran contained the guidelines by which followers of Allah, known as Muslims (i.e., those who practice Islam), were to live. Like the Christians and the Jews, Muslims were a "People of the Book."

After receiving the revelations, Muhammad returned to his home to consult with his wife Khadija. According to tradition, he was severely shaken by his experience, but his wife encouraged him to comply with Gabriel's message. Muhammad then set out to persuade the residents of Mecca of the truth of his revelations. At first, many were convinced that he was mad or a charlatan. Others were undoubtedly concerned that his vigorous

◆ **The Ka'aba in Mecca.** The Ka'aba, a massive black meteorite in the Arabian city of Mecca, is the sacred stone of the Islamic faith. Wherever Muslims pray, they are instructed to face Mecca; each thus becomes a spoke of the Ka'aba, the holy center of the wheel of Islam. If they are able to do so, all Muslims are encouraged to visit the Ka'aba at least once in their lifetime. Called the *hajj*, this pilgrimage to Mecca represents the ultimate in spiritual fulfillment.

◆ **Muhammad and the Sacred Stone.** In pre-Islamic times, the Arabs were polytheistic, with a supreme deity symbolized by a sacred stone. Although each tribe possessed its own stone, all worshiped the black metorite stone at a shrine in Mecca called the Ka'aba. In 630 Muhammad proclaimed the Ka'aba to be the sacred shrine of Islam. In this fourteenth-century miniature, we see Muhammad restoring the black stone to its rightful place in the wall of the Ka'aba.

The Koran and the Spread of the Muslim Faith

The Koran is the sacred book of Islam, holding a place comparable to that of the Bible in Christianity. The Koran contains 114 suras or chapters that were systematically written down after Muhammad's death to preserve the revelation that Allah made to his Prophet. In this selection from Chapter 47, entitled "Muhammad, Revealed at Medina," it is apparent that Islam encourages the spreading of the faith. A garden of paradise quite unlike the arid desert homeland of the Arab warriors awaited all believers who died for Allah.

The Koran: Chapter 47, "Muhammad, Revealed at Medina"

Allah will bring to nothing the deeds of those who disbelieve and debar others from His path. As for the faithful who do good works and believe in what is revealed to Muhammad—which is the truth from their Lord—He will forgive them their sins and ennoble their state.

This, because the unbelievers follow falsehood, while the faithful follow the truth from their Lord. Thus Allah coins their sayings for mankind.

When you meet the unbelievers in the battlefield strike off their heads and, when you have laid them low, bind your captives firmly. Then grant them their freedom or take ransom from them, until War shall lay down her armour.

Thus shall you so. Had Allah willed, He could Himself have punished them; but He has ordained it thus that He might test you, the one by the other.

As for those who are slain in the cause of Allah, He will not allow their works to perish. He will vouchsafe them guidance and ennoble their state; He will admit them to the Paradise He has made known to them.

Believers, if you help Allah, Allah will help you and make you strong. But the unbelievers shall be consigned to perdition. He will bring their deeds to nothing. Because they have opposed His revelations, He will frustrate their works.

Have they never journeyed through the land and seen what was the end of those who have gone before them? Allah destroyed them utterly. A similar fate awaits the unbelievers, because Allah is the protector of the faithful; because the unbelievers have no protector.

Allah will admit those who embrace the true faith and do good works to gardens watered by running streams. The unbelievers take their fill of pleasure and eat as the beasts eat: but Hell shall be their home. . . .

This is the Paradise which the righteous have been promised. There shall flow in it rivers of unpolluted water, and rivers of milk forever fresh; rivers of delectable wine and rivers of clearest honey. They shall eat therein of every fruit and receive forgiveness from their Lord. Is this like the lot of those who shall abide in Hell for ever and drink scalding water which will tear their bowels? . . .

Know that there is no god but Allah. Implore Him to forgive your sins and to forgive the true believers, men and women. Allah knows your busy haunts and resting-places.

attacks on traditional beliefs and the corrupt society around him could severely shake the social and political order. After three years of proselytizing, he had only thirty followers.

Discouraged by the systematic persecution of his followers, which was undertaken with a brutality reminiscent of the cruelties suffered by early Christians, as well as the failure of the Meccans to accept his message, in 622 Muhammad and some of his closest supporters (mostly from his own Hashemite clan) left the city and retreated north to the rival city of Yathrib. The city was later renamed Medina, or "city of the Prophet." That flight, known in history as the Hegira (*Hijrah*), marked the first date of the official calendar of Islam. Muhammad failed in his original purpose—to convert the Jewish community in Medina to his beliefs—but he was successful in winning support from other residents of the city as well as from members of Bedouin tribal groups in the surrounding countryside. From this mixture, he formed the first Muslim community (the *umma*). Returning to his birthplace at the head of a considerable military force, Muhammad conquered Mecca and converted the townspeople to the new faith. In 630 he made a symbolic visit to the Ka'aba, where he declared it a sacred shrine of Islam and ordered the destruction of the idols of the traditional faith. Two years later, Muhammad died, just as the influence of Islam was beginning to spread throughout the peninsula.

⇒ A Pilgrimage to Mecca ⇐

The pilgrimage to Mecca, one of the "five pillars of Islam," is the duty of every Muslim. Ibn Jubayr, a twelfth-century Spanish Muslim, left a description of his trip in his journal. The work is famous for its vivid and abundant detail. In this almost lyrical passage, Ibn Jubayr tells of reaching his final destination, the Ka'aba at Mecca, containing the Black Stone. The Qarmata were an extremist religious sect in ninth- and tenth-century Mesopotamia.

Ibn Jubayr, *Travels*

The blessed Black Stone is encased in the corner [of the Ka'aba] facing east. The depth to which it penetrates it is not known, but it is said to extend two cubits into the wall. Its breadth is two-thirds of a span, its length one span and a finger joint. It has four pieces, joined together, and it is said that it was the Qarmata—may God curse them—who broke it. Its edges have been braced with a sheet of silver whose white shines brightly against the black sheen and polished brilliance of the Stone, presenting the observer a striking spectacle which will hold his gaze. The Stone, when kissed, has a softness and moistness which so enchants the mouth that he who puts his lips to it would wish them never to be removed. This is one of the special favors of Divine Providence, and it is enough that the Prophet—may God bless and preserve him—declare it to be a covenant of God on earth. May God profit us by the kissing and touching of it. By His favor may all who yearn fervently for it be brought to it. In the sound piece of the stone, to the right of him who presents himself to kiss it, is a small white spot that shines and appears like a mole on the blessed surface. Concerning this white mole, there is a tradition that he who looks upon it clears his vision, and when kissing it one should direct one's lips as closely as one can to the place of the mole.

The Teachings of Muhammad

Like Christianity and Judaism, Islam is monotheistic. Allah is the all-powerful being who created the universe and everything in it. Islam is also concerned with salvation and offers the hope of an afterlife. Those who hope to achieve it must subject themselves to the will of Allah. Unlike Christianity, Islam denies the divinity of its founder. Muhammad, like Jesus, Moses, and other figures of the Old Testament, was a prophet, but he was also a man like other men. Because human beings rejected his earlier messengers, Allah sent his final revelation through Muhammad.

At the heart of Islam is the Koran (meaning "recitation"), with its basic message that there is no God but Allah and Muhammad is his Prophet (see the box on p. 234). Consisting of 114 *suras* (chapters) that were drawn together into an integrated whole by a committee established after Muhammad's death, the Koran is not only the sacred book of Islam, but an ethical guidebook and a code of law and political theory combined.

Islam was a direct and simple faith, emphasizing the need to obey the will of Allah. This meant following a basic ethical code that consisted of what are popularly termed the "five pillars" of Islam: belief in Allah and Muhammad as his Prophet; standard prayer five times a day and public prayer on Friday at midday to worship Allah; observation of the holy month of Ramadan including fasting from dawn to sunset; making a pilgrimage, if possible, to Mecca in one's lifetime (see the box above); and giving alms (called the *zakat*) to the poor and unfortunate. The faithful who observed the law were guaranteed a place in an eternal paradise with the sensuous delights so obviously lacking in the midst of the Arabian desert.

Islam was not just a set of religious beliefs, but a way of life as well. After the death of Muhammad, Muslim scholars, known as the *ulama*, drew up a law code, called the *Shari'ah*, to provide believers with a set of prescriptions to regulate their daily lives. Much of the *Shari'ah* was drawn from the Koran, or from the *Hadith*, a collection of the sayings of the Prophet that were used to supplement the revelations contained in the holy scriptures.

Believers were subject to strict behavioral requirements. In addition to the "five pillars," Muslims were forbidden to gamble, to eat pork, to drink alcoholic beverages, and to engage in dishonest behavior. Sexual mores were also strict. Contacts between unmarried men and women were discouraged, and ideally marriages were to be arranged by the parents. In accordance with Bedouin custom, polygyny was permitted, but Muhammad attempted to limit the practice by restricting males to four wives.

The Arab Empire and Its Successors

The death of Muhammad presented his followers with a dilemma. Although Muhammad had not claimed divine qualities, Muslims saw no separation between political and religious authority. Submission to the will of Allah meant submission to his Prophet Muhammad. According to the Koran: "Whoso obeyeth the messenger obeyeth Allah."[2] Muhammad's charismatic authority and political skills had been at the heart of his success. But he never named a successor, and although he had several daughters, he left no sons. In a male-oriented society, who would lead the community of the faithful?

Shortly after Muhammad's death, a number of his closest followers selected Abu Bakr, a wealthy merchant from Medina who was Muhammad's father-in-law and one of his first supporters, as caliph (*khalifa*, literally "successor"), or the temporal leader of the Islamic community. Under Abu Bakr's prudent leadership, the movement succeeded in suppressing factional tendencies among some of the Bedouin tribes in the peninsula and began to direct their attention to wider fields. Muhammad had used the Arabic tribal custom of the *razzia* or raid in the struggle against his enemies. Now his successors turned to the same custom to expand the authority of the movement. The Koran called this activity "striving in the way of the Lord," or *jihad*. Although sometimes translated as "holy war," the *jihad* grew out of the Arabic tradition of tribal raids, which were permitted as a way to channel the warlike energies of the Bedouin tribes.

Once the Arabs had become unified under Muhammad's successor, they began to conduct a *jihad* on a larger scale, directing outward against neighboring peoples the energy they had formerly directed against each other. The Byzantine and the Persian Empires were the first to feel the strength of the newly united Arabs, now aroused to a peak of zeal by their common faith. At Yarmuk in 636, the Muslims defeated the Byzantine army. Four years later, they took possession of the Byzantine province of Syria. To the east, the Arabs defeated a Persian force in 637 and then went on to conquer the entire empire of the Sassanids by 650.

In the meantime, Egypt and other areas of North Africa were also brought under Arab authority (see Chapter 8). Some historians have argued that the ongoing conflict between the Byzantines and the Persians had weakened both powers and made the Arab triumph substantially easier. Although there may be some truth in this assertion, the power of the Bedouin armies should not be overlooked. Led by a series of brilliant generals, the Arabs had put together a large and highly motivated army, whose valor was enhanced by the belief that Muslim warriors were guaranteed a place in paradise if they died in battle.

To some, the advance of the Arabs was a religious war, a *jihad* led by fanatical Muslims determined to impose their faith on nonbelievers. Certainly, Islam did provide a unifying creed that mobilized the enthusiastic support of the Bedouin peoples of the Arabian peninsula. But Muslim scholars contend that Arab administrators did not impose their faith on the conquered population and point to the maxim in the Koran that "there shall be no compulsion in religion."[3]

That contention is essentially correct. In general, Arab administration of conquered areas was relatively tolerant, at least by the standards of the time. Sometimes, due to a shortage of trained Arab administrators, government was left to local officials. Mistreatment of the people by Arab soldiers was rare, and conversion to Islam was voluntary. Those who chose not to convert were required only to submit to Muslim rule and pay a head tax in return for exemption from military service, which was required of all Muslim males. Under such conditions, the local populations often welcomed Arab rule as preferable to Byzantine rule or that of the Sassanid dynasty in Persia. Furthermore, the simple and direct character of the new religion, as well as its egalitarian qualities (all people were viewed as equal in the eyes of Allah), were undoubtedly attractive to peoples throughout the region.

What explains the rapid expansion of the Arabs after the rise of Islam in the early seventh century? Some recent historians have rejected the "holy war" hypothesis and have sought the answer in a long period of drought that may have afflicted the Arabian peninsula. For the moment, however, there is no evidence to support this theory. Others have attempted to show that Arab expansion was not a spontaneous event but a deliberate decision on the part of ruling elites in Mecca to extend trade routes and bring surplus-producing regions under their control. Another consideration may have been the desire to channel the energies of the new converts.

Whatever the case, the main challenge to the growing empire came from within. Some of Muhammad's followers had not agreed with the selection of Abu Bakr as the first caliph and promoted the candidacy of Muhammad Ali, Muhammad's cousin and son-in-law, as an alternative. Ali's claim to legitimacy was ignored by other leaders, however, and after Abu Bakr's death, the office was passed to Umar, another of Muhammad's followers. In 656, Umar's successor Uthman was assassinated, and Ali was finally selected for the position. But Ali's rivals were convinced that he had been implicated in the death of his predecessor, and a factional struggle broke out within the Muslim leadership. In 661 Ali himself was assassinated, and Mu'awiyah, the governor of Syria and one of Ali's chief rivals, replaced him in office. Mu'awiyah thereupon made the caliphate hereditary in his own family, called the Umayyads, who were a branch of the Quraishi clan. The new caliphate, with its capital at Damascus, remained in power for nearly a century.

The Umayyads

The factional struggle within Islam did not bring an end to Arab expansion. At the beginning of the eighth century, new attacks were launched at both the western and the eastern end of the Mediterranean world. Arab armies advanced across North Africa and conquered the Berbers, a primarily pastoral people living along the Mediterranean coast and in the mountains in the interior. Then, around 710 Arab forces, supplemented by Berber allies under their commander Tariq, crossed the Strait of Gibraltar and occupied southern Spain. The Visigothic kingdom, already weakened by internecine warfare, quickly collapsed, and by 725 most of the Iberian peninsula had become a Muslim state with its center in Andalusia. Seven years later, an Arab force, making a

foray into southern France, was defeated by the army of Charles Martel between Tours and Poitiers. Some historians think that internal exhaustion would have forced the invaders to retreat even without their defeat at the hands of the Franks. In any event, the Battle of Tours (or Poitiers) would be the high-water mark of Arab expansion in Europe.

In the meantime, in 717 another Muslim force had launched an attack on Constantinople with the hope of destroying the Byzantine Empire. But the Byzantines' use of Greek fire destroyed the Muslim fleet, thus saving the empire and indirectly Christian Europe, since the fall of Constantinople would have opened the door to an Arab invasion of eastern Europe. The Byzantine Empire and Islam now established an uneasy frontier in southern Asia Minor.

The Arab advance had finally come to an end in western Europe, but not before the southern and eastern parts of the old Roman Empire had been conquered, turning the Mediterranean into what one European historian has called a "Muslim lake." The Umayyad dynasty at Damascus now ruled an enormous empire. While expansion conveyed untold wealth and new ethnic groups into the

✖ **Map 7.2** The Expansion of Islam.

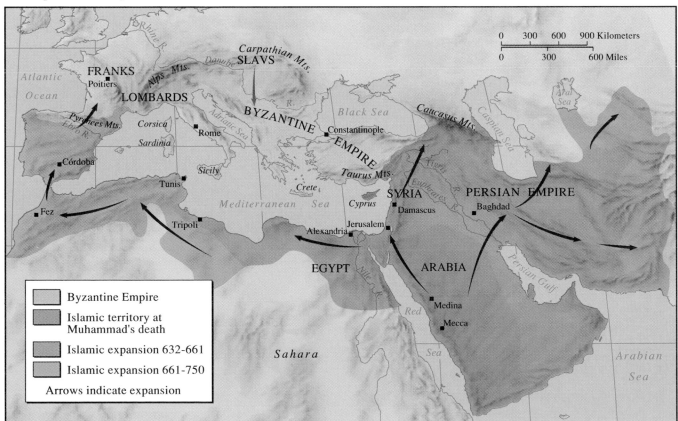

fold of Islam, it also brought increased contacts between the Arab world and Byzantine civilization. Although the relationship was marked by friction, the increased cultural and intellectual contacts would prove fruitful to both societies.

Arab power also extended to the east, consolidating Islamic rule in Mesopotamia and Persia and northward into Central Asia. But factional disputes continued to plague the empire. Many Muslims of non-Arab extraction resented the favoritism shown by local administrators to Arabs. In some cases, resentment led to revolt, as in Iraq, where Ali's second son Hussein disputed the legitimacy of the Umayyads and incited his supporters—to be known in the future as Shi'ites (from the Arabic phrase *shi'at Ali*, or "partisans of Ali")—to rise up against Umayyad rule in 680. Hussein's forces were defeated, but a schism between Shi'ite and Sunnite (usually translated as "orthodox") Muslims had been created that continues to the present.

The Rise of the Abbasids

The Umayyad dynasty of caliphs had established Damascus as the center of an Islamic empire created by Arab expansion in the seventh and eighth centuries. But Umayyad rule, always (in historian Arthur Goldschmidt's words) "more political than pious," created resentment, not only in Mesopotamia, but also in North Africa, where Berber resistance continued, especially in the mountainous areas south of the coastal plains. The Umayyads contributed to their own demise by their decadent behavior. One caliph allegedly swam in a pool of wine and then imbibed enough of the contents to lower the wine level to a significant degree. Finally, in 750 a revolt led by Abu al-Abbas, a descendant of Muhammad's uncle, led to the overthrow of the Umayyads and the establishment of the Abbasid dynasty (750–1258) in what is now Iraq.

The Abbasid caliphs brought political, economic, and cultural change to the world of Islam. While stressing religious orthodoxy, they tried to break down the distinctions between Arab and non-Arab Muslims. All Muslims were now allowed to hold both civil and military offices. This change helped to open Islamic culture to the influences of the occupied civilizations. Many Arabs now began to intermarry with the peoples they had conquered. In many parts of the Islamic world, notably North Africa and the eastern Mediterranean, most Muslim converts began to consider themselves Arabs. In 762, the Abbasids built a new capital city at Baghdad (in Persian,

Map 7.3   The Abbasid Caliphate at the Height of its Power.

"gift of God") on the Tigris River far to the east of the Umayyad capital at Damascus. The new capital was strategically positioned to take advantage of river traffic to the Persian Gulf and also lay astride the caravan route from the Mediterranean to Central Asia. The move eastward allowed Persian influence to come to the fore, encouraging a new cultural orientation. Under the Abbasids, judges, merchants, and government officials, rather than warriors, were viewed as the ideal citizens.

In bringing peace and stability to much of the Middle East, the Abbasids not only consolidated their own empire, but also contributed to a significant increase in the exchange of culture, ideas, and technology from one end of the known world to the other. Paper was introduced from China and eventually passed on to North Africa and Europe. Crops from India and Southeast Asia such as rice, sugar, sorghum, and cotton moved toward the west, while glass, wine, and indigo dye were introduced into China. For the first time, there was a true globalization of ideas, and the seeds of the future world civilization were sown.

The new Abbasid caliphate experienced a period of splendid rule well into the ninth century. Best known of the caliphs of the time was Harun al-Rashid (786–809), or Harun "the upright," whose reign is often described as the golden age of the Abbasid caliphate. His son al-Ma'mun (813–833) was a patron of learning who founded an astronomical observatory and established a foundation for undertaking translations of classical Greek works. This was also a period of growing economic prosperity. After all, the Arabs had conquered many of the richest provinces of the Roman Empire and controlled the routes to the east. Baghdad now became the center of an enormous commercial market that extended into Europe, Central Asia, and Africa, greatly adding to the wealth of the Islamic world.

But an element of instability lurked below the aura of prosperity. Disputes over the succession to the caliphate were common. At Harun's death, the rivalry between his two sons Amin and al-Ma'mun led to civil war and the destruction of Baghdad. As described by the tenth-century Muslim historian al-Mas'udi:

> Mansions were destroyed, most remarkable monuments obliterated; prices soared. . . . Brother turned his sword against brother, son against father, as some fought for Amin, others for Ma'mun. Houses and palaces fueled the flames; property was put to the sack.[4]

Vast wealth also contributed to financial corruption. By awarding important positions to court favorites, the Abbasid caliphs began to undermine the foundations of

CHRONOLOGY

Islam: The First Millennium

Life of Muhammad	570–632
Flight to Medina	622
Conquest of Mecca	630
Fall of Cairo	640
Defeat of Persians	650
Election of Ali to caliphate	656
Muslim entry into Spain	c. 710
Abbasid caliphate	750–1258
Construction of city of Baghdad	762
Reign of Harun al-Rashid	786–809
Founding of Fatimid dynasty in Egypt	973
Capture of Baghdad by Seljuk Turks	1055
Seizure of Anatolia by Seljuk Turks	1071
First crusade	1096
Saladin destroys Fatimid kingdom	1169
Fourth crusade	1204
Mongols seize Baghdad	1258
Ottoman Turks capture Constantinople	1453

their own power and eventually became mere figureheads. Under Harun al-Rashid, members of his Hashemite clan received large pensions from the coffers of the state treasury, while his wife Zubaida was reported to have spent vast sums while shopping on a pilgrimage to Mecca. One powerful family, the Barmakids, amassed vast wealth and power until Harun al-Rashid eliminated the entire clan in a fit of jealousy (see the box on p. 240).

The life of luxury enjoyed by the caliph and other political and economic elites in Baghdad seemingly undermined the stern fiber of Arab society as well as the strict moral code of Islam. Strictures against sexual promiscuity were widely ignored, and caliphs were rumored to maintain thousands of concubines in their harems. Divorce was common, and homosexuality was widely practiced, while alcohol was consumed in public despite Islamic law's prohibition against imbibing spirits.

⇒ The Murder of Ja'far al-Barmaki ⇐

The historian al-Mas'udi is our best source for inside information about the reign of the caliph Harun al-Rashid. In this excerpt, Harun begins to suspect his favorite courtier, the handsome Ja'far of the powerful Barmakid family, of breaking his word. The story illustrates the intense jealousies and personal rivalries that affected court life in the Abbasid era. Some historians suspect that Harun's love for Ja'far was sexual.

al-Mas'udi, The Meadows of Gold:
The Fall of the Barmakids

This is what a certain person, very well versed in the history of the Barmakids, relates:

'Yahya, the son of Khalid ibn Barmak, his two sons Ja'far and Fadl and other members of this family were at the height of their power, which was without limit, and unassailable in their high offices. The days of their rule, it is said, were like a perpetual wedding feast, filled with unending happiness and joy. It was during this time that Harun al-Rashid said to Ja'far:

"Ja'far, there is no one in the world dearer or closer to me than yourself and no one whose conversation is sweeter or more desirable than yours. Now my sister Abbasa holds in my heart a place not inferior to that which I have given you. I have considered the feelings that each of you inspire in me and I have realized that I cannot easily dispense either with you or with my sister. When you are absent no pleasure or satisfaction is perfect in her company and when I am alone with you, her absence inspires the same regrets. I know of only one way to procure myself this double pleasure and to enjoy henceforth the sweetness of both your companies."

Rashid continued thus:

"I wish to have you marry Abbasa and to give you the right, by this marriage, to pass your evenings with her, to see her, to be near her, whenever I am with you both. But your privileges will end there."

[Ja'far accepted these conditions, and after the marriage took place, considered himself bound by his word and did not assert his conjugal rights. Abbasa, however, was secretly fond of Ja'far and determined to win his love. When her advances were spurned, she enlisted the help of Ja'far's mother in a secret plot to have a child by her husband. One day Ja'far's mother went to her son and said:]

"My child, I have been told of a young slave girl who is living in such-and-such a place. She has had a royal education, she is lettered and learned, gracious and charming, her beauty is beyond compare, her figure perfect and she has a winning personality. In fact, she is a constellation of perfections the like of which I have never seen. I resolved to buy her for you and the matter is almost settled with her owner."

[Ja'far was delighted, and pleaded with his mother until she agreed that on a given night she would present him with the pretty slave. Then she told Abbasa of her plan. When the time came, she dressed as a slave girl and went to the house of Ja'far's mother.] That night Ja'far, his head still turning from wine, left the Caliph's palace to come to the tryst. Scarcely had he entered the house than he asked for the slave girl and was told that she had arrived. Abbasa, on going in to her husband, found a man sufficiently drunk not to know her face or figure. Once the marriage had been consummated and her husband's lust satisfied, Abbasa asked:

"What do you think of the ruses of the daughters of kings?"

"Whom do you mean?" he asked, convinced that he was talking to some Byzantine slave girl.

"Of myself!" she answered. "I, your mistress, Abbasa, daughter of Mahdi!"

Ja'far rose in horror, his drunkenness suddenly gone, and returned to his senses. At once he went to his mother and said to her:

"You have sold me cheap and placed me on the edge of an abyss. See what the outcome of my predicament will be!"

[Abbasa became pregnant, and in due course gave birth to a son, whom she later sent to Mecca in the care of two servants to keep Harun al-Rashid from learning of his identity. But the caliph's wife Zubaida found out about the affair and informed her husband. In revenge, Harun ordered his courtier Ja'far to be assassinated. Then, out of remorse, he executed the assassin.]

The process of disintegration was accelerated by changes that were taking place within the armed forces and the bureaucracy of the empire. Given the shortage of qualified Arabs for key positions in the army and the administration, the caliphate began to recruit officials from among the non-Arab peoples within the empire, such as Persians and Turks from Central Asia. Although these people were easily trained to serve the caliphate, they gradually became a dominant force within the army and the administration. Eventually, provincial rulers began to break away from central control and establish their own independent dynasties. Spain had already established its own caliphate when a prince of the Umayyad dynasty had escaped execution and fled there in 750. Morocco became independent, and a new dynasty under the Fatimids was established in Egypt in 973. With increasing disarray in the empire, the Islamic world was held together only by the common commitment to the Koran and the use of Arabic as the prevailing means of communication.

By the mid-tenth century, as the Abbasid empire in Baghdad continued its decline, the Fatimids attempted to establish a new Shi'ite caliphate at their capital in Cairo and advanced into Syria and Arabia. But they were unable to overcome the Abbasids in Mesopotamia, and the Islamic world remained divided.

The Seljuk Turks

Nevertheless, the Fatimid dynasty prospered and soon surpassed the Abbasid caliphate as the dynamic center of Islamic civilization. Benefiting from their position in the heart of the Nile delta, the Fatimids played a major role in the regional trade passing from the Mediterranean to the Red Sea and beyond. They adopted a religious policy based on toleration and created a strong military force by using nonnative peoples as mercenaries. One such group, the Seljuk Turks, soon posed a threat to the Fatimids themselves.

The Seljuk Turks were a nomadic people from Central Asia who had converted to Islam and flourished as military mercenaries for the Abbasid caliphate, where they were known for their ability as mounted archers. Some of them had received tracts of land from the caliphate in return for their service. Moving gradually into Iran and Armenia as the Abbasids weakened, the Seljuk Turks grew in number until by the eleventh century, they were able to occupy the eastern provinces of the Abbasid empire. In 1055, a Turkish leader captured Baghdad and assumed command of the empire with the title of sultan (the term means "holder of power"). While the Abbasid caliph remained the chief representative of Sunni religious au-

thority, the real military and political power of the state was in the hands of the Seljuk Turks. The latter did not establish their headquarters in Baghdad, which now entered a period of decline. As the historian Khatib Baghdadi described:

> There is no city in the world equal to Baghdad in the abundance of its riches, the importance of its business, the number of its scholars and important people, the distinctions of its leaders and its common people, the extent of its districts, the width of its boundaries, the great number of its palaces, inhabitants, streets, avenues, alleys, mosques, baths, docks and caravansaries, the purity of its air, the sweetness of its water, the freshness of its dew and its shade, the temperateness of its summer and winter, the healthfulness of its spring and fall, and its great swarming crowds. The buildings and the inhabitants were most numerous during the time of Harun al-Rashid, when the city and its surrounding areas were full of cooled rooms, thriving places, fertile pastures, rich watering-places for ships. Then the riots began, an uninterrupted series of misfortunes befell the inhabitants, its flourishing conditions came to ruin to such an extent that, before our time and the century preceding ours, it found itself, because of the perturbation and the decadence it was experiencing, in complete opposition to all capitals and in contradiction to all inhabited countries.[5]

⚒ Map 7.4   The Turkish Occupation of Anatolia.

- ▨ Frontier between Byzantine Empire and Abbasid Caliphate, c. 930
- ▨ Frontier of Byzantine Empire, c. 1070
- —— Frontier between Byzantine Empire and Ottoman Turks, 1371 - 1453
- —— Controlled by Seljuk Turks, c. 1080
- - - - Controlled by Seljuk Turks, early 13th century

Baghdad would revive, but it would no longer be the "gift of God" of Harun al-Rashid.

By the last quarter of the eleventh century, the Seljuks were exerting military pressure on Egypt and the Byzantine Empire. In 1071, when the Byzantines foolishly challenged the Turks, their army was routed at Manzikert, near Lake Van in eastern Turkey, and the victors took over most of the Anatolian peninsula. In dire straits, the Byzantine Empire turned to the west for help, setting in motion the papal pleas that led to the crusades.

In Europe, and undoubtedly within the Muslim world itself, the arrival of the Turks was regarded as a disaster. The Turks were viewed as barbarians who destroyed civilizations and oppressed populations. In fact, in many respects Turkish rule in the Middle East was probably beneficial. Converted to Islam, the Turkish rulers temporarily brought an end to the fraternal squabbles between Sunni and Shi'ite Muslims, while supporting the Sunnites. They put their energies to revitalizing Islamic law and institutions and provided much needed political stability to the empire that helped to restore its former prosperity. In one respect, however, their policies may have been detrimental to the later development of Islam. Adopting a narrow interpretation of the Koran and the *Shari'ah*, they encouraged a rigid approach to sacred doctrine that would make it more difficult for the faithful to respond effectively to social changes taking place within Islamic society.

The Crusades

Just before the end of the eleventh century, the Byzantine emperor Alexius I desperately called for assistance from other Christian states in Europe to protect his empire against the invading Seljuk Turks. As part of his appeal, he said that the Christian shrines in the Holy Land had been desecrated by the Muslims who, he claimed, were also molesting Christian pilgrims en route to the shrines. In actuality, the Muslims had not threatened the shrines and had never cut off Christian access to them. But tension between Christendom and the world of Islam was on the rise, and the Byzantine emperor's appeal received a ready response in Europe. Beginning in 1096 and continuing into the thirteenth century, a series of crusades brought the Holy Land and adjacent areas on the Mediterranean coast from Antioch to the Sinai peninsula under Christian rule.

At first, Muslim rulers in the area were taken aback by the invading crusaders, whose armored cavalry presented a new challenge to local warriors, and their response was

ineffectual. The Seljuk Turks by that time were preoccupied with events taking place further to the east and took no action themselves. But in 1169, Sunni Muslims under the leadership of Saladin (Salah al-Din), vizier to the last Fatimid caliph, brought an end to the Fatimid dynasty. Eventually, Saladin proclaimed himself sultan, declared Egypt independent of the Seljuk Turks, and established control over Syria, thereby confronting the Christian states in the area with united Muslim power on two fronts. In 1187 Saladin's army invaded the kingdom of Jerusalem and destroyed the Christian forces concentrated there. Further operations reduced Christian occupation in the area to a handful of fortresses along the northern coast. Unlike the Christians, however, Saladin did not permit a massacre of the civilian population and even tolerated the continuation of Christian religious services in conquered territories (see the box on p. 243).

The Christians returned for another try a few years after the fall of Jerusalem, but the campaign succeeded only in securing some of the coastal cities. Although the Christians would retain a toehold on the coast for much of the thirteenth century (Acre, their last stronghold, fell to the Muslims in 1291), they were no longer a significant force in Middle Eastern affairs. In retrospect, the crusades had only minimal importance in the history of the Middle East and may even have served to unite the forces of Islam against the foreign invaders. Far more important in their impact were the Mongols, a pastoral people who swept out of the Gobi Desert in the early thirteenth century to seize control over much of the known world (see Chapter 12). Beginning with the advances of Genghis Khan in North China, Mongol armies later spread across Central Asia, and in 1258, under the leadership of Hulegu, brother of the more famous Khubilai Khan, they seized Persia and Mesopotamia, bringing an end to the caliphate at Baghdad.

The Mongols

Unlike the Seljuk Turks, the Mongols were not Muslims, and they found it difficult to adapt to the settled conditions that they found in the major cities in the Middle East. Their treatment of the local population in conquered territories was brutal (according to one historian, after conquering a city, they wiped out not only entire families but also their household pets) and destructive to the economy. Cities were razed to the ground, while dams and other irrigation works were destroyed, reducing prosperous agricultural societies to the point of mass starva-

The Crusades in Muslim Eyes

Usamah, an early twelfth-century Muslim warrior and gentleman, had close associations with the crusaders. When he was ninety years old, he wrote his memoirs including many entertaining observations on the crusaders, or "Franks" as he called them. Here Usamah is astounded at the Franks' rudeness to Muslims and at their assumption of cultural superiority.

Usamah, *Book of Reflections*

1. Everyone who is a fresh emigrant from the Frankish lands is ruder in character than those who have become acclimatized and have held long association with the Moslems. Here is an illustration of their rude character.

   Whenever I visited Jerusalem I always entered the Aqsa Mosque, beside which stood a small mosque which the Franks had converted into a church. When I used to enter the Aqsa Mosque, which was occupied by the Templars [al-Æwiyyah], who were my friends, the Templars would evacuate the little adjoining mosque so that I might pray in it. One day I entered this mosque, repeated the first formula, "Allah is great," and stood up in the act of praying, upon which one of the Franks rushed on me, got hold of me and turned my face eastward, saying, "This is the way thou shouldst pray!" A group of Templars hastened to him, seized him and repelled him from me. I resumed my prayer. The same man, while the others were otherwise busy, rushed once more on me and turned my face eastward, saying, "This is the way thou shouldst pray!" The Templars again came in to him and expelled him. They apologized to me, saying, "This is a stranger who has only recently arrived from the land of the Franks and he has never before seen anyone praying except eastward." Thereupon I said to myself, "I have had enough prayer." So I went out, and have ever been surprised at the conduct of this devil of a man, at the change in the color of his face, his trembling, and his sentiment at the sight of one praying towards the *qiblah*.

2. In the army of King Fulk, son of Fulk, was a Frankish reverend knight who had just arrived from their land in order to make the holy pilgrimage and then return home. He was of my intimate fellowship and kept such constant company with me that he began to call me "my brother." Between us were mutual bonds of amity and friendship. When he resolved to return by sea to his homeland, he said to me:

   "My brother, I am leaving for my country and I want thee to send with me thy son (my son, who was then fourteen years old, was at that time in my company) to our country, where he can see the knights and learn wisdom and chivalry. When he returns, he will be like a wise man."

   Thus there fell upon my ears words which would never come out of the head of a sensible man; for even if my son were to be taken captive, his captivity could not bring him a worse misfortune than carrying him into the lands of the Franks.

tion. The Mongols advanced as far as the Red Sea, but their attempt to seize Egypt failed, in part because of the effective resistance posed by the Mamluks (a Turkish military class originally composed of slaves; sometimes written as Mamelukes), who had recently overthrown the administration set up by Saladin and seized power for themselves.

Eventually, the Mongol rulers in the Middle East began to take on the coloration of the peoples that they had conquered. Mongol elites converted to Islam, Persian influence became predominant at court, and the cities began to be rebuilt. By the fourteenth century, the Mongol empire began to split into separate kingdoms and then to disintegrate. In the meantime, however, the old Islamic empire originally established by the Arabs in the seventh and eighth centuries had come to an end. The new center of Islamic civilization was in Cairo, now about to promote a renaissance in Muslim culture under the sponsorship of the Mamluks.

To the north, another new force began to appear on the horizon with the rise of the Ottoman Turks on the Anatolian peninsula. In 1453, Sultan Mehmet II seized Constantinople and brought an end to the decrepit Byzantine Empire. Then the Ottomans began to turn their attention to the rest of the Middle East (see Chapter 16).

◆ **The Destruction of Baghdad by the Mongols.**　In 1258 the Mongols brought an end to the Abbasid caliphate at Baghdad. Their treatment of the local population was brutal. Cities were razed to the ground, while the dams and other irrigation works were destroyed, reducing the people to starvation. Here, in a fourteenth-century miniature, we see Mongol cavalrymen attacking the troops of the last of the Baghdad caliphs.

*I*slamic Civilization

As Thomas Lippman, author of *Understanding Islam*, has remarked, the Muslim religion is based on behavior as well as belief. Although this generalization applies in broad terms to most major religions, it seems to be particularly true of Islam. To be a Muslim is not simply to worship Allah, but also to live according to his law as revealed in the Koran, which is viewed as fundamental and immutable doctrine, not to be revised by human beings.

Thus, in Islamic society there is no rigid demarcation between church and state, between the sacred and the secular. As Allah has decreed, so must human beings behave. Therefore, Islamic doctrine must be consulted to determine questions of politics, economic behavior, civil and criminal law, and social ethics.

To live entirely by God's law is difficult, if not impossible, for all human beings, of course. Moreover, many issues of social organization and human behavior were not addressed in the Koran or in the *Hadith* or *Shari'ah*. There was therefore some room for differing interpretation of holy scripture in accordance with individual preference and local practice. Still, the Islamic world was probably more homogeneous in terms of its political institutions, religious beliefs, and social practices than were most of its contemporary civilizations.

Political Structures

For early converts, establishing political institutions and practices that conformed to Islamic doctrine was a matter of some difficulty. In the first place, the will of Allah, as revealed to his Prophet, was not precise about the relations between religious and political authority, simply decreeing that human beings should "conduct their affairs by mutual consent." On a more practical plane, establishing political institutions for a large and multicultural empire presented a challenge for the Arabs, whose own political structures were relatively rudimentary and relevant only to small pastoral communities.

During the life of Muhammad, the problem could be avoided, since he was generally accepted as both the religious and the political leader of the Islamic community, the *umma*. His death, however, raised the question of how a successor should be chosen and what authority that person should have. As we have seen, Muhammad's immediate successors were called caliphs. Their authority was purely temporal, although they were also considered in general terms to be religious leaders, with the title of *imam*. At first, each caliph was selected informally by leading members of the *umma*. Soon, succession became hereditary in the Umayyad clan, but their authority was still qualified, at least in theory, by the principle of consultation with other leaders.

Under the Abbasids, who seized power in the mid-eighth century, the caliphs became more regal. More kings than spiritual leaders, described by such august phrases as the "caliph of God," they ruled by autocratic means hardly distinguishable from the kings and emperors in neighboring civilizations. A thirteenth-century Chinese author, who compiled a world geography based on accounts by Chinese travelers, left the following description of one of the later caliphs:

> The king wears a turban of silk brocade and foreign cotton stuff (buckram). On each new moon and full moon he puts on an eight-sided flat-topped headdress of pure gold, set with the most precious jewels in the world. His robe is of silk brocade and is bound around him with a jade girdle. On his feet he wears golden shoes. . . . The king's throne is set with pearls and precious stones, and the steps of the throne are covered with pure gold. The various vessels and utensils around the throne are of gold or silver, and precious pearls are knotted in the screen behind it. In great court ceremonies the king sits behind this screen, and on either side, protecting him, the ministers of state surround him bearing golden bucklers and helmets and armed with precious swords.[6]

As the caliph took on more of the trappings of a hereditary autocrat, the bureaucracy assisting him in administering the growing empire grew more complex as well. The caliph was advised by a ministerial council (called a *diwan*) headed by a prime minister, known as a *vizier* (*wazir*). As the Chinese travelers described, the caliph did not attend meetings of the *diwan* in the normal manner, but sat behind a screen and then communicated his divine will to the *vizier*. Some historians have ascribed the change in the caliphate to Persian influence, which permeated the empire after the capital was moved to Baghdad, not far from the ancient city of Babylon. Persian influence was indeed strong during the reign of the Abbasids (the mother of the caliph al-Ma'mun, for example, was a Persian), but more likely, the increase in pomp and circumstance was a natural consequence of the growing power and prosperity of the empire.

In theory, the authority of the caliph in Baghdad was supreme throughout the Islamic world. In reality, rebellious forces in various parts of the empire opposed the rule of the caliph from the very beginning. Sometimes the revolt erupted within the walls of the capital city. As we have seen, after the death of the great Harun al-Rashid, fighting between his two sons led to a bitter civil war that ended in a lengthy siege of Baghdad. Eventually, several of the major segments of the empire, including Persia, Egypt, North Africa, Spain, and the area beyond the Caspian Sea, broke off to become *de facto* independent states. Despite the efforts of the Seljuk Turks and the Mongols, they were not united again.

The Wealth of Araby: Trade and Manufacturing in the Middle East

Despite the sometimes deleterious effects of the internecine struggles within the empire, overall this was probably one of the most prosperous periods in the history of the Middle East. Trade in particular flourished, not only within the Islamic world, but also with China (now in a period of efflorescence during the era of the

◆ **Arab Merchants in a Caravan.**   By land or by sea, Arab trade routes extended over half the globe. The word of Islam and the camel, both portrayed in this thirteenth-century miniature, were essential components of Muslim commercial ventures.

Tang and the Song dynasties—see Chapter 10), with the Byzantine Empire, and with the trading societies in Southeast Asia (see Chapter 9). In his study of trade patterns throughout the Indian Ocean, the historian K. N. Chaudhuri notes that the Arab conquests had created "an enormously powerful zone of economic consumption."[7] Trade goods were carried both by ship and by the "fleets of the desert," the camel caravans that traversed the arid land from Morocco in the far west to the countries beyond the Caspian Sea. From the Sahara came gold and slaves; from China, silk and porcelain; from East Africa, gold, ivory, and rhinoceros horn; and from the lands of southern Asia, sandalwood, cotton, wheat, sugar, and spices. Within the empire, Egypt contributed grain; Iraq linens, dates, and precious stones; Spain leather goods, olives, and wine; and western India various textile goods. The exchange of goods was facilitated by the development of banking and the use of currency and letters of credit.

Under these conditions, urban areas flourished. While the Abbasids were in power, Baghdad was probably the greatest city in the empire, but after the rise of the Fatimids in Egypt, the focus of trade shifted to Cairo, described by the traveler Leo Africanus as "one of the greatest and most famous cities in al [sic] the whole world, filled with stately and admirable palaces and colleges, and most sumptuous temples."[8] Other great commercial cities included Basra at the head of the Persian Gulf, Aden at the southern tip of the Arabian peninsula, Damascus in modern-day Syria, and Marrakech in Morocco. The prime beneficiaries of this activity were the merchants, but descriptions of city life by travelers leave the impression that other people, such as the artisans and farmers producing goods for the market, were able to profit from the general prosperity as well.

The Arab empire was clearly more urbanized than most other areas of the known world at the time. Yet the bulk of the population continued to live in the countryside and supported themselves by farming or herding animals. During the early stages, most of the farmland was owned by independent peasants, but later some concentration of land in the hands of wealthy owners began to take place. Some lands were owned by the state or the court and were cultivated by slave labor, but plantation agriculture was not as common as would be the case later in many areas of the world. In river valleys like the Tigris and Euphrates and the Nile, the majority of the farmers were probably independent peasants. A Chinese account described life along the Nile:

> The peasants work their fields without fear of inundations or droughts; a sufficiency of water for irrigation is supplied by a river whose source is not known. During the season when no cultivation is in progress, the level of the river remains even with the banks; with the beginning of cultivation it rises day by day. Then it is that an official is appointed to watch the river and to await the highest water level, when he summons the people, who then plough and sow their fields. When they have had enough water, the river returns to its former level.[9]

Islamic Society

In some ways, the Arab empire was probably one of the most egalitarian societies of its time. Both the principles of Islam, which held that all were equal in the eyes of Allah, and the importance of trade to the prosperity of the state probably contributed to this egalitarianism. Although there was a fairly well defined upper class, consisting of the ruling families, senior officials, tribal elites, and the wealthiest merchants, there was no hereditary nobility as in many contemporary societies, and the merchants enjoyed a degree of respect that they did not receive in Europe, China, or India.

✦ **A Tangier Spice Market**   For centuries, the spices of the East have passed through Southwestern Asia and North Africa on their way to Europe. Even today, the markets of the region boast a colorful and pungent display of spices, such as the one shown here in a shop in Tangier on the coast of Morocco.

Not all benefited from the high degree of social mobility in the Islamic world, however. Slavery was widespread (see the box on p. 248). Since a Muslim could not be enslaved, the supply came from sub-Saharan Africa or from non-Islamic populations elsewhere in Asia. Most were employed in the army (which was sometimes a road to power as in the case of the Mamluks) or as domestic servants, where they were sometimes permitted to purchase their freedom. The slaves who worked the large estates probably experienced the worst living conditions and rose in revolt on several occasions.

The Islamic principle of human equality also fell short in the treatment of women. Although the Koran instructed men to treat women with respect, and women did have the right to own and inherit property, in general the male was dominant in Muslim society. Polygyny was permitted, and the right of divorce was in practice restricted to the husband, although some schools of legal thought permitted women to stipulate that their husband could have only one wife or to seek a separation in certain specific circumstances. Adultery and homosexuality were stringently forbidden (although such prohibitions were frequently ignored in practice), and Islamic custom required that women be cloistered in their homes (thus the tradition of the harem) and prohibited from social contacts with males outside their own family. The custom of requiring women to cover virtually all parts of their body when appearing in public was common in urban areas and continues to be practiced in many Islamic societies today. It should be noted, however, that these customs owed more to traditional Arab practice than to Koranic law, and the position of women under Islam was probably better than it had been in former times, when they were often treated like slaves.

As might be expected in a region of considerable diversity, housing conditions in the Middle East during this period varied widely according to the region and the economic conditions of the individual family. In the cities, houses were often constructed of stone or brick around a timber frame. The larger houses were often built around an interior courtyard, where the residents could retreat from the dust, noise, and heat of the city streets. Sometimes domestic animals like goats and sheep would be stabled there. The houses of the wealthy were often multistoried with balconies and windows covered with latticework to provide privacy for those inside. The poor in both urban and rural areas lived in simpler houses composed of clay or unfired bricks. The Bedouins, like their nomadic counterparts elsewhere, lived in tents that could be dismantled and moved according to the needs of the day.

Aside from the capitals Baghdad, Damascus, and Cairo, Indian and Chinese travelers did not find the cities of the Middle East especially grand by their standards. Each of the three major cities was the center of administrative, cultural, and economic activity for its region; lesser cities played a similar role on a smaller scale. Usually, the most impressive urban buildings were the palace for the caliph or the local governor and the great mosque. The inhabitants were generally segregated by religion with Jews and Christians living in separate neighborhoods. But all were equally subject to the most common threats to urban life—fire, flood, and disease.

Eating habits varied in accordance with economic standing and religious preference. Muslims did not eat pork, but those who could afford it often served other meats such as mutton, lamb, poultry, or fish. Fruit, spices, and various sweets were delicacies. The poor were generally forced to survive on boiled millet or peas with an occasional lump of meat or fat. Bread—white or whole meal—could be found on tables throughout the region except in the deserts where boiled grain was the staple food.

The Culture of Islam

From the beginning of their empire, Muslim Arabs had demonstrated a willingness to absorb the culture of their conquered peoples. The Arabs were truly heirs to many elements of the remaining Greco-Roman culture of the Roman Empire. Just as readily, they assimilated Byzantine and Persian culture. In the eighth and ninth centuries, numerous Greek, Syrian, and Persian scientific and philosophical works were translated into Arabic. As the chief language in the southern Mediterranean and the Middle East, Arabic became a truly international language. Later, Persian and Turkish also came to be important in administration and culture.

The spread of Islam led to the emergence of a new culture throughout the entire Arab empire. This was true in all fields of endeavor from literature to art and architecture. But pre-Islamic traditions were not extinguished and they frequently combined with Muslim motifs to produce creative works of a high degree of imagination and originality.

PHILOSOPHY AND SCIENCE

During the centuries following the rise of the Arab empire, it was the Islamic world that was most responsible for preserving and spreading the scientific and philosophical achievements of ancient civilizations. At a time

≽ A Consumer's Guide to the Ideal Slave ≼

Slavery was widely practiced in the Middle East under the Abbasid caliphate. In this brief excerpt from a much longer passage, Kai Ka'us, an eleventh-century Persian, instructs his son on what to look for when buying a slave. Clearly, different slaves would serve different purposes, and the ideal qualities would vary according to the individual case. What is striking is that the slaves were evaluated not as human beings but as pieces of merchandise.

A Father's Instructions to His Son

Now let me describe to the best of my ability what is essential in the purchasing of slaves, both white and black, and what their good and bad points are, so that they may be known to you. Understand then that there are three essentials in the buying of slaves; first is the recognition of their good and bad qualities, whether external or internal, by means of physiognomy; second is the awareness of diseases, whether latent or apparent, by their symptoms; third is the knowledge of the various classes and the defects and merits of each.

With regard to the first requirement, that of physiognomy, it consists of close observation when buying slaves. . . . Whoever it may be that inspects the slave must first look at the face, which is always open to view, whereas the body can only be seen as occasion offers. Then look at eyes and eyebrows, followed by nose, lips and teeth, and lastly at the hair. The reason for this is that God placed the beauty of human beings in eyes and eyebrows, delicacy in the nose, sweetness in the lips and teeth and freshness in the skin. To all these the hair of the head has been made to lend adornment, since [God] created the hair for adornment.

You must, consequently, inspect everything. When you see beauty in the eyes and eyebrows, delicacy in the nose, sweetness in the lips and teeth and freshness in the skin, then buy the slave possessing them without concerning yourself over the extremities of the body. If all of these qualities are not present, then the slave must possess delicacy; because, in my opinion, one that is delicate without having beauty is preferable to one that is beautiful but not possessed of delicacy.

The learned say that one must know the indications and signs by which to buy the slaves suited for particular duties. The slave that you buy for your private service and conviviality should be of middle proportions, neither tall nor short, fat nor lean, pale nor florid, thickset nor slender, curly-haired nor with hair over-straight. When you see a slave soft-fleshed, fine-skinned, with regular bones and wine-colored hair, black eyelashes, dark eyes, black eyebrows, open-eyed, long-nosed, slender waisted, round-chinned, red-lipped, with white regular teeth, and all his members such as I have described, such a slave will be decorative and companionable, loyal, of delicate character, and dignified.

The mark of the slave suited for arms-bearing is that his hair is thick, his body tall and erect, his build powerful, his flesh hard, his bones thick, his skin coarse and his limbs straight, the joints being firm. The tendons should be tight and the sinews and blood-vessels prominent and visible on the body. Shoulders must be broad, the chest deep, the neck thick and the head round; also for preference he should be bald. The belly should be concave, the buttocks drawn in and the legs in walking well extended. And the eyes should be black. Any slave who possesses these qualities will be a champion in single combat, brave and successful.

The mark of the slave suited for employment in the women's apartments is that he should be dark-skinned and sour-visaged and have withered limbs, scanty hair, a shrill voice, little [slender] feet, thick lips, a flat nose, stubby fingers, a bowed figure, and a thin neck. A slave with these qualities will be suitable for service in the women's quarters. He must not have a white skin nor a fair complexion; and beware of a ruddy-complexioned man, particularly if his hair is limp. His eyes, further, should not be languorous or moist; a man having such qualities is either over-fond of women or prone to act as a go-between.

when the ancient Greek philosophers were largely unknown in Europe, key works by Aristotle, Plato, Plotinus, Euclid, and Ptolemy were translated into Arabic and stored in a "House of Wisdom" in Baghdad, where they were read and studied by Muslim scholars. Through the writings of the Spanish Muslim philosopher Ibn Rushd (known in the West as Averroës), the contents of many of these works eventually became known in Europe and influenced Christian scholasticism. Texts on mathematics and linguistics were brought from India. The process was undoubtedly stimulated by the introduction of paper manufacturing from China in the eighth century. An understanding of the process was obtained from a Chinese prisoner captured at the Battle of Talas in Central Asia in 751. By the end of the century, the first paper factories had been established in Baghdad, and booksellers and libraries soon followed. The first paper mill in Europe appeared in the Pyrenees Mountains in Spain in the twelfth century.

Although Islamic scholars are justly praised for preserving much of classical knowledge for the West, they also made considerable advances of their own. Nowhere is this more evident than in mathematics and the natural sciences, although early Muslims would have regarded these fields as simply part of the study of philosophy. The list of Muslim achievements in mathematics and astronomy alone is impressive: they adopted and passed on the numerical system of India, including the use of the zero, and a ninth-century Iranian mathematician created the mathematical discipline of algebra (*al-jebr*). In astronomy, Muslims set up an observatory at Baghdad to study the position of the stars. They were aware that the earth was round and in the ninth century produced a world map based on the Greco-Roman tradition of Ptolemy. Muslim fleets and caravans opened up new trading routes connecting the Islamic world with other civilizations, and Muslim travelers such as al-Mas'udi and Ibn Battuta provide modern readers with their most accurate descriptions of political and social conditions throughout the Middle East.

Muslim scholars also made many new discoveries in optics and chemistry and, with the assistance of texts on anatomy by the ancient Greek physician Galen (c. 180–200 C.E.), developed medicine as a distinctive field of scientific inquiry. Especially well known was Ibn Sina (980–1037). Known as Avicenna in the West, he compiled a medical encyclopedia that, among other things, emphasized the contagious nature of certain diseases and showed how they could be spread by contaminated water supplies. After its translation into Latin, Avicenna's work became a basic medical textbook for medieval European university students.

ISLAMIC LITERATURE

The literature of the Middle East is diverse, reflecting the many distinct cultures of the region. The Arabic and Persian works in particular represent a significant contribution to world literature.

An established tradition of Arabic poetry already existed prior to Muhammad. It extolled the Bedouin experience of tribal life, courage in battle, hunting, sports, and respect for the animals of the desert, especially the camel. Because the Arabic language did not possess a written script until the fourth century C.E., poetry was originally passed on by memory. Later, in the eighth and ninth centuries, it was compiled in anthologies. These personal

◆ **Painting from the "Story of the Shahs."**   The conquest of Central Asia by the Mongols in the thirteenth century and the later rule of Tamerlane in the fifteenth century exposed Islamic painters to the art of East Asia. Freed from the limitations of traditional techniques, artists now began to create paintings with a new realism and animated movement. The painting displayed here dates from the fifteenth century and is an illustration from Ferdowzi's *Book of Kings.*

⇒ Love for a Camel ⇐

Early Arabic poetry focused on simple pleasures, such as wine, women, song, and the faithful camel. This excerpt is from a longer work by the sixth-century Arab poet Tarafah. Tarafah was one of a group of seven poets called the "suspended ones." Their poems, having won a prize in an annual competition, were suspended on a wall for all to read.

The Ode of Tarafah

*Ah, but when grief assails me, straightway I ride it off
    mounted on my swift, lean-flanked camel, night and
    day racing, . . .
Her long neck is very erect when she lifts it up calling to
    mind the rudder of a Tigris-bound vessel. Her skull is
    most like an anvil, the junction of its two halves meeting
    together as it might be on the edge of a file.
Her cheek is smooth as Syrian parchment, her split lip
    a tanned hide of Yemen, its slit not bent crooked;
    her eyes are a pair of mirrors, sheltering in the caves of
    her brow-bones, the rock of a pool's hollow, . . .*

*I am at her with the whip, and my she-camel quickens pace
    what time the mirage of the burning stone-tract shim-
    mers; elegantly she steps, as a slave-girl at a party will
    sway, showing her master skirts of a trailing white gown.
I am not one that skulks fearfully among the hilltops, but
    when the folk seek my succor I gladly give it; if you look
    for me in the circle of the folk you'll find me there, and if
    you hunt me in the taverns there you'll catch me.
Come to me when you will, I'll pour you a flowing cup,
    and if you don't need it, well, do without and good luck
    to you!
Whenever the tribe is assembled you'll come upon me at
    the summit of the noble House, the oft-frequented; my
    boon-companions are white as stars, and a singing-
    wench comes to us in her striped gown or her saffron
    robe, wide the opening of her collar, delicate her skin to
    my companions' fingers, tender her nakedness.
When we say, "Let's hear from you," she advances to us
    chanting fluently, her glance languid, in effortless song.*

reflections on wine, sensuous women, good companionship, and the joys of a ride on a fast camel still speak directly to modern readers (see the box above).

Pre-Muslim Persia also boasted a long literary tradition, most of it oral and written down in later centuries in the Arabic alphabet. Lacking the desert tradition of the Arabs, Persian writers focused on legends of past kings, Zoroastrian religious themes, romances, fables, and folktales. The transcendent literary monument of early Persian literature is *The Book of Lords*, an early sixth-century compilation of poetry about Persian myths and legendary heroes. Transmitted orally by generations of poet-musicians, these vivid stories of battles, hunting, and drinking bouts constitute the national epic of ancient Persia, its answer to the Mahabharata.

Islam brought major changes to the culture of the Middle East, not least to literature. Muslims regarded the Koran as their greatest literary work, but pre-Islamic traditions continued to influence writers throughout the region. Poetry is the Persian art par excellence. *The Book of Kings*, a ten-volume epic poem by the Persian poet Ferdowzi (940–1020), is one of the greatest achievements of Persian literature. It traces the history of the country from legendary times to the arrival of Islam. Iranian schoolchildren still learn its verse, which serves to reaffirm pride in their ancient heritage. But love poetry remained popular. Here Rabe'a of Qozdar, Persia's first known woman poet, who wrote in the second half of the tenth century, expresses her anguish at the suffering love brings:

> *The love of him threw me in chains again,
> Struggle against them proved of no avail.*
>
> *Love is a sea of invisible shores,
> How can one swim in it, O clever one?*
>
> *If you want to pursue love to the end,
> Be content to endure much unpleasantness.*
>
> *Ugliness you must see and imagine it is beauty,
> Poison you must take and think it is sugar.*
>
> *Beset with impatience I did not know
> That the more one seeks to pull away, the tighter becomes
>   the rope.[10]*

Writing at about the same time was the Syrian poet al-Mutanabbi (915–965), considered by many Arabs the greatest poet in the Arabic language. Witness these lines on courage:

> *That which souls desire is too small a thing for them to fight*
> *about and perish by each other's hands,*
> *Howbeit a true man will face grim Fate ere he suffer*
> *contumely.*
> *If the life of aught that lives were lasting, we should reckon*
> *the brave the most misguided of us,*
> *But if there is no escape from death, 'tis but weakness to be a*
> *coward.*
> *All that the soul finds hard before it has come to pass is easy*
> *when it comes.*[11]

To Western observers, the most famous works of Middle Eastern literature are undoubtedly the *Rubaiyat* of Omar Khayyam and *The Tales from 1001 Nights* (also called *The Arabian Nights*). Paradoxically, these two works are not as popular with Middle Eastern readers. Both, in fact, were freely translated into Western languages for nineteenth-century European readers, who found themes of wine, women, and hedonistic pleasure more acceptable when set in a quaint foreign disguise.

Unfortunately, very little is known of the life or the poetry of the twelfth-century poet Omar Khayyam. Skeptical, reserved, and slightly contemptuous of his peers, he combined poetry with scientific works on mathematics and astronomy and a revision of the calendar that was more accurate than the Gregorian version devised in Europe hundreds of years later. Omar Khayyam did not write down his poems, but composed them orally over wine with friends at a neighborhood tavern. They were recorded later by friends or scribes. Many poems attributed to him were actually written long after his death. Among them is the well-known couplet translated into English in the nineteenth century: "Here with a loaf of bread beneath the bough, a flask of wine, a book of verse, and thou."

Omar Khayyam's poetry is simple and down to earth. Key themes are the impermanence of life, the impossibility of knowing God, and disbelief in an afterlife. Ironically, recent translations of his work appeal to modern attitudes of skepticism and minimalist simplicity that may make him even more popular in the West:

> *They did not ask me, when they planned my life;*
> *Why then blame me for what is good or bad?*
> *Yesterday and today go on without us;*
> *Tomorrow what's the charge against me, pray?*

> *In youth I studied for a little while;*
> *Later I boasted of my mastery.*
> *Yet this was all the lesson that I learned:*
> *We come from dust, and with the wind are gone.*

> *Of all the travelers on this endless road*
> *No one returns to tell us where it leads,*
> *There's little in this world but greed and need;*
> *Leave nothing here, for you will not return.*

> *When once you hear the roses are in bloom,*
> *Then is the time, my love, to pour the wine;*
> *Houris and palaces and heaven and hell—*
> *These are but fairy-tales, forget them all.*

> *Since no one can be certain of tomorrow,*
> *It's better not to fill the heart with care.*
> *Drink wine by moonlight, darling, for the moon*
> *Will shine long after this, and find us not.*[12]

Like Omar Khayyam's verse, *The Arabian Nights* was loosely translated into European languages and adapted to Western tastes. A composite of folktales, fables, and romances of Indian and indigenous origin, the stories interweave the natural with the supernatural. The earliest stories were told orally and were later transcribed, with many later additions, in Arabic and Persian versions. The famous story of Aladdin and the Magic Lamp, for example, was an eighteenth-century addition. Nevertheless, *The Arabian Nights* has entertained readers for centuries, allowing them to enter a land of wish fulfillment through extraordinary plots, sensuality, comic and tragic situations, and a cast of unforgettable characters (see the box on p. 252).

Sadi (1210–1292), considered the Persian Shakespeare, remains to this day the favorite author in Iran. His *Rose Garden* is a collection of entertaining stories written in prose sprinkled with verse (see the box on p. 253). He is also renowned for his sonnetlike love poems, which set a model for generations to come. He incorporated threads from the Koran, Ferdowzi's *Book of Kings*, and images of nature to skillfully weave in verse the fabric of Persian art. Sadi was a master of the pithy maxim:

> *A cat is a lion in catching mice*
> *But a mouse in combat with a tiger.*

> *He has found eternal happiness who lived a good life,*
> *Because, after his end, good repute will keep his name alive.*

> *When thou fightest with anyone, consider*
> *Whether thou wilt have to flee from him or he from thee.*[13]

⇒ The Tale of Shahrazad ⇐

This characteristic excerpt from The Arabian Nights *describes a wondrous fantasy, an exotic wish fulfillment, blending the extraordinary with the ordinary. Shahrazad, sometimes called Sheherazad, is a vizier's daughter who has been captured by an evil ruler. She saves her life by recounting strange tales to her captor.*

The Arabian Nights

I proceeded immediately to walk until I reached the palace and found it to be exactly as they had described it. The door stood open, and when I entered, I found myself in a spacious and lovely hall as vast as a playground. It was surrounded by forty chambers with doors of sandal and aloewood, covered with plates of red gold and graced with silver handles. At the far end of the hall, I saw forty girls, sumptuously dressed and lavishly adorned. They looked like moons, so lovely that none could tire of gazing on them. When they saw me, they said in one voice, "O lord, welcome, O master, welcome! and good cheer to you lord! We have been expecting one like you for months. Praised be God who has sent us one who is as worthy of us as we are of him." Then they raced toward me and made me sit on a high couch, saying, "This day, you are our lord and master, and we are your maids and servants, at your beck and call." Then while I sat marveling at their behavior, they rose, and some of them set food before me; others warmed water and washed my hands and feet and changed my clothes; others mixed juice and gave me to drink; and they all gathered around me, joyful at my coming. Then they sat down to converse with me and question me till nightfall.

But morning overtook Shahrazad, and she lapsed into silence. Then Dinarzad said, "Sister, what a strange and entertaining story!" Shahrazad replied, "What is this compared with what I shall tell you tomorrow night if the king spares me and lets me live!"

The Fifty-Ninth Night

The following night Dinarzad said to her sister Shahrazad, "Sister, if you are not sleepy, tell us the rest of the story." Shahrazad replied, "Very well":

It is related, O King, that the third dervish said to the girl:

My lady, the girls sat around me, and when night came, five of them rose and set up a banquet with plenty of nuts and fragrant herbs. Then they brought the wine vessels and we sat to drink, with the girls sitting all around me, some singing, some playing the flute, the psalter, the lute, and all other musical instruments, while the bowls and cups went round. I was so happy that I forgot every sorrow in the world, saying to myself, " 'This is the life; alas, that it is fleeting.' " I enjoyed myself with them until most of the night was gone and we were drunk. Then they said to me, "O our lord, choose from among us whomever you wish to spend this night with you and not return to be your bedfellow again until forty days will have passed." I chose a girl who had a lovely face and dark eyes, with black hair, joining brows, and a mouth with slightly parted teeth. Perfect in every way, like a willow bough or a stalk of sweet basil, her beauty struck the eye and bewildered the mind.

Such maxims are typical of the Middle East where the proverb, a one-line witty observation on the vagaries of life, has long been popular. Proverbs are not only a distinctive feature of Middle Eastern verse, especially Persian, but are also a part of daily life—a scholar recently recovered over four thousand in one Lebanese village! The following are some typical examples:

The world has not promised anything to anybody.
    (Moroccan)
An old cat will not learn how to dance. (Moroccan)
Lower your voice and strengthen your argument.
    (Lebanese)

He who has money can eat sherbet in Hell. (Lebanese)
Trust in God, but tie up your camel. (Persian)
What is brought by the wind will be carried away by the
    wind. (Persian)
You can't pick up two melons with one hand. (Persian)

Some Arabic and Persian literature reflected the deep spiritual and ethical concerns of the Koran. Many writers, however, carried Islamic thought in novel directions. The thirteenth-century poet Rumi, for example, embraced Sufism, a form of religious belief that called for a mystical relationship between Allah and human beings (the term *Sufism* stems from the Arabic word for wool, referring to the

≽ Be Thankful for Small Favors ≼

The Rose Garden, an entertaining collection of moral anecdotes and maxims, was written in the thirteenth century by Sadi, considered by many to be Persia's greatest author. Here, in his usual mixture of prose and poetry, Sadi advises his readers to be content with what they have. The second story extols the merits of the generous ruler.

Sadi, The Rose Garden

Story 7

A padshah was in the same boat with a Persian slave who had never before been at sea and experienced the inconvenience of a vessel. He began to cry and to tremble to such a degree that he could not be pacified by kindness, so that at last the king became displeased as the matter could not be remedied. In that boat there happened to be a philosopher, who said: "With thy permission I shall quiet him." The padshah replied: "It will be a great favor." The philosopher ordered the slave to be thrown into the water so that he swallowed some of it, whereon he was caught and pulled by his hair to the boat, to the stern of which he clung with both his hands. Then he sat down in a corner and became quiet. This appeared strange to the king who knew not what wisdom there was in the proceeding and asked for it. The philosopher replied: "Before he had tasted the calamity of being drowned, he knew not the safety of the boat; thus also a man does not appreciate the value of immunity from a misfortune until it has befallen him."

O thou full man, barley-bread pleases thee not.
She is my sweetheart who appears ugly to thee.
To the huris of paradise purgatory seems hell.
Ask the denizens of hell. To them purgatory is paradise.

There is a difference between him whose friend is in his arms
And him whose eyes of expectation are upon the door.

Story 8

A royal prince, having inherited abundant treasures from his father, opened the hand of liberality and satisfied his impulse of generosity by lavishing without stint benefits upon the army and the population.

A tray of lignum aloes will emit no odor.
Place it on fire, it will smell like ambergris.
If thou wishest to be accounted great, be liberal
Because grain will not grow unless it be sown.

One of his courtiers began heedlessly to admonish him, saying: "Former kings have by their exertions accumulated this wealth and deposited it for a useful purpose. Cease this movement because calamities may arise in front and enemies in the rear. It is not meet for thee to be helpless at a time of necessity."

If thou distributest a treasure to the multitude
Each householder will receive a grain of rice.
Why takest thou not from each a barley-corn of silver
That thou mayest accumulate every day a treasure?

The royal prince turned away his face at these words and said: "God the most high has made me the possessor of this country, to enjoy and to bestow, not to guard and to retain."

Qarun, who possessed forty treasure houses, perished.
Nushirvan has not died because he obtained a good reputation.

rough wool garments that its adherents wore). Converted to Sufism by a wandering dervish (dervishes, from the word for "poor" in Persian, sought to achieve a mystical union with Allah through violent dancing and chanting in an ecstatic trance), Rumi abandoned orthodox Islam to embrace God directly through ecstatic love. Realizing that love transcends intellect, he sought to reach God through a trance attained by the whirling dance of the dervish, set to mesmerizing music. As he twirled, the poet extemporized some of the most passionate lyrical verse ever conceived. His faith and art remain an important force in Islamic society today (see the box on p. 255).

The Islamic world also made a major contribution to historical writing, another discipline that was stimulated by the introduction of paper manufacturing. The first great Islamic historian was al-Mas'udi. Born in Baghdad in 896, he wrote about both the Muslim and the non-Muslim world, traveling widely in the process. His *Meadows of Gold* is the source of much of our knowledge about the golden age of the Abbasid caliphate. Translations of his work reveal a wide-ranging mind and a keen intellect, combined with a human touch that practitioners of the art in our century might find reason to emulate (see the box on p. 240). Equaling al-Mas'udi in talent and reputation was the fourteenth-century historian Ibn Khaldun. Combining scholarship with government service, Ibn Khaldun was one of the first historians to attempt a philosophy of history.

ISLAMIC ART AND ARCHITECTURE

The art of Islam is a blend of Arab, Turkish, and Persian traditions. Although local influences can be discerned in Egypt, Anatolia, Spain, and other areas and the Mongols introduced an East Asian accent in the thirteenth century, for a long time Islamic art remained remarkably coherent over a wide area. First and foremost, the Arabs, with their new religion and their writing system, served as a unifying force. Fascinated by the mathematics and astronomy they inherited from the Romans or the Babylonians, they developed a sense of rhythm and abstraction that found expression in their use of repetitive geometric ornamentation. The Turks brought abstraction in figurative and nonfigurative designs, and the Persians added

their lyrical poetical mysticism. Much Islamic painting, for example, consists of illustrations of Persian texts.

The ultimate expression of Islamic art is to be found in the magnificent architectural monuments beginning in the late seventh century. The first great example is the Dome of the Rock, which was built in 691 to proclaim the spiritual and political legitimacy of the new religion to the ancient world. Set in the sacred heart of Jerusalem on Muhammad's holy rock and touching both the Western Wall of the Jews and the oldest Christian church, the Dome of the Rock remains one of the most revered Islamic monuments. Constructed on Byzantine lines with an octagonal shape and marble columns and ornamentation, the interior reflects Persian motifs with mosaics of precious stones. Although rebuilt several times and incorporating influences from both East and West, this first monument to Islam represents the birth of a new art.

At first, desert Arabs, whether nomads or conquering armies, prayed in an open court, shaded along the *kibla* (the wall facing the holy city of Mecca) by a thatched roof supported by rows of palm trunks. There was also a ditch where the faithful could wash off the dust of the desert prior to prayer. As Islam became better established, enormous mosques were constructed, but they were still modeled on the open court, which would be surrounded on all four sides with pillars supporting a wooden roof over the prayer area facing the *kibla* wall. The largest mosque ever built, the Great Mosque of Samarra (848–852), covered ten acres and contained 464 pillars in aisles surrounding the court. Set in the *kibla* wall was a niche, or *mihrab*, containing a decorated panel pointing to Mecca and representing Allah. Remains of

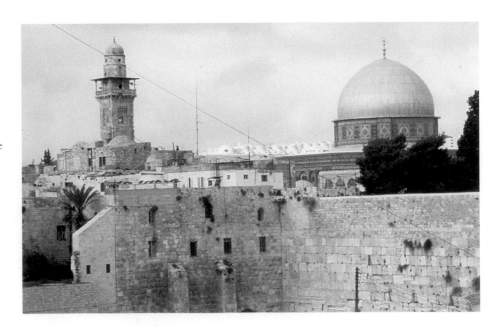

◆ **The Temple Mount at Jerusalem.** The Temple Mount is one of the most sacred sites in the city of Jerusalem. Originally it was the site of a temple built during the reign of Solomon, king of the Jews, about 1,000 B.C.E. The Western Wall of the temple is shown in the foreground. Beyond the Wall is the Dome of the Rock complex, built on the place from which Muslims believe that Muhammad ascended to heaven.

⇝ The Passions of a Sufi Mystic ⇜

*S*ufism was an unorthodox form of Islam that flourished in many parts of the Muslim world. It preached the importance of a highly personal relationship between Allah and the individual believer. Sufi orders began to assume considerable influence by the thirteenth century, perhaps because of the disintegration of the Abbasid empire and the heightened instability throughout the Islamic world. Sufi missionaries played a major role in efforts to spread Islam to India and Central Asia. In this poem, the thirteenth-century Persian poet Rumi describes the mystical relationship achieved by means of passionate music and dance.

Rumi, Call to the Dance

Come!
But don't join us without music.
We have a celebration here.
Rise and beat the drums.

We are Mansur who said "I am God!"

We are in ecstasy—
Drunk, but not from wine made of grapes.

Whatever your thoughts are about us,
We are far, far from them.

This is the night of the same
When we whirl to ecstasy.

There is light now,
There is light, there is light.

This is true love,
Which means farewell to the mind.
There is farewell today, farewell.

Tonight each flaming heart is a friend of music.
Longing for your lips,
My heart pours out of my mouth.

Hush!
You are made of feeling and thought and passion;
The rest is nothing but flesh and bone.
We are the soul of the world,
Not heavy or sagging like the body.
We are the spirit's treasure,
Not bound to this earth, to time or space.

How can they talk to us of prayer rugs and piety?
We are the hunter and the hunted,
Autumn and spring,
Night and day,
Visible and hidden.
Love is our mother.
We were born of Love.

the massive thirty-foot-high outer wall still stand, but the most famous section of the Samarra mosque was its minaret, the tower accompanying a mosque from which the *muezzin* calls the faithful to prayer five times a day. The minaret of Samarra, which was nearly ninety feet in height, was unusual by virtue of its exterior spiral staircase.

Constructed of unfired brick, most of the mosques and palaces of ninth-century Samarra eventually disintegrated, but the Samarra style exerted considerable influence on later Islamic architecture. Cairo's famous Ahmad Ibn Tulun mosque, built in 879, was modeled directly on the Great Mosque of Samarra. Later, the Seljuk Turks were great builders, creating masterpieces

such as the eleventh-century mosque at Isfahan. The original structure consisted of four towering arched gates leading into a central court covered by a high dome. The interior of the mosque was decorated with glazed tile and brick, which were destined to become a highly popular means of ornamentation in the sixteenth century.

No discussion of mosques would be complete without mentioning the famous ninth-century mosque at Córdoba in southern Spain, which is still in remarkable condition. Its 514 columns supporting double horseshoe arches transform this architectural wonder into a unique forest of trees pointing upward, contributing to a light and airy effect. Unique in all of Muslim religious architecture is the elaborate two-story *mihrab* chapel with its delicate carved plasterwork and marble, mosaic, and gold decorations. The unparalleled sumptuousness and elegance make the Córdoba mosque one of the wonders of world art, let alone Islamic art.

Since the Muslim religion combines spiritual and political power in one, palaces also reflected the glory of Islam. Beginning in the eighth century with the spectacular castles of Syria, the rulers constructed large domiciles reminiscent of Roman design, with protective walls,

✦ **An Entrance Portal.** This entrance gate to an Iranian mosque displays the variety and delicacy of the geometrical decorations that often accompanied Islamic architecture. The brilliant blue and white mosaic tile shown here eventually evolved into polychromy by the fifteenth century.

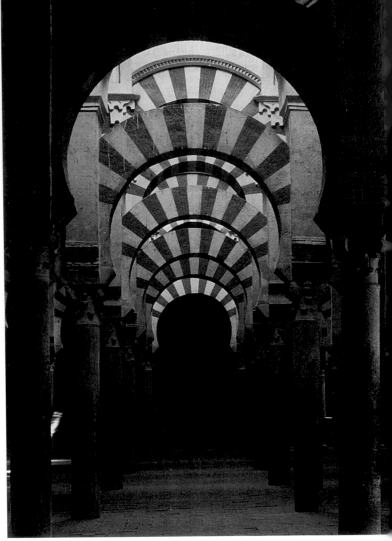

✦ **The Mosque at Córdoba.** Perhaps the most impressive of all Islamic religious structures is the Mosque of Córdoba in southern Spain, which was built between the eighth and tenth centuries. Shown here is the interior of the mosque, showing some of the columns that give the entire structure such an effect of mass as well as lightness.

gates, and baths. Constructed of brick, they unfortunately no longer exist. With a central courtyard surrounded by two-story arcades and massive gate-towers, they resembled a fortress as much as a palace. The remains of the eighth-century palace of Ukhaidir in Iraq still stand and testify to its vastness and grandeur. With its elaborate complex of residential and official rooms in addition to a mosque and a series of courtyards with accompanying rooms for family and guests, the palace resembled a miniature town, completely surrounded by fortified walls. Characteristic of such "desert palaces" was the gallery over the entrance gate with holes through which boiling oil could be poured down on the heads of attacking forces. This architectural feature was exported by the crusaders and was later incorporated repeatedly into medieval European castles.

The ultimate in Islamic palaces, however, is the fourteenth-century Alhambra in Spain. The extensive succession of courtyards, rooms, gardens, and fountains created a fairy-tale castle perched high above the city of Granada and framed by the snowcapped Sierra Nevada. Every inch of surface is decorated in intricate floral and semiabstract patterns; much of the decoration is done in carved plasterwork so fine that it resembles lace. The Lion Court in the center of the harem is world renowned for its lion fountain and surrounding arcade with elegant columns and carvings. With its superb architectural design and exquisite decoration, the Alhambra is considered the most perfect expression of Islamic art.

Out of Islamic architecture arose a variety of art forms related to the palace and especially the mosque. Beautiful glass lamps were needed for reading the Koran. Intricate wood carvings were created to decorate the *mimbar*, or staircase leading to the pulpit from which the Koran was recited. The Seljuk Turks excelled in both wood and stone carving, while the Mamluks in fourteenth-century Egypt developed silver inlaid bronze and brass for basins and ewers into a highly skilled art form.

Introduced to the Middle East by Turkish tribes in the eighth and ninth centuries, the knotted woolen rug became one of the significant contributions of Islamic art. In an attempt to imitate the animal skins that were used as floor and wall coverings in tents, weavers originally knotted their rugs with additional threads resembling animal hairs. Later, these long knotted "hairs" were turned from the underside to the topside and then cut, thus creating the thick pile of the carpet. First and foremost, rugs served as prayer mats, both for individual use and as donations to the mosques by wealthy Muslims. They were also used for wall decorations and warmth in palaces and were given as rewards for political favors by rulers. Highly prized all over the world, Middle Eastern carpets were extremely time-consuming and demanding to produce. A small carpet five feet square, with three hundred knots to the square inch, could take more than a year to make, and the detail was so minute that it was most effectively done by the slender fingers of children.

Most decorations on the rugs, as well as on all forms of Islamic art, consisted of Arabic script and natural plant and figurative motifs. Repeated continuously in naturalistic or semiabstract geometrical patterns called arabesques, these decorations completely covered the surface and left no area undecorated. This dense decor was also evident in brick, mosaic, and stucco ornamentation and culminated in the magnificent tile work of later centuries.

No representation of the Prophet Muhammad ever adorned a mosque, in painting or in any other art form. Although no passage of the Koran forbids representational painting, the *Hadith*, an early collection of the Prophet's sayings, warned against any attempt to imitate God through artistic creation or idolatry. From the time of the Dome of the Rock, no figurative representations appear in Islamic religious art.

Human beings and animals could still be represented in secular art, but relatively little survives from the early centuries aside from a very few wall paintings from the royal palaces. Although the Persians used calligraphy and art to decorate their books, the Arabs had no pictorial tradition of their own and only began to develop the art of book illustration in the late twelfth century to illustrate translations of Greek scientific works. All in all, then, the significant history of Islamic painting did not begin until the Mongol era.

In the thirteenth century, a Mongol dynasty established at Tabriz west of the Caspian Sea offered the Middle East its first direct contact with the art of East Asia. Mongol painting, done in the Chinese manner with a full brush and expressing animated movement and intensity

◆ **The Alhambra in Granada.**   Islamic civilization reached its zenith with the fourteenth-century fairy-tale castle of Alhambra in southern Spain. Perched on a hill high above the city of Granada and framed by snowcapped mountains, the Alhambra is widely considered the most perfect expression of Islamic art. Renowned for its lacelike plaster decorations and imaginative use of reflecting pools and fountains, the Alhambra stands as an exquisite gem of Islam.

(see Chapter 10), freed Islamic painters from traditional confines and enabled them to experiment with new techniques. The most famous paintings of the Tabriz school are found in the illustrations accompanying Ferdowzi's *Book of Kings*. They express a new realistic detail and a concern for individual human qualities.

Chinese art also influenced Islamic art with its sense of space. A new sense of perspective pervaded Islamic painting, leading to some of the great paintings of the Herat School under the fifteenth-century autocrat Tamerlane. Artists working in the Herat style often depicted mounted warriors battling on a richly detailed background of trees and birds. These paintings served as the classical model for later Islamic painting, which culminated in the glorious artistic tradition of sixteenth-century Iran, Turkey, and India (see Chapter 16).

Conclusion

From ancient times, the Middle East has been the site of great empires. Beginning with Sumer, continuing with the Assyrians, the Persians, and the brief but glorious conquests of Alexander the Great, the area has given birth to some of the most powerful and extensive civilizations in history.

In the seventh century, a new force blossomed in the Arabian peninsula and spread rapidly throughout the Middle East. In the eyes of some European writers during the Middle Ages, the Arab empire was a malevolent force that posed a serious threat to the security of Christianity. Indian rajas undoubtedly also felt threatened. The image is not entirely inaccurate, for within half a century after the death of the Prophet, Arab armies overran Christian states in North Africa and the Iberian peninsula, while Turkish Muslims moved eastward onto the fringes of the Indian subcontinent.

But although the teachings of Muhammad brought war and conquest to much of the known world, they also brought hope to millions and a sense of political and economic stability to peoples throughout the region. For many, the arrival of Islam was a welcome event. Islam brought a code of law and a written language to societies that had previously not possessed them. Finally, by creating a revitalized trade network stretching from West Africa to East Asia, it established a vehicle for the exchange of technology and ideas that brought untold wealth to thousands and a better life to millions.

Like other empires in the region, the Arab empire did not last. It fell victim to a combination of internal and external pressures, and by the end of the thirteenth century, it was no more than a memory. But it left a powerful legacy in Islam, which remains one of the great religions of the world. In succeeding centuries, Islam began to penetrate into new areas beyond the fringes of the Sahara and across the Indian Ocean into the islands of the Indonesian archipelago (see Chapters 8 and 9). Some historians assert that the rise of Islam led to the creation of the first global civilization in the known world.

CHAPTER NOTES

1. Quoted in Thomas W. Lippman, *Understanding Islam: An Introduction to the Moslem World* (New York, 1982), p. 40.
2. Mohammed Marmaduke Pickthall, trans., *The Meaning of the Glorious Koran* (New York, 1953), p. 89.
3. Quoted in Lippman, *Understanding Islam*, p. 118.
4. Mas'udi, *The Meadows of Gold: The Abbasids*, ed. Paul Lunde and Caroline Stone (London, 1989), p. 151.
5. Quoted in Gaston Wiet, *Baghdad: Metropolis of the Abassid Caliphate*, trans. Seymour Feiler (Norman, Okla., 1971), pp. 118–19.
6. Friedrich Hirth and W. W. Rockhill, trans., *Chau Ju-kua: His Work on the Chinese and Arab Trade in the Twelfth and Thirteenth Centuries, Entitled Chu-fan-chi* (New York, 1966), p. 115.
7. K. N. Chaudhuri, *Trade and Civilization in the Indian Ocean: An Economic History from the Rise of Islam to 1750* (Cambridge, 1985), p. 36.
8. Leo Africanus, *The History and Description of Africa and of the Notable Things Therein Contained* (New York, n.d.), pp. 820–21.
9. Hirth and Rockhill, *Chau Ju-kua*, p. 116.
10. Ehsan Yarshater, ed., *Persian Literature* (Albany, N.Y., 1988), pp. 125–26.
11. Quoted in James Kritzeck, ed., *Anthology of Islamic Literature* (New York, 1964), pp. 105–6.
12. Yarshater, *Persian Literature*, pp. 154–59.
13. E. Rehatsek, trans., *The Gulistan or Rose Garden of Sa'di* (New York, 1964), pp. 65, 67, 71.

SUGGESTED READINGS

Standard works on the Arab empire and the rise of Islam include B. Lewis, *The Arabs in History* (New York, 1961); and T. Lippman, *Understanding Islam: An Introduction to the Moslem World* (New York, 1982). More up-to-date is G. E. Perry, *The Middle East: Fourteen Islamic Centuries*, 2d ed. (Englewood Cliffs, N.J., 1992). A more detailed treatment can be found in P. M. Holt et al., eds., *The Cambridge History of Islam*, two vols. (Cambridge, 1970). For a popularized history, see A. Nutting, *The Arabs: A Narrative History from Mohammed to the Present* (New York, 1964). For an overview with rich illustrations, see *People and Places of the Past* (National Geographic Society, 1983). For anthropological background, see D. Bates and A. Rassam, *Peoples and Cultures of the Middle East* (Englewood Cliffs, N.J., 1983). On women, see S. Botman et al., *Women in the Middle East* (London, 1987) and N. Keddie et al., eds., *Women in Middle Eastern History: Shifting Boundaries in Sex and Gender* (New Haven, Conn., 1991).

On Islam, see F. Denny, *An Introduction to Islam* (New York, 1985); and J. Esposito, *Islam: the Straight Path* (New York, 1988). Among the various translations of the Koran, two of the best for the introductory student are N. J. Dawood, trans., *The Koran* (Harmondsworth, 1990) and M. M. Pickthall, trans., *The Meaning of the Glorious Koran* (New York, 1953). See also R. W. Bulliet, *Conversion to Islam in the Medieval Period: An Essay in Quantitative History* (Cambridge, 1979).

Specialized works on various historical periods are numerous. For a view of the crusades from an Arab perspective, see A. Maalouf, *The Crusades through Arab Eyes* (London, 1984). On the Mamluks, see R. Irwin, *The Middle East in the Middle Ages: The Early Mamluk Sultanate, 1250–1382* (Carbondale, Ill., 1986).

On the economy, see E. Ashtor, *A Social and Economic History of the Near East in the Middle Ages* (Berkeley, 1976); K. N. Chaudhuri, *Asia before Europe: Economy and Civilization of the Indian Ocean from the Rise of Islam to 1750* (Cambridge, 1990); and C. Issawi, *The Middle East Economy: Decline and Recovery* (Princeton, N.J., Markus Wiener, 1995). On the crucial role of the camel in Middle Eastern society, see the interesting study by R. W. Bulliet, *The Camel and the Wheel* (Cambridge, 1975).

For the best introduction to Islamic literature, consult J. Kritzeck, ed., *Anthology of Islamic Literature* (New York, 1964), with its concise commentaries and introduction. An excellent introduction to Persian literature can be found in E. Yarshater, *Persian Literature* (Albany, N.Y., 1988). Of particular interest are the chapters on Omar Khayyam by L. P. Elwell-Sutton and on Rumi by T .S. Halman. A stimulating analysis of Persian poetry is found in Annemarie Schimmel, *A Two-Colored Brocade: The Imagery of Persian Poetry* (Chapel Hill, N.C., 1992). For the student, H. Haddawy, trans., *The Arabian Nights* (New York, 1990) is the best version. It presents 271 "nights" in a clear and colorful style.

For the best introduction to Islamic art, consult the concise yet comprehensive work by E. J. Grube, *The World of Islam* (New York, 1960). See also D. T. Rice, *Islamic Art*, rev. ed. (London, 1975).

CHAPTER
8

Early Civilizations in Africa

In 1871, the German explorer Karl Mauch began to search South Africa's central Plateau for the colossal stone ruins of a legendary lost civilization. In late August, he found what he had been looking for. According to his diary: "Presently I stood before it and beheld a wall of a height of about 20 feet of granite bricks. Very close by there was a place where a kind of footpath led over rubble into the interior. Following this path I stumbled over masses of rubble and parts of walls and dense thickets. I stopped in front of a towerlike structure. Altogether it rose to a height of about 30 feet." Mauch was convinced that "a civilized nation must once have lived here." Like many other nineteenth-century Europeans, however, Mauch was equally convinced that the Africans who had lived there could never have built such splendid structures like the ones he had found at Great Zimbabwe. To Mauch and other archaeologists, Great Zimbabwe must have been the work of "a northern race closely akin to the Phoenician and Egyptian." It was not until the twentieth century that Europeans could overcome their prejudices and finally admit that Africans south of Egypt had also developed advanced civilizations with spectacular achievements.

The continent of Africa has played a central role in the long evolution of humankind. It was in Africa that the first hominids appeared more than three million years ago. It was probably in Africa that the immediate ancestors of modern human beings—Homo sapiens—emerged for the first time. Both the cultivation of crops and

• • •
Kingship appears
in Nile valley

• •
First states in
West Africa

• •
Kingdom of
Zimbabwe

• • • • •
Kingdom of Kush founded in Nubia

• • •
First
agricultural
settlements

• • •
Desiccation of
Sahara begins

• • •
Iron Age begins in Africa

• • • • • • • • • • • • • • •
Beginning of trans-Saharan trade

• • • • • • • • • • • • •
Nok culture in Nigeria

• • • • • • • • • • • •
Spread of Swahili culture in East Africa

• • •
Christianity arrives in Ethiopia

• • •
Spread of Islam across North Africa

the domestication of animals may have occurred first in Africa. Certainly, one of the first states appeared in Africa, in the Nile valley in the northeastern corner of the continent, in the form of the kingdom of the pharaohs. Recent evidence suggests that Egyptian civilization was significantly influenced by cultural developments taking place to the south, in Nubia in modern-day Sudan.

After the decline of the Egyptian empire during the first millennium B.C.E., the focus of social change began to shift from the lower Nile valley to other areas of the continent: to West Africa, where a series of major trading states began to take part in the caravan trade with the Mediterranean through the vast wastes of the Sahara; to the region of the upper Nile River, where the states of Kush and Axum dominated trade for several centuries; and to the eastern coast from the Horn of Africa to the straits between the continent and the island of Madagascar, where African peoples began to play an active role in the commercial traffic in the Indian Ocean. In the meantime, a gradual movement of agricultural peoples brought Iron Age farming to the central portion of the continent, leading eventually to the creation of several states in the Zaire River basin and the plateau region south of the Zambezi River. When European seafarers began to round the Cape of Good Hope at the end of the fifteenth century C.E., Western historians would herald their voyages as the beginning of an Age of Discovery. That label was a misnomer, however, for the peoples of Africa had played a significant role in the changing human experience since ancient times.

The Land

After Asia, Africa is the largest of the continents. It stretches nearly five thousand miles from the Cape of Good Hope in the south to the Mediterranean in the north and extends a similar distance from Cape Verde at Dakar on the west coast to the Horn of Africa at Cape Guardafui on the Indian Ocean.

Africa is as diverse as it is vast. The old Western image of Africa as a "dark continent" filled with jungles and rain forests is as misleading as the European image of the United States as a land of gangsters and cowboys. Actually, only a small proportion of the continent, in the Congo basin and along the western coast, can be classified as jungle or rain forest.

In fact, Africa includes several distinct geographical zones. The northern fringe, on the coast washed by the Mediterranean Sea, is mountainous through much of its length. South of the mountains lies the greatest desert on earth, the Sahara, which stretches from the Atlantic to the Indian Ocean. To the east is the Nile River, heart of the ancient Egyptian civilization. Beyond that lies the Red Sea, separating Africa from Asia.

The Sahara acts as a great divide separating the northern coast from the rest of the continent. Africa south of the Sahara is itself divided among a number of major regions. In the west is the so-called hump of Africa, which juts like a massive shoulder into the Atlantic Ocean. Here the Sahara gradually gives way to grasslands in the interior and then to tropical jungles along the coast. This region, which is dominated by the Niger River, is rich in natural resources and was the home of many ancient civilizations.

Far to the east bordering the Indian Ocean is a very different terrain of snowcapped mountains, upland plateaus, and lakes. Much of this region is grassland populated by wild beasts, which have given it the modern-day designation of Safari Country. Here, in the East African Rift Valley in the lake district of modern Kenya, early hominids began their long trek to civilization several million years ago.

Further to the south lies the Congo basin, the "darkest Africa" of film and fable, with its jungles watered by the mighty Zaire (formerly Congo) River. The jungles of equatorial Africa then fade gradually into the hills, plateaus, and deserts of the south. This rich land contains some of the most valuable mineral resources known to the world today.

Map 8.1   Ancient Africa.

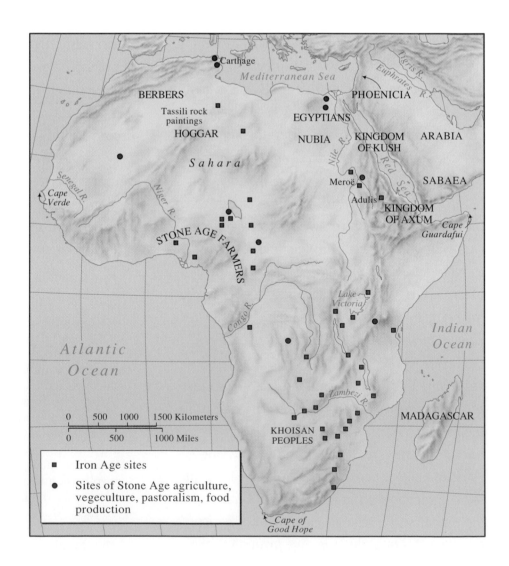

The Emergence of Civilization

It is not certain when agriculture was first practiced on the continent of Africa. Until recently, historians assumed that crops were first cultivated in the lower Nile valley (the northern part near the Mediterranean) about seven or eight thousand years ago, when wheat and barley were introduced, possibly from the Middle East. At first, the local inhabitants may have simply taken advantage of the annual floods to plant crops on the rich lands adjacent to the riverbanks. Eventually, they learned to manipulate the course of the river to divert water and bring additional areas under cultivation. As Chapter 1 explained, this mastery of agriculture provided the foundation for the rise of ancient Egypt, one of the most powerful and sophisticated civilizations of its time.

Kush

Recent evidence suggests that this hypothesis may need some revision. South of Egypt, near the junction of the White and the Blue Nile, is an area known historically as Nubia. Some archaeologists suggest that agriculture may have appeared first in Nubia rather than in the lower Nile valley. Stone Age farmers from Nubia may have begun to cultivate local crops such as sorghum and millet along the banks of the upper Nile (the southern part near the river's source) as early as the eleventh millennium B.C.E.

The origins of the peoples living in this area have long been a matter of speculation. The Greek historian Herodotus described the adult male population of Nubia as "the tallest in the world, the best-looking, and the longest-lived," but he had not personally visited the area and was relying on hearsay.[1] The modern-day population of the area may be descended from a mixture of the descendants of the first agriculturalists who tilled the fields in the eleventh and tenth millennia B.C.E. and new immigrants who began to arrive from the west many thousands of years later as a result of the desiccation of the Sahara.

Recent archaeological finds also imply that the first true African kingdom may have been located in Nubia rather than in Egypt. A drawing on an incense burner dated at about 3100 B.C.E. or earlier depicts a seated ruler with the falcon motif later adopted by the pharaohs of Egypt. Some scholars suggest that the Nubian concept of kingship may have spread to the north, past the cataracts along the Nile, where it eventually gave birth to the better known civilization of Egypt.

Whatever the truth of such conjectures, it is clear that contacts between the upper and lower Nile had been established by the late third millennium B.C.E., when Egyptian merchants traveled to Nubia to obtain ivory, ebony, frankincense, and leopard skins. A few centuries later Nubia had become an Egyptian tributary. With the exception of a brief interval of independence, it remained an Egyptian colony until the end of the second millennium B.C.E., when it profited from the disintegration of the Egyptian New Kingdom to become the independent state of Kush. At one point, Kush briefly conquered the lower Nile valley, but in 663 B.C.E., the Kushite rulers were driven out of Egypt by the Assyrians and returned to their original habitat, establishing themselves on the Nile River north of modern-day Khartoum (see Chapter 1).

Although its economy was probably founded primarily on agriculture and animal husbandry, Kush now emerged as one of the major trading states in the region. Its commercial activities were stimulated by the discovery of iron ore in a floodplain near the river at Meroë. Strategically located at the point where a newly opened land route across the desert to the north intersected the Nile River, Meroë eventually became the capital of the state. For the next several hundred years, Kush was a major commercial empire with links to other states throughout the region. One of its primary functions was to provide goods from Central and East Africa to Rome and its tributary states in the Mediterranean. The major exports of Kush were ivory, gold, ebony, and slaves. At first goods were transported by donkey caravans to the point where the river north was navigable. By the last centuries of the first millennium B.C.E., however, the donkeys were being replaced by camels, newly introduced from the Arabian peninsula.

Many historians once viewed Kush as a mere tributary of the Egyptian empire at its height, and it is true that Kushite culture borrowed extensively from Egypt, including religious beliefs, the practice of interring kings in pyramids, and hieroglyphics. But native elements remained strong in Kushite culture, and eventually Egyptian influence declined after the Greek conquest of Lower Egypt (see Chapter 5). The Kushites devised a phonetic script unrelated to hieroglyphics, but it has not yet been deciphered. Kushite rulers modeled their political institutions after those of the pharaohs, but governmental authority was somewhat more decentralized, and monarchical power was apparently limited by the influence of the priesthood and the local aristocracy. According to a Roman historian:

As for the customs of the Ethiopians [the Kushites], not a few of them are thought to differ greatly from the rest of mankind, this being especially true of those which concern the selection of their kings. The priests first choose out the noblest men, and which from this group the god may select, as he is borne about in a procession in accordance with their practice, him the multitude take for their king, and straightway it both worships and honors him like a god, believing that the sovereignty has been entrusted to him by the divine providence. And the king who has been thus chosen both follows a regimen which has been fixed in accordance with the laws, and performs all his other deeds in accordance with the ancestral customs. . . .[2]

This description implies that only men were selected as monarchs in Kush, but on at least one occasion the throne was occupied by a woman, and there is evidence that females often played an important role in political affairs. Some scholars maintain that the concept of royal legitimacy was based on the principle of matrilinear succession. It is not clear whether this practice was influenced by the customs of Ptolemaic Egypt to the north.

Not much is known about Kushite society, but it seems likely that it was predominantly urban. At first foreign trade was probably a monopoly of the state, but the extensive luxury goods in the numerous private tombs in the vicinity indicate that at one time material prosperity was relatively widespread. This suggests that commercial activities were being conducted by a substantial merchant class. Millet and other grain crops were cultivated along the banks of the river. Beyond the floodplain lived cattle herders and the nomads who took part in the caravan trade across the desert.

Axum, Son of Saba

In the first millennium C.E., the state of Kush declined and was eventually conquered by Axum, a new power located in the highlands of modern-day Ethiopia. This remote area had been one of the original homelands of the ancestors of modern human beings. In the first millennium B.C.E., it began to develop as a colony of the kingdom of Saba (popularly known as Sheba) across the Red Sea on the southern tip of the Arabian peninsula. During antiquity, Saba was a major trading state in the Middle East, serving as a transit point for goods carried from South Asia into the lands surrounding the Mediterranean. Much as the barons along the Rhine River controlled the trade of the Rhine during the Middle Ages, Saba accumulated considerable wealth through its control of the mouth of the Red Sea at the entrance to the Indian Ocean. Biblical sources credited the "queen of Sheba" with vast wealth and resources. In fact, much of that wealth had originated much further to the east and passed through Saba en route to the countries adjacent to the Mediterranean (see Chapters 9 and 10).

◆ **The Pyramids at Meroë.**   The kingdom of Kush borrowed much of its culture from the Egyptian empire to the north, while placing its own imprint on all imports. The pyramids at Meroë, on the banks of the Nile River, are an example. Younger, smaller, unpointed at the top, and more standardized in size and shape than their famous counterparts at Giza, they remain a dramatic reminder of the glory of ancient Kush.

Eventually, people from Saba established a colony at Axum, across the Red Sea in Africa, and began to inter-marry with the local population. When Saba declined, Axum broke away and survived for centuries as an inde-pendent state. Like Saba, Axum owed much of its pros-perity to its location on the commercial trade route be-tween India and the Mediterranean, and Greek ships from the Ptolemaic kingdom in Egypt stopped regularly at the port of Adulis on the Red Sea. Axum exported ivory, frankincense, myrrh, and slaves, while its primary imports were textiles, metal goods, wine, and olive oil. For a time, Axum competed for control of the ivory trade with the neighboring state of Kush, and hunters from Axum armed with imported iron weapons scoured the entire region for elephants. Probably as a result of this competition, in the fourth century C.E., the Axumite ruler, claiming he had been provoked, launched an inva-sion of Kush and conquered it (see the box on p. 267).

The majority of the population of Axum were proba-bly farmers, tilling the soil with the irrigation and terrac-ing techniques they had learned from the early settlers from Saba. Authority in the kingdom was somewhat more dispersed than in the Nile valley, with the rulers of local regions accepting a tributary status to the king in the royal capital.

Perhaps the most distinctive feature of Axumite civi-lization was its religion. Originally, the rulers of Axum (who claimed descent from King Solomon through the visit of the queen of Sheba to Israel in biblical times) fol-lowed the religion of their predecessors in Saba. But in the fourth century C.E., Axumite rulers adopted Chris-tianity from the Egyptians. According to one ancient source, the Axumite king was converted by a ship-wrecked Christian from Syria. More likely the decision was motivated by pecuniary reasons as a means of ce-menting Axum's commercial relationship with Egypt,

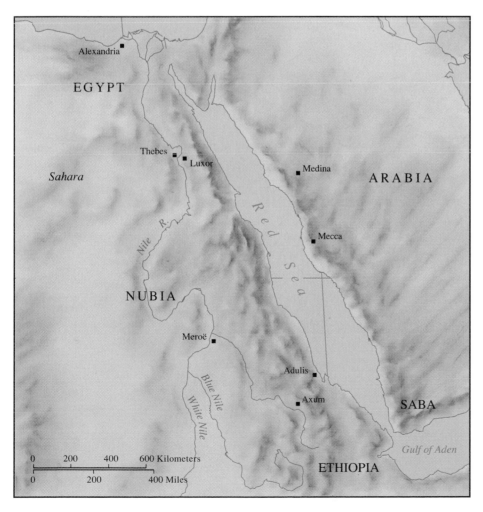

Map 8.2 Ancient Ethiopia and Nubia.

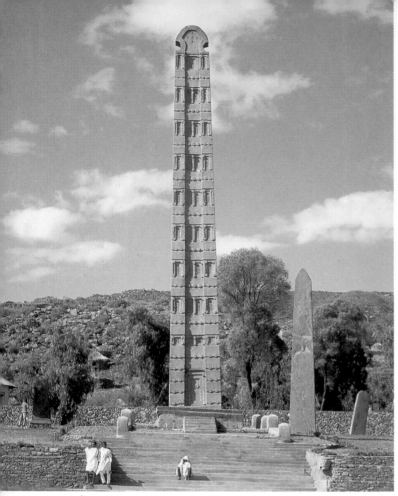

♦ **The Stele at Axum.** Axum was a prosperous trading state by the third century C.E., selling ivory, glass crystal, brass, copper, and frankincense and myrrh. The latter were resins, used in burials and as medicines by the peoples of Egypt and the eastern Roman Empire. In the fourth century, the Axumite rulers erected stelae, or slender columns, to mark the location of the royal tombs. Shown here is the tallest of the still-standing Axum stelae in present-day Ethiopia.

which was then under Christian rule. This commitment to the Egyptian form of Christianity (often called Coptic, from the local language of the day) was retained even after the collapse of Axum and the expansion of Islam through the area in later centuries. Later, Axum (now renamed Ethiopia) would be identified by Europeans as the "hermit kingdom" and the home of Prester John, a legendary Christian king of East Africa. Previously, Prester John had been tentatively identified as a ruler in Central Asia (see Chapter 10).

The Sahara and Its Environs

Kush and Axum were part of the ancient trading network originally established by the Egyptians and were affected in various ways by the cross-cultural contacts that took place throughout that region. Elsewhere in Africa, somewhat different patterns prevailed; they varied from area to area depending on the geography and climate.

At one time, when the climate was much colder than it is today, Central Africa may have been one of the few areas of the world that was habitable for the first hominids. Later, from 8000 to 4000 B.C.E., a warm, humid climate prevailed in the Sahara, creating lakes and ponds, as well as vast grasslands (known as savannahs) replete with game, which became an early source of sustenance. But climatic changes that began to take place in the sixth and fifth millennia B.C.E. eventually dried up the Sahara and turned much of the region into a virtually uninhabitable wasteland.

The desiccation of the Sahara, a process that continues today, had a major impact on the peoples in the area and may have provided the stimulus for the beginnings of agriculture in the savannah region bordering the desert. The peoples of the Sahara had apparently engaged in herding animals—first sheep and goats and later cattle—since 7000 B.C.E. and perhaps even earlier. Information about life in the Sahara at this time is sparse, but rock paintings found in what are today some of the most uninhabitable parts of the region are a clear indication that the environment was much different several thousand years ago.

♦ **Rock Paintings of the Sahara.** Even before the Egyptians built their pyramids at Giza, other peoples far to the west in the vast wastes of the Sahara were creating their own art forms. These rock paintings, some of which date back to the fourth millennium B.C.E., provide a valuable record of a society that supported itself by a combination of farming, hunting, and herding animals.

≽ The Conquest of Kush ≼

One of the few written descriptions of life along the Nile River in ancient times comes from this inscription, which was included in the Periplus, a Greek account probably written in the first century C.E. Here an Axumite king describes his campaign against Meroë, Axum's neighbor to the west in the upper Nile valley.

An Axumite King Proclaims His Victory

With the help of the Lord of Heaven, who in heaven and earth conquers all, Ezana son of Ella Amica, a member of [the group] Halen, king of Axum and of Hemer [Himyar] and of Raydan and of Sab'a and of Salhen and of Tsyamo and of Bega and of Kasu, king of kings . . . never conquered by an enemy . . . by the power of the Lord of the Earth and fought at the Takazi, by the Ford of Kemalke . . . I burnt their towns, those with stone houses and those with straw huts, and [my troops] pillaged their corn and bronze and iron and copper; they destroyed the effigies in their houses [temples], and also their stores of corn and cotton, and threw them in to the river Seda. . . . And I reached the Kasu, whom I fought and made captive at the confluence of the rivers Seda and Takazi; and the next day I sent my troops . . . on a campaign up the Seda to the towns of stone and of straw; the names of the towns of stone are Alwa and Daro. . . . Then I sent troops . . . down the Seda to the four straw villages of the Noba and the king. The stone towns of the Kasu which the Noba took [were] Tabito, Pertoti; and they [my troops] went as far as the Red Noba.

These paintings, which are for the most part five or six thousand years old, depict a culture that relied on a mixture of agriculture and pastoralism. Peoples in the area apparently supplemented their diet by fishing and limited cultivation of local crops, such as millet, sorghum, and a drought-resistant form of dry rice. The importance of agriculture may have increased as the lakes dried up and the opportunities for fishing and food gathering declined.

After 3000 B.C.E., farming began to spread throughout the savannah region on the southern fringes of the desert and eventually into the tropical forest areas to the south. The peoples of this area were not limited to cultivating drought-resistant cereal crops, but could also grow various types of tropical fruit and tubers.

Historians do not know when goods first began to be exchanged across the Sahara. Contacts between the peoples on the southern fringe of the desert and the Berbers, a pastoral people who lived in the mountainous areas along the northern coast from Morocco to Tunisia, may have taken place sporadically since early times. In any event, during the first millennium B.C.E., the level of trade began to increase.

One factor in the rapid expansion of the trans-Sahara trade may have been the emergence of Carthage as a major commercial center on the shores of the Mediterranean. Established originally by Phoenician colonists who later broke away to form their own independent state, Carthage did not carry out the exchange of goods directly, but used the nomadic Berbers as intermediaries. Food products and various manufactured articles were carried south and exchanged for salt, gold and copper, skins, various types of agricultural products, and perhaps slaves.

At first, goods were transported by wheeled chariots or on the backs of oxen along several routes passing through the desert. The introduction of the camel into the area early in the first millennium C.E. provided a major stimulus to trade. With its ability to store considerable amounts of food and water in its hump, the camel was well equipped to handle the arduous conditions of the desert and soon became the standard means by which Berber nomads carried goods from oasis to oasis on the long trek to their eventual destination.

The caravan trade initiated a process of cultural exchange that would exert a significant impact on the peoples of tropical Africa. Among other things, it may have spread the knowledge of iron smelting to the peoples south of the desert. Until recently, historians had thought that the Iron Age did not penetrate to sub-Saharan Africa until the first centuries C.E., when iron smelting was introduced from Meroë in the upper Nile valley. But recent finds suggest that iron smelting took place in the region of the Niger River as early as the middle of the first millennium B.C.E. While some scholars have suggested that the technique may have developed independently in that region, others are convinced that it was introduced by way of the caravan trade with the Mediterranean. The Carthaginians had imported the technique from the Middle East and had already introduced it to the local Berber population in North Africa.

CHRONOLOGY

Early Africa

Origins of agriculture in Africa	c. 7000 B.C.E.
Desiccation of the Sahara	Begins c. 5000 B.C.E.
Kingship appears in the Nile valley	c. 3100 B.C.E.
Kingdom of Kush in Nubia	c. 500 B.C.E.
Iron Age begins	c. sixth century B.C.E.
Beginnings of trans-Sahara trade	c. first millennium B.C.E.
Rise of Axum	First century C.E.
Conquest of Kush by Axum	Fourth century C.E.
Arrival of Bantus in East Africa	Early centuries C.E.
Arrival of Malays on island of Madagascar	Second century C.E.
Origins of Ghana	Fifth century C.E.
Arab takeover of lower Nile valley	641 C.E.
Development of Swahili culture	c. first millennium C.E.
Spread of Islam across North Africa	Seventh century C.E.
Spread of Islam in Horn of Africa	Ninth century C.E.
Decline of Ghana	Twelfth century C.E.
Establishment of Zagwe dynasty in Ethiopia	c. 1150
Rise of Mali	c. 1250
Kingdom of Zimbabwe	c. 1300–c. 1450
Portuguese ships explore West African coast	Mid-fifteenth century

From there, it could have traveled southward across the Sahara.

Whatever the case, the Nok culture in northern Nigeria eventually became one of the most active iron-working societies in Africa. Excavations in the vicinity of the modern settlement of Nok have unearthed numerous terra-cotta and iron figures, as well as stone and iron farm implements, dating back as far as 500 B.C.E. The remains of smelting furnaces confirm that the iron was produced locally.

East Africa, Land of Zanj

South of Axum, along the shores of the Indian Ocean and in the inland plateau that stretches from the mountains of Ethiopia through the lake district of Central Africa, lived a mixture of peoples, some living by hunting and food gathering, and others following pastoral pursuits. There is evidence that cattle were domesticated in the area as early as 5000 B.C.E. and perhaps even earlier.

The coastal region of East Africa, which would later become a major participant in the Indian Ocean trade, was already open to commercial contacts with the states bordering the Mediterranean and the Red Sea by the first century C.E. The author of the *Periplus*, a Greek seaman who probably lived in Alexandria, has provided modern readers with a generally accurate description of the coastline of East Africa from Cape Guardafui (at the tip of the Horn of Africa) to the Strait of Madagascar, thousands of miles to the south. The Greeks called this coastal region Azania, and later the Arabs would call it Zanj.

Although the identity of many of the places mentioned in the text is disputed, it is clear that merchant fleets already sailed through these waters as far as the commercial metropolis of Rhapta (possibly a Greek name for the modern city of Dar es Salaam). Beyond Rhapta was "unexplored ocean." Some contemporary observers like the Greek author of the *Periplus* believed that the Indian Ocean and the Atlantic (which he called the "western ocean") were connected. Others were convinced that the coast of Africa eventually turned eastward and connected with the lands of Southeast Asia. If they were correct, the Indian Ocean was an enclosed sea, and the continent of Africa could not be circumnavigated. But the Greek historian Herodotus raised questions about this theory when he reported that Phoenician sailors had claimed to have sailed directly south from the Red Sea and eventually returned through the Strait of Gibraltar into the Mediterranean (see the box on p. 269).

Beginning in the first millennium B.C.E., new peoples began to migrate into east Africa from the west. Farming peoples speaking dialects of the Bantu family of languages began to move from the region of the Niger River into East Africa and the Zaire River basin. Today Bantu-speaking peoples live throughout the entire region of Central Africa south of the Sahara.

Whether Bantu immigrants were responsible for bringing a knowledge of iron smelting and the widespread cultivation of crops to the peoples living further to the east is not clear. There are some indications that iron working may have been practiced in the region of Lake Victoria as early as the seventh century B.C.E. Whether

≥ *Beyond the Pillars of Hercules* ≤

The first suggestion that seafarers could pass from the Atlantic to the Indian Ocean around the southern tip of Africa came from the Greek historian Herodotus. In the following passage from his History of the Persian Wars, *Herodotus describes a voyage by Phoenician sailors that was recounted to him during his visit to Egypt. The reference to the position of the sun reflects a phenomenon that could only have occurred if the Phoenicians were sailing south of the equator.*

Herodotus, *History of the Persian Wars*

Africa proves to be completely surrounded by water except for as much of it as borders on Asia. Of all men of whom we have any knowledge, the Egyptian king Necho was the first to establish this fact. After he had ceased from trying to dig the canal that extends from the Nile to the Arabian Gulf, he dispatched some Phoenicians in ships with orders to sail back into our northern sea by passing through the Pillars of Hercules and so to return to Egypt.

Accordingly these Phoenicians set out and from the Red Sea sailed into the southern ocean. Whenever autumn came, they went ashore wherever in Africa they chanced to be on their voyage, to sow grain in the earth and await the harvest. On reaping the new grain they put again to sea. In this wise, after two years had elapsed, they rounded the Pillars of Hercules and in the third year reached Egypt.

Now, they told a tale that I personally do not believe (though others may, if they choose), how they had the sun on their right hand as they sailed along the African coast.

that is the case or not, it seems likely that the arrival of Bantu-speaking peoples led to the spread of Iron Age farming throughout the region.

Recent archaeological work has provided us with a better idea of the nature of Bantu society. The communities that arose as a result of these migrations were essentially rural and based on subsistence farming. The primary crops were millet and sorghum, already a staple in the savannah regions to the northwest, along with yams, melons, and beans. The land was often tilled with both iron and stone tools, and the former were usually manufactured in a local smelter. Some people kept domestic animals such as cattle, sheep, goats, or chickens or supplemented their diets by hunting and food gathering. Because the population was still small and an ample supply of cultivable land was available, most settlements were relatively small; each village formed a self-sufficient political and economic entity. It is likely that the inhabitants of most villages were members of a particular lineage group, along with their dependents, although some communities may have consisted of several unrelated families.

Within the family there was apparently a clear division of economic functions between men and women. Women tilled the fields and cared for the children, while the men tended the herds or engaged in such tasks as hunting and trade. Most trade was local and involved necessities such as salt and specialized commodities such as animal products, copper, and iron ore.

On the eastern fringe of the continent, the Bantu-speaking peoples gradually began to take part in the regional trade that moved by sea up and down the East African coast. The author of the *Periplus* notes that the goods exported from the trading port of Rhapta included ivory, rhinoceros horn, and tortoise shell. Imports included manufactured metal goods such as weapons and tools, glass, wine, and cereals. The identity of the peoples taking part in this trade is not clear, but it seems likely that the area was already inhabited by a mixture of local peoples and immigrants from the Arabian peninsula. According to the *Periplus,* the area around Rhapta was under the control of an Arabian kingdom. Out of this mixture would eventually emerge an African-Arabian "Swahili" culture (see East Africa and the Indian Ocean Trade later in this chapter) that continues to exist in coastal areas today.

Trade across the Indian Ocean and down the coast of East Africa, facilitated by the monsoon winds, would gradually become one of the most lucrative sources of commercial profit in the ancient and medieval worlds. Although the origins of the trade remain shrouded in mystery, traders eventually came by sea from as far away as the mainland of Southeast Asia. Early in the first millennium C.E., Malay peoples bringing cinnamon to the Middle East began to cross the Indian Ocean directly and landed on the southeastern coast of Africa. Eventually, a Malay settlement was established on the island of Madagascar, where the population is still of mixed Malay-African origin. Historians suspect that Malay immigrants were responsible for introducing such Southeast Asian foods as the banana and the yam to the African peoples. With its high yield and ability to grow in uncultivated rain forest, the banana often became the preferred crop of the Bantu peoples.

South Africa

South of the East African plateau and the Congo basin is a vast land of hills, grasslands, and arid desert stretching to the Cape of Good Hope at the tip of the continent. As Bantu-speaking farmers spread southward during the final centuries of the first millennium B.C.E., they began to encounter Stone Age peoples in the area who still lived primarily by hunting and foraging. These peoples, many of whom apparently belonged to the Khoisan family of languages (Khoisan languages are distinguished by their numerous "clicking" sounds), were lighter in skin color and generally shorter than the Bantu speakers who were beginning to arrive from the north.

Available evidence suggests that early relations between these two peoples were relatively harmonious. Intermarriage between members of the two groups was apparently not unusual, and many of the Khoisan-speaking peoples were gradually absorbed into what became a dominantly Bantu-speaking pastoral and agricultural society that spread throughout much of southern Africa during the first millennium C.E.

The Coming of Islam

As the previous chapter explained, the rise of Islam in the Arabian peninsula during the first half of the seventh century C.E. did not take long to have an impact on neighboring areas. In 641, Arab forces seized the delta of the Nile River and brought two centuries of Byzantine rule to an end. To guard against attacks from the Byzantine fleet, Arab administrators eventually built a new capital at Cairo, inland from the previous Byzantine capital of Alexandria, and began to consolidate their control over the entire region.

Since the fall of the monarchy of the pharaohs in the fourth century B.C.E., Egypt had been governed by foreign conquerors. First came the Ptolemaic dynasty, which had been founded by Ptolemy, one of the generals of Alexander the Great, who had conquered Egypt in 332 B.C.E. The Ptolemies ruled for three hundred years until Egypt was brought under Roman rule during the time of Antony and Cleopatra in 30 B.C.E. Although the western part of the Roman Empire fell to the Germanic invaders during the fifth and sixth centuries, the eastern part survived as the Byzantine Empire, which continued to control Egypt.

Under the Byzantines, Egypt continued to be a vital part of the political and economic life of the Mediterranean basin. It was a commercial hub and a center for trade, much of which went down the Red Sea and into the Indian Ocean. But the average Egyptian did not share in this prosperity. Tax rates were generally high, and Christians were subjected to periodic persecution by the Byzantines, who viewed the local Coptic faith and other sects in the area as heresies.

As a result, the Arab conquest of the area was probably welcomed by many, if not the majority, of the local inhabitants. Although the new rulers continued to obtain much of their revenue from taxing the local farming population, tax rates were generally lower than they had been under the corrupt Byzantine government, while conversion to Islam brought exemption from taxation. During the next generations, many Egyptians converted to the Muslim faith.

In the meantime, Arab rule was gradually being extended westward along the Mediterranean coast. When the Romans conquered Carthage in 146 B.C.E., they had called their new province Africa, thus introducing a name that would eventually be applied to the entire continent. At first, the Romans penetrated southward into the Sahara in an effort to continue the Carthaginian trade routes. Their caravans and settlements were constantly harassed by the local population, however, and in the third century C.E., the Romans abandoned the area. After the fall of the Roman Empire, much of the area reverted to the control of local Berber chieftains, but the Byzantines captured Carthage in the mid-sixth century C.E. In 690, the city was seized by the Arabs, who now began to consolidate their control over the entire area, which they called Al Maghrib (the west).

At first, the local Berber peoples resisted their new conquerors. The Berbers were tough fighters, and for several generations, Arab rule was limited to the towns and lowland coastal areas. But Arab persistence eventually paid off, and by the early eighth century, the entire coastal region as far west as the Strait of Gibraltar was under Arab rule. The Arabs were now poised to cross the strait and expand into southern Europe and to push south beyond the fringes of the Sahara.

The Kingdom of Ethiopia: A Christian Island in a Muslim Sea

By the end of the sixth century C.E., the kingdom of Axum, long a dominant force in the trade network through the Red Sea, was in a state of decline. Part of this decline may be ascribed to a shift in trade routes. Some of the commerce that had once passed through the Red Sea now went by caravan across the Arabian peninsula and then by sea down the Persian Gulf. The economy of Axum may also have been adversely affected by the overexploitation of farmland, a problem that persists in Ethiopia today. By the beginning of the ninth century, the capital had been moved further into the mountainous interior, and Axum was gradually transformed from a maritime power into an isolated agricultural society.

The rise of Islam on the Arabian peninsula hastened this process, as the Arab world increasingly began to serve as the focus of the regional trade passing through the area. By the eighth century, a number of Muslim trading states had been established on the African coast of the Red Sea, a development that contributed to the transformation of Axum into a landlocked society with primarily agricultural interests. At first relations between Christian Axum and its Muslim neighbors were relatively peaceful, as the larger and more powerful Axumite kingdom attempted with some success to compel the coastal Islamic states to accept a tributary relationship. Axum's role in the local commercial network temporarily revived, and the area became a prime source for ivory, resins like frankincense and myrrh, and slaves. Slaves came primarily from the south, where Axum had been attempting to subjugate restive tribal peoples living in the Amharic plateau beyond its southern border.

Beginning in the twelfth century, however, relations between Axum and its neighbors deteriorated, as the Muslim states along the coast began to move inland to gain control over the growing trade in slaves and ivory. Axum responded with force and at first had some success in reasserting its hegemony over the area. But in the early fourteenth century, the Muslim state of Adal, located at the juncture where the Indian Ocean meets the Red Sea, launched a new attack on the Christian kingdom.

Axum also underwent significant internal change during this period. The Zagwe dynasty, which seized control of the country in the mid-twelfth century, centralized the government and extended the Christian faith throughout the kingdom, now known as Ethiopia. Military commanders or civilian officials who had personal or kinship ties with the royal court established vast landed estates to maintain security and facilitate the collection of taxes from the local population. In the meantime, Christian missionaries established monasteries and churches to propagate the faith in outlying areas. Close relations were reestablished with leaders of the Coptic church in Egypt and with Christian officials in the Holy Land. This process was continued by the Solomonids, who succeeded the Zagwe dynasty in 1270. But by the early fifteenth century, the state had become more deeply involved in an expanding conflict with Muslim Adal to the east, a conflict that lasted for over a century and gradually took on the characteristics of a holy war.

East Africa and the Indian Ocean Trade

The East African coast also began to play a growing role in maritime trade during the seventh and eighth centuries. As we have seen, the east coast had been incorporated into the local trading network by the time of the writing of the *Periplus* in the first century C.E., and there are some indications that Greek sailors had entered the Indian Ocean and explored down the African coast as early as the sixth century B.C.E. Even earlier, during the era of the New Kingdom, Egyptian ships had plied these waters in search of gold, ivory, palm oil, and perhaps slaves.

What little we know about the early history of the peoples living in this area comes from the *Periplus*. The peoples along the coast were seafarers, who used sewn boats and dugout canoes to fish and exchange goods with their neighbors and with merchant ships arriving from distant ports. Evidently, some Arab merchants and government agents lived in the area, but the majority of the population was probably made up of Bantu-speaking peoples who had migrated into the coastal regions as described earlier in this chapter. According to the *Periplus*, some intermarriage was already taking place between the two groups.

With the increase in regional commerce following the rise of Islam during the seventh and eighth centuries, the eastern coast of Africa became a significant part of the trading network throughout the Indian Ocean. Peoples from the Arabian peninsula and the Persian Gulf began to settle at ports along the coast and on the small islands offshore. According to local tradition, this process (called by one standard history of Africa the beginning of the "great age" of the East African coast) began in the eighth century when Muslims from the Arabian peninsula began to settle on the islands scattered up and down the coast. Then, in the middle of the tenth century, a Persian from Shiraz, a city in southern Iran, sailed to the area with his six sons. As his small fleet stopped along the coast, each son disembarked on one of the coastal islands and founded a small community; these settlements later grew into the commercial centers of Mombasa, Pemba, Zanzibar (literally, "the coast of Zanj"), and Kilwa.

Modern historians do not accept the literal truth of such legends, which underestimate the degree to which the area had already become a major participant in local commerce as well as the role of the local inhabitants in the process. Still, the end result was the formation of a string of trading ports stretching from Mogadishu (today the capital of Somalia) in the north to Kilwa (south of present-day Dar es Salaam) in the south. Kilwa became especially important as it was near the southern limit for a ship hoping to complete the round-trip journey in a single season. Merchants in these cities often amassed considerable profit, as evidenced by their lavish stone palaces, some of which still stand in the modern cities of Mombasa and Zanzibar. One of the most magnificent cities of the day, though now in ruins, was Kilwa. The fourteenth-century Arab traveler Ibn Battuta described it as "amongst the most beautiful of cities and most elegantly built. All of it is of wood, and the ceilings of its houses are of *al-dis* [reeds]."[3]

Intermarriage between the immigrants and the local population continued, although a distinct Arab community, made up primarily of merchants, persisted in many areas. The members of the ruling class were often of mixed heritage, but usually traced their genealogy to Arab or Persian ancestors. Al-Mas'udi, a tenth-century visitor from the South Arabian port of Oman, reported that the island of Kanbulu (thought to be the island of Pemba) had a "Muslim population and a royal family"

(see the box on p. 273). Goods such as ivory, gold, and rhinoceros horn were exported to countries as far away as China, while imports included iron goods, glassware, Indian textiles, and Chinese porcelain.

Although some members of the local African population were involved in the local and maritime trade, many others followed traditional pursuits, such as hunting and agriculture. Al-Mas'udi remarked that some of the staple foods of the area included bananas, coconuts, meat, and millet. Commercial activities evidently brought considerable prosperity to the area, at least to the elites. A Portuguese visitor in the early sixteenth century reported:

> The kings of these isles live in great luxury; they are clad in very fine silk and cotton garments, which they purchase at Mombaca [modern-day Mombasa] from the Cambaya merchants [Cambay was a city on the Rann of Kutch, on the northwestern coast of India]. The women of these Moors go bravely decked, they wear many jewels of fine Cofala [Sofala] gold, silver too in plenty, earrings, necklaces, bangles and bracelets, and they go clad in good silk garments. They have many mosques, and honor greatly the Alcoran of Mafamede.[4]

Most of the coastal states were self-governing, although sometimes several towns were grouped together under a single dominant authority. Government revenue came primarily from taxes imposed on commerce. Some trade went on between these coastal city-states and the peoples of the interior, who provided gold and iron, ivory, and various agricultural goods and animal products in return for textiles, manufactured articles, and weapons. Relations apparently varied, and the coastal merchants sometimes resorted to force to obtain goods from the in-

Map 8.3   Trans-Saharan Trade Routes.

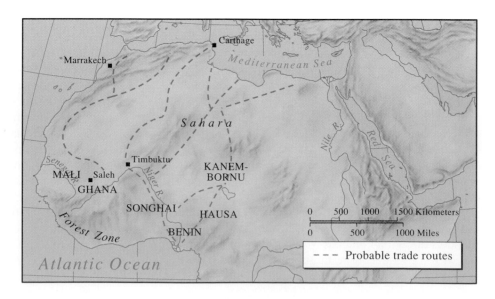

⇒ The Coast of Zanj ⇐

From early times, the people living on the coast of East Africa took an active part in trade along the coast and across the Indian Ocean. This description of the area was written by the Arab traveler al-Mas'udi, who visited the "land of Zanj" in 916.

Al-Mas'udi in East Africa

The land of Zanj produces wild leopard skins. The people wear them as clothes, or export them to Muslim countries. They are the largest leopard skins and the most beautiful for making saddles. . . . They also export tortoise-shell for making combs, for which ivory is likewise used. . . . The Zanj are settled in that area, which stretches as far as Sofala, which is the furthest limit of the land and the end of the voyages made from Oman and Siraf on the sea of Zanj. . . . The Zanj use the ox as a beast of burden, for they have no horses, mules or camels in their land. . . . There are many wild elephants in this land but no tame ones. The Zanj do not use them for war or anything else, but only hunt and kill them for their ivory. It is from this country that come

tusks weighing fifty pounds and more. They usually go to Oman, and from there are sent to China and India. This is the chief trade route. . . .

The Zanj have an elegant language and men who preach in it. One of their holy men will often gather a crowd and exhort his hearers to please God in their lives and to be obedient to him. He explains the punishments that follow upon disobedience, and reminds them of their ancestors and kings of old. These people have no religious law: their kings rule by custom and by political expediency.

The Zanj eat bananas, which are as common among them as they are in India; but their staple food is millet and a plant called kalari which is pulled out of the earth like truffles. They also eat honey and meat. They have many islands where the coconut grows: its nuts are used as fruit by all the Zanj peoples. One of these islands, which is one or two days' sail from the coast, has a Muslim population and a royal family. This is the island of Kanbulu [thought to be modern Pemba].

land peoples. The Portuguese visitor recounted that "the men thereof [of Mombasa] are oft-times at war and but seldom at peace with those of the mainland, and they carry on trade with them, bringing thence great store of honey, wax and ivory."

As time passed, a mixed African-Arabian culture, eventually to be known as Swahili, began to emerge throughout the coastal area. Intermarriage was common among the ruling groups, and the Muslim religion and Middle Eastern urban architectural styles were gradually implanted within a society still predominantly African. The term Swahili (from *sahel*, meaning "coast" in Arabic, thus, "peoples of the coast") was also applied to the major language used in the area. Swahili was a mixed language that combined Bantu grammatical structure with a number of Arabic words and phrases; it is the national language of the countries of Kenya and Tanzania today.

State Building in West Africa

As Muslim traders began to penetrate the Sahara during the eighth century, the area south of the desert was be-

ginning to undergo significant political and social change. A number of major trading states were in the process of creation, and they eventually transformed the Sahara into one of the leading avenues of world trade, crisscrossed by caravan routes leading to destinations as far away as the Atlantic Ocean, the Mediterranean, and the Red Sea.

Ghana

The first of these great commercial states was Ghana, which emerged in the fifth century C.E. in the upper Niger valley, a grassland region between the Sahara and the tropical forests along the West African coast (the modern state of Ghana, which takes its name from the trading society under discussion here, is located in the forest region to the south). The majority of the people in the area were Iron Age farmers living in villages under the authority of a local chieftain. For reasons that are not entirely clear, these localized communities were gradually integrated into a more centralized administrative system that ultimately evolved into the kingdom of Ghana.

Although the people of the region had traditionally lived off the produce of the soil, a primary reason for Ghana's growing importance was gold. The heartland of the state was located near one of the richest gold-producing areas in all of Africa. Ghanaian merchants transported the gold to Morocco, whence it was distributed throughout the known world. This trade began in ancient times, as the Greek historian Herodotus relates:

> The Carthaginians also tell us that they trade with a race of men who live in a part of Libya beyond the Pillars of Heracles [the Strait of Gibraltar]. On reaching this country, they unload their goods, arrange them tidily along the beach, and then, returning to their boats, raise a smoke. Seeing the smoke, the natives come down to the beach, place on the ground a certain quantity of gold in exchange for the goods, and go off again to a distance. The Carthaginians then come ashore and take a look at the gold; and if they think it represents a fair price for their wares, they collect it and go away; if, on the other hand, it seems too little, they go back aboard and wait, and the natives come and add to the gold until they are satisfied. There is perfect honesty on both sides; the Carthaginians never touch the gold until it equals in value what they have offered for sale, and the natives never touch the goods until the gold has been taken away.[5]

Later, Ghana became known to Arab-speaking peoples in North Africa as "the land of gold." Actually, the title was misleading, for the gold did not come from Ghana, but from a neighboring people, who sold it to merchants from Ghana.

Eventually, other exports from Ghana found their way to the bazaars of the Mediterranean coast and beyond—

Map 8.4 The Emergence of States in Africa.

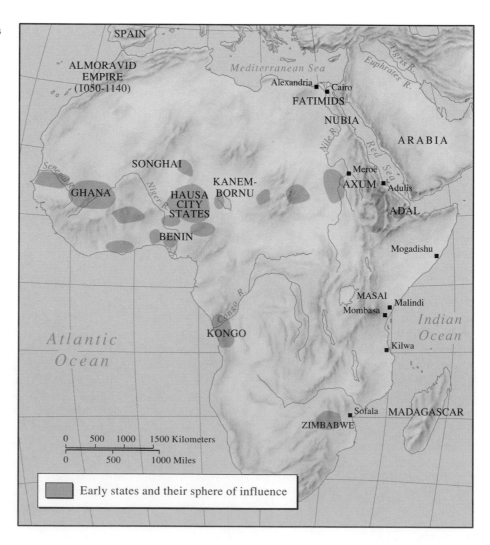

Early states and their sphere of influence

ivory, ostrich feathers, hides, leather goods, and ultimately slaves. The origins of the slave trade in the area probably go back to the pre-Christian era, when Berber tribesmen seized African villagers in the regions south of the Sahara and sold them for profit to buyers in Europe and the Middle East. In return, Ghana imported metal goods (especially weapons), textiles, horses, and salt.

Much of the trade across the desert was still carried by the Berbers, the nomadic peoples whose camel caravans became known as the "fleets of the desert." Ghanaian merchants, however, played an active role as intermediaries, trading tropical products such as bananas, kola nuts, and palm oil from the forest states of Guinea to the south. By the eighth and ninth centuries, much of this trade was carried by Muslim merchants, who purchased the goods from local traders (using iron and copper cash or cowrie shells from Southeast Asia as the primary means of exchange) and then sold them to Berbers who carried them across the desert. The merchants who carried on this trade often became quite wealthy and lived in splendor in cities like Saleh, the capital of Ghana. So did the king, of course, who taxed the merchants as well as the farmers and the producers.

Mali

The state of Ghana flourished for several hundred years, but by the twelfth century, weakened by ruinous wars with Berber tribesmen, it had begun to decline, and it collapsed at the end of the century. In its place rose a number of new trading societies, including large territorial states like Mali and Songhai in the west, Kanem-Bornu in the east, and small commercial city-states like the Hausa, located in what is today northern Nigeria. Along the Atlantic coast to the south were the Guinea forest-states, located at the far end of the African trade routes and isolated from the Mediterranean peoples by the dense forests along the coast. Nevertheless, these forest-states still took part in trade through the intermediary activity of the commercial societies to their north.

The greatest of the states that emerged after the destruction of Ghana was Mali. Extending from the Atlantic coast inland as far as the famous trading metropolis of Timbuktu and Gao, a modern city on the Niger River, Mali built its wealth and power on the gold trade. But the heartland of Mali was situated considerably to the south of the old state of Ghana in the savannah region where sufficient moisture enabled farmers to grow such crops as sorghum, millet, and even rice. The farmers lived in villages ruled by a local chieftain (called a *mansa*), who served as both religious and administrative leader and was responsible for forwarding tax revenues from the village to higher levels of government.

The primary wealth of the country was accumulated in the cities. Here lived the merchants, who were primarily of local origin although many now were practicing Muslims. The court imposed a tax on commercial activities, but unlike its counterparts in many countries in Asia, it was never able to establish a royal monopoly over key items of foreign trade. The gold trade, in particular, remained largely in the hands of local producers, who paid a tax in the form of tribute to the king of Mali, but sold their metal directly to private merchants, who then transported it via the cities of Jenne and Timbuktu to purchasers beyond the Sahara. Still, the kings of Mali had little reason to complain. One of the most powerful, known as Mansa Musa (1312–1337), was so wealthy that when he embarked on a pilgrimage to Mecca in the early fourteenth century, his spending splurge in Egypt depressed the price of gold there for a dozen years.

Mansa Musa's primary contribution to his people was probably not economic prosperity, but the Muslim faith. The kings of Ghana had been followers of traditional African faiths (see the box on p. 276), and early rulers of Mali apparently continued this practice, assuming the role of *mansa* for their subjects from the traditional village chiefs. Later rulers, however, converted to Islam. Mansa Musa strongly encouraged the building of mosques and the study of the Koran in his kingdom and imported scholars and books to introduce his subjects to the message of Allah. One visitor from Europe, writing in the late fifteenth century, reported as follows:

> The rich king of Timbuktu has many plates and scepters of gold, some whereof weigh 1,300 pounds; and he keeps a magnificent and well-furnished court. When he travels anywhere, he rides upon a camel which is led by some of his noblemen: and so he does likewise when he goes to warfare, and all his soldiers ride upon horses. . . . They often have skirmishes with those that refuse to pay tribute and, so many as they may take, they sell unto the merchants of Timbuktu. . . . Here are a great store of doctors, judges, priests and other learned men, that are bountifully maintained at the king's cost and charges. And hither are brought divers manuscripts of written books out of Barbary [North Africa] which are sold for more money than any other merchandise. The coin of Timbuktu is of gold without any stamp or superscription: but in matters of small value they use certain shells [cowrie shells] brought hither out of the kingdom of Persia.[6]

A Description of a Ghanaian Capital

After its first appearance in West Africa in the decades following the death of the Prophet, Islam competed with native African religions for followers. Eventually, several local rulers converted to the Muslim faith. This passage by the Arab geographer al-Bakri shows how both religions flourished side by side in the state of Ghana during the eleventh century.

Al-Bakri's Description of Ghana

The king's residence comprises a palace and conical huts, the whole surrounded by a fence like a wall. Around the royal town are huts and groves of thorn trees where live the magicians who control their religious rites. These groves, where they keep their idols and bury their kings, are protected by guards who permit no one to enter or find out what goes on in them.

None of those who belong to the imperial religion may wear tailored garments except the king himself and the heir-presumptive, his sister's son. The rest of the people wear wrappers of cotton, silk or brocade according to their means. Most of the men shave their beards and the women their heads. The king adorns himself with female ornaments around the neck and arms. On his head he wears gold-embroidered caps covered with turbans of finest cotton. He gives audience to the people for the redressing of grievances in a hut around which are placed 10 horses covered in golden cloth. Behind him stand 10 slaves carrying shields and swords mounted with gold. On his right are the sons of vassal kings, their heads plaited with gold and wearing costly garments. On the ground around him are seated his ministers, whilst the governor of the city sits before him. On guard at the door are dogs of fine pedigree, wearing collars adorned with gold and silver. The royal audience is announced by the beating of a drum, called daba, made out of a long piece of hollowed-out wood. When the people have gathered, his co-religionists draw near upon their knees sprinkling dust upon their heads as a sign of respect, whilst the Muslims clap hands as their form of greeting.

Government and Kingship in West Africa

Like most other major states at the time, West African societies such as Ghana and Mali were monarchies. The king ruled by divine right and was assisted by a hereditary aristocracy composed of the leading members of prominent clans. These powerful hereditary chieftains not only assisted the ruler as a council of advisers, but also served as district chiefs responsible for maintaining law and order and collecting taxes in areas under their control. Villages, in turn, had their headmen and their own councils of elders composed of members of prominent local families who were responsible for carrying out the directives of the government at the local level. In turn, the king was responsible for maintaining the security of his kingdom, serving as an intermediary with local deities, and functioning as the chief law officer to adjudicate disputes (see the box on p. 277).

The origins of this hereditary ruling class are not certain. Local tradition maintains that they were immigrants from the Sahara, and it is possible that pastoral peoples from North Africa conquered the local populations and first organized them into states. For centuries the Berber peoples of West Africa had raided territories south of the Sahara for gold and slaves, and some may have settled permanently in the area. But there is no firm evidence to support this suggestion; nor is it clear that the ruling class was ethnically distinct from the remainder of the population.

Not all the people in West Africa lived in these large commercial empires. In some areas, notably the so-called Hausa states along the Niger River, a decentralized system of small city-states emerged, each with its own government. Like their counterparts in Renaissance Italy, these states lived by commerce and provided protection for farmers living beyond the city walls in return for the payment of taxes.

The expansion of Islam into West Africa had a major impact on the political system. By introducing Arabic as the first written language in the region and Muslim law codes and administrative practices from the Middle East, Islam provided local rulers with the tools to increase their authority and the efficiency of their governments. Moreover, as Islam spread gradually throughout the population, a common religion united previously diverse peoples into a more coherent community sharing common values and beliefs.

⇒ The Kingdom of Borno ⇐

One of our main sources for information about medieval Africa is Leo Africanus, a resident of Spain of Muslim parentage who was captured by Christian corsairs in 1518 and later served under Pope Leo X. Leo Africanus, whose real name was al-Hassan Ibn Mohammed Al-Wezaz Al-Fasi, undertook many journeys to Africa and left us this description of the kingdom of Borno (Bornu). This passage appears in his massive work, The History and Description of Africa.

Leo Africanus, *The History and Description of Africa*

The large province of Borno bordering westward upon the province of Guangana, and from thence extending eastward five hundred miles, is distant from the fountain of Niger almost one hundred and fifty miles, the south part thereof adjoining unto the desert of Set, and the north part unto that desert which lies toward Barca. The situation of this kingdom is very uneven, some part thereof being mountainous, and the residue plain. Upon the plains are sundry villages inhabited by rich merchants, and abounding with corn. The king of this region and all his followers dwell in a certain large village. The mountains inhabited by herdsmen and shepherds do bring forth millet and other grain altogether unknown to us. The inhabitants in summer go all naked save their private members which they cover with a piece of leather: but all winter they are clad in skins, and have beds of skins also. They embrace no religion at all, being neither Christians, Mahumetans [Muslims], nor Jews, nor of any other profession, but living after a brutish manner, and having wives and children in common: and (as I understand among them) they have no proper names at all, but every one is nicknamed according to his length, his fatness, or some other quality. They have a most puissant prince, being lineally descended from the Libyan people called Bardoa. Horsemen he has in a continual readiness to the number of three thousand, and a huge number of footmen; for all his subjects are so serviceable and obedient unto him, that whensoever he commands them, they will arm themselves and follow him whither he pleases to conduct them. They pay unto him none other tribute but the tithes of all their corn; neither has this king any revenues to maintain his estate, but only such spoils as he gets from his next enemies by often invasions and assaults. He is at perpetual enmity with a certain people inhabiting beyond the desert of Sau; who in times past marching with a huge army of footmen over the said desert, wasted a great part of the kingdom of Borno. Whereupon the king of Borno sent for the merchants of Barbary, and willed them to bring him great store of horses; for in this country they use to exchange horses for slaves, and to give fifteen, and sometimes twenty slaves for one horse.

States and Stateless Societies in Southern Africa

In the southern half of the African continent, from the great basin of the Zaire River to the Cape of Good Hope, states formed somewhat more slowly than in the north. Until the eleventh century C.E., most of the peoples in this region lived in what are sometimes called "stateless societies," characterized by autonomous villages organized by clans and ruled by a local chieftain or clan head. Beginning in the eleventh century, in some parts of southern Africa, these independent villages gradually began to consolidate. Out of these groupings came the first states.

One area where this process occurred was the Zaire River valley, where the combination of fertile land and nearby deposits of copper and iron enabled the inhabitants to enjoy an agricultural surplus and engage in regional commerce. Two new states in particular underwent this transition. Sometime during the fourteenth century, the kingdom of Luba was founded in the center of the continent, in a rich agricultural and fishing area near the shores of Lake Kisale. Luba had a relatively centralized government, in which the king appointed provincial governors who, in turn, were responsible for collecting tribute from the village chiefs. At about the same time, the kingdom of Kongo was formed just south of the mouth of the Zaire River on the Atlantic coast.

These new states were primarily agricultural, although both had a thriving manufacturing sector and took an active part in the growing exchange of goods throughout the region. As time passed, both began to expand southward to absorb the mixed farming and pastoral peoples in the area of modern-day Angola. In the drier grassland area to the south, other small communities continued to support themselves by herding, hunting, or food gathering. We know little about these peoples, however, since they possessed no writing system and had few visitors. A Portuguese sailor who encountered them in the late sixteenth century left the following description:

> These people are herdsmen and cultivators. . . . Their main crop is millet which they grind between two stones or in wooden mortars to make flour. From this they make cakes, which they bake under the embers of the fire. Of the same grain they make beer, mixing it with a lot of water, which after being fermented in a clay jar, cooled off and turned sour, they drink with great gusto. Their cattle are numerous, fat, tender, tasty and large, the pastures being very fertile. Their wealth consists mainly in their huge number of dehorned cows. They also subsist on cows' milk and on the butter which they make from it. They live together in small villages, in houses made of reed mats, which do not keep out the rain. The main clothing of these people is a cloak of calf-skin, rubbed with grease to make it soft. On their feet they wear shoes of two or three layers of raw hide, fastened together in a round shape and secured to the foot with thongs. With these they can run with great speed.[7]

Zimbabwe

Further to the east, the situation was somewhat different. In the grassland regions immediately to the south of the Zambezi River, a mixed economy involving farming, cattle herding, and commercial pursuits had begun to develop during the early centuries of the first millennium C.E. Characteristically, villages in this area were constructed inside walled enclosures to protect the animals at night. The most famous of these communities was Zimbabwe, located on the plateau of the same name between the Zambezi and Limpopo Rivers. From about 1300 to the middle of the fifteenth century, Zimbabwe was the most powerful and prosperous state in the region and played a major role in the gold trade with the Swahili trading communities on the eastern coast.

The ruins of Zimbabwe's capital, known as Great Zimbabwe, provide a vivid illustration of the kingdom's power and influence. Modern visitors generally agree that the ruins are the most impressive archaeological site in southern Africa. Located in an area favorable to farming and grazing and strategically situated between substantial gold reserves to the west and a small river leading to the coast, Great Zimbabwe was well placed to benefit from the expansion of trade between the coast and the interior. The town sits on a hill overlooking the river and is surrounded by stone walls, which enclosed an area large enough to hold up to 10,000 residents. The houses of the wealthy were built of cement on stone foundations, while those of the common people were of dried mud with thatched roofs. In the valley below is the royal palace surrounded by a stone wall thirty feet high. Artifacts found at the site include household implements and ornaments made of gold and copper, as well as jewelry and even porcelain imported from China.

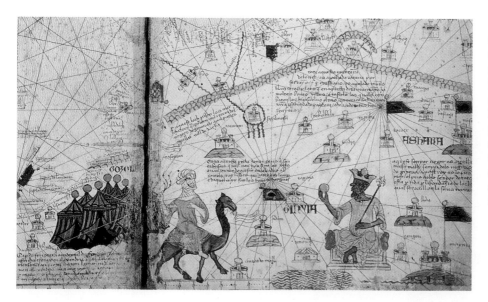

◆ **Mansa Musa.** Mansa Musa (1312–1337), king of the West African state of Mali, was one of the richest and most powerful rulers of his day. During his famous pilgrimage to Mecca, he arrived in Cairo with a hundred camels laden with gold and gave away so much gold that its value depreciated there for several years. His fame spread to Europe as well, evidenced by this Spanish map of 1375, which depicts Mansa Musa seated on his throne in Mali, holding an impressive gold nugget.

Most of the royal wealth probably came from two sources: the ownership of cattle and the king's ability to levy heavy taxes on the gold that passed through the kingdom en route to the coast. By the middle of the fifteenth century, however, the city was apparently abandoned, possibly because of environmental damage caused by overgrazing. With the decline of Zimbabwe, the focus of economic power began to shift northward to the valley of the Zambezi River.

South of the Limpopo River, pastoralism and hunting continued to be the primary means of livelihood. As we saw earlier, some of these peoples had been absorbed by the Iron Age farming communities that spread southward from Central Africa during the first millennium C.E. Others remained independent in isolated villages or small kingdoms, although they often carried on active trade with the growing states to their north.

One such people were the San, called Bushmen by later Europeans. A hunting and foraging people, the San lived in small family communities of twenty to twenty-five members throughout southern Africa from Namibia in the west to the Drakensberg Mountains near the southeastern coast. Scholars have learned about the early life of the San by interviewing their modern descendants and by studying rock paintings found in caves throughout the area. These multicolored paintings, which predate the coming of the Europeans, were drawn with a brush made of small feathers fastened to a reed. They depict various aspects of the San's lifestyle including their hunting techniques and religious rituals.

When the Europeans arrived in the area, they regarded the San as troublesome pests who raided their cattle. One nineteenth-century European missionary dismissed the San contemptuously, saying: "He has no religion, no laws, no government, no recognized authority, no patrimony, no fixed abode."[8] Over time, as the Europeans constantly encroached on their hunting grounds, the San found it virtually impossible to maintain their way of life. Only a few survive today, most of them in the Kalahari Desert in Botswana.

Aspects of African Society

Drawing generalizations about social organization, cultural development, and daily life in this early period of African history is difficult for several reasons. First, Africa was a vast and highly diverse continent that was far less homogeneous than Europe, the Middle East, South Asia, and East Asia during the same period. Sec-

ond, few written records are available. Most African societies did not have written languages, so historians must rely on accounts by the occasional visitor. But those visitors, such as the Arab travelers al-Mas'udi and Ibn Battuta, tended to come into contact mostly with the wealthy and the powerful. Consequently, they say little about the lives of the common people, leaving us to speculate about what life was like for ordinary Africans during this early period.

Urban Life

African towns often began as fortified walled villages and gradually evolved into larger communities serving several purposes. Here, of course, were the center of government and the teeming markets filled with goods from distant regions. Here also were artisans, skilled in metal or wood working, pottery making, and other crafts, as well as some farmers who tilled the soil in the neighboring fields. Unlike the rural areas, where a village was usually composed

◆ **Great Zimbabwe.**   Situated on an important trade route and a center for cattle and agriculture, Great Zimbabwe was once the capital of a prosperous state. Its thirty-foot walls were the first in Africa to be constructed without the use of mortar. The ruins of the walled palace shown here indicate why Great Zimbabwe is generally regarded as the most impressive archaeological site in southern Africa.

of a single lineage group or clan, the towns drew their residents from several clans, although individual clans usually lived in their own compounds and were governed by their own clan heads.

The houses of the wealthy were usually of stone. Often they consisted of two stories and were built around an inner courtyard. The houses of the poor were usually constructed of wood or thatch. One of the most famous cities, the Saharan oasis city of Timbuktu, was described by a traveler from the Mediterranean:

> Here are many shops of artificers and merchants, and especially of such as weave linen and cotton cloth. And hither do the Barbary [North African] merchants bring the cloth of Europe. All the women of this region except maid-servants go with their faces covered, and sell all necessary victuals. The inhabitants, and especially strangers there residing, are exceeding rich, insomuch that the king that now is, married both his daughters to two rich merchants. Here are many wells containing most sweet water. . . . Corn, cattle, milk and butter this region yields in great abundance: but salt is very scarce here, for it is brought hither by land from Taghaza which is five hundred miles distant.[9]

As this description indicates, the relationship between the ruler and the merchant class in West Africa differed from the situation in most Asian societies, where the royal family and the aristocracy were largely isolated from the remainder of the population. In Africa, the chasm between the king and the common people was not so great. Often the ruler would hold an audience to allow people to voice their complaints or to welcome visitors from foreign countries.

This is not to say that the king was not elevated above all others in status. In wealthier states, the walls of the audience chamber would be covered with sheets of beaten silver and gold, and the king would be surrounded by hundreds of armed soldiers and some of his trusted advisers. An audience must have been an awesome experience, as Ibn Battuta describes:

> The blacks are the most humble of men before their king and the most extreme in their self-abasement before him. . . . When he calls one of them while he is in session in his cupola, . . . the man invited takes off his clothes and wears patched clothes, takes off his turban, puts on a dirty cap, and goes in raising his clothes and trousers up his legs halfway to his knees. He advances with humility looking like a beggar. He hits the ground with his elbows, he hits it hard. He stands bowed, like one in the *ruku* position in prayer, listening to what the king says. When one of them speaks to the sultan and he gives him an answer, he removes his clothes from his back and throws dust on his head and back, as a person does when bathing with water. I used to wonder how they do not blind their eyes.[10]

◆ **The City of Timbuktu.** The city of Timbuktu sat astride one of the major trade routes that passed through the Sahara between the kingdoms of West Africa and the Mediterranean Sea. Caravans transported food and various manufactured articles southward in exchange for salt, gold, copper, skins, agricultural goods, and slaves. Salt was at such a high premium in Timbuktu that a young Moroccan wrote in 1513 that one camel's load, brought 500 miles by caravan, sold for 80 gold ducats, while a horse sold for only 40 ducats. Timbuktu became a prosperous city as well as a great center of Islamic scholarship. By 1550, it had three universities connected to its principal mosques and 180 Koranic schools.

Nevertheless, the symbiotic relationship between the ruler and the merchant class served to reduce the gap between the king and his subjects. The relationship was mutually beneficial. The merchants received honors and favors from the palace, while the king's coffers were filled with taxes paid by the merchants. Certainly, it was to the benefit of the king to maintain law and order in his domain so that the merchants could ply their trade. In describing the good qualities of the peoples of West Africa, Ibn Battuta remarks:

> Among these qualities there is also the prevalence of peace in their country, the traveler is not afraid in it nor is he who lives there in fear of the thief or of the robber by violence. They do not interfere with the property of the white man [the Muslim trader] who dies in their country even though it may consist of great wealth, but rather entrust it to the hand of someone dependable among the men until it is taken by the rightful claimant.[11]

Family, Village, and Women

Few Africans, of course, ever had an audience with their monarch or with his key advisers and subordinates. The vast majority of the African people lived in small rural villages. Their identities were established by their membership in a nuclear family and a lineage group. At the basic level was the nuclear family composed of parents and preadult children; sometimes it included an elderly grandparent and other family dependents as well. They lived in small round huts constructed of packed mud and topped with a conical thatch roof. In most African societies, these nuclear family units would in turn be combined into larger kinship communities known as households or lineage groups.

The lineage group was similar in many respects to the clan in China or the caste system in India in that it was normally based on kinship ties, although sometimes outsiders such as friends or other dependents may have been admitted to membership. Throughout the precolonial era, lineages served, in the words of one historian, as the "basic building blocks" of African society. The authority of the leading members of the lineage group was substantial. As in China, the elders had considerable power over the economic functions of the other people in the group, which provided mutual support for all members much as a clan would do in China.

In many traditional African communities, several households would gather together in villages for protection. At the head of the village was the familiar "big man," who was often assisted by a council of representatives of the various households in the community. Often the "big man" was believed to possess supernatural powers, and as the village grew in size and power, he would eventually be transformed into a local chieftain or monarch.

Unlike the situation in India, there were generally no rigid demarcations between different classes and economic functions in African society. Many African communities, however, possessed a local aristocracy, which was separated by status, function, and rights from the remainder of the population.

THE ROLE OF WOMEN

Although generalizations are risky, women were usually subordinate to men in Africa, as they were in most early societies. In some cases, they were valued for the work they could do or for their role in increasing the size of the lineage group. Polygyny was not uncommon, particularly in Muslim societies. Women often worked in the fields while the men of the village tended the cattle or went on hunting expeditions. In some communities, the women specialized in commercial activities. In one area in southern Africa, young girls were sent into the mines to extract gold because of their smaller physiques.

But there were some key differences between the role of women in Africa and elsewhere. In many African societies, lineage was matrilinear rather than patrilinear. In the words of Ibn Battuta, "a man does not pass on inheritance except to the sons of his sister to the exclusion of his own sons." He said he had never encountered this custom before except among the unbelievers of the Malabar coast in India. Women were often permitted to inherit property, and the husband was often expected to move into his wife's house.

Relations between the sexes were also sometimes more relaxed than in China or India, with none of the taboos characteristic of those societies. Again, in the words of Ibn Battuta, himself a Muslim:

> With regard to their women, they are not modest in the presence of men, they do not veil themselves in spite of their perseverance in the prayers. . . . The women there have friends and companions amongst men outside the prohibited degrees of marriage [i.e., others than brothers, fathers, etc.]. Likewise for the men, there are companions from amongst women outside the prohibited degrees. One of them would enter his house to find his wife with her companion and would not disapprove of that conduct.

When Ibn Battuta asked an African acquaintance about these customs, the latter responded: "Women's companionship with men in our country is honorable and takes place in a good way: there is no suspicion about it. They are not like the women in your country." Ibn Battuta noted his astonishment at such a "thoughtless" answer and did not accept further invitations to visit his friend's house.[12]

Such informal attitudes toward the relationship between the sexes were not found everywhere in Africa and were probably curtailed as many Africans converted to Islam. But it is a testimony to the tenacity of traditional customs that the relatively puritanical views about the role of women in society brought by Muslims from the Middle East made little impression even among Muslim families in West Africa.

Slavery

African slavery is often associated with the period after 1500. Indeed, the slave trade did reach enormous proportions in the seventeenth and eighteenth centuries, when European slave ships transported millions of unfortunate victims abroad to Europe or the Americas (see Chapter 14).

Slavery did not originate with the coming of the Europeans, however. It had been practiced in Africa since ancient times and probably originated with prisoners of war who were forced into perpetual servitude. Slavery was common in ancient Egypt and became especially prevalent during the New Kingdom, when slaving expeditions brought back thousands of captives from the upper Nile to be used in labor gangs, for tribute, and even as human sacrifices.

Slavery persisted during the early period of state building in the first and early second millennia C.E. Berber tribes may have regularly raided agricultural communities south of the Sahara for captives who were transported northward and eventually sold throughout the Mediterranean. Some were enrolled as soldiers, while others, often women, were used as domestic servants in the homes of the well-to-do. The use of captives for forced labor or for sale was apparently also common in African societies further to the south and along the eastern coast.

Certainly, life was difficult for the average slave. The least fortunate were probably those who worked on plantations owned by the royal family or other wealthy landowners. Those pressed into service as soldiers were sometimes more fortunate, since in Muslim societies in the Middle East, they might at some point win their freedom. Many slaves were employed in the royal household or as domestic servants in private homes. In general, they probably had the most tolerable existence. Although

they normally were not permitted to purchase their freedom, their living conditions were often decent and sometimes were practically indistinguishable from those of the free individuals in the household. In some societies in North Africa, slaves reportedly made up as much as 75 percent of the entire population. Elsewhere, the percentage was much lower, in some cases less than 10 percent.

Religious Beliefs in Traditional Africa

Like other aspects of African life, early African religious beliefs varied from place to place. Reconstructing them in the absence of written records is difficult, but historians have relied on folk rituals passed down through the centuries to identify certain common characteristics that appear to have been shared by most African societies.

One of these common denominators was a belief in a single creator god. The god of the Yoruba peoples in Nigeria, for example, sent his son Oduduwa down from heaven in a canoe to create the first human beings. The supreme god of the Bantu peoples is a pantheistic force from whom all things come. The Fon peoples of modern Dahomey are an exception to this generalization, however; they believe that the earth resulted from the union of a sun god and a moon goddess, who gave birth to numerous children who rule over all the heavenly bodies in the universe.

Sometimes, as in many other societies, the creator god was accompanied by a whole pantheon of lesser gods. The Ashanti people of Ghana, for example, believed in a supreme being called Nyame, whose sons were lesser gods. Each son served a different purpose: one was the rainmaker, another the compassionate, and a third was responsible for the sunshine. Like the deities of the ancient Greeks, these gods were often capricious, and humans were required to propitiate them to avoid their anger. Some peoples believed that the creator god originally lived on earth, but left in disgust at the behavior of human beings. Yet he was also merciful and could be placated by proper behavior.

One way to communicate with the gods was through ritual, a process usually undertaken by a special class of diviners. Many of these seers were employed by the king to contact the supreme deity in order to guarantee a bountiful harvest or otherwise protect the interests of the ruler and his subjects. Sometimes the heavenly hierarchy paralleled earthly arrangements. Among the Ashanti, worship of Nyame was the exclusive preserve of the king through his priestly retainers, while lesser deities were worshiped by the lower officials and the common people.

These lesser gods, who were believed to reside in the forces of nature, could intercede with Nyame on behalf of ordinary Africans.

Another key element in African religion was the importance of ancestors. Each lineage group could trace itself back to a founding ancestor or group of ancestors. Ritual ceremonies dedicated to ancestors were important not only because the ancestors were believed to be closer to the gods, but also because they had the power to influence, for good or evil, the lives of their descendants. Thus, many African religions shared a belief in a form of afterlife. Human existence was believed to consist of two stages: the first stage was life on earth (*sasa*), during which the individual went through a series of steps from birth to death; the second stage was eternal existence (*zamani*), during which the soul floated in the atmosphere through eternity. Ancestral souls would not be extinguished as long as the lineage group continued to perform rituals in their name.

Some African societies may have believed that the soul of the ruler ascended after death to the realm of the gods. According to one source, in medieval Ghana, after the death of the king, an enormous wooden dome was constructed over the site of his tomb. The body was placed inside the dome, along with ornaments, eating utensils, weapons, and his servants. The dome was then draped with mats and other materials, and the entire edifice was covered with dirt until it resembled a large mound.

Such beliefs were challenged but not always replaced by the arrival of Islam. Islam swept rapidly across the northern coast of Africa in the wake of the Arab conquest, although the Berber peoples living in the mountainous interior of the Maghrib were initially resistant to the new faith. It was even slower to penetrate the lands south of the Sahara. As with Christianity at a later date, the process probably began as a consequence of trade; beginning in the eighth century, merchants from the Maghrib introduced Muslim beliefs to the trading states in the savannah areas south of the desert. At first, conversion took place on an individual basis rather than through official encouragement. The rulers of Ghana, for example, did not convert to Islam themselves, although they welcomed Muslim merchants and apparently did not discourage their subjects from adopting the new faith. The first rulers to convert to Islam were the royal family of Gao at the end of the tenth century. By the end of the fifteenth century, much of the population in the grasslands south of the Sahara had accepted Islam.

The process was even more gradual in East Africa. Egypt was converted during the first phase of expansion during the seventh century, but Muslim beliefs did not move into the upper Nile valley until several hundred years later. As Islam spread southward, it was adopted by many lowland peoples, but had less success in the mountains of Ethiopia, where Coptic Christianity continued to win adherents. Islam was first brought to the coast of East Africa by Muslim merchants from the Arabian peninsula, but did not win many adherents until the twelfth and thirteenth centuries when Swahili culture emerged and many members of the upper class converted to the Muslim faith.

Although Islam's popularity was sometimes simply a matter of personal preference, it had special appeal to the ruling class. With Islam came a theory of statecraft, a code of laws, a system of ethics, and a written language that could legitimize their status and facilitate the administration of their territories. The common people may have converted for reasons of economic convenience or have been impressed by Islam's powerful doctrine of equality and its sanction of polygyny.

In some ways, of course, the tenets of Islam were in conflict with indigenous beliefs and customs. Although the concept of a single transcendent deity presented no problems in many African societies, Islam's rejection of spirit worship and a priestly class ran counter to the beliefs of many Africans and was often ignored in practice. Similarly, as the Muslim traveler Leo Africanus lamented, Islam's puritanical insistence on the separation of the sexes contrasted with the relatively informal relationships that prevailed in many African societies and was probably slow to take root (see the box on p. 284). As elsewhere, imported ideas were synthesized with native beliefs to create a unique brand of Africanized Islam.

African Culture

In early Africa, as in much of the rest of the world at the time, creative expression, whether in the form of painting, literature, or music, was above all a means of serving religion. While to the uninitiated a wooden mask or the bronze and iron statuary of southern Nigeria is simply a work of art, to the artist it was often a means of expressing religious convictions. Some African historians reject the use of the term *art* to describe such artifacts because they were produced for religious rather than aesthetic purposes.

Painting and Sculpture

The earliest extant art forms in Africa are rock paintings. The most famous examples are in the Tassili Mountains

❧ Women and Islam in North Africa ❧

In Muslim societies in North Africa, as elsewhere, women were required to cover their bodies to avoid giving temptations to men. In this excerpt from The History and Description of Africa, *Leo Africanus describes the customs along the Mediterranean coast of Africa.*

Leo Africanus, *The History and Description of Africa*

Their women (according to the guise of that country) go very gorgeously attired: they wear linen gowns dyed black, with exceeding wide sleeves, over which sometimes they cast a mantle of the same color or of blue, the corners of which mantle are very artificially fastened about their shoulders with a fine silver clasp. Likewise they have rings hanging at their ears, which for the most part are made of silver; they wear many rings also upon their fingers. Moreover they usually wear about their thighs and ankles certain scarfs and rings, after the fashion of the Africans. They cover their faces with certain masks having only two holes for the eyes to peep out at. If any man chance to meet with them, they presently hide their faces, passing by him with silence, except it be some of their allies or kinsfolks; for unto them they always discover their faces, neither is there any use of the said mask so long as they be in presence. These Arabians when they travel any journey (as they oftentimes do) they set their women upon certain saddles made handsomely of wicker for the same purpose, and fastened to their camel backs, neither be they anything too wide, but fit only for a woman to sit in. When they go to the wars each man carries his wife with him, to the end that she may cheer up her good man, and give him encouragement. Their damsels which are unmarried do usually paint their faces, breasts, arms, hands, and fingers with a kind of counterfeit color: which is accounted a most decent custom among them.

in the central Sahara, where the earliest paintings may date back as far as c. 5000 B.C.E., though the majority are a millennium or so younger. These paintings depict the evolving livelihood of the peoples of the area as they shifted from hunting to cattle herding and ultimately to engaging in regional commerce. Some of the later paintings depict the two-horse chariots used to transport goods prior to the introduction of the camel. Rock paintings are also found elsewhere in the continent, including the Nile valley and in eastern and southern Africa. Those of the San peoples of southern Africa are especially interesting for their illustrations of ritual ceremonies in which village shamans induce rain, propitiate the spirits, or cure illnesses.

More familiar, perhaps, are African wood carvings and sculpture. Wood carvers throughout the continent produced remarkable masks (actually headpieces) and statuary. The carvings often represent gods, spirits, or ancestral figures and were believed to embody the spiritual powers of the subject in symbolic form. Terra-cotta and metal figurines served a similar purpose. For example, the impressive figures found near the city of Nok in northern Nigeria are believed to have had religious significance. Dating from the first millennium B.C.E., they include human figures and heads in terra-cotta, as well as in iron and stone.

In the thirteenth and fourteenth centuries C.E., metal workers at Ife in what is now southern Nigeria produced handsome bronze and iron statues using the lost-wax method, in which melted wax is replaced in a mold by molten metal. The Ife sculptures, in turn, may have influenced artists in Benin in West Africa who produced equally impressive works in bronze during the same period. The Benin sculptures include bronze heads, relief plaques depicting life at court, ornaments, and figures of various types of animals.

Westerners once regarded African wood carvings and metal sculpture as a form of "primitive art," but the label is not appropriate. The metal sculpture of Benin, for example, is highly sophisticated, and some of the best works are considered masterpieces. Such artistic works were often created by artisans in the employ of the royal court.

Music

Like sculpture and wood carving, African music and dance often served a religious function. African dancing, for example, with its characteristic heavy rhythmic beat

◆ **Nok Pottery Head.**   The Nok peoples of the Niger River are the oldest known culture in West Africa to have created sculpture. This is a typical terra-cotta head from the Nok culture dating from 500 B.C.E. to 200 C.E. Discovered accidentally in the twentieth century by tin miners, these heads exhibit perforated eyes set in triangles or circles, stylized eyebrows, open thick lips, broad noses with wide perforated nostrils, and large ears. Although the function of these statutes is not known for certain, they likely were connected with religious rituals or ancestor devotion.

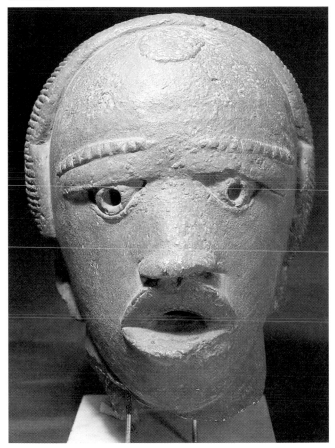

that has had such an impact on modern Western music, was in the words of a well-known African historian, "the great popular art of the African people." But the dances were also a means of communicating with the spirits, and the frenzied movements that are often identified with African dance were intended to represent the spirits acting through humans.

African music during the traditional period varied to some degree from one society to another. A wide variety of instruments were used, including drums and other percussion instruments, xylophones, bells, horns and flutes, and stringed instruments like the fiddle, harp, and zither. Still, the music throughout the continent had sufficient

common characteristics to justify a few generalizations. In the first place, a strong rhythmic pattern was an important feature of most African music, although the desired effect was achieved through a wide variety of means, including gourds, pots, bells, sticks beaten together, and hand-clapping as well as drums.

Another important feature of African music was the integration of voice and instrument into a total musical experience. Musical instruments and the human voice were often woven together to tell a story, and instruments, such as the famous "talking drum," were often used to represent the voice. Choral music and individual voices were frequently used in a pattern of repetition and

◆ **African Metalwork, Benin.**   By 1500 the West African state of Benin had expanded into an extensive and powerful empire with a highly developed official court art, especially in metalwork. Rulers were commemorated with bronze, brass, and copper sculpture, such as the stunning head of a queen mother shown here. These pieces were intended as ancestral memorial portraits and were placed on the altar of the deceased ruler by his successor. The queen mother, who claimed a revered position in Benin culture, would have ordered several such artistic renderings. The delicate attention to detail and the graceful sense of movement of this head attest to the technical excellence and sophistication of Benin bronze casting.

♦ **A Coptic Church in Ethiopia.** In 1200 C.E., Christian monks in Ethiopia began to construct a remarkable series of eleven churches carved out of solid volcanic rock. After a forty-foot trench was formed by removing the bedrock, the central block of stone was hewed into the shape of a Greek cross; then it was hollowed out and decorated. These churches, which are still in use today, testify to the fervor of Ethiopian Christianity.

variation, sometimes known as the "call and response" technique. Through this technique, the audience participated in the music by uttering a single phrase over and over as a choral response to the changing call sung by the soloist. Sometimes instrumental music achieved a similar result.

Finally, African music was not simply for the purpose of aesthetic enjoyment, but served as an integral part of the social fabric of African society. Much music was produced in the context of social rituals, such as weddings and funerals, religious ceremonies, and official inaugurations. It could also serve an educational purpose by passing on to the young people information about the history and social traditions of the community. Music, dance, drama, and art (in the form of costumes) were woven together to produce a desired social experience. In the absence of written languages in sub-Saharan Africa (except for the Arabic script, used in Muslim societies in East and West Africa), music served as the primary means of transmitting folk legends and religious traditions from generation to generation. Storytelling, which was usually undertaken by a priestly class or a specialized class of storytellers, served a similar function.

Architecture

No aspect of African artistic creativity is more varied than architecture. From the pyramids along the Nile to the ruins of Great Zimbabwe south of the Zambezi River, from the Moorish palaces at Zanzibar to the turreted mud mosques of West Africa, African architecture shows a striking diversity of approach and technique that is unmatched in other areas of creative endeavor.

The earliest surviving architectural form found in Africa, of course, is the pyramid (see Chapter 1). Although the Egyptians may have borrowed some aspects of their culture from Nubia, there is no evidence that the pyramid was one of them. On the contrary, the pyramidal form was adopted at Meroë during the last centuries of the first millennium B.C.E. Although used for the same purpose as their earlier counterparts at Giza, the pyramids at Meroë were distinctive in style; they were much smaller and were topped with a flat platform rather than rising to a point. Remains of temples with massive carved pillars at Meroë also reflect Egyptian influence.

Further to the south, the kingdom of Axum was developing its own architectural traditions. Like the Egyptians and the Nubians, the elites at Axum constructed palaces, religious monuments, and tombs for the royal family, all built of stone. Most distinctive were the carved stone pillars, known as stelae, that were used to mark the tombs of dead kings. Some stood as high as a hundred feet.

The advent of Christianity eventually had an impact on Axumite architecture. During the Zagwe dynasty in the twelfth and thirteenth centuries C.E., churches carved out of solid rock were constructed throughout the country. Stylistically, they combined indigenous techniques inherited from the pre-Christian period with elements borrowed from Christian churches in the Holy Land.

In West Africa, buildings constructed in stone were apparently a rarity until the emergence of states during the first millennium C.E. At that time, the royal palace, as well as other buildings of civic importance, were often built of stone or cement, while the houses of the majority of the population continued to be constructed of dried mud. On his visit to the state of Guinea on the West

A Chinese View of Africa

This passage from Chau Ju-kua's thirteenth-century treatise on geography describes various aspects of life along the eastern coast of Africa in what is now Somalia, including the urban architecture. The author was an inspector of foreign trade in the city of Quanzhou (sometimes called Zayton) on the southern coast of China. His account was compiled from reports of seafarers. Note the varied uses that the local people make of a whale carcass.

Chau Ju-kua on East Africa

The inhabitants of the Chung-li country [the Somali coast] go bareheaded and barefooted, they wrap themselves in cotton stuffs, but they dare not wear jackets, for the wearing of jackets and turbans is a privilege reserved to the ministers and the king's courtiers. The king lives in a brick house covered with glazed tiles, but the people live in huts made of palm leaves and covered with grass-thatched roofs. Their daily food consists of baked flour cakes, sheep's and camel's milk. There are great numbers of cattle, sheep and camels. . . .

There are many sorcerers among them who are able to change themselves into birds, beasts, or aquatic animals, and by these means keep the ignorant people in a state of terror. If some of them in trading with some foreign ship have a quarrel, the sorcerers pronounce a charm over the ship so that it can neither go forward nor backward, and they only release the ship when it has settled the dispute. The government has formally forbidden this practice.

When one of the inhabitants dies, and they are about to bury him in his coffin, his kinsfolk from near and far come to condole. Each person, flourishing a sword in his hand, goes in and asks the mourners the cause of the person's death. If he was killed by the hand of man, each one says, we will revenge him on the murderer with these swords. Should the mourners reply that he was not killed by any one, but that he came to his end by the will of Heaven, they throw away their swords and break into violent wailing.

Every year there are driven on the coast a great many dead fish measuring two hundred feet in length and twenty feet through the body. The people do not eat the flesh of these fish, but they cut out their brains, marrow, and eyes, from which they get oil. They mix this oil with lime to caulk their boats, and use it also in lamps. The poor people use the ribs of these fish to make rafters, the backbones for door leaves, and they cut off vertebrae to make mortars with.

African coast, the sixteenth-century traveler Leo Africanus noted that the houses of the ruler and other elites were built of chalk with roofs of straw. Even then, however, well into the state-building period, mosques were often built of mud.

Along the east coast, the architecture of the elite tended to reflect Middle Eastern styles. In the coastal towns and islands from Mogadishu to Kilwa, the houses of the wealthy reflected Moorish influence. As elsewhere, the common people lived in huts of mud, thatch, or palm leaves (see the box above). Mosques were built of stone.

The most famous stone buildings in sub-Saharan Africa are those at Great Zimbabwe. Constructed of carefully cut stones that were set in place without mortar, the great wall and the public buildings at Great Zimbabwe are an impressive monument to the architectural creativity of the peoples of the region.

Literature

Literature in the sense of written works did not exist in sub-Saharan Africa during the early traditional period, except in regions where Islam had brought the Arabic script from the Middle East. But African societies compensated for the absence of a written language with a rich tradition of oral lore. The bard, or professional storyteller, was an ancient African institution by which history was orally transmitted from generation to generation. In many West African societies, bards were highly esteemed and served as counselors to kings as well as protectors of local tradition. Bards were revered for their oratory and singing skills, phenomenal memory, and astute interpretation of history. As one African scholar wrote, the death of a bard was equivalent to the burning of a library.

Bards served several necessary functions in society. They were chroniclers of history, preservers of social

♦ **The Mosque at Jenne, Mali.** With the opening of the gold fields south of Mali, in present-day Ghana, Jenne became an important trading center for gold. Shown here is its distinctive fourteenth-century mosque made of unbaked clay without reinforcements. The projecting timbers offer easy access for repairing the mud exterior, as was regularly required.

customs and proper conduct, and entertainers who possessed a monopoly over the playing of several musical instruments, which accompanied their narratives. Because of their unique position above normal society, bards often played the role of mediator between hostile families or clans in a community. They were also credited with possessing occult powers and could read divinations and give blessings and curses. Traditionally, bards also served as advisers to the king, sometimes inciting him to action (such as going to battle) through the passion of their poetry. When captured by the enemy, bards were often treated with respect and released or compelled to serve the victor with their art.

One of the most famous West African epics, taking its place next to such great works as the Mahabharata and the *Romance of the Three Kingdoms* (see Chapter 10), is *Son-Jara* (also known as *Sunjata* or *Sundiata*). Passed down orally by bards for more than seven hundred years, it relates the heroic exploits of Son-Jara, the founder and ruler (1230–1255) of Mali's empire. Although Mansa Musa is famous throughout the world because of his flamboyant pilgrimage to Mecca in the fourteenth century, Son-Jara is more celebrated in West Africa because of the dynamic and unbroken oral traditions of the West African peoples (see the box on p. 289).

Conclusion

Thanks to the dedicated work of a generation of archaeologists, anthropologists, and historians, we now have a much better understanding of the evolution of human societies in Africa than we did a few decades ago. Intensive efforts by archaeologists have demonstrated beyond reasonable doubt that the first hominids lived there. Recent evidence suggests that farming may have been practiced in Africa more than twelve thousand years ago, while the concept of kingship may have originated not in Sumer or in Egypt, but in the upper Nile valley as long ago as the fourth millennium B.C.E.

Less is known about more recent African history, partly because of the paucity of written records. Still, historians have established that the first civilizations had begun to take shape in sub-Saharan Africa by the first millennium C.E., while the continent as a whole was an active participant in emerging regional and global trade with the Mediterranean world and across the Indian Ocean.

Thus, the peoples of Africa were not as isolated from the main currents of human history as was once assumed. Although the state-building process in sub-Saharan Africa was still in its early stages compared with the ancient civilizations of India, China, and Mesopotamia, in many respects these new states were as impressive and sophisticated as their counterparts elsewhere in the world.

In the fifteenth century, a new factor was added to the equation. Urged on by the tireless efforts of Prince Henry the Navigator, Portuguese fleets began to probe southward along the coast of West Africa. At first their sponsors were in search of gold and slaves, but at the end of the century, Vasco da Gama's voyage around the Cape of Good Hope signaled Portugal's determination to dominate the commerce of the Indian Ocean in the future. The new situation posed a challenge to the peoples of Africa, whose nascent states and technology would be severely tested by the rapacious demands of the Europeans (see Chapter 14).

❧ A West African Oral Tradition ❧

*I*n this passage from the West African Epic of Son-Jara, Son-Jara's sister, Sugulun Kulunkan, offers to seduce his enemy Sumamuru in order to obtain the Manden secret, or magic spell, needed to control the Kingdom of Mali. Sumamuru divulges his all-powerful secret and is rebuked by his mother; both son and mother then disown one another with the trenchant symbols of the slashed breast and cut cloth. After each line of the verse, the bard's assistant would shout the endorsement "true," perhaps the distant origin of today's African-American practice of approving each line of religious oratory with "Amen."

The Epic of Son-Jara

Son-Jara's flesh-and-blood-sister, Sugulun Kulunkan,
She said, "O Magan Son-Jara,
"One person cannot fight this war.
"Let me go seek Sumamuru.
"Were I then to reach him,
"To you I will deliver him,
"So that the folk of the Manden be yours,
"And all the Mandenland you shield."
Sugulun Kulunkan arose,
And went up to the gates of Sumamuru's fortress:
. . .
"Come open the gates, Susu Mountain Sumamuru!
"Come make me your bed companion!"
Sumamuru came to the gates:
"What manner of person are you?"
"It is I Sugulun Kulunkan!"
"Well, now, Sugulun Kulunkan,
"If you have come to trap me,
"To turn me over to some person,

"Know that none can ever vanquish me.
"I have found the Manden secret,
"And made the Manden sacrifice,
"And in five score millet stalks placed it,
"And buried them here in the earth.
"'Tis I who found the Manden secret,
"And made the Manden sacrifice,
"And in a red piebald bull did place it,
"And buried it here in the earth.
"Know that none can vanquish me.
"'Tis I who found the Manden secret
"And made a sacrifice to it,
"And in a pure white cock did place it.
"Were you to kill it,
"And uproot some barren groundnut plants,
"And strip them of their leaves,
"And spread them round the fortress,
"And uproot more barren peanut plants,
"And fling them into the fortress,
"Only then can I be vanquished."
His mother sprang forward at that:
"Heh! Susu Mountain Sumamuru!
"Never tell all to a woman,
"To a one-night woman!
"The woman is not safe, Sumamuru."
Sumamuru sprang towards his mother,
And came and seized his mother,
And slashed off her breast with a knife, magasi!
She went and got the old menstrual cloth.
"Ah! Sumamuru!" she swore.
"If your birth was ever a fact,
"I have cut your old menstrual cloth!"

CHAPTER NOTES

1. Quoted in Basil Davidson, *Africa in History* (New York, 1968), p. 29.
2. Diodorus Siculus, *Bibliotheca Historica*, 3:5, quoted in Roland Oliver and Brian Fagan, *Africa in the Iron Age* (Cambridge, 1975), p. 39.
3. Said Hamdun and Noel King, eds., *Ibn Battuta in Africa* (London, 1975), p. 19.
4. *The Book of Duarte Barbosa* (Nedeln, Liechtenstein, 1967), p. 28.
5. Herodotus, *The Histories*, trans. Aubrey de Sélincourt (Baltimore, 1964), p. 307.
6. Margaret Shinnie, *Ancient African Kingdoms* (London, 1965), p. 60.
7. C. R. Boxer, ed., *The Tragic History of the Sea, 1589–1622* (Cambridge, 1959), pp. 121–22, quoted in Kevin Shillington, *History of Africa* (New York, 1989), p. 155.
8. Quoted in Brian Fagan, *New Treasures of the Past: Fresh Finds That Deepen Our Understanding of the Archaeology of Man* (Leicester, 1987), p. 154.
9. Shinnie, *Ancient African Kingdoms*, p. 60.
10. Hamdun and King, *Ibn Battuta in Africa*, p. 39.
11. Ibid., p. 47.
12. Ibid., pp. 28–30.

SUGGESTED READINGS

In few areas of world history is scholarship advancing as rapidly as in African history. New information is constantly forcing archaeologists and historians to revise their assumptions about the early history of the continent. Standard texts therefore quickly become out-of-date as their conclusions are supplanted by new evidence.

Still, there are several worthwhile general surveys that provide a useful overview of the early period of African history. The dean of African historians, and certainly one of the most readable, is B. Davidson. For a sympathetic portrayal of the African people, see his *African History* (New York, 1968) and *Lost Cities in Africa*, rev. ed. (Boston, 1970). Other respected accounts are R. Oliver and J. D. Fage, *A Short History of Africa* (Middlesex, 1986); J. M. Harris, *Africans and Their History* (New York, 1972); and V. B. Khapoya, *The African Experience: An Introduction* (Englewood Cliffs, N.J., 1994). A more detailed interpretation, by four respected historians, is P. Curtin et al., *African History* (Boston, 1978). For a readable treatment embodying recent scholarly evidence, see K. Shillington, *History of Africa* (New York, 1989). For an overview with maps and illustrations, see J. Barraclough, ed., *The Times Atlas of World History* (Maplewood, N.J., 1978); and *Past Worlds: The Times Atlas of Archaeology* (Maplewood,

N.J., 1988). R. O. Collins, ed., *Problems in African History: The Precolonial Centuries* (New York, 1993) provides a useful collection of scholarly articles on key issues in precolonial Africa.

Specialized studies are beginning to appear with frequency on many areas of the continent. For a popular account of recent archaeological finds, see B. Fagan, *New Treasures of the Past: Fresh Finds That Deepen Our Understanding of the Archaeology of Man* (Leicester, 1987). For a more detailed treatment of the early period, see the early volumes in *The Cambridge History of Africa* (Cambridge, 1976–1986). See also R. Oliver, ed., *The Dawn of African History* (New York, 1968); and R. Oliver and B. Fagan, *Africa in the Iron Age* (Cambridge, 1975). J. D. Clarke and S. A. Brandt, eds., *From Hunters to Farmers* (Berkeley, Calif., 1984), takes an economic approach. For a fascinating account of trans-Sahara trade, see E. W. Bovill, *The Golden Trade of the Moors: West African Kingdoms in the Fourteenth Century*, 2d ed. (Princeton, N.J., 1995). On the cultural background, see R. Olaniyan, ed., *African History and Culture* (Lagos, 1982); and J. Vansina, *Paths in the Rainforest: Toward a History of Political Tradition in Equatorial Africa* (Madison, Wis., 1990). Although there exist many editions of *The Epic of Son-Jara* based on recitations of different bards, the most conclusive edition is by F.-D. Sisòkò, translated and thoroughly annotated by J. W. Johnson (Bloomington, Ind., 1992).

On East Africa, see D. Nurse and T. Spear, *The Swahili: Reconstituting the History and Language of an African Society, 800–1500* (Philadelphia, 1985). The maritime story is recounted with documents in G. S. P. Freeman-Grenville, *The East African Coast: Select Documents from the First to the Earlier Nineteenth Century* (Oxford, 1962). For the larger picture, see K. N. Chaudhuri, *Trade and Civilization in the Indian Ocean: An Economic History from the Rise of Islam to 1750* (Cambridge, 1985). On the early history of Ethiopia, see the classic work by S. H. Sellassie, *Ancient and Medieval Ethiopian History* (1972); and J. D. Fage and R. Oliver, eds., *The Cambridge History of Africa*, vol. 4 (Cambridge, 1977–1985).

For useful general surveys of southern Africa, see N. Parsons, *A New History of Southern Africa* (New York, 1983) and K. Shillington, *A History of Southern Africa* (Essex, 1987), a profusely illustrated account.

CHAPTER 9

The Expansion of Civilization in Southern Asia

As the traveler wandered through the length and breadth of the land, he carefully recorded his impressions of the people, from the king down to his most insignificant subject. Their dress, he remarked, was quite different from that of his own country. People wore loose-fitting clothing gathered at the armpits. Most garments were white and were fashioned of cotton, wool, or silk. The robes of the women fell to the ground and completely covered their shoulders. In some areas, the common people wore garments made of leaves or bark or even went naked.

The visitor was especially impressed with the people's personal cleanliness. All wash themselves before eating, he said, and when they completed their meal, they cleaned their teeth with a willow stick and washed their hands and mouths. After relieving themselves, they washed their bodies and used perfume of sandalwood or turmeric.

The visitor was Xuan Zang (Hsuan Tsang), a Buddhist monk from China who traveled to India in the seventh century C.E. to search for holy scriptures to take back to his own country for translation into Chinese. Because little of the literature of the Indian people from that period survives, Xuan Zang's observations are a valuable resource for our knowledge of the daily lives of the people and show us that the dhoti and the sari, common forms of Indian dress today, have a long history on the subcontinent.

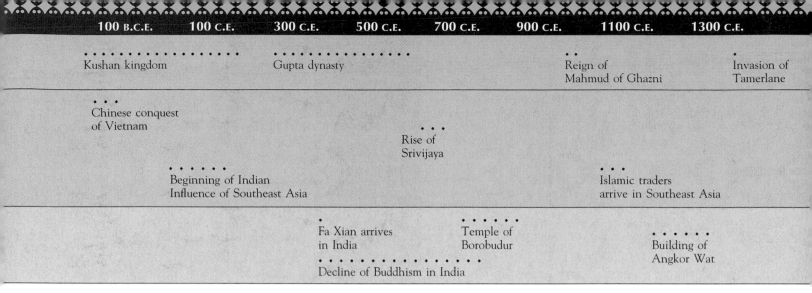

100 B.C.E.	100 C.E.	300 C.E.	500 C.E.	700 C.E.	900 C.E.	1100 C.E.	1300 C.E.

Kushan kingdom

Gupta dynasty

Reign of
Mahmud of Ghazni

Invasion of
Tamerlane

Chinese conquest
of Vietnam

Rise of
Srivijaya

Beginning of Indian
Influence of Southeast Asia

Islamic traders
arrive in Southeast Asia

Fa Xian arrives
in India

Temple of
Borobudur

Building of
Angkor Wat

Decline of Buddhism in India

India from the Mauryas to the Mughals

The India Xuan Zang visited was no longer the unified land it had been under the Mauryan dynasty. The overthrow of the Mauryas in the early second century B.C.E. had been followed by several hundred years of disunity, when the subcontinent was divided into a number of separate kingdoms and principalities. The dominant force in the north was the Kushan state, established by Indo-European–speaking peoples who had been driven out of Central Asia by the Xiongnu. The Kushans penetrated into the mountains north of the Indus River, where they eventually formed a kingdom with its capital at Bactria, not far from modern-day Kabul. Over the next two centuries, the Kushans expanded their supremacy along the Indus River and into the central Ganges valley. Then the dynasty began to weaken, and it collapsed sometime in the third century C.E. After the disintegration of the Kushan state, northern India remained divided until the rise of the Gupta dynasty in the early fourth century. The Guptas revived the ancient tradition of the Mauryas for nearly two hundred years until they too were overthrown in about 500 C.E.

Meanwhile, to the south, a number of kingdoms arose among the Dravidian peoples of the Deccan Plateau, which had been only partly under Mauryan rule. The most famous of these kingdoms was Cola (sometimes spelled "Chola") on the southeastern coast. Cola developed into a major trading power and sent merchant fleets eastward across the Bay of Bengal, where they introduced Indian culture as well as Indian goods to the peoples of Southeast Asia. In the fourth century C.E., Cola was overthrown by the Pallavas, who ruled from their capital at Kanchipuram (known today as Kanchi), just southwest of modern Madras, for the next four hundred years.

Beginning in the eleventh century, much of northern India fell under the rule of Turkic-speaking peoples who penetrated into the subcontinent from the northwest. Eventually, Turkic dynasties were set up in many areas and introduced the peoples of India to Islamic religion and civilization. These dynasties were able to survive attacks by the forces of Tamerlane (Timur the Lame), but by the end of the fifteenth century, they were coming under severe pressure from the Mughals, a powerful new force from the mountains. In the meantime, however, a number of new states established on the Indian model had emerged to the east in Southeast Asia.

The Kushan Kingdom: Linchpin of the Silk Road

The Kushan kingdom, with its power base beyond the Khyber Pass in modern-day Afghanistan, became the dominant political force in northern India in the centuries immediately after the fall of the Mauryas. Sitting astride the main trade routes across the northern half of the subcontinent, the Kushans thrived on the commerce that passed through the area on its way between the Mediterranean Sea and the countries bordering the

Pacific Ocean. The bulk of that trade was between the Roman Empire and China and was transported along the route known as the Silk Road, one segment of which passed through the mountains northwest of India.

Trade between India and Europe had begun even before the rise of the Roman Empire, but it expanded rapidly in the first century C.E., when sailors mastered the pattern of the monsoon winds in the Indian Ocean (from the southwest in the summer and the northeast in the winter). For the first time, goods could be transported reliably from the Mediterranean to seaports on the west coast of the Indian subcontinent. From there, the goods could be carried overland through the forbidding Pamir Mountains and to China.

Contacts between India and China had begun as early as the opening decades of the Han dynasty. Chinese envoys arrived in Bactria to request joint operations against the Xiongnu (see Chapter 3). Although no formal agreement was reached at that time, the expansion of Han authority over Central Asia soon led to an increase in trade between the two regions and between China and Rome as well.

The connection between the Mediterranean and the Indian Ocean, as described in the *Periplus*, a first-century C.E. account by a Greek participant, was extensive and often profitable, and it resulted in the establishment of several small Roman settlements along the Indian coast. Rome imported ivory, indigo, textiles, precious stones, and pepper from India and silk from China. The Romans sometimes paid cash for these goods but also exported silver, wine, perfume, slaves, and glass and cloth from Egypt. Overall, Rome appears to have imported much more than it sold to the Far East, leading Emperor Tiberius to grumble that "the ladies and their baubles are transferring our money to foreigners."

Above all, the Romans desired silk, which came primarily from China. The Silk Road ran from the Han capital at Chang'an westward along the northern and southern fringes of the vast Taklimakan Desert, through the Pamir Mountains into the Indus valley, and then to ports on the Arabian Sea. From there, the silk was shipped to Rome through the Persian Gulf or the Red Sea. At that time, ships from the Mediterranean apparently did not sail as far as the South China Sea. As the author of the *Periplus* reports:

> Beyond this region [presumably Southeast Asia], by now at the northernmost point, where the sea ends somewhere on the outer fringe, there is a very great inland city called Thina from which silk floss, yarn, and cloth are shipped by land via Bactria to Barygaza and via the Ganges River back to Limyrike. It is not easy to get to this Thina; for rarely do people come from it, and only a few.[1]

The author apparently knew little about Thina (China), describing it as adjacent to the Caspian Sea. China would remain the main supplier of silk to the Mediterranean world for centuries, supplying first Rome and later the Byzantine Empire.

The emergence of the Kushan kingdom as a major commercial power in the region was due not only to its role as an intermediary in the Rome-China trade, but also to the rising popularity of Buddhism. Sometime during the second century C.E. (the precise dates of his reign are unknown), Kanishka, the greatest of the Kushan monarchs, began to patronize Buddhism. Followers of the Buddha thus had a major opportunity to propagate his doctrine in the areas under Kushan rule. Under Kanishka and his successors, an intimate and mutually beneficial relationship was established between Buddhist monasteries and the local merchant community in thriving urban centers like Taxila and Varanasi. Merchants were eager to build stupas and donate money to monasteries in return for social prestige and the implied promise of a better life in this world or the hereafter.

For their part, the wealthy monasteries ceased to be simple communities where monks could find a refuge from the material cares of the world; instead they became major consumers of luxury goods provided by their affluent patrons. Monasteries and their inhabitants became increasingly involved in the economic life of society, while Buddhist architecture began to be richly decorated with precious stones and glass purchased from local merchants or imported from abroad. The process was highly reminiscent of the changes that occurred in the church in medieval Europe.

The Gupta Dynasty

The Kushan kingdom came to an end under uncertain conditions sometime in the third century C.E. In 320, a new state was established in the central Ganges valley by a local raja named Chandragupta (no relation to Chandragupta Maurya, the founder of the Mauryan dynasty). Chandragupta located his capital at Pataliputra, the site of the now decaying palace of the Mauryas. Under his successor Samudragupta, the territory under Gupta rule was extended into surrounding areas, and eventually the new kingdom became the dominant political force throughout northern India. It also established a loose suzerainty over the Dravidian state of Pallava, thus becoming the greatest state in the subcontinent since the decline of the Mauryan Empire.

Under a succession of powerful, efficient, and highly cultured monarchs, notably Samudragupta and Chandragupta II, the Gupta Empire established a new "classical age" of Indian civilization. Although written records of the Gupta era are relatively scarce, the greatness of its culture was reported by the famous Chinese pilgrim Fa Xian, who spent several years there in the fifth century C.E. Fa Xian, a fervent Buddhist, could not have been pleased that the Gupta monarchs had adopted the Hindu faith, but he admired the benevolent character of their rule and the prosperity of the country (see the box on p. 296).

Like the Dravidian kingdoms along the southern coast, the Gupta Empire was actively involved in commerce with China, Southeast Asia, and the Mediterranean. It also promoted domestic trade in cloth, salt, and iron. Great cities, notable for their temples and Buddhist monasteries as well as for their economic prosperity, rose along the main trade routes throughout the subcontinent. Much of their wealth apparently came from the religious trade, as pilgrims from across India

and as far away as China came to visit the major religious centers.

India's emergence as a manufacturing and commercial hub also provided a spur to the growth of the state. As in the Mauryan Empire, much of the trade in the Gupta Empire and its counterparts to the south was managed or regulated by the government. The Guptas owned mines and vast crown lands and earned massive profits from their commercial dealings. But there was also a large private sector, dominated by great caste guilds that monopolized key sectors of the economy. A money economy had probably been in operation since the second century B.C.E., when copper and gold coins had been introduced from the Middle East. This in turn led to the development of banking. Nevertheless, there are indications that the circulation of coins was limited. The Chinese missionary Xuan Zang, who visited India early in the

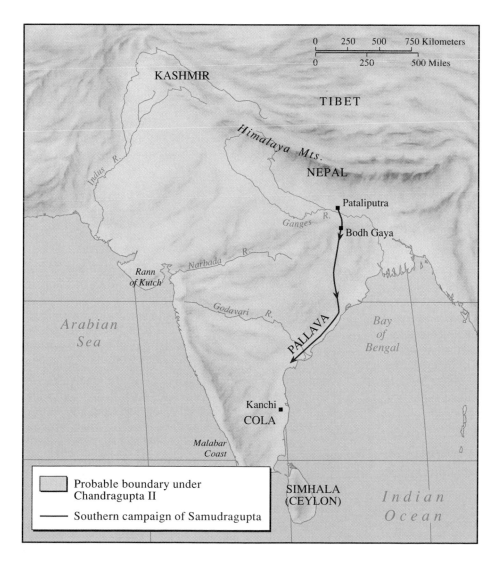

� **Map 9.1**   The Gupta Empire.

≽ The Good Life in Medieval India ≼

Much of what we know about life in medieval India comes from the accounts of Chinese missionaries who visited the subcontinent in search of documents recording the teachings of the Buddha. Here the fifth-century Buddhist monk Fa Xian reports on conditions in the kingdom of Mathura (Mo-tu-lo), a vassal state in western India that was part of the Gupta Empire. He found that the people were contented and prosperous except for the outcastes, whom he called Chandalas.

Fa Xian, *The Travels of Fa Xian*

Going south-east from this somewhat less than 80 *joyanas*, we passed very many temples one after another, with some myriad of priests in them. Having passed these places, we arrived at a certain country. This country is called Mo-tu-lo. Once more we followed the Pu-na river. On the sides of the river, both right and left, are twenty *sangharamas*, with perhaps 3000 priests. The law of Buddha is progressing and flourishing. Beyond the deserts are the countries of Western India. The kings of these countries are all firm believers in the law of Buddha. They remove their caps of state when they make offerings to the priests. The members of the royal household and the chief ministers personally direct the food-giving; when the distribution of food is over, they spread a carpet on the ground opposite the chief seat (the president's seat) and sit down before it.

They dare not sit on couches in the presence of the priests. The rules relating to the almsgiving of kings have been handed down from the time of Buddha till now. Southward from this is the so-called middle-country (Madhyadesa). The climate of this country is warm and equable, without frost or snow. The people are very well off, without poll-tax or official restrictions. Only those who till the royal lands return a portion of profit of the land. If they desire to go, they go; if they like to stop, they stop. The kings govern without corporal punishment; criminals are fined, according to circumstances, lightly or heavily. Even in cases of repeated rebellion they only cut off the right hand. The king's personal attendants, who guard him on the right and left, have fixed salaries. Throughout the country the people kill no living thing nor drink wine, nor do they eat garlic or onions, with the exception of Chandalas only. The Chandalas are named "evil men" and dwell apart from others; if they enter a town or market, they sound a piece of wood in order to separate themselves; then men, knowing who they are, avoid coming in contact with them. In this country they do not keep swine nor fowls, and do not deal in cattle; they have no shambles or wine-shops in their market-places. In selling they use cowrie shells. The Chandalas only hunt and sell flesh.

seventh century, remarked that most commercial transactions were conducted by barter.[2]

But the good fortunes of the Guptas proved to be relatively short-lived. Beginning in the late fifth century C.E., incursions by nomadic warriors from the northwest gradually reduced the power of the empire. It was briefly revived by the conquests of the military commander Harsa in the middle of the seventh century, but after his death, the remnants of the empire fell apart. North India would not be reunited for many centuries.

FEUDALISM, INDIAN STYLE

For many centuries after the fall of the Mauryan Empire, Kautilya's vision of a centralized empire throughout the subcontinent seemed more dream than reality. With the exception of the relatively brief Gupta era, political power tended to be decentralized, in the manner of early Aryan pastoral society. In the seventh century, Xuan Zang reported that India was divided into about seventy countries.[3]

In some respects, the political relationships among Indian states took on the character of the feudal system that emerged in Europe after the fall of Rome. Like medieval European lords, local Indian rajas were technically vassals of the king, but unlike in European feudalism, the relationship was not a contractual one. Still, the Indian model became highly complex with "inner" and "outer" vassals, depending on their physical or political proximity to the king, and "greater" or "lesser" vassals, depending on their power and influence. As in Europe, the vassals themselves often had vassals. The one constant factor was the perennial state of rivalry and civil strife that characterized the vassals' relationships and plagued the lives of ordinary Indians.

Only in the south did a tradition of strong kingship survive. Here kingship had developed along somewhat different lines than in the north. Where Aryan tradition had held that the ruler was a man like other men and thus was obligated to conform to the sacred *dharma,* rulers of some Dravidian kingdoms claimed to possess divine status. Under the Cola dynasty, temples were apparently constructed for the worship of the king. This concept of divine rule (known as the *devaraja,* or god-king, concept) would later be carried across the Bay of Bengal to become the basis for theories of kingship in some Southeast Asian societies down to modern times (see The Indian Model in Southeast Asia later in this chapter).

BUDDHISM AT BAY

For several hundred years after the reign of Asoka, Buddhism retained its popularity among the Indian people. But with popularity came change. Like all great religious and philosophical doctrines, the teachings of Siddhartha Gautama underwent a transformation that altered much of the original meaning. This process occurred in part because the earliest written sources were transcribed two centuries after his death, but also because his message was reinterpreted as it became part of the everyday life of the people. Abstract concepts of a *Nirvana* that cannot be described began to be replaced, at least in the popular mind, with more concrete visions of heavenly salvation, while Siddhartha was increasingly regarded as a divinity rather than as a sage. The Buddha's teachings that all four classes were equal gave way to the familiar Hindu conviction that some people, by reason of previous reincarnations, were closer to *Nirvana* than others.

These developments led to a split in the movement. Purists emphasized what they insisted were the original teachings of the Buddha (describing themselves as the school of Theravada, or "the teachings of the elders"). Followers of Theravada considered Buddhism a way of life, not a salvationist creed. Theravada stressed the importance of strict adherence to personal behavior and the quest for understanding as a means of release from the wheel of life.

In the meantime, another interpretation of Buddhist doctrine was emerging in the northwest. Here Buddhist believers, perhaps hoping to compete with other salvationist faiths circulating in the region, began to promote the view that *Nirvana* could be achieved through devotion and not just through painstaking attention to one's behavior. According to advocates of this school, eventually to be known as Mahayana (greater vehicle), Ther-

avada teachings were too demanding or strict for ordinary people to follow and therefore favored the wealthy, who were more apt to have the time and resources to spend weeks or months away from their everyday occupations. Mahayana Buddhists referred to their rivals as Hinayana, or "lesser vehicle," because in Theravada fewer would reach enlightenment. Mahayana thus attempted to provide hope for the masses in their efforts to reach *Nirvana,* but to the followers of Theravada, it did so at the expense of an insistence on proper behavior.

To advocates of the Mahayana school, salvation could also come from the intercession of a *bodhisattva* (he who possesses the essence of Buddhahood). According to Mahayana beliefs, some individuals who had achieved *bodhi* and were thus eligible to enter the state of *Nirvana* after death chose instead, because of their great compassion, to remain on earth in spirit form to help all human beings achieve release from the life cycle. Followers of Theravada, who believed the concept of *bodhisattva* applied only to Siddhartha Gautama himself, denounced such ideas as "the teaching of demons." But to their proponents, such ideas extended the hope of salvation to the masses. Mahayana Buddhists revered the saintly individuals who, according to tradition, had become *bodhisattvas* at death and erected temples in their honor where the local population could pray and render offerings. The most famous of the *bodhisattvas* was Avalokitesvara, a mythic figure whose name in Sanskrit means "Lord of Compassion." Perhaps because of the identification of Avalokitesvara with the concept of mercy, in China he was gradually transformed into a female figure known as Guan Yin (Kuan Yin).

A final distinguishing characteristic of Mahayana Buddhism was its reinterpretation of Buddhism as a religion rather than as a philosophy. Although Mahayana had philosophical aspects, its adherents increasingly regarded the Buddha as a divine figure, and an elaborate Buddhist cosmology developed. *Nirvana* was not a form of extinction, but a true heaven with many rest stations along the way for the faithful.

Under Kushan rule, Mahayana achieved considerable popularity in northern India and for a while even made inroads in such Theravada strongholds as the island of Sri Lanka. But in the end, neither the Mahayana nor the Theravada sect of Buddhism was able to retain its popularity in Indian society. By the seventh century C.E., Theravada had declined rapidly on the subcontinent, although it retained its foothold in Sri Lanka and across the Bay of Bengal in Southeast Asia, where it remained an influential force to modern times. Mahayana prospered in the northwest for centuries, but eventually it was supplanted by a revived Hinduism and later by a new arrival, Islam. But Mahayana too would find better fortunes abroad, as it was carried by missionaries like Fa Xian and Xuan Zang over the Silk Road or by sea back to China and then to Korea and Japan. In all three countries in East Asia, Buddhism has coexisted with Confucian doctrine and indigenous beliefs to the present.

Why was Buddhism unable to retain its popularity in its native environment, although it became a major force elsewhere in Asia? Some have speculated that in denying the existence of the soul, Buddhism ran counter to traditional Hindu belief in the concept of *atman*. Perhaps, too, one of Buddhism's strengths was also a weakness. In rejecting the class divisions that defined the Indian way of life, Buddhism appealed to those very groups who lacked an accepted place in Hindu society, such as the untouchables. But at the same time, it represented a threat to those with a higher status. Moreover, by emphasizing the responsibility of each person to seek an individual path to *Nirvana*, Buddhism undermined the strong social bonds of the Indian caste system, which, as we have seen, played a useful and perhaps necessary role in Indian society.

◆ Mamallapuram Ocean Temple. The eighth-century remnants of one of the earliest free-standing Hindu temples grace the shore at Mamallapuram, south of Madras. The temple was constructed of granite blocks and was originally covered with ornate carvings, but centuries of wind and sea have softened its surfaces. It would be difficult to conceive of a more romantic temple than this, especially at dawn with the sun and the ocean intensifying its mystery.

⇒ *The Education of a Brahmin* ⇐

Although the seventh-century Chinese traveler Xuan Zang was a Buddhist, he faithfully recorded his impressions of the Hindu religion in his memoirs. Here he describes the education of a brahmin, *the highest class in Indian society.*

Xuan Zang, *Records of Western Countries*

The Brahmans study the four *Veda Sastras*. The first is called *Shau* [longevity]; it relates to the preservation of life and the regulation of the natural condition. The second is called *Sse* [sacrifice]; it relates to the [rules of] sacrifice and prayer. The third is called *Ping* [peace or regulation]; it relates to decorum, casting of lots, military affairs, and army regulations. The fourth is called *Shue* [secret mysteries]; it relates to various branches of science, incantations, medicine.

The teachers [of these works] must themselves have closely studied the deep and secret principles they contain, and penetrated to their remotest meaning. They then explain their general sense, and guide their pupils in understanding the words which are difficult. They urge them on and skillfully conduct them. They add luster to their poor knowledge, and stimulate the desponding. If they find that their pupils are satisfied with their acquirements, and so wish to escape to attend to their worldly duties, then they use means to keep them in their power. When they have finished their education, and have attained thirty years of age, then their character is formed and their knowledge ripe. When they have secured an occupation they first of all thank their master for his attention. There are some, deeply versed in antiquity, who devote themselves to elegant studies, and live apart from the world, and retain the simplicity of their character. These rise above mundane presents, and are as insensible to renown as to the contempt of the world. Their name having spread afar, the rulers appreciate them highly, but are unable to draw them to the court. The chief of the country honors them on account of their [mental] gifts, and the people exalt their fame and render them universal homage. . . . They search for wisdom, relying on their own resources. Although they are possessed of large wealth, yet they will wander here and there to seek their subsistence. There are others who, whilst attaching value to letters, will yet without shame consume their fortunes in wandering about for pleasure, neglecting their duties. They squander their substance in costly food and clothing. Having no virtuous principle, and no desire to study, they are brought to disgrace, and their infamy is widely circulated.

Perhaps a final factor in the decline of Buddhism was the revival of Hinduism. In its early development, Hinduism had been highly elitist. Observance of court ritual had been a monopoly of the *brahmin* class (see the box above), while the major route to individual salvation, asceticism, was hardly realistic for the average Indian. But in the centuries after the fall of the Mauryas, a growing emphasis on devotion (*bhakti*) as a means of religious observance brought the possibility of improving one's *karma* by means of ritual acts within the reach of Indians of all classes. It seems likely that Hindu devotionalism rose precisely to combat the inroads of Buddhism and reduce the latter's appeal among the Indian population. The Chinese Buddhist missionary Fa Xian, who visited India in the mid-Gupta era, reported that mutual hostility between the Buddhists and the *brahmins* was quite strong:

Leaving the southern gate of the capital city, on the east side of the road is a place where Buddha once dwelt. Whilst here he bit (a piece from) the willow stick and fixed it in the earth; immediately it grew up seven feet high, neither more or less. The unbelievers and Brahmans, filled with jealousy, cut it down and scattered the leaves far and wide, but yet it always sprung up again in the same place as before. Here also they raised towers on places where the four Buddhas walked for exercise and sat down. The ruins still exist.[4]

For a while, Buddhism was probably able to stave off the Hindu challenge by its own salvationist creed of Mahayana, which also emphasized the role of devotion in escaping from the cares of this life. But during the Gupta era, Buddhism began to decline in popularity, and although Chinese pilgrims such as Fa Xian and Xuan Zang found Buddhist communities composed of powerful monasteries with thousands of adherents, the days of Buddhism as a dominant faith in the subcontinent were numbered.

Islam on the March

In the seventh century C.E., the entire Middle East was shaken by the birth of a new and dynamic religion. The messenger was Muhammad and the religion was Islam (see Chapter 7). In succeeding generations, the new faith spread rapidly westward from its origins in the Arabian peninsula, advancing across North Africa and crossing the Strait of Gibraltar into Spain. Islam also moved eastward across the arid wastelands of Persia and into the rugged mountains of the Hindu Kush. Finally, in the early eighth century, it penetrated into the northwestern corner of the Indian subcontinent.

The new religion had a major impact on Indian civilization, an impact that is still evident today in the division of the subcontinent into predominantly Hindu India and two Muslim states, Bangladesh and Pakistan. One reason for Islam's success in South Asia is that it arrived at a time when India was in a state of political disunity. The Gupta Empire, which had united most of northern and central India in the fourth century, had collapsed over a century earlier, and sporadic efforts to revive it had failed.

Although Arab merchants had been active along the coasts of the Indian subcontinent for centuries, Arab armies did not reach India until the early eighth century.

Map 9.2   India at the Death of Mahmud of Ghazni.

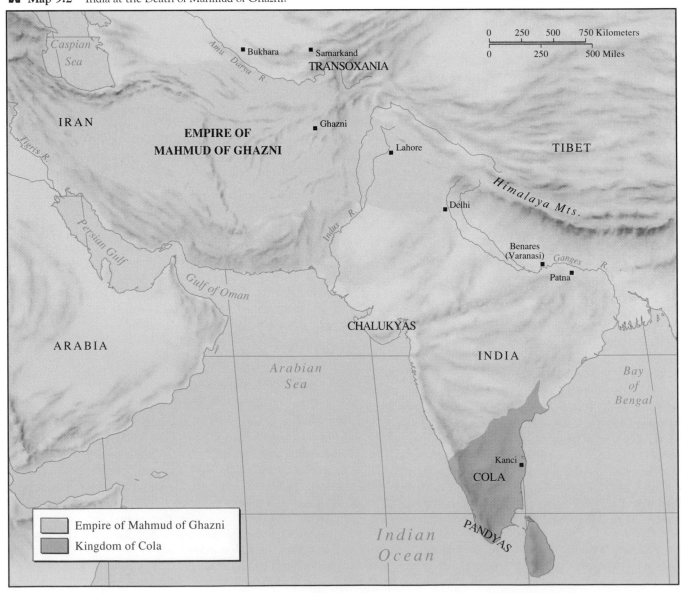

When Indian pirates attacked Arab shipping near the delta of the Indus River, the Muslim ruler in Iraq demanded an apology from the ruler of Sind, a Hindu state in the Indus valley. When the latter refused, Muslim forces conquered lower Sind in 711 and then moved northward into the Punjab, bringing Arab rule into the frontier regions of the subcontinent for the first time.

For the next three centuries, Islam made no further advances into India. But a second phase began at the end of the tenth century with the rise of the state of Ghazni, located in the area of the old Kushan kingdom in present-day Afghanistan. The new kingdom was founded in 962, when Turkic–speaking slaves seized power from the Samanids, a Persian dynasty. When the founder of the new state died in 997, his son, Mahmud of Ghazni (997–1030), succeeded him. Brilliant and ambitious, Mahmud used his patrimony as a base of operations for sporadic forays against neighboring Hindu kingdoms to the southeast. Before his death in 1030, he was able to extend his rule throughout the upper Indus valley and as far south as the Indian Ocean. In wealth and cultural brilliance, his court at Ghazni rivaled that of the Abbasid dynasty in neighboring Baghdad. But his achievements had a dark side. Describing Mahmud's conquests in northwestern India, the contemporary historian al-Biruni wrote:

> Mahmud utterly ruined the prosperity of the country, and performed wonderful exploits by which the Hindus became like atoms scattered in all directions, and like a tale of old in the mouth of the people. Their scattered remains cherish, of course, the most inveterate aversion towards all Muslims. This is the reason, too, why Hindu sciences have retired far away from those parts of the country conquered by us, and have fled to places which our hand cannot yet reach, to Kashmir, Benares, and other places.[5]

Resistance against the advances of Mahmud and his successors into northern India was led by the Rajputs, aristocratic Hindu clans who were probably descended from tribal groups that had penetrated into northwestern India from Central Asia in earlier centuries. The Rajputs, who claimed warrior (*kshatriya*) status, possessed a strong military tradition and fought bravely, but their military tactics, based on infantry supported by elephants, were no match for the fearsome cavalry of the invaders, whose ability to strike with lightning speed contrasted sharply with the slow-footed forces of their adversaries. Moreover, the incessant squabbling among the Rajput leaders put them at a disadvantage against the single-minded intensity and religious fervor of Mahmud's armies. It is no wonder that Mahmud was given the sobriquet "sword of Islam." Although the power of Ghazni declined after his

✦ **Kutub Minar.** To commemorate their religious victory in 1192, the Muslim conquerors of northern India constructed a magnificent mosque on the site of Delhi's largest Hindu temple. Much of the material for the mosque came from twenty-seven local Hindu and Jain shrines. Adjacent to the mosque soars the Kutub Minar, symbol of the new conquering faith. Originally 238 feet high, the tower carries an inscription proclaiming its mission to cast the long shadow of God over the realm of the Hindus.

death, a successor state in the area resumed the advance in the late twelfth century, and by 1200 Muslim power, in the form of a new Delhi sultanate, had been extended over the entire plain of northern India.

South of the Ganges River valley, Muslim power spread more slowly and in fact had little immediate impact. Muslim armies launched occasional forays into the Deccan Plateau, but at first they had little success, even though the area was divided among a number of warring kingdoms, each as large as a modern European state. Most powerful were the Chalukyas, located in the center of the peninsula near the modern city of Hyderabad.

Along the eastern coast were the Colas, and to the south were the Pandyas and the Pallavas. Like the earlier states in the area, many of these Hindu kingdoms flourished as a result of their trade with Southeast Asia, China, and the Middle East.

One reason the Delhi sultanate failed to take advantage of the disarray of its rivals was the threat posed by the Mongols on the northwestern frontier (see Chapter 10). Mongol armies unleashed by the great tribal warrior Genghis Khan occupied Baghdad and destroyed the Abbasid caliphate in the 1250s, while other forces occupied the Punjab around Lahore, from which they threatened Delhi on several occasions. For the next half-century, the attention of the sultanate was focused on the Mongols. That threat finally declined in the early fourteenth century with the gradual breakup of the Mongol Empire, and a new Islamic state emerged in the form of a new Tughluq dynasty (1320–1413), which extended its power into the Deccan Plateau. In praise of his sovereign, the Tughluq monarch Ala-ud-din, the poet Amir Khusrau exclaimed:

> Happy be Hindustan, with its splendor of religion,
> Where Islamic law enjoys perfect honor and dignity;
> In learning Delhi now rivals Bukhara;
> Islam has been made manifest by the rulers.
> From Ghazni to the very shore of the ocean
> You see Islam in its glory.[6]

Such happiness was not destined to endure, however. During the latter half of the fourteenth century, the Tughluq dynasty gradually fell into decline. In 1398, a new military force crossed the Indus River from the northwest, raided the capital of Delhi, and then withdrew. According to some contemporary historians, as many as 100,000 Hindu prisoners were massacred before the gates of the city. Such was India's first encounter with Tamerlane.

Tamerlane (b. 1330s), also known as Timur-i-lang (Timur the Lame), was the ruler of a Mongol khanate based in Samarkand to the north of the Pamir Mountains. His kingdom had been founded on the ruins of the Mongol Empire, which had begun to disintegrate as a result of succession struggles in the thirteenth century. As the power of the Great Khan at Karakorum declined, local Mongol rulers began to rule independently. In Samarkand, Tamerlane, the son of a local aristocrat, seized power in 1369 and immediately launched a program of conquest. During the 1380s, he brought the entire region east of the Caspian Sea under his authority and then conquered Baghdad and occupied Mesopotamia. After his brief foray into northern India, he turned to the west and raided the Anatolian peninsula. Defeating the army of the Ottoman Turks, he advanced almost as far as the Bosporus before withdrawing. "The last of the great nomadic conquerors," as one recent historian

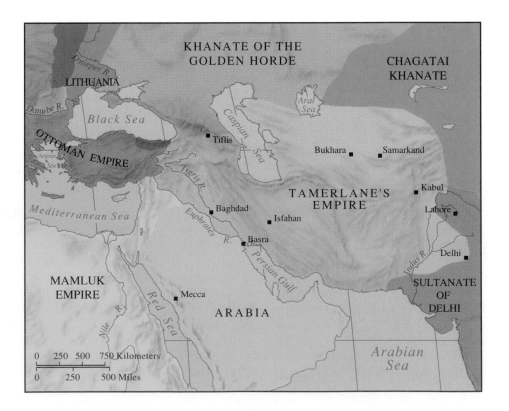

�֎ **Map 9.3** The Empire of Tamerlane.

described him, died in 1405 in the midst of a final military campaign.

The passing of Tamerlane removed a major menace from the diverse states of the Indian subcontinent. But the respite from external challenge was not a long one. By the end of the fifteenth century, two new challenges had appeared from beyond the horizon: the Mughals, a newly emerging nomadic power beyond the Khyber Pass in the north, and the Portuguese traders, who arrived by sea from the eastern coast of Africa in search of gold and spices. Both the Mughals and the Portuguese, in their different ways, would exert a major impact on the later course of Indian civilization.

IMPORTING THE ISLAMIC MODEL

Since ancient times, Indian ideas of governance had incorporated two contradictory themes: the decentralizing legacy of the Aryan conquest and the Mauryan ideal of universal empire (chakravartin), which may have drawn on the experience of neighboring river valley societies. Indian political thought also contained two concepts of kingship, the divine and the contractual. The first possibly originated in Harappa; the second was a legacy of Indo-European traditions. During antiquity, Indian society had vacillated between these contrasting approaches, but during most of the millennium after the Mauryan era, the forces of decentralization were clearly in the ascendant. The only serious effort to establish a universal empire throughout the subcontinent disappeared with the death of Harsa in the seventh century C.E.

At first, the establishment of Islamic power in northern India did not substantially change local methods of government. Muslim rulers simply set up their own states and operated as part of the prevailing interstate system. By the time the Delhi sultanate had been established in northern India, the powers of the caliphate in Baghdad had declined significantly, so its links with Muslim rulers in India were relatively tenuous from the beginning. In general, the latter did not attempt to assume the religious functions of the caliphate or to interpret Islamic law or serve as Defender of the Faith in their dominions except in a limited fashion.

One difference between the Muslim rulers and their Hindu counterparts, however, was that the Muslims continued to view themselves as foreign conquerors and generally maintained a strict separation between the Muslim ruling class and the mass of the Hindu population. Although a few Hindus rose to important positions in the local bureaucracy, in general high posts in the central government and the provinces were reserved for Muslims. At the local level, however, the autonomy traditionally enjoyed by the village hierarchy was preserved.

ISLAM AND INDIAN SOCIETY

Like their counterparts in other areas that came under Islamic rule, many Muslim rulers in India were quite tolerant of other faiths and used peaceful means, if any, to encourage nonbelievers to convert to Islam. Even the more enlightened, however, could be fierce when their religious zeal was aroused. Said one, when faced with reports that a Hindu fair had been held near Delhi, "I ordered that the leaders of these people and the promoters of this abomination should be put to death. I forbade the infliction of any severe punishment on the Hindus in general, but I destroyed their idol temples and instead thereof raised mosques."[7] Eventually, however, even the least tolerant Muslim rulers realized that there were simply too many Hindus to be converted and recognized the necessity of accepting what to them was an alien and repugnant religion.

While Hindu religious practices were generally tolerated, non-Muslims were compelled to pay a tax, called the jizya, to the state. Some Hindus likely converted to Islam to avoid paying the tax, but were then expected to make the traditional charitable contribution (the zakat, or tithe) required of Muslims in all Islamic societies.

Over time, millions of Hindus did turn to the Muslim faith. Some were individuals or groups in the employ of the Muslim ruling class, such as government officials, artisans, or merchants catering to the needs of the court. But many others were probably peasants from the sudra class or even untouchables who found in the egalitarian message of Islam a way of removing the stigma of low-class status in the Hindu social hierarchy.

Seldom have two major religions been so strikingly different. Where Hinduism tolerated a belief in the existence of several deities (although admittedly they were all considered by some to be manifestations of one supreme god), Islam was uncompromisingly monotheistic. Where Hinduism was hierarchical, Islam was egalitarian. Where Hinduism featured a priestly class to serve as an intermediary with the ultimate force of the universe, Islam permitted no one to come between believers and their god. Such differences contributed to the mutual hostility that developed between the adherents of the two faiths in the Indian subcontinent, but more mundane issues, such as the Muslim habit of eating beef and the idolatry and sexual frankness in Hindu art, were probably a greater source of antagonism at the popular level (see the box on p. 304).

In other cases, the two peoples borrowed from each other. Some Muslim rulers found the Indian idea of

The Islamic Conquest of India

One consequence of the Muslim conquest of northern India was the imposition of many Islamic customs on Hindu society. In this excerpt, the fourteenth-century Muslim historian Zia-ud-din Barani describes the attempt of one Muslim ruler, Ala-ud-din, to forbid the use of alcohol and gambling, two practices expressly forbidden in Muslim society. Ala-ud-din had seized power in Delhi from a rival in 1294.

A Muslim Ruler Suppresses Hindu Practices

Thirdly, he forbade wine, beer, and intoxicating drugs to be used or sold; dicing, too, was prohibited. Vintners and beer-sellers were turned out of the city, and the heavy taxes which had been levied from them were abolished. All the china and glass vessels of the Sultan's banqueting room were broken and thrown outside the gate of Badaun, where they formed a mound. Jars and casks of wine were emptied out there till they made mire as if it were the season of the rains. The Sultan himself entirely gave up wine parties. Self-respecting people at once followed his example; but the ne'er-do-wells went on making wine and spirits and hid the leather bottles in loads of hay or firewood and by various such tricks smuggled it into the city. Inspectors and gatekeepers and spies diligently sought to seize the contraband and the smugglers; and when seized the wine was given to the elephants, and the importers and sellers and drinkers flogged and given short terms of imprisonment. So many were they, however, that holes had to be dug for their incarceration outside the great thoroughfare of the Badaun gate, and many of the wine-bibbers died from the rigor of their confinement and others were taken out half-dead and were long in recovering their health. The terror of these holes deterred many from drinking. Those who could not give it up had to journey ten or twelve leagues to get a drink, for at half that distance, four or five leagues from Delhi, wine could not be publicly sold or drunk. The prevention of drinking proving very difficult, the Sultan enacted that people might distill and drink privately in their own homes, if drinking parties were not held and the liquor not sold. After the prohibition of drinking, conspiracies diminished.

divine kingship appealing. In their turn, Hindu rajas learned by bitter experience the superiority of cavalry mounted on horses instead of elephants, the primary assault weapon in early India. Some upper-class Hindu males were attracted to the Muslim tradition of *purdah* and began to keep their women in seclusion (termed locally "behind the curtain") from everyday society. Hindu sources claimed that one reason for adopting the custom was to protect Hindu women from the roving eyes of foreigners. But it is likely that many Indian families adopted the practice for reasons of prestige or because they were convinced that *purdah* was a practical means of protecting female virtue. Adult Indian women had already begun to cover their heads with a scarf during the Gupta era.

All in all, Muslim rule probably did not have a significant impact on the lives of most Indian women. *Purdah* was practiced more commonly among high castes than among the lower castes. Though it was probably of little consolation, sexual relations in poor and low-caste families were relatively egalitarian, as men and women worked together on press gangs or in the fields. Muslim customs apparently had little effect on the Hindu tradition of *sati* (see Chapter 2), which was sometimes described in detail by horrified Europeans in the fifteenth and sixteenth centuries (see the box on p. 305). In fact, in many respects Muslim women had more rights than their Hindu counterparts. They had more property rights than Hindu women and were legally permitted to divorce under certain conditions and to remarry after the death of their husband.

Overall, however, the relationship between Muslim and Hindu was that of conqueror and conquered and was marked by suspicion rather than friendship and understanding. Only with the founding of the Mughal dynasty was a serious effort undertaken to reconcile the differences. One result of this effort was the religion of the Sikhs. Founded by the guru Nanak in the early sixteenth century in the Punjab, Sikhism attempted to integrate the best of the two faiths in a single religion.

Sikhism (the term means "disciple") originated in the devotionalist movement in Hinduism, which taught that God was the single true reality. All else is illusion. But Nanak rejected the Hindu tradition of asceticism and mortification of the flesh and, like Muhammad, taught his disciples to participate in the world. Sikhism achieved considerable popularity in northwestern India

≈ The Practice of Sati ≈

One of the most repugnant aspects of medieval Indian society was the Hindu custom of sati, whereby a widow was immolated on the funeral pyre of her husband during his cremation. Here the Portuguese adventurer Duarte Barbosa describes such a practice in the southern state of Narsyngua.

Duarte Barbosa, On Sati

In this kingdom of Narsyngua there are three classes of Heathen, each one of which has a very distinct rule of its own, and also their customs differ much one from the other.

The principal of these is that the King, the great Lords, the knights and fighting men, who may marry . . . as many women as they wish, and are able to maintain; their sons inherit their estates; the women are bound by very ancient custom, when their husbands die, to burn themselves alive with their corpses which are also burnt. This they do to honor the husband. If such a woman is poor and of low estate, when her husband dies she goes with him to the burning ground, "where there is a great pit" in which a pile of wood burns. When the husband's body has been laid therein and begins to burn she throws herself of her own free will into the midst of the said fire, where both their bodies are reduced to ashes. But if she is a woman of high rank, rich, and with distinguished kindred, whether she be a young maid or an old woman, when her husband dies she accompanies the aforesaid corpse of her husband to the aforesaid burning ground, bewailing him; and there they dig a round pit, very wide and deep, which they fill with wood . . . and, when they have kindled it, they lay the man's body therein, and it is burnt while she weeps greatly. Wishing to do all honor to her husband she then causes all his kindred and her own to be called together, that they may come to feast and honor her thereby, all of whom gather together at the said field for this ceremony, where she spends with them and with her kindred and friends all

that she has in festivities with music and singing and dancing and banquets. Thereafter she attires herself very richly with all the jewels she possesses, and then distributes to her sons, relatives and friends all the property that remains. Thus arrayed she mounts on a horse, light gray or quite white if possible, that she may be the better seen of all the people. Mounted on this horse they lead her through the whole city with great rejoicings, until they come back to the very spot where the husband has been burnt, where, they cast a great quantity of wood into the pit itself and on its edge they make a great fire. When it has burnt up somewhat they erect a wooden scaffold with four or five steps where they take her up just as she is. When she is on the top she turns herself round thereon three times, worshipping towards the direction of sunrise, and, this done, she calls her sons, kindred and friends, and to each she gives a jewel, whereof she has many with her, and in the same way every piece of her clothing until nothing is left except a small piece of cloth with which she is clothed from the waist down. All this she does and says so firmly, and with such a cheerful countenance, that she seems not about to die. Then she tells the men who are with her on the scaffold to consider what they owe to their wives who, being free to act, yet burn themselves alive for the love of them, and the women she tells to see how much they owe to their husbands, to such a degree as to go with them even to death. Then she ceases speaking, and they place in her hands a pitcher full of oil, and she puts it on her head, and with it she again turns round thrice on the scaffold and again worships towards the rising sun. Then she casts the pitcher of oil into the fire and throws herself after it with as much goodwill as if she were throwing herself on a little cotton, from which she could receive no hurt. The kinsfolk all take part at once and cast into the fire many pitchers of oil and butter which they hold ready for this purpose, and much wood on this, and therewith bursts out such a flame that no more can be seen.

where Islam and Hinduism confronted each other directly and eventually evolved into a militant faith that fiercely protected its adherents against its two larger rivals. In the end, Sikhism did not reconcile Hinduism and Islam, but provided an alternative to both.

One complication for both Muslims and Hindus as they tried to come to terms with the existence of a mixed society was the problem of caste. Could non-Hindus form castes, and if so, how were these castes related to the Hindu castes? Where did the Turkic-speaking elites who made up the ruling class in many of the Islamic states fit into the equation?

The problem was resolved in a pragmatic manner that probably followed an earlier tradition of assimilating non-Hindu tribal groups into the system. Descendants of the invading Turkic ruling groups formed themselves into social groups that were roughly equivalent to the Hindu castes and were identified in terms of *varna* to either the *brahmin* or the *kshatriya* caste. During the Delhi sultanate in the north, members of the local Rajput nobility who converted to Islam were occasionally permitted to join such caste groupings.

Ordinary Indians who converted to Islam also formed themselves into Muslim castes, although at a lower level on the social scale. Many who did so were probably artisans whose skills were required by the Muslim nobility. Many members of such caste groupings probably converted en masse to obtain the privileges that conversion could bring. Although orthodox Hindus viewed all such groups as untouchables, in reality their social status reflected their power and importance in Indian society.

In most of India, then, Muslim rule did not substantially disrupt the caste system. Early European visitors to India, most of whom traveled primarily in the southern part of the subcontinent, reported at considerable length on the social distinctions that they encountered there. Although they were often confused by the differences between caste and class, their accounts reveal the tenacity of the traditional system and the degree to which it still defined the various economic functions of Indian society. One perceptive visitor in the early sixteenth century reported that in Malabar, along the southwestern coast, there were separate castes for fishing, pottery making, weaving, carpentry and metal working, salt mining, sorcery, and labor on the plantations. There were separate castes for doing the laundry, one for the elite and the other for the common people (see the box on p. 307).

Economy and Daily Life

In the medieval era, most Indians lived on the land. In contrast to China, which had a complex system of land

ownership including landed gentry, peasants who owned their own lands, and sharecroppers, the vast majority of Indian peasants tilled their tiny plots in return for paying a percentage of their harvest annually to a landlord. The landlord in turn forwarded part of the payment to the local ruler. In effect, the landlord functioned somewhat as a tax collector for the king, who retained ultimate ownership of all farmland in his domain. Under Muslim rule, the landlord's family often lost control of the land at his death, and the right to collect rents from the tenants was bestowed on another individual.

But although the vast majority of Indians were farmers, reports by visitors, from the Chinese missionaries during the Gupta era to the European merchants who began to arrive at the end of the fifteenth century, indicate that a substantial minority of the population lived in the cities. It was here that the landed and commercial elites lived, often in conditions of considerable opulence. The rulers, of course, possessed the most wealth. One maharaja of a relatively small state in southern India, for example, had over 100,000 soldiers in his pay along with 900 elephants and 20,000 horses. Another maintained a thousand high-caste women to serve as sweepers of his palace. Each carried a broom and a brass basin containing a mixture of cow dung and water, and "when the King goes from one house to another, or to a house of prayer, he goes on foot, and these women go before him with their brooms and basins in their hands, plastering the path where he is to tread."[8] Most urban dwellers, of course, did not live in such style. Xuan Zang, the Chinese Buddhist missionary who visited India in the early seventh century, left us a description of ordinary homes in urban areas:

> Their houses are surrounded by low walls, and form the suburbs. The earth being soft and muddy, the walls of the towns are mostly built of brick or tiles. The towers on the walls are constructed of wood or bamboo; the houses have balconies and belvederes, which are made of wood, with a coating of lime or mortar, and covered with tiles. The different buildings have the same form as those in China; rushes, or dry branches, or tiles, or boards are used for covering them. The walls are covered with lime and mud, mixed with cow's dung for purity. At different seasons they scatter flowers about. Such are some of their different customs.[9]

For ordinary Indian peasants in the countryside, life may not have been as difficult in some respects as it is for their counterparts today. The population of the subcontinent was much smaller then than it is now (India's population during the first millennium C.E. has been estimated at slightly over 100 million, compared to over 700 mil-

⇒ *Untouchables in South India* ⇐

Some of the best descriptions of Indian society in the late medieval era came from European merchants and missionaries. The following passage was written by the Portuguese traveler Duarte Barbosa and describes an untouchable caste on the southwestern coast of India in the early sixteenth century. The Nayres mentioned in this excerpt were a higher caste in the region.

Duarte Barbosa, *From the Land of Malabar*

And there is yet another caste of Heathen lower than these whom they call Poleas, who among all the rest are held to be accursed and excommunicate; they dwell in the fields and open campaigns [plots] in secret lurking places, whither folk of good caste never go save by mischance, and live in huts very strait and mean. They are tillers of rice with buffaloes and oxen. They never speak to the Nayres save from afar off, shouting so that they may hear them, and when they go along the roads they utter loud cries, that they may be let past, and whosoever hears them leaves the road, and stands in the wood till they have passed by; and if anyone, whether man or woman, touches them his kinsfolk slay him forthwith, and in vengeance therefore they slay Poleas until they weary without suffering any punishment. In certain months of the year they do their utmost to touch some Nayre woman by night as secretly as they can, and this only for the sake of doing evil. They go by in order to get into the houses of the Nayres to touch women, and during these months the women guard themselves carefully, and if they touch any woman, even though none have seen it, and there may be no witnesses, yet she declares it at once, crying out, and she will stay no longer in her house that her caste may not be destroyed; in general she flees to the house of some other low caste folk, and hides herself, that her kinsfolk may not slay her; and that thence she may help herself and be sold to foreigners, which is ofttimes done. And the manner of touching is this, even though no words are exchanged, they throw something at her, a stone or a stick, and if it touches her she is touched and ruined. These people are also great sorcerers and thieves; they are a very evil race.

---

lion today), and plots may therefore have been larger. Moreover, the land may have been more fertile than it is today, since rainfall patterns may have been more favorable and the soil had not yet been leached of its nutrients by heavy use. Accounts by foreign visitors to India indicate that many farmers were able to harvest two crops a year from their land, often without the use of irrigation. In the north and in the upland regions of the Deccan Plateau, the primary grain crops were wheat and barley. In the Ganges valley and the southern coastal plains, the main crop was rice.

According to Xuan Zang, the most common foods were milk and other dairy products, cornbread, fish, mutton, and venison. Eating the meat of cattle, elephants, pigs, and dogs was prohibited, and those who did so were universally despised and scorned. The use of alcohol apparently varied according to class, with *brahmins* abstaining from fermented drinks. Xuan Zang noted with surprise that Indians used no spoons, cups, or even chopsticks.[10] Vegetables were grown everywhere, while southern India produced many spices, sugarcane, fruits, and cotton goods. The cotton plant had apparently originated in the Indus River valley and spread from there. Although cotton reached Spain and North Africa in the eighth and ninth centuries C.E., India remained the primary producer of cotton goods. Tropical products such as cinnamon, pepper, ginger, sandalwood, cardamon, and cumin were among the area's major exports.

Still, life was undoubtedly hard for the average Indian peasant. As is the case today, most farmers tilled their small plots of land with a small wooden plow pulled by oxen and paid a high percentage of the harvest to the landlord. These rents, obtained from the sweat of millions of toiling Indian peasants, funded the sumptuous lifestyle, the fratricidal wars, and the grandiose temples of the wealthy and the highborn. At best, most peasants lived at the subsistence level. At worst, they were forced into debt and fell victim to moneylenders who regularly charged exorbitant rates of interest.

Agriculture, of course, was not the only source of wealth in India. Since ancient times, the subcontinent had served as a major entrepôt for trade between the Middle East and the Pacific basin, as well as the source for other goods shipped throughout the known world. Some historians believe that the level of manufacturing and commercial activity in India declined during the medieval era, at least in terms of trade within the subcontinent. If that is the case, one reason may have been the disappearance of centralized empires in India. Internal civil strife and piracy, heavy taxation of the business community by local rulers to finance their fratricidal wars, and increased customs duties between principalities may all have contributed to the decline in internal trade.

The level of foreign trade, however, remained high, particularly in the Dravidian kingdoms in the south and along the northwestern coast, which were located along the traditional trade routes to the Middle East and the Mediterranean Sea. Much of this foreign trade was carried on by wealthy Hindu castes with close ties to the royal courts. But there were other participants as well, including such non-Hindu minorities as the Muslims, the Parsis, and the Jain community. European visitors frequently noted the presence of what they termed "Moorish traders" in port cities along the coast. The Parsis, expatriates from Persia who practiced the Zoroastrian religion, dominated banking and the textile industry in the cities bordering the Rann of Kutch. Later they would become a dominant economic force in the modern city of Bombay. The Jains became prominent in trade and manufacturing even though their faith emphasized simplicity and the rejection of materialism. Perhaps like Chinese merchants living in Southeast Asia at a later time, their thrifty habits and tendency to clannishness gave them a decided advantage in competition with the Indian population at large.

If accounts by early European travelers can be believed, merchants often lived quite well. One Portuguese observer described the "Moorish" population in Bengal as follows:

> They have girdles of cloth, and over them silk scarves, they carry in their girdles daggers garnished with silver and gold, according to the rank of the person who carries them; on their fingers many rings set with rich jewels, and cotton turbans on their heads. They are luxurious, eat well and spend freely, and have many other extravagances as well. They bathe often in great tanks which they have in their houses. Everyone has three or four wives or as many as he can maintain. They keep them carefully shut up, and treat them very well, giving them great store of gold, silver and apparel of fine silk.[11]

Outside these relatively small, specialized trading communities, most manufacturing and commerce were in the hands of petty traders and artisans, who generally were limited to local markets. This failure to build on the promise of antiquity has led some historians to ask why India failed to produce an urban revolution similar to the growth of cities that began in Europe during the High Middle Ages or even in China during the Song dynasty

(see Chapter 10). Some have pointed to the traditionally low status of artisans and merchants in Indian society, a status symbolized by the comment in the *Arthasastra* that merchants were "thieves that are not called by the name of thief."[12] Yet commercial activities were frowned upon in many countries in Europe throughout the feudal period, a fact that did not prevent the emergence of capitalist societies throughout much of the West.

Another factor may have been the monopoly on foreign trade held by the government in many areas of India. According to the author of the *Periplus*, at Barbarikon, a seaport near the delta of the Indus River, "all the cargoes are taken up the river to the king at the metropolis," suggesting that the government maintained a tight control over the importation of goods. Later rulers made similar efforts to enhance their wealth through the establishment of state trading monopolies, although with only limited success.[13]

More important, perhaps, was the impact of the caste system, which reduced the ability of entrepreneurs to expand their activities and have dealings with other members of the commercial and manufacturing community. Successful artisans, for example, could not normally set up as merchants to market their products, nor could merchants compete for buyers outside their normal area of operations. The complex interlocking relationships among the various castes in a given region were a powerful factor inhibiting the development of a thriving commercial sector in medieval India.

The Wonder of Indian Culture

The era between the Mauryas and the Mughals in India was a period of cultural evolution, as Indian writers and artists built on the literary and artistic achievements of their predecessors. This is not to say, however, that Indian culture rested on its ancient laurels. To the contrary, it was an era of tremendous innovation in all fields of creative endeavor. This era can legitimately be called the golden age of traditional Indian culture.

ART AND ARCHITECTURE

At the end of antiquity, the primary forms of religious architecture were the Buddhist cave temples and monasteries. The next millennium witnessed the evolution of religious architecture from underground cavity to monumental structure.

The twenty-eight caves of Ajanta in the Deccan Plateau are one of India's greatest artistic achievements. They are as impressive for their sculpture and painting as for their architecture. Except for a few examples from the second century B.C.E., most of the caves were carved out of solid rock over an incredibly short period of seventeen years, from 460 to 478 C.E. In contrast to the early unadorned temple halls, these temples were exuberantly decorated with ornate pillars, friezes, beamed ceilings, and statues of the Buddha and *bodhisattvas*. Several caves served as monasteries, which by then had been transformed from simple holes in the wall to large complexes with living apartments, halls, and shrines to the Buddha. Here the monks resided and studied the life and teachings of the Buddha.

All of the inner surfaces of the caves, including the ceilings, sculptures, walls, door frames, and pillars, were painted in vivid colors. The caves of Ajanta are perhaps best known, however, for their wall paintings, which illustrate the various lives and incarnations of the Buddha. These paintings are in an admirable state of preservation, making it possible to reconstruct the customs, dress, house interiors, and physical characteristics of the peoples of fifth-century India. These paintings are of more than mere historical and religious significance, however, and are considered some of the greatest art in all India.

Near Ajanta are the equally famous rock temples at Ellora. These temples, carved out of a mountain of solid rock, were originally built by Buddhists during the seventh century C.E. Later, however, they were taken over by Hindus and at one time were used by followers of Jainism. While the complex consists of several temples, the most famous is the Hindu temple of Kailasantha, dedicated to Siva. The floor of the temple is similar in size to the Parthenon in Greece, but the building is three stories high and required the excavation of an estimated three million cubic feet of stone. Unlike earlier temples, which were constructed in the form of caves, the Kailasantha temple at Ellora was open to the sky (although many of the free-standing shrines are covered with roofs), while the walls are festooned with some of India's finest sculptures. The overall impression is one of wonder and massive grandeur.

◆ **Rock paintings at Sigiriya, Sri Lanka.** Closely linked to Indian art and culture are these surviving paintings at the sixth-century rock fortress at Sigiriya, on the island of Sri Lanka. Portraits of serving girls from the king's harem were painted high up along the cliff wall. Many were destroyed by Buddhist monks when they reclaimed the area after the king's sudden death. Thankfully, a few of these graceful, languid maidens were left unharmed to captivate viewers over the centuries.

✦ **Rock Temple at Ellora.** An estimated 3 million cubic feet of stone were excavated out of solid rock to build the massive eighth-century Kailasantha Rock Temple at Ellora. Renowned for its elaborate sculptures dedicated to the legends of the Hindu deities, Ellora is one of India's greatest architectural sites.

Two other rock temples are worthy of mention. The first is the sixth-century cave temple at Elephanta, just outside Bombay, with its colossal triple-headed statue of Siva. This eighteen-foot-high monument depicts Siva's three roles as creator, preserver, and destroyer. The central face of the statue is recognized worldwide as one of the most serenely beautiful representations of Siva ever created. Another sculpture worthy of note is the hermaphrodite (that is, half male and half female) statue of Siva expressing the Hindu concept that only through the fusion of the active female with the inactive male can an individual achieve wholeness.

Among the most impressive rock carvings in southern India are the cave temples at Mamallapuram (also known as Mahabalipuram), south of the modern city of Madras. The sculpture called the Descent of the Ganges River, which depicts the role played by Siva in intercepting the heavenly waters of the Ganges and allowing them to fall gently on the earth, is among India's finest. Also at Mamallapuram are nine monolithic seventh-century temples dedicated to Siva, four of which were cut from a single boulder. Each is ornately decorated both inside and out. Three large statues of a lion, an elephant, and a bull sit nearby. Mamallapuram also boasts an eighth-century shore temple, which is considered to be one of the earliest surviving free-standing structures in the subcontinent. It would be difficult to conceive of a more romantic temple than this, especially at dawn with the sun and the ocean intensifying its mystery.

From the eighth century until the time of the Mughals, Indian architects built a multitude of magnificent Hindu temples, now constructed exclusively above ground. Each temple consisted of a central shrine surmounted by a sizable tower, a hall for worshipers, a vestibule, and a porch, all set in a rectangular courtyard that might also contain other minor shrines. Temples became progressively more ornate until the eleventh century, when the sculpture began to dominate the structure itself. The towers became higher and the temple complexes more intricate, some becoming virtual walled compounds set one within the other and resembling a town in themselves.

Among the best examples of temple art are those in the eastern state of Orissa. The temples of Bhubaneswar (750–1000 C.E.) elicit admiration with their massive, beehive-shaped towers and their strong horizontal effect. But it is the Sun Temple at Konarak, standing at the edge of the sea and covered with intricate carvings, that is generally considered the masterpiece of its genre. Although now in ruins, the Sun Temple still boasts some of India's most memorable sculptures. Especially renowned are the twelve pairs of carved wheels, each ten feet high and seated on a raised platform. Each represents one of the twelve signs of the zodiac and leaves the viewer with the impression that the whole might have represented a chariot for the Sun God. Of equal artistic merit are the erotic carvings that adorn the temple walls. In every physical position possible, these frenzied lovers symbolize the ecstasy of human beings reunited with the divine.

✦ **Descent of the Ganges River.** One of India's most outstanding sculptures is found at Mamallapuram, an eighth-century site on the eastern coast south of Madras. This open relief, known as the Descent of the Ganges River, is about twenty feet high and eighty feet long. It portrays Siva's effort to deflect the waters of the heavenly River Ganges on his head to spare the earth from destruction. Although it presents a rich panorama of gods, animals, and men, the gentle elephant in particular delights one and all.

The greatest example of medieval Hindu temple art, however, is probably Khajuraho. Of the original eighty temples, dating from the tenth century, twenty remain standing today. All of the towers are buttressed at various levels on the sides, giving the whole a sense of unity and creating a vertical movement similar to Mount Kailasa in the Himalayas, sacred to Hindus. Everywhere the viewer is entertained by voluptuous temple dancers bringing life to the massive structures. Frozen in stone, they still mesmerize us with their innocent and intimate pastimes. One is removing a thorn from her foot, another is applying eye makeup, and yet another is wringing out her hair.

In the Deccan Plateau, a different style prevailed. The southern temple style was marked by the erection of massive oblong stone towers, some as much as two hundred feet high. The towers were often covered with a profusion of sculpted figures and were visible for miles. The walls surrounding the temple complex were also surmounted with impressive gate towers, known as *gopuras*. Certainly, the temple is one of India's most significant contributions to world art.

The delicate bronze statues of the Cola dynasty are yet another achievement of the medieval period. The most famous are the Natarajas, or four-armed dancing Sivas, in which the god is shown destroying the universe so that it can be reborn again. Another stunning bronze is the hermaphrodite Siva, whose stone counterpart can be found in the caves at Elephanta. These Cola bronzes, dating from the tenth to the twelfth centuries, are much admired and are represented in museums all over the world.

LITERATURE

Indian art has often been described as sensuous, vigorous, humorous, innocent, bawdy, lyrical, and tender. The same adjectives can be applied to the literature of this period. During this period, Indian authors produced a prodigious number of written works, both secular and religious. Regrettably, many have been lost due to the climate or to the destructive force of the Muslim occupation of the north. Ninety percent of extant Sanskrit literature belongs to the period after 1200. This chapter deals with the remaining 10 percent, which testifies to the vitality and diversity of literary achievement during the period.

Essential to any discussion of Indian literature is the concept of the *rasa*, which was delineated 2,500 years ago and codified in the fifth century C.E. The *rasa* is an aesthetic mood created in a work of art to produce a distilled emotive response in the reader. The purpose of the aroused emotion is not the Western sense of catharsis, but a calmer, more detached experience in which the reader forgets him- or herself. Each work is designed to contain one or more of the nine *rasas*: the erotic, the heroic, the loathsome, the wrathful, the comic, the terrifying, the compassionate, the marvelous, and the peaceful.

The tradition of Indian poetry, which had begun orally during the Vedic period with the Vedas and the Mahabharata, continued with the religious and secular verse of later centuries. Both types were moralistic and passionately physical and reflected a deep love of nature.

A phenomenal amount of Indian religious poetry was written, both in Sanskrit and in the languages of southern India. As Hinduism was transformed from a contemplative to a more devotional religion, its poetry became more ardent and erotic and prompted a sense of divine ecstacy. Much of the religious verse extolled the lives and heroic acts of Siva, Vishnu, Rama, and Krishna by repeating the same themes over and over, which is also a characteristic of Indian art. These themes represent Truth, and as such, they validate the generations of Indian artists who re-created and elaborated on these verities.

The great secular literature of traditional India was also written in Sanskrit in the form of poetry, drama, and prose. Sanskrit court poetry was narrative, interweaving history and the epics. Its extensive ornamentation, such as punning, double entrendres, alliteration, and the incantation of words and phrases, may seem florid to Western taste, but with a single line of verse, the poetry could induce a series of ideas and emotions, a world beyond itself. Metrically, Sanskrit poetry was rigidly regulated and generally unrhymed. A normal stanza consisted of four lines, varying from eight to twenty-eight syllables. Above all Sanskrit poetry was sonorous. Unfortunately, its versification and ornamentation are not easily translated. As an example of its sonorous ingenuity, note the following stanza in Sanskrit by the seventh-century poet Maha, which made use of only one consonant:

Dadado dudda-dud-dadi
dadado duda-di-da-doh
dud-dadam dadade dudde
dad-adada-dodo da-dah.[14]

Some of the best medieval Indian poetry is found in single-stanza poems, which create an entire emotional scene in just four lines. Witness this poem by the poet Amaru:

We'll see what comes of it, I thought,
*   and I hardened my heart against her.*

♦ **Sculptural Decorations at Khajuraho.** This Hindu temple, one of the greatest in India, is literally covered with the statues of temple dancers who bring life to its massive architecture. Frozen in stone, they mesmerize the viewer. Many represent the ideal couple or divine lovers, who symbolize the union of the worshipers with the deity, thus blending physical and spiritual beauty.

> What, won't the villain speak to me? she
>   thought, flying into a rage.
> And there we stood, sedulously refusing to look one
>   another in the face,
> Until at last I managed an unconvincing laugh,
>   and her tears robbed me of my resolution.[15]

A stunning example of the erotic *rasa* is the fifty-stanza poem entitled *Caurapancasika*, which is attributed to the eleventh-century Kashmiri poet Bilhana. Each stanza begins with the same phrase:

> Even now,
>   if I see her again,

> a lotus-eyed girl
> weary from bearing her own heavy breasts,
> I'll crush her in my arms
> and drink her mouth like a madman,
> a bee insatiably drinking a lotus!
>
> Even now,
> I remember her in love.
> Her body was weak with fatigue,
> swarms of curling hair
> fell on pale cheeks.
> As if to keep between us
> the secret of our guilt,
> her soft arms
> clung
> like vines on my neck.[16]

One of India's most famous authors was Kalidasa, who lived during the Gupta dynasty. Although little is known of him, including his dates, he probably wrote for the court of Chandragupta II (375–415 C.E.). Even today Kalidasa's hundred-verse poem, *The Cloud Messenger*, remains one of the most popular Sanskrit poems (see the box on p. 313).

In addition to being a poet, Kalidasa was also a great dramatist. He wrote three plays, all dramatic romances that blend the erotic with the heroic and the comic. *Shakuntala*, perhaps the best-known play in all Indian literature, tells the story of a king who, while out hunting, falls in love with the maiden Shakuntala. He asks her to marry him and offers her a ring of betrothal, but is suddenly recalled to his kingdom on urgent business. Shakuntala, who is pregnant, goes to him, but the king has been cursed by a hermit and no longer recognizes her. With the help of the gods, the king eventually does recall their love and is reunited with Shakuntala and their son.

Each of Kalidasa's plays is propelled by the magic powers of a love-speech goddess, and each ends in affirmation and unity. Another interesting aspect of Kalidasa's plays is that they combine several languages as well as poetry and prose. The language and form of the characters' speeches correspond to their position in the social hierarchy. Thus, the king speaks in Sanskrit poetry, while the other characters in the play use prose in three different vernaculars. The dramas thus incorporate the spectrum of literary expression from the language of the court to the vernacular of everyday life.

Kalidasa was one of the greatest Indian dramatists, but he was by no means the only one. The genre predated the Gupta era, but did not emerge in its sophisticated form until the fourth and fifth centuries C.E. Sanskrit plays

❧ An Indian Love Poem ❧

Kalidasa, who lived during the Gupta period, was India's greatest dramatist and poet. This is a brief excerpt from The Cloud Messenger, one of the most popular and beautiful poems in the Sanskrit language. It describes the anguish of a young Indian who has been sent into exile and misses his wife. In the poem he watches clouds drifting northward and describes to them the route to his home in the Himalaya Mountains.

Kalidasa, *The Cloud Messenger*

Stay for a while over the thickets, haunted by the girls of
    the hill-folk, then press on with faster pace, having shed
    your load of water,
and you'll see the Narmada river, scattered in torrents, by
    the rugged rocks at the foot of the Vindhyas,
looking like the plastered pattern of stripes on the flank of
    an elephant.

Note by the banks the flowers of the nipa trees, greenish
    brown, with their stamens half developed,
    and the plantains, displaying their new buds.
Smell the most fragrant earth of the burnt out woodlands,
    and as you release your raindrops the deer will show you
    the way.

. . . where the wind from the Sipra river prolongs the shrill
    melodious cry of the cranes,

fragrant at early dawn from the scent of the opening lotus,
    and, like a lover, with flattering requests,
dispels the morning languor of women, and refreshes their
    limbs.

Your body will grow fat with the smoke of incense from
    open windows where women dress their hair.
You will be greeted by palace peacocks, dancing to welcome
    you, their friend.
If your heart is weary from travel you may pass the night
    above mansions fragrant with flowers,
whose pavements are marked with red dye from the feet of
    lovely women.

. . . where yaksas dwell with lovely women in white man-
    sions, whose crystal terraces reflect the stars like flowers.
They drink the wine of love distilled from magic trees,
    while drums beat softly, deeper than your thunder.

I see your body in the sinuous creeper, your gaze in the
    startled eyes of deer,
your cheek in the moon, your hair in the plumage of
    peacocks,
and in the tiny ripples of the river I see your sidelong
    glances,
but alas, my dearest, nowhere do I find your whole
    likeness!

typically contained one to ten acts. They were performed in theaters in the palaces or in court temples by troupes of actors of both sexes who were trained and supported by the royal family. The plots were usually taken from Indian legends of gods and kings. No stage curtain, scenery, or props were used, but costumes and makeup were elaborate. The theaters had to be small because much of the drama was conveyed through intricate gestures and dance conventions. There were many different positions for various parts of the body, including one hundred for the hands alone. Another important aspect of the actor's trade was the expression of emotion through such means as tears, a trembling voice, or fainting. Much of this mimetic drama can be viewed today in the paintings of Ajanta and temple sculptures.

Like poetry, prose developed in India from the Vedic period. The use of prose was well established by the sixth and seventh centuries C.E. This is truly astonishing considering that the novel did not appear until the tenth century in Japan and until the seventeenth century in Europe.

One of the greatest masters of Sanskrit prose was Dandin, who lived during the seventh century. In *The Ten Princes*, he created a fantastic and exciting world that fuses history and fiction. His keen powers of observation, details of low life, and humor give his writing considerable vitality.

MUSIC

Another area of Indian creativity that developed during this era was music. Ancient Indian music had come from the chanting of the Vedic hymns and thus inevitably had a strong metaphysical and spiritual flavor. The actual physical vibrations of music (*nada*) were considered to be related to the spiritual world. An off-key or sloppy rendition of a sacred text could upset the harmony and balance of the entire universe. Understandably, then, great composers in traditional India were often regarded as saints.

Although Indian music in later times was more complex than these early forms, the Vedic traditions were maintained through elaborate texts dealing with musical performance and dance. Consequently, an understanding of the classical musical tradition requires some knowledge of the basic concepts and terminologies of the Vedic hymns themselves.

In form, Indian classical music is based on a scale, called a *raga*. There are dozens, if not hundreds, of separate scales, which are grouped into separate categories depending on the time of day during which they are to be performed. The performers use a stringed instrument called a *sitar* and various types of wind instruments and drums. The performers select a basic *raga* and then are free to improvise the melodic structure and rhythm. The music begins slowly at the lower end of the scale, and then the performers explore all the notes and combinations in the scale as they move up the register. A good performer never performs a particular *raga* the same way twice. The audience is concerned not so much with faithful reproduction, but with the performer's own creativity, as is the case with jazz music in the West.

The Golden Region: Early Southeast Asia

Between China and India lies the region that today is called Southeast Asia. It has two major components: a mainland region extending southward from the Chinese border down to the tip of the Malay peninsula and an extensive archipelago, most of which is part of present-day Indonesia and the Philippines.

Located between the highly advanced and densely populated civilizations of India and China, Southeast Asia is a melting pot, a vast mixture of races, cultures, and religions similar to the Middle East. During the Ice Age, when the sea level was much lower than it is today, the islands of Southeast Asia were connected to the

Asian mainland, and prehistoric peoples were able to roam freely between them. Even later, after the water levels rose, travel between the islands and regions to the west, north, and east was not difficult, in part because some of the seafaring peoples of the area had already mastered the art of navigating by the stars and by minute observation of the movements of the waves. As a result, Southeast Asia has historically served as a vast land bridge for the movement of peoples between China, the Indian subcontinent, and the more than 25,000 islands of the South Pacific, which are spread over one-third of the earth's surface.

Hominids have apparently lived in Southeast Asia for several hundred thousand years. *Homo sapiens* gradually appeared in the region during the Paleolithic period. By the Neolithic era, the migration of peoples into the area began to increase and has continued, although at a reduced rate, to the present day. One reason for this continuous migration is the ecological environment. Although the soil in some areas is poor, water is plentiful, and the climate is predictable and conducive to the cultivation of rice.

Another factor is the configuration of the land. Due to the massive collision between the Asian tectonic plate and the subcontinent of South Asia millions of years ago, mainland Southeast Asia consists of several mountain ranges. All of them originate in southern China and then extend southward into the Bay of Bengal or the South China Sea. Between these north-south ranges are several river valleys that run in a southerly or southeasterly direction. Many early peoples came down these river valleys from China or Tibet in search of a new homeland. Once in Southeast Asia, most of these migrants settled in the fertile deltas of the rivers—the Irrawaddy and the Salween in Burma, the Chao Phraya in Thailand, and the Red River and the Mekong in Vietnam—or in lowland areas in the islands to the south.

In contrast, lateral movement between east and west on the Southeast Asian mainland was relatively difficult. The mountains are densely forested and often infested with malaria-bearing mosquitoes. Consequently, the lowland peoples in the river valleys were often isolated from each other and had only limited contacts with the upland peoples living in the mountains.

These geographical barriers may help explain why Southeast Asia is one of the few regions in Asia that was never unified under a single government. This division into isolated compartments may also be a reason for the region's relatively slow development. Although wet rice agriculture was practiced in lowland areas as early as 7000 B.C.E., advanced civilizations apparently did not develop in the region until late in the first millennium B.C.E., more than 2,000 years after similar societies had emerged in India, China, and the Middle East.

While human settlements were beginning to appear in various parts of the mainland and islands of Southeast Asia, other peoples were migrating further southward and eastward. Migrants from continental Asia apparently arrived on the island of New Guinea at the eastern end of the Indonesian archipelago as early as 50,000 years ago. The sea level was lower at that time, and New Guinea was probably joined with Australia, forming a continent called Sahul. Some migrants thus were able to continue on to Australia and from there to Tasmania. Descendants of these early settlers reached the nearby Solomon Islands by 11,000 B.C.E.

A second wave of migration began sometime during the fourth millennium B.C.E., when peoples from South China crossed the South China Sea to Taiwan and the Philippines and thence to Indonesia. In time, they ventured beyond the Solomon Islands into the more remote reaches of the South Pacific. Traveling by outrigger canoes, they sailed as far as Fiji, Tonga, Samoa, and New Zealand and became the ancestors of today's Polynesian peoples. By the first millennium C.E., some had ventured as far as Easter Island, about 2,500 miles west of South America. To support themselves on some of the relatively barren islands, they brought with them crops from Asia such as the banana, breadfruit, and the yam, as well as pigs, dogs, and chickens.

The Beginnings of Civilization

Students of human society regard Southeast Asia as one of the most complex regions in the world. It has been said that more different languages are spoken in Southeast Asia than in any area of comparable size on earth. As we have seen, much of this complexity stems from the numerous migrations into and through the area that have taken place since prehistoric times. The earliest migration that historians know much about was the movement of the Malay peoples (the Malayo-Polynesians), which apparently took place in two major waves. The first group entered the region about 2500 B.C.E. and then were conquered or driven into the mountains by a later flow arriving about a thousand years later. The original habitat of the Malay peoples is a matter of dispute, but they speak tongues that are part of a larger family of languages known as Malayo-Polynesian that is spread throughout the region. Most of the later immigrants eventually settled on the Malay peninsula or on the islands to the south and east and are considered to be the ancestors of

CHRONOLOGY

Early Southeast Asia

Malayo-Polynesian migration	c. 2500–1500 B.C.E.
Chinese conquest of Vietnam	111 B.C.E.
Rise of Funan	c. first century C.E.
Arrival of Burman peoples	c. seventh century
Formation of Srivijaya	c. 670
Construction of Borobudut	c. eighth century
Creation of Angkor kingdom	c. ninth century
Thai migrations into Southeast Asia	c. thirteenth century
Rise of Majapahit empire	1292
Foundation of sultanate of Malacca	1402
Fall of Angkor kingdom	1432

the present-day majority population in Malaysia, Indonesia, and the Philippines.

When the Malayo-Polynesians arrived, they found peoples already living in Southeast Asia. Some had settled in lowland regions where they engaged in agriculture. Others lived in the mountains or on remote islands and survived by hunting or foraging. Among the farming communities were two distinct language groups who may well have been in the area prior to the arrival of the Malayo-Polynesians—the Vietnamese in the Red River delta and the Mon-Khmer peoples in lowland regions from lower Burma to the mouth of the Mekong River. Both would be responsible for early steps toward civilization in Southeast Asia. Because the Vietnamese were conquered by the Han dynasty in the second century B.C.E. and remained in the Chinese Empire for more than a millennium, their early history will be discussed later in Chapter 11.

EARLY CONTACTS WITH INDIA

Another element in the early civilizations of Southeast Asia came from India. The precise date for the beginning of Indian contacts with Southeast Asia is uncertain, although it seems clear that the process was well underway by the first century C.E. Archaeologists working at various sites on the Malay peninsula and the Indonesian islands have unearthed relics in Indian style that date from

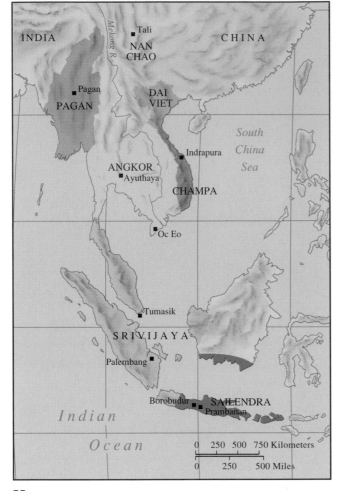

�֍ Map 9.4   Southeast Asia in the Thirteenth Century.

classes of Southeast Asia, who may have been just emerging from tribal status into more complex forms of social organization, Indian culture must have seemed an appealing way of enhancing their lifestyles and their social status.

In general, Indian influence penetrating into northern mainland areas tended to come from the Gupta dynasty, whereas the Indonesian islands such as Sumatra and Java drew upon the Dravidian states of southern India. Why Buddhist influence predominated at certain periods and in certain areas and Hindu influence in others is not clear. Most of the early Southeast Asian kingdoms adopted some aspects of both doctrines.

The first society in Southeast Asia to show the effects of Indian influence was the kingdom of Funan, located on the lower Mekong River in present-day Cambodia. The kingdom of Funan (apparently a Chinese transliteration of Phnom, the Cambodian word for "mountain") is the first historically confirmed state in Southeast Asia. First mentioned in written sources by a Chinese traveler in the third century C.E., Funan was both an agricultural and a trading society and possessed commercial ties with both India to the west and China to the northeast. Roman coins found at the Funanese port of Oc Eo on the Gulf of Siam indicate that the kingdom had at least indirect contact with Rome. The identity of the inhabitants of Funan is not entirely clear, but they probably were the ancestors of the modern Cambodian people, known as the Khmer. According to local legend, the first king of Funan was an Indian *brahmin* named Kaundinya who married a local water princess, thus symbolizing the mixture of Indian and indigenous culture in Funan society.

We do not know a great deal about Funanese political or social institutions, since few records of the period are available except reports by Chinese visitors to the area. The Funanese rulers were apparently familiar with Indian cosmology and concepts of statecraft and may have used rituals associated with the worship of Siva and Vishnu to build up royal power. But they showed little desire to create a centralized kingdom in the manner of Kautilya's description of the Mauryan Empire in India (see Chapter 2). More likely, Funan was a collection of autonomous principalities held together by the shifting power of a local potentate.

The Formation of States

Between the sixth and the fifteenth century C.E., several other larger and more complex civilizations emerged in Southeast Asia. By the end of the fifteenth century, organized states had developed throughout mainland and island Southeast Asia.

the first centuries C.E. Not long after that, Chinese missionaries in transit to or from Buddhist centers in India left brief descriptions of Hinduized kingdoms in the lower Mekong River valley and in the Indonesian archipelago, not far from the Strait of Malacca, the body of water that separates the Malay peninsula from the island of Sumatra.

Historians once believed that Indian culture was introduced into Southeast Asia when invaders from India conquered the local peoples and established themselves as a new ruling class, complete with *brahmin* priests and princely rulers (see Chapter 2). But in recent decades that theory has been replaced by a more nuanced view that Indian culture was first introduced to mainland Southeast Asia by merchants from the east coast of India. They were followed by Buddhist and Hindu missionaries, some of whom were probably invited to serve the local rulers as political advisers and then married into the local aristocracy. To the relatively unsophisticated ruling

♦ **Angkor Wat.**   The Khmer rulers of Angkor constructed a number of remarkable temples and palaces. Devised as either Hindu or Buddhist shrines, the temples also reflected the power and sanctity of the king. This twelfth-century temple known as Angkor Wat is renowned both for its spectacular architecture and for the thousands of fine bas-reliefs relating Hindu legends and Khmer history. Most memorable are the heavenly dancing maidens and the royal processions with elephants and soldiers.

One reason for this development was the region's expanding role in the trade that passed through the area en route between the Indian Ocean and the South China Sea. As trading contacts with states outside the region increased, local societies ceased to be just intermediate stops in the shipment of goods and began to produce goods for export themselves. The demands posed by this new role provided the initial stimulus for the creation of more complex forms of political and social organization throughout the region.

The introduction of foreign ideas also contributed to the development of Southeast Asian civilizations. Chinese armies and administrators carried Chinese institutions with them into Vietnam. Foreign merchants and sailors brought information about Indian institutions and cultural achievements to peoples elsewhere in the region. Not surprisingly, when the peoples of Southeast Asia began to form states, they looked to the more complex political and social institutions of China and the Indian subcontinent as models, while adapting those institutions to their own needs and preferences.

ANGKOR AND OTHER MAINLAND STATES

The most powerful state to emerge in mainland Southeast Asia before the sixteenth century was the kingdom of Angkor, which took shape in the ninth century after the kingdom of Funan had collapsed. The kingdom was founded by a powerful figure called Jayavarman who drove out invaders from Java and established his capital

≥ The Kingdom of Angkor ≤

Angkor (known to the Chinese as Chon-la) was the greatest kingdom of its time in Southeast Asia. This passage, probably written in the thirteenth century by the Chinese port official Chau Ju-kua, includes a brief description of the capital city, Angkor Thom, which is still one of the great archaeological sites of the region. Angkor was already in decline when Chau Ju-kua described the kingdom, and the capital was abandoned soon afterward in 1432.

Chau Ju-kua, Records of Foreign Nations

Chon-la [Angkor] lies to the south of Chan-ch'ong [Annam].

From Ts'uan-chou [Chuanzhou] a ship, with a good wind, can reach this country within a month or more.

The country covers altogether fully 7000 square li. The capital of the kingdom is called Lu-wu. There is no cold weather.

The king's clothing is in all respects similar to that of the king of Chan-ch'ong, but the ceremonial at his court is more elaborate. When he goes out in his carriage of state it is drawn by a pair of horses or he has oxen. . . .

The officials and the common people dwell in houses with sides of bamboo matting and thatched with reeds. Only the king resides in a palace of hewn stone. It has a granite lotus pond of extraordinary beauty with golden bridges, some three hundred odd feet long. The palace buildings are solidly built and richly ornamented. The throne on which the king sits is made of gharu-wood and the seven precious substances; the dais is jewelled, with supports of veined wood [ebony?]; the screen [behind the throne] is of ivory.

When all the ministers of state have audience, they first make three full prostrations at the foot of the throne; they then kneel and remain thus, with hands crossed on their breasts, in a circle round the king, and discuss the affairs of state. When they have finished, they make another prostration and retire. . . .

[The people] are devout Buddhists. There are serving [in the temples] some three hundred foreign women; they dance and offer food to the Buddha. They are called *a-nan* or slave dancing-girls.

As to their customs, lewdness is not considered criminal; theft is punished by cutting off a hand and a foot and by branding on the chest.

The incantations of the Buddhist and Taoist priests [of this country] have magical powers. Among the former those who wear yellow robes may marry, while those who dress in red lead ascetic lives in temples. The Taoists clothe themselves with leaves; they have a deity called P'o-to-li which they worship with great devotion.

[The people of this country] hold the right hand to be clean, the left unclean, so when they wish to mix their rice with any kind of meat broth, they use the right hand to do so and also to eat with.

The soil is rich and loamy; the fields have no bounds. Each one takes as much as he can cultivate. Rice and cereals are cheap; for every tael of lead one can buy two bushels of rice.

The native products comprise elephants' tusks, the *chan* and *su* [varieties of gharu-wood], good yellow wax, kingfisher's feathers, . . . resin, foreign oils, ginger peel, gold colored incense, . . . raw silk and cotton fabrics.

The foreign traders offer in exchange for these gold, silver, porcelainware, sugar, preserves and vinegar.

in the flatlands north of the great lake called the Tonle Sap. For the next several hundred years, Angkor (as the kingdom came to be known from its capital city Angkor Thom) was the most powerful state in mainland Southeast Asia (see the box above).

Like its predecessor Funan, Angkor was a commercial as well as an agricultural society, although much of the regional trade that had passed through the area now traveled further south, through the Strait of Malacca. But above all, the wealth of Angkor was based on agriculture, the result of an extensive system of irrigation throughout much of what is now Cambodia. Like Funan and the contemporary kingdoms in the Indonesian archipelago, Angkor made fruitful use of symbols and institutions brought from India. It also maintained trade relations with China, but its proud rulers refused to accept a tributary relationship as the Mongols demanded.

Although Angkor was a major force on the Southeast Asian mainland for several hundred years, it is doubtful that its rulers ever felt totally secure, for the kingdom faced enemies on all sides. Angkor fought with the kingdom of Champa to the east and with the Vietnamese, who had regained their independence from China in the tenth century (see Chapter 11). By the fourteenth century, Angkor had begun to decline. One of the reasons was the arrival of new peoples from the north, known today as the

Thai. The Thai, whose original homeland was probably in southwestern China, first appeared in the sixth century C.E. as a frontier people only partly assimilated into Chinese civilization. But beginning in the eleventh or twelfth century, Thai tribes began migrating southward, a process that was accelerated by the Mongol invasion of China in the mid-thirteenth century. At first these migrating peoples settled in the mountains just south of the Chinese border, where they set up the kingdom of Sukhothai. But later they moved further south into the broad valley of the Chao Phraya River, where they came into conflict with Angkor. In 1432 they destroyed Angkor's capital and forced the remnants of the kingdom's ruling class to flee to the southeast where they set up a new capital near Phnom Penh, the capital of present-day Cambodia.

The Thai did not occupy Angkor itself, but set up their own capital further to the west at Ayuthaya, on the Chao Phraya River. There they remained as a major force in the region for the next four hundred years. From their neighbors they absorbed Indian religious and political institutions in a unique blend that would evolve into modern-day Thai culture.

As they expanded southward into the rich Chao Phraya delta, the Thai began to come into contact with other peoples living in the area. Their main competition came from the west, where the Burman peoples had formed their own agricultural society in the valleys of the Salween and Irrawaddy Rivers. Like the Thai, the Burmans were relatively recent arrivals in the area, having migrated southward from the highlands of Tibet beginning in the seventh century C.E.

Although the Burmans were originally pastoral peoples, they adopted irrigated agriculture after their arrival in Southeast Asia. After subjugating weaker societies already living in the area, in the eleventh century they founded the first great Burman state, the kingdom of Pagan. Like the Thai, they quickly converted to Buddhism and adopted Indian political institutions and culture. During the next two hundred years, Pagan became a major force in the western segment of Southeast Asia. The kingdom expanded down the Malay peninsula and took an active part in the maritime trade throughout the region. But attacks from the Mongols in the late thirteenth century weakened Pagan, and the resulting vacuum may have benefited the Thai as they moved into areas occupied by Burman migrants in the Chao Phraya valley.

THE MALAY WORLD

In the Malay peninsula and the Indonesian archipelago, a different pattern emerged. For centuries, this area had been linked to the trade that passed from East Asia into the In-dian Ocean, and much of its wealth had come from the export of tropical products to China, India, and the Middle East. The area had never been united under a single state, however. Although the vast majority of the inhabitants of the region were of Malay ethnic stock, culturally and linguistically as well as politically, the peoples of the area were divided into numerous separate communities.

The first signs of organized societies in the area appear in Chinese records of trading contacts with states on the islands of Java and southern Sumatra. In the eighth century, the trading state of Srivijaya, located along the eastern coast of Sumatra, became a powerful commercial state that dominated the trade route passing through the Strait of Malacca. At approximately the same time, the kingdom of Sailendra emerged in eastern Java. Although both states were influenced by Indian culture and took part in the maritime trade throughout the region, Srivijaya was predominantly a trading society, while the wealth of Sailendra was based primarily on agriculture.

Like the mainland states, these island kingdoms were plagued with mutual rivalries, not only between themselves but also with nearby mainland states. Srivijaya in particular inspired resentment because of its aggressive efforts to control the passage of trade through the Strait of Malacca, the most convenient route at the time from East Asia into the Indian Ocean. In 1025, Srivijaya was attacked and defeated by the South Indian kingdom of Cola. Srivijaya was able to recover from the defeat, but never managed to regain its former dominance over the area. One reason for its decline may have been that maritime commerce through the region began to flow increasingly to the east, through the Strait of Sunda and directly out into the Indian Ocean.

In the late thirteenth century, this shift in trade patterns led to the founding of a new kingdom of Majapahit on the island of Java. According to contemporary historical accounts, Majapahit became the greatest empire the region had yet seen. In the mid-fourteenth century, under a talented leader named Gaja Madah, the kingdom united most of the archipelago and perhaps even parts of the mainland under a single rule. The memory of Majapahit is still very much alive in modern Indonesia. President Sukarno, the prominent Indonesian nationalist and founder of the modern Republic of Indonesia, referred to this fourteenth-century empire to support his claim that all the Indonesian islands should be encompassed within a single state.

THE INDIAN MODEL IN SOUTHEAST ASIA

During the first stage of state formation in Southeast Asia, political institutions and symbols of authority came primarily from the Indian subcontinent across the Bay of Bengal. The first major society in the region to adopt the Indian model had been Funan, in the lower region of the Mekong valley. Many later kingdoms in the area, from Pagan and Ayuthaya on the mainland to Srivijaya and Majapahit on the Indonesian islands, followed Funan's lead.

Some historians have maintained that one of the key elements of Indian statecraft that was appropriated by Southeast Asian rulers was the *devaraja*, or god-king concept, first brought to the region by travelers from the Dravidian states in southern India. In this type of kingship, the ruler possessed divine powers and godlike status, and historians assumed that rulers of Indianized societies in Southeast Asia used the concept as a means of enhancing their authority and prestige among their subjects. Recent evidence, however, brings this assumption into question and suggests that Southeast Asian rulers were not regarded literally as gods, but rather as individuals who possessed distinctive characteristics that enabled them to serve as a link between human beings on earth and the transcendent world of the deities.

Whatever the truth in this debate, the ruler was considered to possess special qualities that raised him above the level of ordinary men. This special aura—sometimes called charisma—was often given a physical manifestation by placing the imperial palace on a hill in the capital city. Some historians have identified this practice with Mount Meru, the legendary home of the gods in Hindu tradition, but others have pointed out that mountains were considered sacred places in many Southeast Asian societies and have suggested that this is a good example of the blending of local and foreign traditions in Southeast Asia.

The king was also viewed as the high priest in a fertility cult, a role that was sometimes symbolized by the use of a phallic symbol called the *linga*. The *linga* appeared in stylized form in Indianized architecture throughout the region, but its characteristic location was in a royal temple (often devoted to Siva, known as the "God of the Mountain") where the ruler performed fertility rites as a normal part of his royal functions.

The charisma of the ruler rubbed off on those around him. Key positions in the central bureaucracy and the territorial administration were reserved for members of the hereditary nobility. In theory, all such positions were subject to appointment by the ruler himself, but in practice many were probably passed on within a particular noble family. Many of the most prominent royal advisers were *brahmins* serving as priests. Some of these may have come from India or were descendants of *brahmins* who had come to Southeast Asia at an earlier date. In some Southeast Asian societies, such as Angkor, a *brahmin*

class on the Indian model was created to differentiate these individuals from the remainder of the population, while the ruling family was assigned the status of *kshatriya* (warrior).

Spices and Paddy Fields: The Economy of Southeast Asia

The traditional states of Southeast Asia can be generally divided between agricultural societies and trading societies. The distinction between farming and trade was undoubtedly a product of the environment. Vietnam, Angkor, and Pagan were situated in rich river deltas that were conducive to the development of a wet rice economy. Although all produced some items of value for the regional markets, none was tempted to turn to commerce as the prime source of national income. In fact, none was situated astride the main trade routes that crisscrossed the region. Funan, one of the predecessors of Angkor, had dominated the regional trade of its time, which passed through Funan en route to or from the Isthmus of Kra, the land route between the Gulf of Thailand and the Bay of Bengal. But by the seventh century C.E., the regional trade route had shifted to the Strait of Malacca to the south, and Funan lost its central position to the new state of Srivijaya with its capital at Palembang in eastern Sumatra.

The rulers of Srivijaya had helped to bring about the relocation of the trade routes by controlling the pirates who had once plagued shipping in the Strait of Malacca. Another factor was the deepwater port at Palembang where sailors could wait out the change in the monsoon season before making their return voyage. But the new route was not without costs. Like barons on the Rhine and Danube Rivers or Arab princes along the Red Sea, Srivijaya's rulers exacted stiff payments for shipping through the strait.

Srivijaya's attack on the pirates also facilitated the passage of goods between East Asia and the Middle East. As we have seen, this trade dated back to ancient times. The author of the *Periplus* had referred to a place called Chryse ("golden peninsula" or "golden region"), which he described as "an island in the ocean, the furthest extremity towards the east of the inhabited world, lying under the rising sun itself. . . ."[17] Roman and Indian accounts of the first centuries C.E. had distinguished between a golden peninsula and a silver island, possibly Malaya and Sumatra.

The emergence of states in Southeast Asia contributed significantly to the expansion of trade, as did the rise in demand for spices. As the wealth of Europe and the Middle East increased, demand for the tropical products of East Asia grew correspondingly, and merchant fleets from India and the Arabian peninsula sailed to the Indonesian islands to buy cloves, pepper, nutmeg, cinnamon, precious woods, and other tropical products popular among the wealthy in China and the West. India and Africa provided textile goods, indigo, metals, and such specialty items as rhinoceros horn. From China came silk, porcelain, and salt.

At first, much of the trade through the region was conducted by private merchants living in port cities in Sumatra, Java, and the Malay peninsula. Traders from outside the area like the Arabs, Indians, and Chinese were restricted to the carrying trade between their home countries and Southeast Asian ports. But eventually the outsiders sought to increase their profits by taking a more active role in local trade. Muslim merchants from India in particular began to play a more aggressive role in the political arena.

By no means did all the inhabitants of Southeast Asia live in the large agricultural or trading states. In the mountains surrounding the river valleys and deltas and on thousands of islands scattered throughout the Indonesian archipelago and the South China Sea, other peoples lived in small communities independent of any higher authority. Some lived by hunting, fishing, or food gathering; others practiced slash-and-burn agriculture or cultivated wet rice. A few, such as the Bugis of the Indonesian island of Sulawesi, lived by piracy or regional trade.

By virtue of their remote locations and the diversity of their inhabitants' ethnic and linguistic backgrounds, such communities were not united, nor for the most part did they have many direct contacts with the larger societies around them. Some, like the aboriginal peoples in central Borneo and parts of the Philippines and the Batak peoples in the mountainous spine of the island of Sumatra, lived in almost total isolation from the outside world. Like the peoples living on the periphery of ancient civilizations in China, India, and the Middle East, some were gradually absorbed into the larger states taking root in the region. But other, more isolated peoples continued to live beyond the fringes of civilization in Southeast Asia throughout the traditional period. Only in the twentieth century were many of them brought inexorably into the vortex of the modern world.

Daily Life

Because of the diversity of ethnic backgrounds, religions, and cultures, making generalizations about daily life in Southeast Asia during the early historical period is difficult. Nevertheless, it appears that Southeast Asian societies did not always apply the social distinctions that

were sometimes imported from India. For example, although the local population, as elsewhere, was divided according to a variety of economic functions, the dividing lines between classes were not as rigid and imbued with religious significance as they were in the Indian subcontinent.

Still, traditional societies in Southeast Asia had some clearly hierarchical characteristics. At the top of the social ladder were the hereditary aristocrats, who monopolized both political power and economic wealth and enjoyed a borrowed aura of charisma by virtue of their proximity to the ruler. Most aristocrats lived in the major cities, which were the main source of power, wealth, and foreign influence. The best surviving example of such a city in Southeast Asia is probably Angkor Thom, located north of the Tonle Sap in northern Cambodia. Although not fully restored, the site clearly shows the magnificence of Angkor civilization at its zenith, with royal palaces and parks, a massive parade ground, crematoria, reservoirs, and numerous temples (see the box on p. 318). The city itself formed a square two miles on each side. Its massive stone walls were several feet thick and were surrounded by a moat. Four main gates led into the city, which at its height had a substantial population.

Beyond the major cities lived the mass of the population, composed of farmers, fishermen, artisans, and merchants. In most Southeast Asian societies, the vast majority were probably rice farmers, living at a bare level of subsistence and paying heavy rents or taxes to a landlord or a local ruler.

The average Southeast Asian peasant was not actively engaged in commerce except as a consumer of various necessities. But accounts by foreign visitors indicate that in the Malay world some were involved in growing or mining products for export, such as tropical food products, precious woods, tin, and precious gems. Most of the regional trade was carried on by local merchants, who purchased products from local growers and then transported them to the major port cities. During the early state-building era, roads were few and relatively primitive, so most of the trade was transported by small boats down rivers to the major ports along the coast. There the goods were loaded onto larger ships for delivery outside the region. Growers of export goods in areas near the coast were thus indirectly involved in the regional trade network, but received few economic benefits from the relationship.

As we might expect from an area of such ethnic and cultural diversity, social structures differed significantly from country to country. In the Indianized states on the mainland, the tradition of a hereditary tribal aristocracy was probably accentuated by the Hindu practice of dividing the population into separate classes, called *varna* in imitation of the Indian model. In Angkor and Pagan, for example, the divisions were based on occupation or ethnic background. Some people were considered free subjects of the king, although there may have been legal restrictions against changing occupations. Others, however, may have been indentured to an employer. Each community was under a chieftain, who in turn was subordinated to a higher official responsible for passing on the tax revenues of each group to the central government.

In the kingdoms in the Malay peninsula and the Indonesian archipelago, social relations were generally less formal. Most of the people in the region, whether farmers, fishermen, or artisans, lived in small *kampongs* (the Malay word for village) in wooden houses built on stilts to avoid flooding during the monsoon season. Some of the farmers were probably sharecroppers who paid a part of their harvest to a landlord, who was often a member of the aristocracy. But in other areas the tradition of free farming was strong. In some cases, some of the poorer land belonged to the village as a collective unit and was assigned for use by the neediest families.

Most societies in Southeast Asia accorded greater rights to women than their counterparts in China and India. Women worked with men side by side in the fields and, as in Africa, often played an active role in trading activities. Family relationships were also less hierarchical and formalized, and the nuclear family was generally more common than the joint family system practiced in China and the Indian subcontinent.

The relative availability of cultivable land in the region may help explain the absence of joint families. Joint families under patriarchal leadership tend to be found in

◆ **Mount Agung in Bali.** In Southeast Asia as in many other cultures, mountains are considered to be the abode of the gods. This was notably the case on the island of Bali, where beautiful Mount Agung is still viewed by Hindus as the local equivalent of Mt. Meru in India. In Balinese cosmology, the sea is the home of evil spirits, while humans occupy the profane world in between. An active volcano, Mount Agung has not always been grateful for its exalted status. In 1964 it erupted, killing thousands of islanders in a cloud of volcanic ash.

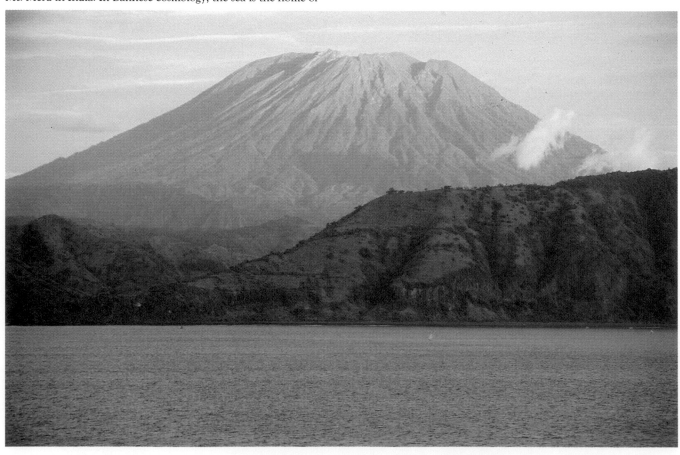

areas where land is scarce and individual families must work together to conserve resources and maximize income. With the exception of a few crowded river valleys, few areas in Southeast Asia had a high population density per acre of cultivable land. Throughout most of the area, water was plentiful, and the land was relatively fertile. In parts of Indonesia, it was possible to survive by living off the produce of wild fruit trees—bananas, coconuts, mangoes, and a variety of other tropical fruits. One participant in Admiral Zhenghe's voyages to Southeast Asia in the fifteenth century (see Chapter 10) noted that the food products available in the port city of Malacca included sugarcane, bananas, jackfruit, wild lichees, and a host of vegetables. Meat was fairly rare and therefore costly.

It is tempting to conclude from this picture that life was easier in much of Southeast Asia than it was elsewhere in Asia. Food and land were relatively plentiful, local products brought a handsome profit in trade with merchants from across the sea, and social relations were less rigid and formalized than they were in the more crowded and less naturally endowed regions of East and South Asia.

World of the Spirits: Religious Belief

Before the introduction of Indian religious ideas into Southeast Asia early in the first millennium C.E., religious belief in Southeast Asia took the familiar form of spirit worship and animism that we have seen in other cultures in the area. Southeast Asians believed that spirits dwelled in the mountains, rivers, streams, and other sacred places in their environment. Mountains were probably particularly sacred, since they were considered to be the abode of ancestral spirits, the place to which the souls of all the departed would retire after death.

When Hindu and Buddhist ideas began to penetrate the area early in the first millennium C.E., they exerted a strong appeal among local elites. Not only did the new doctrines offer a more convincing explanation of the nature of the cosmos, but they also provided local rulers with a means of enhancing their prestige and power and conferred an aura of legitimacy on their relations with their subjects. In the Javanese kingdoms and in Angkor, Hindu gods like Vishnu and Siva provided a new and more sophisticated veneer for existing beliefs in nature deities and ancestral spirits. In Angkor, the king's duties included performing sacred rituals on the mountain in the capital city; in time the ritual became a state cult uniting Hindu gods with local nature deities and ancestral spirits in a complex pantheon.

♦ **The Bayon at Angkor.** Whereas Angkor Wat was dedicated to Hindu mythology, the Bayon Temple was a Buddhist structure. In addition to its extraordinary bas-reliefs, which illuminate the everyday life of thirteenth-century Cambodia, the Bayon is known for its huge heads of the Bodhisattva of Mercy. These 172 giant heads, looking in all four cardinal directions for souls to save, are reputedly modeled after the monarch Jayavarman, whose conversion from Hinduism to Buddhism as an adult contributed to the mixture of architectural styles in the temple. The faces are mesmerizing with their haunting smiles, reflecting the mystery of enlightenment.

This state cult, financed by the royal court, eventually led to the construction of temples throughout the country. Many of these temples housed thousands of priests and retainers and amassed great wealth, including vast estates farmed by local peasants. It has been estimated that there were as many as 300,000 priests in Angkor at the height of its power. This vast wealth, which was often exempt from taxes, may be one explanation for the gradual decline of Angkor in the thirteenth and fourteenth centuries. Nevertheless, the spread of Hindu doctrines was essentially an elite phenomenon. Although the common people participated in the state cult and helped construct the temples, they did not give up their traditional beliefs in local deities and ancestral spirits.

The introduction of Buddhism into the region did not immediately affect this situation. In fact, during the early state-building period, Hindu and Mahayana Buddhist state cults competed for influence in many states throughout the region. In some instances, ruling elites may have shifted from one religion to the other as a means of gaining political advantage over their rivals. Thus, for example, in the eighth and ninth centuries, central Java shifted from Buddhism to Hinduism, a conversion marked in stone by the construction of a Buddhist temple at Borobudur and a later Hindu temple at

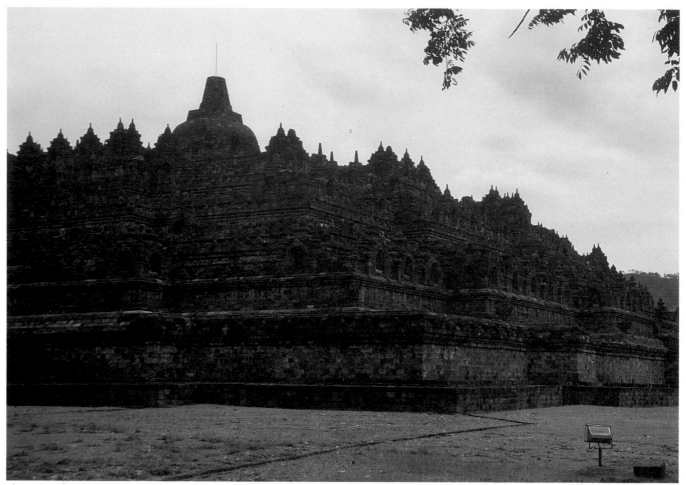

◆ **The Temple of Borobudur.** The colossal pyramid temple at Borobudur, on the island of Java, is one of the greatest Buddhist monuments. Constructed in the eighth century, it depicts the path to spiritual enlightenment in stone. The reliefs along the lowest walls depict the world of desire, while the higher levels represent the world of the spirit, culminating at the summit with the empty and closed stupa, signifying the state of Nirvana. After the decline of Buddhism in the ninth century, Borobudur was abandoned. Buried for a thousand years under volcanic ash and jungle, it was rediscovered in the nineteenth century and recently restored to its former splendor.

neighboring Prambanan near the modern-day city of Jokjakarta.

A major transformation began in the eleventh century, however, when Theravada Buddhism began to penetrate mainland Southeast Asia from the island of Sri Lanka. In the eleventh century, Theravada was introduced to the peoples of Burma by monks returning to Pagan from a visit to the island. From Pagan, it spread rapidly to other areas in Southeast Asia and eventually became the religion of the masses throughout the mainland west of the Annamite Mountains.

Theravada's appeal to the peoples of Southeast Asia is reminiscent of the original attraction of Buddhist thought centuries earlier on the Indian subcontinent. By teaching that individuals could seek *Nirvana* through their own actions rather than through the intercession of the ruler or a priest, Theravada was more accessible to the masses than were the state cults promoted by the rulers. During the next centuries, Theravada gradually undermined the influence of state-supported religions and became the dominant faith in several mainland societies, including Burma, Thailand, Laos, and Cambodia. In the process, however, it was gradually appropriated by local rulers, who portrayed themselves as "immanent Buddhas," higher than ordinary mortals on the scale of human existence.

Theravada did not penetrate far into the Malay peninsula or the Indonesian island chain, perhaps because it entered Southeast Asia through Burma further to the north. But the Malay world found its own popu-

◆ **Followers of the Buddha Borobudur.** Although the primary purpose of the stone carvings on the walls of the temple at Borobudur was to transmit the life of the Buddha, to modern viewers they are an important source of information about life in early Southeast Asia. Intricate bas-relief sculptures decorating the lower levels of the temple reveal the customs and costumes of eighth-century Java. Here followers of Siddhartha Gautama seek enlightenment under the Bodhi tree.

lar alternative to state religions when Islam began to enter the area in the thirteenth and fourteenth centuries. Like Theravada Buddhism, Islam became a religion of the masses. But as Marco Polo observed during a visit in the thirteenth century, Islam, like its predecessors, had difficulty penetrating into the rural areas. Because Islam's expansion into Southeast Asia took place for the most part after 1500, its emergence as a major force in the region will be discussed in a later chapter.

The Cultural World of Southeast Asia

When the first states began to form in Southeast Asia, not surprisingly their culture showed considerable Indian influence. Perhaps the most visible example was in architecture. Temple architecture reflecting Gupta or South Indian styles began to appear in Southeast Asia during the first centuries C.E. While Indian influence was clear, local artists soon began to follow their own creative urge and produced religious structures of astonishing size and grace. Most famous is the Buddhist temple at Borobudur in central Java. Begun in the late eighth century at the behest of a king of Sailendra, Borobudur is a massive stupa with nine terraces. Sculpted on the sides of each terrace are bas-reliefs depicting the nine stages in the life of Siddhartha Gautama from childhood to his final release from the chain of human existence. Surmounted by hollow bell-like towers containing representations of the Buddha and capped by a single stupa, the entire structure dominates the landscape for miles around.

Second only to Borobudur in technical excellence and even more massive in size are the ruins of the old capital city of Angkor Thom, near the modern-day city of Siem Reap in northern Cambodia. Abandoned in 1432 after the defeat by the Thai, Angkor Thom sank into the jungle and was not rediscovered until the mid-nineteenth century when a wandering French archaeologist stumbled upon it by accident. Most of what remains are the temples, the royal crematoria, and the city walls (see the box on p. 318). The temple of Angkor Wat is the most famous and arguably the most beautiful of all the existing structures at Angkor Thom. Built on the model of the legendary Mount Meru, it combines Indian architectural techniques with native inspiration in a structure of impressive delicacy and grace.

With its over six hundred years of existence, Angkor Thom serves as a bridge between the Hindu and Buddhist architectural styles. The last of its great temples, known as the Bayon, followed the earlier Hindu model, but was topped with sculpted towers containing four-sided representations of a *bodhisattva*, searching, it is said, for souls to save. Shortly after the Bayon was built, Theravada Buddhist societies in Burma and Thailand began to create a new Buddhist architecture based on the concept of a massive stupa surmounted by a spire. Most famous, perhaps, is the Shwedagon Pagoda in Rangoon, Burma, which is covered with gold leaf contributed by devout Buddhists from around the country.

Indianized areas of Southeast Asia have not left much of a literary legacy, in part because they did not possess written scripts for their own native languages prior to the arrival of Indian influence. India not only provided Southeast Asians with a system of phonetic symbols to record their own spoken languages, it also introduced them to popular Indian themes, such as stories from the Buddhist scriptures, tales from the classic Hindu epic, the Ramayana, and so forth. Eventually, however, literary works began to appear that reflected native inspiration, such as the classical epic *Nagarkertagama* by the Indonesian poet Prapanca (see the box on p. 327).

At first, court literature was probably inscribed in Sanskrit or other South Asian tongues, but eventually Southeast Asians developed written forms of their own languages from scripts already in use in the Indian subcontinent. For the common people, entertainment came not from the written word, but from popular theater, known in the Indonesian islands as *wayang*. The earliest form of such entertainment was probably *wayang beber*, in which the narrator unfolded a long horizontal scroll while describing events portrayed sequentially on the painted panels of the scroll. This technique gave way to the *wayang kulit*, also known as the shadow play.

In *wayang kulit* (literally, leather shadows), flat leather puppets were manipulated behind a screen illuminated from the rear, while the narrator, sometimes accompanied by music, recited events from the Indian classics. In daylight performances, three-dimensional puppets would sometimes replace the leather ones. The shadow play probably came originally from India or possibly from China, but it became a highly popular and distinctive art form in Java and other islands in the Indonesian archipelago. As in many other traditional societies, the original motives were probably religious rather than aesthetic. Shamans, who often served as narrators, used the popular theater to instruct the audience in religious verities and perhaps to solicit the presence of the gods. Eventually, the shadow theater came increasingly to be used for entertainment purposes. Although elite observers may occasionally have viewed it condescendingly as entertainment for the masses (one eleventh-century poet remarked sarcastically that the audience often seemed to forget that the figures behind the screen were simply leather puppets), it appears to have retained its popularity not only in rural villages but at court as well.

As in many traditional societies, theater, painting, and music in Indonesian societies were often integrated into a single art form. Little remains in the way of painting because of the ravages of the tropical climate, but traditional music survives in the modern gamelan orchestra. Relief sculptures on temple architecture from Borobudur to Angkor depict a court culture that was fond of music and dance.

Although Indian traditions probably influenced musical development in many Southeast Asian societies, gamelan, a type of music performed by an orchestra composed primarily of a variety of percussion instruments, is apparently Javanese in inspiration. According to tradition, gamelan (meaning "hammer") originated when a Javanese deity sounded a gong to assemble all of the other spirits in the vicinity to a conference. Today the gamelan orchestra uses kettles, drums, xylophones, and various string and wind instruments as well as gongs to create a unique type of music. Its basic purpose is to instill a sense of restraint and refined emotion in the mind of the performer rather than the listener. Gamelan music is essentially polyphonic (that is, the parts are related melodically, not harmonically) and traditionally included a number of separate styles, depending on whether the purpose was to encourage intimacy or to supplement a ceremonial occasion. Gamelan often accompanied performances of shadow plays and today is sometimes employed to summon the Muslim faithful to the mosque.

Conclusion

During the long period from the fall of the Mauryas to the rise of the Mughals, an interval of more than 1,500

The Legendary Grandeur of Majapahit

The Nagarkertagama, written by the court poet Prapanca in 1365, was the national epic of the kingdom of Majapahit. This passage describes the relationship between the kingdom and neighboring countries in the region.

Prapanca, *Nagarkertagama*

Such is the excellence of His Majesty the Prince who reigns at Majapahit as absolute monarch. His is praised like the moon in autumn, since he fills all the world with joy. The evil-doers are like the red lotus, the good—who love him wholeheartedly—are like the white lotus. His retinue, treasures, chariots, elephants, horses, etc., are (immeasurable) like the sea.

The land of Java is becoming more and more famous for its blessed state throughout the world. "Only Jambudwipa [India] and Java," so people say, "are mentioned for their superiority, good countries as they are, because of the multitude of men experienced in the doctrine . . . ; whatever 'work' turns up, they are very able to handle it."

First comes the Illustrious Brahmaraja, the excellent brahmin, an irreproachable, great poet and expert of the religious traditions; he has complete knowledge of the speculative as well as all the other philosophies, . .

. the system of dialectical (logic), etc. And (then) the holy Shamana, very pious, virtuous, experienced in the Vedas and the six pure activities. And also the Illustrious Vishnu, powerful in Samaveda incantations, with which he aims to increase the country's prosperity.

For this reason all kinds of people have continually come from other countries, in multitudes. There are Cambudwipa, Kamboja [Cambodia], China, Yawana [Annam], Champa, Kannataka [in South China], etc., Goda [Guar] and Siam—these are the places whence they come from. They come by ship with numerous merchants; monks and brahmins are the principal ones who as they come are regaled and are well pleased during their stay.

And in each month of Phalguna [February-March] His Majesty the Prince is honored and celebrated in his residence. Then the high state officials come from all over Java, the heads of districts, and the judicial officials . . . ; also the (people from) other islands, Bali, etc., all come with tributes so numerous that they are uninterrupted, to honor him. Traders and merchants fill the market in dense crowds with all their wares in great variety.

---

years, Indian civilization faced a number of severe challenges to the ideal of universal monarchy originally set forth in the *Arthasastra*. One challenge was primarily external in nature and took the form of a continuous threat from beyond the mountains in the northwest while a second was generated by internal causes and stemmed from the tradition of factionalism and internal rivalry (the "war of the fishes") that had marked relations within the aristocracy since the Aryan invasion in the second millennium B.C.E. (see Chapter 2). Despite the abortive efforts of the Guptas, that tradition continued almost without interruption down to the founding of the Mughal Empire in the sixteenth century.

The third challenge was primarily cultural and appeared in the religious divisions between Hindus and Buddhists, and later between Hindus and Muslims, that took place throughout much of this period. It is a measure of the strength and resilience of Hindu tradition that it was able to surmount the challenge of Buddhism and by the late first millennium C.E. had managed to reassert

its dominant position in Indian society. But that triumph was short-lived. One result of the foreign conquest of northern India was the introduction of Islam into the region. As we shall see later, the new religion was about to become a serious rival to traditional beliefs among the Indian people.

During the same period that Indian civilization faced these challenges at home, it was having a profound impact upon the emerging states of Southeast Asia. Situated at the crossroads between two oceans and two great civilizations, Southeast Asia has long served as a bridge linking peoples and cultures, and as complex societies began to develop in the area, it is not surprising that they were strongly influenced by the older civilizations of neighboring China and India. But this tendency to import ideas and institutions from abroad should not necessarily be viewed as a disadvantage. In many instances, the borrowings probably enriched the local society and improved the overall life of the general population. At the same time, the Southeast Asian peoples put their own unique stamp on the ideas that they adopted and eventually rejected those that were inappropriate to local conditions.

The result was a region characterized by an almost unparalleled cultural richness and diversity, reflecting influences from as far away as the Middle East, yet preserving indigenous elements that were deeply rooted in the local culture. Unfortunately, that very diversity posed potential problems for the peoples of Southeast Asia as they faced a new challenge from beyond the horizon. We shall deal with that challenge when we return to the region in a later chapter. In the meantime, we must turn our attention to the other major civilization that spread its shadow over the societies of southern Asia—that of China.

CHAPTER NOTES

1. *The Periplus Maris Erythraei*, with commentary by Lionel Casson (Princeton, N.J., 1989), 64:21.13–14, p. 91, with discussion on pp. 238–39.
2. Hiuen Tsiang, *Si-Yu-Ki: Buddhist Records of the Western World*, trans. Samuel Beal (London, n.d.), pp. 89–90.
3. Ibid., p. 70.
4. Fo-Kwo-Ki (Travels of Fa Xian), in ibid., Chapter 20, xliii.
5. E. C. Sachau, *Alberoni's India* (London, 1914), 1:22, quoted in S. M. Ikram, *Muslim Civilization in India* (New York, 1964), pp. 31–32.
6. Ibid., p. 68.
7. Quoted in Vincent A. Smith, *The Oxford History of India* (Oxford, 1958), p. 259.

8. Duarte Barbosa, *The Book of Duarte Barbosa* (Nedeln, 1967), 2:19.
9. Hiuen Tsiang, *Si-Yu-Ki*, pp. 73–74.
10. Hiuen Tsiang, *Si-Yu-Ki*, 2:88–89.
11. Barbosa, *Book of Duarte Barbosa*, pp. 147–48.
12. Quoted in Richard Lannoy, *The Speaking Tree: A Study of Indian Culture and Society* (London, 1971), p. 232.
13. *The Periplus*, 39:13.5–6, with discussion on p. 33.
14. Cited in A. L. Basham, *The Wonder That Was India* (London, 1954), p. 423.
15. Ibid., p. 426.
16. From B. S. Miller, *Phantasies of a Love-Thief* (New York, 1971).
17. *The Periplus*, p. 91.

SUGGESTED READINGS

The period from the decline of the Mauryas to the rise of the Mughals in India is not especially rich in terms of materials in English. Still, a number of the standard texts on Indian history contain useful sections on the period. Particularly good are A. L. Basham, *The Wonder That Was India* (London, 1954) and S. Wolpert, *New History of India* (New York, 1989). See also V. A. Smith, *The Oxford History of India* (Oxford, 1958) and H. H. Dodwell, ed. *The Cambridge History of India*, 6 vols. (Cambridge, 1922–1953). An overview with illustrations can be found in *Past Worlds: The Times Atlas of Archaeology* (Maplewood, N.J., 1988).

A number of studies of Indian society and culture deal with this period. See, for example, R. Lannoy, *The Speaking Tree* (Oxford, 1971) for a sophisticated interpretation of Indian culture during the medieval period. On Buddhism, see H. Nakamura, *Indian Buddhism: A Survey with Bibliographical Notes* (Delhi, 1987) and H. Akira, *A History of Indian Buddhism from Sakyamuni to Early Mahayana* (Hawaii, 1990). For an interesting treatment of the Buddhist influence on commercial activities that is reminiscent of the role of Christianity in Europe, see L. Xinru, *Ancient India and Ancient China: Trade and Religious Changes A.D. 1–600* (Delhi, 1988).

The most up-to-date treatment of the Indian economy and, in particular, the regional trade throughout the Indian Ocean is K. N. Chaudhuri, *Trade and Civilization in the Indian Ocean: An Economic History from the*

Rise of Islam to 1750 (Cambridge, 1985), a ground-breaking comparative study. See also his more recent and massive *Asia before Europe: Economy and Civilization of the Indian Ocean from the Rise of Islam to 1750* (Cambridge, 1990), which owes a considerable debt to F. Braudel's classical work on the Mediterranean Sea.

The Islamic period in Indian history is treated in S. M. Ikram, *Muslim Civilization in India* (New York, 1964) and C. E. Bosworth, *The Later Ghaznavids: Splendour and Decay* (New York, 1977). On the career of Tamerlane, see B. F. Manz, *The Rise and Rule of Tamerlane* (Cambridge, 1989).

For Indian art during the medieval period, see the concise volume by R. C. Craven, *Indian Art* (London, 1976). A more detailed analysis is S. Huntington, *The Art of Ancient India: Buddhist, Hindu and Jain* (New York, 1985). For a detailed description of archaeological sites with maps and magnificent photographs of monuments and sculptures, consult M. Bussagli, *5000 Years of the Art of India* (New York, n.d.).

For a brief introduction to Indian literature, see A. L. Basham, *A Cultural History of India* (Oxford, 1975). See also E. C. Dimock, *The Literature of India: An Introduction* (Chicago, 1974) and A. K. Warder, *Indian Kavya Literature*, 5 vols. (Delhi, 1972–1988). For Kalidasa, consult B. S. Miller, ed., *Theater of Memory: The Plays of Kalidasa* (New York, 1984) and *The Cloud Messenger* (Ann Arbor, Mich., 1964). For the *Caurapancasika* of Bilhana, see B. S. Miller, *Phantasies of a Love-Thief* (New York, 1971). For Dandin's prose, see A. W. Ryder, *The Ten Princes* (Chicago, 1927).

The early history of Southeast Asia is not as well documented as that of China or India. Except for Vietnam, where histories written in Chinese appeared shortly after the Chinese conquest, written materials on societies in the region are relatively sparse. Historians have therefore been compelled to rely on stone inscriptions and the accounts of travelers and historians from other countries. Very useful in this regard is the Chinese port official Chau Ju-kua's *Records of Foreign Nations*. For a translation, see F. Hirth and W. W. Rockhill, *Chau Ju-kua: His Work on the Chinese and Arab Trade in the Twelfth and Thirteenth Centuries, entitled Chu-fan-chi* (New York, 1966). See also *The Travels of Marco Polo* (New York, n.d.); I-tsing, *A Record of the Buddhist Religion as Practiced in India and the Malay Archipelago* (Oxford, 1896); and A. Cortesao, ed. and trans., *The Suma Oriental of Tome Pires and the Book of Francisco Rodrigues* (London, 1944).

A number of useful general surveys of early Southeast Asian history are available. Many of them are now dated in the light of recent information, but still provide a useful overview. The most detailed is D. G. E. Hall, *A History of South-east Asia* (New York, 1966). See also J. F. Cady, *Southeast Asia: Its Historical Development* (New York, 1964). For a more recent account, see D. R. SarDesai, *Southeast Asia: Past and Present* (Boulder, Colo., 1989). For a useful survey of the ethnographic background, see R. Provencher, *Mainland Southeast Asia: An Anthropological Perspective* (Pacific Palisades, Calif., 1975). R. Burling, *Hill Farms and Padi Fields: Life in Mainland Southeast Asia* (Englewood Cliffs, N.J., 1965) provides a short discussion of the dynamic forces that have shaped the mainland societies in the region. See also P. Wheatley, *The Golden Khersonese: Studies in the Historical Geography of the Malay Peninsula before A.D. 1500* (Kuala Lumpur, 1961).

Working with limited resources, modern scholars are bringing out some fascinating interpretations of the early history of the region. An extensive analysis of the "Indianized" states of mainland Southeast Asia is available in G. Coedes, *The Making of Southeast Asia* (Berkeley, Calif., 1966). More recently, some scholars have tended to emphasize the role of indigenous forces in the evolution of the region. See, for example, O. W. Wolters, *Early Indonesian Commerce: A Study of the Origins of Sri Vijaya* (Ithaca, N.Y., 1967) and *The Fall of Srivijaya in Malay History* (Ithaca, N.Y., 1970). See also J. C. Van Leur, *Indonesian Trade and Society: Essays in Asian Social and Economic History* (The Hague, 1955).

The role of commerce has recently been highlighted as a key aspect in the development of the region. For two fascinating accounts, see K. R. Hall, *Maritime Trade and State Development in Early Southeast Asia* (Honolulu, 1985) and A. Reid, *Southeast Asia in the Era of Commerce, 1450–1680: The Lands below the Winds* (New Haven, Conn., 1989).

The nature of kingship has attracted attention from scholars in recent years. K. R. Hall and J. K. Whitmore, eds., *Explorations in Early Southeast Asian History: The Origins of Southeast Asian Statecraft* (Ann Arbor, Mich., 1976) and L. Gesick, ed., *Centers, Symbols, and Hierarchies: Essays on the Classical States of Southeast Asia* (New Haven, Conn., 1983) provide interesting essays on the subject. See also L. Castles and A. Reid, eds., *Pre-Colonial State Systems in Southeast Asia* (Kuala Lumpur, 1975).

For further information on the art and culture of Southeast Asia, see T. Bodrogi, *The Art of Indonesia* (New York, 1972). See also E. H. Schafer, *The Vermilion Bird: T'ang Images of the South* (Berkeley, Calif., 1967).

CHAPTER 10

From the Tang to the Mongols: The Flowering of Traditional China

On his first visit to the city, the traveler was mightily impressed. Its streets were so straight and wide that he could see through the city from one end to the other. Along the wide boulevards were beautiful palaces and inns in great profusion. The city was laid out in squares "like a chessboard," and within each square were spacious courts and gardens. Truly, said the visitor, this must be one of the largest and wealthiest cities on earth—a city so splendid that "it is impossible to give a description that should do it justice."[1]

The visitor was Marco Polo, and the city was Khanbaliq (later known as Beijing), capital of the Yuan dynasty (1279–1368) and one of the great commercial centers of the Chinese Empire. Marco Polo was an Italian merchant who had traveled to China in the late thirteenth century and then served as an official at the court of Khubilai Khan. His diary, published after his return to Italy almost twenty years later, astonished readers with tales of this magnificent but unknown civilization far to the east.

When Marco Polo arrived, China was ruled by the Mongols, a nomadic people from Central Asia who had overthrown the Song (Sung) dynasty and assumed control of the Chinese Empire. The Yuan dynasty, as the Mongol rulers were called, was only one of a succession of dynasties to rule China after the collapse of the Han dynasty in the third century C.E. The end of the Han had led to a period of internal division and civil war that lasted nearly four hundred years and was aggravated by the threat posed by

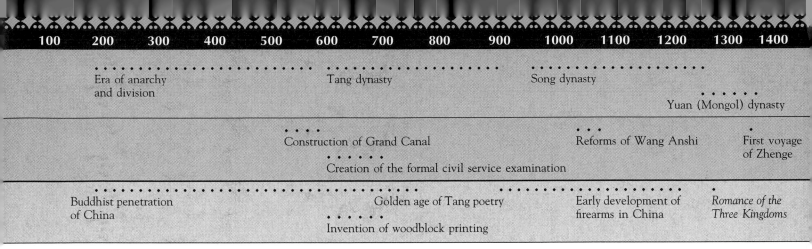

Era of anarchy and division

Tang dynasty

Song dynasty

Yuan (Mongol) dynasty

Construction of Grand Canal

Reforms of Wang Anshi

First voyage of Zhenge

Creation of the formal civil service examination

Buddhist penetration of China

Golden age of Tang poetry

Early development of firearms in China

Romance of the Three Kingdoms

Invention of woodblock printing

nomadic peoples from the north. This time of troubles ended in the early seventh century C.E., however, when the dynamic Tang dynasty led China to some of its finest achievements.

To this point, Chinese history appeared to be following a pattern similar to that of India. There, as we have seen, the passing of the Mauryan dynasty in the second century B.C.E. unleashed a period of internal division that lasted for several hundred years. Although the Guptas were able to revive the magnificence of India's first golden age, their glorious era soon flickered and died, and it was not until the rise of the Mughal Empire in the early sixteenth century that unity returned to the subcontinent.

But China did not recapitulate the Indian experience. The Tang dynasty collapsed in 907, but after a brief interregnum, China was reunified under the Song, who ruled most of China for nearly three hundred years. The Song in turn were overthrown by the Mongols in the late thirteenth century, and they in turn gave way to a powerful new native dynasty, the Ming, in 1368. Dynasty followed dynasty, with periods of extraordinary cultural achievement alternating with periods of internal disorder, but in general Chinese society continued to build on the political and cultural foundations of the Zhou and the Han.

Chinese historians, viewing this vast process as it evolved over time, began to hypothesize that Chinese history was cyclical in nature, driven by the dynamic interplay of the forces of good and evil, yang and yin, growth and decay. Beyond the forces of conflict and change lay the essential continuity of Chinese history, based on the timeless principles established by Confucius and other thinkers during the Zhou dynasty in antiquity. If India often appeared to be a politically and culturally diverse entity, only sporadically knit together by ambitious rulers spurred by the Kautilyan vision of the universal monarch, China, at least in the eyes of its historians, was a coherent civilization struggling to relive the glories of its ancient golden age while contending against the divisive forces of yin and yang operating throughout the cosmos. In actuality, this picture of a succession of dynasties each seeking to replicate the glories of China's golden age under the early Zhou dynasty disguises the reality that under the surface Chinese society was undergoing significant changes and bore scant resemblance to the kingdom that had been founded by the house of Zhou more than twenty centuries earlier.

◆ **The Buddhist Pilgrim Xuan Zang.**   Although the first recorded Buddhist pilgrimage from China across Central Asia to India was that of Fa Xian in 399 C.E., the seventh century was the golden age of these religious pilgrimages. The most famous was that of Xuan Zang, whose sixteen-year journey was recorded by a disciple: "Alone and abandoned he traversed the sandy waste . . . following the heaps of bones and horse-dung." Here Xuan Zang holds a fly whisk in his left hand to drive away demons, while in his right he brandishes the khakkhara, a symbol of the Buddhist monk. With sacred texts on his back and a hat against the desert sun, Xuan Zang proceeds on his pilgrimage protected by the image of the Lord Buddha.

China after the Han

After the collapse of the Han dynasty at the beginning of the third century C.E., China fell into an extended period of division and civil war. In the chaos that accompanied the collapse of the empire, the warlord Cao Cao (Ts'ao Ts'ao) had attempted to emulate the great Liu Bang (Liu Pang) and unify the country under his own authority (see Chapter 3). But Cao Cao was unable to consolidate his power, and for the next three centuries China was in a state of almost constant anarchy and internal division. Taking advantage of the absence of organized government in China, nomadic forces from the Gobi Desert penetrated south of the Great Wall and established their own rule over northern China. In the Yangtze valley and further to the south, native Chinese rule was maintained, but constant civil war and instability led later historians to refer to the period as the "era of the six dynasties."

The decline and fall of the Han Empire had a marked effect on the Chinese psyche. The Confucian principles that emphasized hard work, the subordination of the individual to community interests, and belief in the essentially rational order of the universe came under severe challenge, and many Chinese began to turn to more messianic creeds that emphasized the supernatural or the promise of earthly or heavenly salvation. Intellectuals began to reject the stuffy moralism and complacency of State Confucianism and sought emotional satisfaction in hedonistic pursuits or philosophical Daoism (see the box on p. 333).

One example of such attitudes was the poet Juan Chi, who lived in the middle of the third century C.E. A biographical sketch described him as follows:

> Handsome and imposing in appearance, and of open and far-ranging mind, Juan Chi was fiercely independent and did exactly as he pleased. Neither joy nor anger was ever expressed on his face. Sometimes he stayed shut up in his room studying books for several months on end, without ever going out; sometimes he went up into the mountains or to the waterside, forgetting for several days to return home. He read an enormous amount and had a special love for Chuang-tzu [a well-known Daoist philosopher of the third century B.C.E.] and Lao-tzu. He was a great drinker, an accomplished performer on the lute, and skilled in whistling. While he was following a train of thought, he would quite forget about the outside world. His contemporaries often called him a madman.[2]

Eccentric behavior and a preference for philosophical Daoism became a common response to a corrupt age. A group of writers known as the "seven sages of the bamboo

≽ A Daoist Critique of Confucianism ≼

This document is a biting Daoist attack on the type of pompous and hypocritical Confucian "gentleman" who feigned high moral principles while secretly engaging in corrupt and licentious behavior. It was written during the chaotic period following the collapse of the Han dynasty in the third century C.E.

The Biography of a Great Man

What the world calls a gentleman [chun-tzu] is someone who is solely concerned with moral law [fa], and cultivates exclusively the rules of propriety [li]. His hand holds the emblem of jade [authority], his foot follows the straight line of the rule. He likes to think that his actions set a permanent example; he likes to think that his words are everlasting models. In his youth, he has a reputation in the villages of his locality, in his later years he is well known in the neighboring dis-

tricts. Upward, he aspires to the dignity of the Three Dukes; downward, he does not disdain the post of governor of the nine provinces.

Have you ever seen the lice that inhabit a pair of trousers? They jump into the depths of the seams, hiding themselves in the cotton wadding, and believe they have a pleasant place to live. Walking, they do not risk going beyond the edge of the seam; moving, they are careful not to emerge from the trouser leg; and they think they have kept to the rules of etiquette. But when the trousers are ironed, the flames invade the hills, the fire spreads, the villages are set on fire and the towns burned down; then the lice that inhabit the trousers cannot escape.

What difference is there between the gentleman who lives within a narrow world and the lice that inhabit trouser legs?

---

forest" exemplified the period. Among the best known was the poet Liu Ling, whose odd behavior is described in this oft-quoted passage:

> Liu Ling was an inveterate drinker and indulged himself to the full. Sometimes he stripped off his clothes and sat in his room stark naked. Some men saw him and rebuked him. Liu Ling said, "Heaven and earth are my dwelling, and my house is my trousers. Why are you all coming into my trousers?"[3]

Popular beliefs in the supernatural and philosophical Daoism provided a temporary antidote to the patent weaknesses of a stale Confucianism. But neither could satisfy deeper emotional needs or provide solace in time of sorrow or the hope of a better life in the hereafter. Instead, Buddhism filled that gap.

Buddhism, of course, did not originate in China (see Chapter 2). It was brought to China in the first or second century C.E., probably by missionaries traveling over the Silk Road. The concept of rebirth was probably unfamiliar to most Chinese, and the intellectual hairsplitting that often accompanied discussion of Buddha's message in India was somewhat too esoteric for the Chinese taste. Still, in the difficult years surrounding the decline of the Han dynasty, Buddhist ideas, especially those of the Mahayana school, began to find adherents among intellectuals and ordinary people alike. As Buddhism increased in

popularity, it was frequently attacked by supporters of Confucianism and Daoism for its foreign origins. Some even claimed that Gautama Buddha had been a disciple of Lao Tzu. But such sniping did not halt the progress of Buddhism, and eventually the new faith was assimilated into Chinese culture, assisted by the efforts of such tireless advocates as the missionaries Fa Xian and Xuan Zang and the support of ruling elites in both northern and southern China (see The Rise and Decline of Buddhism and Daoism later in this chapter).

China Reunified: The Sui, the Tang, and the Song

After nearly four centuries of internal division, China was unified once again in 581 when Yang Jian (Yang Chien), a member of a respected aristocratic family in North China, founded a new dynasty, known as the Sui (581–618 C.E.). Yang Jian (who is also known by his reign title of Sui Wendi, or Sui Wen Ti) established his capital at the historic metropolis of Chang'an and began to extend his authority throughout the heartland of China.

Like his predecessors, the new emperor sought to create a unifying ideology for the state to enhance its efficiency. But where Liu Bang, the founder of the Han dynasty, had adopted Confucianism as the official doctrine to hold the empire together, Yang Jian turned to Daoism and Buddhism. He founded monasteries for both doctrines in the capital and appointed Buddhist monks to key positions as political advisers. Given Buddhism's popularity at the time, Yang Jian's use of Buddhist advisers helped to foster a sense of unity throughout the country. Buddhism would continue to influence state policy for the next two centuries.

Yang Jian was a builder as well as a conqueror, ordering the construction of a new canal from the capital to the confluence of the Wei and the Yellow Rivers nearly one hundred miles to the east. His son, the emperor Sui Yangdi (Sui Yang Ti), continued the process, and the famous Grand Canal, linking the two great rivers of China, the Yellow and the Yangtze, was completed during his reign. The new waterway, which was 1,400 miles long, was dug with conscript labor on the foundations of earlier canals dating back as far as the Zhou dynasty. The new

canal facilitated the shipment of grain and other commodities from the rice-rich southern provinces to the densely populated north. In fact, the canal symbolized the emergence of the lower Yangtze region as a pivotal area in the economy of medieval China. The canal also served other purposes, such as speeding communications between the two regions and permitting the rapid dispatch of troops to troubled provinces. Sui Yangdi also used the canal as an imperial highway for inspecting his empire. One imperial procession from the capital to the central Yangtze region was described as follows:

> Moreover the emperor caused to be built dragon boats, phoenix vessels, war boats of the "Yellow dragon" style, red battle cruisers, multi-decked transports, lesser vessels of bamboo slats. Boatmen hired from all the waterways . . . pulled the vessels by ropes of green silk on the imperial progress to Chiang-tu [Yangzhou]. The Emperor rode in the dragon boat, and civil and military officials of the fifth

�֍ Map 10.1 China under the Tang.

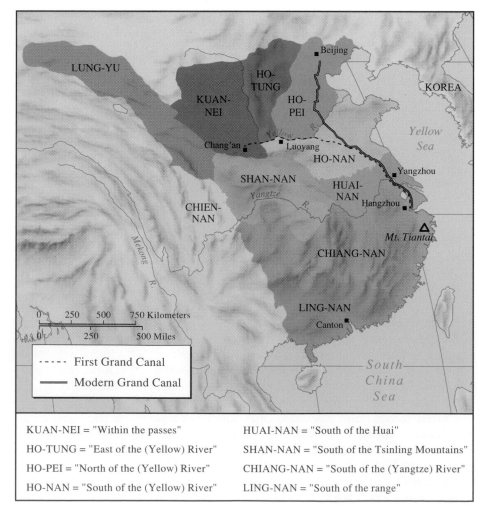

KUAN-NEI = "Within the passes"

HO-TUNG = "East of the (Yellow) River"

HO-PEI = "North of the (Yellow) River"

HO-NAN = "South of the (Yellow) River"

HUAI-NAN = "South of the Huai"

SHAN-NAN = "South of the Tsinling Mountains"

CHIANG-NAN = "South of the (Yangtze) River"

LING-NAN = "South of the range"

grade and above rode in the multi-decked transports; those of the ninth grade and above were given the vessels of yellow bamboo. The boats followed one another poop to prow for more than 200 leagues [about 65 miles]. The prefectures and counties through which they passed were ordered to prepare to offer provisions. Those who made bountiful arrangements were given an additional office or title; those who fell short were given punishments up to the death penalty.[4]

Despite such efforts to project the majesty of the imperial personage, the Sui dynasty came to an end immediately after Sui Yangdi's death. The Sui emperor was a tyrannical ruler, and his expensive campaigns against nomadic tribesmen in the north and against the state of Champa in Southeast Asia (see Chapter 11) aroused widespread unrest. But it was his campaign against the Korean kingdom of Koguryo that caused his downfall. The Korean peninsula had long been under Chinese influence, and several of its kings had paid tribute to China in the past (see Chapter 11). But the current ruler of Koguryo refused Sui Yangdi's peremptory demand to present his submission in person. Three attempts to conquer the kingdom failed, and on his return from the last effort in 618, the emperor was murdered in his palace. One of his generals, Li Yuan, took advantage of the instability that ensued and declared the foundation of a new dynasty, known as the Tang (T'ang). Building on the successes of its predecessor, the Tang lasted for three hundred years, until 907.

Li Yuan ruled for a brief period and then was elbowed aside by his son, Li Shimin (Li Shih-min), who assumed the reign title Tang Taizong (T'ang T'ai-tsung). Under his vigorous leadership, the Tang launched a program of internal renewal and external expansion that would make it one of the greatest dynasties in the long history of China. Li Shimin and his immediate successors attempted to strengthen the central government by streamlining its political institutions. A formal civil service examination system was established to serve as the primary method of recruiting officials for the civilian bureaucracy. The court also tried to solve the problem of land shortage and inequality of holdings that had brought down the proud Han by setting up an "equal lands" policy to distribute land to the peasants and break up the power of the large estates.

Tang rulers were equally energetic in trying to restore the power and majesty of China in regional affairs. During its first decades, the dynasty followed the pattern of the Han and attempted to secure the Chinese heartland by subduing the nomadic peoples beyond the Great Wall. Under the Tang, the northwest was pacified and given

the name of Xinjiang, or "new region." A long conflict with the Tibetan kingdom led for the first time to the extension of Chinese control over the vast and desolate plateau north of the Himalaya Mountains. With reason, China now claimed to be the foremost power in East Asia, and the emperor demanded fealty and tribute from all his fellow rulers beyond the frontier.

In some cases, the prestige and influence of the Tang traveled by peaceful means. During the Tang, for example, the Japanese first became closely acquainted with their neighbor to the west and dispatched official missions to China to learn more about its customs and institutions as a means of promoting the unification of the Japanese islands. Other neighboring states like Korea—now unified under the Silla dynasty—accepted tribute status and attempted to adopt the Chinese model (see Chapter 11). Also during the Tang, the southern provinces below the Yangtze were fully assimilated into the Chinese Empire, while the imperial court established commercial and diplomatic relations with the states of Southeast Asia.

Finally, the Tang dynasty witnessed a flowering of Chinese culture. Many modern observers feel that the era represents the apogee of Chinese creativity in poetry and sculpture and perhaps in painting as well, although the

✖ Map 10.2 Chang'an under the Sui and the Tang.

The Good Life in the High Tang

At the height of the Tang dynasty, China was at the apex of its power and magnificence. Here the Tang poet Du Fu describes a gala festival in the capital of Chang'an (Ch'ang-an) attended by the favored elite. The author's distaste for the spectacle of arrogance and waste is expressed in muted sarcasm.

Du Fu, A Poem

Third day of the third month
The very air seems new
In Ch'ang-an along the water
Many beautiful girls . . .
Firm, plump contours,
Flesh and bone proportioned.
Dresses of gauze brocade
Mirror the end of spring
Peacocks crimped in thread of gold
Unicorns in silver. . . .
Some are kin to the imperial favorite
Among them the Lady of Kuo and the Lady of Ch'in
  [Qin].
Camel-humps of purple meat

Brought in shining pans
The white meat of raw fish
Served on crystal platters
Don't tempt the sated palate.
All that is cut with fancy and
Prepared with care—left untouched.
Eunuchs, reins a-flying
Disturb no dust
Bring the "eight chef d'oeuvres"
From the palace kitchens.
Music of strings and pipes . . .
Accompanying the feasting
Moving the many guests
All of rank and importance.
Last comes a horseman
See him haughtily
Dismount near the screen
And step on the flowery carpet. . . .
The chancellor is so powerful
His mere touch will scorch
Watch you don't come near
Lest you displease him.

physical evidence for the latter is scarce. One reason for this explosion of culture was the influence of Buddhism, which affected art, literature, and philosophy, as well as religion and politics. Monasteries sprang up throughout China, and (as under the Sui) Buddhist monks served as advisers at the Tang imperial court. The city of Chang'an, now restored to the glory it had known as the capital of the Han dynasty, once again became the seat of the empire. It was possibly the greatest city in the world of its time, with an estimated population of nearly two million. The city was filled with temples and palaces, and its markets teemed with goods from all over the known world, as befit the eastern terminus of the Silk Road (see the box above).

But the Tang, like the Han, sowed the seeds of their own destruction. Tang rulers could not prevent the rise of internal forces that would ultimately weaken the dynasty and bring it to an end. Two ubiquitous problems were court intrigues and official corruption. Xuanzong (Hsuan

Tsung, who reigned from 712 to 756), one of the great Tang emperors and a renowned patron of the arts, was dominated in later life by one of his favorite concubines, the beautiful Yang Guifei (Yang Kuei-fei). One of her protégés launched a rebellion in 755 and briefly seized power in the capital of Chang'an. The revolt was eventually suppressed, and Yang Guifei, who is viewed as one of the great villains of Chinese history, was put to death. But the Tang never fully recovered from the catastrophe. The loss of power by the central government led to increased influence by great landed families inside China and chronic instability along the northern and western frontiers, where local military commanders ruled virtually without central government interference. It was an eerie repetition of the final decades of the Han.

The end finally came in the early tenth century, when border troubles with northern nomadic peoples increased, leading to the final collapse of the dynasty in 907. The Tang had followed a classical pattern of "using a barbarian to oppose a barbarian" by allying with a new nomadic people called the Uighurs (a Turkic-speaking people whose descendants continue to live throughout Central Asia) against their old rivals. But yet another nomadic people called the Kirghiz defeated the Uighurs and then turned on the Tang government in its moment of weakness and overthrew it.

For two generations, China slipped once again into chaos. This time, the period of foreign invasion and division was much shorter. In 960 a new dynasty, known as the Song (960–1279), rose to power. From the start, however, the Song (Sung) rulers encountered more problems than their predecessors. Although the founding emperor Song Taizu (Sung T'ai-tsu) was able to co-opt many of the powerful military commanders whose rivalry had brought the Tang dynasty to an end, he was unable to reconquer the northwestern part of the country from the nomadic Khitan peoples, who had formed their own Liao dynasty. The emperor therefore established his capital further to the east, at Kaifeng, where the Grand Canal intersected the Yellow River. Later, when pressures from the nomads in the north increased, the court was forced to move the capital even further south to Hangzhou (Hangchow) on the coast just south of the Yangtze River delta. The Song also lost control over Tibet. Despite their political and military weaknesses, which prevented both the northern and the southern Song from exerting the influence throughout the region that the Tang had displayed, the dynasty nevertheless ruled during a period of economic expansion, prosperity, and cultural achievement and is therefore considered among the more successful Chinese dynasties.

Yet the Song dynasty was never able to surmount the external challenge from the north, and that failure eventually brought about the end of the dynasty. During its final decades, the Song rulers were forced to pay tribute to the Jin (Chin) dynasty, ruled by the so-called Jurchen peoples from Manchuria. In the early thirteenth century, the Song, ignoring precedent and the fate of the Tang, formed an alliance with the Mongols, a new and obscure nomadic people from the Gobi Desert. As under the Tang, the decision proved to be a disaster. Within a few years, the Mongols had become a much more serious threat to China than the Jurchen. After defeating the Jin, the Mongols turned their attention to the Song, advancing on Song territory from both the north and the west. By this time, the Song empire had been weakened by internal factionalism and a loss of tax revenue to wealthy families. After a series of river battles and sieges marked by the use of catapults and gunpowder, the Song were defeated and the conquerors announced the cre-

CHRONOLOGY

Medieval China

Arrival of Buddhism in China	c. first century C.E.
Fall of the Han dynasty	220 C.E.
Sui dynasty	581–618
Tang dynasty	618–907
Li Bo and Du Fu	700s
Emperor Xuanzong	712–756
Song dynasty	960–1279
Wang Anshi	1021–1086
Southern Song dynasty	1127–1279
Mongol conquest of China	1279
Reign of Khubilai Khan	1260–1294
Fall of the Yuan dynasty	1368
Ming dynasty	1369–1644

ation of a new Yuan (Mongol) dynasty. Ironically, the Mongols had first learned about gunpowder from the Chinese (see Explosion in Central Asia: The Mongol Empire later in this chapter).

Political Structures: The Triumph of Confucianism

During the long era from the Sui to the end of the Song, a period of nearly seven hundred years, a mature political system based on principles originally established during the Qin and Han dynasties gradually emerged in China. In many respects, the institutions of the Song dynasty resembled those that had emerged centuries earlier during the Qin and the Han. As in the Han era, China was still a monarchy employing a large bureaucracy. At least in principle, officials were selected primarily on merit, rather than on the accident of birth. The tripartite division among the civil, military, and censorate authorities within the central government was retained. Beyond the capital, government was based on three echelons: provinces, districts or counties, and, at the lowest level, the rural village. After the Tang dynasty's brief flirtation with Buddhism, State Confucianism became the ideological cement that held the system together. The development of this system took several centuries, and it did not reach its height until the period of the Song dynasty.

EQUAL OPPORTUNITY IN CHINA:
THE CIVIL SERVICE EXAMINATION

At the apex of the government hierarchy was a Grand Council, assisted by a secretariat and a chancellery; it included representatives from all three authorities—civil, military, and censorate. Under the Grand Council was a Department of State Affairs composed of six ministries responsible for justice, military affairs, personnel, public works, revenue, and rites (ritual). This department was in effect the equivalent of a modern cabinet.

The Chinese army was divided into frontier forces, local units, and a capital guard. In theory, soldiers were recruited through a conscript system, but in practice the army was composed primarily of career troops, sometimes described as mercenaries.

The Tang dynasty continued the effort begun by the Qin dynasty to transform the basis of the bureaucracy from heredity to merit. During the Tang, a formal civil service examination system was established at several levels to recruit worthy candidates to the bureaucracy. To provide potential candidates with training in classical subjects, the court set up training academies at Chang'an (the capital) and Luoyang (a later capital). But the Tang never carried the new system to its logical conclusion. Despite efforts by the Tang rulers, the large aristocratic clans maintained considerable political influence at both the central and local levels. Members of the wealthy clans dominated the bureaucracy and the national university as well.

Like their governmental institutions, the Tang approach to State Confucianism as a set of principles governing Chinese political behavior represents a transitional phase between antiquity and the more fully developed institutions of the Song period. Under the early Tang rulers, Confucianists were forced to share pride of place at court with Buddhist and Daoist monks. Even the civil service examination asked questions relating to all three doctrines. Only after the Tang began to curb the power of influential Buddhist monasteries in the ninth century (see The Rise and Decline of Buddhism and Daoism later in this chapter) did Confucianism rise to the dominant position that it had achieved earlier during the Han.

Under the Song, Tang political institutions began to reach full maturity. For one thing, the Song brought an end to the influence of the aristocratic clans in the central administration. The power of the nobility had been irreparably weakened during the final years of the Tang dynasty and did not recover during the interregnum that followed its collapse. Early Song rulers took advantage of

that opportunity to strengthen the power of the imperial court and the central administration.

One way of doing this was to make the civil service examination system into the primary route to an official career. To reduce the power of the noble families, relatives of individuals serving in the imperial court, as well as eunuchs, were prohibited from taking the examinations. But if the Song rulers' objective was to make the bureaucracy more subservient to the court, they may have been disappointed. The rising professionalism of the bureaucracy provided it with an esprit de corps and an influence that sometimes enabled it to resist the whims of individual emperors.

Nevertheless, under the Song, the examination system attained the form that it would retain in later centuries. In general, three levels of examinations were administered. The first was a qualifying examination given annually at the provincial capital. Candidates who succeeded in this first stage (called *xiu cai*, or "received talents") were considered qualified to take the next examinations, but normally were not given positions in the bureaucracy except at the local level. Many stopped at this level and accepted positions as village teachers to train other candidates. Candidates who wished to go on could take a second examination given at the provincial capital every three years. Successful candidates (called *zhu ren*, or "elevated men") could apply for an official position. Some went on to take the final examination, which was given in the imperial capital, including a session at the imperial palace, once every three years. Those who passed (called *zhin shi*, or "presented scholars") were eligible for high positions in the central bureaucracy or for appointments as district magistrates.

The content of the examinations provided the final element of uniformity to the system. During the early Tang the subject matter included Buddhist and Daoist as well as Confucian texts (sometimes called the "three doctrines"), but by Song times examinations were based entirely on the Confucian classics. Candidates were expected to memorize passages and to be able to define the moral lessons they contained. The system guaranteed that successful candidates—and therefore officials—would have received a full dose of Confucian political and social ethics. Whether they followed those ethics, of course, was another matter. Many students complained about the rigors of memorization and the irrelevance of the process. Others brought crib notes into the examination hall (one enterprising candidate concealed an entire Confucian text in the lining of his cloak). One famous Tang scholar complained that if Mencius and other Confucian worthies had lived in his own day, they would have refused to sit for the examinations.

The Song authorities ignored such criticisms, but they did open the system to more people by allowing all males except criminals or members of certain restricted occupations to take the examinations. To provide potential candidates with schooling, training academies were set up at the provincial and district level. Without such academies, only individuals fortunate enough to receive training in the classics in family-run schools would have had the expertise to pass the examinations. Such policies represented a considerable improvement over earlier times, when most candidates came from the ranks of the elite. According to one historian, more than half of the successful candidates during the mid-Song period came from families that had not previously had a successful candidate for at least three generations.

But certain aspects of the system still prevented it from truly providing equal opportunity to all. In the first place, only males were eligible. Then again, the Song did not attempt to establish a system of universal elementary education. In practice, only those who had been given a basic education in the classics at home were able to enter the state-run academies and compete for a position in the bureaucracy. The poor had little chance.

Despite such weaknesses, the civil service examination system was an impressive achievement for its day and probably provided a more efficient government and more opportunity for upward mobility than were found in any other civilization of its time. Most Western governments, for example, only began to recruit officials on the basis of merit in the nineteenth century. Furthermore, by regulating the content of the examinations, the system helped provide China with a cultural uniformity lacking in empires elsewhere in Asia.

Whether the system resulted in an honest, efficient bureaucracy that governed with the talent and the virtue called for by Confucius and his disciples is another question. No system can eliminate all the quirks in human nature, and the Chinese bureaucracy suffered under many of the same limitations as modern government bureaucracies. Official arrogance, bureaucratic infighting, corruption, and legalistic interpretations of government regulations were as prevalent in medieval China as in bureaucracies the world over.

One chronic weakness of Chinese officialdom was actually a consequence of one of its strengths. Because of the strength and importance of the family system, officials were expected to use their position to help relatives. In fact, many wealthy families would provide an education to promising young men from poorer families within the clan in the hope of placing them in the bureaucracy. As we observed earlier, even Confucius pointed out that filial duty transcends loyalty to the community. What is nepotism in Western eyes was simply proper behavior in China. Chinese rulers attempted to circumvent this problem by assigning officials outside their home region (called the "law of avoidance"), but this policy met with only limited success.

The court also attempted to curb official misbehavior through the censorate. These specially trained officials were assigned to investigate possible cases of official wrongdoing and report directly to the court. The censorate was supposed to be independent of outside pressures to ensure that its members would feel free to report wrongdoing wherever it occurred. In practice, censors who displeased high court officials were often removed or even subjected to more serious forms of punishment, which reduced the effectiveness of the system.

LOCAL GOVERNMENT

The Song dynasty maintained the local government institutions that it had inherited from its predecessors. At the base of the government pyramid was the district (or county), governed by a magistrate. The magistrate, assisted by his staff, was responsible for maintaining law and order and collecting taxes within his jurisdiction. As the Chinese population grew to well above its pre-Tang levels, a district could exceed 100,000 people. Below the district was the basic unit of Chinese government, the village. Because villages were so numerous in China, the central government did not appoint an official at that level and allowed the villages to administer themselves. Village government was normally in the hands of a village council of elders, usually assisted by a village chief. The duties of the council were to maintain the local irrigation and transportation network, adjudicate local disputes, organize and maintain a militia, and assist in collecting taxes and delivering them to the district magistrate.

Village leaders were selected in various ways, but often the council of elders was made up of the heads of influential families in the village. Since many villages included members of several large clans, often the heads of the most influential clans comprised the council. Sometimes they were elected, but often the position was virtually hereditary. Individual families not belonging to larger clan groupings were often not represented, which meant that small families and unmarried members of the community had no one to speak for them, since they usually were in no position to represent their own interests.

As a rule, most Chinese had little involvement with government matters. When they had to deal with the government, they almost always turned to their village officials. Although the district magistrate was empowered to settle local civil disputes, most villagers preferred to resolve the problem among themselves, since referring the issue to the district would result in additional costs and bring unwanted attention to the village and its problems. It was expected that the magistrate and his staff would supplement their income by charging for such services, a practice that reduced the costs of the central government but also provided an opportunity for "squeeze," or the taking of bribes, a problem that plagued the Chinese bureaucracy down to modern times.

Economy and Society

During the long period between the Sui and the Song, the Chinese economy, like the government, grew considerably in size and complexity. China was still an agricultural society, but major changes were taking place within the economy and the social structure. The urban sector of the economy was becoming increasingly important, new social classes were beginning to appear, and the economic focus of the empire was beginning to shift from the Yellow River valley in the north to the Yangtze River valley in the center—a process that was encouraged both by the expansion of cultivation in the Yangtze delta and by the control exerted over the north by nomadic peoples during the Song.

The economic revival began shortly after the rise of the Tang. During the long period of internal division, land had become concentrated in the hands of aristocratic families, while most peasants were reduced to serfdom or slavery. Under the early Tang, the government tried to reduce the power of the landed nobility and maximize tax revenue by adopting the ancient "equal field" system (*zhun tian*, or *chun t'ien*), according to which land was allocated to farmers for life in return for an annual tax payment and three weeks of conscript labor.

At first the new system was vigorously enforced and led to increased rural prosperity and government revenue. But eventually the rich and the politically influential learned to manipulate the system for their own benefit, while the court began to reward government officials with large grants of land for their permanent use. Some received grants of up to 10,000 *mou* each (a *mou* is one-sixth of an acre), more than a hundred times larger than the average family plot. Meanwhile additional lands were concentrated in the hands of large Buddhist monasteries. The growing population, caused by a rise in food production and the extended period of social stability, also put steady pressure on the system. Eventually, the government abandoned the effort to equalize landholdings and returned the land to private hands, while attempting to prevent inequalities through the tax system. The failure to resolve the land problem was one of the primary reasons for the decline and fall of the Tang dynasty in the early tenth century.

The Song tried to resolve the land problem by returning to the successful programs of the early Tang and reducing the power of the wealthy landed aristocrats. During the late eleventh century, the reformist official Wang Anshi (Wang An-shih) attempted to limit the size of landholdings through progressive land taxes and provided cheap credit to poor peasants to help them avoid bankruptcy. His reforms met with some success, but other developments probably contributed more to the general agricultural prosperity under the Song. These included the opening of new lands in the Yangtze River valley, improvements in irrigation techniques such as the chain pump (a circular chain of square pallets on a treadmill that enabled farmers to lift considerable amounts of water or mud to a higher level), and the introduction of a new strain of quick-growing rice from Southeast Asia, which permitted farmers in warmer regions to plant and harvest two crops each year.

A COMMERCIAL REVOLUTION?

Major changes also took place in the Chinese urban economy, which witnessed a significant increase in trade and manufacturing. This process began under the Tang dynasty, but it was not entirely a product of deliberate state policy. In fact, early Tang rulers shared some of the traditional prejudice against commercial activities that had been prevalent under the Han and enacted a number of regulations that restricted trade. As had been the case under the Han, the state maintained monopolies over key commodities such as salt, tea (first introduced from Southeast Asia during the Han and popularized during the Tang era), and liquor (the Chinese had developed various techniques for distilling alcohol several centuries before similar developments in Europe). The government also initiated a number of large-scale projects, such as the construction of "ever-normal granaries" (i.e., always sufficient to meet the need) to provide food for the needy in times of shortage. The funds from these activities helped compensate the government for the loss of agricultural tax revenue.

Despite the restrictive policies of the state, the urban sector grew steadily larger and more complex, helped by several new technological developments. During the Tang, the Chinese mastered the art of manufacturing steel by mixing cast iron and wrought iron. The blast furnace was heated to a high temperature by burning coal, which had been used as a fuel in China from about the fourth century C.E. The resulting product was used in the manufacture of swords, sickles, and even suits of armor. By the eleventh century, more than 35,000 tons of steel were being produced annually. The introduction of cotton offered new opportunities in textile manufacturing. Gunpowder, invented by the Chinese during the Tang dynasty and used primarily for explosives and a primitive form of flamethrower, reached the West via the Arabs in the twelfth century.

By the late Tang and the Song, the nature of trade was also changing. In the past, most long-distance trade had been undertaken by state monopoly. By the time of the Song, private commerce was being actively encouraged, and many merchants engaged in shipping as well as in wholesale and retail trade.

As the pace of economic life quickened, guilds began to appear, along with a new money economy. Paper currency began to be used in the eighth and ninth centuries. Credit (at first called "flying money") also made its first appearance during the Tang. With the increased circulation of paper money, banking began to develop, as merchants found that strings of copper coins were too cumbersome for their increasingly complex operations. Unfortunately, early issues of paper currency were not backed by metal coinage and led to price inflation. Equally useful, if more prosaic, was the invention of the abacus, an early form of calculator that shortened the time needed for completing commercial transactions.

Long-distance trade, both overland and by sea, expanded under the Tang and the Song. Trade with countries and peoples to the west had been carried on for centuries (see Chapter 3), but it had declined dramatically between the fourth and the sixth century C.E. as a result of the collapse of the Han and the Roman Empire. It began to revive with the rise of the Tang and the simultaneous unification of much of the Middle East under the Arabs. During the Tang era, the Silk Road, whose eastern segment thrust through the wastes of what is now China's Xinjiang province, revived and then reached its zenith. Much of the trade was carried by the Turkic-speaking Uighurs. During the Tang, Uighur caravans of two-humped Bactrian camels (a hardy variety native to Iran and regions to the northeast) carried goods back and forth between China and the countries of South Asia and the Middle East.

In actuality, the Silk Road was composed of a number of separate routes. The first to be used, probably because of the jade found in the mountains south of Khotan, ran along the southern rim of the Taklimakan Desert via Kashgar and thence through the Pamir Mountains into Bactria. The first Buddhist missionaries traveled this route from India to China.

Eventually, however, this area began to dry up, and traders were forced to seek other routes. From a climatic standpoint, the best route for the Silk Road was to the north of the Tian Shan (Heavenly Mountains), where moisture-laden northwesterly winds created pastures where animals could graze. But the area was frequently infested by bandits who preyed on unwary travelers. Most caravans therefore followed the southern route, which passed along the fringes of the Taklimakan Desert to Kashgar and down into northwestern India. Travelers avoided the direct route through the desert (in the Uighur language, the name means "go in, and you won't come out") and trudged from oasis to oasis along the southern slopes of the Tian Shan. The oases were created

◆ **Tang Camel.** During the Tang dynasty, trade between China, India, and the Middle East along the famous Silk Road increased rapidly and introduced new Central Asian motifs to Chinese culture. As seen in this sturdy example, the Bactrian two-humped camel played a major role in carrying goods along the trade route, since its ability to withstand long periods without water enabled it to survive the grueling trek across the Central Asian deserts. Created as tomb figures, and therefore preserved for us today, are numerous ceramic studies of horses and camels, along with officials, court ladies, and servants painted in brilliant gold, green, and blue lead glazes.

◆ The Heavenly Mountains. Of the three possible routes over the Silk Road between China and Central Asia, the most satisfactory, from an ecological point of view, was along the northern slopes of the Heavenly Mountains, where moist north-westerly winds and runoff from the showy peaks of the mountains provided lush grasses for the camels to feed on, and water for parched and weary merchants. Unfortunately, this region, shown above, also harbored nomadic peoples who preyed on merchant caravans for their livelihood.

by the water runoff from winter snows in the mountains, which then dried up in the searing heat of the desert.

The Silk Road was so hazardous that shipping goods by sea became increasingly popular, creating what one historian has described as "the first period of great oceanic commerce in the history of the world." China had long been engaged in sea trade with other countries in the region, but most of the commerce was originally in the hands of Korean, Japanese, or Southeast Asian merchants. Chinese maritime trade, however, was stimulated by the invention of the compass and technical improvements in shipbuilding such as the widespread use of the sternpost rudder and the lug sail (which enabled ships to sail close to the wind). If Marco Polo's observations can be believed, by the thirteenth century Chinese junks had multiple sails and weighed up to two thousand tons, much larger than contemporary ships in the West. The Chinese governor of Canton in the early twelfth century remarked:

> According to the government regulations concerning sea-going ships, the larger ones can carry several hundred men, and the smaller ones may have more than a hundred men on board. . . . The ship's pilots are acquainted with the configuration of the coasts; at night they steer by the stars, and in the day-time by the Sun. In dark weather they look at the south-pointing needle. They also use a line a hundred feet long with a hook at the end, which they let down to take samples of mud from the sea-bottom; by its appearance and smell they can determine their whereabouts.[5]

Regional trade increased substantially during the era of the Tang and the Song. The Chinese exported tea, silk, and porcelain to the countries beyond the South China Sea, receiving exotic woods, precious stones, and various tropical goods in exchange. Seaports on the South China coast exported sweet oranges, lemons, and peaches in return for grapes, walnuts, and pomegranates. Along the Silk Road to China came raw hides, furs, and horses. Chinese aristocrats, their appetite for material consumption stimulated by the affluence of Chinese society during much of the Tang and the Song periods, were fascinated by the exotic goods and the flora and the fauna of the desert and the tropical lands of the South Seas. As we have seen, the city of Chang'an became the eastern terminus of the Silk Road and perhaps the wealthiest city in the world during the Tang era. The major port of exit in southern China was Canton, where an estimated 100,000 merchants lived. Their activities were controlled by an imperial commissioner sent from the capital.

Some of this trade was a product of the tribute system, which the Chinese rulers used as an element of their foreign policy. The Chinese viewed the outside world as they viewed their own society—in a hierarchical manner. Rulers of smaller countries along the periphery were viewed as "younger brothers" of the Chinese emperor; they owed fealty to him in a manner reminiscent of the feudal system in medieval Europe. Foreign rulers who accepted the relationship were required to pay tribute to their "liege lord" and to promise not to harbor enemies of the Chinese Empire. But the foreign rulers also benefited from the relationship. Not only did it confer legitimacy upon them, but they often received magnificent gifts from their "elder brother" as a reward for good behavior. Merchants from their countries also gained access to the vast Chinese market.

In the long run, perhaps the most important consequence of China's growing trade relationship with other countries was the importation of Buddhism, which was brought to China along the Silk Road by Indian missionaries. Later, Chinese pilgrims like Fa Xian and Xuan Zang traveled to India to bring back more information about the exciting new doctrine (see The Rise and Decline of Buddhism and Daoism later in this chapter). In the early fifth century, Syrian merchants introduced Christianity to China, and a Nestorian monastery was established in the Tang capital of Chang'an.

These political and economic changes also affected Chinese society during the Tang and Song era. For one thing, it became much more complex. Whereas previously China had been almost exclusively rural, with a small urban class of merchants, artisans, and workers almost entirely dependent upon the state, the cities had now grown into an important, if statistically still insignificant, part of the population. Urban life, too, had changed. Cities were no longer primarily administrative centers dominated by officials and their families, but now included a much broader mix of officials, merchants, artisans, touts, and entertainers. Although many were still employed by the government, increasing numbers were operating within the private sector. For the more fortunate city dwellers, it was indeed an age of affluence.

In the countryside, equally significant changes were taking place, as the relatively rigid demarcation between the landed aristocracy and the mass of the rural population gave way to a more complex mixture of landed gentry, free peasants, sharecroppers, and landless laborers. Perhaps the most significant development was the rise of the landed gentry—often called the scholar-gentry because they were both an economic and an educated elite—as the most influential force in Chinese society. The gentry class controlled much of the wealth in the rural areas and produced the majority of the candidates for the bureaucracy. The gentry were also the repository of the sacred doctrine of Confucianism and the primary producers and consumers of Chinese culture.

By virtue of their possession of land and specialized knowledge of the Confucian classics, the gentry had replaced the aristocracy as the political and economic elite of Chinese society. Unlike the aristocracy, however, the gentry did not form an exclusive class separated by the accident of birth from the remainder of the population. Upward and downward mobility between the scholar-gentry class and the remainder of the population was not uncommon and may have been a key factor in the stability and longevity of the system. A position in the bureaucracy opened the doors to wealth and prestige for the individual and his family, but it was no guarantee of success, and the fortunes of individual families might experience a rapid rise and fall. The soaring ambitions and arrogance of China's landed gentry are vividly described in the following wish list set in poetry by a young bridegroom of the Tang dynasty:

> *Chinese slaves to take charge of treasury and barn,*
> *Foreign slaves to take care of my cattle and sheep.*
> *Strong-legged slaves to run by saddle and stirrup when I ride,*
> *Powerful slaves to till the fields with might and main,*
> *Handsome slaves to play the harp and hand the wine;*
> *Slim-waisted slaves to sing me songs, and dance;*
> *Dwarfs to hold the candle by my dining-couch.*[6]

DAILY LIFE IN TRADITIONAL CHINA

Much more is known about the daily lives of ordinary Chinese during this era than during antiquity. Literature and the visual arts provide us with a much clearer picture

◆ **Spring Festival on the River.**   Besides being an artistic masterpiece, this Chinese scroll, known as *Spring Festival on the River,* is one of the most remarkable social documents of early twelfth-century China. Nearly thirty-three feet in length, it records with encyclopedic detail various aspects of Chinese soci- ety from the imperial court down to the lowliest peasants as they prepare for the spring festival. The viewer is expected to unfold the scroll slowly from right to left and linger on each segment as the scroll follows the path along the Yellow River to the Song capital of Kaifeng, then the most sophisticated city in the world.

of living conditions from the Tang to the Ming than for the period before the Han. For affluent Chinese, life offered many more pleasures than had been available to their ancestors. There were new forms of entertainment, such as playing cards and chess (brought from India, although an early form had been invented in China during the Zhou dynasty); new forms of transportation, such as the paddle-wheel boat and horseback riding (made possible by the introduction of the stirrup); better means of communication (block printing was first invented in the eighth century C.E.); and new tastes for the palate introduced from lands beyond the frontier. Tea had been introduced from the Burmese frontier by monks as early as the Han dynasty, and brandy and other concentrated spirits produced by the distillation of alcohol were invented in the seventh century.

The vast majority of the Chinese people still lived off the land in villages scattered from the dusty hills north of the Yellow River to the lush flatlands of the Yangtze delta and the hills of southern China. Villages ranged in size from a few dozen residents to several thousand. A group of villages would be linked to a larger market town in the vicinity and, beyond that, to the district capital.

The life of the peasants was bounded by their village. Although many communities were connected to the outside world by roads or rivers, the average Chinese rarely left the confines of their native village except for an occasional visit to a nearby market town. This isolation was psychological as well as physical, for most Chinese identified with their immediate environment and had difficulty envisioning themselves living beyond the bamboo hedges or mud walls that marked the limit of their horizon.

An even more basic unit than the village in the lives of most Chinese, of course, was the family. The ideal was the joint family—with at least three generations under one roof. Because of the heavy labor requirements of rice farming, the tradition of the joint family was especially prevalent in the south. When a son married, he was expected to bring his new wife back to live in his parents' home. Often the parents added a new wing to the house for the new family. If a woman married, she went to live with her husband; women who did not marry remained as spinsters in the home where they grew up.

Chinese village architecture reflected these traditions. Most family dwellings were simple, consisting of one or at most two rooms. They were usually constructed of dried mud, stone, or brick, depending on available materials and the prosperity of the family. Roofs were of thatch or tile, and the floors were usually of packed dirt. Large houses were often built in a square around an inner courtyard, thus guaranteeing privacy from the outside world.

Within the family unit, the eldest male theoretically ruled as an autocrat. He was responsible for presiding over ancestral rites at an altar, usually in the main room of the house. He had traditional legal rights over his wife, and if she did not provide him with a male heir, he was permitted to take a second wife. She, on the other hand, had no recourse to divorce (see the box on p. 346). As the old saying went, "Marry a chicken, follow the chicken; marry a dog, follow the dog." Wealthy Chinese might keep concubines, who lived in a separate room in the house and sometimes competed with the legal wife for precedence.

In accordance with Confucian tradition, children were expected, above all, to obey their parents, who not only determined their children's careers but normally selected their marriage partners. Filial piety was viewed as an absolute moral good, above virtually all other moral obligations. Even today duty to one's parents is considered important in traditional Chinese families, and the tombstones of deceased Chinese are often decorated with tile paintings depicting the filial acts that they performed during their lifetime.

The tradition of male superiority continued from ancient times into the medieval era, especially under the southern Song when it was reinforced by Neo-Confucianism. Female children were considered to be less desirable than males, because they could not undertake heavy work in the fields or carry on the family traditions.

In addition, a girl's parents were expected to provide a dowry to her husband when she married. Poor families often sold their daughters to wealthy villagers to serve as concubines, and female infanticide was not uncommon in times of famine to ensure there would be food for the remainder of the family. Concubines had few legal rights, and female domestic servants even fewer.

As in most traditional societies, there were exceptions to the low status of women in Chinese society. Women had substantial property rights and retained control over their dowries even after divorce or the death of the husband. Wives were frequently an influential force within the home, often handling the accounts and taking primary responsibility for raising the children. Some were active in politics. The outstanding example was Wu Zhao (625?–706?), popularly known as Empress Wu. Selected by Emperor Tang Taizong as a concubine, after his death she rose to a position of supreme power at court. At first she was content to rule through her sons, but in 690 she declared herself empress of China. To bolster her claim of legitimacy, she cited a Buddhist sutra to the effect that a woman would rule the world seven hundred years after the death of Gautama Buddha. For her presumption, she has been vilified by later Chinese historians, but she was actually quite a capable ruler. She was responsible for giving meaning to the civil service examination system and was the first to select graduates of the examinations for the highest positions in government. During her last years, she reportedly fell under the influence of courtiers and was deposed in 705, at the age of eighty.

*E*xplosion in Central Asia: The Mongol Empire

The Mongols, who succeeded the Song as the rulers of China in the late thirteenth century, rose to power in Asia with stunning rapidity. When Genghis Khan (also known as Chinggis Khan), the founder of Mongol greatness, was born, the Mongols were a relatively obscure pastoral people in the region of modern-day Outer Mongolia. Like most of the nomadic peoples in the region, they were organized loosely into clans and tribes and even lacked a common name for themselves. Rivalry among the various tribes over pasture land, livestock, and booty was intense and increased at the end of the twelfth century as a result of a growing population and the consequent overgrazing of pastures. Since they had no source of subsistence besides their herds, the Mongols were, in the words of one historian, in a "state of stress."

❧ *The Saintly Miss Wu* ❧

The idea that a wife should sacrifice her wants to the needs of her husband and family was deeply embedded in traditional Chinese society. Widows in particular had few rights, and their remarriage was strongly condemned. In this account from a story by Hung Mai, a twelfth-century writer, the widowed Miss Wu wins the respect of the entire community by faithfully serving her mother-in-law.

Hung Mai, A Song Family Saga

Miss Wu served her mother-in-law very filially. Her mother-in-law had an eye ailment and felt sorry for her daughter-in-law's solitary and poverty-stricken situation, so suggested that they call in a son-in-law for her and thereby get an adoptive heir. Miss Wu announced in tears, "A woman does not serve two husbands. I will support you. Don't talk this way." Her mother-in-law, seeing that she was determined, did not press her. Miss Wu did spinning, washing, sewing, cooking, and cleaning for her neighbors, earning perhaps a hundred cash a day, all of which she gave to her mother-in-law to cover the cost of firewood and food. If she was given any meat, she would wrap it up to take home.

Miss Wu was honest by nature. She did not chat idly, and even if other people's things were right in front of her, she did not look at them, wanting only what was her own. Thus neighbors often engaged her, and they helped out her and her mother-in-law, so they managed to avoid dying of hunger or cold.

Once when her mother-in-law was cooking rice, a neighbor called to her, and to avoid overcooking the rice she dumped it into a pan. Owing to her bad eyes, however, she mistakenly put it in the dirty chamber pot. When Miss Wu returned and saw it, she did not say a word. She went to a neighbor to borrow some cooked rice for her mother-in-law and took the dirty rice and washed it to eat herself.

One day in the daytime neighbors saw [Miss Wu] ascending into the sky amid colored clouds. Startled, they told her mother-in-law, who said, "Don't be foolish. She just came back from pounding rice for someone, and is lying down on the bed. Go and look." They went to the room and peeked in and saw her sound asleep. Amazed, they left.

When Miss Wu woke up, her mother-in-law told her what happened, and she said, "I just dreamed of two young boys in blue clothes holding documents and riding on the clouds. They grabbed my clothes and said the Emperor of Heaven had summoned me. They took me to the gate of heaven and I was brought in to see the emperor, who was seated beside a balustrade. He said 'Although you are just a lowly ignorant village woman, you are able to serve your old mother-in-law sincerely and work hard. You really deserve respect.' He gave me a cup of aromatic wine and a string of cash, saying, 'I will supply you. From now on you will not need to work for others.' I bowed to thank him and came back, accompanied by the two boys. Then I woke up."

There was in fact a thousand cash on the bed, and the room was filled with a fragrance. They then realized that the neighbors' vision had been a spirit journey. From this point on even more people asked her to work for them, and she never refused. But the money that had been given to her she kept for her mother-in-law's use. Whatever they used promptly reappeared, so the thousand cash was never exhausted. The mother-in-law also regained her sight in both eyes.

This challenge was met by the great Mongol chieftain Genghis Khan. Born sometime during the 1160s, Genghis Khan (his original name was Temuchin, or Temujin) was the son of one of the more impoverished nobles of his tribe. When Temuchin was still a child, his father was murdered by a rival, and the young boy was temporarily forced to seek refuge in the wilderness. Described by one historian as tall, adroit, and vigorous, young Temuchin gradually unified the Mongol tribes through his prowess and the power of his personality. In 1206 he was elected Genghis Khan (universal ruler) at a massive tribal meeting somewhere in the Gobi Desert. From that time on, he devoted himself to military pursuits. Mongol nomads were now forced to pay taxes and were subject to military conscription. "Man's highest joy," Genghis Khan reportedly remarked, "is in victory: to conquer one's enemies, to pursue them, to deprive them of their possessions, to make their beloved weep, to ride on their horses, and to embrace their wives and daughters."[7]

The army that Genghis Khan unleashed on the world was not exceptionally large—totaling less than 130,000 in 1227, at a time when the total Mongol population numbered between one and two million. But their mastery of military tactics set the Mongols apart from their rivals. Their tireless flying columns of mounted warriors surrounded their enemies and harassed them like cattle, luring them into pursuit, then ambushing them with flank attacks. John Plano Carpini, a contemporary Franciscan friar, remarked:

> As soon as they discover the enemy they charge and each one unleashes three or four arrows. If they see that they can't break him, they retreat in order to entice the enemy to pursue, thus luring him into an ambush prepared in advance. If they conclude that the enemy army is stronger, they retire for a day or two and ravage neighboring areas. . . . Or they strike camp in a well chosen position, and when the enemy army begins to pass by, they appear unexpectedly. . . . Their military stratagems are numerous. At the moment of an enemy cavalry attack, they place prisoners and foreign auxiliaries in the forefront of their own position, while positioning the bulk of their own troops on the right and left wings to envelop the adversary, thus giving the enemy the impression that they are more numerous than in reality. If the adversary defends himself well, they open their ranks to let him pass through in flight, after which they launch in pursuit and kill as many as possible.[8]

In the years after the election of Temuchin as universal ruler, the Mongols defeated tribal groups to their west and then turned their attention to the seminomadic non-Chinese kingdoms in northern China. There they discovered that their adversaries were armed with a weapon called a fire-lance, an early form of flamethrower. Gunpowder had been invented in China during the late Tang period, and by the early thirteenth century a type of fire-lance had been developed that could spew out a combination of flame and projectiles that could travel as far as thirty or forty yards and inflict considerable damage on the enemy. The following account of a battle in the 1230s between Mongol forces and the army of the state of Jin (Chin) in northern China describes the effects of this weapon:

> On the fifth day of the fifth month they sacrificed to Heaven, secretly prepared fire-lances, and embarked 450 Chin soldiers outside the south gate, whence they sailed first east and then north. During the night they killed the enemy guards outside the dikes, and reached the Wang family temple. . . . Kuan-Nu divided his small craft into squadrons of five, seven and ten boats, which came out from behind the defenses and caught the Mongols both from front and rear, using the fire-spouting lances. The

Mongols could not stand up to this and fled, losing more than 3500 men drowned. Finally their stockades were burnt, and our force returned.[9]

Before the end of the thirteenth century, the fire-lance had evolved into the much more effective hand gun and cannon. These inventions came too late to save China from the Mongols, however, and were transmitted to Europe by the early fourteenth century by foreigners employed by the Mongol rulers of China.

While some Mongol armies were engaged in the conquest of northern China, others traveled farther afield and advanced as far as central Europe (see the box on p. 348). Only the death of the Great Khan may have prevented an all-out Mongol attack on western Europe. In 1231 they attacked Persia and then defeated the Abbasids at Baghdad in 1258 (see Chapter 7). Mongol forces attacked the Song from the west in the 1260s and finally defeated the remnants of the Song navy in 1279.

By then, the Mongol Empire was quite different from what it had been under its founder. Prior to the conquests of Genghis Khan, the Mongols had been purely nomadic. They spent their winters in the southern plains where they found suitable pastures for their cattle and traveled north in the summer to wooded areas where the water was sufficient. They lived in round tents covered with felt (called yurts), which were lightly constructed so that they could be easily transported. For food, the Mongols depended on milk and meat from their herds and game from hunting.

To administer the new empire, Genghis Khan set up a capital city at Karakorum in present-day Outer Mongolia, but prohibited his fellow Mongols from practicing sedentary occupations or living in cities. But under his successors, the Mongols began to adapt to their conquered areas. As one khan remarked, quoting his Chinese adviser, "Although you inherited the Chinese Empire on horseback, you cannot rule it from that position." Mongol aristocrats began to enter administrative positions, while commoners took up sedentary occupations as farmers or merchants.[10]

The territorial nature of the empire also changed. Following tribal custom, at the death of the ruling khan, the territory was distributed among his heirs. The once-united empire of Genghis Khan was thus divided into several separate khanates, each under the autonomous rule of one of his sons by his principal wife. One of his sons was awarded the khanate of Chaghadai in Central Asia with its capital at Samarkand; another ruled Persia from the conquered city of Baghdad; a third took charge of the khanate of Kipchak (commonly known as the

⇝ A Letter to the Pope ⇜

In 1243 Pope Innocent IV dispatched the Franciscan friar John Plano Carpini to the Mongol headquarters at Karakorum to appeal to the great khan to cease his attacks on Christians. After a considerable wait, Carpini was given the following reply, which could not have pleased the pope. The letter was discovered recently in the Vatican archives.

A Letter from Kuyuk Khan to Pope Innocent IV

"By the power of the Eternal Heaven, We are the all-embracing Khan of all the Great Nations. It is our command:

"This is a decree, sent to the great Pope that he may know and pay heed.

"After holding counsel with the monarchs under your suzerainty, you have sent us an offer of subordination, which we have accepted from the hands of your envoy.

"If you should act up to your word, then you, the great Pope, should come in person with the monarchs to pay us homage and we should thereupon instruct you concerning the commands of the Yasak.

"Furthermore, you have said it would be well for us to become Christians. You write to me in person about this matter, and have addressed to me a request. This, your request, we cannot understand.

"Furthermore, you have written me these words: 'You have attacked all the territories of the Magyars and other Christians, at which I am astonished. Tell me, what was their crime?' These, your words, we likewise cannot understand. Jenghiz Khan and Ogatai Khakan revealed the commands of Heaven. But those whom you name would not believe the commands of Heaven. Those of whom you speak showed themselves highly presumptuous and slew our envoys. Therefore, in accordance with the commands of the Eternal Heaven the inhabitants of the aforesaid countries have been slain and annihilated. If not by the command of Heaven, how can anyone slay or conquer out of his own strength?

"And when you say: 'I am a Christian. I pray to God. I arraign and despise others,' how do you know who is pleasing to God and to whom He allots His grace? How can you know it, that you speak such words?

"Thanks to the power of the Eternal Heaven, all lands have been given to us from sunrise to sunset. How could anyone act other than in accordance with the commands of Heaven? Now your own upright heart must tell you: 'We will become subject to you, and will place our powers at your disposal.' You in person, at the head of the monarchs, all of you, without exception, must come to tender us service and pay us homage, then only will we recognize your submission. But if you do not obey the commands of Heaven, and run counter to our orders, we shall know that you are our foe.

"That is what we have to tell you. If you fail to act in accordance therewith, how can we foresee what will happen to you? Heaven alone knows."

Golden Horde). But it was one of his grandsons, named Khubilai Khan (1260–1294), who completed the conquest of the Song and established a new Chinese dynasty, called the Yuan (from a phrase in the *Book of Changes* referring to the "original creative force" of the universe). Khubilai moved the capital of China northward to Khanbaliq (the city of the Khan), which was located on a major trunk route from the Great Wall to the plains of northern China. Later the city would be known by the Chinese name Beijing, or Peking (Northern Capital).

Mongol Rule in China

At first China's new rulers exhibited impressive vitality. Under the leadership of the talented Khubilai Khan, the Yuan continued to flex their muscles by attempting to expand their empire. Mongol armies advanced into the Red River valley and reconquered Vietnam, which had declared its independence after the fall of the Tang three hundred years earlier. Mongol fleets were launched against Malay kingdoms in Java and Sumatra and twice against the islands of Japan. Only the expedition against Vietnam succeeded, however, and even there success was temporary. The Vietnamese counterattacked and eventually drove the Mongols back across the border. The attempted conquest of Japan was even more disastrous. On one occasion, a massive storm destroyed the Mongol fleet, killing thousands (see Chapter 11).

Logistics may explain why the Mongol armies failed elsewhere after succeeding in China. The Mongol attacks on Japan, Vietnam, and the Indonesian kingdoms were too far afield for the army to be easily supported and resupplied. The terrain may also have contributed to their defeats. Mongol tactics, such as cavalry charges and siege warfare, were less effective in tropical terrain and hilly regions than they were closer to the arid Mongol heartland.

The Mongols had more success in governing China. After a failed attempt to administer their conquest as they had ruled their own tribal society (some advisers reportedly even suggested that the plowed fields be transformed into pasture), Mongol rulers adapted to the Chinese political system and made use of local talents in the bureaucracy. The tripartite division of the administration into civilian, military, and censorate was retained, as were the six ministries. The civil service system, which had been abolished in the north in 1237 and in the south forty years later, was revived in the early fourteenth century. Eventually, even the civil service system was revived, as was the state cult of Confucius, although Khubilai Khan himself was a Buddhist.

But there were some key differences. Culturally, the Mongols were strikingly different from the Chinese and remained apart as a separate class with their own laws. The highest positions in the bureaucracy were usually staffed by Mongols. Although some leading Mongols followed their ruler in converting to Buddhism, most commoners retained their traditional religion. Even those who adopted Buddhism chose the Lamaist variety from Tibet, which emphasized divination and magic.

Despite these differences, some historians believe that the Mongol dynasty won considerable support from the majority of the Chinese. The people of the north, after all, were used to foreign rule, and although those living further to the south may have resented their alien conquerors, they may have gradually come to respect the stability, unity, and economic prosperity that the Mongols initially brought to China.

Indeed, the Mongols' greatest achievement may have been the prosperity they fostered. At home, they continued

✂ Map 10.3 Asia under the Mongols.

⇒ *How Khubilai Khan Chooses His Consorts* ⇐

All Chinese emperors had a number of concubines in addition to their formal wives. Although this practice helped ensure that there would be one or more potential heirs to the throne, it also often led to disputes over the succession. In this passage, the Italian adventurer Marco Polo describes how the great Mongol ruler Khubilai Khan selected members of his harem. Since all of the official wives had large numbers of courtiers in their entourage, rivalry within the imperial court was not uncommon. Although some historians doubt that Marco Polo was ever in China, his account is generally viewed as a reliable description of thirteenth-century China.

Marco Polo, *The Travels of Marco Polo*

The personal appearance of the great Khan, lord of lords, whose name is Kublai, is such as I shall now tell you. He is of a good stature, neither tall nor short, but of a middle height. He has a becoming amount of flesh, and is very shapely in all his limbs. His complexion is white and red, the eyes black and fine, the nose well formed and well set on. He has four wives, whom he retains permanently as his legitimate consorts. . . .

When the emperor desires the society of one of these four consorts, he will sometimes send for the lady to his apartment and sometimes visit her at her own. He has also a great number of concubines, and I will tell you how he obtains them.

You must know that there is a tribe of Tartars called Kungurat, who are noted for their beauty. The great Khan sends his commissioners to the province to select four or five hundred, or whatever number may be or-dered, of the most beautiful young women, according to the scale of beauty enjoined upon them. . . . The commissioners on arriving assemble all the girls of the province, in the presence of appraisers appointed for the purpose. These carefully survey the points of each girl in succession, as for example her hair, her complexion, eyebrows, mouth, lips, and the proportion of all her limbs. . . . And whatever standard the great Khan may have fixed for those that are to be brought to him, . . . the commissioners select the required number from those who have attained that standard, and bring them to him. And when they reach his presence he has them appraised anew by other parties, and has a selection made of thirty or forty of those, who then get the highest valuation. Now every year a hundred of the most beautiful maidens of this tribe are sent to the great Khan, who commits them to the charge of certain elderly ladies dwelling in his palace. And these old ladies make the girls sleep with them, in order to ascertain if they have sweet breath and do not snore, and are sound in all their limbs. Then such of them as are of approved beauty, and are good and sound in all respects, are appointed to attend on the emperor by turns. Thus six of these damsels take their turn for three days and nights, and wait on him when he is in his chamber and when he is in his bed, to serve him in any way, and to be entirely at his orders. At the end of the three days and nights they are relieved by another six. And so throughout the year, there are reliefs of maidens by six and six, changing every three days and nights.

the relatively tolerant economic policies of the southern Song, and by bringing the entire Eurasian landmass under a single rule, they encouraged long-distance trade, particularly along the Silk Road, now dominated by Muslim merchants from Central Asia. To promote trade, the Grand Canal was extended from the Yellow River to the capital. Adjacent to the canal, a paved highway was constructed that extended all the way from the Song capital of Hangzhou to its Mongol counterpart at Khanbaliq.

The capital was a magnificent city. According to the Italian merchant Marco Polo, who resided there during the reign of Khubilai Khan, it was twenty-four miles in diameter and surrounded by thick walls of earth penetrated by twelve massive gates. He described the old Song capital of Hangzhou as a noble city where "so many pleasures may be found that one fancies himself to be in Paradise."

Ironically, while many of their subjects prospered, the Mongols themselves often did not. Burdened by low salaries and heavy military obligations that left them little time for their herds, many Mongol warriors became so impoverished that they were forced to sell their sons and daughters into slavery. Eventually, the Yuan government had to provide funds from the imperial treasury to buy them back and return them to their families.

The magnificence of the empire impressed foreign visitors, including Marco Polo, whose tales of the glories of

Cathay (a name adapted from Kitai, the Russian word for China) were not believed when he returned to Europe (see the box on p. 350). But the Yuan eventually fell victim to the same fate that had afflicted other powerful dynasties in China. In fact, it was one of the most short-lived of the great dynasties, lasting less than one hundred years. Excessive spending on foreign conquest, inadequate tax revenues, factionalism and corruption at court and in the bureaucracy, and growing internal instability, brought about in part by a famine in central China in the 1340s, all contributed to the dynasty's demise. Khubilai Khan's successors lacked his administrative genius, and by the middle of the next century, the Yuan dynasty in China, like the Mongol khanates elsewhere in Central Asia, had begun to decline rapidly.

The immediate instrument of Mongol defeat was Zhu Yuanzhang (Chu Yuan-chang), the son of a poor peasant in the lower Yangtze valley. After losing most of his family in the famine of the 1340s, Zhu became an itinerant monk and then the leader of a band of bandits. In the 1360s, unrest spread throughout the country, and after defeating a number of rivals, Zhu Yuanzhang put an end to the disintegrating Yuan regime and declared the foundation of a new Ming (Bright) dynasty (1369–1644).

The Mongols' Place in History

The Mongols were the last, and arguably the greatest, of the nomadic peoples who came thundering out of the steppes of Central Asia, pillaging and conquering the territories of their adversaries. What caused this extraordinary burst of energy, and why were the Mongols so much more successful than their predecessors? Historians are divided. Some have suggested that drought and overpopulation may have depleted the available pasture on the steppes. Others have cited the ambition and genius of Genghis Khan, who was able to arouse a sense of personal loyalty unusual in a society where commitments were ordinarily tribal in nature. Still others point to his reliance on the organizational unit known as the *ordos*, described by the historian S. A. M. Adshead as "a system of restructuring tribes into decimal units whose top level of leadership was organized on bureaucratic lines." Although the *ordos* system had been used by the Xiongnu and other nomadic peoples before them, the Mongols applied it to create disciplined military units that were especially effective against the relatively freewheeling tactics of their rivals on the steppes and devastating against the relatively immobile armies of the sedentary states in their path. Once organized, the Mongols used their superior horsemanship and blitzkrieg tactics effectively, while taking advantage of divisions within the enemy ranks and borrowing more advanced military technology.

Once in power, however, the Mongols' underlying weaknesses eventually proved fatal. Unlike some of their predecessors, the Mongols had difficulty making the transition from the nomadic life of the steppes to the sedentary life of the villages, while their unwieldy system of royal succession led to instability in the leadership ranks. Still, although the Mongol era was just a brief interlude in the long sweep of human history, it was rich in consequences.

The era of Mongol expansion has usually been portrayed as a tragic period in human history. Their conquests resulted in widespread death and suffering throughout the civilized world. Nations and empires were humbled, cities destroyed, and irrigation systems laid waste. Then, just when the ravages of the era appeared to come to an end, the Black Death, probably carried by lice hidden in the saddlebags of Mongol horsemen, decimated the populations of Europe and the Middle East. Some regions lost as much as one-third of their population with severe economic consequences.

Few modern historians would dispute the brutality that characterized Mongol expansion. But some are now beginning to point out that beyond its legacy of death and destruction, the Mongol era also brought widespread peace (known as the Pax Mongolica) and inaugurated what one scholar has described as "the idea of the unified conceptualization of the globe," creating a "basic information circuit" that spread commodities, ideas, and inventions from one end of the Eurasian supercontinent to the other. We shall return to this question at the close of Part II. In the meantime, let us examine the consequences of the Mongol conquest in one of its primary victims—imperial China.

The Ming Dynasty

The new dynasty had an auspicious beginning. Its founder, who assumed the reign title of Ming Hongwu (Ming Hung Wu, or the Ming Martial Emperor), was a man of enormous energy and imagination. He abolished slavery, launched an extensive land reform program, strengthened the powers of the central government, and even pacified the border regions. After his death, his son Yongle (Yung Lo, or Perpetual Happiness) moved the imperial capital from Nanjing, where Hongwu had located it, back to Beijing, where it would remain until the end of the dynastic system early in the twentieth century. Yongle (1402–1424) continued to consolidate the empire internally and extended it to the north through a series of campaigns beyond the Great Wall. He also ordered the reconstruction of the section of the wall north of Beijing that is now commonly visited by tourists.

Yongle also took a more aggressive policy in the south, restoring Chinese rule over Vietnam and sponsoring a series of naval expeditions into the Indian Ocean that sailed as far west as the eastern coast of Africa. The voyages not only extended Chinese trade relations far to the west, but also enhanced the empire's prestige throughout the area, as many of the local kingdoms in Southeast Asia declared their fealty to the emperor in far-off Beijing.

Ming Hongwu: The People's Emperor

In founding the new dynasty, Ming Hongwu consciously strove to return China to the native traditions that had marked the era of the Tang and the Song. Yet in certain key respects, he rejected those traditions and ruled according to his own instincts. In the first place, although compassionate and paternalistic in his concern for the common people, he was suspicious by nature and harbored an immense resentment against the scholar-gentry class, whom he viewed with the primordial suspicion of the rural peasant. Many of them reportedly ridiculed the emperor for his lack of erudition and his peculiar facial features (one historian has described him as "physically ugly," with a high forehead, a thick nose, and a protruding jaw). As he wrote on one occasion:

> The "outstanding" scholar-gentry sit in the market or village, pride themselves on their capability, and listen to people flatter and praise them. Yet all they know is writing on paper. They have never had any practical experience of affairs. They write books to establish doctrine, but all this amounts to is chewing on phrases and biting on words to the ruination of their students. When you examine what they do, it is nothing. They make grand discussions and thus consider themselves capable in affairs. They are of no benefit.[11]

It is little wonder that the emperor relied on aristocratic appointments for the majority of his advisers and only approved a return to the civil service examinations in the mid-1380s.

Ming Hongwu was also a man of immense energy and interest in public affairs. He brought about a substantial

✴ **Map 10.4**   The Voyages of Zhenghe.

TAKLIMAKAN DESERT
KOREA
Kaifang
Yellow R.
East China Sea
Nanjing
PERSIA
TIBET
Hangzhou
Hormuz
CHINA
Jidda
Mecca
Ganges R.
Chittagong
Canton
ARABIA
INDIA
South China Sea
Dhofar
Arabian Sea
SIAM
Ayuthaya
PHILIPPINE ISLANDS
Aden
Calicut
Cochin
CAMBODIA
Colombo
AFRICA
Indian Ocean
Malacca
BORNEO
Mogadishu
SUMATRA
JAVA   Surabaya
Malindi

— Outward journey (Jan. 1431 - Jan. 1433)
→ Return voyage (Mar. - Jul. 1433)
--➤ Ancillary voyages

increase in central government control, ordering the abolition of the imperial secretariat, which he viewed as a collection of bureaucrats resisting his will, and attempting to rule directly. Eventually, a new grand secretariat evolved that operated as a kind of "supercabinet" over the traditional six ministries. The Ming also extended the tentacles of the central government down to the village, setting up the so-called *Li-jia* (Li-chia) system, which grouped ten to one hundred families together in each village to organize tax payments and conscript labor services.

The Ming Turn Inward

Many historians have viewed Yongle's decision to launch naval expeditions into the southern seas as a culmination of the process of opening China to the wider world that had begun with the Tang, continued during the Song, and come to a temporary climax under the Yuan, when China was part of the global trading network that operated within the widespread territories under Mongol domination. Yongle's seven expeditions were impressive in scope. On the first voyage in 1405, nearly 28,000 men embarked on 62 ships; the largest ship was over 440 feet long and displaced 3,100 tons. The fleet passed through Southeast Asia and eventually visited ports as far away as the western coast of India.

Why the expeditions were undertaken has been a matter of some debate. Some assume that economic profit was the main reason. Others point to Yongle's native curiosity and note that the fleet returned not only with goods, but also with a plethora of information about the outside world as well as with some items unknown in China (the emperor was especially intrigued by the giraffes and placed them in the imperial zoo, where they were identified by soothsayers with the coming of good government). Others speculate that the emperor was seeking to ascertain the truth of rumors that his immediate predecessor, Emperor Jianwen or Chien Wen (1398–1402), had escaped to Southeast Asia to live in exile.

Whatever the case, the voyages resulted in massive profits for their sponsors, including individuals connected with the eunuch admiral Zhenghe (Cheng Ho) at court. This aroused resentment among conservatives within the bureaucracy, some of whom viewed commercial activities with a characteristic measure of Confucian disdain. One commented that an end to the voyages would provide the Chinese people with a respite "so that they can devote themselves to husbandry [agriculture] and schooling." Shortly after Yongle's death, the voyages

were discontinued, never to be revived. The decision had long-term consequences and in the eyes of many modern historians marks a turning inward of the Chinese state, away from commerce and toward a more traditional emphasis on agriculture, away from the exotic lands to the south and toward the heartland of the country in the Yellow River valley.

Ironically, the move toward the Yellow River had been initiated by Yongle himself, when he had decided to move the Ming capital from Nanjing in central China (where the ships were built, and the voyages were launched) back to Beijing (where official eyes were firmly focused on the threat from beyond the Great Wall to the north). As a means of reducing that threat, Yongle ordered the resettlement of thousands of families from the rich Yangtze valley. The emperor had presumably not intended to set forces in motion that would divert the country from its growing contacts with the external world. After all, he had been the driving force behind Zhenghe's voyages. But the end result was a shift in the balance of power from central China (where it had been since the southern Song dynasty) back to northern China, where it had originated and would remain for the rest of the Ming era. China would not look outward again for more than four centuries.

In Search of the Way

By the time of the Sui and the Tang dynasties, Buddhism and Daoism had emerged as major rivals of Confucianism as the ruling ideology of the state. But in the eighth and ninth centuries, during the last half of the Tang dynasty, Confucianism revived and once again became dominant at court, a position it would retain to the end of the dynastic period in the early twentieth century. Buddhist and Daoist beliefs, however, remained popular at the local level.

The Rise and Decline of Buddhism and Daoism

As noted earlier, Buddhism arrived in China with merchants from India and found its first adherents among the merchant community and among intellectuals intrigued by the new ideas. Then, during the centuries following the collapse of the Han dynasty, the chaotic social conditions and the inability of Confucianism to satisfy people's emotional and spiritual needs in troubled times helped to make Buddhism and Daoism more attractive to many people. Both faiths reached beyond the common people and found support among the ruling classes as well,

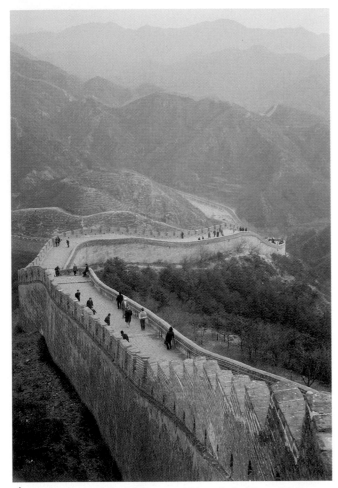

◆ **The Great Wall of China.** Although the Great Wall is popularly believed to be over 2,000 years old, in actuality that part of the wall that is most frequently visited by tourists was a reconstruction undertaken during the early Ming Dynasty as a means of protection against invasion from the north. Part of that wall appears here.

particularly in the north, where non-Chinese dynasties often established Buddhism as a state religion and subsidized the foundation of great monasteries.

The burgeoning popularity of Buddhism continued into the early years of the Tang dynasty and may have won over some adherents of Daoism, as the following sarcastic passage from the pen of a contemporary Confucian scholar suggests:

> In the eastern streets, in the western streets
> They preach the Buddhist sutras
> They embroider and exaggerate tales of retribution and
>   reward

> The listening crowd shoves and pushes
> Jostling each other like clotted water-plants
> A yellow-robed Taoist monk
> Also preaches his theories
> But below his platform
> The listeners are few
> Like a few bright stars in an empty sky.

Early Tang rulers lent their support to Buddhist monasteries established throughout the country. Buddhist scriptures were regularly included in the civil service examinations, and Buddhist and Daoist advisers replaced shamans and Confucian scholar-officials as advisers at court.

As Buddhism grew, it began to take on Chinese characteristics and divided into a number of separate sects. Some, like the *Chan* (Zen in Japanese) sect, called for mind training and a strict regimen as a means of seeking enlightenment, a technique that reflected Daoist ideas and appealed to many intellectuals (see the box on p. 355). Others, like the Pure Land sect, stressed the role of devotion, an approach that was more appealing to ordinary Chinese who lacked the time and inclination for strict monastic discipline. Still others were attracted to mystical sects like Tantrism, which emphasized the importance of magical symbols and ritual in seeking a preferred way to enlightenment.

Some Buddhist sects, like their Daoist counterparts, had political overtones. The White Lotus sect, founded in 1133, often adopted the form of a rebel movement, seeking political reform or the overthrow of a dynasty and forecasting a new era when a "savior Buddha" (known popularly as the Maitreya Buddha) would come to earth to herald the advent of a new age. Most believers, however, assimilated Buddhism into their daily lives, where it joined Confucian ideology and spirit worship as an element in the highly eclectic and tolerant Chinese worldview.

During the early Tang, Buddhist and Daoist beliefs at the popular level received encouragement from the state. For a time, Tang rulers apparently even believed that their family was descended from the old master Lao Zi. But ultimately, Buddhism and Daoism lost favor at court and were increasingly subjected to official persecution. Part of the reason was xenophobia. Envious Daoists and Confucianists made a point of criticizing the foreign origins of Buddhist doctrines, which one prominent Confucian scholar characterized as nothing but "silly relics." To deflect such criticism, Buddhists attempted to make the doctrine more Chinese, equating the Indian concept of *dharma* (law) with the Chinese concept of *Dao* (the

⇒ The Way of the Great Buddha ⇐

According to Buddhists, it is impossible to describe the state of Nirvana, which is sometimes depicted as an extinction of self. Yet Buddhist scholars found it difficult to avoid trying to interpret the term for their followers. The following passage by the Chinese monk Shen-Hui, one of the leading exponents of Chan Buddhism, dates from the eighth century and attempts to describe the means by which an individual may hope to seek enlightenment. There are clear similarities with philosophical Daoism.

Shen-Hui, *Elucidating the Doctrine*

"Absence of thought" is the doctrine.
"Absence of action" is the foundation.
True Emptiness is the substance.
And all wonderful things and beings are the function.
True Thusness is without thought; it cannot be known
  through conception and thought.
The True State is noncreated—can it be seen in matter
  and mind?
There is no thought except that of True Thusness.
There is no creation except that of the True State.
Abiding without abiding, forever abiding in Nirvana.
Acting without acting, immediately crossing to the Other
  Shore.
Thusness does not move, but its motion and functions are
  inexhaustible.

In every instant of thought, there is no seeking; the seeking
  itself is no thought.
Perfect wisdom is not achieved, and yet the Five Eyes all
  become pure and the Three Bodies are understood.
Great Enlightenment has no knowledge, and yet the Six
  Supernatural Powers of the Buddha are utilized and the
  Four Wisdoms of the Buddha are made great.
Thus we know that calmness is at the same time no calmness, wisdom at the same time no wisdom, and action at
  the same time no action.
The nature is equivalent to the void and the substance is
  identical with the Realm of Law.
In this way, the Six Perfections are completed.
None of the ways to arrive at Nirvana is wanting.
Thus we know that the ego and the dharmas are empty in
  reality and being and nonbeing are both obliterated.
The mind is originally without activity; the Way is always
  without thought.
No thought, no reflection, no seeking, no attainment;
No this, no that, no coming, no going.
With such reality one understands the True Insight [into
  previous and future mortal conditions and present mortal suffering].
With such a mind one penetrates the Eight Emancipations
  [through the eight stages of mental concentration].
By merits one accomplishes the Ten Powers of the Buddha.

Way). Emperor Tang Taizong ordered the Buddhist monk Xuan Zang to translate Lao Zi's classic *The Way of the Dao* into Sanskrit, reportedly to show visitors from India that China had its own equivalent to the Buddhist scriptures. But another reason for this change of heart may have been financial. The great monasteries had accumulated thousands of acres of land and serfs that henceforth were exempt from paying taxes to the state. As in Europe, wealth contributed to the corruption of the monks and other Buddhist officials, and this corruption in turn aroused popular resentment and official disapproval. As the state attempted to eliminate the great landholdings of the aristocracy, the large monasteries also attracted its attention. During the later Tang, countless temples and monasteries were destroyed, and over 100,000 monks

were compelled to leave the monasteries and return to secular life.

Yet there were probably deeper political and ideological reasons for the growing antagonism between Buddhism and the state. By preaching the illusory nature of the material world, Buddhism was denying the very essence of Confucian teachings—the necessity for filial piety and hard work. These were virtues that the Chinese state had reason to support. By encouraging young Chinese to abandon their rice fields and seek refuge and wisdom in the monasteries, Buddhism was undermining the foundation stones of Chinese society—the family unit and the work ethic. In the last analysis, Buddhism was incompatible with the activist element in Chinese society, an orientation that was most effectively expressed by

State Confucianism. In the competition with Confucianism for support by the state, Buddhism, like Daoism, was almost certain to lose, at least in the more this-worldly, secure, and prosperous milieu of late Tang and Song China. The two doctrines continued to win converts at the local level (partly in competition with each other, as Daoists disparaged Buddhists and adopted a more religious orientation), but official support ceased, although officials often turned to Buddhist or Daoist ideas as an alternative to the constraining tenets of State Confucianism.

In the meantime, Buddhism was under attack in Central Asia as well. In the eighth century, the Uighur kingdom adopted Manichaeanism, an offshoot of the ancient Zoroastrian religion with some influence from Christianity. Manichaeanism spread rapidly throughout the area and may have been a reason for the European belief that a Christian king (the legendary Prester John) ruled somewhere in Asia. By the tenth century, Islam was beginning to move east along the Silk Road, posing a severe threat to both Manichaean and Buddhist centers in the area.

Neo-Confucianism: The Investigation of Things

Into the vacuum left by the decline of Buddhism and Daoism stepped a revived Confucianism. From the late Tang to the end of the dynastic system in the twentieth century, Confucianism served as the bulwark of the state. But it was a different kind of Confucianism than the state ideology established during the Han dynasty. Confucian doctrine was significantly altered by its competition with Buddhist and Daoist teachings. Before and during the Han dynasty, Confucianism had served above all as a system of social ethics and a set of political principles. Its metaphysical structure was limited to primitive ideas about the interaction between the forces of *yin* and *yang* and the "five elements" (the ancient Chinese notion that the universe was composed of earth, wood, fire, water, and metal), supplemented by a heavy dose of Confucian skepticism.

Now, challenged by Buddhist and Daoist ideas about the nature of the universe, Confucian thinkers began to flesh out the spare metaphysical structure of classical Confucian doctrine with a set of sophisticated theories about the nature of the cosmos and humans' place in it. Although the origins of this effort can be traced to the early Tang period, it reached fruition during the intellectually prolific Song dynasty when it became the dominant ideology of the state.

The fundamental purpose of Neo-Confucianism, as the new doctrine was called, was to unite the metaphysical speculations of Buddhism and Daoism with the pragmatic Confucian approach to society and thus provide a cosmological basis for a set of beliefs that would reaffirm the reality and significance of the material world and a lifestyle of active participation in the effort to build a better society. Neo-Confucianism thus served as a Confucian response to Buddhism and Daoism: the world is real, not illusory, and fulfillment comes from participation, not withdrawal.

The primary contributor to this intellectual effort was the philosopher Zhu Xi (Chu Hsi). Raised during the southern Song era, Zhu Xi accepted the division of the world into a material world and a transcendent world (called by Neo-Confucianists the Supreme Ultimate, or *Tai Ji*). The latter was roughly equivalent to the *Dao*, or Way, in classical Confucian philosophy. To Zhu Xi, this Supreme Ultimate was a set of abstract principles governed by the law of *yin-yang* and the five elements.

Human beings served as a link between the two halves of this bifurcated universe. Although human beings live in the material world, each individual has an identity that is linked with the Supreme Ultimate, and the goal of individual action is to transcend the material world in a Buddhist sense to achieve an essential identity with the Supreme Ultimate. According to Zhu Xi and his followers, the means of transcending the material world is self-cultivation, which is achieved by the "investigation of things" (see the box on p. 357).

The Neo-Confucian emphasis on the "investigation of things" has led some Western observers to compare the concept with the scientific attitude that developed in Europe during and after the Italian Renaissance of the fourteenth and fifteenth centuries (discussed in Chapter 13). But there were key differences in the attitudes toward "things" in the two cultures, differences that help to explain why the Italian Renaissance led ultimately to the Industrial Revolution in Europe, while a similar process did not occur in China. In the West, the "investigation of things" meant an empirical and experimental attitude of curiosity about the impersonal forces of nature. In Confucianism, it tended to focus not on an expansion of scientific knowledge, but on the need to elucidate the moral principles that permitted individuals to transcend the material universe to a common identity with the Supreme Ultimate. As a consequence, while Europeans studied nature, the Chinese examined questions of social ethics, which led them back into the Confucian classics. The emphasis on the investigation of things also led to the view that there was a proper principle for everything, a belief that contributed to the increasing rigidity in social thinking in late imperial China.

came more gentle and refined and the artist moved in closer to the subject.

In the meantime, a new school of expressionist and experimental painting appeared. These so-called literati artists were scholars and administrators, highly educated and adept in music, poetry, and painting. Being scholars first and artists second, however, they believed that the purpose of painting was not representation but expression. Painting, like handwriting, should express the inner quality of the artist. No longer did painters wish to evoke the feeling of wandering in nature. Instead they tried to reveal to the viewer their own mind and feelings. Like many Western painters in the nineteenth and twentieth centuries, many of these artists were misunderstood by the public and painted only for themselves and one another. They even developed a style of pointillism. Witness the incredibly "modern" painting of the Tang poet, Li Bo, created by the thirteenth-century artist Liang Kai. With just a few bold black strokes, he managed to convey the whole man, standing calmly but poised, with inner intensity.

The Yuan dynasty was a time of turmoil in art as well as in politics. Many artists shared the humility of China's defeat and blamed it on the weakness and effete character of life under the Song. Yuan painting therefore sought to achieve a total break from the sweetness and romanticism of Song art and strove for plainness, as witnessed by Huang Kung-wang's *Dwelling in the Fu-ch'un Mountains*, one of the most influential and imitated of all Chinese paintings. The tradition of bamboo painting also became popular. Representing resilience and beauty under stress, bamboo became a focus of expression for exiled artists under Mongol domination. After the fall of the Mongols, court painting revived, but it began to lose the vitality and freshness that had been achieved under earlier dynasties, as artists clung to classical styles without the inspiration of their predecessors.

Second only to painting in creativity was the field of ceramics, notably, the manufacture of porcelain. Made of fine clay baked at unusually high temperatures in a kiln, porcelain was first produced during the period after the fall of the Han and became popular during the Tang era. As an Arab traveler in 851 C.E. described: "There is in China a very fine clay from which are made vases having the transparency of glass bottles; water in these vases is visible through them, and yet they are made of clay."[15] The technique did not reach Europe until the eighteenth century.

During the Song, porcelain came into its own. Most renowned perhaps are the celadons, in a delicate gray-green, but Song artists also excelled in other colors and

◆ **Li Bo Chanting a Poem.** Li Bo, one of the most celebrated Tang poets, wrote about the changing seasons, the joys of friendship and drink, and his sadness at the brevity of life, old age, and parting. The legend of his death undoubtedly added to his reputation. Reportedly, he drowned while reaching out in a drunken stupor to embrace the reflection of the moon in the water. Here he is portrayed by the thirteenth century painter Liang Kai, who gave up a promising career as an official to retreat to a Buddhist monastery near Hangzhou.

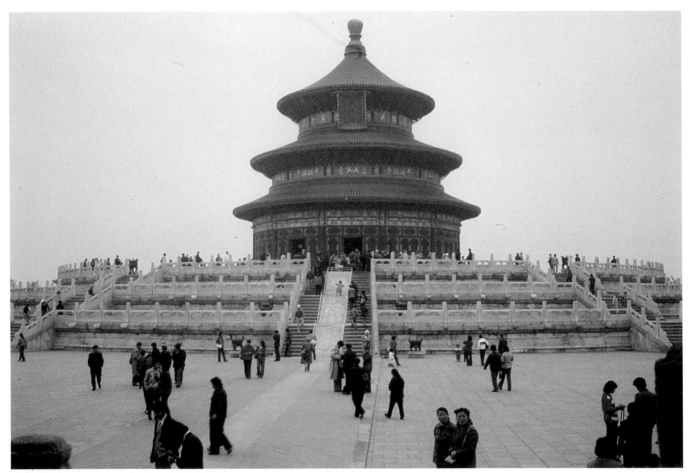

◆ **The Temple of Heaven.**   This temple, located in the capital Beijing, is one of the most important historical structures in China. Built in 1420 at the order of the Ming emperor Yongle, it served as the location for the emperor's annual ceremony appealing to Heaven for a good harvest. Yongle's temple burned to the ground in 1889, but was immediately rebuilt according to the original design.

techniques. As in painting, Song delicacy and grace contrasted with the bold and often crude styles popular under the Tang. During the Yuan and the Ming, new styles appeared. Most notable is the cobalt blue and white porcelain usually identified with the Ming dynasty, but which originated during the Yuan (the cobalt was originally brought from Iran by the Mongols and is therefore called "Mohammedan blue" by the Chinese). The Ming also produced a multicolored porcelain—often in green, yellow, and red—covered with exotic designs.

Other outlets for Chinese artistic creativity were lacquerware, jade carving, and wood carving. Curiously, Chinese architecture appeared to change little over the centuries from the Tang to the Ming. Although influenced to a degree by Buddhism, where the Indian stupa gave way in China to a multitiered pagoda, the basic form of Chinese temple architecture has remained essentially unchanged since antiquity. Nevertheless, some of the greatest examples of traditional Chinese architecture date from this period, including (among countless examples) the Temple of the Forest of the Clouds (*Ling Yin Shi*) near West Lake in Hangzhou and the Big Goose Pagoda in Xian.

Conclusion

Traditionally, Chinese historians believed that Chinese history tended to be cyclical in nature. The pattern of history was marked by the rise and fall of great dynasties, interspersed with periods of internal division and foreign invasion. Underlying the waxing and waning of dynasties was the essential continuity of Chinese civilization.

This view of the dynamic forces of Chinese history was long accepted as valid by historians in China and in the West and led many to assert that Chinese history was unique and could not be placed within a European or universal framework. Whereas Western history was linear, leading steadily away from the past, China's always returned to its moorings and was rooted in the values and institutions of antiquity.

In recent years, however, this traditional view of a changeless China has come under increasing challenge from historians who see patterns of change that made the China of 1500 a very different place from the country that had existed at the rise of the Tang dynasty in the seventh century C.E. To such scholars, China had passed through its own version of the "middle ages" and was on the verge of beginning a linear evolution into a posttraditional society.

As we have seen, China under the Ming had advanced in many ways since the end of the great Han dynasty over a thousand years earlier. The industrial and commercial sector had grown considerably in size, complexity, and technological capacity, while in the countryside the concentration of political and economic power in the hands of the aristocracy had been replaced by a more stable and equitable mixture of landed gentry, freehold farmers, and sharecroppers. In addition, Chinese society had achieved a level of stability and social tranquillity that not only surpassed conditions during the final years of the Han, but was the envy of observers from other lands, near and far. The civil service provided an avenue of upward mobility that was virtually unknown elsewhere in the world, while the state tolerated a diversity of beliefs that responded to the emotional needs and preferences of the Chinese people. In many respects, China's achievements were unsurpassed throughout the world and marked a major advance beyond the world of antiquity.

Yet there were also some key similarities between the China of the Ming and the China of late antiquity. Ming China was still a predominantly agrarian society, with wealth based primarily on the ownership of land. Commercial activities flourished, but remained under a high level of government regulation and by no means represented a major proportion of the national income. China also remained a relatively centralized empire based on an official ideology that stressed the virtue of hard work, social conformity, and hierarchy. In foreign affairs, the long frontier struggle with the nomadic peoples along the northern and western frontiers continued unabated.

Thus, the significant change that China experienced during its medieval era can probably be best described as change within continuity, an evolutionary working out of trends that had first become visible during the Han dynasty or even earlier. The result was a civilization that was the envy of its neighbors and of the world. It also influenced other states in the region, including Japan, Korea, and Vietnam. It is to these societies along the Chinese rimlands that we now turn.

CHAPTER NOTES

1. *The Travels of Marco Polo* (New York, n.d.), p. 119.
2. Quoted in Etienne Balazs, *Chinese Civilization and Bureaucracy* (New Haven, Conn., 1964), p. 236.
3. Quoted in Arthur F. Wright, *Buddhism in Chinese History* (Stanford, Calif., 1959), p. 30.
4. Quoted in Arthur F. Wright, *The Sui Dynasty* (New York, 1978), p. 180.
5. Chu-yu, *P'ing chow Table Talks*, quoted in Robert Temple, *The Genius of China: 3,000 Years of Science, Discovery, and Invention* (New York, 1986), p. 150.
6. Quoted in Edward H. Schafer, *The Golden Peaches of Samerkand: A Study of T'ang Exotics* (Berkeley, Calif., 1963), p. 43.
7. Quoted in John K. Fairbank, Edwin O. Reischauer, and Albert M. Craig, *East Asia: Tradition and Transformation* (Boston, 1973), p. 164.
8. John Plano Carpini, quoted in Rene Grousset, *L'Empire des Steppes* (Paris, 1939), p. 285.
9. Temple, *The Genius of China*, pp. 242–43.

10. A.M. Khazanov, *Nomads and the Outside World* (Cambridge, 1983), p. 241.

11. Quoted in Edward L. Dreyer, *Early Ming China* (Stanford, Calif., 1982), p. 67.

12. Temple, *The Genius of China*, pp. 83–84.

13. Steve Owen, *The Great Age of Chinese Poetry: The High T'ang* (New Haven, Conn., 1981), p. 200.

14. Liu Wu-chi, *An Introduction to Chinese Literature* (Bloomington, Ind., 1966), p. 187.

15. Temple, *The Genius of China*, p. 91.

SUGGESTED READINGS

A number of general histories of China provide a good overview of this period. See, for example, C.O. Hucker, *China's Imperial Past: An Introduction to Chinese History and Culture* (Stanford, Calif., 1975) and C. Schirokauer, *A Brief History of Chinese and Japanese Civilizations*, revised ed. (San Diego, Calif., 1989). For an interpretative treatment, see M. Elvin, *The Pattern of the Chinese Past* (Stanford, Calif., 1973). A global perspective is presented in S. A. M. Adshead, *China in World History* (New York, 1988).

A vast body of material is available on almost all periods of early Chinese history. For the post-Han period, see A. E. Dien, ed., *State and Society in Early Medieval China* (Stanford, Calif., 1990); E. Balazs, *Chinese Civilization and Bureaucracy: Variations on a Theme* (New Haven, Conn.; 1964); and D. Twitchett and M. Loewe, *Cambridge History of China*, vol. 3, *Medieval China* (Cambridge, 1986).

For a readable treatment of the brief but tempestuous Sui dynasty, see A. F. Wright, *The Sui Dynasty* (New York, 1978). See also A. F. Wright and D. Twitchett, *Perspectives on the Tang* (New Haven, Conn., 1973). For a popularized treatment of one of China's most controversial female figures, see C. P. Fitzgerald, *The Empress Wu* (London, 1968).

The Song dynasty has been studied in considerable detail by Chinese historians. For a new and exciting interpretation, see J. T. C. Liu, *China Turning Inward: Intellectual Changes in the Early Twelfth Century* (Cambridge, Mass., 1988). Song problems with the northern frontier are chronicled in Tao Jing-shen, *Two Sons of Heaven: Studies in Sung-Liao Relations* (Tucson, Ariz., 1988).

There are a number of recent studies on the Mongol period in Chinese history. See, for example, W. A. Langlois, *China under Mongol Rule* (Princeton, N.J., 1981) and J. W. Dardess, *Conquerors and Confucians: Aspects of Political Change in Late Yuan China* (New York, 1973). M. Rossabi, *Khubilai Khan: His Life and Times* (Berkeley, Calif., 1988) is a recent biography of the dynasty's greatest emperor, while M. Rossabi, ed., *China among Equals: The Middle Kingdom and Its Neighbors* (Berkeley, Calif., 1983) deals with foreign affairs. For the rise of the Mongols, see M. Prawdin, *The Mongol Empire: Its Rise and Legacy* (New York, 1966). A more analytic account of the dynamics of nomadic society is A. M. Khazanov, *Nomads and the Outside World* (Cambridge, 1983). For a provocative new interpretation of Chinese relations with nomadic peoples, see T. J. Barfield, *The Perilous Frontier: Nomadic Empires and China* (Cambridge, 1989).

The Ming dynasty will be discussed in part in a later chapter, but see E. L. Dreyer, *Early Ming China: A Political History, 1355–1435* (Stanford, Calif., 1982) for a readable survey of the early period. See also L. Levathes, *When China Ruled the Seas: The Treasure Fleet of the Dragon Throne* (New York, 1994) and T. Huff, *The Rise of Early Modern Science: Islam, China, and the West* (Cambridge, 1993).

On Central Asia, two popular accounts are J. Myrdal, *The Silk Road* (New York, 1979) and N. Marty, *The Silk Road* (Methuen, Mass., 1987). A more interpretive approach is found in S. A. M. Adshead, *Central Asia in World History* (New York, 1993).

The period from the fall of the Han to the early Ming was an important period in Chinese intellectual history. For developments in Confucianism, see Fung Yu-lan, *A Short History of Chinese Philosophy*, ed. D. Bodde (New York, 1948); and Carsun Chang, *The Development of Neo-Confucian Thought*, 2 vols. (New Haven, Conn., 1963). For a more scholarly study, see W. T. de Bary, *Self and Society in Ming Thought* (New York, 1970). A classic survey of the role of Buddhism in Chinese society is A. F. Wright, *Buddhism in Chinese History* (Stanford, Calif., 1959). See also E. O. Reischauer, *Ennin's Diary:*

The Record of a Pilgrimage to China in Search of the Law (New York, 1955).

The best introduction to Chinese literature is Liu Wu-chi, *An Introduction to Chinese Literature* (Bloomington, Ind., 1966). Also of interest is Ch'en Shou-yi, *Chinese Literature: A Historical Introduction* (New York, 1961). Many anthologies of Chinese literature cover this period. See C. Birch, ed., *Anthology of Chinese Literature: From Early Times to the 14th century,* vol. 1 (New York, 1965). See also Liu Wu-chi and I. Yucheng Lo, *Sunflower Splendor: Three Thousand Years of Chinese Poetry* (Bloomington, Ind., 1975) and K. Rexroth, *One Hundred Poems from the Chinese* (New York, 1971). For an anthology with the poems in both Chinese and Eng-lish, consult S. Owen, *The Great Age of Chinese Poetry: The High T'ang* (New Haven, Conn., 1981). For anthologies of prose works, consult *A Treasury of Chinese Literature: A New Prose Anthology Including Fiction and Drama* (New York, 1965) and *Traditional Chinese Stories: Themes and Variations* (Boulder, Colo., 1978).

For a comprehensive introduction to Chinese art, see M. Sullivan, *The Arts of China,* 3d ed. (Berkeley, Calif., 1984) and M. Tregear, *Chinese Art* (New York, 1980). A concise introduction to Chinese painting can be found in J. Cahill, *Chinese Painting* (New York, 1985). See also the classic six-volume work by O. Siren, *Chinese Painting: Leading Masters and Principles* (New York, 1956–1958).

CHAPTER
11

The East Asian Rimlands: Early Japan, Korea, and Vietnam

These people, the exasperated official complained, are like birds and beasts. "They wear their hair tied up and go barefoot, while for clothing they simply cut a hole in a piece of cloth for their head or they fasten their garments on the left side [in barbarian style]." Their women are untrustworthy "and promiscuously wander about." In some areas, "men and women go naked without shame" and are little better than bugs.[1]

The speaker was Xue Tong, a Chinese administrator stationed in northern Vietnam at the end of the Han dynasty. His comments vividly reflected the frustration of Chinese bureaucrats faced with what they regarded as the uncivilized behavior of the untutored peoples living along the frontiers of the Chinese Empire. To Xue Tong and other upright Confucian officials like him, it was hopeless to try to civilize them.

Such comments should not surprise us. During ancient times, China was the most technologically advanced society in East Asia. To the north and west were nomadic pastoral peoples whose military exploits were often impressive, but whose political and cultural attainments were still limited, at least by comparison with the great river valley civilizations of the day. In inland areas south of the Yangtze River were scattered clumps of rice farmers and hill peoples, most of whom had not yet entered the era of state building, and certainly had little knowledge of the niceties of Confucian ethics.

But Xue Tong and officials like him were being a little too hasty in their judgments. Along the

| 300 | 400 | 500 | 600 | 700 | 800 | 900 | 1000 | 1100 | 1200 | 1300 | 1400 |

Jimmu's migration
to central Japan

Rise of Yamato
state

Heian (Kyoto) era

Kamakura shogunate

Era of Three Kingdoms
in Korea

Restoration of Vietnamese
independence

Koryo Dynasty in Korea

Vietname
conquest
Champa

Shotoku Taishi

Mongol
invasions
of Japan and Korea

Onin War

Era of Taika reforms

Arrival of Buddhism
in Vietnam

Arrival of Buddhism in Japan and Korea

Life of
Murasaki Shikibu

Minamoto
Yoritomo

Foundation of Yi
Dynasty in Korea

Nara period in Japanese culture

Construction of Temple of
Literature in Hanoi

fringes of Chinese civilization were a number of other agricultural societies that were beginning to follow a pattern of development similar to that of China, although somewhat later in time. One of these was in the islands of Japan, where an organized agricultural society was beginning to take shape just about the time Xue Tong was complaining abut the barbarian peoples in the south. These developments may have been hastened by events on the Korean peninsula, where an advanced Neolithic society had begun to develop a few centuries earlier. Even in the Red River valley, where Xue Tong viewed the local inhabitants with such disdain, a relatively advanced civilization had been in existence for several hundred years before the area was conquered by the Han dynasty in the second century B.C.E.

All of these early agricultural societies were eventually influenced to some degree by their great neighbor China. Vietnam remained under Chinese rule for a thousand years. Korea retained its separate existence but was for long a tributary state of China and in many ways followed the cultural example of its larger patron. Only Japan retained both its political independence and its cultural uniqueness. Yet even the Japanese were strongly influenced by the glittering culture of their powerful neighbor, and even today many Japanese institutions and customs bear the imprint of several centuries of borrowing from the Middle Kingdom. In this chapter, we will take a closer look at those emerging societies along the Chinese rimlands and consider how their cultural achievements reflected or contrasted with those of the Chinese Empire

Japan: Land of the Rising Sun

One of the reasons for the historical differences between Chinese and Japanese society is the influence of the geographical environment. While China is a continental civilization, Japan is an island country. It consists of four main islands: Hokkaido in the north, the main island of Honshu in the center, and the two smaller islands of Kyushu and Shikoku in the southwest. Its total land area is about 146,000 square miles (378,000 square kilometers), about the size of the state of Montana. Japan's main islands extend from about 31 degrees to 46 degrees north latitude, placing it approximately at the same latitude as the eastern seaboard of the United States from Maine to northern Florida.

Like the eastern seaboard of the United States, Japan is blessed with a temperate climate. It is slightly warmer on the east coast, which is washed by the Pacific Current that sweeps up from the south. The east coast also has a number of natural harbors that provide protection from the winds and high waves of the Pacific Ocean. As a consequence, in recent times the majority of the Japanese people have tended to live along the east coast, especially in the flat plains surrounding the cities of Tokyo, Osaka, and Kyoto. In these favorable environmental conditions, Japanese farmers have been able to harvest two crops of rice annually since early times.

By no means, however, is Japan an agricultural paradise. Like China, much of the country is mountainous, with only about 20 percent of the total land area susceptible to cultivation. These mountains are volcanic in origin, since the Japanese islands are located at the juncture between the Asian and Pacific tectonic plates. This location is both an advantage and a disadvantage. Volcanic soils are extremely fertile, which helps to explain the exceptionally high productivity of Japanese farmers. On the other hand, the area is prone to earthquakes, such as the famous earthquake of 1923, which destroyed almost the entire city of Tokyo.

The fact that Japan is an island country had a significant impact on Japanese history. As we have seen, the continental character of Chinese civilization, with its constant threat of invasion from the north, had a number of consequences for the history of the country. One effect was to make the Chinese more sensitive to the preservation of their culture from destruction at the hands of non-Chinese invaders. Proud of their own considerable cultural achievements and their dominant position throughout the region, the Chinese have traditionally been reluctant to dilute the purity of their culture with foreign innovations. Culture more than race is a determinant of the Chinese sense of identity.

By contrast, the island character of Japan probably had the effect of strengthening the Japanese sense of ethnic and cultural distinctiveness. In this regard, the Japanese are often compared with the people of Great Britain. Both peoples shared many racial and cultural characteristics with the inhabitants of the adjacent continent, but because of their relative geographical isolation, they developed a number of unique qualities that contributed to their image of themselves as having a separate destiny from the peoples of the continent.

Although the Japanese view of themselves as the most ethnically homogeneous people in East Asia may not be entirely accurate (the modern Japanese probably represent a mix of peoples much as do their neighbors on the continent), their sense of racial and cultural homogeneity has enabled them to import ideas from abroad without the risk of destroying the uniqueness of their own culture. At the same time, it has also contributed to a reluctance on the part of the modern Japanese government to permit foreigners to migrate to Japan in large numbers. The only substantial racial minority in Japan today are the Koreans, most of whom are descended from migrants who arrived in Japan prior to World War II to work in low-paying jobs. To most Americans, the "melting pot" quality of the United States is a source of strength, providing an influx of talent and cultural enrichment from abroad. The Japanese, to the contrary, see their racial and cultural homogeneity as an advantage, since all share a common dedication to creating a prosperous and efficient society through hard work and cooperation.

A Gift from the Gods: Prehistoric Japan

According to an ancient legend recorded in historical chronicles written in the eighth century C.E., the islands of Japan were formed as a result of the marriage of the god Izanagi and the goddess Izanami. After giving birth to Japan, Izanami gave birth to a sun goddess whose name was Amaterasu. A descendant of Amaterasu later descended to earth and became the founder of the Japanese nation. According to the *Kojiki* (*Records of Ancient Matters*), an early history written in the eighth century: "When the primeval matter had congealed but breath and form had not yet appeared, there were no names and no action. Who can know its form? However, when heaven and earth were first divided, the three deities became the first of all creation. The Male and Female here began, and the spirits (Izanagi and Izanami) were the ancestors of all creation. . . ."[2]

The Japanese creation myth is reminiscent of similar beliefs in other ancient societies, which often saw themselves as the product of a union of deities. What is interesting about the Japanese version is that it has survived into modern times as an explanation for the uniqueness of the Japanese people and a foundation for the divinity of the Japanese emperor, who is still believed by some Japanese to be a direct descendant of the sun goddess Amaterasu (see the box on p. 373).

Modern scholars have a more prosaic explanation for the origins of Japanese civilization. According to archaeological evidence, the Japanese islands have been occu-

The Eastern Expedition of Emperor Jimmu

Japanese myths maintained that the Japanese nation could be traced to the sun goddess Amaterasu, who was the ancestor of the founder of the Japanese imperial family, the Emperor Jimmu. This passage from the Nihon Shoki *(The Chronicles of Japan) describes the campaign in which Jimmu occupied the central plains of Japan, symbolizing the founding of the Japanese nation.*

The Chronicles of Japan

Emperor Jimmu was forty-five years of age when he addressed the assemblage of his brothers and children: "Long ago, this central land of the Reed Plains was bequeathed to our imperial ancestors by the heavenly deities, Takamimusubi-no-Kami and Amaterasu Omikami. . . . However, the remote regions still do not enjoy the benefit of our imperial rule, with each town having its own master and each village its own chief. Each of them sets up his own boundaries and contends for supremacy against other masters and chiefs."

"I have heard from an old deity knowledgeable in the affairs of the land and sea that in the east there is a beautiful land encircled by blue mountains. This must be the land from which our great task of spreading our benevolent rule can begin, for it is indeed the center of the universe. . . . Let us go there, and make it our capital. . . ."

In the winter of that year. . . the Emperor personally led imperial princes and a naval force to embark on his eastern expedition. . . .

When Nagasunehiko heard of the expedition, he said: "The children of the heavenly deities are coming to rob me of my country." He immediately mobilized his troops and intercepted Jimmu's troops at the hill of Kusaka and engaged in a battle. . . . The imperial forces were unable to advance. Concerned with the reversal, the Emperor formulated a new divine plan and said to himself: "I am the descendant of the Sun Goddess, and it is against the way of heaven to face the sun in attacking my enemy. Therefore our forces must retreat to make a show of weakness. After making sacrifice to the deities of heaven and earth, we shall march with the sun on our backs. We shall trample down our enemies with the might of the sun. In this way, without staining our swords with blood, our enemies can be conquered.". . . So, he ordered the troops to retreat to the port of Kusaka and regroup there. . . .

[After withdrawing to Kusaka, the imperial forces sailed southward, landed at a port in the present-day Kita peninsula, and again advanced north toward Yamato.]

The precipitous mountains provided such effective barriers that the imperial forces were not able to advance into the interior, and there was no path they could tread. Then one night Amaterasu Omikami appeared to the Emperor in a dream: "I will send you the Yatagarasu, let it guide you through the land." The following day, indeed, the Yatagarasu appeared flying down from the great expanse of the sky. The Emperor said: "The coming of this bird signifies the fulfillment of my auspicious dream. How wonderful it is! Our imperial ancestor, Amaterasu Omikami, desires to help us in the founding of our empire. . . ."

pied by human beings for at least 100,000 years. Unfortunately, little is known about Paleolithic times, because many of the early sites were submerged by the rise of the sea level after the last Ice Age. But the earliest known Neolithic inhabitants, known as the Jomon people from the so-called cord pattern of their pottery, lived in the islands as much as 10,000 years ago. They lived by hunting, fishing, and food gathering and probably had not mastered the techniques of agriculture.

Agriculture probably first appeared in Japan sometime during the first millennium B.C.E., although some archaeologists believe that the Jomon people had already learned how to cultivate some food crops considerably earlier than that. Rice cultivation was introduced about 400 B.C.E. and, according to present evidence, was probably brought to Japan by immigrants from the mainland by way of the Korean peninsula. Like Japan, the Korean peninsula at that time was occupied by fishing and hunting peoples who gradually mastered techniques of agriculture. Such techniques may have been brought by new arrivals who were migrating from Manchuria to escape the expanding power of the Xiongnu (see Chapter 10).

Until recently, historians believed that these immigrants from the continent dominated the existing inhabitants of the area and gave rise to the emerging Yayoi culture (from the site near Tokyo where pottery from the period was found). It is now thought, however, that Yayoi culture was a product of the Jomon people, enriched by ideas such as the introduction of wet rice agriculture that had been brought by small numbers of immigrants from the mainland. In any event, it seems clear that the Yayoi peoples were the ancestors of the vast majority of present-day Japanese.

At first the Yayoi lived primarily on the southern island of Kyushu, but eventually they moved northward onto the main island of Honshu, conquering, assimilating, or driving out the previous inhabitants of the area (including the Ainu, whose descendants still live in the northern islands) and eventually settling in the Yamato plain in the vicinity of the modern-day cities of Osaka and Kyoto. Japanese legend recounts the story of a "divine warrior" (in Japanese, Jimmu) who led his people eastward from the island of Kyushu to establish a kingdom in the Yamato plain in 660 B.C.E. (see the box on p. 373). Modern historians believe that the migration took place at a much later time (perhaps as late as the fourth century C.E.) and that the story of the "divine warrior" may represent an effort by Japanese chroniclers to find a local equivalent to the great Sage Kings of prehistoric China.

In central Honshu, the Yayoi set up a tribal society based on a number of clans called *uji*, which resembled the clans of Shang dynasty China in many respects. Each *uji* was ruled by a hereditary chieftain, who traced his lineage back to an original creator-deity. The population itself was divided between a small aristocratic class and the majority of the population, composed of rice farmers, artisans, and other household servants of the aristocrats. These tribal chieftains provided protection to the local population in return for a proportion of the annual harvest. Yayoi society was highly decentralized, although eventually the chieftain of the dominant clan in the Yamato region, who claimed to be descended from the sun goddess Amaterasu, achieved a kind of titular primacy. There is no evidence of a central ruler equivalent in power to the Chinese rulers of the Shang and the Zhou eras, however.

The Rise of the Japanese State

The Yamato state arose at a momentous time in Japanese history. The Japanese had known of China for centuries as the result of the sporadic migration of peoples of Yayoi stock into Japan from the mainland. Further knowledge came from contact with Korea, which had come under Chinese rule at the height of the Han dynasty. The first written account of Japan comes from a dynastic history of the early Han period, which describes a society of small communities that had dispatched tribute missions to the Han imperial court.

During the period of division after the fall of the Han, the Chinese posed no threat to Japan and even lost their hold on Korea. The rise of the centralized and expansionistic Tang dynasty in the early seventh century provided a new challenge to both the Koreans and the Japanese, however. The Tang soon began to meddle in the affairs of the Korean peninsula, conquering the southwestern coast and arousing anxiety in Japan.

Yamato rulers attempted to deal with the potential threat posed by the Chinese in two ways. First, they sought to form alliances with the remaining Korean states. Secondly, they attempted to centralize their authority so that they could mount a more effective resistance in the event of a Chinese invasion. The key figure in this effort was Shotoku Taishi (572–622), a leading aristocrat in one of the dominant clans in the Yamato region. Prince Shotoku sent missions to the Tang capital of Chang'an in order to adopt political institutions already in use in the relatively centralized Tang kingdom.

EMULATING THE CHINESE MODEL

Shotoku Taishi then launched a series of reforms to create a new system based roughly on the Chinese model. In the so-called seventeen-article constitution (either writ-

Map 11.1 Japan, China, and Korea, 600–800.

The Seventeen-Article Constitution

The following excerpt from the Nihon Shoki (The Chronicles of Japan) *is a passage from the seventeen-article constitution promulgated in 604 C.E. While the opening section reflects Chinese influence in its emphasis on social harmony, there is also a strong focus on obedience and hierarchy. The constitution was put into practice during the reign of the famous Prince Shotoku. Shotoku was the nephew of Empress Suiko, who had been placed on the throne by her uncle, the leader of the Soga clan that controlled the Yamato plain at that time. Appointed regent by the Soga, Shotoku thereupon embarked on a series of major reforms.*

The Chronicles of Japan

Summer, 4th month, 3rd day [12th year of Empress Suiko, 604 C.E.]. The Crown Prince personally drafted and promulgated a constitution consisting of seventeen articles, which are as follows:

I. Harmony is to be cherished, and opposition for opposition's sake must be avoided as a matter of principle. Men are often influenced by partisan feelings, except a few sagacious ones. Hence there are some who disobey their lords and fathers, or who dispute with their neighboring villages. If those above are harmonious and those below are cordial, their discussion will be guided by a spirit of conciliation, and reason shall naturally prevail. There will be nothing that cannot be accomplished.

II. With all our heart, revere the three treasures. The three treasures, consisting of Buddha, the Doctrine, and the Monastic Order, are the final refuge of the four generated beings, and are the supreme objects of worship in all countries. Can any man in any age ever fail to respect these teachings? Few men are utterly devoid of goodness, and men can be taught to follow the teachings. Unless they take refuge in the three treasures, there is no way of rectifying their misdeeds.

III. When an imperial command is given, obey it with reverence. The sovereign is likened to heaven, and his subjects are likened to earth. With heaven providing the cover and earth supporting it, the four seasons proceed in orderly fashion, giving sustenance to all that which is in nature. If earth attempts to overtake the functions of heaven, it destroys everything. . . . If there is no reverence shown to the imperial command, ruin will automatically result. . . .

VII. Every man must be given his clearly delineated responsibility. If a wise man is entrusted with office, the sound of praise arises. If a wicked man holds office, disturbances become frequent. . . . In all things, great or small, find the right man, and the country will be well governed. . . . In this manner, the state will be lasting and its sacerdotal functions will be free from danger.

ten by Shotoku or at a later time by scribes attempting to reconstruct the original), he called for the creation of a centralized government under a supreme ruler and a merit system for selecting and ranking public officials (see the box above). His objective was to limit the powers of the hereditary nobility and enhance the prestige and authority of the Yamato ruler, now emerging as a divine figure and the symbol of the Japanese nation.

The constitution set up a centralized government subject to the will of the ruler. "When an imperial command is given," announced the constitution, "obey it with reverence. The sovereign is likened to heaven, and his subjects are likened to earth." Yet the new government was designed to be benevolent on the Confucian model.

"The way of the minister is to turn away from private motives and to uphold public good." Evil was to be punished, and good rewarded. Major decisions "must not be made by one person alone, but must be deliberated with many."[3]

After Shotoku Taishi's death in 622, his successors continued to introduce reforms based on the Chinese model to make the government more efficient. In a series of so-called Taika (great change) reforms that began in the mid-seventh century, a Grand Council of State was established, which presided over a cabinet of eight ministries. To the traditional six ministries of Tang China were added ministers representing the central secretariat and the imperial household. The territory of Japan was

♦ **Samurai.** During the Kamakura period, painters began to depict the adventures of the new warrior class. Here is an imposing mounted samurai warrior, the Japanese equivalent of the medieval knight in feudal Europe. Like his European counterpart, the samurai was supposed to live by a strict moral code and was expected to maintain an unquestioning loyalty to his liege lord. Above all, a samurai's life was one of simplicity and self-sacrifice.

divided into administrative districts on the Chinese pattern, with the senior official of each district selected from local nobles "of unblemished character, strong and upright, who can discharge the duties of the time effectively." The rural village, composed ideally of fifty households, was the basic unit of government. The village chief was responsible for "the maintenance of the household registers, the assigning of the sowing of crops and the cultivation of mulberry trees, the prevention of offenses, and the requisitioning of taxes and forced labor. . . ." A law code was introduced, and a new tax system was established; now all farmland technically belonged to the state, so taxes were paid directly to the central government rather than through the local nobility, as had previously been the case.

Along with its political institutions, Japan developed a strong interest in Buddhism as a result of its new acquaintance with China. Some of the first Japanese to travel to China during this period were Buddhist pilgrims hoping to learn more about the exciting new doctrine and bring back scriptures for their compatriots to peruse

and study in Japan. As in China, however, the importation of Buddhism aroused resistance within Japanese society. Some argued that the worship of foreign spirits would offend the national spirits. Probably, at least partly to respond to the challenge of Buddhism, traditional forms of Japanese spirit belief were transformed into a more systematic faith known as Shinto (in Chinese, *shen dao*, or the Way of the Spirits).

Eventually, the early resistance was overcome, and during the Nara period (710–784 C.E.)., Buddhism received official encouragement, and a national temple was erected in the capital city. Buddhism became quite popular among the aristocrats, who endowed wealthy monasteries that became quite active in Japanese politics. At first the new faith did not penetrate to the masses, but eventually popular sects such as the Pure Land Sect, an import from China, won many adherents among the common people.

Japan may have acquired one final import from the continent during this period. Prior to the establishment of regular contacts with China, Japan had been relatively isolated from the mainland and therefore may have been spared the effects of diseases, such as smallpox and measles, that ravaged other parts of Asia. But some recent historians believe that Japanese monks returning from the mainland may have brought such diseases to the islands and set off a series of epidemics that severely reduced the local population. Not until the rise of the Heian state (794–1185), when people had built up immunities that curbed the worst effects of the diseases, did Japan enjoy a period of sustained population growth.

THE NARA AND HEIAN PERIODS

At first the effort to build a new state modeled roughly after the Tang state was successful. After Shotoku Taishi's death in 622, political influence fell into the hands of the powerful Fujiwara clan, which managed to marry into the ruling family and continue the reforms Shotoku had begun. In 710, a new capital, laid out on a grid similar to the great Tang city of Chang'an, was established at Nara on the eastern edge of the Yamato plain. The Yamato ruler began to use the title "son of Heaven" in the Chinese fashion. In deference to the allegedly divine character of the ruling family, the mandate remained in perpetuity in the imperial house rather than being bestowed on an individual who was selected by Heaven because of his talent and virtue, as was the case in China.

Had these reforms succeeded, Japan might have followed the Chinese pattern and developed a centralized bureaucratic government. But as time passed, the central government was unable to undermine the power of the court aristocrats in the capital, who were able to dominate the ranks of the public officials. Unlike Tang China, the civil service examinations were not open to all, but were restricted to individuals of noble birth. An academy was established to train candidates for official positions, but only aristocrats were eligible for entrance.

Perhaps more important, the central authorities were unable to undermine the power of the landed nobility in the countryside. As had been the case during the Tang dynasty in China, leading officials were awarded large tracts of land, and they and other powerful families were able to keep the taxes from the lands for themselves. Increasingly starved for revenue, the central government steadily lost power and influence.

In 794, the emperor moved the capital to his family's original power base at nearby Heian on the site of present-day Kyoto. The new capital was laid out in the now familiar Chang'an checkerboard pattern, but on a larger scale than at Nara. Now increasingly self-confident, the rulers ceased to emulate the Tang and sent no more missions to Chang'an. At Heian, the emperor—as the royal line descended from the sun goddess was now styled—continued to rule in name, but actual power was in the hands of the Fujiwara clan, which had managed through intermarriage to link its fortunes closely with the imperial family. A senior member of the clan began to serve as regent (in practice, the chief executive of the government) for the emperor.

In fact, what was happening was a return to the decentralized system that had existed prior to Shotoku Taishi. Attempts to strengthen the power of the central government by imposing taxes directly on the rice lands failed, and powerful families whose wealth was based on the ownership of tax-exempt farmland (called *shoen*) rose in rural areas. To avoid paying taxes, peasants would often surrender their lands to a local aristocrat, who then would allow the peasants to cultivate the lands in return for the payment of rent. To obtain protection from government officials, these local aristocrats in turn might grant title of their lands to a more powerful aristocrat with influence at court. In return, these individuals would receive inheritable rights to a portion of the income from the estate.

In its hierarchical character, the *shoen* system is reminiscent of the relationships that developed between lords and peasants in medieval Europe, but there were some key differences. The landed estates were usually not unified tracts surrounding the manor house of a single lord,

CHRONOLOGY

The Formation of the Japanese State

Shotoku Taishi	572–622
Era of Taika reforms	Mid-seventh century
Nara period	710–784
Heian (Kyoto) period	794–1185
Murasaki Shikibu	978–1016?
Minamoto Yoritomo	1142–1199
Kamakura shogunate	1185–1333
Mongol invasions	Late thirteenth century
Ashikaga period	1333–1600
Onin War	1462–1477

but were made up of small parcels of land scattered throughout the region. Moreover, unlike European serfs, Japanese peasants were not legally bound to their lord's land even after they had surrendered title to their lands.

With the decline of central power at Heian, local aristocrats tended to take justice into their own hands and turned increasingly to military force as a means of protecting their interests. A new class of military retainers emerged whose purpose it was to protect the security and property of their patron. They frequently drew their leaders from disappointed aristocratic office seekers who thus began to occupy a prestigious position in local society, where they often served an administrative as well as a military function. Called the samurai (retainer), these warriors resembled the knights of medieval Europe. Like the knights, the samurai fought on horseback (although a samurai carried a sword and a bow and arrows rather than lance and shield) and were supposed to live by a strict warrior code, known in Japan as *Bushido* (the way of the warrior). As time went on, they became a major force and almost a pseudo-government in much of the Japanese countryside (see the box on p. 378).

THE KAMAKURA SHOGUNATE AND AFTER

By the end of the twelfth century, as rivalries among noble families led to almost constant civil war, once again centralizing forces asserted themselves. This time the instrument was a powerful noble from a warrior clan named Minamoto Yoritomo (1142–1199) who defeated several rivals and set up his power base on the Kamakura

❧ Japan's Warrior Class ❧

*T*he samurai was the Japanese equivalent of the medieval European knight. Like the knight, he was expected to adhere to a strict moral code. Although this passage comes from a document dating only to the seventeenth century, it shows the importance of hierarchy and duty in a society influenced by the doctrine of Confucius. Note the similarity with Krishna's discourse on the duties of an Indian warrior in Chapter 2.

The Way of the Samurai

The master once said: The generation of all men and of all things in the universe is accomplished by means of the marvelous interaction of the two forces [yin and yang]. Man is the most highly endowed of all creatures, and all things culminate in man. Generation after generation men have taken their livelihood from tilling the soil, or devised and manufactured tools, or produced profit from mutual trade, so that peoples' needs were satisfied. Thus the occupations of farmer, artisan, and merchant necessarily grew up as complementary to one another. However, the samurai eats food without growing it, uses utensils without manufacturing them, and profits without buying or selling. What is the justification for this? When I reflect today on my pursuit in life [I realize that] I was born into a family whose ancestors for generations have been warriors, and whose pursuit is service at court. The samurai is one who does not cultivate, does not manufacture, and does not engage in trade, but it cannot be that he has no function at all as a samurai. He who satisfied his needs without performing any function at all would more properly be called an idler. Therefore one must devote all one's mind to the detailed examination of one's calling.

If one deeply fixes his attention on what I have said and examines closely one's own function, it will become clear what the business of the samurai is. The business of the samurai consists in reflecting on his own station in life, in discharging loyal service to his master if he has one, in deepening his fidelity in associations with friends, and, with due consideration of his own position, in devoting himself to duty above all. However, in one's own life, one becomes unavoidably involved in obligations between father and child, older and younger brother, and husband and wife. Though these are also the fundamental moral obligations of everyone in the land, the farmers, artisans, and merchants have no leisure from their occupations, and so they cannot constantly act in accordance with them and fully exemplify the Way. The samurai dispenses with the business of the farmer, artisan, and merchant and confines himself to practicing this Way; should there be someone in the three classes of the common people who transgresses against these moral principles, the samurai summarily punishes him and thus upholds proper moral principles in the land. It would not do for the samurai to know the martial and civil virtues without manifesting them. Since this is the case, outwardly he stands in physical readiness for any call to service and inwardly he strives to fulfill the Way of the lord and subject, friend and friend, father and son, older and younger brother, and husband and wife. Within his heart he keeps to the ways of peace, but without he keeps his weapons ready for use. The three classes of the common people make him their teacher and respect him. By following his teachings, they are enabled to understand what is fundamental and what is secondary.

Herein lies the Way of the samurai, the means by which he earns his clothing, food, and shelter; and by which his heart is put at ease, and he is enabled to pay back at length his obligation to his lord and the kindness of his parents. Were there no such duty, it would be as though one were to steal the kindness of one's parents, greedily devour the income of one's master, and make one's whole life a career of robbery and brigandage. This would be very grievous.

peninsula, south of the modern city of Tokyo. To strengthen the state, he created a more centralized government (the *bakufu,* or "tent government") under a powerful military leader, known as the shogun (general). The shogun attempted to increase the powers of the central government while reducing rival feudal clans to vassal status. This "shogunate system," in which the emperor was the titular authority while the shogun exercised actual power, served as the political system in Japan until the last half of the nineteenth century.

At first the system worked effectively, and it was fortunate that it did, because during the next century Japan faced the most serious challenge it had confronted yet. The threat came from the Mongols, who had destroyed the Song dynasty in China and were now attempting to assert their hegemony throughout all of Asia (see Chapter 10). In 1266 Emperor Khubilai Khan demanded tribute from Japan. When the Japanese refused, he invaded with an army of over 30,000 troops. Bad weather and difficult conditions forced a retreat, but the Mongols tried again in 1281. An army nearly 150,000 strong landed on the northern coast of Kyushu. The Japanese were able to contain them for two months, until virtually the entire Mongol fleet was destroyed by a massive typhoon, a "divine wind" (*kamikaze*) that had protected the Japanese people and their divine emperor from their enemies. Japan would not face a foreign invader again until American forces landed on the Japanese islands in the summer of 1945.

The resistance to the Mongols had put a heavy strain on the system, however, and in 1333 the Kamakura shogunate was overthrown by a coalition of powerful clans. A new shogun, supplied by the Ashikaga family, arose in Kyoto and attempted to continue the shogunate system. But the Ashikaga were unable to restore the centralized power of their predecessors. With the central government reduced to a shell, the power of the local landed aristocracy increased to an unprecedented degree. Heads of great noble families, now called daimyo (great names), controlled vast landed estates that owed no taxes to the government or to the court in Kyoto. As clan rivalries continued, the daimyo relied increasingly on the samurai for protection, and political power came into the hands of a loose coalition of noble families.

By the end of the fifteenth century, Japan was again close to anarchy. A disastrous civil conflict known as the Onin War (1467–1477) led to the virtual destruction of the capital city of Kyoto and the disintegration of the shogunate. With the disappearance of any central authority, powerful aristocrats in rural areas now seized total control over large territories and ruled as independent great lords. Territorial rivalries and claims of precedence led to almost constant warfare in this period of "warring states," as it is called (in obvious parallel with a similar era during the Zhou dynasty in China). The trend back toward central authority did not begin until the last quarter of the sixteenth century.

As this brief description shows, Japanese political history was characterized by the same tensions between the center and the periphery that marked Chinese history. The forces that undermined and ultimately destroyed Shotoku Taishi's centralized state were reminiscent of

◆ **The Burning of the Palace.** The Kamakura era is represented in this thirteenth-century action-packed scene from the *Scroll of the Heiji Period,* which depicts the burning of a retired emperor's palace in the middle of the night. Servants and ladies of the court flee in vain from the massive flames. Confusion and violence reign. The determined faces of the warriors only add to the ferocity of the attack.

�֎ Map 11.2   Early Japan.

Economic and Social Structures

From the time the Yayoi culture was first established on the Japanese islands, Japan was a predominantly agrarian society. Although Japan lacked the spacious valleys and deltas of most ancient and medieval river valley societies, its inhabitants were able to take advantage of their limited amount of tillable land and plentiful rainfall to create a society based on the cultivation of wet rice.

As we have seen, in the beginning landholding patterns were organized on a tribal or clan basis, as in Shang and early Zhou China. In China, this system was gradually replaced by a more bureaucratic model based on centralized rule and private ownership of land. But in Japan, the effort by Shotoku Taishi and his successors to establish a similar pattern failed. Noble families were able to seize control of most *uji* land, and gradually many were able to obtain exemptions to prevent taxes from the land from going to the central government. At first, leading noble families at court or in urban areas were able to keep the lands in their own hands by hiring local managers who retained a portion of the taxes paid by the peasants and sent the remainder to their absentee patron. Later, when central authority had almost entirely collapsed, powerful local lords, assisted by their military retainers, the samurai, were able to control large tracts of land (the *shoen*) somewhat similar to the manors of medieval Europe. At the local level, agricultural work was organized by estate managers hired by the aristocratic patron or manorial lord. These managers, who might be civilians or local members of warrior clans, collected the taxes from the peasants and forwarded them to the patron or the lord of the manor. The managers, in turn, were exempt from taxes and the obligation to provide labor services.

During the early period, most of the wealth of Japanese society came from agriculture, particularly from the cultivation of wet rice. The bulk of it passed into the hands of the wealthy landowners, although as the *shoen* system developed, a significant portion began to be accumulated by the local managers. As time passed, agricultural productivity began to rise with the opening of new lands, improved irrigation, and the cultivation of new crops. In turn, manufacturing and trade began to increase.

As in China, commerce was slow to develop in Japan. During ancient times, each *uji* had a local artisan class, composed of weavers, carpenters, and iron workers, but trade was essentially local and was regulated by the local clan leaders. With the rise of the Yamato state, a money economy gradually began to develop, although most trade was still conducted through barter until the twelfth

those that weakened and destroyed the Tang. But in China, central power eventually reasserted itself, and during the Song dynasty, the power of the noble clans was forever eliminated. That process did not take place in Japan until well into the modern era.

One reason for this difference may have been the absence of a foreign threat in Japan. The Song rulers, for example, living under the constant threat of tribal invasions from the north, were able to suppress the power of the landed nobility in China. In Japan, external threats—from Tang China or from the Mongols—also stimulated a temporary growth of central power. But when the threat subsided, divisive forces reasserted themselves. Only in the nineteenth century, when a new and even more serious threat appeared in the form of Western imperialism, did the Japanese ruling classes finally realize that the central government must be endowed with adequate powers if it was to protect the interests of the entire nation.

Furthermore, whereas Chinese political thought evolved from the aristocratic principle to that of rule by merit, a similar process did not take place in Japan until modern times. While the Japanese borrowed liberally from China, they applied Confucian concepts in their own way. As we have seen, access to official careers through the civil service examinations was limited to those of aristocratic birth. Perhaps this was also a consequence of the failure of the central government to assert its dominance over the landed nobility until the nineteenth century. And the lateness of this development, in turn, may be a consequence of Japan's relative isolation from the turbulent history of mainland Asia.

century, when metal coins introduced from China became more popular.

Trade and manufacturing began to develop more rapidly during the Kamakura period, with the appearance of trimonthly markets in the larger towns and the emergence of such industries as paper, iron casting, and porcelain. Intraregional trade, in which goods were transported in horse-drawn carts, by boats on rivers or along the coast, or on human backs, became increasingly common. Foreign trade, mainly with Korea and China, began during the eleventh century. Japan exported raw materials, paintings, swords, and other manufactured items in return for silk, porcelain, books, and copper cash. Some Japanese traders were so aggressive in pressing their interests that authorities in China and Korea attempted to limit the number of Japanese commercial missions that could visit each year. Such restrictions were often ignored, however, and encouraged some Japanese traders to turn to piracy.

Significantly, manufacturing and commerce developed rapidly during the more decentralized period of the Ashikaga shogunate and the era of the "warring states," perhaps because of the rapid growth in the wealth and autonomy of local daimyo families. Market towns, now

operating on a full money economy, began to appear, and local manufacturers formed guilds to protect their mutual interests. Sometimes local peasants would sell products made in their homes, such as clothing made of silk or hemp, household items, or food products, at the markets. In general, however, trade and manufacturing remained under the control of the local daimyo, who would often provide tax breaks to local guilds in return for other benefits. Although Japan remained a primarily agricultural society, it was on the verge of a major advance in manufacturing.

DAILY LIFE

As in other early societies, we have much more evidence for aristocratic culture than for the lives of the common people. In general, there was a sharp distinction between the aristocracy and the common people, as had been the case in China until the middle of the Zhou dynasty. The existence of class differences apparently goes back to ancient times. A Chinese dynastic history of the third century C.E. referred to clear class distinctions in the country of Wa (as Japan was known to the Chinese) and added: "When plebeians meet the high-echelon men on

◆ **Scene of Urban Life.** Although traditional Japan was largely an agricultural society, trade and manufacturing began to develop during the Kamakura period, sparked by the rapid growth of local daimyo families and market towns. Portrayed here is a detail from a thirteenth-century scroll depicting the bustle and general confusion of the city of Edo (now Tokyo).

The Seduction of the Akashi Lady

The Tale of Genji, *Japan's most famous novel, is a panoramic portrayal of court life in tenth-century Japan. In this excerpt, the courtier Genji has just seduced a lady at court and now feels misgivings at having betrayed his child bride. A koto is a Japanese string instrument similar to a zither.*

The Tale of Genji

A curtain string brushed against a koto, to tell him that she had been passing a quiet evening at her music.

"And will you not play for me on the koto of which I have heard so much?"

"Would there were someone with whom I might share my thoughts
And so dispel some part of these sad dreams."
"You speak to one for whom the night has no end.
How can she tell the dreaming from the waking?"

The almost inaudible whisper reminded him strongly of the Rokujo lady.

This lady had not been prepared for an incursion and could not cope with it. She fled to an inner room. How she could have contrived to bar it he could not tell, but it was very firmly barred indeed. Though he did not exactly force his way through, it is not to be imagined that he left matters as they were. Delicate, slender—she was almost too beautiful. Pleasure was mingled with pity at the thought that he was imposing himself upon her. She was even more pleasing than reports from afar had had her. The autumn night, usually so long, was over in a trice. Not wishing to be seen, he hurried out, leaving affectionate assurances behind.

Genji called in secret from time to time. The two houses being some distance apart, he feared being seen by fishermen, who were known to relish a good rumor,

and sometimes several days would elapse between his visits. . . .

Genji dreaded having Murasaki [his bride] learn of the affair. He still loved her more than anyone, and he did not want her to make even joking reference to it. She was a quiet, docile lady, but she had more than once been unhappy with him. Why, for the sake of brief pleasure, had he caused her pain? He wished it were all his to do over again. The sight of the Akashi lady only brought new longing for the other lady.

He got off a more earnest and affectionate letter than usual, at the end of which he said: "I am in anguish at the thought that, because of foolish occurrences for which I have been responsible but have had little heart, I might appear in a guise distasteful to you. There has been a strange, fleeting encounter. That I should volunteer this story will make you see, I hope, how little I wish to have secrets from you. Let the gods be my judges.

"It was but the fisherman's brush with the salty sea pine
Followed by a tide of tears of longing."

Her reply was gentle and unreproachful, and at the end of it she said: "That you should have deigned to tell me a dreamlike story which you could not keep to yourself calls to mind numbers of earlier instances.

"Naive of me, perhaps; yet we did make our vows.
And now see the waves that wash the Mountain of Waiting!"

It was the one note of reproach in a quiet, undemanding letter. He found it hard to put down, and for some nights he stayed away from the house in the hills.

the road, they withdraw to the grassy area [presumably to the side of the road] hesitantly. When they speak or are spoken to, they either crouch or kneel with both hands on the ground to show their respect."[4]

The origins of these class differences are not clear, although the Chinese dynastic history suggests that they may have been based on a combination of political and religious functions. The Japanese ruling elite was composed of the hereditary rulers of the various clans. The rise of the

centralized Yamato state in the sixth and seventh centuries saw the emergence of a court aristocracy, whose wealth was obtained primarily from rents from their estates.

Court life is described in considerable detail in some of the early Japanese literary classics, such as *The Tale of Genji* by Lady Murasaki (978–c. 1016), whose formal name was Murasaki Shikibu. In many ways, the courtiers resembled their counterparts in Europe or in India under the Mughals (see Chapter 16). They enjoyed a life of

leisure and refinement, aesthetic pleasures and elaborate court ritual. Though far removed from the concerns of ordinary Japanese, this lifestyle left its mark on Japanese culture (see the box on p. 382).

There was another side to the Japanese aristocracy, however. Like the aristocrats of medieval Europe, their roots were in the countryside, in their landed estates, and, for some, in military combat. Although this more vigorous and rustic aspect of the aristocracy was submerged during the Fujiwara period, it returned to prominence after the collapse of central authority in the fourteenth century and became a leading element in Japanese culture from that point on until the nineteenth century. The samurai, who were considered members of the minor nobility, were the symbol of the rural aristocracy. Many samurai may have come from the local aristocracy, although some scholars have recently argued that many were descendants of pre-Yayoi peoples living on the Japanese islands (such as the Ainu) who were hired to protect the lands of the nobility.

The samurai lived by a strict warrior code, the *Bushido* (see the box on p. 378). They lived a life of simplicity and self-sacrifice and were expected to maintain an intense and unquestioning loyalty to their lord. Bonds of loyalty were also quite strong among members of the samurai class, and homosexuality was quite common, as it was among monks in Buddhist monasteries. In early days, the samurai fought on horseback. Later, as the nature of warfare changed, they led infantry into battle or, in times of peace, became estate administrators, the closest Japanese equivalent, perhaps, of the Confucian scholar-officials in medieval China.

Below the hereditary nobility in social status were the masses of the population. One of the first descriptions of the life of the Japanese people comes from the Chinese dynastic history quoted earlier. It describes lords and peasants living in an agricultural society that was based on the cultivation of wet rice. Laws had been enacted to punish offenders, local trade was conducted in markets, and government granaries stored the grain that was paid as taxes (see the box on p. 384).

Life for the common people probably changed very little over the next several hundred years. Most were peasants, who worked on land owned by their manorial lord or, in some cases, by the state or by Buddhist monasteries. By no means, however, were all peasants equal either economically or socially. Although in ancient times all land was owned by the state and peasants working the land were taxed at an equal rate depending on the nature of the crop, after the Yamato era variations began to develop. At the top were local officials who were often well-to-do peasants. They were responsible for organizing collective labor services and collecting tax grain from the peasants and in turn were exempt from such obligations themselves.

The mass of the peasants were under the authority of these local officials. In general, peasants were free to dispose of their harvest as they saw fit after paying their tax quota, but in practical terms their freedom was limited. Those who were unable to pay the tax sank to the level of *genin*, or landless laborers, who could be bought and sold by their proprietors like slaves along with the land on which they worked. Some fled to escape such a fate and attempted to survive by clearing plots of land in the mountains or by becoming bandits.

In addition to the *genin*, the bottom of the social scale was occupied by the *eta*, a class of hereditary slaves who were responsible for what were considered degrading occupations, such as curing leather and burying the dead. The origins of the *eta* are not entirely clear, but they probably were descendants of prisoners of war, criminals, or mountain dwellers who were not related to the dominant Yamato peoples. As we shall see, the *eta* are still a distinctive part of Japanese society, and although their full legal rights are guaranteed under the current constitution, discrimination against them is not uncommon.

Daily life for ordinary people in early Japan resembled that of their counterparts throughout much of Asia. The vast majority lived in small villages, several of which normally made up a single *shoen*. Housing was simple. Most lived in small two-room houses of timber, mud, or thatch, with dirt floors covered by straw or woven mats (the origin, perhaps, of the well-known *tatami*, or woven mat floor, of more modern times). Their diet consisted of rice (if some was left after the payment of the grain tax), wild grasses, millet, roots, and some fish and birds. Festivals, folk dramas, jugglers, and acrobats broke the monotony of the daily routine. Such entertainment was often produced by wandering troupes, who were sponsored by the local *shoen* or perhaps by a Buddhist temple in the vicinity. Still, life must have been difficult at best, as it was for their contemporaries throughout Asia (see the box on p. 385).

Evidence about the relations between men and women in early Japan presents a mixed picture. The Chinese dynastic history reports that "in their meetings and daily living, there is no distinction between father and son, or between men and women." It notes that a woman "adept in the ways of shamanism" had briefly ruled Japan in the third century C.E. But it also remarks that polygyny was common, with nobles normally having four to five wives, and commoners two or three.[5]

⇒ Life in the Land of Wa ⇐

Some of the earliest descriptions of Japan come from Chinese sources. The following passage from the History of the Wei Dynasty *was written in the late third century* C.E. *The term Wa is a derogatory word meaning "dwarf" and was frequently used in China to refer to the Japanese people. The author of this passage, while remarking on the strange habits of the Japanese, writes without condescension.*

History of the Wei Dynasty

The people of Wa make their abode in the mountainous islands located in the middle of the ocean to the southeast of the Taifang prefecture. Formerly there were more than one hundred communities. During the Han dynasty their envoys appeared in the court. Today, thirty of their communities maintain communication with us through their envoys. . . .

All men, old or young, are covered by tattoos. Japanese fishers revel in diving to catch fish and shellfish. Tattoos are said to drive away large fish and water predators. They are considered an ornament. Tattoos differ from community to community. Some place tattoos on the left, and others on the right, some place large ones and others small ones. Tattoos also differ in accordance with the social position. . . . Men allow their hair to cover both of their ears and wear headbands. They wear loin cloth wrapped around their bodies and seldom use stitches. Women gather their hair at the ends and tie it in a knot and then pin it to the top of their heads. They make their clothes in one piece, and cut an opening in the center for their heads. They plant wet-field rice, China-grass [a type of nettle], and mulberry trees. They raise cocoons and reel the silk off the cocoons. They produce clothing made of China-grass, of coarse silk, and of cotton. In their land, there are no cows, horses, tigers, leopards, sheep or swan. They fight with halberds, shields and wooden bows. . . . Their arrows are made of bamboo and iron and bone points make up the arrowhead.

The land of Wa is warm and mild. The people eat raw vegetables and go about barefoot in winter as in summer. They live in houses. Father and mother, older and younger, sleep separately. They paint their bodies with vermilion and scarlet, just as the Chinese apply powder. They serve food on bowl-shaped stemware, and eat with their fingers. When a person dies, he is placed in a coffin (which is buried directly in the grave) without an outer protective layer. The grave is then covered with earth to make a mound. When death occurs, the family observes mourning for more than ten days, during which period no meat is eaten. The head mourner wails and cries, while others sing, dance and drink liquor (probably *sake*, the Japanese rice wine). When the funeral is over, the entire family goes into the water to cleanse themselves in a manner similar to the Chinese in their rites of purification.

In their meetings and daily living, there is no distinction between father and son, men and women. People enjoy liquor. . . . They live long, some reaching one hundred years of age, and others to eighty or ninety years. Normally men of high echelon have four or five wives, and the plebeians may have two or three. Women are chaste and not given to jealousy. They do not engage in thievery, and there is very little litigation. When the law is violated, the light offender loses his wife and children by confiscation, and the grave offender has his household and kinsmen exterminated. There are class distinctions within the nobility and the base, and some are vassals of others. There are mansions and granaries erected for the purpose of collecting taxes. Each community has a market place where commodities are exchanged under the supervision of an official of Wa. . . .

When plebeians meet the high-echelon men on the road, they withdraw to the grassy area (side of the road) hesitantly. When they speak or are spoken to, they either crouch or kneel with both hands on the ground to show their respect. When responding they say "aye," which corresponds to our affirmative "yes."

A Lament of the Common Man

The lives of the common people often passed unrecorded in medieval Japan. This passage from the Japanese poem *Manyoshu* dates from the mid-eighth century. Unlike many written works from the period, many passages of *Manyoshu* describe everyday life and display a strong sense of sympathy for the trials of the poor.

Manyoshu

On the night when the rain beats,
Driven by the wind,
On the night when the snowflakes mingle
With the sleety rain,
I feel so helplessly cold.
I nibble at a lump of salt,
Sip the hot, oft-diluted dregs of sake;
And coughing, sniffing,
And stroking my scanty beard,
I say in my pride,
"There's none worthy, save I!"
But I shiver still with cold.
I pull up my hempen bedclothes,
Wear what few sleeveless clothes I have,
But cold and bitter is the night!
As for those poorer than myself,
Their parents must be cold and hungry,

Their wives and children beg and cry.
Then, how do you struggle through life?
Wide as they call the heaven and earth,
For me they have shrunk quite small,
Bright though they call the sun and moon,
They never shine for me.
Is it the same with all men,
Or for me alone?
By rare chance I was born a man
And no meaner than my fellows,
But, wearing unwadded sleeveless clothes
In tatters, like weeds waving in the sea,
Hanging from my shoulders,
And under the sunken roofs,
Within the leaning walls,
Here I lie on straw
Spread on bare earth,
With my parents at my pillow,
My wife and children at my feet,
All huddled in grief and tears.
No fire sends up smoke
At the cooking-place,
And in the cauldron
A spider spins its web.

The introduction of Confucian ideas had an impact on women's position in Japanese society. Still, the tradition of relative equality appeared to survive. An eighth-century law code guaranteed the inheritance rights of women, while wives abandoned by their husbands were permitted to obtain a divorce and to remarry. A husband could divorce his wife if she did not produce a male child, committed adultery, disobeyed her parents-in-law, talked too much, engaged in theft, was jealous, or had a serious illness.[6]

Women also suffered from sexual discrimination in Buddhist teachings and practices (for the introduction of Buddhism to Japan, see In Search of the Pure Land: Religion in Early Japan on the next page). Although women were permitted to take up monastic life—in fact, many widows entered a monastery at the death of their husbands—they were not permitted to visit the holy places and buildings of the Buddhist faith, nor were they even (in the accepted wisdom) equal with men in the afterlife. As one Buddhist commentary written in the late thirteenth century put it:

> We must admit that there are great hindrances in the way of woman's attaining enlightenment . . . the reason is that her sin is grievous, and so she is not allowed to enter the lofty palace of the great Brahma, nor to look upon the clouds which hover over his ministers and people. She is always taken down to a lower seat than the soft-cushioned one of the divine, Indra, and she can never behold the flowers in his thirty-three-citied Heaven. . . .[7]

Such disabilities eventually drew the attention of compassionate observers. The author of this commentary, a leading figure in the Pure Land sect, went on to lament:

Alas! Woman! Though thou has two feet, there are mountains of the Law which thou mayst not ascend, and courtyards of the Buddha which thou mayst not tread. Shame though it be, while possessed of two eyes, there are sacred places upon which thou mayst not look, and holy images which thou mayst not worship! . . . How then, can you ever possibly draw near to the Buddha of the ten thousand transcendent virtues in the Pure Land of countless treasures?

In a treatise written in the thirteenth century, a Zen priest argued in favor of equality between the sexes in the search for Buddhahood:

When we speak of the wicked there are certainly men among them. When we speak of noble persons, these surely include women. Learning the Law of Buddha and achieving release from illusion have nothing to do with whether one happens to be a man or a woman.

A nun who has attained the Way is entitled to receive the homage of all the arhats, pratyeka-buddhas and bodhisattvas who would seek to learn the Dharma from her. What is so sacred about the status of a man?[8]

In response to such views, women for the first time were given the right to participate actively in Buddhist activities in medieval Japan.

Although women did not possess the full legal and social rights of their male counterparts, they played an active role at various levels of Japanese society. Aristocratic women were prominent at court, and some, such as the author Lady Murasaki, became renowned for their artistic or literary talents. Though few commoners could aspire to such prominence, women often appear in the scroll paintings of the period along with men, doing the spring planting, threshing and hulling the rice, and acting as carriers, peddlers, salespersons, and entertainers.

In Search of the Pure Land: Religion in Early Japan

In Japan, as elsewhere, religious belief began with the worship of nature spirits. Early Japanese worshiped spirits, called *kami*, who resided in trees, rivers and streams, and mountains. They also believed in ancestral spirits who were present in the atmosphere. In Japan, these beliefs eventually evolved into a kind of state religion called Shinto (the Sacred Way or the Way of the Gods) that is still practiced today. Shinto still serves as an ideological and emotional force that knits the Japanese into a single people and a single nation.

Shinto does not have a complex metaphysical superstructure or an elaborate moral code. It does require certain ritual acts, usually undertaken at a shrine, and a process of purification, which may have originated in primitive concerns about death, childbirth, illness, and menstruation. This traditional concern about physical purity may help to explain the strong Japanese concern for personal cleanliness and the practice of denying women entrance to the holy places.

Another feature of Shinto is its stress on the beauty of nature and the importance of nature itself in Japanese life. Shinto shrines are usually located in places of exceptional beauty and are often dedicated to a nearby physical feature. As time passed, such primitive beliefs contributed to the characteristic Japanese love of nature. In this sense, early Shinto beliefs have been incorporated into the lives of all Japanese.

In time, Shinto evolved into a state doctrine that was linked with belief in the divinity of the emperor and the sacredness of the Japanese nation. A national shrine was established at Ise, north of the early capital of Nara, where the emperor annually paid tribute to the sun goddess. But although Shinto had evolved well beyond its primitive origins, like its counterparts elsewhere it could not satisfy all the religious and emotional needs of the Japanese people. For those needs, the Japanese turned to Buddhism.

Buddhism was introduced into Japan during the sixth century C.E. by missionary monks from China. At first it was primarily a court religion, but by the eighth century it began to spread rapidly among the remainder of the population. As in China, most Japanese saw no contradiction between worshiping both the Buddha and their local nature gods, many of whom were considered to be later manifestations of the Buddha. Most of the Buddhist sects that had achieved popularity in China were established in Japan, and many of them attracted powerful patrons at court. Great monasteries were established that competed in wealth and influence with the noble families that had traditionally ruled the country.

Perhaps the two most influential Buddhist sects were the Pure Land (Jodo) sect and Zen (in Chinese, Chan or Ch'an). The Pure Land sect, which taught that devotion alone could lead to enlightenment and release, was very popular among the common people, for whom monastic life was one of the few routes to upward mobility. Among the aristocracy, the most influential school was Zen, which exerted a significant impact on Japanese life and culture during the era of the warring states. In its emphasis on austerity, self-discipline, and communion with nature, Zen complemented many traditional beliefs in Japanese society and became an important component of the samurai warrior's code.

In Zen teachings, there were various ways to achieve enlightenment (*satori* in Japanese). Some stressed that it could be achieved suddenly. One monk, for example, reportedly achieved *satori* by listening to the sound of a bamboo striking against roof tiles, another by carefully watching the opening of peach blossoms in the spring. But other practitioners, sometimes called adepts, said that enlightenment could come only through studying the scriptures and arduous self-discipline (known as *zazen*, or "seated Zen"). Seated Zen involved a lengthy process of meditation that cleansed the mind of extraneous thoughts, so that it could concentrate on the essential.

Sources of Traditional Japanese Culture

Nowhere is the Japanese genius for blending indigenous and imported elements into an effective whole better demonstrated than in culture. In such widely diverse fields as art, architecture, sculpture, and literature, the Japanese from early times showed an impressive capacity to borrow selectively from abroad without destroying essential native elements tracing back to the origins of Japanese society.

Unfortunately, our knowledge of both the Neolithic Jomon people and the subsequent Yayoi culture is limited. The Yayoi peoples had apparently not mastered the art of writing and left no written records. Nor were they given to grandiose architecture except for burial mounds for the tombs of the elite. Of most interest are the clay figurines—known as *haniwa*—that have been found in the burial mounds. These figurines, usually of animals, were probably sacrificial objects meant to accompany the deceased on the journey to the next world.

Growing contact with China during the period of the rise of the Yamato state stimulated Japanese artists. Missions sent to China and Korea during the seventh and eighth centuries returned with examples of Tang literature, sculpture, and painting, all of which influenced the Japanese.

LITERATURE

Borrowing from Chinese models was somewhat complicated for Japanese authors, however. The early Japanese had no writing system for recording their own spoken language and initially adopted the Chinese written language for writing after frequent contacts were established with China during the sixth and seventh centuries C.E. But resourceful Japanese soon began to adapt the Chinese written characters so they could be used for record-

◆ **Portrait of a Zen Master.** Reflecting the chaos of the fourteenth century, the art of portraiture flourished, and artists produced a full gallery of warriors and holy men in startlingly realistic detail. This painting of a Zen master, complete with crooked mouth, stubble, and worry lines, is an unflattering one. Nevertheless, with economy of line, the artist has managed to convey the master's spiritual and mental intensity.

ing the Japanese language. Spoken Japanese, however, is strikingly different from Chinese—Japanese is polysyllabic rather than monosyllabic and has no tones. In some cases, Chinese characters were borrowed and given Japanese pronunciations. But Chinese characters ordinarily could not be used to record Japanese words, which normally contain more than one syllable. Sometimes the Japanese simply used Chinese characters as phonetic symbols that were combined to form Japanese words. Later they simplified the characters into phonetic symbols called *kana* that were used alongside Chinese characters. This hybrid system continues to be used today.

At first, many educated Japanese preferred to write in Chinese, and a court literature—consisting of essays, poetry, and official histories—appeared in the classical Chinese language. But the native Japanese spoken language never totally disappeared among the educated classes and eventually became the instrument of a unique literature. During the Nara period, Japan produced an anthology of 4,500 poems composed between the fourth and the mid-eighth centuries. Although written in Chinese characters, these poems exhibited little Chinese influence in form or sentiment. At the beginning of the Heian period in the ninth century, however, poets began

to adhere strictly to Chinese rules for writing poetry. In fact, learning Chinese poems and composing in the Chinese manner were prerequisites for acceptance and promotion at court. With the lessening of Chinese political and cultural influence in the tenth century, Japanese verse resurfaced. Now all courtiers tried to learn the poems in both the Chinese and Japanese verse anthologies. Quotations from and improvisations on these poems became a standard part of oral and written communications for all official functions as well as for intimate personal moments. Knowledge of poetry testified to one's breeding, sensitivity, and high moral character. Between the tenth and the fifteenth centuries, twenty imperial anthologies of poetry were compiled. Initially, they were written primarily by courtiers, but with the fall of the Heian court and the rise of the warrior and merchant classes, all literate segments of society began to produce poetry.

Japanese poetry is unique. It expresses its themes in a simple form, a characteristic stemming from traditional Japanese aesthetics, Zen religion, and the language itself. In Japanese, each syllable ends in a vowel, and there are no consonant clusters, meter, or rhyme in poetry. Until the seventh century, the traditional Japanese poem contained thirty-one syllables divided into lines of five, seven, five, seven, and seven syllables each. Poets tried to express and evoke the emotions of the passage of time and the evanescence of the material world. Because the Japanese language contains only a small number of sounds, many words have two or more meanings. Thus, a single word could allude to several ideas or emotions simultaneously. Furthermore, poets often alluded to earlier poems by repeating their images with small changes, a technique that reminded the reader of the themes of the first poem, while calling attention to the new form. This was viewed not as plagiarism, but as an elaboration on the meaning of the earlier poem. The following poems in English translation illustrate this technique; the first poem is by Fujiwara no Michimune; the second is by Lady Sagami:

The under leaves
In the autumn wind
Must have become cold:
In the moor of little lespedezas
The quail are crying.

The under leaves of the lespedeza
When the dew is gathering
Must be cold:

In the autumn moor
The young deer are crying.[9]

The aim of the Japanese poet was to create a mood, perhaps the melancholic effect of gently falling cherry blossoms or leaves. With a few specific references, the poet suggested a whole world, just as Zen Buddhism sought enlightenment from a sudden perception. These twelfth-century poems by the priest Jakuren and Fujiwara no Yasusue focus attention on such prosaic subjects as raindrops and footprints:

The hanging raindrops
Have not dried from the needles
Of the fir forest
Before the evening mist
Of autumn rises.

Nothing whatsoever
Remains of you in this grass
We once used to tread;
How long ago it was we came—
The garden now is a wilderness.

Poetry served a unique function at the Heian court where it was the initial means of communication between lovers. By custom, aristocratic women were isolated from all contact with men outside their immediate family and spent their days hidden behind screens. Some amused themselves by learning how to write poetry. When courtship began, poetic exchanges were the only means a woman had to attract her prospective lover, who would be enticed solely by her poetic art. If her poetry excited him, he stepped beyond the screen to possess her. Even then, her physical attributes were considered less important than her breeding, refinement, the delicacy of her poetic expression, and the proper coloring and arrangement of her clothing.

By the fourteenth century, the technique of the "linked verse" had become the most popular form of Japanese poetry. Known as haiku, it is composed of seventeen syllables divided into lines of five, seven, and five syllables. The poems usually focused on images from nature and the mutability of life. Often the poetry was written by several individuals alternatively composing verses and linking them together into long sequences of hundreds and even thousands of lines (see the box on p. 389).

During the Heian period, male courtiers wrote in Chinese, believing that Chinese civilization was superior and

A Sample of Linked Verse

One of the distinctive features of medieval Japanese literature was the technique of "linked verse." In a manner similar to haiku poetry today, such poems, known as renga, were written by groups of individuals who would join together to compose the poem, verse by verse. The following example, by three famous poets named Sogi, Shohaku, and Socho, is one of the most famous of the period.

The Three Poets at Minase

Snow clinging to slope,   Sogi
 On mist-enshrouded mountains
 At eveningtime.
In the distance flows   Shohaku
 Through plum-scented villages.

Willows cluster   Socho
 In the river breeze
 As spring appears.
The sound of a boat being poled   Sogi
 In the clearness at dawn
Still the moon lingers   Shohaku
As fog o'er-spreads
 The night.
A frost-covered meadow;   Socho
 Autumn has drawn to a close.
Against the wishes   Sogi
 Of droning insects
 The grasses wither.

---

worthy of emulation. Like the Chinese, they viewed prose fiction as "vulgar gossip." Consequently, from the ninth to the twelfth century, Japanese women were the most prolific writers of prose fiction in Japanese. Excluded from school, they learned to read and write at home and wrote diaries, stories, and novels to pass the time. Some of the most talented women were invited to court as authors in residence.

From this tradition of female prose appeared one of the world's truly great novels, *The Tale of Genji*, written by the diarist and court author Murasaki Shikibu around the year 1000. Through a mist of nostalgia, she re-created the golden age of the tenth-century Fujiwara court. The novel has a cast of 430 realistic characters and covers a span of seventy-five years in 2,500 pages. It still touches the reader with its intimate psychological realism and themes of beauty and sorrow (see the box on p. 382).

The novel traces the life and loves of the courtier Genji as he strives to remain in favor with those in power while at the same time pursuing his cult of love and beauty. Polygamy and sexual promiscuity were prominent at the Heian court. Genji himself had several wives and numerous affairs, which are described in vivid detail. The essential element in the story line, however, is the artistic refinement and sensitivity of the characters. The most important aspect of their lives is the style with which they write letters and poetry, sing songs, dance, or play the flute or the zither. In Fujiwara Japan, artistic sensitivity and performance were more highly prized than moral conduct. Indeed, beauty was equated with goodness.

Considered the world's first psychological novel and the greatest of all Japanese novels, *The Tale of Genji* has inspired more than 20,000 analytical studies. Above all, it is the psychological complexity of the characters that makes them so realistic. The many facets of Genji's personality are explored in detail, as he progresses from youthful escapades to an attitude of compassion and melancholy in his later years.

After the refined and gentle sadness of the era of Genji, Japanese fiction entered the increasingly pessimistic world of the warring states of Kamakura (1185–1333). Typically, the novels of this period focus on a solitary figure, who is aloof from the refinements of the court and faces battle and possibly death. Understandably, a new genre, that of the heroic war tale, developed out of the new warrior class. Such works described the military exploits of warriors, coupled with an overwhelming sense of sadness and loneliness. A classic of this genre, *The Tale of the Heike*, relates the story of a twelfth-century assault on Kyoto during a struggle for

✦ **Guardian Kings.** Larger than life and intimidating in its presence, this thirteenth-century wooden statue departs from the refined atmosphere of the Heian court and pulsates with the masculine energy of the Kamakura period. Placed strategically at the entrance to Buddhist shrines, guardian kings such as this one protected the temple and the faithful.

domination between two rival clans. Underlying the story is the Buddhist philosophy of the transience of existence. The story opens with a lyrical passage, expressing the spirit of the era:

> In the sound of the bell of the Gion Temple echoes the impermanence of all things. The pale hue of the flowers of the teak-tree shows the truth that they who prosper must fall. The proud ones do not last long, but vanish like a spring-night's dream. And the mighty ones too will perish in the end, like dust before the wind.[10]

During this period, the famous classical Japanese drama known as *No* also originated. *No* developed out of

a variety of entertainment forms such as dancing and juggling that were part of the native tradition or had been imported from China and other regions of Asia. The plots were normally based on stories from Japanese history or legend. Eventually, *No* evolved into a highly stylized drama in which the performers wore masks and danced to the accompaniment of instrumental music. In some respects, *No* is reminiscent of classical Greek drama in that both incorporated text, music, dance, a chorus, and masks. Unlike Greek drama, however, the chorus did not participate in the action taking place on stage. Like much of Japanese culture, *No* was restrained, graceful, and refined. With hardly any scenery, the performers, garbed in elaborate costumes, mimed the story through dance and declaimed Japanese verse. *No* plays tended to be short, and often as many as five were presented in a single evening.

ART AND ARCHITECTURE

In art and architecture, as in literature, the Japanese pursued their interest in beauty, simplicity, and nature. To some degree, Japanese artists and architects were influenced by Chinese forms. Prior to the sixth century, for example, Japanese Shinto shrines had been characterized by a simplicity of form and materials. As they became familiar with Chinese architecture, Japanese rulers and aristocrats tried to emulate the splendor of Tang civilization and began constructing their palaces and temples in Chinese style. Often the buildings were designed by Chinese or Korean architects. Eventually, however, Japanese architects changed the layout inside the traditional Buddhist temple from the vertical axis used by the Chinese, where the structures aligned in a straight line, to a more asymmetrical alignment in which all of the buildings were visible simultaneously as the visitor entered the compound gate.

During the Heian period (794–1185), the search for beauty was reflected in various art forms, such as narrative hand scrolls, screens, sliding door panels, fans, and lacquer decoration. As in the case of literature, nature themes dominated, such as seashore scenes, a spring rain, moon and mist, or flowering wisteria and cherry blossoms. All were intended to evoke an emotional response on the part of the viewer. Japanese painting suggested the frail beauty of nature by presenting it on a smaller scale. The majestic mountain in a Chinese painting became a more intimate Japanese landscape with rolling hills and a rice field.

Very popular at the Heian court were hand scrolls that used painting and calligraphy to narrate works such as

The Tale of Genji. Painted by multiple artists, the scrolls were unrolled slowly to be admired and read aloud to an audience. Because of the rigid court etiquette for body comportment, emotion was demonstrated by body position. Faces were rarely shown, and human drama was indicated by a woman lying prostrate or hiding her face in her sleeve. Tension was shown by two people talking at a great distance or with their backs to one another.

During the Kamakura period (1185–1333), the hand scroll with its physical realism and action-packed paintings of the new warrior class achieved great popularity. Reflecting these chaotic times, the art of portraiture flourished, and a scroll would include a full gallery of warriors and holy men in starkly realistic detail, including such unflattering features as stubble, worry lines on a forehead, and crooked teeth. Japanese sculptors also produced naturalistic wooden statues of generals, nobles, and saints. By far the most distinctive, however, were the fierce heavenly "guardian kings," who still intimidate the viewer today. In contrast to the refined atmosphere of the Fujiwara court, the Kamakura era was a warrior's world.

The next 250 years, sometimes known as the Muramachi era because the ruling clan established its headquarters in the Muramachi section of Kyoto, witnessed a phenomenal level of artistic activity. In an effort to rival the Ming dynasty, shoguns acquired great quantities of Chinese art and commanded Japanese artists to imitate it. Many of the latter became mesmerized by the monochrome black ink washes of the Song period and adopted this medium. Others created "impressionist" landscapes or experimented with the splattered ink method. Nevertheless, Japanese painters continued to reject the grandeur of the Chinese landscape in favor of more intimate and tranquil Japanese scenes.

Zen Buddhism, an import from China in the thirteenth century, further refined Japanese aesthetics. With its emphasis on immediate enlightenment without recourse to intellectual analysis and elaborate ritual, Zen reinforced the Japanese predilection for simplicity and self-discipline. During this era, Zen philosophy found expression in the Japanese garden, the tea ceremony, the art of flower arranging, pottery and ceramics, and miniature plant display (the famous *bonsai*, literally "pot scenery").

Landscape served as an important means of expression in both Japanese art and architecture. Like so much of Japanese artistic expression, Japanese gardens were initially modeled on Chinese examples. Early court texts during the Heian period emphasized the importance of including water in either a stream or a pond when creating a garden. The landscape surrounding the fourteenth-century Golden Pavilion in Kyoto displays a harmony of garden, water, and architecture that makes it one of the treasures of the world. Because of the shortage of water in the city, later gardens concentrated on rock composition, using white pebbles to represent water. In the Ryoanji Temple on the outskirts of the city, seventeen rocks are arranged in five groups surrounded by wavy raked pebbles meant to suggest mountains emerging from the sea. Here we experience the quintessential Japanese aesthetic expression of allusion, simplicity, restraint, and tranquillity.

Like the Japanese garden, the tea ceremony represents the fusion of Zen and aesthetics. Developed in the fifteenth century, it was practiced in a simple room devoid of external ornament except for a *tatami* floor, sliding doors, and an alcove with a writing desk and asymmetrical shelves. The participants could therefore focus completely on the activity of pouring and drinking tea. "Tea

♦ **A seated Buddha.** Buddhist statuary, which originated in India and China, evolved as a popular art form in Japan from the seventh century on. Characteristic of these statues are the *mudras*, or hand and body positions by which the Buddha communicated with his followers. Here, his connected fingers indicate meditation. Whereas earlier Japanese sculptors worked in bronze, the depletion of metal reserves eventually necessitated the use of wood. This remarkable eleventh-century gilded wood carving, over ten feet in height, is composed of fifty-three pieces of cypress and exudes a feeling of stability and calm, expressing the Buddha's deep spirituality.

♦ **The Golden Pavilion in Kyoto.** The landscape surrounding the Golden Pavilion displays a harmony of garden, water, and architecture that makes it one of the treasures of the world. Constructed in the fourteenth century as a retreat for the shoguns to withdraw from their administrative chores, the pavilion is named for the gold foil that covered its exterior. Completely destroyed by an arsonist in 1950 as a protest against the commercialism of modern Buddhism, it was rebuilt and reopened in 1987.

and Zen have the same flavor," goes the Japanese saying. Considered the ultimate symbol of spiritual deliverance, the tea ceremony had great aesthetic value and moral significance in traditional times as well as today.

Japan and the Chinese Model

Few societies in Asia have historically been as isolated as Japan. Cut off from the mainland by 120 miles of frequently turbulent ocean, the Japanese had only minimum contact with the outside world during most of their early development.

Whether this isolation was ultimately beneficial to Japanese society cannot be determined. The lack of knowledge of developments taking place elsewhere probably delayed the process of change in Japan. On the other hand, the Japanese were spared the destructive invasions that afflicted other ancient civilizations. What is apparent is that once the Japanese became acquainted with Chinese culture at the height of the Tang era, they were quick to take advantage of the opportunity. In the space of a few decades, the young state adopted many aspects of Chinese society and culture and thereby introduced major changes into the Japanese way of life.

Had things gone as some Japanese rulers wanted, Japanese political institutions might have followed the Chinese pattern. In fact, however, they did not. Despite Prince Shotoku's effort to make effective use of the imperial traditions of Tang China, the decentralizing forces inside Japanese society remained dominant throughout the period under discussion in this chapter. Adoption of the Confucian civil service examination did not lead to a breakdown of Japanese social divisions; instead, the examination was administered in a manner that preserved and strengthened them. Although Buddhist and Daoist doctrines made a significant contribution to Japanese religious practices, Shinto beliefs continued to play a major role in shaping the Japanese worldview.

Why Japan did not follow the Chinese road to centralized authority has been the subject of some debate among historians. Some argue that the answer lies in differing cultural traditions, while others suggest that Chinese institutions and values were introduced too rapidly to be assimilated effectively by Japanese society. A recent view holds that diseases imported inadvertently from China led to a marked decline in the population of the islands, reducing the food output and preventing the population from coalescing in more compact urban centers.

In any event, Japan was not the only society in Asia to assimilate ideas from abroad while at the same

♦ **Ryoanji Temple Garden in Kyoto.** As the result of a water shortage in the fifteenth century, Japanese landscape designers began to make increasing use of rocks and pebbles to represent water. In the Ryoanji Temple in the hills west of Kyoto, seventeen rocks surrounded by wavy raked pebbles are arranged in five groups to suggest mountains emerging from the sea. Here we experience the quintessential Japanese aesthetic expression of allusion, simplicity, restraint, and tranquillity.

time preserving customs and institutions inherited from the past. Across the Sea of Japan to the west and several thousand miles to the south, other Asian peoples were embarked on a similar journey. We now turn to their experience.

Korea

No society in East Asia was more strongly influenced by the Chinese model than was that of Korea. Slightly larger in size than the state of Minnesota, the Korean peninsula was probably first settled by Altaic-speaking fishing and hunting peoples from neighboring Manchuria during the Neolithic Age. Because the area is relatively mountainous (only about one-fifth of the peninsula is adaptable to cultivation), farming was apparently not practiced until about 2000 B.C.E. Dry crops were probably grown first, but wet rice agriculture was introduced a few hundred years later and spread from the peninsula to the Japanese islands (see A Gift from the Gods: Prehistoric Japan earlier in this chapter).

As with many other peoples living in the region, the origins of the first organized society on the peninsula are heavily encrusted in myth. One account asserts that the first Korean state was established in the late second millennium B.C.E. by a member of the Shang royal family who had been ousted by the rising power of the Zhou state (see Chapter 3). While the story may be apocryphal, it does suggest the possibility that the founders of the first organized society on the peninsula may have been refugees from China. Evidently, sometime in the early second century B.C.E., migrants from Manchuria established the kingdom of Chosun with its capital at Pyongyang, the modern-day capital of North Korea. About this time, iron working was also introduced.

In 109 B.C.E., the northern part of the peninsula came under direct Chinese rule. During the next several generations, the area was ruled by the Han dynasty, which divided the territory into provinces and introduced Chinese institutions. With the decline of the Han in the third century C.E., power gradually shifted to local tribal leaders, who drove out the Chinese administrators, but continued to absorb Chinese cultural influence. Eventually, three separate kingdoms emerged on the peninsula: Koguryo in the north, Paekche in the southwest, and Silla in the southeast. The Japanese, who had recently established their own state on the Yamato plain near modern-day Kyoto, maintained a small colony on the southern coast.

◆ **Silla Sword Handle and Sheath.**   The Silla dynasty was renowned for the high quality of its gold jewelry. Shown here is an agate-inlaid sword handle and sheath excavated from a royal tomb. Although much Silla artwork reflects Chinese influence, royal crowns located in Silla tombs often contain antler-like motifs, reflecting the animistic traditions of Korea's pre-Chinese past.

The Three Kingdoms

From the fourth to the seventh centuries, the three kingdoms were bitter rivals for influence and territory on the peninsula. At the same time, all began to absorb Chinese political and cultural institutions. Chinese influence was most notable in Koguryo, where Buddhism was introduced in the late fourth century C.E., and the first Confucian academy on the peninsula was established in the capital at Pyongyang. All three kingdoms also appear to have accepted a tributary relationship with one or another of the squabbling states that emerged in China after the fall of the Han. The kingdom of Silla, less exposed than its two rivals to Chinese influence, was at first the weakest of the three, but eventually its greater internal cohesion—perhaps a consequence of the tenacity of its tribal traditions—enabled it to become the dominant power on the peninsula. When first the Sui dynasty and then the Tang tried to reassert Chinese control over the area, the rulers of Silla took advantage of the confusion caused by the invading armies to establish their control over the entire peninsula. Then they forced the Chinese to withdraw their forces from all but the area adjacent to the Yalu River. To pacify the haughty Chinese, Silla accepted tributary status under Tang dynasty. The remaining Japanese colonies in the south were eliminated.

With the country unified for the first time, the rulers of Silla attempted to use Chinese political institutions and ideology to forge a centralized state. Buddhism, now rising in popularity, became the state religion, and Korean monks followed the paths of their Japanese counterparts on journeys to the Middle Kingdom. Chinese architecture and art became dominant in the capital at Kyongju and other urban centers, and the written Chi-

nese language became the official means of communication at court. But powerful aristocratic families, long dominant in the southeastern part of the peninsula, were still influential at court. They were able to prevent the adoption of the Tang civil service examination system and resisted the distribution of manorial lands to the poor. The failure to adopt the Chinese model was fatal. Squabbling among noble families steadily increased, and after the assassination of the King of Silla in 780, the country sank into civil war.

Unification

The decline of Silla provided an opportunity for elements elsewhere in the peninsula to fill the vacuum, and in the early tenth century a new dynasty called Koryo (the root of the modern word for Korea) arose in the north. Following the example of its founder Taejo, the new kingdom adopted Chinese political institutions to strengthen the power of the state and unify the territory under its control. The civil service examination system

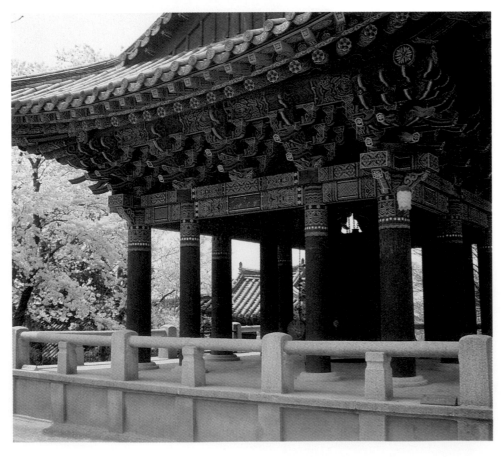

◆ **Pulguksa Bell Tower.**
Among the greatest architectural achievements on the Korean peninsula is the Pulguksa (Monastery of the Land of Buddha), built near the ancient capital of Silla in the eighth century C.E. Shown here is the Bell Tower, located in the midst of beautiful parklands on the monastery grounds. Young Korean couples often come to this monastery after their weddings to be photographed in the stunning surroundings.

⇝ The Flower Garden Scripture ⇜

By the eighth century, Buddhism had come to Korea from China, and like their counterparts in Christian Europe, Korean monks could accumulate merit toward salvation by copying the scriptures. In this passage, the eighth-century Master Yongi of Hwangyong monastery has volunteered to copy a scripture as a way of expressing gratitude for the love of his parents and assisting others in following the Buddhist eightfold path to wisdom. Note the careful attention to ritual as the process is brought to realization. This scripture, which was discovered in 1979, consisted of two scrolls of thirty white papers joined together, with characters in black ink. Each scroll was fourteen meters long.

An Eighth-Century Buddhist Scripture

The scripture is made as follows: First scented water is sprinkled around the roots of a paperbark mulberry tree to quicken its growth; the bark is then peeled and pounded to make paper with a clean surface. The copyists, the artisans who make the centerpiece of the scroll, and the painters who draw the images of buddhas and bodhisattvas all receive the bodhisattva ordination and observe abstinence. After relieving themselves, sleeping, eating, or drinking, they take a bath in scented water before returning to the work. Copyists are adorned with new pure garments, loose trousers, a coarse crown, and a deva crown. Two azure-clad boys

sprinkle water on their heads and . . . azure-clad boys and musicians perform music. The processions to the copying site are headed by one who sprinkles scented water on their path, another who scatters flowers, a dharma master who carries a censer, and another dharma master who chants Buddhist verses. Each of the copyists carries incense and flowers and invokes the name of the Buddha as he progresses.

Upon reaching the site, all take refuge in the Three Jewels (the Buddha, the Dharma, and the Order), make three bows, and offer the *Flower Garland Scripture* and others to buddhas and bodhisattvas. Then they sit down and copy the scripture, make the centerpiece of the scroll, and paint the buddhas and bodhisattvas. Thus, azure-clad boys and musicians cleanse everything before a piece of relic is placed in the center.

Now I make a vow that the copied scripture will not break till the end of the future—even when a major chilicosm is destroyed by the three calamities, this scripture shall be intact as the void. If all living beings rely on this scripture, they shall witness the Buddha, listen to his dharma, worship the relic, aspire to enlightenment without backsliding, cultivate the vows of the Universally Worthy Bodhisattva, and achieve Buddhahood.

was introduced in 958, but as in Japan, the bureaucracy continued to be dominated by influential aristocratic families.

The Koryo dynasty remained in power for four hundred years, protected from invasion by the absence of a strong dynasty in neighboring China, as well as by a "great wall" that stretched across the peninsula from the mouth of the Yalu River to the Sea of Japan. Under the Koryo, industry and commerce slowly began to develop, but as in China, agriculture was the prime source of wealth. In theory, all land was the property of the king, but in actuality noble families controlled their holdings in much the same way that medieval European nobles maintained their hereditary fiefdoms. The lands were worked by peasants who were subject to burdens similar to those of European serfs. At the bottom of society was a class of "base people" (*chonmin*), composed of slaves, artisans, and other specialized workers.

From a cultural point of view, the Koryo era was one of high achievement. Buddhist monasteries, run by sects introduced from China like the Pure Land and Zen (Chan), controlled vast territories, while their monks served as royal advisers at court. At first Buddhist themes dominated in Korean art and sculpture, and the entire Tripitaka (the "three baskets" of the Buddhist canon) was printed by wooden blocks (see the box above). Eventually, however, with the appearance of landscape painting and porcelain, Confucian themes began to predominate.

Under the Mongols

Like its predecessor in Silla, the kingdom of Koryo was unable to overcome the power of the nobility and the absence of a reliable tax base. After the eleventh century, military elements began to dominate at court in a manner reminiscent of the rise of the *bakufu* in Japan. One

⇌ The Chinese Conquest of Vietnam ⇍

In the third century B.C.E., the armies of the Chinese state of Qin [Ch'in] invaded the Red River delta to launch an attack on the small Vietnamese state located there. As this passage by a Chinese historian shows, the Vietnamese were not easy to conquer, and the new state soon declared its independence from the Qin. It was a lesson that was too often forgotten by would-be conquerors in later centuries.

The Huai Nan Tzu

Ch'in Shih Huang Ti was interested in the rhinoceros horn, the elephant tusks, the kingfisher plumes, and the pearls of the land of Yueh [Viet]; he therefore sent Commissioner T'u Sui at the head of five hundred thousand men divided into five armies. . . . For three years the sword and the crossbow were in constant readiness. Superintendent Lu was sent; there was no means of assuring the transport of supplies so he employed soldiers to dig a canal for sending grain, thereby making it possible to wage war on the people of Yueh. The lord of Western Ou, I Hsu Sung, was killed; consequently, the Yueh people entered the wilderness and lived there with the animals; none consented to be a slave of Ch'in; choosing from among themselves men of valor, they made them their leaders and attacked the Ch'in by night, inflicting on them a great defeat and killing Commissioner T'u Sui; the dead and wounded were many. After this, the emperor deported convicts to hold the garrisons against the Yueh people.

The Yueh people fled into the depths of the mountains and forests, and it was not possible to fight them. The soldiers were kept in garrisons to watch over abandoned territories. This went on for a long time, and the soldiers grew weary. Then the Yueh came out and attacked; the Ch'in soldiers suffered a great defeat. Subsequently, convicts were sent to hold the garrisons against the Yueh.

---

explanation of the growing power of the army may have been increased pressure from Manchuria, where the nomadic Liao Khitan and then the Jurchen periodically harassed the frontier. In the thirteenth century, the Mongols attacked Koryo and, despite sporadic resistance from guerrilla forces, eventually seized control over the northern part of the country and assimilated it into the Yuan empire. The weakened kingdom of Koryo became a tributary of the great khan in Khanbaliq (see Chapter 10).

The era of Mongol rule was one of profound suffering for the Korean people, especially the thousands of peasants and artisans who were compelled to perform corvée labor to help build the ships in preparation for Khubilai Khan's invasion of Japan. On the positive side, the Mongols introduced many new ideas and technology from China and further afield. The Koryo dynasty had managed to survive, but only by accepting Mongol authority, and when the power of the Mongols declined, the kingdom declined with it. With the rise to power of the Ming in China, Koryo collapsed, and power was seized by the military commander Yi Song-gye, who declared the founding of the new Yi dynasty in 1392. Once again, the Korean people were in charge of their own destiny.

Vietnam: The Smaller Dragon

While the Korean people were attempting to establish their own identity in the shadow of the powerful Chinese empire, the peoples of Vietnam, on China's southern frontier, were trying to do the same. Little evidence about the original homeland of the Vietnamese people is available. When they first appear in history during the late second or early first millennium B.C.E., they were already settled in the region of the Red River delta in what is today northern Vietnam. They were the southernmost fringe of a vast spreading of peoples called the Viets who inhabited the coastal regions from the Yangtze River to the Red River delta.

The Vietnamese began to practice irrigated agriculture in the flooded regions of the Red River delta at an early date and entered the Bronze Age sometime during the second millennium B.C.E. By about 200 B.C.E., a young state had begun to form in the area, but immediately encountered the expanding power of the Qin empire under Qin Shi Huangdi (see Chapter 3). The Vietnamese were not easy to subdue, however (see the box above), and the collapse of the Qin dynasty temporarily enabled them to preserve their independence. Nevertheless, a century later, they were absorbed into the Han empire.

At first, the Han were satisfied to rule the delta as an autonomous region under the administration of the local landed aristocracy. But Chinese taxes were oppressive, and in 39 C.E. a revolt led by the Trung Sisters (widows of local nobles who had been executed by the Chinese) briefly brought Han rule to an end. The Chinese soon suppressed the rebellion, however, and began to rule the area directly through officials dispatched from China. In time, however, these foreign officials began to intermarry with the local nobility and form a Sino-Vietnamese ruling class who, though trained in Chinese culture, began to identify with the cause of Vietnamese autonomy.

For nearly a thousand years, Vietnam underwent a rigorous process of sinification (the introduction of Chinese culture and institutions), as the Han dynasty attempted to integrate the area culturally as well as politically and administratively into the Chinese empire. After all, no less an authority than Mencius had remarked that it was the duty of a good Confucian to educate the barbarians. During this period, the Vietnamese were exposed to Chinese art, architecture, literature, philosophy, and even the Chinese written language. To all intents and purposes, the Red River delta, then known to the Chinese as the "pacified South" (Annam), became a part of China.

The communal ownership of land that had been prevalent in Vietnamese villages throughout the fertile Red River delta was replaced by a system of private ownership. Traditional informal Vietnamese family relations in which couples did not undergo a formal marriage ceremony were also forced to conform to the Chinese model. In one case, a Confucian official was reported to have presided over the marriage of a thousand Vietnamese couples on a single occasion. One can only imagine the frustration of upright Confucian officials faced with subjects who did not follow prescribed rules for Confucian family behavior and chewed betel nut—a favorite form of stimulant in Southeast Asia.

Another consequence of Chinese rule was the spread of Buddhist, Daoist, and Confucian ideas, which supplemented the Viets' traditional belief in nature spirits. Soon, Buddhist precepts had become popular among the local population, who integrated the new faith into their existing belief system by founding Buddhist temples dedicated to the local village deity in the hope of guaranteeing an abundant harvest.

As in China, Buddhist, Daoist, and Confucian themes often intermingled. Upper-class Vietnamese educated in

CHRONOLOGY

Early Korea and Vietnam

Formation of kingdom of Chosun	Second century B.C.E.
Chinese conquest of Korea and Vietnam	First century B.C.E
Trung Sisters' Revolt	39 C.E.
Foundation of Champa	192
Era of Three Kingdoms in Korea	Fourth–seventh centuries C.E.
Restoration of Vietnamese independence	939
Mongol invasion of Korea and Vietnam	1257–1285
Foundation of Yi Dynasty in Korea	1392
Vietnamese conquest of Champa	1471

the Confucian classics tended to follow the more agnostic Confucian doctrine, but some joined the Buddhist monasteries that began to proliferate after the fall of the Han dynasty. Daoism also flourished at all levels of society and, as in China, provided a structure for animistic beliefs and practices that still predominated at the village level.

The Rise of Great Viet

For ten centuries, the Chinese attempted to assimilate Vietnam as they had other peoples south of the Yangtze River. The Vietnamese sense of ethnic and cultural identity proved inextinguishable, however, and in the tenth century, after many previous abortive attempts, the Vietnamese took advantage of the collapse of the Tang dynasty in China to overthrow Chinese rule in the Red River delta. But the restoration of Vietnamese independence did not mean an end to Chinese influence. Like Prince Shotoku in Japan, Vietnamese rulers were astute enough to see that Confucian institutions could be helpful in creating a centralized kingdom and were quick to pattern their own political system after the Chinese model.

The sense of identity of the Vietnamese people, combined with the organizational genius of State Confucianism, made the new Vietnamese state, which called itself Dai Viet (Great Viet), a dynamic new force on the

✦ **The Temple of Literature, Hanoi.** When the Vietnamese regained their independence from China in the tenth century C.E.., they retained Chinese institutions that they deemed beneficial. A prime example was the establishment of the Temple of Literature, Vietnam's first university, in 1076. Here the sons of mandarins were educated in the Confucian classics in preparation for an official career. Beginning in the fifteenth century, those receiving doctorates had stelae erected to identify their achievements. Shown here is the central hall of the temple where advanced students took the metropolitan examinations for the doctorate.

Southeast Asian mainland. As the population of the Red River delta expanded, Dai Viet soon came into conflict with Champa, its neighbor to the south. Located along the central coast of modern-day Vietnam, Champa was a trading society based on Indian cultural traditions. It had strong links to the commercial network throughout the region and was a bitter rival of the Vietnamese. Over a period of several centuries, the two states fought on numerous occasions. At times the Cham were victorious and occasionally raided the Red River delta, even occupying the Vietnamese capital of Thang Long (now known as Hanoi). But eventually the martial abilities of the Vietnamese proved decisive, and by the end of the fifteenth century, they had conquered Champa. The Vietnamese then resumed their march southward, establishing agricultural settlements in newly conquered territory. By the seventeenth century, the Vietnamese "March to the South," as they called their version of Manifest Destiny, had reached the Gulf of Siam.

The Vietnamese faced even more serious challenge from the north. The Song dynasty in China, beset with its own problems on the northern frontier and convinced that the "pestilential place" in the Red River delta was not worth occupying, eventually accepted the Dai Viet ruler's offer of tribute status. But the Chinese imperial vision of total control over the former "pacified South"

died hard, and later dynasties attempted to reintegrate the Red River delta into the Chinese Empire. The first effort was made in the late thirteenth century by the Mongols, who attempted on two occasions to conquer the Vietnamese (see Chapter 10). After a series of bloody battles, during which the Vietnamese displayed an impressive capacity for guerrilla warfare, the invaders were driven out. A little over a century later, the Ming dynasty tried again, and for twenty years Vietnam was once more under Chinese rule. In 1428, the Vietnamese evicted the Chinese again, but the experience had contributed to the strong sense of Vietnamese identity.

THE CHINESE LEGACY

Despite their stubborn resistance to Chinese rule, after the restoration of independence in the tenth century, Vietnamese rulers quickly discovered the convenience of the Confucian model in administering a river valley society and therefore attempted to follow Chinese practice in forming their own state. The ruler styled himself an emperor like his counterpart to the north (although he prudently termed himself a king in his direct dealings with the Chinese court), adopted Chinese court rituals, claimed the Mandate of Heaven, and arrogated to himself the same authority and privileges in his dealings with his subjects.

Like his Chinese counterpart, the Vietnamese ruler fought to preserve his authority from the challenges of powerful aristocratic families and turned to the Chinese bureaucratic model, including the concept of the civil service examination, as a means of doing so. At first, candidates for official careers were in practice restricted to members of noble families, but under the pressure of strong monarchs, the concept of merit eventually took hold, and the power of the landed aristocracy was weakened if not entirely broken. The Vietnamese adopted much of the Chinese administrative structure, including the six ministries, the censorate, and the various levels of provincial and local administration. Officials at the local level were appointed by higher authorities and accountable to them. At the lowest level of the hierarchy was the village. As in China, it was essentially autonomous, a status symbolized by the popular Vietnamese saying: "The authority of the emperor stops at the village gate."

In all these respects, Vietnam was indeed a "smaller dragon," to use the apt phrase of a recent Western historian of Vietnam. But if Vietnamese government and politics differed little from the Chinese model in theory, there were some significant departures in practice. Perhaps the most important was the relationship between the king and his subjects. In China, the emperor was a distant figure who represented the Chinese people in a spiritual sense as a "Son of Heaven" but had no particular symbolic role as defender of the Chinese people or Chinese culture. In fact, the emperor was frequently not an ethnic Chinese and ruled his kingdom from an imperial court dominated by a foreign aristocracy.

In Vietnam, the monarch was viewed, above all, as the symbol and defender of Vietnamese independence. A number of the great dynasties of medieval Vietnam were founded in the crucible of a common struggle against invaders from China, and although most Vietnamese rulers accepted a tributary relationship with the Chinese Empire, to their subjects their legitimacy was based on their role as defenders of the Vietnamese state.

During the early period of independence, Vietnamese culture also borrowed liberally from its larger neighbor. Educated Vietnamese tried their hand at Chinese poetry, wrote dynastic histories in the Chinese style, and followed Chinese models in sculpture, architecture, and porcelain. Many of the notable buildings of the medieval period, such as the Temple of Literature and the famous One-Pillar Pagoda in Hanoi, are classic examples of Chinese architecture.

But there were signs that Vietnamese creativity would eventually transcend the bounds of Chinese cultural norms. While most classical writing was undertaken in literary Chinese, the only form of literary expression deemed suitable by Confucian conservatives, an adaptation of Chinese written characters, called *Chu Nom* (southern characters), was devised to provide a written system for spoken Vietnamese. In use by the early ninth century, it eventually began to be used for the composition of essays and poetry in the Vietnamese language. Such pioneering efforts would lead in later centuries to the emergence of a vigorous national literature totally independent of Chinese forms.

Society and Family Life

Vietnamese social institutions and customs were also strongly influenced by those of China. As in China, the introduction of a Confucian system and the adoption of civil service examinations undermined the role of the old landed aristocrats and led eventually to their replacement by the scholar-gentry class. Also as in China, the examinations were open to most males, regardless of family background, and certainly opened the door to a degree of social mobility unknown in most of the Indianized states elsewhere in the region. Candidates for the bureau-

cracy read many of the same Confucian classics and absorbed the same ethical principles as their counterparts in China. At the same time, they were also exposed to the classic works of Vietnamese history, which strengthened their sense that Vietnam was a distinct culture similar to, but separate from, that of China.

Below the ruling elite was the mass of the population. As in China, the vast majority of the Vietnamese people were peasants. Virtually all lived in tiny villages in the Red River valley or on the narrow ledge of flatland between the Annamite Mountains and the South China Sea. Most Vietnamese peasants were small landholders or sharecroppers, who rented their plots from wealthier farmers, but large estates were rare due to the systematic efforts of the central government to prevent the rise of a powerful local landed elite. Those who lacked land altogether could sometimes work communal land made available by the village, although these lands were often appropriated by wealthy families with influence in the village council of elders.

Family life in Vietnam was similar in many respects to that of China. Although according to Chinese reports the Vietnamese did not have a strong family tradition prior to the Chinese conquest in the second century B.C.E., the Confucian concept of family took hold during the period of Chinese rule, along with the related concepts of filial piety and gender inequality. Perhaps the most striking difference between family traditions in China and Vietnam was that Vietnamese women possessed more rights both in practice and by law. Whether Vietnam had ever been a matriarchal society is not certain, but since ancient times wives had been permitted to own property and to initiate divorce proceedings against their husbands. One consequence of Chinese rule was a growing emphasis on male dominance, but the tradition of women's rights was never totally extinguished and was legally recognized in a law code promulgated in 1460.

Moreover, Vietnam had a strong historical tradition associating heroic women with the defense of the homeland. The Trung Sisters were the first but by no means the only example. In the following passage, a Vietnamese historian of the eighteenth century recounts their story:

> The imperial court was far away; local officials were greedy and oppressive. At that time the country of one hundred sons was the country of the women of Lord To. The ladies [the Trung Sisters] used the female arts against their irreconcilable foe; skirts and hairpins sang of patriotic righteousness, uttered a solemn oath at the inner door of the ladies' quarters, expelled the governor, and seized the capital. . . . Were they not grand heroines? . . . Our two ladies

◆ **The One-Pillar Pagoda, Hanoi.**
This eleventh-century pagoda was built at the order of a Vietnamese monarch who had dreamed that the Buddhist goddess of mercy, while seated on a lotus, had promised him a son. Shortly after the dream, the emperor fathered a son. In gratitude he constructed this distinctive pagoda on one pillar, resembling a lotus blossom, the Buddhist symbol of purity, rising out of the mud.

brought forward an army of all the people, and, establishing a royal court that settled affairs in the territories of the sixty-five strongholds, shook their skirts over the Hundred Yueh [the Vietnamese people].[11]

Conclusion

There are some tantalizing similarities among the three countries we have examined in this chapter. All borrowed liberally from the Chinese model. At the same time, all adapted Chinese institutions and values to the conditions prevailing in their own societies. While all expressed admiration and respect for China's achievement, all sought to keep Chinese power at a distance.

As an island nation, Japan was the most successful of the three in protecting its political sovereignty and its cultural identity. Both Korea and Vietnam were compelled on various occasions to defend their independence by force of arms. That experience may have shaped their strong sense of national distinctiveness, which we shall discuss further in a later chapter.

The appeal of Chinese institutions can undoubtedly be explained by the fact that Japan, Korea, and Vietnam were all agrarian societies, much like their larger neighbor. But it is undoubtedly significant that the aspect of Chinese political culture that was least amenable to adoption abroad was the civil service examination system. The Confucian concept of meritocracy ran directly counter to the strong aristocratic tradition that flourished in all three societies during their early stage of development. Even when the system was adopted, it was put to quite different uses. Only in Vietnam did the concept of merit eventually triumph over that of birth, as strong rulers of Dai Viet attempted to initiate the Chinese model as a means of creating a centralized system of government.

CHAPTER NOTES

1. Keith W. Taylor, *Ancient Vietnam* (Berkeley, Calif., 1983), p. 75.
2. From the *Kojiki*, preface, quoted in David John Lu, *Sources of Japanese History*, vol. 1 (New York, 1974), p. 33.
3. From the "Seventeen Article Constitution," quoted in ibid., pp. 21–23.
4. From "The History of Wei," quoted in ibid., p. 10.
5. Ibid.
6. From "The Law of Households," quoted in ibid., p. 32.

7. From "On the Salvation of Women," quoted in ibid., p. 127.

8. Quoted in Barbara Ruch, "The other side of culture in medieval Japan," in Kozo Yamamura, ed., *The Cambridge History of Japan*, vol. 3, *Medieval Japan* (Cambridge, 1990), p. 506.

9. From Donald Keene, *Anthology of Japanese Literature* (New York, 1955), p. 24.

10. Ibid., p. 192.

11. Quoted in Tayler, *Ancient Vietnam*, pp. 336–37.

SUGGESTED READINGS

Some of the standard treatments of the rise of Japanese civilization appear in textbooks dealing with the early history of East Asia. Two of the best are J. K. Fairbank, E. O. Reischauer, and A. M. Craig, *East Asia: Tradition and Transformation* (Boston, 1973) and C. Schirokauer, *A Brief History of Chinese and Japanese Civilizations* (San Diego, Calif., 1989). A number of historical works deal specifically with early Japan. G. Sansom, *A History of Japan to 1334* (Stanford, Calif., 1958) is now somewhat out of date but is still informative and very well written. For the latest scholarship on the early period, see the first three volumes of *The Cambridge History of Japan*, edit. J. W. Hall, M. B. Jansen, M. Kanai, and D. Twitchett (Cambridge, 1988).

The best available collections of documents on the early history of Japan are D. J. Lu, ed., *Sources of Japanese History*, vol. 1 (New York, 1974) and Ryusaku Tsunoda et al., eds., *Sources of Japanese Tradition*, vol. 1 (New York, 1958). For some stunning illustrations with a brief text, see *Peoples and Places of the Past: The National Geographic Illustrated Cultural Atlas of the Ancient World* (Rockville, Md., 1983).

For specialized books on the early historical period, see R. J. Pearson, ed., *Windows on the Japanese Past: Studies in Archaeology and Prehistory* (1986). J. W. Hall, *Government and Local Power in Japan, 500–1700* (1966) provides a detailed analysis of the development of Japanese political institutions. The relationship between disease and state building is analyzed in W. W. Farris, *Population, Disease, and Land in Early Japan, 645–900* (Cambridge, 1985). The Kamakura period is covered in J. P. Mass, ed., *Court and Bakufu in Japan: Essays in Kamakura History* (1982). See also H. P. Varley, *The Onin War* (1977). For Japanese Buddhism, see W. T. de Bary, ed., *The Buddhist Tradition in India, China, and Japan* (New York, 1972).

The most comprehensive and helpful anthology of Japanese literature is still D. Keene, *Anthology of Japanese Literature* (New York, 1955). A more recent contribution is J. T. Rimer, ed., *A Reader's Guide to Japanese*

Literature: From the Eighth Century to the Present (Tokyo and New York, 1988). Still the best introduction for college students is the concise and insightful D. Keene, *Japanese Literature: An Introduction for Western Readers* (London, 1953). A good all-round presentation is found in E. Putzar, *Japanese Literature: A Historical Outline* (Tucson, Ariz., 1973).

For the text of *The Tale of Genji*, see A. Waley's translation (New York, 1935) and a more recent one by E. Seidensticker (Tokyo 1977). The best translation for college students is the latter's abridged Vintage Classics edition of 1990, which captures the spirit of the original in 360 pages. Of the many works on the novel, a most accessible and stimulating presentation is I. Morris, *The World of the Shining Prince: Court Life in Ancient Japan* (New York, 1964).

For the most comprehensive and accessible introduction to Japanese art, consult P. Mason, *History of Japanese Art* (New York, 1993). Also see the concise J. Stanley-Baker, *Japanese Art* (London, 1984). For a stimulating text with magnificent illustrations, see D. and V. Elisseeff, *Art of Japan* (New York, 1985). See also J. E. Kidder, Jr., *The Art of Japan* (London, 1985) for an insightful text accompanied by beautiful photographs.

For an informative and readable history of Korea that emphasizes the early period, see W. E. Henthorn, *A History of Korea* (New York, 1971). P. H. Lee, ed., *Sourcebook of Korean Civilization*, vol. 1 (New York, 1993) is a rich collection of documents dating from the period prior to the sixteenth century.

Vietnam often receives little attention in general studies of Southeast Asia because it was part of the Chinese Empire for much of the traditional period. For a detailed investigation of the origins of Vietnamese civilization, see K. W. Taylor, *The Birth of Vietnam* (Berkeley, Calif., 1983). T. Hodgkin, *Vietnam: The Revolutionary Path* (New York, 1981) provides an overall survey of Vietnamese history to modern times. See also J. Buttinger, *The Smaller Dragon: A Political History of Vietnam* (New York, 1966).

CHAPTER

12

The Making of Europe and the World of the Byzantine Empire, 500–1300

In 800, Charlemagne, the king of the Franks, journeyed to Rome to help Pope Leo III, head of the Catholic church, who was barely clinging to power in the face of rebellious Romans. On Christmas Day, Charlemagne and his family, attended by Romans, Franks, and even visitors from the Byzantine Empire, crowded into St. Peter's Basilica to attend mass. Quite unexpectedly, according to a Frankish writer, "as the king rose from praying before the tomb of the blessed apostle Peter, Pope Leo placed a golden crown on his head." In keeping with ancient tradition, the people in the church shouted, "Long life and victory to Charles Augustus, crowned by God the great and peace-loving Emperor of the Romans." Seemingly, the Roman Empire in the West had been reborn, and Charles had become the first Roman emperor since 476. But this "Roman emperor" was actually a German king, and he had been crowned by the head of the western Christian church. In truth, the coronation of Charlemagne was a sign not of the rebirth of the Roman Empire, but of the emergence of a new European civilization that came into being in western Europe after the collapse of the Western Roman Empire.

This new civilization—European civilization—was formed by the coming together of three major elements: the Germanic peoples who moved in and settled the western empire, the legacy of the Romans, and the Christian church. By 800, the contours of a new European civilization were beginning to emerge in western Europe. Increasingly, Europe would become the

Germanic kingdoms

Reign of Charlemagne

Pope Gregory VII and Investiture Controversy

Magna Carta

Emergence of English Parliament

Benedictine order established

Growth of trade and towns

Innocent III and papal power

Pope Gregory the Great

First Crusade

Reign of Justinian

Carolingian Renaissance

Byzantine "Golden Age"

Rise of universities

Thomas Aquinas and scholasticism

---

focus and center of Western civilization. European civilization developed during a period that historians call the Middle Ages, or the medieval period, which lasted from about 500 to 1500. To the historians who first used the title, the Middle Ages were a middle period between the ancient world and the modern world.

At the same time that medieval European civilization was emerging in the west, the eastern part of the old Roman Empire, increasingly Greek in culture, continued to survive as the Byzantine Empire. While serving as a buffer between Europe and the peoples to the east, the Byzantine or Eastern Roman Empire also preserved the intellectual and legal accomplishments of the Greeks and Romans.

The Transformation of the Roman World

The Germanic peoples were an important component of the new European civilization. Already by the third century C.E., they had begun to move into the lands of the Roman Empire. As imperial authority vanished in the fifth century, a number of German kings set up new states. By 500, the Western Roman Empire had been replaced politically by a series of states ruled by German kings.

The New Germanic Kingdoms

The fusion of Romans and Germans took different forms in the various Germanic kingdoms. The kingdom of the Ostrogoths in Italy managed to preserve the Roman tradition of government. After establishing his control over Italy, the Ostrogothic king Theodoric (493–526) kept the entire structure of imperial Roman government, although he used separate systems of rule for Romans and Ostrogoths. The Roman population of Italy lived under Roman law administered by Roman officials. The Ostrogoths were governed by their own customs and their own officials.

Like the kingdom of the Ostrogoths in Italy, the kingdom of the Visigoths in Spain inherited and continued to maintain much of the Roman structure of government. In both states, the Roman population was allowed to maintain Roman institutions while being largely excluded from power as a Germanic warrior caste came to dominate the considerably larger native population. Over time, however, the Visigoths and the Hispano-Roman peoples began to fuse together.

Roman influence was weaker in Britain. When the Roman armies abandoned Britain at the beginning of the fifth century, the Angles and Saxons, Germanic tribes from Denmark and northern Germany, moved in and settled there. Eventually, these peoples succeeded in carving out small kingdoms throughout the island, Kent in southeastern England being one of them.

THE KINGDOM OF THE FRANKS

Only one of the German states on the European continent proved long-lasting—the kingdom of the Franks. The establishment of a Frankish kingdom was the work of Clovis (c. 482–511), a member of the Merovingian dynasty. Initially the leader of only one group of Franks, he eventually became king of them all.

Clovis became a Catholic Christian around 500. He was not the first German king to convert to Christianity, but the others had joined the Arian sect of Christianity, a group who believed that Christ had been human and thus not truly God. The Christian church in Rome, which had become known as the Roman Catholic church, regarded the Arians as heretics, or people who believed in teachings different from the official church doctrine. To Catholics, Christ was human, but of the "same substance" as God and therefore also truly God.

Clovis found that his conversion to Catholic Christianity gained him the support of the Roman Catholic church, which was only too eager to obtain the friendship of a major Germanic ruler who was a Catholic Christian. The conversion of the king also paved the way for the conversion of the Frankish peoples.

By 510, Clovis had established a powerful new Frankish kingdom stretching from the Pyrenees in the west to German lands in the east (modern-day France and western Germany). After Clovis's death, however, his sons divided his newly created kingdom, as was the Frankish custom. During the sixth and seventh centuries, the once-united Frankish kingdom came to be divided into

◆ **Map 12.1**   The New Kingdoms of the Old Western Empire.

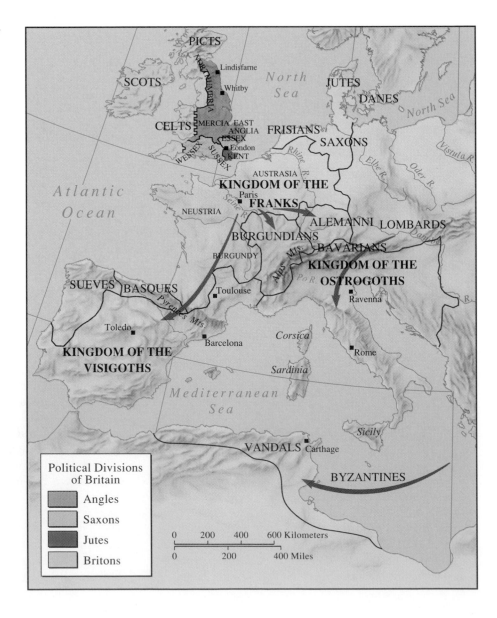

three major areas: Neustria in northern Gaul; Austrasia, consisting of the ancient Frankish lands on both sides of the Rhine; and the former kingdom of Burgundy.

THE SOCIETY OF THE GERMANIC PEOPLES

As Germans and Romans intermarried and began to create a new society, some of the social customs of the Germanic peoples came to play an important role. The crucial social bond among the Germanic peoples was the family, especially the extended family of husbands, wives, children, brothers, sisters, cousins, and grandparents. In addition to working the land together and passing it down to future generations, the extended family also provided protection, which was sorely needed in the violent atmosphere of Merovingian times.

The German conception of family affected the way Germanic law treated crime and punishment. In the Roman system, as in our own, a crime such as murder was considered an offense against society or the state and was handled by a court that heard evidence and arrived at a decision. Germanic law was personal. An injury by one person against another could lead to a blood feud in which the family of the injured party took revenge on the family of the wrongdoer. Feuds could lead to savage acts of revenge, such as hacking off hands or feet, gouging out eyes, or slicing off ears and noses. Because this system could easily get out of control, an alternative system arose that made use of a fine called *wergeld*, which was paid by a wrongdoer to the family of the person he had injured or killed. *Wergeld*, which means "money for a man," was the value of a person in monetary terms. That value varied considerably according to social status. An offense against a nobleman, for example, cost considerably more than one against a freeman or a slave.

Germanic law provided two common means of determining guilt: compurgation and the ordeal. Compurgation involved the swearing of an oath by the accused person, backed up by a group of twelve or twenty-five "oathhelpers," who would also swear that the accused was telling the truth. The ordeal was based on the idea of divine intervention; divine forces (whether pagan or Christian) would not allow an innocent person to be harmed (see the box on p. 406).

The Role of the Christian Church

By the end of the fourth century, Christianity had become the predominant religion of the Roman Empire. As the official Roman state disintegrated, the Christian church played an increasingly important role in the emergence and growth of the new European civilization.

♦ **The Baptism of Clovis.** The conversion of Clovis to Catholic Christianity was an important factor in gaining papal support for his Frankish kingdom. In this illustration from a medieval manuscript, bishops and nobles look on while Clovis is baptized. One of the nobles holds a crown while a dove, symbol of the Holy Spirit, descends from heaven bringing sacred oil for the ceremony.

❧ Germanic Customary Law: The Ordeal ❧

In Germanic customary law, the ordeal was used as a means by which accused persons might clear themselves. Although the ordeal took different forms, all involved a physical trial of some sort, such as holding a red-hot iron. It was believed that God would protect the innocent and allow them to come through the ordeal unharmed. This sixth-century account by Gregory of Tours describes an ordeal by hot water.

Gregory of Tours, An Ordeal of Hot Water (c. 580)

An Arian presbyter disputing with a deacon of our religion made venomous assertions against the Son of God and the Holy Ghost, as is the habit of that sect [the Arians]. But when the deacon had discoursed a long time concerning the reasonableness of our faith and the heretic, blinded by the fog of unbelief, continued to reject the truth, . . . the former said: "Why weary ourselves with long discussions? Let acts approve the truth; let a kettle be heated over the fire and someone's ring be thrown into the boiling water. Let him who shall take it from the heated liquid be approved as a follower of the truth, and afterward let the other party be converted to the knowledge of the truth. And do you also understand, O heretic, that this our party will fulfill the conditions with the aid of the Holy Ghost; you shalt confess that there is no discordance, no dissimilarity in the Holy Trinity." The heretic consented to the proposition and they separated after appointing the next morning for the trial. But the fervor of faith in which the deacon had first made this suggestion began to cool through the instigation of the enemy. Rising with the dawn he bathed his arm in oil and smeared it with ointment. But nev-

ertheless he made the round of the sacred places and called in prayer on the Lord. . . . About the third hour they met in the market place. The people came together to see the show. A fire was lighted, the kettle was placed upon it, and when it grew very hot the ring was thrown into the boiling water. The deacon invited the heretic to take it out of the water first. But he promptly refused, saying, "You who did propose this trial are the one to take it out." The deacon all of a tremble bared his arm. And when the heretic presbyter saw it besmeared with ointment he cried out: "With magic arts you have thought to protect yourself, that you have made use of these salves, but what you have done will not avail." While they were thus quarreling there came up a deacon from Ravenna named Iacinthus and inquired what the trouble was about. When he learned the truth he drew his arm out from under his robe at once and plunged his right hand into the kettle. Now the ring that had been thrown in was a little thing and very light so that it was thrown about by the water as chaff would be blown about by the wind; and searching for it a long time he found it after about an hour. Meanwhile the flame beneath the kettle blazed up mightily so that the greater heat might make it difficult for the ring to be followed by the hand; but the deacon extracted it at length and suffered no harm, protesting rather that at the bottom the kettle was cold while at the top it was just pleasantly warm. When the heretic beheld this he was greatly confused and audaciously thrust his hand into the kettle saying, "My faith will aid me." As soon as his hand had been thrust in all the flesh was boiled off the bones clear up to the elbow. And so the dispute ended.

THE ORGANIZATION OF THE CHURCH

During the course of the fourth century, the Christian church had undergone significant organizational and structural changes. For some time, the Christian community in each city had been headed by a bishop, whose area of jurisdiction was known as a bishopric, or diocese; the bishoprics of each Roman province were joined together under the direction of an archbishop. The bishops of four great cities—Rome, Jerusalem, Alexandria, and Antioch—held positions of special power in church affairs because the churches in these cities all asserted that they had been founded by the original apostles sent out by Christ. Soon, however, one of them—the bishop of Rome—claimed even more, that he was the leader of the western Christian church. According to church tradition, Christ had given the keys to the kingdom of heaven to Peter, who was considered the chief apostle and the first bishop of Rome. Subsequent bishops of Rome were considered Peter's successors and came to be known as popes (from the Latin word *papa*, meaning father) of the Catholic church.

Although western Christians came to accept the bishop of Rome as head of the church in the fourth and fifth centuries, there was certainly no unanimity on the extent of the powers the pope possessed as a result of his position. Nevertheless, in the sixth century, a strong pope, Gregory I, known as Gregory the Great, strengthened the power of the papacy and the Roman Catholic church. As pope, Gregory I (590–604) assumed direction of Rome and its surrounding territories, thus giving the papacy a source of political power in a territorial unit that eventually came to be known as the Papal States. Gregory also extended papal authority over the Christian church in the west and was especially active in converting the pagan peoples of Germanic Europe. His primary instrument was the monastic movement.

THE MONKS AND THEIR MISSIONS

A monk (Latin *monachus*, meaning "someone who lives alone") was one who sought to live a life divorced from the world, cut off from ordinary human society, in order to pursue an ideal of godliness, or total dedication to the will of God. At first, Christian monasticism was based on the model of the solitary hermit who gives up all civilized society to pursue a spiritual life. Saint Simeon the Stylite, for example, lived for thirty years in a basket atop a pillar more than sixty feet high.

These early monks, however, soon found themselves unable to live in solitude. Their feats of holiness attracted followers on a wide scale, and as the monastic ideal spread, a new form of monasticism based upon living together in a community soon became the dominant form. Monastic communities came to be seen as the ideal Christian society that could provide a moral example to the wider society around them.

Saint Benedict (c. 480–c. 543), who founded a monastic house for which he wrote a set of rules, established the basic form of monastic life in the western Christian church. The Benedictine rule came to be used by other monastic groups and was crucial to the growth of monasticism in the western Christian world.

Benedict's rule divided each day into a series of activities with primary emphasis upon prayer and manual labor. All monks were required to perform physical work of some kind for several hours a day because idleness was "the enemy of the soul." At the very heart of community practice was prayer, the proper "Work of God." While this included private meditation and reading, all monks in the monastery gathered together seven times during the day for common prayer and chanting of psalms. A Benedictine life was a communal one. Monks ate, worked, slept, and worshiped together.

Each Benedictine monastery was strictly ruled by an abbot, or "father" of the monastery, who had complete authority over his fellow monks. Unquestioning obedience to the will of the abbot was expected of each monk. Each Benedictine monastery held lands that enabled it to be a self-sustaining community, isolated from and independent of the world surrounding it. Within the monastery, however, monks were to fulfill their vow of poverty: "Let all things be common to all, as it is written, lest anyone should say that anything is his own."[1] The first monks were men, but women (called nuns) also began to withdraw from the world to dedicate themselves to God.

Monasticism played an indispensable role in early medieval civilization. Monks became the new heroes of Christian civilization, and their dedication to God became the highest ideal of Christian life. They were the social workers of their communities: monks provided schools for the young, hospitality for travelers, and hospitals for the sick. Monks also copied Latin works and passed on the legacy of the ancient world to the new European civilization. Monasteries became centers of learning wherever they were located. Moreover, the monks were important in spreading Christianity to the entire European world. English and Irish monks were particularly enthusiastic missionaries, who undertook the conversion of pagan peoples, especially in Germany.

Women, too, played an important role in the monastic missionary movement and the conversion of the Germanic kingdoms. Many of the abbesses (an abbess was the head of a monastery or convent for nuns) belonged to royal houses, especially in Anglo-Saxon England. In the kingdom of Northumbria, for example, Saint Hilda founded the monastery of Whitby in 657. As abbess, she was responsible for giving learning an important role in the life of the monastery. Five future bishops were educated under her direction.

Charlemagne and the World of the Carolingians

During the seventh and eighth centuries, within the Frankish kingdom of western Europe, the mayors of the palace of Neustria and Austrasia had expanded their power at the expense of the Merovingian dynasty. One of these mayors, Pepin, finally took the logical step of deposing the decadent Merovingians and assuming the kingship of the Frankish state for himself and his family. Upon his death in 768, his son came to the throne of the Frankish kingdom.

This new king was the dynamic and powerful ruler known to history as Charles the Great or Charlemagne (from the Latin *Carolus magnus*). Charlemagne was a

⇒ The Achievements of Charlemagne ⇐

Einhard, the biographer of Charlemagne, was born in the valley of the Main River in Germany about 775. Raised and educated in the monastery of Fulda, an important center of learning, he arrived at the court of Charlemagne in 791 or 792. Although he did not achieve high office under Charlemagne, he served as private secretary to Louis the Pious, Charlemagne's son and successor. Einhard's Life of Charlemagne *was modeled on Suetonius's* Lives of the Caesars, *especially his biography of Augustus. Einhard's work, written between 817 and 830, was the "first medieval biography of a lay figure." In this selection, he discusses some of Charlemagne's accomplishments.*

Einhard, *Life of Charlemagne*

Such are the wars, most skillfully planned and successfully fought, which this most powerful king waged during the forty-seven years of his reign. He so largely increased the Frank kingdom, which was already great and strong when he received it at his father's hands, that more than double its former territory was added to it. . . . He subdued all the wild and barbarous tribes dwelling in Germany between the Rhine and the Vistula, the Ocean and the Danube, all of which speak very much the same language, but differ widely from one another in customs and dress. . . .

He added to the glory of his reign by gaining the good will of several kings and nations; so close, indeed, was the alliance that he contracted with Alfonso, King of Galicia and Asturias, that the latter, when sending letters or ambassadors to Charles, invariably styled himself his man. . . . The Emperors of Constantinople [the Byzantine emperors] sought friendship and alliance with Charles by several embassies; and even when the Greeks [the Byzantines] suspected him of designing to take the empire from them, because of his assumption of the title Emperor, they made a close alliance with him, that he might have no cause of offense. In fact, the power of the Franks was always viewed with a jealous eye, whence the Greek proverb, "Have the Frank for your friend, but not for your neighbor."

This King, who showed himself so great in extending his empire and subduing foreign nations, and was constantly occupied with plans to that end, undertook also very many works calculated to adorn and benefit his kingdom, and brought several of them to completion. Among these, the most deserving of mention are the basilica of the Holy Mother of God at Aix-la-Chapelle [Aachen], built in the most admirable manner, and a bridge over the Rhine River at Mainz, half a mile long, the breadth of the river at this point. . . . Above all, sacred buildings were the object of his care throughout his whole kingdom; and whenever he found them falling to ruin from age, he commanded the priests and fathers who had charge of them to repair them, and made sure by commissioners that his instructions were obeyed. . . . Thus did Charles defend and increase as well as beautify his kingdom. . . .

He cherished with the greatest fervor and devotion the principles of the Christian religion, which had been instilled into him from infancy. Hence it was that he built the beautiful church at Aix-la-Chapelle, which he adorned with gold and silver and lamps, and with rails and doors of solid brass. He had the columns and marbles for this structure brought from Rome and Ravenna, for he could not find such as were suitable elsewhere. He was a constant worshiper at this church as long as his health permitted, going morning and evening, even after nightfall, besides attending mass. . . .

He was very forward in caring for the poor, so much so that he not only made a point of giving in his own country and his own kingdom, but when he discovered that there were Christians living in poverty in Syria, Egypt, and Africa, at Jerusalem, Alexandria, and Carthage, he had compassion on their wants, and used to send money over the seas to them. . . . He sent great and countless gifts to the popes, and throughout his whole reign the wish that he had nearest at heart was to reestablish the ancient authority of the city of Rome under his care and by his influence, and to defend and protect the Church of St. Peter, and to beautify and enrich it out of his own store above all other churches.

determined and decisive man, highly intelligent and inquisitive. A fierce warrior, he was also a strong statesman (see the box above). Unable to read and write, he was nevertheless a wise patron of learning. He greatly expanded the territory of the Carolingian Empire during his lengthy rule from 768 to 814.

In the tradition of the Germanic kings, Charlemagne was a determined warrior who undertook fifty-four military campaigns, which took him to many areas of Europe. His most successful campaigns were in Germany, especially against the Saxons located between the Elbe River and the North Sea. As Einhard, Charlemagne's biographer, recounted: "No war ever undertaken by the Frank nation was carried on with such persistence and bitterness, or cost so much labor, because the Saxons, like almost all the tribes of Germany, were a fierce people."[2] At its height, Charlemagne's empire covered much of western and central Europe; not until the time of Napoleon in the nineteenth and Hitler in the twentieth century would an empire its size be seen again in Europe.

Charlemagne continued the efforts of his father in organizing the Carolingian kingdom. To administer the empire, Charlemagne depended both upon his household staff and upon the counts who were his chief representatives in local areas. The counts were members of the nobility that had already existed under the Merovingians. They had come to control government functions in their own lands and thus acted as judges, military leaders, and agents of the king. As an important check on the power of the counts, Charlemagne established the *missi dominici* ("messengers of the lord king"), two men, one lay lord and one church official, who were sent out to local districts to ensure that the counts were executing the king's

wishes. Each count also had assistants, but they were members of his household, not part of a bureaucratic office.

The last point reminds us that we should not think of Carolingian administration in the modern sense of government offices run by officials committed to an impersonal ideal of state service. The Carolingian system was glaringly inefficient. Great distances had to be covered on horseback, making it impossible for Charlemagne and his household staff to exercise much supervision over local affairs. What held the system together was personal loyalty to a king who was strong enough to ensure loyalty by force when necessary. The Carolingian system worked as long as it had a powerful and energetic ruler like Charlemagne.

CHARLEMAGNE AS EMPEROR

As Charlemagne's power grew, so too did his prestige as the most powerful Christian ruler; one monk even wrote that he ruled the "kingdom of Europe." In 800,

♦ **Map 12.2**   The Carolingian Empire.

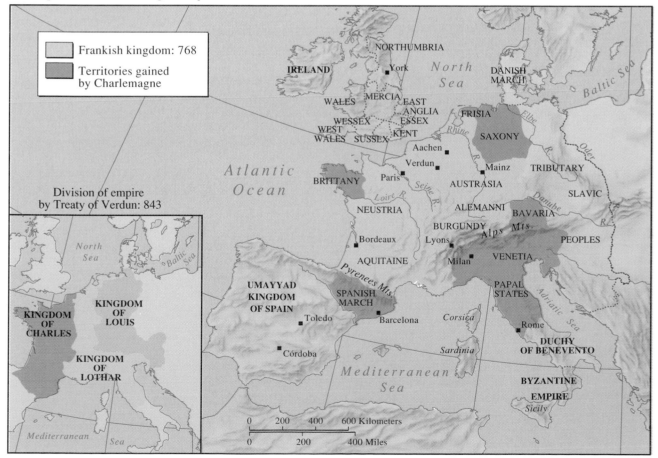

Charlemagne acquired a new title—emperor of the Romans. Charlemagne welcomed the new title; after all, as an emperor, he was now on a level of equality with the Byzantine emperor (see The Byzantine Empire and the Crusades later in this chapter). Moreover, the coronation also meant that the papacy now had a defender of great stature.

Charlemagne's coronation as Roman emperor demonstrated the strength, even after three hundred years, of the concept of an enduring Roman Empire. More importantly, it symbolized the fusion of those Roman, Christian, and Germanic elements that constituted the foundation of European civilization. A Germanic king had been crowned emperor of the Romans by the spiritual leader of western Christendom. A new civilization had emerged.

AN INTELLECTUAL RENEWAL

Charlemagne had a strong desire to revive learning in his kingdom, an attitude that stemmed from his own intellectual curiosity as well as the need to provide educated clergy for the church and literate officials for the government. His efforts led to a revival of learning and culture that some historians have labeled a Carolingian Renaissance or "rebirth" of learning.

For the most part, the revival of classical studies and the efforts to preserve Latin culture took place in the monasteries, many of which had been established by Irish and English missionaries in the seventh and eighth centuries. By the ninth century, the "work" required of Benedictine monks was the copying of manuscripts. Monasteries established *scriptoria*, or writing rooms, where monks copied not only the works of early Christianity, such as the Bible, but also the works of Latin classical authors. The copying of manuscripts in Carolingian monastic *scriptoria* was a crucial factor in the preservation of the ancient legacy. About eight thousand manuscripts survive from Carolingian times. Virtually 90 percent of the ancient Roman works that we have today exist because they were copied by Carolingian monks.

✦ **The Coronation of Charlemagne.** After rebellion in 799 forced Pope Leo III to seek refuge at Charlemagne's court, Charlemagne went to Rome to settle the affair. There, on Christmas Day 800, he was crowned emperor of the Romans by the pope. This manuscript illustration shows Leo III placing a crown on Charlemagne's head.

The World of Feudalism

The Carolingian Empire began to disintegrate soon after Charlemagne's death in 814, and less than thirty years later, in 843, it was divided among his grandsons into three major sections: Charles the Bald (843–877) obtained the west Frankish lands, which formed the core of the eventual kingdom of France; Louis the German (843–876) took the eastern lands, which became Germany; and Lothair (840–855) received the title of emperor and a "Middle Kingdom" extending from the North Sea to Italy, including the Netherlands, the Rhineland, and northern Italy. The division did not lead to peace, however, for the rulers and their heirs engaged in almost incessant struggles—squabbles that allowed powerful aristocrats to acquire even more power in their own local territories at the expense of the rulers. In the meantime, the process of disintegration was further hastened by invasions of different parts of the old Carolingian world.

Invasions of the Ninth and Tenth Centuries

In the ninth and tenth centuries, western Europe was beset by several waves of invasions. The Muslims raided the southern coast of Europe and sent raiding parties into southern France. The Magyars, a people from western Asia, moved into central Europe at the end of the ninth century and settled on the plains of Hungary; from there they made raids into western Europe. After suffering a crushing defeat at the Battle of Lechfeld in Germany in 955, the Magyars converted to Christianity and settled down to create the kingdom of Hungary.

By far, the most far-reaching attacks of the time came from the Northmen or Norsemen of Scandinavia, also known to us as the Vikings. The Vikings were a Germanic people based in Scandinavia. Their great love of adventure and their search for booty and new avenues of trade may have led them to invade other areas of Europe.

Two features of Viking society help to explain the Vikings' success. First of all, they were warriors. Secondly, they were superb shipbuilders and sailors. Their ships were the best of the period. Long and narrow with beautifully carved arched prows, the Viking dragon ships carried about fifty men. Their shallow draft enabled the Vikings to sail up European rivers and attack places at some distance inland. In the ninth century, Vikings sacked villages and towns, destroyed churches, and easily defeated small local armies.

Early Viking raids were largely limited to the summer, but by the mid-ninth century, the Northmen had begun to build settlements and spend the winter in different areas of Europe. By 850, Norsemen from Norway had set-

◆ **The Vikings Attack England.** This illustration from an eleventh-century English manuscript depicts a band of armed Vikings invading England. Two ships have already reached the shore, and a few Vikings are shown walking down a long gangplank onto English soil.

tled in Ireland, while the Danes occupied northeastern England by 878. Beginning in 911, the ruler of the western Frankish lands gave one band of Vikings land at the mouth of the Seine river in the section of France that came to be known as Normandy. This policy of settling the Vikings and converting them to Christianity was a deliberate one; by their conversion to Christianity, the Vikings were soon made a part of European civilization.

The Development of Feudalism

The disintegration of all central authority in the Carolingian world and the invasions by Muslims, Magyars, and Vikings led to the emergence of a new type of political order. When royal governments could no longer defend their subjects, people turned to the local landed aristocrats or nobles who could offer protection in return for service. This practice led to a new system of rule known as feudalism.

At the heart of feudalism was the idea of vassalage. In Germanic society, warriors swore an oath of loyalty to their leader. They fought for their chief, and he in turn took care of their needs. By the eighth century, an individual who served a lord in a military capacity was known as a vassal.

With the breakdown of royal governments, powerful nobles took control of large areas of land. They needed men to fight for them, so the practice arose of giving grants of land to vassals who in return would fight for their lord. The Frankish army had originally consisted of foot soldiers, dressed in coats of mail and armed with swords. But in the eighth century, when larger horses and the stirrup were introduced, a military change began to occur. Earlier, horsemen had been throwers of spears. Now they wore armored coats of mail (the larger horse could carry the weight) and wielded long lances that enabled them to act as battering rams (the stirrups kept them on their horses). For almost five hundred years, warfare in Europe would be dominated by heavily armored cavalry or knights as they came to be called. The knights came to have the greatest social prestige and formed the backbone of the European aristocracy.

Of course, a horse, armor, and weapons were expensive to purchase and maintain, and learning to wield these instruments skillfully from a horse took much time and practice. Consequently, lords who wanted men to fight for them had to grant each vassal a piece of land that provided for the support of the vassal and his family. In return for the land, the vassal provided his lord with one major service, his fighting skills. Each needed the other. In the society of the Early Middle Ages (the period between 400 and 1000), where there was little trade and wealth was based primarily on land, land became the most important gift a lord could give to a vassal in return for military service.

The relationship between lord and vassal was made official by a public ceremony. To become a vassal, a man performed an act of homage to his lord, as described in this passage from a medieval treatise on feudal practice:

> The man should put his hands together as a sign of humility, and place them between the two hands of his lord as a token that he vows everything to him and promises faith to him; and the lord should receive him and promise to keep faith with him. Then the man should say: "Sir, I en-

ter your homage and faith and become your man by mouth and hands [i.e., by taking the oath and placing his hands between those of the lord], and I swear and promise to keep faith and loyalty to you against all others, and to guard your rights with all my strength.[3]

As in the earlier Germanic band, loyalty to one's lord was the chief virtue.

By the ninth century, the land granted to a vassal in return for military service had come to be known as a fief. In time, many vassals who held such grants of land came to exercise rights of jurisdiction or political and legal authority within their fiefs. As the Carolingian world disintegrated politically under the impact of internal dissension and invasions, an increasing number of powerful lords arose. Instead of a single government, many people were now responsible for keeping order.

Feudalism also became increasingly complicated with the development of subinfeudation. The vassals of a king, who were themselves great lords, might also have vassals who would owe them military service in return for a grant of land from their estates. Those vassals, in turn, might likewise have vassals, who at this low level would be simple knights with barely enough land to provide their equipment. The lord-vassal relationship, then, bound together both greater and lesser landowners. At all levels, the lord-vassal relationship was always an honorable relationship between free men and did not imply any sense of servitude. Since kings could no longer provide security in the midst of the breakdown created by the invasions of the ninth century, the system of feudalism became ever more widespread.

Feudalism was basically a product of the Carolingian world, but it also spread to England, Germany, and central Europe and in some form to Italy. Feudalism came to be characterized by a set of practices—known as the feudal contract—that determined the relationship between a lord and his vassal. The major obligation of a vassal to his lord was to perform military service, usually about forty days a year. A vassal was also required to appear at his lord's court when summoned to give advice to the lord. He might also be asked to sit in judgment in a legal case because the important vassals of a lord were peers and only they could judge each other. Finally, vassals were also responsible for aids, or financial payments to the lord upon a number of occasions, including the knighting of the lord's eldest son, the marriage of his eldest daughter, and the ransom of the lord's person in the event he was captured.

In turn, a lord had responsibilities toward his vassal. His major obligation was to protect his vassal, either by defending him militarily or by taking his side in a court of law if necessary. The lord was also responsible for the maintenance of the vassal, usually by granting him a fief.

The Nobility of the Middle Ages

In the High Middle Ages (the period between 1000 and 1300), European society was dominated by a group of men whose primary preoccupation was warfare. King Alfred of Wessex (871–899) in England had said that a "well-peopled land" must have "men of prayer, men of war, and men of work," and medieval ideals held to a tripartite division of society into these three basic groups. The "men of war" were the lords and vassals of medieval society.

The lords were the kings, dukes, counts, barons, and viscounts (and even bishops and archbishops) who held extensive lands and considerable political power. They formed an aristocracy or nobility that consisted of people who held real political, economic, and social power. As warriors united by the institution of knighthood, the great lords and ordinary knights came to form a common group, albeit a group with social divisions based on extremes of wealth and landholdings.

Medieval theory maintained that the warlike qualities of the nobility were justified by their role as defenders of society, and the growth of the European nobility in the High Middle Ages was made visible by an increasing number of castles scattered across the landscape. Although castle architecture varied considerably, castles did possess two common features: they were permanent residences for the noble family, its retainers, and servants, and they were defensible fortifications. For defensive purposes, castles were surrounded by open areas and large stone walls. At the heart of the castle was the keep, a large, multistoried building that housed kitchens, stables, storerooms, a great hall for visitors, dining, and administrative business, and numerous rooms for sleeping and living. The growing wealth of the High Middle Ages made it possible for the European nobility to build more elaborate castles with thicker walls and better furnished and decorated interiors. As castles became more elaborate and securely built, they proved to be more easily defended and harder to seize by force.

THE WAY OF THE WARRIOR

At the age of seven or eight, the sons of the nobility were sent either to a clerical school to pursue a religious career or to another nobleman's castle where they prepared for the life of a noble. Their chief lessons were military; they learned how to joust, hunt, ride, and handle weapons properly. Occasionally, aristocrats' sons might also learn the basic fundamentals of reading and writing. After his apprenticeship in knighthood, at about the age of twenty-one, a young man formally entered the adult world in a ceremony of "knighting." A sponsor girded a sword on the young candidate and struck him on the cheek or neck with an open hand (or later touched him three times on the shoulder with the blade of a sword), possibly signifying the passing of the sponsor's military valor to the new knight.

In the eleventh and twelfth centuries, under the influence of the church, an ideal of civilized behavior called chivalry gradually evolved among the nobility. Chivalry represented a code of ethics that knights were supposed to uphold. In addition to defending the church and the defenseless, knights were expected to treat captives as honored guests instead of putting them in dungeons. Chivalry also implied that knights should fight only for glory, but this account of a group of English knights by a medieval writer reveals another motive for battle: "The whole city was plundered to the last farthing, and then they proceeded to rob all the churches throughout the city, . . . and seizing gold and silver, cloth of all colors, women's ornaments, gold rings, goblets, and precious stones . . . they all returned to their own lords rich men."[4] Apparently, not all the ideals of chivalry were taken seriously.

After his formal initiation into the world of warriors, a young man returned home to find himself once again subject to his parents' authority. Young men were discouraged from marrying until their fathers died, at which time they could marry and become lords of the castle. Trained to be warriors, but with no adult responsibilities, young knights naturally gravitated toward military activities and often furthered the private warfare endemic to the noble class. In the twelfth century, tournaments began to appear as an alternative to the socially destructive fighting that the church was increasingly trying to curb. Initially, tournaments consisted of the "melee," in which warriors on horseback fought with blunted weapons in free-for-all combat. The goal was to take prisoners who would then be ransomed, making success in tournaments a path to considerable gain. By the late twelfth century, the melee was preceded by the joust or individual combat between two knights. Gradually, the joust became the main part of the tournament. No matter how much the church condemned tournaments, knights themselves continued to see them as an excellent way to train for war. As one knight explained: "A knight cannot distinguish himself in that [war] if he has not trained for it in tourneys. He must have seen his blood flow, heard his teeth crack under fist blows, felt his opponent's weight bear down upon him as he lay on the ground and, after being twenty times unhorsed, have risen twenty times to fight."[5]

ARISTOCRATIC WOMEN

Although women could legally hold property, most women remained under the control of men—of their fathers until they married and their husbands after they married. Nevertheless, aristocratic women had many opportunities for playing important roles. Because the lord was often away at war or court, the lady of the castle had to manage the estate. A household could include large numbers of officials and servants, so this was no small responsibility. Maintaining the financial ac-

counts alone took considerable financial knowledge. The lady of the castle was also responsible on a regular basis for overseeing the food supply and maintaining all the other supplies needed for the smooth operation of the household.

Although women were expected to be subservient to their husbands, there were many strong women who advised and sometimes even dominated their husbands. Perhaps the most famous was Eleanor of Aquitaine (c. 1122–1204), heiress to the duchy of Aquitaine in southwestern France. Married to King Louis VII of France (1137–1180), Eleanor accompanied her husband on a crusade, but her alleged affair with her uncle during the crusade led Louis to have their marriage annulled. Eleanor then married Henry, duke of Normandy and count of Anjou, who became King Henry II of England (1154–1189). She took an active role in politics, even

◆ **The Tournament.**   The tournament arose as a socially acceptable alternative to the private warfare that plagued the nobility. This illustration from *The Book of Tourneys* by King René of Anjou shows opposing teams behind ropes.

At the top center, red-robed judges prepare to signal the men waiting below to cut the cords, at which point the two sides will begin their mock battle. Female supporters of the two sides look on.

assisting her sons in rebelling against Henry in 1173–1174. Imprisoned for her activities, after Henry's death she again assumed an active political life, providing both military and political support for her sons.

The Growth of European Kingdoms

The domination of society by the nobility reached its apex in the High Middle Ages. During the same period, however, kings began the process of extending their power in more effective ways. Out of these growing monarchies would eventually come the European states that dominated much of later European history.

In theory, a king was regarded as the head of his kingdom and was expected to lead his vassals and subjects into battle. The king's power was strictly limited, however. He had to honor the rights and privileges of his vassals and was expected to resolve any disputes by principles of established law. If he failed to observe his vassals' rights, they could and did rebel. Kings, however, did possess some sources of power that other feudal lords did not. Usually, kings had greater opportunities to increase their lands through war and marriage alliances and then could use their new acquisitions to reward their followers and bind powerful nobles to them. In the High Middle Ages, kings found new ways to extend their powers. The growth of cities, the revival of commerce, and the emergence of a money economy, all of which we will examine in the next sections, enabled monarchs to hire soldiers and officials and to rely less on their vassals.

England in the High Middle Ages

In 1066, an army of heavily armed knights under William of Normandy landed on the coast of England and soundly defeated King Harold and the Anglo-Saxon foot soldiers at the Battle of Hastings on October 14. William (1066–1087) was crowned king of England at Christmas time in London and then began the process of combining Anglo-Saxon and Norman institutions to create a new England. Many of the Norman knights were given parcels of land that they held as fiefs from the new English king. William made all nobles swear an oath of loyalty to him as sole ruler of England and insisted that all people owed loyalty to the king.

The Norman ruling class spoke French, but as the Norman-French and the Anglo-Saxon nobility intermarried, Anglo-Saxon and French gradually merged to form a new English language. The Normans also took over existing Anglo-Saxon institutions, such as the office of sheriff. William took a census and more fully developed the system of taxation and royal courts begun by the Anglo-Saxon kings of the tenth and eleventh centuries. All in all, William of Normandy created a strong, centralized monarchy.

The Norman conquest of England had other repercussions as well. Because the new king of England was still the duke of Normandy, he was both a king (of England) and at the same time a vassal to a king (of France), but a vassal who was now far more powerful than his lord. This connection with France kept England heavily involved in European affairs throughout the High Middle Ages.

In the twelfth century, the power of the English monarchy was greatly enlarged during the reign of Henry II (1154–1189), the founder of the Plantagenet dynasty. The new king was particularly successful in strengthening the power of the royal courts. Henry expanded the number of criminal cases tried in the king's court and also devised ways of taking property cases from local courts to the royal courts. Henry's goals were clear: expanding the power of the royal courts expanded the king's power and, of course, brought revenues into his coffers. Moreover, because the royal courts were now found throughout England, a body of common law (law that was common to the whole kingdom) began to replace the different law codes that often varied from place to place.

Henry was less successful at imposing royal control over the church and became involved in a famous struggle between church and state in medieval England. Henry claimed the right to punish clergymen in church courts, but Thomas Becket, archbishop of Canterbury, the highest ranking English cleric, claimed that only church courts could try clerics. Attempts at compromise failed, and the angry king publicly expressed the desire to be rid of Becket: "Who will free me of this priest?" he screamed. Four knights took the challenge, went to Canterbury, and murdered the archbishop in the cathedral (see the box on p. 416). Faced with public outrage, Henry was forced to allow the right of appeal from English church courts to the papal court.

Many English nobles came to resent the ongoing growth of the king's power and rose in rebellion during the reign of Henry's son, King John (1199–1216). At Runnymeade in 1215, John was forced to seal the Magna Carta (the Great Charter) of feudal liberties. Magna Carta was, above all, a feudal document. Feudal custom had always recognized that the relationship between king and vassals was based on mutual rights and obligations. Magna Carta gave written recognition to that fact and was used in later years to strengthen the idea that the monarch's power was limited, not absolute.

⇛ *Murder in the Cathedral* ⇚

The most famous church-state controversy in medieval England arose between Henry II and Thomas Becket, archbishop of Canterbury, the highest ranking English cleric. Conflict erupted over the issue of whether the king had the right to punish clerics in royal courts. Attempts at compromise failed, and the king in exasperation publicly expressed the desire to be rid of Becket. Four knights who had taken the king's words literally went to Canterbury and murdered the archbishop in the cathedral. This excerpt is from a letter by John of Salisbury who served as secretaty to Theobald, archbishop of Canterbury, and his successor, Thomas Becket. John was present at the murder of the archbishop in 1170.

John of Salisbury to John of Canterbury, Bishop of Poitiers

The martyr [Becket] stood in the cathedral, before Christ's altar, as we have said, ready to suffer; the hour of slaughter was at hand. When he heard that he was sought—heard the knights who had come for him shouting in the throng of clerks and monks 'Where is the archbishop?'—he turned to meet them on the steps which he had almost climbed, and said with steady countenance: 'Here am I! What do you want?' One of the knight-assassins flung at him in fury: 'That you die now! That you should live longer is impossible.' No martyr seems ever to have been more steadfast in his agony than he . . . and thus, steadfast in speech as in spirit, he replied: 'And I am prepared to die for my God, to preserve justice and my church's liberty. If you seek my head, I forbid you on behalf of God almighty and on pain of anathema to do any hurt to any other man, monk, clerk or layman, of high or low degree. Do not involve them in the punishment, for they have not been involved in the cause: on my head not on theirs be it if any of them have supported the Church in its troubles. I embrace death readily, so long as peace and liberty for the Church follow from the shedding of my blood. . . . ' He spoke, and saw that the assassins had drawn their swords; and bowed his head like one in prayer. His last words were 'To God and St. Mary and the saints who protect and defend this church, and to the blessed Denis, I commend myself and the church's cause.' No one could dwell on what followed without deep sorrow and choking tears. A son's affection forbids me to describe each blow the savage assassins struck, spurning all fear of God, forgetful of all fealty and any human feeling. They defiled the cathedral and the holy season [Christmas] with a bishop's blood and with slaughter; but that was not enough. They sliced off the crown of his head, which had been specially dedicated to God by anointing with holy chrism—a fearful thing even to describe; then they used their evil swords, when he was dead, to spill his brain and cruelly scattered it, mixed with blood and bones, over the pavement. . . . Through all the agony the martyr's spirit was unconquered, his steadfastness marvelous to observe; he spoke not a word, uttered no cry, let slip no groan, raised no arm nor garment to protect himself from an assailant, but bent his head, which he had laid bare to their swords with wonderful courage, till all might be fulfilled. Motionless he held it, and when at last he fell his body lay straight; and he moved neither hand nor foot.

During the reign of Edward I (1272–1307), an institution of great importance in the development of representative government—the English Parliament—emerged. Originally, the word *parliament* was applied to meetings of the king's Great Council, in which the greater barons and chief prelates of the church met with the king's judges and principal advisers to deal with judicial affairs. But in his need for money, Edward I in 1295 invited two knights from every county and two residents from each town to meet with the Great Council to consent to new taxes. This was the first Parliament.

The English Parliament, then, came to be composed of two knights from every county and two burgesses from every borough as well as the barons and ecclesiastical lords. Eventually, barons and church lords formed the House of Lords; knights and burgesses, the House of Commons. The Parliaments of Edward I granted taxes, discussed politics, passed laws, and handled judicial business. Although not as yet the important body it would eventually become, the English Parliament had clearly emerged as an institution by the end of the thirteenth century. The law of the realm was beginning to be determined not by the king alone, but by the king in consultation with representatives of various groups that constituted the community.

The Growth of the French Kingdom

In 843, the Carolingian Empire had been divided into three major sections. The west Frankish lands formed the core of the eventual kingdom of France. In 987, after the death of the last Carolingian king, the west Frankish nobles chose Hugh Capet as the new king, thus establishing the Capetian dynasty of French kings. Although they carried the title of kings, the Capetians had little real power. They controlled as the royal domain (the lands of the king) only the lands around Paris known as the Ile-de-France. As kings of France, the Capetians were formally the overlords of the great lords of France, such as the dukes of Normandy, Brittany, Burgundy, and Aquitaine. In reality, however, many of the dukes were considerably more powerful than the Capetian kings. All in all, it would take the Capetian dynasty hundreds of years to create a truly centralized monarchical authority in France.

The reign of King Philip II Augustus (1180–1223) was an important turning point. Philip II waged war against the Plantagenet rulers of England, who also ruled the French territories of Normandy, Maine, Anjou, and Aquitaine, and was successful in gaining control of most of these territories. Through these conquests, Philip II quadrupled the income of the French monarchy and greatly enlarged its power. To administer justice and collect royal revenues in his new territories, Philip appointed new royal officials, thus inaugurating a French royal bureaucracy in the thirteenth century.

Capetian rulers after Philip II continued to add lands to the royal domain. Although Philip had used military force, other kings used both purchase and marriage to achieve the same end. Philip IV the Fair (1285–1314)

♦ **Map 12.3**   Europe in the High Middle Ages.

The European Kingdoms

England	
Norman Conquest	1066
William the Conqueror	1066–1087
Henry II, founder of Plantagenet dynasty	1154–1189
John	1199–1216
Magna Carta	1215
Edward I	1272–1307
First Parliament	1295
France	
Philip II Augustus	1180–1223
Philip IV	1285–1314
First Estates-General	1302
Germany and the Empire	
Otto I	936–973
Henry IV	1056–1106
Frederick I Barbarossa	1152–1190
Northern Italian cities defeat Frederick	1176
Frederick II	1212–1250
The Eastern World	
Mongol conquest of Russia	1230s
Alexander Nevsky, prince of Novgorod	c. 1220–1263

was especially effective in strengthening the French monarchy. The machinery of government became even more specialized. French kings going back to the early Capetians had possessed a household staff for running their affairs. Over time, however, this household staff was enlarged and divided into three groups to form three major branches of government: a council for advice, a chamber of accounts for finances, and a *parlement* or royal court. By the beginning of the fourteenth century, the Capetians had laid the firm foundations for a royal bureaucracy.

Philip IV also brought a French parliament into being by asking representatives of the three estates—or classes—the clergy (first estate), the nobles (second estate), and the townspeople (third estate) to meet with him. They did so in 1302, inaugurating the Estates-

General, the first French parliament, although it had little real power. By the end of the thirteenth century, France was the largest, wealthiest, and best-governed monarchical state in Europe.

The Lands of the Holy Roman Empire

In the tenth century, the powerful dukes of the Saxons became kings of the eastern Frankish kingdom (or Germany, as it came to be called). The best known of the Saxon kings of Germany was Otto I (936–973), who intervened in Italian politics and for his efforts was crowned emperor of the Romans by the pope in 962, reviving a title that had not been used since the time of Charlemagne. Otto's creation of a new "Roman Empire" in the hands of the eastern Franks (or Germans, as they came to be called) added a tremendous burden to the king of Germany who now took on the onerous task of ruling Italy as well.

In the eleventh century, German kings created a strong monarchy and a powerful empire by leading armies into Italy. To strengthen their power, they relied upon their ability to control the church and select bishops whom they could then use as royal administrators. But the struggle between church and state during the reign of Henry IV (1056–1106) weakened the king's ability to use church officials in this way (see Reform of the Papacy later in this chapter). The German kings also tried to bolster their power by using their position as emperors to exploit the resources of Italy. But this strategy tended to backfire; many a German king lost armies in Italy in pursuit of a dream of empire, and no German dynasty demonstrates this better than the Hohenstaufens.

The two most famous members of the Hohenstaufen dynasty, Frederick I (1152–1190) and Frederick II (1212–1250), tried to create a new kind of empire. Previous German kings had focused on building a strong German kingdom, to which Italy might be added as an appendage. Frederick I, however, planned to get his chief revenues from Italy as the center of a "holy empire," as he called it (hence the name Holy Roman Empire). But his attempt to conquer northern Italy ran into severe problems. The pope opposed him, fearful that the emperor wanted to include Rome and the Papal States as part of his empire. The cities of northern Italy, which had become used to their freedom, were also not willing to be Frederick's subjects. An alliance of these northern Italian cities, with the support of the pope, defeated the emperor's forces in 1176.

The main goal of Frederick II was the establishment of a strong centralized state in Italy dominated by the kingdom in Sicily he had inherited from his mother. Frederick's major task was to gain control of northern Italy. In attempting to conquer Italy, however, he became involved in a deadly struggle with the popes who feared that a single ruler of northern and southern Italy would mean the end of papal power in central Italy. The northern Italian cities were also unwilling to give up their freedom. Frederick waged a bitter struggle in northern Italy, winning many battles but ultimately losing the war.

The struggle between popes and emperors had dire consequences for the Holy Roman Empire. While they were fighting in Italy, the German emperors left Germany in the hands of powerful German feudal lords who ignored the emperor and created their own independent kingdoms. This ensured that the German monarchy would remain weak and incapable of maintaining a centralized monarchical state; thus, the German Holy Roman emperor had no real power over either Germany or Italy. Unlike France and England, neither Germany nor Italy created a unified national monarchy in the Middle Ages. Both Germany and Italy consisted of many small, independent states, and both had to wait until the nineteenth century to form united states.

The Slavic Peoples of Central and Eastern Europe

East of the Carolingian Empire lay a spacious plain through which a number of Asian nomads, such as the Huns, Bulgars, Avars, and Magyars, had pushed their way westward. Eastern Europe was ravaged by these successive waves of invaders who found it relatively easy to create large empires that, in turn, were overthrown by the next invaders. Over time, the invaders themselves were largely assimilated with the native Slavic peoples of the area.

The Slavic peoples were originally a single people in central Europe, but they gradually divided into three major groups: the western, southern, and eastern Slavs. The western Slavs eventually formed the Polish and Bohemian kingdoms. German Christian missionaries converted both the Czechs in Bohemia and the Slavs in Poland by the tenth century. The non-Slavic kingdom of Hungary, which emerged after the Magyars settled down after their defeat in 955, was also converted to Christianity by German missionaries. The Poles, Czechs, and Hungarians all accepted Catholic or western Christianity and

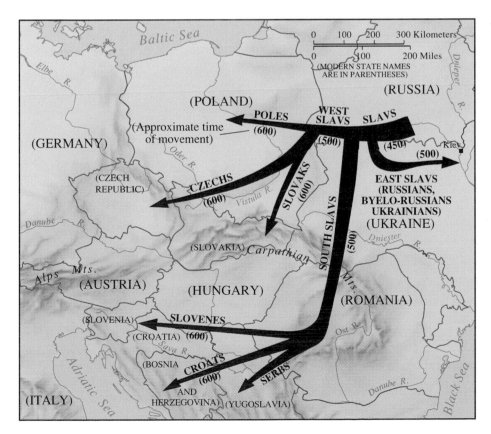

◆ **Map 12.4**   The World of the Slavs.

⇒ A Muslim's Description of the Rus ⇐

Despite the difficulties that travel presented, early medieval civilization did witness some contact among the various cultures. This might occur through trade, diplomacy, or the conquest and migration of peoples. This document is a description of the Swedish Rus who eventually merged with the native Slavic peoples to form the principality of Kiev, commonly regarded as the first Russian state. It was written by Ibn Fadlan, a Muslim diplomat sent from Baghdad in 921 to a settlement on the Volga River. His comments on the filthiness of the Rus reflect the Muslim preoccupation with cleanliness.

Ibn Fadlan, Description of the Rus

I saw the Rus folk when they arrived on their trading-mission and settled at the river Atul (Volga). Never had I seen people of more perfect physique. They are tall as date-palms, and reddish in color. They wear neither coat nor kaftan, but each man carried a cape which covers one half of his body, leaving one hand free. No one is ever parted from his axe, sword, and knife. Their swords are Frankish in design, broad, flat, and fluted. Each man has a number of trees, figures, and the like from the finger-nails to the neck. Each woman carried on her bosom a container made of iron, silver, copper or gold—its size and substance depending on her man's wealth.

They [the Rus] are the filthiest of God's creatures. They do not wash after discharging their natural func-tions, neither do they wash their hands after meals. They are as lousy as donkeys. They arrive from their distant lands and lay their ships alongside the banks of the Atul, which is a great river, and there they build big houses on its shores. Ten or twenty of them may live together in one house, and each of them has a couch of his own where he sits and diverts himself with the pretty slave girls whom he had brought along for sale. He will make love with one of them while a comrade looks on; sometimes they indulge in a communal orgy, and, if a customer should turn up to buy a girl, the Rus man will not let her go till he has finished with her.

They wash their hands and faces every day in incredibly filthy water. Every morning the girl brings her master a large bowl of water in which he washes his hands and face and hair, then blows his nose into it and spits into it. When he has finished the girl takes the bowl to his neighbor—who repeats the performance. Thus the bowl goes the rounds of the entire household. . . .

If one of the Rus folk falls sick they put him in a tent by himself and leave bread and water for him. They do not visit him, however, or speak to him, especially if he is a serf. Should he recover he rejoins the others; if he dies they burn him. But if he happens to be a serf they leave him for the dogs and vultures to devour. If they catch a robber they hang him to a tree until he is torn to shreds by wind and weather. . . .

became closely tied to the Roman Catholic church and its Latin culture.

The southern and eastern Slavic populations largely took a different path because of their proximity to the Byzantine Empire. The Slavic peoples of Moravia were converted to the Orthodox Christianity of the Byzantine Empire by two Byzantine missionary brothers, Cyril and Methodius, who began their activities in 863. They created a Slavonic (Cyrillic) alphabet, translated the Bible into Slavonic, and developed Slavonic church services. Although the southern Slavic peoples accepted Christianity, a split eventually developed between the Croats who accepted the Roman Catholic church and the Serbs who remained loyal to Orthodox Christianity.

Much of the Balkan peninsula was conquered by the Bulgars, who were originally an Asian people, but were eventually absorbed by the larger native south Slavic population. Together, they formed a largely Slavic Bulgarian kingdom that embraced the church services developed earlier by Cyril and Methodius. The acceptance of Eastern Orthodoxy by the southern Slavic peoples, the Serbs and Bulgarians, meant that their cultural life was linked to the Byzantine state.

The eastern Slavic peoples, from whom the modern Russians and Ukrainians are descended, had settled in the territory of present-day Ukraine and European Russia. There, beginning in the late eighth century, they began to encounter Swedish Vikings who moved down the extensive network of rivers into the lands of the eastern Slavs in search of booty and new trade routes (see the box on p. 420). These Vikings built trading settlements and eventually came to dominate the native peoples who called them "the Rus," from which the name Russia is derived.

THE DEVELOPMENT OF RUSSIA

One Viking leader named Oleg (c. 873–913) settled in Kiev at the beginning of the tenth century and created the Rus state known as the principality of Kiev. His successors extended their control over the eastern Slavs and expanded the territory of Kiev until it included all the lands between the Baltic and Black Seas and the Danube and Volga Rivers. By marrying Slavic wives, the Viking ruling class was gradually assimilated into the Slavic population.

The growth of the principality of Kiev attracted religious missionaries, especially from the Byzantine Empire. One Rus ruler, Vladimir (c. 980–1015), married the Byzantine emperor's sister and officially accepted Christianity for himself and his people in 987. From the end of the tenth century, Byzantine Christianity became the model for Russian religious life.

The Kievan Rus state prospered and reached its high point in the first half of the eleventh century. Kievan society was dominated by a noble class of landowners known as the boyars while Kievan merchants carried on a regular trade with Scandinavia to the north and the Islamic and Byzantine worlds to the south. But civil wars and new invasions by Asian nomads caused the principality of Kiev to collapse, and the sack of Kiev by north Russian princes in 1169 brought an end to the first Russian state. That state had remained closely tied to the Byzantine Empire, not to the new Europe. Its Christianity had been Orthodox Christianity, not the Catholicism of Europe. In the thirteenth century, the Mongols conquered Russia and cut it off even more from Europe.

The Mongols had exploded upon the scene in the thirteenth century, moving east into China and west into the Middle East and central Europe. Although they conquered Russia, they were not numerous enough to occupy all of its vast lands. Instead, they required the Russian princes to pay tribute to them. One Russian prince soon emerged as more powerful than the others. Alexander Nevsky (c. 1220–1263), prince of Novgorod, defeated a German invading army in northwestern Russia in 1242. His cooperation with the Mongols won him their favor. The khan, leader of the western part of the Mongol empire, rewarded Alexander Nevsky with the title of grand-prince, enabling his descendants to become the princes of Moscow and eventually leaders of all Russia.

The World of the Peasants

In the Early Middle Ages, Europe had a relatively small population, but in the High Middle Ages, the population increased dramatically. The number of people in Europe almost doubled between 1000 and 1300, rising from 38 million to 74 million. Why this dramatic increase in population? For one thing, conditions in Europe were more settled and peaceful after the invasions of the Early Middle Ages had stopped. Then, too, agricultural production also expanded dramatically after 1000. Whether this new productivity was a cause or effect of the population increase is uncertain, but without such a significant rise in food supplies, the growth in population could never have been sustained.

The New Agriculture

During the High Middle Ages, Europeans began to farm in new ways. Although an improvement in climate produced better growing conditions, another important factor in increasing the output of food was the expansion of cultivated or arable land, accomplished primarily by clearing forested areas for cultivation. Eager for land, peasants of the eleventh and twelfth centuries cut down trees and drained swamps. By the thirteenth century, the total acreage available for farming in Europe was greater than the amount tilled at any time before or since.

Technological changes also furthered the development of farming. The Middle Ages witnessed an explosion of labor-saving devices, many of which were made from iron, which was mined in different areas of Europe. Iron was in demand to make swords and armor, but it was also used to make scythes, axes, and hoes for use on farms as well as saws, hammers, and nails for building purposes. Iron was crucial in making the *carruca*, a heavy-wheeled plow with an iron plowshare, which could turn over the heavy clay soil north of the Alps and allow for its drainage.

Because of the *carruca's* weight, six or eight oxen were needed to pull it, but oxen were slow. Two new inventions for the horse made it possible to plow even faster. A new horse collar, which appeared in the tenth century, distributed the weight around the shoulders and chest, rather than the throat, and could be used to hitch up a series of horses, enabling them to pull the new heavy plow faster and cultivate more land. The use of the horseshoe, an iron shoe nailed to the horse's hooves, made it easier for horses to pull the heavy plow through the rocky and heavy clay soil of northern Europe.

The use of the heavy-wheeled plow also led to the growth of agricultural villages where people had to work together. Because iron was expensive, a heavy-wheeled plow had to be purchased by the entire community. Likewise an individual family could not afford a team of animals so villagers shared their beasts. Moreover, the size and weight of the plow made it necessary to plow the land in long strips to minimize the amount of turning that would have to be done.

Besides using horsepower, the High Middle Ages harnessed the power of water and wind to do jobs formerly done by human or animal power. Located along streams, mills powered by water were used to grind grains and produce flour. Dams were constructed to increase waterpower. Where rivers were not available or not easily dammed, Europeans developed windmills to harness the power of the wind. By the end of the twelfth century, they were beginning to dot the European landscape. Like the watermill, the windmill was first used for grinding grains. The watermill and windmill were the most important devices for harnessing power before the invention of the steam engine in the eighteenth century. Their spread had revolutionary consequences in enabling Europeans to produce more food.

The shift from a two-field to a three-field system also contributed to the increase in food production. In the Early Middle Ages, farmers commonly planted one field while allowing another of equal size to lie fallow to regain its fertility. Now estates were divided into three parts. One field was planted in the fall with winter grains, such as rye and wheat, while spring grains, such as oats or barley, and vegetables, such as peas, beans, or lentils, were planted in the second field. The third was allowed to lie fallow. By rotating the fields, only one-third rather than one-half of the land lay fallow at any time. The rotation of crops also kept the soil from being exhausted so quickly, and more crops could now be grown.

The Manorial System

The system of feudalism that we examined rested upon an economic system known as manorialism. A manor was an agricultural estate operated by a lord and worked by peasants; it was the fundamental unit of rural organization in the Middle Ages. Manorialism grew out of the unsettled conditions of the Early Middle Ages, when small farmers often needed protection or food in a time of bad harvests. Free peasants gave up their freedom to the lords of large landed estates in return for protection and use of the lord's land. While a large class of free peasants continued to exist, increasing numbers of free peasants became serfs—peasants bound to the land and required to pro-

◆ **Map 12.5**   A Manor.

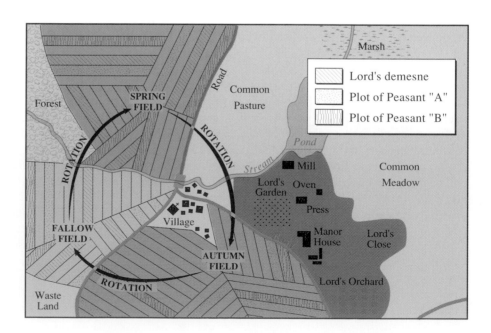

vide labor services, pay rents, and be subject to the lord's jurisdiction. By the ninth century, probably 60 percent of the population of western Europe had become serfs.

Labor services consisted of working the lord's demesne, the land retained by the lord, which might consist of one-third to one-half of the cultivated lands scattered throughout the manor. The rest would be used by the peasants for themselves. Building barns and digging ditches were also part of the labor services. Serfs usually worked about three days a week for their lord.

The serfs paid rents by giving the lord a share of every product they raised. Moreover, serfs paid the lord for the use of the manor's common pasturelands, streams, ponds, and surrounding woodlands. For example, if a serf fished in the pond or stream on a manor, he turned over part of the catch to his lord. Peasants were also obliged to pay a tithe (a tenth of their produce) to their local village church.

Lords possessed a variety of legal rights over their serfs as a result of their unfree status. Serfs were legally bound to the lord's lands and could not leave without his permission. Although free to marry, serfs could not marry anyone outside their manor without the lord's approval. Moreover, lords sometimes exercised public rights or political authority on their lands, which gave them the right to try peasants in their own courts. In fact, the manorial court provided the only law that most peasants knew. Peasants also had to pay the lord for certain services; for example, they might be required to bring their grain to the lord's mill and pay a fee to have it ground into flour.

As the growing towns and cities needed more food, food prices tended to rise in the thirteenth century. This led lords to try to grow more food for profit. One way to do so was to lease their demesne land to their serfs. Labor services were then transformed into money payments or fixed rents, thereby converting many unfree serfs into free peasants. Although many peasants still remained economically dependent on their lords, they were no longer legally tied to the land. Lords, in turn, became collectors of rents, rather than operators of a manor with both political and legal privileges. The political and legal powers formerly exercised by lords were increasingly reclaimed by the monarchical states.

Daily Life of the Peasantry

Peasant activities were largely determined by the seasons of the year. Each season brought a new round of tasks appropriate for the time, although some periods were considerably more hectic than others, especially harvest time in August and September. The peasant diet was based on bread, so an adequate harvest of grains was crucial to survival in the winter months. A new cycle began in October when the peasants prepared the ground for planting winter crops. In November came the slaughter of excess livestock because there was usually insufficient fodder to keep animals all winter. The meat would be salted to preserve it for winter use. In February and March, the land was plowed for spring crops—oats, barley, peas, beans, and lentils. Early summer was a comparatively relaxed

◆ **Peasants in the Manorial System.** In the manorial system, peasants were required to provide labor services for their lord. This thirteenth-century illustration shows a group of English peasants harvesting grain. Overseeing their work is a bailiff, or manager, who supervised the work of the peasants.

time, although there was still weeding and sheepshearing to be done. In every season, the serfs worked not only their own land, but also the lord's demesne. They also tended the small gardens next to their dwellings where they grew the vegetables that made up part of their diet.

But peasants did not face a life of constant labor thanks to the feast days or holidays of the Catholic church, which commemorated the great events of the Christian faith or the lives of Christian saints or holy persons. The three great feasts of the Catholic church were Christmas (celebrating the birth of Christ), Easter (celebrating the resurrection of Christ), and Pentecost (celebrating the descent of the Holy Spirit on Christ's disciples fifty days after his resurrection). Numerous other feasts dedicated to saints or the Virgin Mary, the mother of Christ, were also celebrated, making a total of over fifty days that were essentially holidays.

Religious feast days, Sunday mass, baptisms, marriages, and funerals all brought peasants into contact with the village church, a crucial part of manorial life. The village priest instructed the peasants in the basic elements of Christianity so that they would attain the Christian's ultimate goal—salvation. But village priests were often barely literate peasants themselves, and it is difficult to know how much church doctrine the peasants actually understood. Very likely, they regarded God as an all-powerful force who needed to be appeased by prayer to bring good harvests.

The lifestyle of the peasants was quite simple. Their cottages consisted of wood frames covered by sticks with the space between them filled with straw and rubble and then plastered over with clay. Roofs were simply thatched. The houses of poorer peasants consisted of a single room, but others had at least two rooms—a main room for cooking, eating, and other activities and another room for sleeping. There was little privacy in a medieval peasant household.

Peasant women occupied both an important and a difficult position in manorial society. They were expected to carry and bear their children and at the same time fulfill their obligation to labor in the fields. Their ability to manage the household might determine whether a peasant family would starve or survive in difficult times.

Though simple, a peasant's daily diet was adequate when food was available. The staple of the peasant diet, and the medieval diet in general, was bread. While women made the dough for the bread, the loaves were usually baked in community ovens, which were owned by the lord of the manor. Peasant bread was highly nutritious because it contained not only wheat and rye, but also barley, millet, and oats, giving it a dark appearance and a very heavy, hard texture. Bread was supplemented by numerous vegetables from the household gardens, cheese from cow's or goat's milk, nuts and berries from woodlands, and fruits, such as apples, pears, and cherries. Chickens provided eggs and sometimes meat. Peasants usually ate meat only on the great feast days, such as Christmas, Easter, and Pentecost.

Grains were important not only for bread, but also for making ale. In northern European countries, ale was the most common drink of the poor. If records are accurate, enormous quantities of ale were consumed. A monastery in the twelfth century records a daily allotment to the monks of three gallons a day, far above the weekend consumption of many present-day college students. Peasants in the field undoubtedly consumed even more. This high consumption of alcohol might help to explain the large number of accidental deaths recorded in medieval court records.

The New World of Trade and Cities

Medieval Europe was overwhelmingly an agrarian society with most people living in small villages. In the eleventh and twelfth centuries, however, new elements were introduced that began to transform the economic foundation of European civilization: a revival of trade, the emergence of specialized craftsmen and artisans, and the growth and development of towns. These changes were made possible by the new agricultural practices and subsequent increase in food production, which freed part of the European population from producing their own food. Merchants and craftsmen could now buy their necessities.

The Revival of Trade

The revival of trade was a gradual process. During the chaotic conditions of the Early Middle Ages, large-scale trade had declined in western Europe except for Byzantine contacts with Italy and the Jewish traders who moved back and forth between the Muslim and Christian worlds. By the end of the tenth century, however, people with both the skills and the products for commercial activity were emerging in Europe. Cities in Italy took the lead in this revival of trade. By the end of the eighth century, for example, Venice had emerged as a town with close trading ties to the Byzantine Empire. It developed a mercantile fleet and by the end of the tenth century had become the chief western trading center for Byzantine and Islamic commerce.

the late Roman Empire. Basilicas were simply rectangular buildings with flat wooden roofs. While using this basic plan, Romanesque builders made a significant innovation by replacing the flat wooden roof with a long, curved stone vault called a barrel vault or a cross vault where two barrel vaults intersected. The latter was used when a transept was added to create a church plan in the shape of a cross. Although barrel and cross vaults were difficult to build, they were considered aesthetically more pleasing and technically more proficient and were also less apt to catch fire.

Because stone roofs were extremely heavy, Romanesque churches required massive pillars and walls to hold them up. This left little space for windows, and the churches were correspondingly dark on the inside. Their massive walls and pillars gave Romanesque churches a sense of solidity and almost the impression of a fortress. Indeed, massive walls and slit windows were also characteristic of the castle architecture of the same period.

The Gothic Cathedral

Begun in the twelfth century and brought to perfection in the thirteenth, the Gothic cathedral remains one of the greatest artistic triumphs of the High Middle Ages. Soaring skyward, almost as if to reach heaven, it was a fitting symbol for medieval people's preoccupation with God.

Two fundamental innovations of the twelfth century made Gothic cathedrals possible. The combination of ribbed vaults and pointed arches replaced the barrel vault of Romanesque churches and enabled builders to make Gothic churches higher than their Romanesque counterparts. The use of pointed arches and ribbed vaults created an impression of upward movement, a sense of weightless upward thrust that implied the energy of God. Another technical innovation, the flying buttress, basically a heavy arched pier of stone built onto the outside of the wall, made it possible to distribute the weight of the church's vaulted ceilings outward and down and thus eliminate the heavy walls used in Romanesque churches to hold the weight of the massive barrel vaults. Thus, Gothic cathedrals could be built with thin walls that were filled with magnificent stained glass windows, which created a play of light inside that varied with the sun at different times of the day. This preoccupation with colored light in Gothic cathedrals was not accidental, but was executed by people who believed that natural light was a symbol of the divine light of God.

The first fully Gothic church was the abbey church of Saint-Denis near Paris, inspired by its famous abbot

♦ **The Gothic Cathedral.** The Gothic cathedral was one of the great artistic triumphs of the High Middle Ages. Seen here is the cathedral of Notre Dame in Paris. Begun in 1163, it was not completed until the beginning of the fourteenth century.

Suger (1122–1151) and built between 1140 and 1150. Although the Gothic style was a product of northern France, by the mid-thirteenth century, French Gothic architecture had spread to England, Spain, Germany— virtually all of Europe. By the mid-thirteenth century, French Gothic architecture was displayed most brilliantly in cathedrals in Paris (Notre Dame), Reims, Amiens, and Chartres.

A Gothic cathedral was the work of an entire community. All classes contributed to its construction. Money was raised from wealthy townspeople who had profited from the new trade and industries as well as from kings and nobles. Master masons who were both architects and engineers designed the cathedrals. They drew up the plans and supervised the work of construction. Stonemasons and other craftsmen were paid a daily wage and

◆ The Emperor Justinian Surrounded by His Court. The church of San Vitale at Ravenna contains some of the finest examples of sixth-century Byzantine mosaics. This mosaic depicts the Byzantine emperor Justinian and his court dressed in their elaborate court robes.

provided the skilled labor to build the cathedrals. The building of cathedrals often became highly competitive as communities vied with one another to build the highest tower. Most importantly, a Gothic cathedral symbolized the chief preoccupation of a medieval Christian community, its dedication to a spiritual ideal. As we have observed before, the largest buildings of an era reflect the values of its society. The Gothic cathedral with its towers soaring toward heaven gave witness to an age when a spiritual impulse still underlay most of existence.

The Byzantine Empire and the Crusades

In the fourth century, a noticeable separation between the western and eastern parts of the Roman Empire began to develop. In the course of the fifth century, the Germanic tribes moved into the western part of the empire and established their states while the Roman Empire in the east, centered on Constantinople, continued to exist.

The Reign of Justinian (527–565)

When he became emperor of the Eastern Roman Empire, Justinian was determined to reestablish the Roman Empire in the entire Mediterranean world. His army, commanded by Belisarius, probably the best general of the late Roman world, sailed to North Africa and quickly destroyed the Vandals in two major battles. From North Africa Belisarius led his forces onto the Italian peninsula and defeated the Ostrogoths. By 552, Justinian appeared to have achieved his goals. He had restored the Roman Empire in the Mediterranean. His empire included Italy, part of Spain, North Africa, Asia Minor, Palestine, and Syria. But the reconquest of the western empire proved fleeting. Only three years after Justinian's death, the Lombards conquered much of Italy. Although the eastern empire maintained the fiction of Italy as a province, its forces were limited to southern and central Italy, Sicily, and some coastal areas.

Justinian's most important contribution was his codification of Roman law. The eastern empire had inherited a vast quantity of legal materials connected to the development of Roman law, which Justinian wished to simplify. The result was the Code of Law, the first part of the *Corpus Iuris Civilis (The Body of Civil Law)*, completed in 529. Four years later, two other parts of the *Corpus* appeared: the *Digest*, a compendium of writings of Roman jurists, and the *Institutes*, a brief summary of the chief principles of Roman law. The fourth part of the *Corpus* was the *Novels*, a compilation of the most important new edicts issued during Justinian's reign.

Justinian's codification of Roman law remained the basis of imperial law in the Eastern Roman Empire until its end in 1453. More importantly, however, because it was written in Latin (it was, in fact, the last product of eastern Roman culture to be written in Latin, which was soon replaced by Greek), it was also eventually used in the west and, in fact, became the basis of the legal systems of all of continental Europe.

From Eastern Roman to Byzantine Empire

Justinian's accomplishments had been spectacular, but he left the Eastern Roman Empire with serious problems: too much territory to protect far from Constantinople, an empty treasury, a decline in population after a plague, and renewed threats to its frontiers. In the first half of the seventh century, the empire was attacked by the Persians to the east and the Slavs to the north. The empire survived, only to face a new series of threats.

The most serious challenge to the Eastern Roman Empire came from the rise of Islam, which unified the Arab tribes and created a powerful new force that swept through the east (see Chapter 8). The defeat of an eastern Roman army at Yarmuk in 636 meant the loss of the provinces of Syria and Palestine. Problems arose along the northern frontier as well, especially in the Balkans, where the Bulgars had arrived earlier in the sixth century.

◆ **Map 12.6**   The Byzantine Empire in the Time of Justinian.

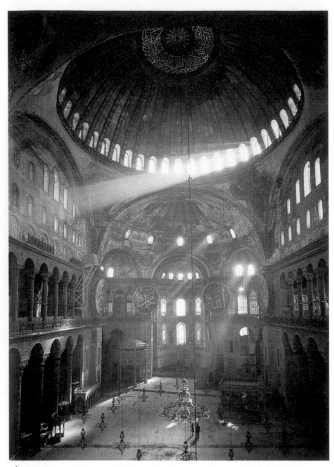

✦ **Interior View of Hagia Sophia.** Pictured here is the interior of the Church of the Holy Wisdom, constructed under Justinian by Anthemius of Tralles and Isidore of Milan. The pulpits and the great plaques bearing inscriptions from the Koran were introduced when the Turks converted this church into a mosque in the fifteenth century.

In 679, the Bulgars defeated the eastern Roman forces and took possession of the lower Danube valley, creating a strong Bulgarian kingdom.

By the beginning of the eighth century, the Eastern Roman Empire was greatly diminished in size. Consisting only of the eastern Balkans and Asia Minor, it was no longer an eastern Mediterranean state. The external challenges had important internal repercussions as well. By the eighth century, the Eastern Roman Empire had been transformed into what historians call the Byzantine Empire, a civilization with its own unique character that would last until 1453.

The Byzantine Empire was both a Greek and a Christian state. Increasingly, Latin fell into disuse as Greek became both the common and the official language of the empire. The Byzantine Empire was also a Christian state. The empire was built on a faith in Christ that was shared in a profound way by almost all of its citizens. An enormous amount of artistic talent was poured into the construction of churches, church ceremonies, and church decoration. Spiritual principles deeply permeated Byzantine art.

The emperor occupied a crucial position in the Byzantine state. Portrayed as chosen by God, the emperor was crowned in sacred ceremonies, and his subjects were expected to prostrate themselves in his presence. His power was considered absolute and was limited in practice only by deposition or assassination. Since the emperor appointed the head of the church (known as the patriarch), he also exercised control over both church and state. The Byzantines believed that God had commanded their state to preserve the true Christian faith. Emperor, clergy, and state officials were all bound together in service to this ideal. It can be said that spiritual values truly held the Byzantine state together.

LIFE IN CONSTANTINOPLE

After riots destroyed much of Constantinople in 532, Emperor Justinian rebuilt the city and gave it the appearance it would keep for almost a thousand years. With a population estimated in the hundreds of thousands, Constantinople was the largest city in Europe during the Middle Ages. It viewed itself as the center of an empire and a special Christian city.

Until the twelfth century, Constantinople was Europe's greatest commercial center, the chief marketplace where western and eastern products were exchanged. Highly desired in Europe were the products of the East: silk from China, spices from Southeast Asia and India, jewelry and ivory from India (the latter used by Byzantine craftsmen for church items), wheat and furs from southern Russia, and flax and honey from the Balkans. Many of these eastern goods were then shipped to the Mediterranean area and northern Europe. Some imported raw materials were used in Constantinople for local industries. During Justinian's reign, two Christian monks smuggled silkworms from China to begin a Byzantine silk industry. The state controlled the production of silk cloth, and the workshops themselves were housed in Constantinople's royal palace complex. European demand for silk cloth made it the city's most lucrative product.

Before Justinian's program of rebuilding in the sixth century, Emperor Theodosius II (408–450) in the mid-fifth century had erected an enormous defensive wall to protect the city on its land side. The city was dominated by an immense palace complex, hundreds of churches, and a huge arena known as the Hippodrome. No residential district was particularly fashionable; palaces, tenements, and slums ranged alongside one another. Justinian added many new buildings. His public works projects included roads, bridges, walls, public baths, law courts, and colossal underground reservoirs to hold the city's water supply. He also built hospitals, schools, monasteries, and churches. The latter were his special passion, and in Constantinople alone he built or rebuilt thirty-four of them. His greatest achievement was the famous Hagia Sophia—the Church of the Holy Wisdom.

Completed in 537, Hagia Sophia was designed by a Greek architect who did not use the simple, flat-roofed basilica of western architecture. The center of Hagia Sophia consisted of four large piers crowned by an enormous dome, which seemed to be floating in space. In part, this impression was created by ringing the base of the dome with forty-two windows, which allowed an incredible play of light within the cathedral. Light served to remind the worshipers of God. As invisible light illuminates darkness, so too it was believed invisible spirit illuminates the world.

The Hippodrome was a huge amphitheater, constructed of brick covered by marble, holding between 40,000 and 60,000 spectators. Although gladiator fights were held there, the main events were the chariot races; twenty-four would usually be presented in one day. The citizens of Constantinople were passionate fans of chariot racing. Successful charioteers were acclaimed as heroes and honored with public statues.

New Heights and New Problems

By 750, the Byzantine Empire consisted only of Asia Minor, some lands in the Balkans, and the southern coast of Italy. Although Byzantium was beset with internal dissension and invasions in the ninth century, it was able to deal with them and not only endured, but even expanded, reaching its high point in the tenth century, which some historians have called "the golden age of Byzantine civilization."

A new dynasty of Byzantine emperors known as the Macedonians (867–1081) was chiefly responsible for the empire's renewed strength. This line of emperors managed to beat off the empire's external enemies, go over to the offensive, and reestablish domestic order. The empire was expanded to include Bulgaria in the Balkans, the islands of Crete and Cyprus, and Syria. By 1025, the

Byzantine Empire was the largest it had been since the beginning of the seventh century.

The Macedonian emperors also fostered a burst of economic prosperity by expanding trade relations with western Europe, especially by selling silks and metalwork. Thanks to this prosperity, the city of Constantinople flourished. Foreign visitors continued to be astounded by its size, wealth, and physical surroundings. To western Europeans, it was the stuff of legends and fables (see the box on p. 440).

Although the Macedonians had restored much of the power of the Byzantine Empire in the tenth and eleventh centuries, their incompetent successors reversed most of the gains as struggles for power between ambitious military leaders and aristocratic families led to political and social disorder in the late eleventh century. The Byzantine Empire had also been troubled by the growing split between the Catholic church of the west and the Eastern Orthodox church of the Byzantine Empire. The Eastern Orthodox church was unwilling to accept the pope's claim that he was the sole head of the church. In 1054, Pope Leo IX and Patriarch Michael Cerularius, head of the Byzantine church, formally excommunicated each other, initiating a schism between the two great branches of Christianity that has not been completely healed to this day.

The Byzantine Empire faced threats from abroad as well. The greatest challenge came from the advance of the Seljuk Turks (see Chapter 8) who had moved into Asia Minor—the heartland of the empire and its main source of food and manpower. In 1071, a Turkish army disastrously defeated the Byzantine forces under Emperor

⇒ *A Western View of the Byzantine Empire* ⇐

Bishop Liudprand of Cremona undertook diplomatic missions to Constantinople on behalf of two western kings, Berengar of Italy and Otto I of Germany. This selection is taken from his description of his mission to the Byzantine emperor Constantine VII in 949 as an envoy for Berengar, king of Italy from 950 until his overthrow by Otto I of Germany in 964. Liudprand had mixed feelings about Byzantium: admiration, yet also envy and hostility because of its superior wealth.

Liudprand of Cremona, Antapodosis

Next to the imperial residence at Constantinople there is a palace of remarkable size and beauty which the Greeks call Magnavra . . . the name being equivalent to "Fresh breeze." In order to receive some Spanish envoys, who had recently arrived, as well as myself . . . , Constantine gave orders that this palace should be got ready. . . .

Before the emperor's seat stood a tree, made of bronze gilded over, whose branches were filled with birds, also made of gilded bronze, which uttered different cries, each according to its varying species. The throne itself was so marvelously fashioned that at one moment it seemed a low structure, and at another it rose high into the air. It was of immense size and was guarded by lions, made either of bronze or of wood covered over with gold, who beat the ground with their tails and gave a dreadful roar with open mouth and quivering tongue. Leaning upon the shoulders of two eunuchs I was brought into the emperor's presence. At my approach the lions began to roar and the birds to cry out, each according to its kind; but I was neither terrified nor surprised, for I had previously made enquiry about all these things from people who were well ac-

quainted with them. So after I had three times made obeisance to the emperor with my face upon the ground, I lifted my head, and behold! The man whom just before I had seen sitting on a moderately elevated seat had now changed his raiment and was sitting on the level of the ceiling. How it was done I could not imagine, unless perhaps he was lifted up by some such sort of device as we use for raising the timbers of a wine press. On that occasion he did not address me personally, . . . but by the intermediary of a secretary he enquired about Berengar's doings and asked after his health. I made a fitting reply and then, at a nod from the interpreter, left his presence and retired to my lodging.

It would give me some pleasure also to record here what I did then for Berengar. . . . The Spanish envoys . . . had brought handsome gifts from their masters to the emperor Constantine. I for my part had brought nothing from Berengar except a letter and that was full of lies. I was very greatly disturbed and shamed at this and began to consider anxiously what I had better do. In my doubt and perplexity it finally occurred to me that I might offer the gifts, which on my account I had brought for the emperor, as coming from Berengar, and trick out my humble present with fine words. I therefore presented him with nine excellent cuirasses, seven excellent shields with gilded bosses, two silver gilt cauldrons, some swords, spears and spits, and what was more precious to the emperor than anything, four carzimasia; that being the Greek name for young eunuchs who have had both their testicles and their penis removed. This operation is performed by traders at Verdun, who take the boys into Spain and make a huge profit.

Romanus IV Diogenes at Manzikert. Lacking the resources to undertake new campaigns against the Turks, the new emperor, Alexius I Comnenus (1081–1118), turned to Europe for military assistance. It was the positive response of Europeans to the emperor's request that led to the crusades. The Byzantine Empire lived to regret it.

The Crusades

The crusades were based upon the idea of a holy war against the infidels or unbelievers. The wrath of Chris-

tians was directed against the Muslims, and at the end of the eleventh century, Christian Europe found itself with a glorious opportunity to attack them. The immediate impetus for the crusades came when the Byzantine emperor Alexius I asked Pope Urban II for help against the Seljuk Turks, who were Muslims. The pope saw a golden opportunity to provide papal leadership for a great cause: to rally the warriors of Europe for the liberation of Jerusalem and the Holy Land from the infidel. At the Council of Clermont in southern France near the end of 1095, Urban II challenged Christians to take up their weapons and join in a holy war to recover the Holy Land.

✦ Map 12.7   The Early Crusades.

The pope promised remission of sins: "All who die by the way, whether by land or by sea, or in battle against the pagans, shall have immediate remission of sins. This I grant them through the power of God with which I am invested."[13] The enthusiastic crowd cried out in response: "It is the will of God, it is the will of God."

The warriors of western Europe, particularly France, formed the first crusading armies. The knights who made up this first crusading host were motivated by religious fervor, but there were other attractions as well. Some sought adventure and welcomed a legitimate opportunity to pursue their favorite pastime—fighting. Others saw an opportunity to gain territory, riches, and possibly a title. From the perspective of the pope and European monarchs, the crusades offered the potential of freeing Europe of contentious young nobles who disturbed the peace and wasted lives fighting each other.

Three organized crusading bands of noble warriors, most of them French, made their way to the east. The crusading army probably numbered several thousand cavalry and as many as 10,000 infantry. After the capture of Antioch in 1098, much of the crusading host proceeded down the Palestinian coast, evading the well-defended coastal cities, and reached Jerusalem in June 1099. After a five-week siege, the Holy City was taken amidst a horrible massacre of the inhabitants, men, women, and children.

After further conquest of Palestinian lands, the crusaders ignored the wishes of the Byzantine emperor (who foolishly believed the crusaders were working on his behalf) and organized four Latin crusader states. Because the crusader states were surrounded by Muslims, they grew increasingly dependent upon the Italian commercial cities for supplies from Europe. Some Italian cities, such as Genoa, Pisa, and, above all, Venice, grew rich and powerful in the process.

But it was not easy for the crusader states to maintain themselves in the east. Already by the 1120s, the Muslims had begun to strike back. In 1144, Edessa became the first of the four Latin states to be recaptured. Its fall led to renewed calls for another crusade, especially from the monastic firebrand Saint Bernard of Clairvaux. He exclaimed: "Now, on account of our sins, the enemies of the cross have begun to show their faces. . . . What are you doing, you servants of the cross? Will you throw to the dogs that which is most holy? Will you cast pearls before swine?"[14] Bernard aimed his message at knights and even managed to enlist two powerful rulers, King Louis VII of France (1137–1180) and Emperor Conrad III of Germany (1138–1152). Their Second Crusade, however, proved to be a total failure.

The Third Crusade was a reaction to the fall of the Holy City of Jerusalem in 1187 to the Muslim forces under Saladin. Now all of Christendom was ablaze with calls for a new crusade. Three major monarchs agreed to lead their forces in person: Emperor Frederick Barbarossa of Germany (1152–1190), Richard I the Lionhearted of England (1189–1199), and Philip II Augustus of France (1180–1223). Some of the crusaders finally arrived in the east by 1189 only to encounter problems. Frederick Barbarossa drowned while swimming in a local river, and his army quickly disintegrated. The English and French arrived by sea and met with success against the coastal cities where they had the support of their fleets, but when they moved inland, they failed miserably. Eventually, after Philip went home, Richard the Lionhearted negotiated a settlement whereby Saladin agreed to allow Christian pilgrims free access to Jerusalem.

After the death of Saladin in 1193, Pope Innocent III initiated a Fourth Crusade. On its way to the east, the crusading army became involved in a dispute over the succession to the Byzantine throne. The Venetian leaders of the Fourth Crusade saw an opportunity to neutralize their greatest commercial competitor: the Byzantine Empire. Diverted to Constantinople, the crusaders sacked the great capital city of Byzantium in 1204 and created a new Latin Empire of Constantinople. Not until 1261 did a Byzantine army recapture Constantinople. The Byzantine Empire had been saved, but it was no longer a great Mediterranean power. The restored empire now comprised only the city of Constantinople and its surrounding lands as well as some lands in Asia Minor. Though reduced in size, the empire limped along for another 190 years, until its weakened condition finally enabled the Ottoman Turks to conquer it in 1453.

Despite the failures, the crusading ideal was not yet completely lost. In Germany in 1212, a youth known as Nicholas of Cologne announced that God had inspired him to lead a "children's crusade" to the Holy Land. Thousands of young people joined Nicholas and made their way down the Rhine and across the Alps to Italy where the pope told them to go home. Most tried to do so. At about the same time, a group of about 20,000 French children made their way to Marseilles where two shipowners agreed to transport them to the Holy Land. Seven ships packed with hymn-singing youths soon left the port. Two of the ships perished in a storm near Sardinia; the other five sailed to North Africa where the children were sold into slavery. The next crusades of adult warriors were hardly more successful.

All in all, the crusades had failed to accomplish their primary goal of holding the Holy Land for the Christian west. Whether the crusades had much effect on European civilization is widely debated. Did the crusades help to stabilize European society by removing large numbers of young warriors who would have fought each other in Europe? Some historians think so and believe that western monarchs established their control more easily as a result. There is no doubt that the Italian seaports, especially Genoa, Pisa, and Venice, benefited economically from the crusades, but even without the crusades, Italian merchants would have pursued new trade contacts with the eastern world. The crusades did have unfortunate side effects that would afflict European society for generations. The first widespread attacks on the Jews occurred during the crusades. Some Christians argued that to undertake holy wars against infidel Muslims while the "murderers of Christ" ran free at home was unthinkable. The massacre of Jews became a regular feature of medieval European life (see the box on p. 443).

Conclusion

After the collapse of the Western Roman Empire and the establishment of the Germanic states, a new European civilization slowly began to emerge in the Early Middle Ages. The coronation of Charlemagne, descendant of a Germanic tribe converted to Christianity, as Roman emperor in 800 symbolized the fusion of the three chief components of the new European civilization: the German tribes, the Roman legacy, and the Christian church. In the long run, the creation of Charlemagne's empire fostered the idea of a distinct European identity. The lands north of the Alps now became the political center of Europe.

With the disintegration of the Carolingian Empire, new forms of political institutions began to develop in Europe. The feudal system put power into the hands of many different lords, who came to constitute a powerful

⇒ *Treatment of the Jews* ⇐

The development of new religious sensibilities in the High Middle Ages also had a negative side, turning Christians against their supposed enemies. Although the crusades provide the most obvious example, Christians also turned on the Jews as the "murderers of Christ." As a result, Jews suffered increased persecution. These two documents show different sides of the picture. The first is a chronicler's account of the most absurd charge levied against the Jews—that they were guilty of the ritual murder of Christian children to obtain Christian blood for the passover service. This charge led to the murder of many Jews. The second document, taken from a list of regulations issued by the city of Avignon, France, illustrates the contempt Christian society held for the Jews.

The Jews and the Ritual Murder of Christian Children

[. . . The eight-year-old boy] Harold, who is buried in the Church of St. Peter the Apostle, at Gloucester . . . is said to have been carried away secretly by Jews, in the opinion of many, on Feb. 21, and by them hidden till March 16. On that night, on the sixth of the preceding feast, the Jews of all England coming together as if to circumcise a certain boy, pretend deceitfully that they are about to celebrate the feast [Passover] appointed by law in such case, and deceiving the citizens of Gloucester with that fraud, they tortured the lad placed before them with immense tortures. It is true no Christian was present, or saw or heard the deed, nor have we found that anything was betrayed by any Jew. But a little while after when the whole convent of monks of Gloucester and almost all the citizens of that city, and innumerable persons coming to the spectacle, saw the wounds of the dead body, scars of fire, the thorns fixed on his head, and liquid wax poured into the eyes and face, and touched it with the diligent examination of their hands, those tortures were believed or guessed to have been inflicted on him in that manner. It was clear that they had made him a glorious martyr to Christ, being slain without sin, and having bound his feet with his own girdle, threw him into the river Severn.

The Regulations of Avignon, 1243

Likewise, we declare that Jews or whores shall not dare to touch with their hands either bread or fruit put out for sale, and that if they should do this they must buy what they have touched.

---

group of nobles that dominated the political, economic, and social life of Europe. But quietly and surely, within this world of castles and private power, kings gradually began to extend their public power. Though they could not know it then, their actions laid the foundations for the European kingdoms that in one form or another have dominated the European political scene ever since.

European civilization began to flourish in the High Middle Ages. The revival of trade, the expansion of towns and cities, and the development of a money economy did not mean the end of a predominantly rural European society, but they did open the door to new ways to make a living and new opportunities for people to expand and enrich their lives. At the same time, the High Middle Ages also gave birth to an intellectual and spiritual revival that transformed European society. The intellectual revival led to new centers of learning in the cathedral schools and universities and to the use of reason to systematize the study of theology and develop whole new ways of thought. Spiritual renewal in the High Middle Ages led to numerous and even divergent paths: revived papal leadership, the crusading "holy warriors" who killed for God, a dramatic increase in the number and size of churches, and new dimensions to the religious life of the clergy and laity.

While a new civilization arose in Europe, the Byzantine Empire created its own unique civilization in the eastern Mediterranean. While Europe struggled in the Early Middle Ages, the Byzantine world continued to prosper and flourish. The crusades to Palestine, however, ostensibly for religious motives, eventually had the result of weakening the Christian power that had initiated the whole process: the Byzantine Empire.

Growth and optimism seemed to characterize the High Middle Ages, but underneath the calm exterior lay seeds of discontent and change. By the fourteenth century, as we shall see in the next chapter, Europe would begin to experience a real time of troubles.

CHAPTER NOTES

1. Norman F. Cantor, ed., *The Medieval World: 300–1300* (New York, 1963), pp. (in order of quotations) 104, 101, 108, 103.
2. Einhard, *The Life of Charlemagne*, trans. Samuel Turner (Ann Arbor, Mich., 1960), p. 30.
3. Quoted in Oliver Thatcher and Edgar McNeal, eds., *A Source Book for Medieval History* (New York, 1905), p. 363.
4. Quoted in Joseph and Frances Gies, *Life in a Medieval Castle* (New York, 1974), p. 175.
5. Quoted in Robert Delort, *Life in the Middle Ages*, trans. Robert Allen (New York, 1972), p. 218.
6. Quoted in Jean Gimpel, *The Medieval Machine* (Harmondsworth, 1977), p. 92.
7. Ernest F. Henderson, ed., *Select Historical Documents of the Middle Ages* (London, 1892), p. 365.
8. Thatcher and McNeal, *A Source Book for Medieval History*, p. 208.
9. Quoted in R. H. C. Davis, *A History of Medieval Europe from Constantine to Saint Louis*, 2d ed. (London and New York, 1988), p. 252.
10. Quoted in Rosalind and Christopher Brooke, *Popular Religion in the Middle Ages* (London, 1984), p. 19.
11. Helen Waddell, *The Wandering Scholars* (New York, 1961), p. 222.
12. Quoted in John W. Baldwin, *The Scholastic Culture of the Middle Ages, 1000–1300* (Lexington, Mass., 1971), p. 15.
13. Thatcher and McNeal, *A Source Book for Medieval History*, p. 517.
14. Quoted in Hans E. Mayer, *The Crusades*, trans. John Gillingham (New York, 1972), pp. 99–100.

SUGGESTED READINGS

Good general histories of the entire medieval period can be found in B. Tierney and S. Painter, *Western Europe in the Middle Ages, 1300–1475* (New York, 1983); E. Peters, *Europe and the Middle Ages*, 2d ed. (Englewood Cliffs, N.J., 1989); and G. Holmes, ed., *The Oxford Illustrated History of Medieval Europe* (Oxford, 1988). For a good general survey of the social history of the Middle Ages, see C. B. Bouchard, *Life and Society in the West: Antiquity and the Middle Ages* (San Diego, 1988). A brief history of the Early Middle Ages can be found in R. Collin, *Early Medieval Europe, 300–1000* (New York, 1991).

Surveys of Carolingian Europe include H. Fichtenau, *The Carolingian Empire* (Oxford, 1957) and R. McKitterick, *The Frankish Kingdoms under the Carolingians, 751–987* (London, 1983). On Charlemagne, see H. R. Loyn and J. Percival, *The Reign of Charlemagne* (New York, 1976).

Two important introductory works on feudalism are F. L. Ganshof, *Feudalism* (London, 1952) and the classic work by M. Bloch, *Feudal Society* (London, 1961).

Works on the function and activities of the nobility in the High Middle Ages include S. Reynolds, *Kingdoms and Communities in Western Europe, 900–1300* (Oxford, 1984); M. Keen, *Chivalry* (London, 1984); and G. Duby, *The Chivalrous Society* (Berkeley, Calif., 1977). G. Duby discusses the theory of medieval social order in *The Three Orders* (Chicago, 1980).

There are numerous works on the various feudal principalities. On England, see F. Barlow, *The Feudal Kingdom of England, 1042–1216*, 3d ed. (New York, 1972). On Germany, see H. Fuhrmann, *Germany in the High Middle Ages, c. 1050–1250* (Cambridge, 1986), an excellent account, and A. Haverkamp, *Medieval Germany* (Oxford, 1988). On France, see J. Dunbabib, *France in the Making, 843–1180* (Oxford, 1985). On Italy, see D. J. Herlihy, *Cities and Society in Medieval Italy* (London, 1980). On eastern Europe, see N. Davies, *God's Playground: A History of Poland*, vol. 1 (Oxford, 1981).

On economic conditions in the Middle Ages, see N. J. G. Pounds, *An Economic History of Medieval Europe* (New York, 1974) and R. S. Lopez, *The Commercial*

Revolution of the Middle Ages: 950–1350 (Englewood Cliffs, N.J., 1971); Urban history is covered in E. Ennen, *The Medieval Town* (Amsterdam, 1978). A good short introduction to medieval society is C. Brooke, *The Structure of Medieval Society* (London, 1971). On peasant life, see R. Fossier, *Peasant Life in the Medieval West* (New York, 1988).

For a general survey of church life, see R. W. Southern, *Western Society and the Church in the Middle Ages* (Baltimore, 1970). On the papacy in the High Middle Ages, see C. Morris, *The Papal Monarchy* (Oxford, 1989) and I. S. Robinson, *The Papacy* (Cambridge, 1990). Good works on monasticism include B. Bolton, *The Medieval Reformation* (London, 1983); C. H. Lawrence, *Medieval Monasticism* (London, 1984), a good general account; and H. Leyser, *Hermits and the New Monasticism* (London, 1984). The new monastic orders of the thirteenth century are examined in R. B. Brooke, *The Coming of the Friars* (New York, 1975). For a good introduction to popular religion in the eleventh and twelfth centuries, see R. and C. N. L. Brooke, *Popular Religion in the Middle Ages* (London, 1984). On the Inquisition, see B. Hamilton, *The Medieval Inquisition* (New York, 1981).

The development of universities is covered in S. Ferruolo, *The Origin of the University* (Stanford, 1985); and the brief, older work by C. H. Haskins, *The Rise of Universities* (Ithaca, N.Y., 1957). Various aspects of the intellectual and literary developments of the High Middle Ages are examined in J. W. Baldwin, *The Scholastic Culture of the Middle Ages, 1000–1300* (Lexington, Mass., 1971); J. Weisheipl, *Friar Thomas d'Aquino: His Life, His Thought and Work* (New York, 1974); and H. Waddell, *The Wandering Scholars* (New York, 1961). A good introduction to Romanesque style is G. Künstler, *Romanesque Art in Europe* (New York, 1973). On the Gothic movement, see G. Henderson, *Gothic* (Baltimore, 1967). A good book on the construction of Gothic cathedrals is J. Gimpel, *The Cathedral Builders* (New York, 1961).

Brief but good introductions to Byzantine history can be found in H. W. Haussig, *A History of Byzantine Civilization* (New York, 1971) and C. Mango, *Byzantium: The Empire of New Rome* (London, 1980). The best single political history is G. Ostrogorsky, *A History of the Byzantine State*, 2d ed. (New Brunswick, N.J., 1968). The zenith of Byzantine civilization is examined in R. Jenkins, *Byzantium: The Imperial Centuries, 610–1071* (New York, 1969).

The best general surveys on the crusades are H. E. Mayer, *The Crusades* (London, 1970) and J. Riley-Smith, *The Crusades: A Short History* (New Haven, Conn., 1987).

CHAPTER

13

Crisis and Rebirth: Europe in the Fourteenth and Fifteenth Centuries

The High Middle Ages in Europe had reached its pinnacle in the thirteenth century, but by 1300, the energy of medieval civilization seemed to be dissipating. At mid-century, one of the most destructive natural disasters in history erupted— the Black Death. One contemporary observer named Henry Knighton, a canon of Saint Mary-of-the-Meadow Abbey in Leicester, England, was simply overwhelmed by the magnitude of the catastrophe. Knighton began his account of the great plague with these words: "In this year [1348] and in the following one there was a general mortality of people throughout the whole world." Few were left untouched; even in isolated monasteries, the plague struck: "At Montpellier, there remained out of a hundred and forty friars only seven." Animals, too, were devastated: "During this same year, there was a great mortality of sheep everywhere in the kingdom; in one place and in one pasture, more than five thousand sheep died and became so putrefied that neither beast nor bird wanted to touch them." Knighton was also stunned by the economic and social consequences of the Black Death. Prices dropped: "And the price of everything was cheap, because of the fear of death; there were very few who took any care for their wealth, or for anything else." Laborers became scarce, and their wages increased: "In the following autumn, one could not hire a reaper at a lower wage than eight pence with food, or a mower at less than twelve pence with food. Because of this, much grain rotted in the fields for lack of harvesting." So many people died that some towns were deserted

Hundred Years' War   Turks capture Constantinople

Black Death devastates Europe   Medici rule in Florence

Popes at Avignon   Great Schism   Johannes Gutenberg's printing press

Peasant revolts

Dante, *The Divine Comedy*   Masaccio's frescoes   Machiavelli's *The Prince*

High Renaissance (Leonardo, Raphael, Michelangelo)

and some villages disappeared altogether: "Many small villages and hamlets were completely deserted; there was not one house left in them, but all those who had lived in them were dead." To some people, the end of the world seemed at hand.

Plague was not the only disaster in the fourteenth century, however. Signs of disintegration were everywhere: famine, economic depression, war, social upheaval, a rise in crime and violence, and a decline in the power of the universal Catholic church. Periods of disintegration, however, are often fertile grounds for change and new developments. Out of the dissolution of medieval civilization came a rebirth of culture that many historians have labeled the Renaissance. Although the disintegrative patterns of the fourteenth century continued into the fifteenth, at the same time elements of recovery made the fifteenth century a period of significant political, economic, artistic, and intellectual change. The humanists or intellectuals of the age called their period (from the mid-fourteenth to the mid-sixteenth century) an age of rebirth, believing that they had restored arts and letters to new glory

after they had been "neglected" or "dead" for centuries. The humanists' view of their age as a rebirth of the classical civilization of the Greeks and Romans ultimately led historians to use the word Renaissance to identify this period. Although recent historians have emphasized the many elements of continuity between the Middle Ages and the Renaissance, the latter age was also distinguished by its own unique characteristics.

✣ Time of Troubles: Black Death and Social Crisis

Well into the thirteenth century, Europe had experienced good harvests and an expanding population. By the end of the thirteenth century, however, a period of disastrous changes had begun.

Famine and the Black Death

By the end of the thirteenth and beginning of the fourteenth centuries, Europe entered a period that has been called a "little ice age." A small shift in overall temperature patterns resulted in shortened growing seasons and disastrous weather conditions, including heavy storms and constant rain. Between 1315 and 1317, northern Europe experienced heavy rains that destroyed harvests and caused serious food shortages, resulting in extreme hunger and starvation. The great famine of 1315–1317 in northern Europe became an all-too-familiar pattern.

Southern Europe, for example, seems to have been struck by similar conditions, especially in the 1330s and 1340s. Hunger became widespread, and the scene described by this chronicler became common:

> We saw a larger number of both sexes, not only from nearby places but from as much as five leagues away, barefooted and maybe even, except for women, in a completely nude state, together with their priests coming in procession at the Church of the Holy Martyrs, their bones bulging out, devoutly carrying bodies of saints and other relics to be adorned hoping to get relief.[1]

Some historians have pointed out that famine could have led to chronic malnutrition, which in turn contributed to increased infant mortality, lower birthrates, and higher susceptibility to disease because malnourished people are less able to resist infection. This, they argue, helps to explain the virulence of the great plague known as the Black Death.

The Black Death of the mid-fourteenth century was the most devastating natural disaster in European history, ravaging Europe's population and causing economic, social, political, and cultural upheaval. A chronicler wrote that "father abandoned child, wife husband, one brother another, for the plague seemed to strike through breath and sight. And so they died. And no one could be found to bury the dead, for money or friendship."[2] People were horrified by an evil force they could not understand and by the subsequent breakdown of all normal human relations.

The Black Death was all the more horrible because it was the first major epidemic disease to strike Europe since

✚ Map 13.1 Spread of the Black Death.

the seventh century, an absence that helps explain medieval Europe's remarkable population growth. This great plague originated in Central Asia. It was spread, it is believed, both by the Mongols as they expanded across Asia and by ecological changes that caused Central Asian rodents to move westward.

Bubonic plague, which was the most common and most important form of plague in the diffusion of the Black Death, was spread by black rats infested with fleas who were host to the deadly bacterium *Yersinia pestis*. Symptoms of bubonic plague include high fever, aching joints, swelling of the lymph nodes, and dark blotches caused by bleeding beneath the skin. Bubonic plague was actually the least toxic form of plague, but nevertheless killed 50 to 60 percent of its victims. In pneumonic plague, the bacterial infection spread to the lungs, resulting in severe coughing, bloody sputum, and the relatively easy spread of the bacillus from human to human by coughing. Fortunately, since it was more deadly, this form of the plague occurred less frequently than bubonic plague.

The plague reached Europe in October of 1347 when Genoese merchants brought it from the Middle East to the island of Sicily off the coast of southern Italy. It quickly spread to southern Italy and southern France by the end of 1347. Usually, the diffusion of the Black Death followed commercial trade routes. In 1348, the plague spread through Spain, France, and the Low Countries and into Germany. By the end of that year, it had moved to England, ravaging it in 1349. By the end of 1349, the plague had reached northern Europe and Scandinavia. Eastern Europe and Russia were affected by 1351, although mortality rates were never as high in eastern Europe as they were in western and central Europe.

Overall, mortality figures for the Black Death were incredibly high. Italy was especially hard hit. Its crowded cities suffered losses of 50 to 60 percent. In northern France, farming villages suffered mortality rates of 30 percent, while cities such as Rouen were more severely affected and experienced losses of 30 to 40 percent. In England and Germany, entire villages simply disappeared from history. In Germany, of approximately 170,000 inhabited locations, only 130,000 were left by the end of the fourteenth century.

It has been estimated that the European population declined by 25 to 50 percent between 1347 and 1351. If we accept the recent scholarly assessment of a European population of 75 million in the early fourteenth century, this means a death toll in four years of 19 to 38 million people. And the plague did not end in 1351. There were major outbreaks again in 1361–1362 and 1369 and then regular recurrences during the remainder of the fourteenth century and all of the fifteenth century. The European population did not start to recover until the end of the fifteenth century; not until the mid-sixteenth century did Europe begin to regain its thirteenth-century population levels. Even then, recurrences of the plague did not end until the beginning of the eighteenth century when a new species of brown rat began to replace the black rat.

The attempt of contemporaries to explain the Black Death and mitigate its harshness led to extreme sorts of behavior. To many, the plague had either been sent by God as a punishment for humans' sins or caused by the evil one, the devil. Some—the flagellants—resorted to extreme asceticism to gain God's forgiveness and emerged as a popular movement in 1348, especially in Germany. Groups of flagellants, both men and women,

◆ Mass Burial of Plague Victims. The Black Death had spread to northern Europe by the end of 1348. Shown here is a mass burial of victims of the plague in Tournai, located in modern Belgium. As is evident in the illustration, at this stage of the plague, there was still time to make coffins for the victims' burial. Later, as the plague intensified, the dead were thrown into open pits.

❧ A Medieval Holocaust: The Cremation of the Strasbourg Jews ❧

In their attempt to explain the widespread horrors of the Black Death, medieval Christian communities looked for scapegoats. As at the time of the Crusades, the Jews were accused of poisoning wells and hence spreading the plague. This selection by a contemporary chronicler, written in 1349, gives an account of how Christians in the town of Strasbourg in the Holy Roman Empire dealt with their Jewish community. It is apparent that financial gain was also an important factor in killing the Jews.

Jacob von Königshofen, "The Cremation of the Strasbourg Jews"

In the year 1349 there occurred the greatest epidemic that ever happened. Death went from one end of the earth to the other.... And from what this epidemic came, all wise teachers and physicians could only say that it was God's will.... This epidemic also came to Strasbourg in the summer of the above-mentioned year, and it is estimated that about sixteen thousand people died.

In the matter of this plague the Jews throughout the world were reviled and accused in all lands of having caused it through the poison which they are said to have put into the water and the wells—that is what they were accused of—and for this reason the Jews were burnt all the way from the Mediterranean into Germany....

[The account then goes on to discuss the situation of the Jews in the city of Strasbourg.]

On Saturday ... they burnt the Jews on a wooden platform in their cemetery. There were about two thousand people of them. Those who wanted to baptize themselves were spared. [Some say that about a thousand accepted baptism.] Many small children were taken out of the fire and baptized against the will of their fathers and mothers. And everything that was owed to the Jews was canceled, and the Jews had to surrender all pledges and notes that they had taken for debts. The council, however, took the cash that the Jews possessed and divided it among the working-men proportionately. The money was indeed the thing that killed the Jews. If they had been poor and if the feudal lords had not been in debt to them, they would not have been burnt....

Thus were the Jews burnt at Strasbourg, and in the same year in all the cities of the Rhine, whether Free Cities or Imperial Cities or cities belonging to the lords. In some towns they burnt the Jews after a trial, in others, without a trial. In some cities the Jews themselves set fire to their houses and cremated themselves.

It was decided in Strasbourg that no Jew should enter the city for a hundred years, but before twenty years had passed, the council and magistrates agreed that they ought to admit the Jews again into the city for twenty years. And so the Jews came back again to Strasbourg in the year 1368 after the birth of our Lord.

wandered from town to town, flogging each other with whips to win the forgiveness of a God who they felt had sent the plague to punish humans for their sinful ways. One contemporary chronicler described their activities:

> The penitents went about, coming first out of Germany. They were men who did public penance and scourged themselves with whips of hard knotted leather with little iron spikes. Some made themselves bleed very badly between the shoulder blades and some foolish women had cloths ready to catch the blood and smear it on their eyes, saying it was miraculous blood. While they were doing penance, they sang very mournful songs about the nativity and the passion of Our Lord. The object of this penance was to put a stop to the mortality, for in that time ... at least a third of all the people in the world died.[3]

The flagellants attracted attention and created mass hysteria wherever they went. The Catholic church, however, became alarmed when flagellant groups began to kill Jews and attack the clergy who opposed them. Pope Clement VI condemned the flagellants in October 1349 and urged the public authorities to crush them. By the end of 1350, most of the flagellant movements had been destroyed.

An outbreak of virulent anti-Semitism also accompanied the Black Death. Jews were accused of causing the plague by poisoning town wells. Although Jews were persecuted in Spain, the worst pogroms against this minority were carried out in Germany, where more than sixty major Jewish communities were exterminated by 1351 (see the box above). Many Jews fled eastward to Russia and especially to Poland where the king offered them protection. Eastern Europe became home to large Jewish communities.

Economic Dislocation and Social Upheaval

The population collapse of the fourteenth century had dire economic and social consequences, as economic dislocation was accompanied by social upheaval. Both peasants and noble landlords were affected by the demographic crisis of the fourteenth century. Most noticeably, Europe experienced a serious labor shortage that caused a dramatic rise in the price of labor. At the same time, the decline in population depressed the demand for agricultural produce, resulting in falling prices for output. Because landlords were having to pay more for labor at the same time that their rents or income was declining, they began to experience considerable adversity and lower standards of living.

Landed aristocrats responded to adversity by seeking to lower the wage rate. The English Parliament passed the Statute of Laborers (1351), which attempted to limit wages to preplague levels and forbid the mobility of peasants as well. Although such laws proved largely unworkable, they did keep wages from rising as high as they might have in a free market. Overall, the position of noble landlords continued to deteriorate during the late fourteenth and early fifteenth centuries. At the same time, the position of peasants improved, though not uniformly throughout Europe.

The decline in the number of peasants after the Black Death accelerated the process of converting labor services to rents, freeing peasants from the obligations of servile tenure. But there were limits to how much the peasants could advance. They faced the same economic hurdles as the lords while the latter also attempted to impose wage restrictions and reinstate old forms of labor service. New governmental taxes also hurt. Peasant complaints became widespread and soon gave rise to rural revolts.

In 1358, a peasant revolt, known as the *Jacquerie*, broke out in northern France. The destruction of normal order by the Black Death and the subsequent economic dislocation were important contributors to the revolt, but the French peasantry were also affected by the ravages created by the Hundred Years' War (see The Hundred Years' War later in this chapter). Both the French and the English forces followed a deliberate policy of laying waste to peasants' lands while bands of mercenaries lived off the land by taking peasants' produce as well. Thus, the *Jacquerie* was a revolt of desperation; it was linked to the political ambitions of townspeople in Paris who were also upset with the conduct of the war and wished to limit monarchical power.

The outburst of peasant anger led to savage confrontations. Castles were burned and nobles murdered (see the box on p. 452). Such atrocities did not go unanswered, however. The *Jacquerie* soon failed as the privileged classes closed ranks, savagely massacred the rebels, and ended the revolt.

The English Peasants' Revolt of 1381 was the most prominent of all. It was not a revolt caused by desperation but was a product of rising expectations. After the Black Death, the English peasants had enjoyed improved conditions with greater freedom and higher wages or lower rents. Aristocratic landlords had fought back with legislation to depress wages and an attempt to reimpose old feudal dues. The most immediate cause of the revolt, however, was the monarchy's attempt to raise revenues by imposing a poll tax or a flat charge on each adult member of the population. Peasants in eastern England, the wealthiest part of the country, refused to pay the tax and expelled the collectors forcibly from their villages.

This action produced a widespread rebellion of both peasants and townspeople led by a well-to-do peasant called Wat Tyler and a preacher named John Ball. The revolt was initially successful as the rebels burned down

◆ **Peasant Rebellion.** The fourteenth century witnessed a number of revolts of the peasantry against noble landowners. Although the revolts were initially successful, they were soon crushed. This illustration shows nobles massacring the rebels in the French *Jacquerie*.

❧ A Revolt of French Peasants ❧

In 1358, French peasants rose up in a revolt known as the Jacquerie. The relationship between aristocrats and peasants had degenerated as a result of the social upheavals and privations caused by the Black Death and the Hundred Years' War. This excerpt from the chronicle of an aristocrat paints a horrifying picture of the barbarities that occurred during the revolt.

Jean Froissart, Chronicles

Not long after the King of Navarre had been set free, there were very strange and terrible happenings in several parts of the kingdom of France. . . . They began when some of the men from the country towns came together in the Beauvais region. They had no leaders and at first they numbered scarcely a hundred. One of them got up and said that the nobility of France, knights and squires, were disgracing and betraying the realm, and that it would be a good thing if they were all destroyed. At this they all shouted: "He's right! He's right! Shame on any man who saves the gentry from being wiped out!"

They banded together and went off, without further deliberation and unarmed except for pikes and knives, to the house of a knight who lived near by. They broke in and killed the knight, with his lady and his children, big and small, and set fire to the house. Next they went to another castle and did much worse; for, having seized the knight and bound him securely to a post, several of them violated his wife and daughter before his

eyes. Then they killed the wife, who was pregnant, and the daughter and all the other children, and finally put the knight to death with great cruelty and burned and razed the castle.

They did similar things in a number of castles and big houses, and their ranks swelled until there were a good six thousand of them. Wherever they went their numbers grew, for all the men of the same sort joined them. The knights and squires fled before them with their families. They took their wives and daughters many miles away to put them in safety, leaving their houses open with their possessions inside. And those evil men, who had come together without leaders or arms, pillaged and burned everything and violated and killed all the ladies and girls without mercy, like mad dogs. Their barbarous acts were worse than anything that ever took place between Christians and Saracens. Never did men commit such vile deeds. They were such that no living creature ought to see, or even imagine or think of, and the men who committed the most were admired and had the highest places among them. I could never bring myself to write down the horrible and shameful things which they did to the ladies. But, among other brutal excesses, they killed a knight, put him on a spit, and turned him at the fire and roasted him before the lady and her children. After about a dozen of them had violated the lady, they tried to force her and the children to eat the knight's flesh before putting them cruelly to death.

---

the manor houses of aristocrats, lawyers, and government officials and murdered several important officials, including the archbishop of Canterbury. After the peasants marched on London, the young king Richard II (1377–1399) promised to accept the rebels' demands if they would return to their homes. They accepted the king's word and began to disperse, but the king reneged and with the assistance of the aristocrats brutally crushed the rebels. The poll tax was eliminated, however.

Revolts also erupted in the cities where commercial and industrial activity suffered almost immediately from the Black Death. Bourgeois merchants and manufacturers responded to the decline in trade and production by attempting to restrict competition and resisting the demands of the lower classes. As capitalist industrialists

paid low wages and prevented workers from forming organizations to help themselves, industrial revolts broke out in urban areas throughout Europe. Ghent experienced one in 1381, Rouen in 1382. Most famous was the revolt of the *ciompi* in Florence in 1378. The *ciompi* were woolworkers in Florence's most prominent industry. In the 1370s, the woolen industry was depressed, and woolworkers saw their real wages decline as a result of the debasement of the coinage in which they were paid. Their revolt won them some concessions from the municipal government, including the right to form guilds and be represented in the government. But their newly won rights were short-lived. A counterrevolution by government authorities brought an end to *ciompi* participation in the government by 1382.

Although the peasant and urban revolts sometimes resulted in short-term gains for the participants, the uprisings were relatively easily crushed and their gains quickly lost. Geographically dispersed, rural and urban rebels were not united and had no long-range goals. Immediate gains were uppermost in their minds. Accustomed to ruling, the established classes easily combined and crushed dissent when faced with social uprising. Nevertheless, the revolts of the fourteenth century had introduced a new element to European life; henceforth social unrest would be a characteristic of European history.

FAMILY LIFE AND GENDER ROLES IN LATE MEDIEVAL CITIES

The effects of plague were also felt in other areas of medieval urban life. The basic unit of the late medieval urban environment was the nuclear family of husband, wife, and children. Especially in wealthier families, there might also be servants, apprentices, and other relatives, including widowed mothers and the husband's illegitimate children.

Before the Black Death, late marriages were common for urban couples. It was not unusual for husbands to be in their late thirties or forties and wives in their early twenties. The expense of setting up a household probably necessitated the delay in marriage. But the situation changed dramatically after the plague, as the survivors found new economic opportunities and were reluctant to postpone living after experiencing so much death. The economic difficulties of the fourteenth century also tended to strengthen the development of gender roles and to set new limits on employment opportunities for women. Based on the authority of Aristotle, Thomas Aquinas and other thirteenth-century scholastic theologians had advanced the belief that according to the natural order, men were active and domineering while women were passive and submissive. As more and more lawyers, doctors, and priests, who had been trained in universities where these notions were taught, entered society, these ideas of the different natures of men and women became widely acceptable. Increasingly, women were expected to forgo any active functions in society and remain subject to direction from males. A fourteenth-century Parisian provost commented on glass cutters that "no master's widow who keeps working at his craft after her husband's death may take on apprentices, for the men of the craft do not believe that a woman can master it well enough to teach a child to master it, for the craft is a very delicate one."[4] Although this statement suggests that some women were in fact running businesses, it also reveals that they were viewed as incapable of undertaking all of men's activities. Based on this view of gender, Europeans created a division of labor roles between men and women that persisted until the Industrial Revolution of the eighteenth and nineteenth centuries.

Economic Recovery

After the severe economic reversals and social upheavals of the second half of the fourteenth century, the European economy gradually recovered during the fifteenth century as manufacturing and trade increased in volume. Economic growth varied from area to area, however, and despite the improvement Europe did not experience the economic boom of the High Middle Ages.

Before the plague, Italian merchants were already carrying on a flourishing commerce throughout the Mediterranean and had also expanded their lines of trade north along the Atlantic seaboard. The great galleys of the Venetian Flanders Fleet maintained a direct sea route from Venice to England and the Netherlands, where Italian merchants came into contact with the increasingly powerful Hanseatic League of merchants. Hard hit by the plague, the Italians lost their commercial preeminence in the second half of the fourteenth century while the Hanseatic League continued to prosper.

As early as the thirteenth century, a number of north German coastal towns had formed a commercial and military league known as the Hansa or Hanseatic League to protect themselves from marauding pirates and competition from Scandinavian merchants. By 1500, more than eighty cities belonged to the league, which established settlements and commercial bases in northern Europe and England. For almost two hundred years, the Hansa had a monopoly on northern European trade in timber, fish, grain, metals, honey, and wines. Its southern outlet in Flanders, the city of Bruges, became the economic crossroads of Europe in the fourteenth century because it served as the meeting place between Hanseatic merchants and the Flanders Fleet of Venice. In the fifteenth century, however, Bruges slowly began to decline, paralleling the decline of the Hanseatic League itself as it proved increasingly unable to compete with the developing larger territorial states.

Overall, trade recovered dramatically from the economic contraction of the fourteenth century. The Italians and especially the Venetians continued to maintain a wealthy commercial empire. Not until the sixteenth century, when the overseas discoveries gave new importance to the states facing the Atlantic, did the small Italian city-states begin to suffer from the competitive

Harbor Scene at Hamburg. This illustration from a fifteenth-century treatise on the laws of Hamburg shows a busy port with ships of all sizes. At the left, a crane is used to unload barrels. In the building at the right, customs officials collect their dues. Merchants and townspeople are shown talking at dockside.

advantages of the ever-growing and more powerful national territorial states.

The economic depression of the fourteenth century also affected patterns of manufacturing. The woolen industries of Flanders and the northern Italian cities had been particularly devastated. By the beginning of the fifteenth century, however, the Florentine woolen industry was experiencing a recovery. At the same time, the Italian cities began to develop and expand luxury industries, especially lace and silk, glassware, and handworked items in metal and precious stones. Unfortunately, these luxury industries employed fewer people than the woolen industry and contributed less to overall prosperity. Indeed, the concentration of wealth in the hands of fewer people seems to characterize the prosperity of the fifteenth century.

Other new industries, especially printing, mining, and metallurgy, began to rival the textile industry in importance in the fifteenth century. New machinery and techniques for digging deeper mines and for separating metals from ore and purifying them were put into operation. When rulers began to transfer their titles to underground mineral rights to financiers as collateral for loans, these entrepreneurs quickly developed large mining operations to produce copper, iron, and silver. Especially valuable were the rich mineral deposits in central Europe, Hungary, the Tyrol, Bohemia, and Saxony. Expanding iron production and new skills in metalworking, in turn, contributed to the development of firearms that were more effective than the crude weapons used in the fourteenth century.

The city of Florence regained its preeminence in banking in the fifteenth century, primarily due to the Medici family. In its best days (in the fifteenth century), the House of Medici was the greatest banking house in Europe with branches in Venice, Milan, Rome, Avignon, Bruges, London, and Lyons. Moreover, the family had controlling interests in industrial enterprises for wool, silk, and the mining of alum, which was used in dyeing textiles. The Medici were also the principal bankers for the papacy, a position that produced big profits and influence at the papal court. Despite its great success in the early and middle part of the fifteenth century, the Medici bank declined suddenly at the end of the century due to poor management and a series of bad loans, especially uncollectible loans to rulers. In 1494, when the French expelled the Medici from Florence and confiscated their property, the Medicean financial edifice collapsed.

Political Instability and Political Renewal

Famine, plague, economic turmoil, social upheaval, and violence were not the only problems of the fourteenth century. War and political instability must also be added to the list. Of all the struggles that ensued in the fourteenth century, the Hundred Years' War was the most violent.

The Hundred Years' War

In 1259, the English king, Henry III, had relinquished his claims to all the French territories previously held by the English monarchy in France except for one relatively small possession known as the duchy of Gascony. As duke of Gascony, the English king pledged loyalty as a vassal to the French king. But this territory gave rise to numerous disputes between the kings of England and France. By the end of the thirteenth century, the Capetian monarchs had greatly increased their power over their most important vassals, the great lords of France. Royal officials interfered regularly in the affairs of their vassals' fiefs, and although this policy irritated all the vassals, it especially annoyed the king of England who considered himself the peer of the French king. When King Philip VI of France (1328–1350) seized Gascony in 1337, the duke of Gascony—King Edward III of England (1327–1377)—declared war on Philip. The attack on Gascony was a convenient excuse; Edward III had already laid claim to the throne of France after the senior branch of the Capetian dynasty had become extinct in 1328.

The Hundred Years' War began in a burst of knightly enthusiasm. Trained to be warriors, knights viewed the clash of battle as the ultimate opportunity to demonstrate their chivalric qualities. The Hundred Years' War proved to be an important watershed, however, because peasant foot soldiers, not knights, decided the chief battles of the war. The French army of 1337 with its heavily armed noble cavalry resembled its twelfth- and thirteenth-century forebears. Considering themselves a fighting elite, the noble cavalry looked with contempt upon the foot soldiers and crossbowmen whom they regarded as social inferiors. The English army, however, had evolved differently and made use of paid foot soldiers. Armed with pikes, many of these foot soldiers had also adopted the longbow, invented by the Welsh. The longbow had greater striking power, longer range, and more rapid speed of fire than the crossbow. Although the English also used heavily armed cavalry, they relied even more on their large numbers of foot soldiers.

Edward III's early campaigns in France were indecisive and achieved little. In 1346, Edward was forced to fight at Crécy, just south of Flanders. The larger French army followed no battle plan but simply attacked the English lines in a disorderly fashion. The arrows of the English archers decimated the French cavalry. As the chronicler Froissart described it, "[with their longbows] the English continued to shoot into the thickest part of the crowd, wasting none of their arrows. They impaled or wounded horses and riders, who fell to the ground in great distress, unable to get up again without the help of several men."[5] It was a stunning victory for the English.

The Battle of Crécy was not decisive, however. The English simply did not possess the resources to subjugate all France, and hostilities continued intermittently for another fifty years until a twenty-year truce was negotiated in 1396, seemingly bringing an end to this pro-

tracted series of struggles. In 1415, however, the English king, Henry V (1413–1422), renewed the war. At the Battle of Agincourt (1415), the heavily armored French knights attempted to attack across a field turned to mud by heavy rain; the result was a disastrous French defeat and the death of 1,500 French nobles. Henry went on to forge an alliance with the duke of Burgundy, making the English masters of northern France.

The seemingly hopeless French cause fell into the hands of the dauphin Charles, the heir to the throne, who governed the southern two-thirds of France. Charles's cause seemed doomed until a French peasant woman quite unexpectedly saved the timid prince. Born in 1412, the daughter of well-to-do peasants, Joan of Arc was a deeply religious person who experienced visions and came to believe that her favorite saints had commanded her to free France. In February 1429, Joan made her way to the dauphin's court, where her sincerity and simplicity persuaded Charles to allow her to accompany a French army to Orléans. Apparently inspired by the faith of the peasant woman who called herself "the Maid," the French armies found new confidence in themselves and liberated Orléans. Within a few weeks, the entire Loire valley had been freed of the English. Joan had brought the war to a decisive turning point.

But she did not live to see the war concluded. Captured by the Burgundian allies of the English in 1430, Joan was turned over first to the English and then to the Inquisition to face charges of witchcraft (see the box on p. 457). In the fifteenth century, spiritual visions were thought to be inspired either by God or the devil. Joan was condemned to death as a heretic and burned at the stake in 1431. To the end, as the flames rose up around her, she declared "that her voices came from God and had not deceived her." Twenty-five years later, a new ecclesiastical court exonerated her of these charges, and

CHRONOLOGY

The Hundred Years' War

Outbreak of hostilities	1337
Battle of Crécy	1346
Henry V renews the war	1415
Battle of Agincourt	1415
French recovery under Joan of Arc	1429–1431
End of the war	1453

✦ **Joan of Arc.** Pictured here in a suit of armor, Joan of Arc is holding aloft a banner that shows Christ and two angels. This miniature portrait is believed to be a good likeness of Joan.

five centuries later, in 1920, she was made a saint of the Roman Catholic church. Joan of Arc's accomplishments proved decisive. Although the war dragged on for another two decades, defeats of English armies in Normandy and Aquitaine led to French victory by 1453.

Political Instability

The fourteenth century was a period of adversity for the internal political stability of European governments. Although government bureaucracies grew even larger, at the same time the question of who should control the bureaucracies led to internal conflict and instability. This instability was part of a general breakdown of customary feudal institutions. Traditional feudal loyalties were disintegrating rapidly and had not yet been replaced by the national loyalties of the future. Like the lord and serf relationship, the lord and vassal relationship based on land and military service was being replaced by a contract

based on money. Especially after the Black Death, money payments were increasingly substituted for military service. Monarchs welcomed this development since they could now hire professional soldiers who tended to be more reliable anyway. As lord and vassal relationships became less personal and less important, new relationships based on political advantage began to be formed, opening up new avenues for political influence—and for corruption as well. Especially noticeable, as the landed aristocrats suffered declining rents and social uncertainties with the new relationships, was the formation of factions of nobles who looked for opportunities to advance their power and wealth at the expense of other noble factions and of their monarchs. At the same time, two other developments, related to the rise of factions, added to the instability of governments in the fourteenth century.

First, dynasties in the fourteenth century seemed unable to produce male heirs. By the mid-fifteenth century, reigning monarchs in many European countries were not the direct male descendants of those ruling in 1300. The founders of these new dynasties had to struggle for their positions as factions of nobles vied to gain material advantages for themselves. At the end of the fourteenth century and beginning of the fifteenth, there were two claimants to the throne of France, and two aristocratic factions fought for control of England; in Germany, three princes struggled to be recognized as emperor.

Fourteenth-century monarchs, whether of old or new dynasties, found themselves with financial problems as well. The shift to using mercenary soldiers left monarchs perennially short on cash. Traditional revenues, especially rents from property, increasingly proved insufficient to meet their needs. Monarchs attempted to generate new sources of revenues, especially through taxes, which often meant going through parliaments. This opened the door for parliamentary bodies to gain more power by asking for favors first. Although unsuccessful in most cases, the role of parliaments simply added another element of uncertainty and confusion to fourteenth-century politics.

Political Recovery: The "New Monarchies"

In the first half of the fifteenth century, European states continued the disintegrative patterns of the previous century. In the second half of the fifteenth century, however, recovery set in, and attempts were made to reestablish the centralized power of monarchical governments. To characterize the results, some historians have spoken of the "new monarchies" of the end of the fifteenth century, especially those of France, England, and Spain. Al-

❧ The Trial of Joan of Arc ❧

Feared by the English and Burgundians, Joan of Arc was put on trial on charges of witchcraft and heresy after her capture. She was condemned for heresy and burned at the stake on May 30, 1431. This excerpt is taken from the records of Joan's trial, which presented a dramatic confrontation between the judges, trained in the complexities of legal questioning, and a nineteen-year-old woman who relied only on the "voices" of saints who gave her advice. In this selection, Joan describes what these voices told her to do.

The Trial of Joan of Arc

Afterward, she declared that at the age of thirteen she had a voice from God to help her and guide her. And the first time she was much afraid. And this voice came towards noon, in summer, in her father's garden. . . . She heard the voice on her right, in the direction of the church; and she seldom heard it without a light. This light came from the same side as the voice, and generally there was a great light. . . .

Asked what instruction this voice gave her for the salvation of her soul: she said it taught her to be good and to go to church often. . . . She said that the voice told her to come, and she could no longer stay where she was; and the voice told her again that she should raise the siege of the city of Orléans. She said moreover that the voice told her that she, Joan, should go to Robert de Baudricourt, in the town of Vaucouleurs of which he was captain, and he would provide an escort for her. And the said Joan answered that she was a poor maid, knowing nothing of riding or fighting. She said she went to an uncle of hers, and told him she wanted to stay with him for some time; and she stayed there about eight days. And she told her uncle she must go to the said town of Vaucouleurs, and so her uncle took her.

Then she said that when she reached Vaucouleurs she easily recognized Robert de Baudricourt, although she had never seen him before; and she knew him through her voice, for the voice had told her it was he. . . . The said Robert twice refused to hear her and repulsed her; the third time he listened to her and gave her an escort. And the voice had told her that it would be so.

---

though appropriate, the term *new monarch* can also be misleading. These monarchs were new in their concentration of royal authority, their attempts to suppress the nobility, their efforts to control the church in their lands, and their insistence upon having the loyalty of people living within definite territorial boundaries. The new monarchs were often crafty men obsessed with the acquisition and expansion of political power. Of course, none of these characteristics was entirely new since a number of medieval monarchs, especially in the thirteenth century, had also exhibited them. Nevertheless, the fifteenth century does mark a further extension of royal centralized authority, although the degree to which monarchs were successful in extending their political authority varied from area to area. Unlike western Europe, in central and eastern Europe, decentralization rather than centralization of political authority remained the rule.

WESTERN EUROPE

The Hundred Years' War left France prostrate. Depopulation, desolate farmlands, ruined commerce, and independent and unruly nobles made it difficult for the kings to assert their authority. But the war had also developed a strong degree of French national feeling toward a common enemy that the kings could use to reestablish monarchical power. The process of developing a French territorial state was greatly advanced by King Louis XI (1461–1483), known as the Spider because of his wily and devious ways. Louis strengthened the use of the *taille*—an annual direct tax usually on land or property—as a permanent tax imposed by royal authority, giving him a sound, regular source of income. Louis was not completely successful in repressing the French nobility whose independence posed a threat to his own state building. A major problem was his supposed vassal, Charles the Bold, duke of Burgundy (1467–1477), who tried to create a middle kingdom between France and Germany, stretching from the Low Countries in the north to Switzerland. Louis opposed this scheme, and when Charles was killed in 1477 fighting the Swiss, Louis added part of Charles's possessions, the duchy of Burgundy, to his own lands. Three years later, the provinces of Anjou, Maine, Bar, and Provence were brought under royal control. Many historians believe that Louis created a base for the later development of a strong French monarchy.

The Hundred Years' War had also strongly affected the other protagonist in that conflict—the English. The cost of the war in its final years and the losses in manpower strained the English economy. Moreover, with the end of the war, England experienced even greater domestic turmoil as a civil war erupted and aristocratic factions fought over the monarchy until 1485, when Henry Tudor established a new dynasty.

As the first Tudor king, Henry VII (1485–1509) worked to reduce internal dissension and establish a strong monarchical government. Henry eliminated the private wars of the nobility by abolishing their private armies. The new king was particularly successful in obtaining sufficient income from the traditional financial resources of the English monarch, such as crown lands, judicial fees and fines, and customs duties. By using diplomacy to avoid wars, which are always expensive, the king

avoided having to call Parliament on any regular basis to grant him funds. By not overburdening the landed gentry and middle class with taxes, Henry won their favor, and they provided much support for his monarchy. Henry's policies enabled him to leave England with a stable and prosperous government and an enhanced status for the monarchy itself.

Spain, too, experienced the growth of a strong national monarchy by the end of the fifteenth century, a development that might have seemed unlikely at the beginning of the century. During the Middle Ages, several independent Christian kingdoms had emerged in the course of the long reconquest of the Iberian peninsula from the Muslims. Aragon and Castile were the strongest Spanish kingdoms; in the west was the independent monarchy of Portugal; in the north the small kingdom of Navarre; and in the south the Muslim kingdom of

✶ Map 13.2 Europe in the Fifteenth Century.

Granada. Few people at the beginning of the fifteenth century could have predicted the national unification of Spain.

A major step in that direction was taken with the marriage of Isabella of Castile (1474–1504) and Ferdinand of Aragon (1479–1516) in 1469. This marriage was a dynastic union of two rulers, not a political union. Both kingdoms maintained their own parliaments (Cortes), courts, laws, coinage, speech, customs, and political organs. Nevertheless, the two rulers worked to strengthen royal control of government, especially in Castile. The royal council, which was supposed to supervise local administration and oversee the implementation of government policies, was stripped of aristocrats and filled primarily with middle-class lawyers. Trained in the principles of Roman law, these officials operated on the belief that the monarchy embodied the power of the state.

The towns were also enlisted in the policy of state building. Medieval town organizations known as *hermandades* ("brotherhoods"), which had been organized to maintain law and order, were revived. Ferdinand and Isabella transformed them into a kind of national militia whose primary goal was to stop the wealthy landed aristocrats from disturbing the peace. The *hermandades* were disbanded by 1498 when the royal administration became strong enough to deal with lawlessness.

Ferdinand and Isabella reorganized the military forces of Spain, seeking to replace the undisciplined feudal levies they had inherited with a more professional royal army. The development of a strong infantry force as the heart of the new Spanish army made it the best in Europe by the sixteenth century, and Spain emerged as an important power in European affairs.

Recognizing the importance of controlling the Catholic church with its vast power and wealth, Ferdinand and Isabella secured from the pope the right to select the most important church officials in Spain, virtually making the clergy an instrument for the extension of royal power. Ferdinand and Isabella also pursued a policy of strict religious uniformity. Spain possessed two large religious minorities, the Jews and Muslims, both of whom had generally been tolerated in medieval Spain. Increased persecution in the fourteenth century, however, led the majority of Spanish Jews to convert to Christianity. But complaints that these Jewish converts were not always faithful to Christianity prompted Ferdinand and Isabella to ask the pope to introduce the Inquisition into Spain in 1478. Under royal control, the Inquisition worked with cruel efficiency to guarantee the orthodoxy of the converts, but had no authority over practicing

Jews. Consequently, in 1492, flush with the success of the conquest of Muslim Granada, Ferdinand and Isabella took the drastic step of expelling all professed Jews from Spain. It is estimated that 150,000 out of possibly 200,000 Jews fled. Muslims, too, were then "encouraged" to convert to Christianity, and in 1502, Isabella issued a decree expelling all professed Muslims from her kingdom. To a very large degree, the "Most Catholic" monarchs had achieved their goal of absolute religious orthodoxy as a basic ingredient of the Spanish state. To be Spanish was to be Catholic, a policy of uniformity enforced by the Inquisition.

CENTRAL EUROPE: THE HOLY ROMAN EMPIRE

Unlike France, England, and Spain, the Holy Roman Empire failed to develop a strong monarchical authority. The failure of the Hohenstaufens in the thirteenth century ended any chance of centralized monarchical authority, and Germany became a land of hundreds of virtually independent states. These varied in size and power and included princely states, such as the duchies of Bavaria and Saxony; free imperial city-states, such as Nuremberg; modest territories of petty imperial knights; and ecclesiastical states in which a high church official, such as a bishop, archbishop, or abbot, served in a dual capacity as an administrative official of the Catholic church and secular lord over the territories of his ecclesiastical state. Although all of the rulers of these various states had some obligations to the German king and Holy Roman emperor, increasingly they acted independently of the German ruler. After 1438, the position of Holy Roman emperor was in the hands of the Habsburg dynasty. Having gradually acquired a number of possessions along the Danube, known collectively as Austria, the house of Habsburg had become one of the wealthiest landholders in the empire and by the mid-fifteenth century began to play an important role in European affairs. Much of the Habsburg success in the fifteenth century was due not to military prowess, but to a well-executed policy of dynastic marriages. So successful were the Habsburgs in matrimonial arrangements that at the beginning of the sixteenth century, one of their members, Charles, succeeded in inheriting the traditional lands of the Habsburg, Burgundian, and Spanish monarchical lines, making him the leading monarch of his age (see Chapter 15).

EASTERN EUROPE

In eastern Europe, rulers struggled to achieve the centralization of their territorial states but faced serious obstacles to that goal. Although the population was mostly Slavic, there were islands of other ethnic groups who caused untold difficulties. Religious differences also troubled the area, as Roman Catholics, Greek Orthodox Christians, and pagans confronted each other.

Much of Polish history revolved around a bitter struggle between the crown and the landed nobility until the end of the fifteenth century when the preoccupation of the Polish monarchy with problems in Bohemia and Hungary as well as war with the Russians and Turks enabled the aristocrats to reestablish their power. Through their control of the *Sejm* or national diet, the magnates reduced the peasantry to serfdom by 1511 and established the right to elect their kings. The Polish kings proved unable to establish a strong royal authority.

Since the conversion of Hungary to Roman Catholicism by German missionaries, its history had been closely tied to that of central and western Europe. The church became a large and prosperous institution. Wealthy bishops, along with great territorial lords, became powerful, independent political figures. For a brief while, however, Hungary developed into an important European state, the dominant power in eastern Europe. King Matthias Corvinus (1458–1490) broke the power of the wealthy lords and created a well-organized central administration. After his death, Hungary returned to weak rule, however, and the work of Corvinus was largely undone.

Since the thirteenth century, Russia had been under the domination of the Mongols. Gradually, the princes of Moscow rose to prominence by using their close relationship to the Mongol khans to increase their wealth and expand their possessions. During the reign of the great prince Ivan III (1462–1505), a new Russian state was born. Ivan III annexed other Russian principalities and took advantage of dissension among the Mongols to throw off their yoke by 1480.

The Ottoman Turks and the End of the Byzantine Empire

Eastern Europe was increasingly threatened by the steadily advancing Ottoman Turks. The Byzantine Empire had served as a buffer between the Muslim Middle East and the Latin West for centuries, but it was severely weakened by the sack of Constantinople in 1204 and its occupation by the west. Although the Paleologus dynasty (1260–1453) had tried to reestablish Byzantine power in the Balkans after the overthrow of the Latin Empire, the threat from the Turks finally doomed the long-lasting empire.

Beginning in northeastern Asia Minor in the thirteenth century, the Ottoman Turks spread rapidly, seizing the lands of the Seljuk Turks and the Byzantine Empire (see Chapter 16). In 1345, they bypassed Constantinople and moved into the Balkans, which they conquered by the end of the century. Finally in 1453, the great city of Constantinople fell to the Turks after a siege of several months. After consolidating their power, the Turks prepared to exert renewed pressure on the west, both in the Mediterranean and up the Danube valley toward Vienna. By the end of the fifteenth century, they were threatening Hungary, Austria, Bohemia, and Poland.

The Italian States

As we have seen, by the end of the fifteenth century, many European rulers had begun to rebuild their governments by restraining turbulent nobles, curbing violence, and establishing internal order. But like the Holy Roman

Empire, Italy failed to develop a centralized monarchical state. Papal opposition to the Hohenstaufens in the thirteenth century had virtually guaranteed that. Moreover, the kingdom of Naples in the south was dominated by the French house of Anjou (Sicily was ruled by the Spanish house of Aragon) while the papacy remained in shaky control of much of central Italy as rulers of the Papal States. Lack of centralized authority had enabled numerous city-states in northern and central Italy to remain independent of any political authority. Three of them—Milan, Venice, and Florence—managed to become fairly well centralized territorial states. Some historians view the Italian states, in their preoccupation with political power, as the first true examples of the modern secular state.

Located in the rich land of the Po valley at the intersection of the chief trade routes from the Italian coastal cities to the Alpine passes, Milan was one of the richest city-states in Italy. Politically, it was also one of the most agitated until members of the Visconti family established themselves as hereditary dukes of Milan and extended

their power over all of Lombardy. After the death of the last Visconti ruler of Milan in 1447, Francesco Sforza, one of the leading *condottieri* (a *condottiere* was a leader of a mercenary band) of the time, turned on his Milanese

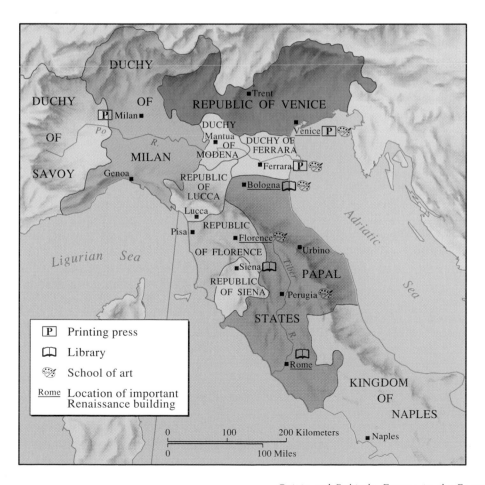

Map 13.3 The Italian States in the Fifteenth Century.

◆ **Piero della Francesca, *Duke and Duchess of Urbino*.**
Federigo da Montefeltro and his wife, Battista Sforza, ruled the small central Italian principality of Urbino. These profile portraits

by Piero della Francesca gave a realistic rendering of the two figures. Visible in the background are the hills and valleys of Urbino.

employers, conquered the city, and became its new duke. Both the Visconti and the Sforza rulers worked to create the institutions of a strongly centralized territorial state. They were especially successful in devising systems of taxation that generated enormous revenues for the government.

The second major northern Italian state was the maritime republic of Venice, which had grown rich from commercial activity throughout the eastern Mediterranean and into northern Europe. Venice remained an extremely stable political entity governed by a small oligarchy of merchant-aristocrats who had become extremely wealthy through their trading activities. Venetian government was respected by contemporaries for its stability. Venice's commercial empire brought in enormous revenues and gave it the status of an international

power. At the end of the fourteenth century, Venice embarked upon the conquest of a territorial state in northern Italy to protect its food supply and its overland trade routes.

The republic of Florence dominated the region of Tuscany. In the course of the fourteenth century, a small but wealthy merchant oligarchy took control of the Florentine government, led the Florentines in a series of successful wars against their neighbors, and established Florence as a major territorial state in north-central Italy. In 1434, Cosimo de' Medici (1434–1464) assumed control of the ruling oligarchy. Although the wealthy Medici family maintained republican forms of government for appearance's sake, they ran the government from behind the scenes. Through their lavish patronage and careful courting of political allies, the Medici were successful in dominating the city at a time when Florence was the cultural center of Italy.

A number of independent city-states under the control of powerful ruling families also became brilliant centers of culture in the fifteenth century. Perhaps the most famous was Urbino, ruled by the Montefeltro dynasty. Federigo da Montefeltro, who ruled Urbino from 1444 to 1482, received a classical education. He had also learned the skills of fighting, since the Montefeltro family compensated for the poverty of Urbino by hiring themselves out as *condottieri*. Federigo was not only a good ruler, but a rather unusual *condottiere* by fifteenth-century standards. Although not a brilliant general, he was reliable and honest. He did not break promises, even when urged to do so by a papal legate. At the same time, Duke Federigo was one of the greatest patrons of Renaissance culture. Under his direction, Urbino became a well-known cultural and intellectual center. Though despotic, he was also benevolent. It was said that he could walk safely through the streets of Urbino, unaccompanied by a bodyguard, a feat few Italian rulers dared to emulate.

A noticeable feature of these smaller Italian courts was the important role played by women. The most famous of the Italian ruling women was Isabella d'Este (1474–1539), daughter of the duke of Ferrara, who married Francesco Gonzaga, marquis of Mantua. Their court was another important center of art and learning in the Renaissance. Educated at the brilliant court of Ferrara, Isabella was known for her intelligence and political wisdom. Called the "first lady of the world," she attracted artists and intellectuals to the Mantuan court and was responsible for amassing one of the finest libraries in all of Italy. Her numerous letters to friends, family, princes, and artists all over Europe disclose her political acumen as well as a good sense of humor (see the box on p. 464). Both before and after the death of her husband Francesco, she effectively ruled Mantua and was well known as a clever negotiator.

The growth of powerful monarchical states led to trouble for the Italians and brought an end to the independence of the Italian states. Attracted by the riches of Italy, the French king Charles VIII (1483–1498) led an army of 30,000 men into Italy and occupied the kingdom of Naples. Other Italian states turned for help to the Spanish, who gladly complied. For the next thirty years, the French and Spanish competed to dominate Italy, which was only a pawn for the two great powers, a convenient arena for fighting battles. The terrible sack of Rome in 1527 by the armies of the Spanish king Charles I brought a temporary end to the Italian wars. Hereafter, the Spaniards dominated Italy.

Machiavelli and the New Statecraft

No one gave better expression to the Italians' preoccupation with political power than Niccolò Machiavelli (1469–1527). He entered the service of the Florentine republic in 1498, four years after the Medici family had been expelled from the city. As a secretary to the Florentine Council of Ten, he went on numerous diplomatic missions, including trips to France and Germany, and saw the workings of statecraft firsthand. Since Italy had been invaded in 1494, Machiavelli was active during a period of Italian tribulation and devastation. In 1512, French defeat and Spanish victory led to the reestablishment of Medici power in Florence. Staunch republicans, including Machiavelli, were sent into exile. Forced to give up politics, the great love of his life, Machiavelli now reflected on political power and wrote books, including *The Prince* (1513), one of the most famous treatises on political power in the Western world.

Machiavelli's ideas on politics stemmed from two major sources, his preoccupation with Italy's political problems and his knowledge of ancient Rome. His major concerns in *The Prince* were the acquisition, maintenance, and expansion of political power as the means to restore and maintain order in his time. Machiavelli was aware that his own approach to political power was different from that of previous political theorists. Late medieval political theory conceived of the state as a necessary creation for humankind's spiritual, material, and social well-being. A ruler was justified in his exercise of political power only if it contributed to the common good of the people he served. The ethical side of a prince's activity—how a ruler ought to behave based on Christian moral principles—was the focus of many late medieval treatises on politics. Machiavelli bluntly contradicted this approach:

> But my hope is to write a book that will be useful, at least to those who read it intelligently, and so I thought it sensible to go straight to a discussion of how things are in real life and not waste time with a discussion of an imaginary world. . . for the gap between how people actually behave and how they ought to behave is so great that anyone who ignores everyday reality in order to live up to an ideal will soon discover he had been taught how to destroy himself, not how to preserve himself.[6]

Machiavelli considered his approach far more realistic than that of his medieval forebears.

In Machiavelli's view, a prince's attitude toward power must be based on an understanding of human nature,

❧ *The Letters of Isabella d'Este* ❧

Many Italian and European rulers at the beginning of the sixteenth century saw Isabella d'Este as an important political figure. In these excerpts from her letters, Isabella reveals her political skills and her fierce determination. After her husband was taken prisoner by the Venetians in 1509, she refused to accept the condition for his release—namely, that her son Federico would be kept as a hostage by the Venetians or the Holy Roman emperor. She wrote to both the emperor and her husband, refusing to agree to their demands.

Letter of Isabella d'Este to the Imperial Envoy

As to the demand for our dearest first-born son Federico, besides being a cruel and almost inhuman thing for any one who knows the meaning of a mother's love, there are many reasons which render it difficult and impossible. Although we are quite sure that his person would be well cared for and protected by His Majesty [the Holy Roman emperor], how could we wish him to run the risk of this long and difficult journey, considering the child's tender and delicate age? And you must know what comfort and solace, in his father's present unhappy condition, we find in the presence of this dear son, the hope and joy of all our people and subjects. To deprive us of him, would be to deprive us of life itself, and of all we count good and precious. If you take Federico away you might as well take away our life and state. . . . Once for all, we will suffer any loss rather than part from our son, and this you may take to be our deliberate and unchanging resolution.

Letter of Isabella d'Este to Her Husband [who had ordered her to send the boy to Venice]

If in this matter Your Excellency were to despise me and deprive me of your love and grace, I would rather endure such harsh treatment, I would rather lose our State, than deprive us of our children. I am hoping that in time your own prudence and kindness will make you understand that I have acted more lovingly toward you than you have to yourself.

Have patience! You can be sure that I think continuously of your liberation and when the time comes I will not fail you, as I have not relaxed my efforts. As witness I cite the Pope, the Emperor, the King of France, and all the other reigning heads and potentates of Christendom. Yes, and the infidels as well [she had written to the Turkish sultan for help]. If it were *really* the only means of setting you free, I would not only send Federico but all the other children as well. I will do everything imaginable. Some day I hope I can make you understand. . . .

Pardon me if this letter is badly written and worse composed, but I do not know if I am dead or alive.

> Isabella, who desires the best for Your Excellency, written with her own hand

[Isabella's husband was not pleased with her response. His angry reaction was: "That whore of my wife is the cause of it all. Send me into battle alone, do what you like with me. I have lost in one blow my state, my honor and my freedom. If she does not obey, I'll cut her vocal cords."]

which he perceived as basically self-centered. He said, "For of men one can, in general, say this: They are ungrateful, fickle, deceptive and deceiving, avoiders of danger, eager to gain." Political activity, therefore, could not be restricted by moral considerations. The prince acts on behalf of the state, and for the sake of the state, he must be willing to let his conscience sleep. As Machiavelli put it:

You need to understand this: A ruler, and particularly a ruler who is new to power, cannot conform to all those rules that men who are thought good are expected to respect, for he is often obliged, in order to hold on to power, to break his word, to be uncharitable, inhumane, and irreligious. So he must be mentally prepared to act as circumstances and changes in fortune require. As I have said, he should do what is right if he can; but he must be prepared to do wrong if necessary.[7]

In Cesare Borgia, the son of Pope Alexander VI, who used ruthless measures to achieve his goal of carving out a new state in central Italy, Machiavelli found a good example of the new Italian ruler. As he said, "So anyone who decides that the policy to follow when one has newly acquired power is to destroy one's enemies, to secure some allies, to win wars, whether by force or by fraud, to make oneself both loved and feared by one's subjects, . . . cannot hope to find, in the recent past, a better model to imitate than Cesare Borgia." Machiavelli was among the first to abandon morality as the basis for the analysis of political activity.

The Decline of the Church

The papacy of the Roman Catholic church reached the height of its power in the thirteenth century. Theories of papal supremacy included a doctrine of "fullness of power" as the spiritual head of Christendom and claims to universal temporal authority over all secular rulers. But the growing secular monarchies of Europe presented a challenge to papal claims of temporal supremacy that led the papacy into a conflict with these territorial states that it was unable to win. Papal defeat, in turn, led to other crises that brought into question and undermined not only the pope's temporal authority over all Christendom, but his spiritual authority as well.

Boniface VIII and the Conflict with the State

The struggle between the papacy and the secular monarchies began during the pontificate of Pope Boniface VIII (1294–1303). One major issue appeared to be at stake between the pope and King Philip IV (1285–1314) of France. Looking for a source of new revenues, Philip asserted the right to tax the clergy of France. Boniface VIII claimed that the clergy of any state could not pay taxes to their secular ruler without the pope's consent. Underlying this issue, however, was a basic conflict between the claims of the papacy to universal authority over both church and state, which necessitated complete control over the clergy, and the claims of the monarchs that all subjects, including ecclesiastics, were under the jurisdiction of the crown and subject to the king's authority on matters of taxation and justice. In short, the fundamental issue was the universal sovereignty of the papacy versus the royal sovereignty of the monarchs.

Boniface VIII asserted his position in a series of papal bulls or letters, the most important of which was *Unam Sanctam*, issued in 1302. It was the strongest statement ever made by a pope on the supremacy of the spiritual authority over the temporal authority (see the box on p. 466). When it became apparent that the pope had decided to act upon his principles by excommunicating Philip IV of France, the latter sent a small contingent of French soldiers to capture Boniface and bring him back to France for trial. The pope was captured in Anagni, although Italian nobles from the surrounding countryside soon rescued him. Boniface died shortly thereafter from the shock of this experience, however. Philip's strong-arm tactics had produced a clear victory for the national monarchy over the papacy since no later pope dared renew the extravagant claims of Boniface VIII. To ensure his position and avoid any future papal threat, Philip IV brought enough pressure on the college of cardinals to achieve the election of a Frenchman, Clement V (1305–1314), as pope. Using the excuse of turbulence in the city of Rome, the new pope took up residence in Avignon on the east bank of the Rhone River. Although Avignon was located in the Holy Roman Empire and was not a French possession, it lay just across the river from the territories of King Philip IV and was French in culture.

The Papacy at Avignon (1305–1378)

The residency of the popes in Avignon for almost three-quarters of the fourteenth century led to a decline in papal prestige and a growing antipapal sentiment. The city of Rome was the traditional capital of the universal church. The pope was the bishop of Rome, and his position was based upon being the successor to the apostle Peter, the first bishop of Rome. It was quite unseemly that the head of the Catholic church should reside in Avignon instead of Rome. Although the Avignonese popes frequently announced their intention to return to Rome, the political turmoil in the Papal States in central Italy always gave them an excuse to postpone their departure. In the decades of the 1330s, the popes began to construct a stately palace in Avignon, a clear indication that they intended to stay for some time.

Other factors also led to a decline in papal prestige during the Avignonese residency. Many contemporaries believed that the popes at Avignon were captives of the French king. Although questionable, since Avignon did not belong to the French monarchy, it was easy to believe in view of Avignon's proximity to French lands. Moreover, during the seventy-three years of the Avignonese papacy, of the 134 new cardinals created by the popes, 113 of them were French. At the same time, the popes attempted to find new sources of revenue to compensate

❧ Boniface VIII's Defense of Papal Supremacy ❧

One of the more remarkable documents of the four-teenth century was the exaggerated statement of papal supremacy issued by Pope Boniface VIII in 1302 in the heat of his conflict with the French king Philip IV. Ironically, this strongest statement ever made of papal supremacy was issued at a time when the rising power of the secular monarchies made it increasingly difficult for the premises to be accepted. Not long after issuing it, Boniface was taken prisoner by the French. Although freed by his fellow Italians, the humiliation of his defeat brought his death a short time later.

Pope Boniface VIII, *Unam Sanctam*

We are compelled, our faith urging us, to believe and to hold—and we do firmly believe and simply confess—that there is one holy catholic and apostolic church, outside of which there is neither salvation nor remission of sins. . . . In this church there is one Lord, one faith and one baptism. . . . Therefore, of this one and only church there is one body and one head . . . Christ, namely, and the vicar of Christ, St. Peter, and the successor of Peter. For the Lord himself said to Peter, feed my sheep. . . .

We are told by the word of the gospel that in this His fold there are two swords—a spiritual, namely, and a temporal. . . . Both swords, the spiritual and the material, therefore, are in the power of the church; the one, indeed, to be wielded for the church, the other by the church; the one by the hand of the priest, the other by the hand of kings and knights, but at the will and sufferance of the priest. One sword, moreover, ought to be under the other, and the temporal authority to be subjected to the spiritual. . . .

Therefore if the earthly power err it shall be judged by the spiritual power; but if the lesser spiritual power err, by the greater. But if the greatest, it can be judged by God alone, not by man, the apostle bearing witness. A spiritual man judges all things, but he himself is judged by no one. This authority, moreover, even though it is given to man and exercised through man, is not human but rather divine, being given by divine lips to Peter and founded on a rock for him and his successors through Christ himself whom he has confessed; the Lord himself saying to Peter: "Whatsoever thou shalt bind, etc." Whoever, therefore, resists this power thus ordained by God, resists the ordination of God. . . .

Indeed, we declare, announce and define, that it is altogether necessary to salvation for every human creature to be subject to the Roman pontiff.

for their loss of revenue from the Papal States. Their imposition of new taxes on the clergy, frequently enforced by the threat of excommunication if they were not paid, did not improve people's opinion of the popes' use of their spiritual authority. Furthermore, the splendor in which the pope and cardinals were living in Avignon led to a highly vocal criticism of both clergy and papacy. Avignon had become a powerful symbol of abuses within the church. At last, Pope Gregory XI, perceiving the disastrous decline in papal prestige, returned to Rome in 1377. His untimely death shortly afterward, however, soon gave rise to an even greater crisis for the Catholic church.

The Great Schism

Gregory XI (1370–1378) died in Rome in the spring of 1378. When the college of cardinals met in conclave to elect a new pope, the citizens of Rome, fearful that the French majority would choose another Frenchman who would return the papacy to Avignon, threatened that the cardinals would not leave Rome alive unless a Roman or Italian was elected pope. Wisely, the terrified cardinals duly elected the Italian archbishop of Bari as Pope Urban VI (1378–1389). Five months later, a group of dissenting cardinals—the French ones—declared Urban's election null and void and chose one of their number, a Frenchman, who took the title of Clement VII and promptly returned to Avignon. Since Urban remained in Rome, there were now two popes, initiating what has been called the Great Schism of the church. Europe became divided in its loyalties: France, Spain, Scotland, and southern Italy supported Clement, while England, Germany, Scandinavia, and most of Italy supported Urban. These divisions generally followed political lines. Since the French supported the Avignonese, so did their allies; their enemies, particularly England and its allies, supported the Roman pope. The need for political support caused both popes to subordinate their policies to the policies of these states.

The Great Schism badly damaged the faith of Christian believers. The pope was widely believed to be the true leader of Christendom and, as Boniface VIII had pointed out, held the keys to the kingdom of heaven. Since both lines of popes denounced the other as the antichrist, such a spectacle could not help but undermine the institution that had become the very foundation of the church. The Great Schism introduced uncertainty into the daily lives of ordinary Christians.

As dissatisfaction with the papacy grew, so also did the calls for a revolutionary approach to solving the church's institutional problems. Final authority in spiritual matters must reside not with the popes, reformers claimed, but with a general church council representing all members. The Great Schism led large numbers of serious churchmen to take up the theory of conciliarism in the belief that only a general council of the church could end the schism and bring reform to the church in its "head and members." In desperation, a group of cardinals from both lines of popes finally heeded these theoretical formulations and convened a general council. This Council of Pisa, which met in 1409, deposed the two popes and elected a new one. The council's action proved disastrous when the two deposed popes refused to step down. There were now three popes and the church seemed more hopelessly divided than ever.

Leadership in convening a new council now passed to the Holy Roman emperor Sigismund, and as a result of his efforts, a new ecumenical church council met at Constance from 1414 to 1418. It had three major objectives: to end the schism, to eradicate heresy, and to reform the church in "head and members." The ending of the schism proved to be the Council of Constance's easiest task. After the three competing popes either resigned or were deposed, a new conclave elected a Roman cardinal, a member of a prominent Roman family, as Pope Martin V (1417–1431). The council was much less successful in dealing with the problems of heresy and reform.

The Problems of Heresy and Reform

Heresy was, of course, not a new problem, and in the thirteenth century, the church had developed inquisitorial machinery to deal with it. But widespread movements in the early fifteenth century—especially Hussitism—posed new threats to the church. A group of Czech reformers led by the chancellor of the university of Prague, John Hus (1374–1415), called for an end to the worldliness and corruption of the clergy, criticized the sale of in-

CHRONOLOGY

The Decline of the Church

Pope Boniface VIII	1294–1303
Unam Sanctam	1302
The papacy at Avignon	1305–1378
Pope Gregory XI returns to Rome	1377
The Great Schism begins	1378
Pope Urban VI	1378–1389
Failure of Council of Pisa to end schism	1409
Council of Constance	1414–1418
End of the Great Schism	1417
The Renaissance papacy	
Sixtus IV	1471–1484
Alexander VI	1492–1503
Julius II	1503–1513
Leo X	1513–1521

dulgences, and attacked the excessive power of the papacy within the Catholic church. Hus's objections fell on receptive ears because there was already widespread criticism of the Catholic church as one of the largest landowners in Bohemia. Moreover, many clergymen were German, and the native Czechs' strong resentment of the Germans who dominated Bohemia also contributed to Hus's movement.

The Council of Constance attempted to deal with the growing problem of heresy by summoning John Hus to the council. Granted a safe conduct by Emperor Sigismund, Hus went in the hope of receiving a free hearing for his ideas. Instead he was arrested, condemned as a heretic, and burned at the stake in 1415. This action turned the unrest in Bohemia into revolutionary upheaval, and the resulting Hussite wars wracked the Holy Roman Empire until a truce was arranged in 1436.

The reform of the church in "head and members" was even less successful than the attempt to eradicate heresy. The Council of Constance passed two startling reform decrees. One boldly stated that a general council of the church received its authority from God; hence, every Christian, including the pope, was subject to its authority. The other decree provided for the regular holding of general councils in order to maintain an ongoing reform of the church. Decrees alone, however, proved insufficient to reform the church. Councils could issue decrees, but popes had to execute them, and popes would not cooperate with councils that diminished their absolute authority. Beginning already in 1417, successive popes worked steadfastly for the next thirty years to defeat the conciliar movement.

By the mid-fifteenth century, the popes had reasserted their supremacy over the Catholic church. No longer, however, did they have any possibility of asserting supremacy over temporal governments as the medieval papacy had. The papal monarchy had been maintained, although it had lost much moral prestige. In the fifteenth and early sixteenth centuries, the Renaissance popes contributed to an even further decline in the moral leadership of the papacy.

◆ **A Renaissance Pope: Sixtus IV.** The Renaissance popes allowed secular concerns to overshadow their spiritual duties. They became concerned with territorial expansion, finances, and Renaissance culture. Pope Sixtus IV built the Sistine Chapel and later had it decorated by some of the leading artists of his day. This fresco by Melozzo da Forlì shows the pope on his throne receiving the humanist Platina (kneeling), who was keeper of the Vatican Library.

The Renaissance Papacy

The phrase *Renaissance papacy* refers to the line of popes from the end of the Great Schism (1417) to the beginnings of the Reformation in the early sixteenth century. The primary concern of the papacy is governing the Catholic church as its spiritual leader. But as heads of the church, popes had temporal preoccupations as well, and the story of the Renaissance papacy is really an account of how the latter came to overshadow the pope's spiritual functions.

The preoccupation of the popes with the territory of the Papal States and Italian politics was not new in the fifteenth century. Popes had been temporal as well as spiritual rulers for centuries. But the manner in which Renaissance popes pursued their temporal interests, especially their use of intrigue, deceit, and open bloodshed, seemed shocking. Of all the Renaissance popes, Julius II (1503–1513) was most involved in war and politics. The fiery "warrior-pope" personally led armies against his enemies, much to the disgust of pious Christians who viewed the pope as a spiritual leader. As one intellectual wrote at the beginning of the sixteenth century: "How, O bishop standing in the room of the Apostles, dare you teach the people the things that pertain to war?"

To further their territorial aims in the Papal States, the popes needed loyal servants. Because they were not hereditary monarchs, popes could not build dynasties over several generations and came to rely on the practice of nepotism to promote their families' interests. Pope Sixtus IV (1471–1484), for example, made five of his nephews (the word *nepotism* is, in fact, derived from *nepos*, meaning nephew) cardinals and gave them an abundance of church offices to build up their finances. The infamous Borgia pope, Alexander VI (1492–1503), known for his debauchery and sensuality, raised one son, one nephew, and the brother of one mistress to the cardinalate. Alexander scandalized the church by encouraging his son Cesare to carve a territorial state out of the territories of the Papal States in central Italy.

The Renaissance popes were great patrons of Renaissance culture, and their efforts made Rome a cultural leader at the beginning of the sixteenth century. For the warrior-pope Julius II, the patronage of Renaissance culture was mostly a matter of policy as he endeavored to add to the splendor of his pontificate by tearing down the old basilica of Saint Peter and beginning construction of what was to be the greatest building in Christendom, Saint Peter's Basilica. Julius's successor, Leo X (1513–1521), was also a patron of Renaissance culture, not as a matter of policy, but as a deeply involved participant. A member of the Medici family, he was made a cardinal at the age of thirteen and acquired a refined taste in art, manners, and social life among the Florentine elite. He became pope at the age of thirty-seven, supposedly remarking to the Venetian ambassador, "Let us enjoy the papacy, since God has given it to us." Raphael was commissioned to do paintings, and the construction of St. Peter's was accelerated as Rome became the literary and artistic center of the Renaissance.

Meaning and Characteristics of the Italian Renaissance

The word *Renaissance* means "rebirth." A number of people who lived in Italy between c. 1350 and c. 1550 believed that they had witnessed a rebirth of antiquity or Greco-Roman civilization, which marked a new age. To them, the approximately thousand years between the end of the Roman Empire and their own era was a middle period (hence the "Middle Ages"), characterized by darkness because of its lack of classical culture. Historians of the nineteenth century later used similar terminology to describe this period in Italy. The Swiss historian and art critic, Jacob Burckhardt, created the modern concept of the Renaissance in his celebrated work, *Civilization of the Renaissance in Italy*, published in 1860. He portrayed Italy in the fourteenth and fifteenth centuries as the birthplace of the modern world and saw the revival of antiquity, the "perfecting of the individual," and secularism ("worldliness of the Italians") as its distinguishing features. No doubt, Burckhardt exaggerated the individuality and secularism of the Renaissance and failed to recognize the depths of its religious sentiment. Nevertheless, he established the framework for all modern interpretations of the Renaissance. Although contemporary scholars do not believe that the Renaissance represents a sudden or dramatic cultural break with the Middle Ages (as Burckhardt argued)—there was after all much continuity between the two periods in economic, political, and social life—the Renaissance can still be viewed as a distinct period of European history that manifested itself first in Italy and then spread to the rest of Europe. What, then, are the characteristics of the Italian Renaissance?

Renaissance Italy was largely the product of an urban society. The city-states became the centers of Italian political, economic, and social life. Within this new urban society, a secular spirit emerged as increasing wealth created new possibilities for the enjoyment of worldly things.

Above all, the Renaissance was an age of recovery from the "calamitous fourteenth century." Italy and Europe began a slow process of recuperation from the effects of the Black Death, political disorder, and economic recession. By the end of the fourteenth and beginning of the fifteenth centuries, Italians were using the words *recovery* and *revival* and were actively involved in a rebuilding process.

Recovery was accompanied by rebirth, specifically, a rebirth of classical antiquity. Increasingly aware of their own historical past, Italian intellectuals became intensely interested in the Greco-Roman culture that had informed the ancient Mediterranean world. This new revival of classical antiquity (the Middle Ages, after all, had preserved much of ancient Latin culture) affected activities as diverse as politics and art and led to new attempts to reconcile the pagan philosophy of antiquity with Christian thought, as well as to see human beings in a new light.

Though not entirely new, a revived emphasis on individual ability became characteristic of the Italian Renaissance. As the fifteenth-century Florentine architect, Leon Battista Alberti, expressed it, "Men can do all things if they will."[8] A high regard for human dignity and worth and a realization of individual potentiality created a new social ideal of the well-rounded personality or universal person (*l'uomo universale*) who was capable of achievements in many areas of life.

These general features of the Italian Renaissance were not characteristic of all Italians, but were primarily the preserve of the wealthy upper classes who constituted a small percentage of the total population. The Italian Renaissance was an elitist, not a mass, movement, although indirectly it did have some impact on ordinary people, especially in the cities where so many of the intellectual and artistic accomplishments of the period were most apparent.

Social Changes in the Renaissance

The Renaissance inherited a tripartite division of society from the Middle Ages. Society was fundamentally divided into three estates: the clergy, whose preeminence was grounded in the belief that people should be guided to spiritual ends; the nobility, whose privileges rested on the principle that the nobles provided security and justice for society; and the third estate, which consisted of the peasants and inhabitants of the towns and cities. This social order experienced certain adaptations in the Renaissance, which we can see by examining the second and third estates (the clergy will be examined in Chapter 15).

The Social Classes: The Nobility

Throughout much of Europe, the landholding nobles were faced with declining real incomes during the greater part of the fourteenth and fifteenth centuries, while the expense of maintaining noble status was rising. But members of the old nobility survived, while new blood infused their ranks. A reconstruction of the aristocracy was well underway by 1500. As a result of this reconstruction, the nobles, old and new, who constituted between 2 and 3 percent of the population in most countries, managed to dominate society as they had done in the Middle Ages, holding important political posts and serving as advisers to the king.

By 1500, certain ideals came to be expected of the noble or aristocrat. These were best expressed in *The Book of the Courtier* by the Italian Baldassare Castiglione (1478–1529). First published in 1528, Castiglione's work soon became popular throughout Europe, and it remained a fundamental handbook for European aristocrats well into the twentieth century.

In *The Book of the Courtier*, Castiglione described the three basic attributes of the perfect courtier. First, nobles should possess fundamental native endowments, such as impeccable character, grace, talents, and noble birth. The perfect courtier must also cultivate certain achievements. Primarily, he should participate in military and bodily exercises because the principal profession of a courtier was arms. For a medieval knight, military skill had been the only requirement, but this was not true of the Renaissance courtier who must seek a classical education and adorn his life with the arts by playing a musical instrument, drawing, and painting. In Castiglione's hands, the Renaissance ideal of the well-developed personality became a social ideal of the aristocracy. Finally, the aristocrat was expected to follow a certain standard of conduct. Nobles were expected to make good impressions; while being modest, they should not hide their accomplishments, but show them off with grace.

But what was the purpose of these courtly standards? Castiglione said:

> Therefore, I think that the aim of the perfect Courtier, which we have not spoken of up to now, is so to win for himself, by means of the accomplishments ascribed to him by these gentlemen, the favor and mind of the prince whom he serves that he may be able to tell him, and always

will tell him, the truth about everything he needs to know, without fear or risk of displeasing him; and that when he sees the mind of his prince inclined to a wrong action, he may dare to oppose him . . . so as to dissuade him of every evil intent and bring him to the path of virtue.[9]

This ideal of service to the prince reflected the secular ethic of the active life espoused by the earlier civic humanists (see Italian Renaissance Humanism later in this chapter). Castiglione put the new moral values of the Renaissance into a courtly, aristocratic form that was now acceptable to the nobility throughout Europe. Nobles would adhere to his principles for hundreds of years while they continued to dominate European life socially and politically.

The Social Classes: The Third Estate of Peasants and Townspeople

Traditionally, peasants made up the overwhelming mass of the third estate and indeed continued to constitute as much as 85 to 90 percent of the total European population, except in the highly urbanized areas of northern Italy and Flanders. The most noticeable trend produced by the economic crisis of the fourteenth century was the decline of the manorial system and the continuing elimination of serfdom. The contraction of the peasantry after the Black Death simply accelerated the process of converting servile labor dues into rents paid in money. By the end of the fifteenth century, serfdom was declining, especially in western Europe, and more and more peasants were becoming legally free.

The remainder of the third estate centered around the people of the towns and cities, originally the merchants and artisans who formed the so-called middle class. The town or city of the fifteenth century actually possessed a multitude of inhabitants widely separated socially and economically.

At the top of urban society were the patricians, whose wealth from capitalistic enterprises in trade, industry, and banking enabled them to dominate their urban communities economically, socially, and politically. Below them were the petty burghers, the shopkeepers, artisans, guildmasters, and guildsmen, who were largely concerned with providing goods and services for local consumption. Below these two groups were the propertyless workers earning pitiful wages and the unemployed, who lived squalid and miserable lives. These people constituted as much as 30 or 40 percent of the urban population. Everywhere in Europe in the late fourteenth and fifteenth centuries, urban poverty had increased dramatically. One rich merchant of Florence wrote:

➢ *Marriage Negotiations* ⬅

Marriages were so important in maintaining families in Renaissance Italy that much energy was put into arranging them. Parents made the choices for their children, most often for considerations that had little to do with the modern notion of love. This selection is taken from the letters of a Florentine matron of the illustrious Strozzi family to her son Filippo in Naples. The family's considerations were complicated by the fact that the son was in exile.

Alessandra Strozzi to Her Son Filippo in Naples

[April 20, 1464] . . . Concerning the matter of a wife [for Filippo], it appears to me that if Francesco di Messer Tanagli wishes to give his daughter, that it would be a fine marriage. . . . Now I will speak with Marco [Parenti, Alessandra's son-in-law], to see if there are other prospects that would be better, and if there are none, then we will learn if he wishes to give her [in marriage]. . . . Francesco Tanagli has a good reputation, and he has held office, not the highest, but still he has been in office. You may ask: "Why should he give her to someone in exile?" There are three reasons. First, there aren't many young men of good family who have both virtue and property. Secondly, she has only a small dowry, 1,000 florins, which is the dowry of an artisan [although not a small sum, either—senior officials in the government bureaucracy earned 300 florins a year]. . . . Third, I believe that he will give her away, because he has a large family and he will need help to settle them. . . .

[July 26, 1465] . . . Francesco is a good friend of Marco and he trusts him. On S. Jacopo's day, he spoke to him discreetly and persuasively, saying that for several months he had heard that we were interested in the girl and . . . that when we had made up our

minds, she will come to us willingly. [He said that] you were a worthy man, and that his family had always made good marriages, but that he had only a small dowry to give her, and so he would prefer to send her outside of Florence to someone of worth, rather than to give her to someone here, from among those who were available, with little money. . . . We have information that she is affable and competent. She is responsible for a large family (there are twelve children, six boys and six girls), and the mother is always pregnant and isn't very competent. . . .

[August 31, 1465] . . . I have recently received some very favorable information [about the Tanagli girl] from two individuals. . . . They are in agreement that whoever gets her will be content. . . . Concerning her beauty, they told me what I had already seen, that she is attractive and well-proportioned. Her face is long, but I couldn't look directly into her face, since she appeared to be aware that I was examining her . . . and so she turned away from me like the wind. . . . She reads quite well . . . and she can dance and sing. . . .

So yesterday I sent for Marco and told him what I had learned. And we talked about the matter for a while, and decided that he should say something to the father and give him a little hope, but not so much that we couldn't withdraw, and find out from him the amount of the dowry. . . . May God help us to choose what will contribute to our tranquility and to the consolation of us all.

[September 13, 1465] . . . Marco came to me and said that he had met with Francesco Tanagli, who had spoken very coldly, so that I understand that he had changed his mind. . . . [Filippo Strozzi eventually married Fiametta di Donato Adimari in 1466.]

Those that are lazy and indolent in a way that does harm to the city, and who can offer no just reason for their condition, should either be forced to work or expelled from the Commune. The city would thus rid itself of that most harmful part of the poorest class. . . . If the lowest order of society earn enough food to keep them going from day to day, then they have enough.[10]

But even this large group was not at the bottom of the social scale; beneath them stood a significantly large group of slaves, especially in the cities of Italy.

Family and Marriage in Renaissance Italy

The family bond was a source of great security in the dangerous urban world of Renaissance Italy. To maintain the family, careful attention was given to marriages, which were arranged by parents, often to strengthen business or family ties. Details were worked out well in advance, sometimes when children were only two or three, and reinforced by a legally binding marriage contract (see the box above). The important aspect of the contract was the size of the dowry, a sum of money presented by the wife's

◆ **Wedding Banquet.** Parents arranged marriages in Renaissance Italy to strengthen business or family ties. A legally binding marriage contact was considered a necessary part of the marital arrangements. So, too, was a wedding feast. This painting by Botticelli shows the wedding banquet in Florence that celebrated the marriage of Nastagio degli Onesti and the daughter of Paulo Traversaro.

family to the husband upon marriage. He would control this money thereafter. The dowry could involve large sums of money and was expected of all families. Because poor families often had difficulty providing a dowry, wealthy families established societies to provide dowries for poor girls.

The father-husband was the center of the Italian family. He gave it his name, was responsible for it in all legal matters, managed all finances (his wife had no share in his wealth), and made the crucial decisions that determined his children's lives. A father's authority over his children was absolute until he died or formally freed his children. In Renaissance Italy, children did not become adults on reaching a certain age; instead adulthood came only when the father went before a judge and formally emancipated them. The age of emancipation varied from early teens to late twenties.

The mother managed the household, a position that gave women a certain degree of autonomy in their daily lives. Considering that marriages had been arranged, marital relationships ran the gamut from deep emotional attachments to purely formal ties. The lack of emotional attachment from arranged marriages did encourage extramarital relationships, especially for those groups whose lifestyle offered special temptations. While sexual license for males was the norm for princes and their courts, women were supposed to follow different guidelines. The first wife of Duke Filippo Maria Visconti of Milan had an affair with the court musician and was executed for it.

The Intellectual Renaissance in Italy

The emergence and growth of individualism and secularism as characteristics of the Italian Renaissance were most noticeable in the intellectual and artistic realms. Italian culture had matured by the fourteenth century. For the next two centuries, Italy was the cultural leader of Europe. This new Italian culture was primarily the product of a relatively wealthy, urban lay society. The most important literary movement associated with the Renaissance was humanism.

Italian Renaissance Humanism

Renaissance humanism was a form of education and culture based upon the study of the classics. Humanism was not so much a philosophy of life as it was an educational program that revolved around a clearly defined group of intellectual disciplines or "liberal arts"—grammar, rhetoric, poetry, moral philosophy or ethics, and history—all based on an examination of classical writers.

The central importance of literary preoccupations in Renaissance humanism is evident in the professional status or occupations of the humanists. Some of them were teachers of the humanities in secondary schools and universities, where they either gave occasional lectures or held permanent positions, often as professors of rhetoric. Others served as secretaries in the chancelleries of Italian city-states or at the courts of princes or popes. All of these occupations were largely secular, and many humanists were laymen rather than members of the clergy.

Petrarch (1304–1374) has often been called the father of Italian Renaissance humanism. He did more than any other individual in the fourteenth century to foster the development of Renaissance humanism. He was the first intellectual to characterize the Middle Ages as a period of darkness, promoting the mistaken belief that medieval culture was ignorant of classical antiquity. Petrarch condemned the scholastic philosophy of the Middle Ages for its "barbarous" Latin and use of logic rather than rhetoric to harmonize faith and reason. Philosophy, he argued, should be the "art of virtuous living," not a science of logic chopping. Petrarch's interest in the classics led him on a passionate search for forgotten Latin manuscripts and set in motion a ransacking of monastic libraries throughout Europe. In his preoccupation with the classics and their secular content, Petrarch doubted at times whether he was sufficiently attentive to spiritual ideals. His qualms, however, did not prevent him from inaugurating the humanist emphasis on the use of pure classical Latin, making it fashionable for humanists to use Cicero as a model for prose and Virgil for poetry. As Petrarch said, "Christ is my God; Cicero is the prince of the language." Humanists would always have a tendency to emphasize style, often at the expense of content.

Petrarch's humanistic pursuits found their most enthusiastic reception in Florence. By the end of the fourteenth century, a whole circle of humanistic scholars had emerged in that city. Although some were connected to monastic orders, many were simply laymen. In fact, the latter were responsible for humanism gaining a powerful momentum at the beginning of the fifteenth century when it became closely tied to Florentine civic spirit and pride, giving rise to what one modern scholar has called "civic humanism."

Fourteenth-century humanists such as Petrarch had glorified intellectual activity pursued in a life of solitude and had rejected a life of action in the community and family. In the busy civic world of Florence, intellectuals began to take a new view of their role as intellectuals, a trend that intensified when the city's liberty was threatened at the beginning of the fifteenth century by the Milanese tyrant, Giangaleazzo Visconti. Cicero, the classical Roman statesman and intellectual, became their model. Leonardo Bruni (1370–1444), a humanist, Florentine patriot, and chancellor of the city, wrote a biography of Cicero entitled the *New Cicero*, in which he waxed enthusiastically about the fusion of political action and literary creation in Cicero's life. Cicero's literary and political activities were simply two sides of the same task, the work of a Roman citizen on behalf of his state. From Bruni's time on, Cicero served as the inspiration for the Renaissance ideal that one must live an active life for one's state, and everything, including riches, must be considered good if it increases one's power of action. An active civic life does not distract from, but actually stimulates the highest intellectual energies. An individual only "grows to maturity—both intellectually and morally—through participation" in the life of the state.

Civic humanism emerged in Florence but soon spread to other Italian cities and beyond. It reflected the values of the urban society of the Italian Renaissance. Civic humanism intensified the involvement of humanist intellectuals in government and guaranteed that the rhetorical discipline they praised would be put to the service of the state. It is no accident that humanists served the state as chancellors, councillors, and advisers. Rhetoricians had become diplomats.

Also evident in the humanism of the first half of the fifteenth century was a growing interest in classical Greek civilization. One of the first Italian humanists to gain a thorough knowledge of Greek was Leonardo Bruni, who became an enthusiastic pupil of the Byzantine scholar Manuel Chrysoloras, who taught in Florence from 1396 to 1400. Humanists eagerly perused the works of Plato as well as Greek poets, dramatists, historians, and orators, such as Thucydides, Euripides, and Sophocles, all of whom had been neglected by the scholastics of the High Middle Ages.

HUMANISM AND PHILOSOPHY

The second half of the fifteenth century saw a dramatic upsurge of interest in the works of Plato. Cosimo de' Medici, the de facto ruler of Florence, encouraged this development by commissioning a translation of Plato's dialogues by Marsilio Ficino (1433–1499), who dedicated his life to the translation of Plato and the exposition of the Platonic philosophy known as Neoplatonism.

In two major works, Marsilio Ficino undertook the synthesis of Christianity and Platonism into a single system. His Neoplatonism was based upon two primary ideas, the Neoplatonic hierarchy of substances and a theory of spiritual love. The former postulated a hierarchy of substances, or great chain of being, from the lowest form of physical matter (plants) to the purest spirit (God), in which humans occupied a central or middle position. They were the link between the material world (through the body) and the spiritual world (through the soul), and their highest duty was to apprehend higher things and ascend toward that union with God that was the true end of human existence. Ficino's theory of spiritual or Platonic love maintained that just as all people are bound together in their common humanity by love, so too are all parts of the universe held together by bonds of sympathetic love.

Renaissance Hermeticism was another product of the Florentine intellectual environment of the late fifteenth century. Upon the request of Cosimo de' Medici, Marsilio Ficino translated into Latin a Greek manuscript entitled the *Corpus Hermeticum*. This work contained two kinds of writings. One type stressed the occult sciences with emphasis on astrology, alchemy, and magic. The other focused on theological and philosophical beliefs and speculations. For Renaissance intellectuals, the Hermetic revival offered a new view of humankind. They believed that human beings had been created as divine beings endowed with divine creative power, but had freely chosen to enter the material world (nature). They could recover their divinity, however, through a regenerative experi-

❧ Pico della Mirandola and the Dignity of Man ❧

Giovanni Pico della Mirandola was one of the foremost intellects of the Italian Renaissance. Pico boasted that he had studied all schools of philosophy, which he tried to demonstrate by drawing up nine hundred theses for public disputation at the age of twenty-four. As a preface to his theses, he wrote his famous oration, On the Dignity of Man, in which he proclaimed the unlimited potentiality of human beings.

Pico della Mirandola, *Oration on the Dignity of Man*

At last the best of artisans [God] ordained that that creature to whom He had been able to give nothing proper to himself should have joint possession of whatever had been peculiar to each of the different kinds of being. He therefore took man as a creature of indeterminate nature, and assigning him a place in the middle of the world, addressed him thus: "Neither a fixed abode nor a form that is yours alone nor any function peculiar to yourself have we given you, Adam, to the end that according to your longing and according to your judgment you may have and possess what abode, what form, and what functions you yourself shall desire. The nature of all other beings is limited and constrained within the bounds of laws prescribed by Us. You, constrained by no limits, in accordance with your own free will, in whose hand We have placed you,

shall ordain yourself the limits of your nature. We have set you at the world's center that you may from there more easily observe whatever is in the world. We have made you neither of heaven nor of earth, neither mortal nor immortal, so that with freedom of choice and with honor, as though the maker and molder of yourself, you may fashion yourself in whatever shape you shall prefer. You shall have the power to degenerate into the lower forms of life, which are brutish. You shall have the power, out of your soul's judgment, to be reborn into the higher forms, which are divine."

O supreme generosity of God the Father, O highest and most marvelous felicity of man! To him it is granted to have whatever he chooses, to be whatever he wills. Beasts as soon as they are born bring with them from their mother's womb all they will ever possess. Spiritual beings, either from the beginning or soon thereafter, become what they are to be for ever and ever. On man when he came into life the Father conferred the seeds of all kinds and the germs of every way of life. Whatever seeds each man cultivates will grow to maturity and bear in him their own fruit. If they be vegetative, he will be like a plant. If sensitive, he will become brutish. If rational, he will grow into a heavenly being. If intellectual, he will be an angel and the son of God.

---

ence or purification of the soul. Thus regenerated, they became true sages or magi, as the Renaissance called them, who had knowledge of God and of truth. In regaining their original divinity, they reacquired an intimate knowledge of nature and the ability to employ its powers for beneficial purposes. Serious Renaissance magi believed in humans' ability to control nature and became involved in the practice of magic as a means of organizing and controlling experience.

In Italy, the most prominent magi in the late fifteenth century were Ficino and his friend and pupil, Giovanni Pico della Mirandola (1463–1494). Pico produced one of the most famous writings of the Renaissance, the *Oration on the Dignity of Man*. Pico combed diligently through the writings of many philosophers of different backgrounds for the common "nuggets of universal truth" that he believed were all part of God's revelation to humanity. In the *Oration* (see the box above), Pico offered a ringing statement of unlimited human potential: "To him it is

granted to have whatever he chooses, to be whatever he wills."[11] Like Ficino, Pico took an avid interest in Hermetic magic, accepting it as the "science of the Divine," which "embraces the deepest contemplation of the most secret things, and at last the knowledge of all nature."[12]

Education in the Renaissance

The humanist movement had a profound effect on education. Genuinely optimistic about the educability of human beings, Renaissance humanists produced treatises on educational theory and developed secondary schools based on their educational philosophy. Most famous was the one founded in 1423 by Vittorino da Feltre (1378–1446) at Mantua, where the ruler of that small Italian state, Gian Francesco I Gonzaga, wished to provide a humanist school for his children. Vittorino based much of his educational system on the ideas of classical authors, particularly Cicero and Quintilian.

At the core of the academic training Vittorino offered were the "liberal studies." The Renaissance view of the value of the liberal arts was most strongly influenced by a treatise on education called *Concerning Character* by Pietro Paolo Vergerio (1370–1444). This work stressed the importance of the liberal arts as the key to true freedom, enabling individuals to reach their full potential. According to Vergerio, "we call those studies liberal which are worthy of a free man; those studies by which we attain and practice virtue and wisdom; that education which calls forth, trains, and develops those highest gifts of body and mind which ennoble men, and which are rightly judged to rank next in dignity to virtue only. . . ."[13] What, then, were the "liberal studies"?

Amongst these I accord the first place to History, on grounds both of its attractiveness and of its utility, qualities which appeal equally to the scholar and to the statesman. Next in importance ranks Moral Philosophy, which indeed is, in a peculiar sense, a "Liberal Art," in that its purpose is to teach men the secret of true freedom. History, then, gives us the concrete examples of the precepts inculcated by Philosophy. The one shows what men should do, the other what men have said and done in the past, and what practical lessons we may draw therefrom for the present day. I would indicate as the third main branch of study, Eloquence. . . . By philosophy we learn the essential truth of things, which by eloquence we so exhibit in orderly adornment as to bring conviction to differing minds.[14]

The remaining liberal studies included letters (grammar and logic), poetry, mathematics, astronomy, and music. Crucial to all liberal studies was the mastery of Greek and Latin because it enabled students to read the great classical authors who were the foundation stones of the liberal arts. In short, the purpose of a liberal education was to produce individuals who followed a path of virtue and wisdom and possessed the rhetorical skills to persuade others to take it.

Following the Greek precept of a sound mind in a sound body, Vittorino's school at Mantua stressed the need for physical education. Pupils were taught the arts of javelin throwing, archery, and dancing and encouraged to run, wrestle, hunt, and swim frequently. Nor was Christianity excluded from Vittorino's school. His students were taught the Scriptures and the works of the church fathers, especially Saint Augustine.

Humanist schools such as Vittorino's were primarily geared for the education of an elite, the ruling classes of their communities. Largely absent from such schools were females. Vittorino's only female pupils were the two daughters of the Gonzaga ruler of Mantua. While these few female students studied the classics and were encouraged to know some history and to ride, dance, sing, play the lute, and appreciate poetry, they were discouraged from learning mathematics and rhetoric. In the educational treatises of the time, religion and morals were thought to "hold the first place in the education of a Christian lady."

Vittorino and other humanist educators considered a humanist education to be a practical preparation for life. The aim of humanist education was not the creation of a great scholar but a complete citizen. As Vittorino said, "Not everyone is obliged to excel in philosophy, medicine, or the law, nor are all equally favored by nature; but all are destined to live in society and to practice virtue."[15] Humanist schools, combining the classics and Christianity, provided the model for the basic education of the European ruling classes until the twentieth century.

The Development of Vernacular Literature

The humanist emphasis on classical Latin led to its widespread use in the fifteenth and sixteenth centuries, especially among scholars, lawyers, and theologians. Nevertheless, a written vernacular literature had produced some notable works in early versions of French and German in the High Middle Ages. In the fourteenth century, the works of Dante and Chaucer were instrumental in transforming regional dialects into national languages, and in the late fifteenth and early sixteenth centuries, vernacular languages became broad enough in scope to create national literary forms that could compete with and eventually replace Latin.

Dante (1265–1321) came from an old Florentine noble family that had fallen upon hard times. His masterpiece in the Italian vernacular was the *Divine Comedy*, written between 1313 and 1321. Cast in a typical medieval framework, the *Divine Comedy* is basically the story of the soul's progression to salvation, a fundamental medieval preoccupation. The lengthy poem was divided into three major sections corresponding to the realms of the afterworld: hell, purgatory, and heaven or paradise. In the "Inferno," Dante is led on an imaginary journey through hell by his guide, the classical author Virgil (see the box on p. 476). Symbolically, the "Inferno" reflects despair, while "Purgatory," the second stage of his journey, reflects hope. In "Paradise," Dante is eventually guided by Saint Bernard, a symbol of mystical contemplation. The saint turns Dante over to the Virgin Mary because grace is necessary to achieve the final step of

❧ Dante's Vision of Hell ❧

The Divine Comedy of Dante Alighieri is regarded as one of the greatest literary works of all time. Many consider it the supreme summary of medieval European thought. It combines allegory with a remarkable amount of contemporary history. Indeed, forty-three of the seventy-nine people consigned to hell in the "Inferno" were Florentines. This excerpt is taken from Canto XVIII of the "Inferno," in which Dante and Virgil visit the eighth circle of hell, which is divided into ten trenches containing those who had committed malicious frauds upon their fellow human beings.

Dante, "Inferno," The Divine Comedy

We had already come to where the walk
crosses the second bank, from which it lifts
another arch, spanning from rock to rock.

Here we heard people whine in the next chasm,
and knock and thump themselves with open palms,
and blubber through their snouts as if in a spasm.

Steaming from that pit, a vapor rose
over the banks, crusting them with a slime
that sickened my eyes and hammered at my nose.

That chasm sinks so deep we could not sight
its bottom anywhere until we climbed
along the rock arch to its greatest height.

Once there, I peered down; and I saw long lines
of people in a river of excrement
that seemed the overflow of the world's latrines.

I saw among the felons of that pit
one wraith who might or might not have been tonsured—
one could not tell, he was so smeared with shit.

He bellowed: "You there, why do you stare at me
more than at all the others in this stew?"
And I to him: "Because if memory

serves me, I knew you when your hair was dry.
You are Alessio Interminelli da Lucca.
That's why I pick you from this filthy fry."

And he then, beating himself on his clown's head:
"Down to this have the flatteries I sold
the living sunk me here among the dead."

And my Guide prompted then: "Lean forward a bit
and look beyond him, there—do you see that one
scratching herself with dungy nails, the strumpet

who fidgets to her feet, then to a crouch?
It is the whore Thäis who told her lover
when he sent to ask her, 'Do you thank me much?'

'Much? Nay, past all believing!' And with this
Let us turn from the sight of this abyss."

entering the presence of God, where one beholds "The love that moves the sun and the other stars."[16] Allegorically, "Paradise" reflects perfection or salvation.

Geoffrey Chaucer (c. 1340–1400) brought a new level of sophistication to the English vernacular language in his famous work *The Canterbury Tales*. His beauty of expression and clear, forceful language were important in transforming his East Midland dialect into the chief ancestor of the modern English language. Although Chaucer's materials were taken from a typically medieval literary tradition, he placed much emphasis on individual characters.

The Canterbury Tales are the stories told by a group of twenty-nine pilgrims journeying from Southwark to the tomb of Saint Thomas at Canterbury. This format gave Chaucer the chance to portray an entire range of English society, both high and low born. Among others, he presented the Knight, the Squire, the Yeoman, the Prioress, the Monk, the Merchant, the Student, the Lawyer, the Carpenter, the Cook, the Doctor, the Plowman, and, of course, "A Good Wife was there from beside the city of Bath—a little deaf, which was a pity." The stories these pilgrims told to while away the time on the journey were just as varied as the storytellers themselves: knightly romances, fairy tales, saints' lives, sophisticated satires, and crude anecdotes.

The Impact of Printing

The period of the Renaissance witnessed the development of printing, one of the most important technological innovations of civilization. The art of printing made an immediate impact on European intellectual life and thought. Printing from hand-carved wooden blocks had been present in the West since the twelfth century and in China even before that. What was new in the fifteenth century in Europe was multiple printing with movable metal type. The development of printing from movable type was a gradual process that culminated sometime between 1445 and 1450; Johannes Gutenberg of Mainz played an important role in bringing the process to completion. Gutenberg's Bible, completed in 1455 or 1456, was the first real book produced from movable type.

The new printing spread rapidly throughout Europe in the last half of the fifteenth century. Printing presses were established throughout the Holy Roman Empire in the 1460s and within ten years had spread to Italy, France, the Low Countries, Spain, and eastern Europe. Especially well known as a printing center was Venice, home by 1500 to almost one hundred printers who had produced almost two million volumes.

By 1500, there were over a thousand printers in Europe who had published almost 40,000 titles (between eight and ten million copies). Probably 50 percent of these books were religious in character—Bibles and biblical commentaries, books of devotion, and sermons. Next in importance were the Latin and Greek classics, medieval grammars, legal handbooks, works on philosophy, and an ever-growing number of popular romances.

Printing became one of the largest industries in Europe, and its effects were soon felt in many areas of European life. Although some humanists condemned printing because they believed that it vulgarized learning, the printing of books actually encouraged the development of scholarly research and the desire to attain knowledge. Moreover, printing facilitated cooperation among scholars and helped produce standardized and definitive texts. Printing also stimulated the rise of an ever-expanding lay reading public, a development that had an enormous impact on European society. Indeed, the new religious ideas of the Reformation would never have spread as rapidly as they did in the sixteenth century without the printing press.

The Artistic Renaissance

Leonardo da Vinci, one of the great Italian Renaissance artists, once explained: "Hence the painter will produce pictures of small merit if he takes for his standard the pictures of others, but if he will study from natural objects he will bear good fruit . . . those who take for their standard any one but nature . . . weary themselves in vain."[17] Renaissance artists considered the imitation of nature to be their primary goal. Their search for naturalism became an end in itself: to persuade onlookers of the reality of the object or event they were portraying. At the same time, the new artistic standards reflected a new attitude of mind as well, one in which human beings became the focus of attention, the "center and measure of all things," as one artist proclaimed.

The frescoes by Masaccio (1401–1428) in the Brancacci Chapel have long been regarded as the first masterpieces of Early Renaissance art. With his use of monumental figures, the demonstration of a more realistic relationship between figures and landscape, and the visual representation of the laws of perspective, a new realistic style of painting was born. Onlookers become aware of a world of reality that appears to be a continuation of their own.

This new or Renaissance style was absorbed and modified by other Florentine painters in the fifteenth century. Especially important was the development of an experimental trend that took two directions. One emphasized the mathematical side of painting, the working out of the laws of perspective and the organization of outdoor space and light by geometry and perspective. The other aspect of the experimental trend involved the investigation of movement and anatomical structure. Indeed, the realistic portrayal of the human nude became one of the foremost preoccupations of Italian Renaissance art. The fifteenth century, then, was a period of experimentation and technical mastery. By the end of the century, Italian painters had created a new artistic environment. Many artists had mastered the new techniques for a scientific observation of the world around them and were now ready to move into individualistic forms of creative expression. This marked the shift to the High Renaissance.

The High Renaissance was dominated by the work of three artistic giants, Leonardo da Vinci (1452–1519),

◆ **Masaccio, *Tribute Money*.** With the frescoes of Masaccio, regarded by many as the first great works of Early Renaissance art, a new realistic style of painting was born. The *Tribute Money* was one of a series of frescoes that Masaccio painted in the Brancacci Chapel in the church of Santa Maria del Carmine in Florence. In illustrating a story from the Bible, Masaccio used a rational system of perspective to create a realistic relationship between the figures and their background.

Raphael (1483–1520), and Michelangelo (1475–1564). Leonardo represents a transitional figure in the shift to High Renaissance principles. He carried on the fifteenth-century experimental tradition by studying everything and even dissecting human bodies in order to better see how nature worked. But Leonardo stressed the need to advance beyond such realism and initiated the High Renaissance's preoccupation with the idealization of nature, or the attempt to generalize from realistic portrayal to an ideal form. Leonardo's *Last Supper* is a brilliant summary of fifteenth-century trends in its organization of space and use of perspective to depict subjects three-dimensionally in a two-dimensional medium. But it is also more. The figure of Philip is idealized, and there are profound psychological dimensions to the work. The words of Christ that "one of you shall betray me" are experienced directly as each of the apostles reveals his personality and his relationship to the Savior. In one of his notebooks, Leonardo wrote that the highest and most difficult aim of painting is to depict "the intention of man's soul." Through gestures and movement, Leonardo hoped to reveal a person's inner life.

Raphael blossomed as a painter at an early age; at twenty-five, he was already regarded as one of Italy's best painters. Well known for his frescoes in the Vatican Palace, Raphael was especially acclaimed for his numerous madonnas, in which he attempted to achieve an ideal of beauty far surpassing human standards. His *Alba Madonna* reveals a world of balance, harmony, and order—basically, the underlying principles of the art of the classical world of Greece and Rome.

Michelangelo, an accomplished painter, sculptor, and architect, was another giant of the High Renaissance. Fiercely driven by his desire to create, he worked with great passion and energy on a remarkable number of projects. Michelangelo was influenced by Neoplatonism, especially evident in his figures on the ceiling of the Sistine Chapel. These muscular figures reveal an ideal type of human being with perfect proportions. In good Neoplatonic fashion, their beauty is meant to be a reflection of divine beauty; the more beautiful the body, the more God-like the figure.

The Northern Artistic Renaissance

In trying to provide an exact portrayal of their world, the artists of the north (especially the Low Countries) and Italy took different approaches. In Italy, the human form became the primary vehicle of expression as Italian artists sought to master the technical skills that allowed them to portray humans in realistic settings. The large wall spaces of Italian churches had given rise to the art of fresco painting, but in the north, the prevalence of Gothic cathedrals with their stained glass windows resulted in more emphasis on illuminated manuscripts and wooden panel painting for altarpieces. The space avail-

♦ **Leonardo da Vinci, *The Last Supper*.** Leonardo da Vinci was the impetus behind the High Renaissance concern for the idealization of nature, moving from a realistic portrayal of the human figure to an idealized form. Evident in Leonardo's *Last Supper* is his effort to depict a person's character and inner nature by the use of gesture and movement. Unfortunately, Leonardo used an experimental technique in this fresco, which soon led to its physical deterioration.

able in these works was limited, and great care was required to depict each object, leading northern painters to become masters at rendering details.

The most influential northern school of art in the fifteenth century was centered in Flanders. Jan van Eyck (1380?–1441) was among the first to use oil paint, a medium that enabled the artist to use a varied range of colors and make changes to create fine details. In his *Giovanni Arnolfini and Bride*, van Eyck's attention to detail is staggering: precise portraits, a glittering chandelier, a mirror reflecting the objects in the room, and the effects of light filtering through the window. Although each detail was rendered as observed, it is evident that van Eyck's comprehension of perspective was still uncertain. His work is truly indicative of northern Renaissance painters, who, in their effort to imitate nature, did so not by mastery of the laws of perspective and proportion, but by empirical observation of visual reality and the accurate portrayal of details. Moreover, northern painters placed great emphasis on the emotional intensity of religious feeling. Michelangelo summarized the difference between northern and Italian Renaissance painting in these words:

> In Flanders, they paint, before all things, to render exactly and deceptively the outward appearance of things. The painters choose, by preference, subjects provoking transports of piety, like the figures of saints or of prophets. But

♦ **Raphael, *The Alba Madonna*.** Although he died at the age of thirty-seven, Raphael achieved in his own lifetime a fame comparable to that of Michelangelo and Leonardo da Vinci. In his madonnas, Raphael sought an idealized beauty that was typical of the High Renaissance. His serene *Alba Madonna* illustrates his mastery of the classical principles of balance, harmony, clarity, and rational composition.

♦ **Michelangelo, *Creation of Adam*.** In 1508, Pope Julius II recalled Michelangelo to Rome and commissioned him to decorate the ceiling of the Sistine Chapel. This colossal project was not completed until 1512. Michelangelo attempted to tell the story of the Fall of Man by depicting nine scenes from the biblical book of Genesis. In this scene, the well-proportioned figure of Adam, meant by Michelangelo to be a reflection of divine beauty, awaits the divine spark.

most of the time they paint what are called landscapes with plenty of figures. Though the eye is agreeably impressed, these pictures have neither choice of values nor grandeur. In short, this art is without power and without distinction; it aims at rendering minutely many things at the same time, of which a single one would have sufficed to call forth a man's whole application.[18]

By the end of the fifteenth century, however, artists from the north began to study in Italy and were visually influenced by what artists were doing there.

One northern artist of this later period who was greatly affected by the Italians was Albrecht Dürer (1471–1528) from Nuremberg. Dürer made two trips to Italy and absorbed most of what the Italians could teach, as is evident in his mastery of the laws of perspective and Renaissance theories of proportion. He wrote detailed treatises on both subjects. At the same time, as in his famous *Adoration of the Magi*, Dürer did not reject the use of minute details characteristic of northern artists. He did try, however, to integrate those details more harmoniously into his works and, like the Italian artists of the High Renaissance, tried to achieve a standard of ideal beauty by a careful examination of the human form.

Conclusion

In the High Middle Ages, European civilization developed many of its fundamental features. Territorial states, parliaments, capitalist trade and industry, banks, cities, and vernacular literatures were all products of that fertile period. During the same time, the Catholic church under the direction of the papacy reached its apogee. Fourteenth-century European society, however, was challenged by an overwhelming number of disintegrative forces. Devastating plague, decline in trade and industry, bank failures, peasant revolts pitting lower classes against the upper classes, seemingly constant warfare, aristocratic factional conflict that undermined political stability, the absence of the popes from Rome, and even the spectacle of two popes condemning each other as the antichrist all seemed to overpower Europeans in this "calamitous century." Not surprisingly, much of the art of the period depicted the Four Horsemen of the Apocalypse described in the New Testament book of Revelation: Death, Famine, Pestilence, and War. No doubt, to some people it appeared that the last days of the world were at hand.

♦ **Jan van Eyck,** *Giovanni Arnolfini and His Bride.*
Northern painters took great care in depicting each object and became masters at rendering details. This emphasis on a realistic portrayal is clearly evident in this oil painting, supposedly a portrait of Giovanni Arnolfini, an Italian merchant who had settled in Bruges, and his wife, Giovanna Cenami.

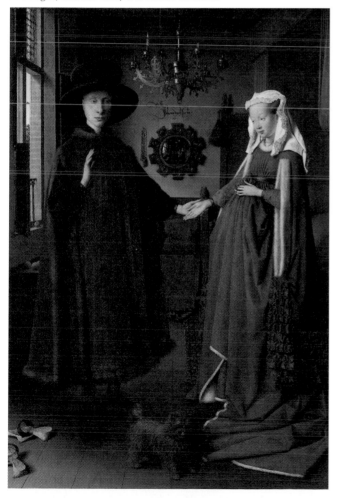

♦ **Albrecht Dürer,** *Adoration of the Magi.* By the end of the fifteenth century, northern artists began studying in Italy and adopting many of the techniques used by Italian painters. As is evident in this painting, which was the central panel for an altarpiece done for Frederick the Wise in 1504, Albrecht Dürer masterfully incorporated the laws of perspective and the ideals of proportion into his works. At the same time, he did not abandon the preoccupation with detail typical of northern artists.

The new European society, however, proved remarkably resilient. Periods of disintegration are usually paralleled by the emergence of new ideas and new practices. The Renaissance was a period of transition that witnessed a continuation of the economic, political, and social trends that had begun in the High Middle Ages. It was also a new age in which intellectuals and artists proclaimed a new vision of humankind and raised fundamental questions about the value and importance of the individual.

Europeans were also engaging in new adventures in the age of the Renaissance. The discovery of new trade routes to the East and the "accidental" discovery of the Americas encouraged Europeans to venture outside the medieval world in which they had been enclosed for virtually a thousand years. A new era of world history was beginning to dawn, and it is to that story that we must now turn.

482 CHAPTER 13

CHAPTER NOTES

1. Quoted in H. S. Lucas, "The Great European Famine of 1315, 1316, and 1317," *Speculum* 5 (1930): 359.
2. Quoted in Robert Gottfried, *The Black Death* (New York, 1983), p. xiii.
3. Jean Froissart, *Chronicles*, ed. and trans. Geoffrey Brereton (Harmondsworth, 1968), p. 111.
4. Quoted in Susan Stuard, "Dominion of Gender: Women's Fortunes in the High Middle Ages," in Renate Bridenthal, Claudia Koonz, and Susan Stuard, eds., *Becoming Visible: Women in European History*, 2d ed. (Boston, 1987), p. 169.
5. Froissart, *Chronicles*, p. 89.
6. Niccolò Machiavelli, *The Prince*, trans. David Wootton (Indianapolis, 1995), p. 48.
7. Ibid., p. 55.
8. Quoted in Jacob Burckhardt, *The Civilization of the Renaissance in Italy*, trans. S. G. C. Middlemore (London, 1960), p. 81.
9. Baldassare Castiglione, *The Book of the Courtier*, trans. Charles S. Singleton (Garden City, N.Y., 1959), pp. 288–89.
10. Quoted in De Lamar Jensen, *Renaissance Europe* (Lexington, Mass., 1981), p. 94.
11. Giovanni Pico della Mirandola, *Oration on the Dignity of Man*, in E. Cassirer, P. O. Kristeller, J. H. Randall, Jr., eds., *The Renaissance Philosophy of Man* (Chicago, 1948), p. 225.
12. Ibid., pp. 247–49.
13. W. H. Woodward, *Vittorino da Feltre and Other Humanist Educators* (Cambridge, 1897), p. 102.
14. Ibid., pp. 106–7.
15. Quoted in Iris Origo, "The Education of Renaissance Man," in *The Light of the Past* (New York, 1959), p. 136.
16. Dante Alighieri, *The Divine Comedy*, trans. Dorothy Sayers (New York, 1962), "Paradise," Canto XXXIII, line 145.
17. Quoted in Elizabeth G. Holt, ed., *A Documentary History of Art* (Garden City, N.Y., 1957), 1:286.
18. Quoted in Johan Huizinga, *The Waning of the Middle Ages* (Garden City, N.Y., 1956), p. 265.

SUGGESTED READINGS

For a general introduction to the fourteenth and fifteenth centuries, see D. Hay, *Europe in the Fourteenth and Fifteenth Centuries* (New York, 1966) and G. Holmes, *Europe: Hierarchy and Revolt, 1320–1450* (New York, 1975).

On the Black Death, see P. Ziegler, *The Black Death* (New York, 1969) and R. S. Gottfried, *The Black Death: Natural and Human Disaster in Medieval Europe* (New York, 1983). On the peasant and urban revolts of the fourteenth century, see M. Mollat and P. Wolff, *The Popular Revolutions of the Late Middle Ages* (Winchester, Mass., 1973). Brief but basic works on economic matters are H. A. Miskimin, *The Economy of Early Renaissance Europe, 1300–1460* (New York, 1975) and *The Economy of Later Renaissance Europe, 1460–1600* (New York, 1978).

The classic work on the Hundred Years' War is E. Perroy, *The Hundred Years War* (New York, 1951). A more recent account is C. Allmand, *The Hundred Years's War: England and France at War, c. 1300–1450* (New York, 1988). On Joan of Arc, see M. Warner, *Joan of Arc: The Image of Female Heroism* (New York, 1981). On the political history of the fourteenth and fifteenth centuries, see B. Guenée, *States and Rulers in Later Medieval Europe*, trans. J. Vale (Oxford, 1985). Works on individual countries and their rulers include P. M. Kendall, *Louis XI: The Universal Spider* (New York, 1971); J. R. Lander, *Crown and Nobility, 1450–1509* (London, 1976); F. R. H. Du Boulay, *Germany in the Later Middle Ages* (London, 1983); and J. N. Hillgarth, *The Spanish Kingdoms, 1250–1516*, vol. 2, *Castilian Hegemony 1410–1516* (New York, 1978). Some good works on eastern Europe include P. W. Knoll, *The Rise of the Polish Monarchy* (Chicago, 1972) and C. A. Macartney, *Hun-*

gary: *A Short History* (Edinburgh, 1962). On the fall of Constantinople, see the classic work by S. Runciman, *The Fall of Constantinople, 1453* (Cambridge, 1965).

The best overall study of the Italian states is L. Martines, *Power and Imagination: City-States in Renaissance Italy* (New York, 1979), although D. Hay and J. Law, *Italy in the Age of the Renaissance* (London, 1989) is also a good, up-to-date survey. The best introduction to Renaissance Florence is G. A. Brucker, *Renaissance Florence*, rev. ed. (New York, 1983). On the Medici period, see J. R. Hale, *Florence and the Medici: The Pattern of Control* (London, 1977). A popular biography of Isabella d'Este is G. Marek, *The Bed and the Throne* (New York, 1976). On the *condottieri*, see M. Mallett, *Mercenaries and Their Masters: Warfare in Renaissance Italy* (Totowa, N.J., 1974). Machiavelli's life can be examined in J. R. Hale, *Machiavelli and Renaissance Italy* (New York, 1960).

Good general studies of the church in the fourteenth century can be found in F. P. Oakley, *The Western Church in the Later Middle Ages* (Ithaca, N.Y., 1980) and S. Ozment, *The Age of Reform, 1250–1550: An Intellectual and Religious History of Late Medieval and Reformation Europe* (New Haven, Conn., 1980). On the Avignonese papacy, see Y. Renouard, *The Avignon Papacy, 1305–1403* (London, 1970). Aspects of the Renaissance papacy can be examined in E. Lee, *Sixtus IV and Men of Letters* (Rome, 1978); M. Mallet, *The Borgias* (New York, 1969); and P. Partner, *Renaissance Rome, 1500–1559: A Portrait of a Society* (Berkeley, Calif., 1976).

The classic study of the Italian Renaissance is J. Burckhardt, *The Civilization of the Renaissance in Italy* (London, 1960), first published in 1860. General works on the Renaissance in Europe include D. L. Jensen, *Renaissance Europe*, 2d ed. (Lexington, Mass., 1991); E. Breisach, *Renaissance Europe, 1300–1517* (New York,

1973); J. Hale, *The Civilization of Europe in the Renaissance* (New York, 1994); and the classic work by M. P. Gilmore, *The World of Humanism, 1453–1517* (New York, 1962). A new approach to the culture of Renaissance Italy can be found in P. Burke, *The Italian Renaissance* (Princeton, N.J., 1986).

Numerous facets of social life in the Renaissance are examined in J. R. Hale, *Renaissance Europe: The Individual and Society* (London, 1971); B. Pullan, *Rich and Poor in Renaissance Venice* (Cambridge, Mass., 1971); and G. Ruggiero, *The Boundaries of Eros: Sex Crime and Sexuality in Renaissance Venice* (Oxford, 1985). A wealth of material on everyday life is provided in the second volume of *A History of Private Life* edited by G. Duby, *Revelations of the Medieval World* (Cambridge, Mass., 1988). On family and marriage, see D. Herlihy, *The Family in Renaissance Italy* (St. Louis, 1974) and the valuable C. Klapisch-Zuber, *Women, Family, and Ritual in Renaissance Italy* (Chicago, 1985). Women are examined in M. L. King, *Women of the Renaissance* (Chicago, 1991).

Brief introductions to Renaissance humanism can be found in D. Kelley, *Renaissance Humanism* (Boston, 1991) and C. G Nauert, Jr., *Humanism and the Culture of Renaissance Europe* (Cambridge, 1995). A more detailed analysis of various aspects of Renaissance humanism is contained in C. Trinkaus, *The Scope of Renaissance Humanism* (Ann Arbor, 1983). The fundamental work on fifteenth-century civic humanism is H. Baron, *The Crisis of the Early Italian Renaissance*, 2d ed. (Princeton, N.J., 1966). The impact of printing is exhaustively examined in E. Eisenstein, *The Printing Press as an Agent of Change*, 2 vols. (New York, 1978). Good surveys of Renaissance art include M. Levy, *Early Renaissance* (Harmondsworth, 1967) and L. Murray, *The High Renaissance* (New York, 1967). Also of value is B. Cole, *The Renaissance Artist at Work from Pisano to Titian* (London, 1983).

REFLECTION

New Patterns of Civilization

*I*n Part II of this book, we examined the period that followed the collapse of the civilizations of antiquity down to the end of the fifteenth century, a date that marks the beginning of the European Age of Exploration and the inauguration of a new stage of world history. During this period of over one thousand years, a number of significant forces were at work in human society. The concept of civilization gradually spread from such heartland regions as the Middle East, the Mediterranean basin, the South Asian subcontinent, and China into new areas of the world—to sub-Saharan Africa, to central and western Europe, to Southeast Asia, and even to the islands of Japan, off the eastern edge of the Eurasian landmass. Across the oceans, unique but advanced civilizations began to take shape in the Americas. In the meantime, the vast migration of peoples continued, leading not only to bitter conflict but also to increased cultural interchange of technology as well as ideas. The end result was the transformation of separate and distinct cultures and civilizations into an increasingly complex and vast world system embracing not only technology and trade, but also ideas and religious beliefs. Although this world system did not by any means include all the peoples and societies in the world—the Amerindian civilizations in the New World were almost certainly totally isolated from it, as were peoples living in stateless societies in various parts of Africa and Asia—its network of goods and ideas extended from the Atlantic to the Pacific and created an interdependent world, in which the economic livelihood, the physical well-being, and even the religious beliefs of one people were linked to the fate of other peoples often living thousands of miles away.

What explains this explosion in human activity? Certainly, one answer is the advance in technology. Better technology, in the form of improved irrigation methods, the introduction of new crops, and the increased use of the iron plow, led to a substantial rise in food production, thus creating wealth that could be used for the purchase of other goods. Improved technology also contributed to advances in ship construction and navigational techniques. Other factors were the mastery of monsoon patterns in the Indian Ocean and the introduction of the camel into North Africa and the Middle East. The wealth brought about by increased trade undoubtedly helped to stimulate the demand for new luxury goods and other commodities, many of which could only be imported from foreign countries. During the first millennium C.E., the great trade routes of the traditional world—the Silk Road from China to the Middle East and then to the Mediterranean, the caravan trade across the Sahara, and the maritime network that stretched across the Indian Ocean—all reached their maturity.

As had been the case during antiquity, the Middle East was at the heart of this activity. During the first centuries of the first millennium C.E., trade passing through the region declined as a result of the collapse of the Han dynasty and the Roman Empire, but it began to revive in the sixth century and then spurted forward with the rise of the Tang in China and the gradual revival of societies in the Mediterranean. The Arab Empire, which took shape after the death of Muhammad in the early seventh century, provided the key link in the trade routes reappearing through the region. Muslim traders—both Arab and Berber—opened contacts with West African societies south of the Sahara, while their ships followed the monsoon winds eastward as far as the Spice Islands in Southeast Asia. Nomads from Central Asia carried goods back and forth along the Silk Road between the Middle East and China. For the next several hundred years, the great cities of the Middle East—Mecca, Damascus, and Baghdad—became among the wealthiest in the known world. The Chinese city of Chang'an lay at the eastern extremity of the Silk Road of Central Asia.

Islam's contributions to the human experience during this period were cultural and technological as well as economic. Muslim philosophers preserved the works of the ancient Greeks for posterity, Muslim scientists and mathematicians made discoveries about the nature of the universe and the human body, and Arab cartographers and historians mapped the known world and speculated about the fundamental forces in society. The mosques of Córdoba and Cairo were built with techniques unknown to medieval European architects and engineers.

But the Middle East was not the only or necessarily

even the primary contributor to world trade and civilization during this period. While the Arab Empire became the linchpin of trade between the Mediterranean and eastern and southern Asia, a new center of primary importance in world trade was emerging in East Asia and focused on China. China had been a major participant in regional trade during the Han dynasty, when its silks were already being transported to Rome via Central Asia, but its role had declined after the fall of the Han. Now, with the rise of the great Tang and Song dynasties, China reemerged as a major commercial power in East Asia, trading by sea with Southeast Asia and Japan and by land with the nomadic peoples of Central Asia. In general, overland trade was carried on by non-Chinese peoples in Central Asia, but the Chinese themselves became directly involved in the maritime trade with the countries in the South Seas.

By now, China was not only a regional economic power, but a global one as well. The Silk Road through Turkestan became one of the most important trade routes of the era, and during the Ming dynasty, Chinese fleets briefly sailed across the Indian Ocean as far as the Red Sea and the eastern coast of Africa.

Like the Middle East, China was also a prime source of new technology. From China came paper, printing, and the compass as well as gunpowder. The double-hulled Chinese junks that entered the Indian Ocean during the Ming dynasty were slow and cumbersome, but extremely seaworthy and capable of carrying substantial quantities of goods over long distances. Among China's other contributions were porcelain, chess, and the iron stirrup. Many of these inventions arrived in Europe by way of India or the Middle East, and therefore their Chinese origins were unknown in the West.

Increasing trade on a regional or global basis also led to the exchange of ideas. Buddhism was brought to China by merchants, and Islam first arrived in sub-Saharan Africa and the Indonesian archipelago in the same manner. In their new environments, these religions initially had an impact mainly on other merchant groups and in the cities, but in some cases they gradually gained favor in the countryside. Sometimes this was the result of support from kings or princes, who viewed conversion to the new faith as politically or economically advantageous. Not all religions, of course, succeeded in transplanting themselves. Although a small community of Nestorian Christians established roots in Central Asia and China, their religion was never able to make the transition to a mass faith.

Merchants were not the only way religious and cultural ideas spread, however. Sometimes migration, conquest, or relatively peaceful processes played a part. The case of the Bantu-speaking peoples in Central Africa is apparently an example of peaceful expansion, while Islam sometimes followed the path of Arab warriors, although it apparently was rarely imposed by force on the local population. In some instances, as with the Mongols, the conquerors made no effort to convert others to their religions. Christian monks, motivated by missionary fervor, converted many of the peoples of central and eastern Europe. Roman Catholic monks brought Latin Christianity to the Germanic and western Slavic peoples while monks from the Byzantine Empire largely converted the southern and eastern Slavs to Eastern Orthodox Christianity.

How precisely did the exchange of ideas and beliefs work during this period? According to Jerry Bentley, author of *Old World Encounters: Cross-cultural Contacts and Exchanges in Pre-Modern Times*, the process was quite complex and varied considerably, depending on the time and place. When conversion to a different religion did occur, it usually took place over a protracted period of time and was undertaken primarily for practical reasons. Those who attempted to promote conversions often used incentives or various forms of punishment for noncompliance, such as tax exemption for Muslims. One way to facilitate conversions was the syncretic technique—to relate or identify new beliefs and rituals to familiar ones, as the Buddhists did by adopting Daoist concepts in China.

Attempts at conversion did not always work. Sometimes new religions were resisted fiercely, as the Christians in the Balkans and Spain resisted Islam. Conversion to Christianity was resisted in the Middle East during the crusades and in Central Asia during the Mongol era. In general, Islam and Buddhism were the most successful. Islam spread throughout the Middle East and Central Asia as well as in much of North Africa, while Buddhism took root in China, Japan, and Southeast Asia.

Why were conversion efforts successful in some areas but not in others? In the case of Islam, successful conversion was often the result of strong state sponsorship, as well as a variety of incentives such as exemption from the poll tax and access to various means of livelihood. Islam also undoubtedly benefited from its egalitarian character and its association with material rewards. This was apparently the case in Africa as well as in much of Central Asia. The success of Buddhism in China and Southeast Asia can be partly ascribed to state support, but also to its salvationist message in societies not possessing any other form of universal world religion. In general, it seems clear that conversion was much more likely to succeed in societies not already possessing a world religion. Where such religions already existed, as in India and much of Europe, conversion to Islam was less likely. Followers of Gautama Buddha had the same experience in India.

In any event, as Bentley points out, conversion was an extended process, even when it did occur. Although the conversion to Islam in much of the Middle East was relatively rapid, it took longer among the Berbers. Buddhism took several hundred years to spread beyond the urban community in China and the Mongol tribal peoples.

Even when conversion did take place, key elements of the core doctrine were often changed to adapt to new circumstances. Buddhism in China took on a strong local character, as did Islam in Southeast Asia, where it was forced to coexist with existing spirit beliefs. The practice of Christianity was much different in the Byzantine Empire than in areas controlled by the pope in Rome. In the end, religion took on much of the color of local society.

The same can be said about the transfer of political and social institutions from one society to another. As the cases of Japan, Korea, and Vietnam make clear, Confucian values were affected by the environment when exported abroad, as were Indian ones after crossing the Bay of Bengal to the rising states of Southeast Asia.

Another characteristic of the period between 500 and 1500 C.E. was the almost constant migration of nomadic and seminomadic peoples. Dynamic forces in the Gobi Desert, Central Asia, the Arabian peninsula, and Central Africa provoked vast numbers of peoples to abandon their homelands and seek their livelihood elsewhere. Sometimes the migration was peaceful, as was apparently the case with the Bantu-speaking peoples in Central Africa. More often than not, however, migration produced violent conflict and sometimes invasion and subjugation. Peoples had been moving since the earliest times, as human communities shifted their habitat in search of grazing lands, herds, or fertile lands for agriculture, and migration continued to be a major factor in this period. As had been the case during antiquity, the most active source of migration was Central Asia. From here, Turkic-speaking peoples spilled over the Hindu Kush into northern India, southwest into Persia, and farther west into the Balkans in southeastern Europe. Later, Central Asia gave birth to an even more fearsome force in the form of the Mongols. Mongol expansion began with the unification of Mongol tribes in the Gobi Desert by Genghis Khan and culminated in the advance of Mongolian armies to the gates of central Europe and the conquest of China in the thirteenth century. Wherever they went, they left a train of enormous destruction and loss of life. Contemporaries recount that entire cities were laid waste, and their populations massacred and irrigation networks destroyed. Inadvertently, the Mongols were also the source of a new wave of epidemics that swept through much of Europe and the Middle East in the fourteenth century. The spread of the plague—known at the time as the Black Death—took much of the population of Europe to an early grave before it finally passed.

But there was another side to the era of invasions. Often, as historian Thomas J. Barfield has noted, the nomadic peoples had a symbiotic relationship with the sedentary societies, propping up governments like the Tang dynasty in China in order to protect their source of income. Once nomadic warriors completed their conquests, they settled down to become administrators. Often the results were constructive. The spread of Islam across the Middle East and North Africa not only introduced millions of people to a dynamic new faith but brought a measure of political stability and economic prosperity to the area that it had not possessed since the fall of the Persian Empire. German migrations and Viking incursions contributed to the creation of dynamic societies in Europe, while Turkish invasions led to the rise of states in the Anatolian peninsula and North India.

Even the invasions of the Mongols—the "scourge of God" as Europeans of the thirteenth and fourteenth centuries called them—had constructive as well as destructive consequences. After their initial conquests, for a brief period of three generations, the Mongols provided an avenue for trade throughout the most extensive empire the world had yet seen. When the pope dispatched envoys to the imperial court in Mongolia in the mid-thirteenth century, it was the first time Europeans had traveled the entire distance by land to eastern Asia.

What had caused this vast movement of peoples? Probably a number of factors were involved, but perhaps the major ones were ecological—changes in the climate or the exhaustion of the land by population pressure. Desiccation of pasturelands in the Gobi Desert may have been a major stimulus for Mongol expansion. Exhaustion of the land may have driven the Bantu peoples from their original habitat in the Niger River valley and forced the Aztecs and related Amerindian communities into the Valley of Mexico. Other peoples, such as the Thai and the Burmese, may have been forced to move into Southeast Asia because they in turn had been displaced by new arrivals in their own territories.

Thus, the approximately thousand-year period following the destruction of the ancient empires brought about enormous changes in society. It led to a significant expansion in the technological and material capacity of societies and in the depth of contact among them. During this period, the concept of civilization spread, and the way was prepared for a new stage of world history.

Index

Document Credits

Map Credits

The authors wish to acknowledge their use of the following books as reference in preparing the maps listed here:

Map 2.2   Geoffrey Barraclough, ed., *Times Atlas of World History*, (Maplewood, N.J.: Hammond Inc., 1978), p. 65.

Map 3.2   Geoffrey Barraclough, ed., *Times Atlas of World History*, (Maplewood, N.J.: Hammond Inc., 1978), p. 63.

Map 3.3   Conrad Schirokauer, *A Brief History of Chinese and Japanese Civilizations*, 2d ed. (San Diego: Harcourt Brace Jovanovich, 1989), p. 52.

Map 3.4   Hammond Past Worlds: *The Times Atlas of Archeology*, (Maplewood, N.J.: Hammond Inc. 1988), pp. 190–191.

Map 6.1   A & B Geoffrey Barraclough, ed., *Times Atlas of World History*, (Maplewood, N.J.: Hammond Inc., 1978), p. 47.

Map 6.3   Michael Coe, Dean Snow and Elizabeth Benson, *Atlas of Ancient America* (New York: Facts on File, 1988), p. 144.

Map 6.4   Phillipa Fernandez-Arnesto, *Atlas of World Exlporation*, (New York: Harper Collins, 1991), p. 35.

Map 7.3   Geoffrey Barraclough, ed., *Times Atlas of World History*, (Maplewood, N.J.: Hammond Inc., 1978), p. 134–135.

Map 7.4   Geoffrey Barraclough, ed., *Times Atlas of World History*, (Maplewood, N.J.: Hammond Inc., 1978), p. 135.

Map 8.1   Geoffrey Barraclough, ed., *Times Atlas of World History*, (Maplewood, N.J.: Hammond Inc., 1978), pp. 44–45.

Map 8.4   Geoffrey Barraclough, ed., *Times Atlas of World History*, (Maplewood, N.J.: Hammond Inc., 1978), p. 136–137.

Map 9.1   Michael Edwardes, *A History of India* (London: Thames and Hudson, 1961), p. 79.

Map 10.1   John K. Fairbank, Edwin O. Reischauer, and Albert M. Craig, *East Asia: Tradition and Transformation* (Boston: Houghton Mifflin, 1973), p. 103

Map 10.2   Albert Hermann, *An Historical Atlas of China* (Chicago: Aidine, 1966), p. 13.

Map 10.4   Map 6.4 Phillipa Fernandez-Arnesto, *Atlas of World Exlporation*, (New York: Harper Collins, 1991), p. 22.

Map 11.1   John K. Fairbank, Edwin O. Reischauer, and Albert M. Craig, *East Asia: Tradition and Transformation* (Boston: Houghton Mifflin, 1973), p. 363.

Photo Credits

CHAPTER 1

6 © British Museum, London, reproduced by Courtesy of the Trustees of the British Museum 9 Francois Ducasse/Photo Researchers, Inc. 12 © British Museum, London, reproduced by Courtesy of the Trustees of the British Museum 15 Babylonian, *Stele of Hammurabi*, Musée du Louvre, © Photo R.M.N. 23 *Pair Statue of King Mycerinus and His Queen; From Giza, Dynasty IV, 2599–1571 B.C. Slate Schist, 54½ in. Harvard MFA Expedition. Courtesy, Museum of Fine Arts, Boston 25 © Will & Deni McIntyre, Photo Researchers, Inc. 28 Erich Lessing/Art Resource, NY 29 ©Adam Woolfitt/Robert Harding Picture Library 32 © British Museum, London, reproduced by Courtesy of the Trustees of the British Museum 37 © British Museum, London, reproduced by Courtesy of the Trustees of the British Museum 40 *Archers of the Persian Guard*, Musée du Louvre, © Photo R.M.N.

CHAPTER 2

44 Borromeo/Art Resource, NY 48 *top* © Royal Smeets Offset, Weert 48 *bottom* Scala/Art Resource, NY 49 © Royal Smeets Offset, Weert 50 Borromeo/Art Resource, NY 60 Courtesy of the British Library, Oriental & India Office Collection 63 © Royal Smeets Offset, Weert 66 Borromeo/Art Resource, NY 70 Borromeo/Art Resource, NY 73 Robert Harding Picture Library 74 Robert Harding Picture Library 75 © Royal Smeets Offset, Weert

CHAPTER 3

78 Robert Harding Picture Library 81 Werner Forman Archive, British Library/Art Resource, NY 85 Art Resource, NY 97 Robert Harding Picture Library 98 Courtesy of William J. Duiker 100 *Detail of Pediment*, right: five male figures, *Lintel and Pediment of Tomb*, 50 B.C.–50 A.D. Artist unknown, China, (Han Dynasty), Earthenware, hollow tiles painted in ink and colors on a white/washed background, 73.8 x 204.7 cm, Denman Waldo Ross Collection, Courtesy of Museum of Fine Arts, Boston 102 Robert Harding Picture Library 103 Courtesy of William J. Duiker 105 Michael Holford, London 107 Robert Harding Picture Library 108 Eric Lessing/Art Resource, NY 108 Robert Harding Picture Library 109 O. Louis Mazzatenta/National Geographic Society Image Collection

CHAPTER 4

114 © Michael Holford, London 116 © Dimitrios Harissiadis, Athens 117 Eric Lessing/Art Resource, NY 121 Scala/Art Resource, NY 128 © British Museum, reproduced by Courtesy of the Trustees of the British Museum 132 © Michael Holford, London 133 Scala/Art Resource, NY 136 The Metropolitan Museum of Art, Fletcher Fund, 1931(31.11.10) 138 *Bust of Alexander*, Musée du Louvre, © Photo R.M.N. 145 The Metropolitan Museum of Art, Fletcher Fund, 1920 (20.2.21) 146 The Metropolitan Museum of Art, Fletcher Fund, 1909 (09.39) 149 Leonard von Matt/Photo Researchers, Inc.

CHAPTER 5

152 Photo © Eberhard Thiem, Lotos-Film, Kaufbeuren, Germany 154 Art Resource, NY 159 British Museum, Photo © Michael Holford, London 164 Scala/Art Resource, NY 167 Photo Vatican Museums 171 Photo © Eberhard Thiem, Lotos-Film, Kaufbeuren, Germany 172 Leonard von Matt/Photo Researchers, Inc. 175 © Thomas S. England/Photo Researchers, Inc. 177 The Metropolitan Museum of Art/Rogers Fund, 1903 (03.14.5) 181 Roger Wood/Corbis-Bettmann 183 Scala/Art Resource, NY

CHAPTER 6

202 Courtesy of William J. Duiker 206 Richard A Cooke III/Tony Stone Images 208 Detail—Mural Room 2, Bonampak, Chiapas, Mexico. © Pres. and fellows of Harvard College, 1988, All rights reserved. Peabody Museum, Harvard, Photography by Hillel Burger 210 *From Atlas of Ancient America* by Michael Coe, Dean Snow and Elizabeth Benson/Andromeda Oxford Limited, Oxford, England 211 Lee Boltin Picture Library 212 Courtesy of William J. Duiker 216 Courtesy of William J. Duiker 218 Lee Boltin Picture Library 222 Courtesy of William J. Duiker 226 Kevin Schafer/Tony Stone Images 227 Robert Harding Picture Library 228 Courtesy of William J. Duiker

CHAPTER 7

230 E.U.L.M.S. 20, fol.25r, reproduced by permission of the Edinburgh University Library 233, *top* Mehmet Biber/Photo Researchers, Inc. 233, *bottom* E.U.L.M.S. 20, fol.25r, reproduced by permission of the Edinburgh University Library 244 OR MS 20 folio 111V, reproduced by permission of the Edinburgh University Library 245 Bibliotheque Nationale, Paris 246 Courtesy of William J. Duiker 249 © Giraudon-Orion Press/Art Resource, NY 254 Courtesy of William J. Duiker 256, *top* Robert Frerck/Odyssey Productions/Chicago 256, *bottom* Fred J. Maroon/Photo Researchers, Inc. 257 Courtesy of William J. Duiker

CHAPTER 8

260 10095 i3; drawing by Caillie of Timbuktu; reproduced by permission of the British Library **264** Robert Harding Picture Library **266, top** Werner Forman/Art Resource, NY **266, bottom** Eric Lessing/Art Resource, NY **278** Atlas Catalan, Bibliotheque Nationale, Paris **279** Ian Tomlinson/Robert Harding Picture Library **280** 10095 i3; drawing by Caillie of Timbuktu; reproduced by permission of the British Library **285, left** Michael Holford, London **285, right** Werner Forman/British Museum/Art Resource, NY **286** Werner Forman/Art Resource, NY **288** Angela Fisher/Robert Estall Photographs

CHAPTER 9

292 Courtesy of William J. Duiker **298** Courtesy of William J. Duiker **301** Earl Young/Tony Stone Images **309** S. Fiore/Explorer **310, top** Courtesy of William J. Duiker **310, bottom** Courtesy of William J. Duiker **312** Marcello Berntinetti/Photo Researchers, Inc. **317** Courtesy of William J. Duiker **322** Courtesy of William J. Duiker **323** Courtesy of William J. Duiker **324** Courtesy of William J. Duiker **325** Courtesy of William J. Duiker

CHAPTER 10

330 Courtesy of the Board of Trustees of the Victoria and Albert Museum **332** Pelliot Chinois 4518(39) Bibliotheque Nationale, Paris **341** Robert Harding Picture Library **342** Courtesy of William J. Duiker **344** *Spring Festival on the River*; Detail, The Metropolitan Museum of Art, Fletcher Fund, 1947, The A. W. Bahr collection, (47.18.1) **354** Courtesy of William J. Duiker **359** Courtesy of the Board of Trustees of the Victoria and Albert Museum **363** Courtesy of William J. Duiker **364** National Palace Museum, Taipei, Taiwan, Republic of China **365** Courtesy of the Tokyo National Museum **366** Courtesy of William J. Duiker

CHAPTER 11

370 Courtesy of William J. Duiker **376** Michael Holford, London **379** Detail—troops fighting as palace burns, scroll w/depictions of the night attack on the Sanjo Palace, from the "Illustrated scrolls of the events of the Heiji Period" 2nd half of the 13th c., Unknown, Japanese, Kamakura Period, Hand scroll; ink and colors on paper, Fenollosa-Weld Collection, Courtesy of the Museum of Fine Arts, Boston **381** Courtesy of the Tokyo National Museum **387** Courtesy of the Tokyo National Museum **390** Courtesy of the Freer Gallery of Art, Smithsonian Institution, Washington, D. C. **391** Robert Harding Picture Library **392, top** Will & Deni McIntyre/Photo Researchers, Inc. **392, bottom** Charles Gupton/Tony Stone Images **393** H. Edward Kim/National Geographic Society **394** Courtesy of William J. Duiker **398** Courtesy of William J. Duiker **400** Courtesy of William J. Duiker

CHAPTER 12

402 Bibliotheque Nationale, Paris, Ms. Nouv. Acq. Fr. 1098 **405** Bibliotheque Nationale, Paris, Ms. Nouv. Acq. Fr. 1098 **410** The Granger Collection **411** The Pierpont Morgan Library/Art Resource, NY M.736, f.9v **414** Bibliotheque Nationale, Paris **423** E.T. Archive, London, from the collections of the British Library, Psalter, Calendar, c.1250–1260 **426** Bibliotheque Nationale, Paris **431** © Biblioteque royale Albert ler (Ms IV 119, fol.72 verso) **432** Staatliche Museen, Berlin, Photo © Bildarchiv Preussischer **434** © C. Dagli Orti **435** © Sylvain Grandadam/Photo Researchers, Inc. **436** Scala/Art Resource, NY **438** © Erich Lessing/Art Resource, NY

CHAPTER 13

446 Private Collection/The Bridgeman Art Library **449** © Biblioteque royale Albert ler, Bruxelles (Ms. 13076-77, f. 12v) **451** Bibliotheque Nationale, Paris **454** Staatliche Landesbildstelle Hamburg **456** Giraudon/Art Resource, NY **462, left** Scala/Art Resource, NY **462, right** Scala/Art Resource, NY **468** Photo Vatican Museums **472** Private Collection/The Bridgeman Art Library **478** Scala/Art Resource, NY **479, top** Scala/Art Resource, NY **479, bottom** National Gallery of Art, Washington, Andrew W. Mellon Collection **480** Photo Vatican Museums **481** Reproduced by Courtesy of the Trustees; The National Gallery, London **481, right** Alinari/Art Resource, NY